Tsunamis in the World Ocean

Past, Present and Future
Volume I

Edited by
Kenji Satake
Alexander Rabinovich
Utku Kânoğlu
Stefano Tinti

Previously published in *Pure and Applied Geophysics*
(PAGEOPH), Volume 168, Nos. 6–7, 2011

Editors

Kenji Satake
Earthquake Research Institute
University of Tokyo
1-1-1 Yayoi, Bunkyo-ku
Tokyo 113-0032
Japan
satake@eri.utokyo.ac.jp

Alexander Rabinovich
Department of Fisheries and Oceans
Institute of Ocean Sciences
9860 West Saanich Road
Sidney, BC V8L 4B2
Canada
A.B.Rabinovich@gmail.com

Utku Kânoğlu
Department of Engineering Sciences
Middle East Technical University
06531 Ankara
Turkey
kanoglu@metu.edu.tr

Stefano Tinti
Department of Physics, Sector of Geophysics
University of Bologna
40127 Bologna
Italy
stefano.tinti@unibo.it

ISBN 978-3-0348-0187-4   e-ISBN 978-3-0348-0188-1
DOI 10.1007/978-3-0348-0188-1

Library of Congress Control Number: 2011930526

Cover illustration: Based on a photograph from "Field Survey of the March 28, 2005 Nias-Simeulue Earthquake and Tsunami" by J. C. Borrero, B. McAdoo, B. Jaffe, L. Dengler, G. Gelfenbaum, B. Higman, R. Hidayat, A. Moore, W. Kongko, Lukijanto, R. Peters, G. Prasetya, V. Titov, and E. Yulianto.

Cover design: deblik, Berlin.

Printed on acid-free paper

Springer Basel AG is part of Springer Science+Business Media

www.birkhauser-science.com

Contents

Contents

Pure Appl. Geophys. 168 (2011), 963–968
© 2011 Springer Basel AG
DOI 10.1007/s00024-011-0304-4

Introduction to "Tsunamis in the World Ocean: Past, Present, and Future. Volume I"

Kenji Satake,[1] Alexander Rabinovich,[2,3] Utku Kânoğlu,[4] and Stefano Tinti[5]

Abstract—Eighteen papers are included in Volume 1 of a PAGEOPH topical issue *Tsunamis in the World Ocean: Past, Present, and Future*. These papers are briefly introduced. They are grouped into three categories: case studies of earthquake-generated tsunamis; tsunami forecast and hazard assessments; and theoretical and computational modeling of tsunami generation, propagation, and coastal behavior. Most of the papers were presented at the 24th International Tsunami Symposium held 14–16 July 2009 in Novosibirsk, Russia, and reflect the current state of tsunami science.

Key words: Tsunami, tsunamigenic earthquake, field survey, tsunami numerical modeling, forecast and warning system, runup.

1. Introduction

The Tsunami Commission was established under the International Union of Geodesy and Geophysics (IUGG) following the 1960 Chilean tsunami, which was caused by the largest (M 9.5) earthquake in the twentieth century and affected many regions around the Pacific Ocean. The Tsunami Commission has since held biannual International Tsunami Symposia and published special volumes of selected papers (e.g., Satake *et al.*, 2007; Cummins *et al.*, 2008, 2009). Tsunami science, as well as warning and

hazard mitigation systems, have dramatically developed and improved as a result of the catastrophic 2004 Indian Ocean tsunami, which was generated by the Sumatra–Andaman earthquake (M 9.3) and was one of the worst tsunami disasters in human history (Stein and Okal, 2005). Furthermore, Intergovernmental Coordination Groups have been established for the Indian Ocean (ICG/IOWTS), the Northeastern Atlantic, the Mediterranean and connected seas (ICG/NEAMTWS), and the Caribbean Sea and adjacent regions (ICG/CARIBEEWS), in addition to the existing group for the Pacific Tsunami Warning System (ICG/PTWS). Thus, scientific and operational communities have interacted closely. Also, the number of participants, their backgrounds, and the range of topics presented at the International Tsunami Symposia have become widespread.

This volume includes 18 papers that reflect the current state of tsunami science. Most of the papers were presented at the 24th International Tsunami Symposium (14–16 July 2009, Novosibirsk, Russia) with 100 participants from 17 countries attendance the symposium. This volume also includes additional papers reporting recent tsunamis that occurred after the symposium. The papers are grouped into three categories: case studies of earthquake-generated tsunamis; tsunami forecasting and hazard assessments; and theoretical and computational studies of tsunami generation, propagation, and coastal behavior. Each paper is briefly introduced in the following sections.

2. Earthquake Tsunamis: Case Studies

This volume starts with a comprehensive review of tsunamigenic earthquakes by Okal (2011). He first describes some major historical tsunamigenic earthquakes such as the 1700 Cascadia, 1755 Lisbon, 1868

[1] Earthquake Research Institute, University of Tokyo, 1-1-1 Yayoi, Bunkyo-ku, Tokyo 113-0032, Japan. E-mail: satake@eri.u-tokyo.ac.jp

[2] Department of Fisheries and Oceans, Institute of Ocean Sciences, 9860 West Saanich Road, Sidney, BC V8L 4B2, Canada. E-mail: a.b.rabinovich@gmail.com

[3] Russian Academy of Sciences, P.P. Shirshov Institute of Oceanology, 36 Nakhimovsky Pr., Moscow 117997, Russia.

[4] Department of Engineering Sciences, Middle East Technical University, 06531 Ankara, Turkey. E-mail: kanoglu@metu.edu.tr

[5] Department of Physics, Sector of Geophysics, University of Bologna, Bologna, Italy. E-mail: stefano.tinti@unibo.it

Peru, and 1896 Sanriku earthquakes and associated tsunamis. Then, he introduces the 1923 Kamchatka and 1946 Aleutian earthquakes, for which far-field tsunami warnings were issued in Hawaii. The 1952 Kamchatka, 1960 Chile, and 1964 Alaska earthquakes were the three largest earthquakes in the twentieth century, and all three caused large trans-Pacific tsunamis. He further discusses several recent smaller earthquakes (i.e., the 1979 Mexico, 1987 and 1988 Gulf of Alaska, 1992 Nicaragua, 1995 Mexico, 1998 Papua New Guinea, 1999 Vanuatu, and 2003 Aleutian) that were epoch-making for recent tsunami research. For the 2004 Sumatra–Andaman earthquake and the associated Indian Ocean tsunami, he lists five particular features that were responsible for the worst tsunami disaster, which impacted the community, and that resulted in the adoption of new devices for tsunami observations. He grades the seven tsunamigenic earthquakes that occurred after 2004, based on forecast and disaster mitigation performance. The 2007 Bengkulu, 2007 Solomon, and 2005 Nias (at least near-field) events receive relatively good evaluations; the 2006 Kuril and 2007 Peru events receive warning alerts; and the 2009 Samoa and 2006 Java earthquakes receive failing grades, as they caused more than 100 casualties.

Geological studies of tsunami deposits have made significant progress in the last few decades. In this issue, TACHIBANA and TSUJI (2011) describe tsunami boulders of the Miocene age (17 million years old) probably deposited at the water depth of 200–400 m. In addition to describing the geology, they report simple model calculations to estimate the minimum current speed (2–3 m/s) needed to transport these boulders. They also carried out tsunami numerical simulation and found that the current speed at a 300 m water depth would be large enough to transport the boulders for several kilometers, if the originating earthquake was extremely large (M ~ 9). They conclude that the boulders were transported by tsunami currents from a giant earthquake along the Nankai Trough, where the Philippine Sea plate subducts beneath southwestern Japan.

The 1 November 1755 Lisbon earthquake (M ~ 8.5) was the most devastating earthquake in Europe, with >70,000 total casualties. The earthquake generated a tsunami that affected not only the Portuguese and Spanish coasts but also coastal areas across the Atlantic Ocean. ROGER et al. (2011) introduce the tsunami data in the Lesser Antilles, particularly Martinique Island, and successfully reproduce the observed tsunami with numerical modeling, using high-resolution bathymetric data. Their modeling results, with tsunami inundation up to 3 m, can be used for tsunami hazard mapping indicating vulnerability for a future tsunami at Martinique Island. OMIRA et al. (2011) also examine the vulnerability of the Gulf of Cadiz coast to tsunamis; this region was exposed to the Atlantic tsunamis and was heavily impacted by the 1755 Lisbon event. They consider two tsunami scenarios generated by earthquakes with M 8.1–8.3 for two different thrust fault ruptures identified in the assumed 1755 source area. Based on numerical modeling results, the maximum expected inundation height on the Gulf of Cadiz coast was 7 m, while the maximum computed flow speed was 8 m/s. These results might enable local authorities and emergency planners to mitigate the damaging effects of future tsunamis and develop tsunami-resilient communities in the region.

The 13 October 1963 Kuril earthquake (M 8.5) was one of the largest plate-boundary earthquakes along the Kuril–Kamchatka subduction zone in the Northwest Pacific. A similar great plate-boundary earthquake (M 8.3) occurred on 15 November 2006, and an outer-rise earthquake (M 8.1) occurred on 13 January 2007 just to the north of the 1963 earthquake source region. IOKI and TANIOKA (2011) collected the tsunami waveforms from 21 tide gauges along the Kuril–Kamchatka Arc, as well as the Aleutians, Hawaii, and the western Pacific Ocean. They used the tsunami waveform inversion results to estimate the slip distribution on a 300 km-long fault. The seismic moment estimated from the tsunami data corresponds to $M_w = 8.3$. They conclude that there is no seismic gap between the 1963 and 2006 Kuril earthquake source areas.

The 27 March 1964 Alaska earthquake (M 9.2) triggered a series of subaerial and submarine failures around nearby fjords, which produced a number of locally destructive slide-generated tsunamis. The town of Seward was severely hit by both tectonic and landslide-generated tsunamis. SULEIMANI et al. (2011) applied a recently developed and validated tsunami numerical model to study the 1964 Alaska tsunami inundation in Resurrection Bay and the town of Seward. The calculated tsunami runup and horizontal inundation in the Seward area caused by the total effect of local slide-generated tsunamis and a tectonically generated tsunami was in good agreement with the actual observations of the inundation zone.

On 28 March 2005, 3 months after the 2004 Indian Ocean tsunami, another great earthquake (M 8.6) occurred near Nias Island off west Sumatra, Indonesia, just to the southeast of the source area of the 2004 Sumatra–Andaman earthquake. BORRERO et al. (2011) report the tsunami field survey results on the Sumatra coast and nearby small islands. On Simeulue Island, located at the boundary between the 2004 and 2005 earthquakes, large tsunami runup heights (>4 m), as well as large coastal uplift (>1 m), were observed. The tsunami was also large (>3 m) at Banyak and Nias islands, but smaller on Sumatra Island, unlike the 2004 tsunami. They found that oral history from the 1907 tsunami and community education significantly helped to mitigate the tsunami disaster at these islands. They also introduce some eyewitness reports indicating that the extreme nature of the 2004 tsunami skewed the perception of a tsunami. The eyewitness told them that there was no tsunami, but that the sea level rose, flooded their land and caused severe damage.

In West Papua, Indonesia, two successive large earthquakes (M 7.7 and 7.4) occurred on 3 January 2009; they were 3 h apart and both caused noticeable tsunamis. A tsunami warning was issued for the coasts of Indonesia and Japan. The maximum tsunami runup height was almost 2 m on the Indonesian coast, and the maximum amplitude was 0.4 m in Japan, but no significant damage was caused in either region. FUJII et al. (2011) conducted a numerical simulation that reproduced the large tsunami that traveled towards Japan, in a direction perpendicular to the fault strike. Some of the tsunami energy was trapped on a shallow Izu-Bonin ridge system to produce large amplitudes. Inversion of the tsunami waveforms recorded by coastal tide gauges, offshore GPS stations, and bottom pressure gauges indicates that the seismic moment of the fault model corresponds to $M_w = 7.3$. ABE (2011) uses spectral

analysis of the 2009 Papua tsunami records from the southwest coast of Japan, and explains the results by applying the "synthesis" method. This method, which is based on joint analysis of tsunami and background spectra observed at a number of stations, is a generalization of the method proposed by RABI-NOVICH (1997) to separate source and topography effects in recorded tsunamis. The "synthesized spectra" explained well the observed spectral amplitudes and their frequency distribution for the region with complicated topography and numerous bays and inlets.

On 29 September 2009, a great earthquake (M 8.1) occurred near the Samoa Islands and generated a major tsunami. The maximum tsunami runup was more than 20 m (OKAL et al., 2010) and caused nearly 2,000 casualties in American Samoa, Western Samoa, and Tonga. The semi-automated routine analysis of this earthquake showed that the main shock was a normal fault type, indicating an outer-rise earthquake. TONINI et al. (2011) model the tsunami generation based on the focal mechanism solutions provided by the USGS and global CMT (GCMT) projects, and compare the calculated tsunami waveforms with those observed at the coastal tide gauge stations at Apia and Pago Pago in the Samoa Islands and three nearby Deep-ocean Assessment and Reporting of Tsunamis (DART) stations operated by the US National Oceanic and Atmospheric Administration (NOAA). They demonstrate that the observed tsunami waveforms at Apia are well-reproduced by a model based on the GCMT model, and that those at Pago Pago can be matched if a time shift, which is probably due to the incomplete knowledge of nearshore bathymetry around the tide gauge station, is considered. However, they cannot successfully model the tsunami waveforms observed at the DART stations.

3. Tsunami Forecast and Hazard Assessments

After the 2004 Indian Ocean tsunami, warning systems were established in many countries, and forecast and hazard assessment systems have been evaluated on global scales. In this issue, four papers are grouped in this category.

3

POWER and GALE (2011) describe the National Tsunami Warning System of New Zealand, which involves multiple organizations (e.g., Pacific Tsunami Warning Center, Ministry of Civil Defense and Emergency Management, GNS Science, and Civil Defense and Emergency Management). The tsunami sources for New Zealand are classified into three categories: local (tsunami travel time <1 h), regional (travel times between 1 and 3 h), and distant (travel time >3 h). For distant tsunamis, a scenario database has been constructed using tsunami numerical modeling and is currently used for forecasts. The New Zealand tsunami monitoring system includes 20 sea-level measurement stations. During the 2009 Samoa tsunami, 10 of these stations recorded the tsunami waveforms.

GREENSLADE et al. (2011) introduce a tsunami scenario database, T2, which was developed and operational at the Joint Australian Tsunami Warning Centre. The T2 scenario consists of more than 500 earthquake sources in the Pacific, Indian, and South Atlantic oceans, ranging in magnitude from 7.5 to 9.0. The coastal (at 20 m water depth) and offshore (at DART stations) tsunami heights from these scenarios are compared with the actual records from recent tsunamis (i.e., the 2006 and 2009 Tonga, 2007 Sumatra, and 2009 Kuril tsunamis). These comparisons indicate that the scenario database generally forecast the observed tsunami heights and waveforms fairly well.

OKAL et al. (2011) present potential tsunami scenarios in the South China Sea and adjoining basins. Their results indicate that the South China, Sulu, and Sulawesi seas are three independent basins: a tsunami generated in one does not leak into another, and the Sunda Arc is an efficient barrier to tsunamis originating in the Indian Ocean. The tsunami amplitude is dampened significantly by the shallow continental shelves in the Java Sea, the Gulf of Thailand, and the western part of the South China Sea. They also discuss the existence of significant tsunami risk from underwater landslides in the South China Sea Basin (e.g., the Brunei Slide), as documented in both modern and geological history. They emphasize that even moderate earthquakes can trigger submarine slides, creating locally catastrophic tsunamis such as the 1998 Papua New Guinea disaster (SYNOLAKIS

et al., 2002). They conclude that a tsunami in the region will have a near-field character, and emphasize the importance of awareness and education in reducing human losses (FRITZ and KALLIGERIS, 2008; OKAL et al., 2010).

Crescent City, California, has been historically impacted by tsunamis more than any other location on the US West Coast. The 15 November 2006 earthquake (M 8.3) in the Kuril Islands generated a moderate Pacific-wide tsunami, but Crescent City experienced structural damage costing more than 20 million US dollars. DENGLER and USLU (2011) first examine how modifications to Crescent City's harbor since the early twentieth century may have affected its vulnerability to the 2006 tsunami. In addition, they examine the 1933 Sanriku tsunami, which occurred before the small boat basin was constructed and did not result in any damage. Their results suggest that harbor modifications increased peak currents produced by a modest tsunami by a factor of at least three within the small boat basin, and pushed the speed over the damage threshold near the harbor entrance. Their results imply that modification of coastal structures along tsunami-prone regions could affect the tsunami vulnerability.

4. Studies of Tsunami Generation, Propagation and Coastal Behaviors

Besides earthquakes, volcanic eruptions and both subaerial and submarine landslides can generate tsunamis. In rare cases, asteroid impacts also generate tsunamis. The best-known example is a huge (10 km) asteroid that impacted Chicxulub 65.5 million years ago and caused a gigantic earthquake and a tsunami, which led to mass extinction at the Cretaceous–Paleogene boundary (SCHULTE et al., 2010). While smaller impacts, which occur more frequently, have also been known to generate tsunamis, the numerical simulation of GISLER et al. (2011) indicates that small (<0.5 km) asteroids do not produce craters or generate tsunamis. They carried out numerical simulation for various asteroid diameters (100–1,000 m) and various water depths (500–5,000 m), and examined the characteristics of the waves generated. They found that, for most asteroid impacts, the generated waves differ from those of a typical tsunami, i.e., shallow-water waves.

Tsunami inundation modeling has evolved through careful and explicit validation and verification, comparing computed predictions with analytical solutions, laboratory experiments, and field measurements. Specific steps are recommended by SYNOLAKIS et al. (2008). NICOLSKY et al. (2011) present a numerical model to solve nonlinear shallow-water wave equations to simulate tsunami propagation and inundation; this model adopts a staggered leap-frog finite-difference scheme to calculate depth-averaged water fluxes in spherical coordinates and a free-surface moving boundary algorithm to calculate the temporal position of the shoreline. They applied their model to several benchmark problems identified by SYNOLAKIS et al. (2008). They also parallelized the solution methodology employing a domain-decomposition technique for large-scale problems. They summarize their model's strengths and limits, and illustrate some possible improvements. Clearly, additional criteria will evolve as the field progresses, and we emphasize that model testing must remain a continuous process.

For earthquake-generated tsunamis, vertical displacement on the surface of an elastic medium due to faulting (e.g., OKADA, 1985) has been traditionally used as the initial water-surface deformation. This is based on the long-wave (shallow-water) assumption that displacements on the water surface and bottom can be considered the same. NOSOV and KOLESOV (2011) examine this classical problem with a historical review, and propose an optimum method to incorporate three-dimensional effects that have been ignored in the traditional approach. The effects include horizontal motion of a sloping seafloor. They also propose a smoothing method to filter out components with short wavelength, and apply this method to the 2006 and 2007 Kuril tsunamis.

DIDENKULOVA and PELINOVSKY (2011) report their analytical study on the shoaling and runup of tsunamis in narrow U-shaped bays and underwater canyons based on the shallow-water wave theory. They first studied wave shoaling in bays using an asymptotic approach when the bottom profile varies smoothly along the channel axis, and report that the

shoaling effects are more significant than the reflection. However, they confirm that for certain bay shapes where depth changes significantly, traveling waves do exist and can propagate a large distance without reflection. As a result, such waves transfer all their energy to the coast and cause anomalous wave amplification and runup. In addition, they demonstrate that the maximum runup heights resulting from both linear and nonlinear analytical solutions are identical for a linearly inclined channel with a parabolic cross-section. They suggest that basins with a non-reflecting bottom configuration lead to significant wave amplification and should be taken into account when evaluating tsunami hazards.

Acknowledgments

The editors of this topical volume thank the authors and reviewers of all the papers for their contributions and efforts. We also thank Renata Dmowska, editor of the topical issue, for her continuous encouragement in the editorial process.

REFERENCES

ABE, K. (2011), *Synthesis of a tsunami spectrum in a semi-enclosed basin using its background spectrum*, Pure Appl Geophys *168*, This issue.

BORRERO, J., McADOO, B., JAFFE, B., DENGLER, L., GELFENBAUM, G., HIGMAN, B., HIDAYAT, R., MOORE, A., KONGKO, W., LUKIJANTO, PETERS, R., PRASETYA, G., TITOV, V., and YULIANTO, E. (2011), *Field survey of the March 28, 2005 Nias-Simeulue earthquake and tsunami*, Pure Appl Geophys *168*, This issue.

CUMMINS, P.R., KONG, L.S.L., and SATAKE, K. (2008), *Tsunami science four years after the 2004 Indian Ocean tsunami. Part I: modelling and hazard assessment*, Pure Appl Geophys *165*, Topical Issue.

CUMMINS, P.R., KONG, L.S.L., and SATAKE, K. (2009), *Tsunami science four years after the 2004 Indian Ocean tsunami. Part II: observation and data analysis*, Pure Appl Geophys *166*, Topical Issue.

DENGLER, L., and USLU, B. (2011), *Effects of harbor modification on Crescent City, California's tsunami vulnerability*, Pure Appl Geophys *168*, This issue.

DIDENKULOVA, I., and PELINOVSKY, E. (2011), *Runup of tsunami waves in U-shaped bays*, Pure Appl Geophys *168*, This issue.

FRITZ, H. M., and KALLIGERIS, N. (2008), *Ancestral heritage saves tribes during 1 April 2007 Solomon Islands tsunami*, Geophys Res Lett *35*, L01607.

FUJII, Y., SATAKE, K., and NISHIMAE, Y. (2011), *Observation and modeling of the January 2009 West Papua, Indonesia tsunami*, Pure Appl Geophys *168*, This issue.

GISLER, G., WEAVER, R., and GITTINGS, M. (2011), *Calculations of asteroid impacts into deep and shallow water*, Pure Appl Geophys *168*, This issue.

GREENSLADE, D.J.M., ALLEN, S.C.R., and SIMANJUNTAK, M.A. (2011), *An evaluation of tsunami forecasts from the T2 scenario database*, Pure Appl Geophys *168*, This issue.

IOKI, K., and TANIOKA, Y. (2011), *Slip distribution of the 1963 great Kurile earthquake estimated from tsunami waveforms*, Pure Appl Geophys *168*, This issue.

NICOLSKY, D.J., SULEIMANI, E.N., and HANSEN, R.A. (2011), *Validation and verification of a numerical model for tsunami propagation and runup*, Pure Appl Geophys *168*, This issue.

NOSOV, M.A., and KOLESOV, S.V. (2011), *Optimal initial conditions for simulation of seismotectonic tsunamis*, Pure Appl Geophys *168*, This issue.

OKADA, Y. (1985), *Surface deformation due to shear and tensile faults in a half-space*, Bull Seism Soc Am *75*, 1135-1154.

OKAL, E.A. (2011), *Tsunamigenic earthquakes: past and present milestones*, Pure Appl Geophys *168*, This issue.

OKAL, E.A., FRITZ, H.M., SYNOLAKIS, C.E., BORRERO, J.C., WEISS, R., LYNETT, P.J., TITOV, V.V., FOTEINIS, S., JAFFE, B.E., LIU, P.L.-F., and CHAN, I. (2010), *Field survey of the Samoa tsunami of 29 September 2009*, Seism Res Lett *81*, 577–591.

OKAL, E.A., SYNOLAKIS, C.E., and KALLIGERIS, N. (2011), *Tsunami simulations for regional sources in the South China and adjoining seas*, Pure Appl Geophys *168*, This issue.

OMIRA, R., BAPTISTA, M.A., and MIRANDA, J.M. (2011), *Evaluating tsunami impact on the Gulf of Cadiz coast (Northeast Atlantic)*, Pure Appl Geophys *168*, This issue.

POWER, W., and GALE, N. (2011), *Tsunami forecasting and monitoring in New Zealand*, Pure Appl Geophys *168*, This issue.

RABINOVICH, A.B. (1997), *Spectral analysis of tsunami waves: Separation of source and topography effects*, J Geophys Res *102*, 12, 663–12,676.

ROGER, J., BAPTISTA, M.A., SAHAL, A., ACCARY, F., ALLGEYER, S., and HÉBERT, H. (2011), *The transoceanic 1755 Lisbon tsunami in Martinique*, Pure Appl Geophys *168*, This issue.

SATAKE, K., OKAL, E.A., and BORRERO, J.C. (2007), *Tsunami and its hazards in the Indian and Pacific Oceans*, Pure Appl Geophys *164*, Topical Issue.

SCHULTE, P., ALEGRET, L., ARENILLAS, I., ARZ, J.A., BARTON, P.J., BOWN, P.R., BRALOWER, T.J., CHRISTESON, G.L., CLAEYS, P., COCKELL, C.S., COLLINS, G.S., DEUTSCH, A., GOLDIN, T.J., GOTO, K., GRAJALES-NISHIMURA, J.M., GRIEVE, R.A. F., GULICK, S.P.S., JOHNSON, K.R., KIESSLING, W., KOEBERL, C., KRING, D.A., MACLEOD, K.G., MATSUI, T., MELOSH, J., MONTANARI, A., MORGAN, J.V., NEAL, C. R., NICHOLS, D.J., NORRIS, R.D., PIERAZZO, E., RAVIZZA, G., REBOLLEDO-VIEYRA, M., REIMOLD, W.U., ROBIN, E., SALGE, T., SPEIJER, R.P., SWEET, A.R., URRUTIA-FUCUGAUCHI, J., VAJDA, V., WHALEN, M.T., and WILLUMSEN, P.S. (2010), *The Chicxulub asteroid impact and mass extinction at the Cretaceous-Paleogene boundary*, Science *327*, 1214–1218.

STEIN, S., and OKAL, E.A. (2005), *Size and speed of the Sumatra earthquake*, Nature *434*, 581–582.

SULEIMANI, E., NICOLSKY, D., HAEUSSLER, P.J., and HANSEN, R. (2011), *Combined effects of tectonics and landslide-generated tsunami runup at Seaward, Alaska during the Mw 9.2 1964 earthquake*, Pure Appl Geophys *168*, This issue.

SYNOLAKIS, C.E., BARDET, J.-P., BORRERO, J.C., DAVIES, H.L., OKAL, E.A., SILVER, E.A., SWEET, S., and TAPPIN, D.R. (2002), *The slump origin of the 1998 Papua New Guinea tsunami*, Proc Roy Soc (London), Ser A, *58*, 763–789.

SYNOLAKIS, C.E., BERNARD, E.N., TITOV, V.V., KÂNOĞLU, U., and GONZÁLEZ, F.I. (2008), *Validation and verification of tsunami numerical models*, Pure Appl Geophys *165*, 2197–2228.

TACHIBANA, T., and TSUJI, Y. (2011), *Geological and hydrodynamical examination of bathyal tsunamigenic origin of Miocene conglomerates in Chita Peninsula, central Japan*, Pure Appl Geophys *168*, This issue.

TONINI, R., ARMIGLIATO, A., and TINTI, S. (2011), *The 29th September 2009 Samoa Islands tsunami: simulations based on the first focal mechanism solutions and implications on tsunami early warning strategies*, Pure Appl Geophys *168*, This issue.

(Received September 11, 2010, Published online April 14, 2011)

Pure Appl. Geophys. 168 (2011), 969–995
© 2010 Springer Basel AG
DOI 10.1007/s00024-010-0215-9

Tsunamigenic Earthquakes: Past and Present Milestones

EMILE A. OKAL[1]

Abstract—We review a number of events which, taken individually, have significantly affected our understanding of the generation of tsunamis by earthquake sources and our efforts at mitigating their hazards, notably through the development of warning algorithms. Starting with the 1700 Cascadia earthquake, we examine how significant tsunamis have changed our views in fields as diverse as seismotectonics, the diversity of earthquake cycles, the development of warning algorithms, the response of communities at risk to warnings, and their education, the latter being either formal or rooted in ancestral heritage. We discuss in detail lessons from the 2004 Sumatra disasters and review the performance of warning centers and the response of affected populations during the nine significant tsunamis which have taken place since 2004.

1. Introduction

This paper examines a number of earthquakes whose tsunamis can be regarded as milestones in the development of our understanding and mitigation of the hazards posed by this form of disaster. The events selected for this discussion do not necessarily derive from a ranking in terms of size (expressed as seismic moment) or tsunami death toll, although the record holders in both categories, the 1960 Chilean and 2004 Sumatran earthquakes, are included. Rather, we compile events which, taken individually, have added an incremental element to our command of one or more aspects of tsunami science in disciplines as diverse as seismological source theory, numerical hydrodynamics, the development of ocean-bottom pressure sensors, and the societal aspects of the mitigation of tsunami hazards.

The milestone events are described in chronological order of their occurrence. In the case of historical tsunamis (e.g., 1700, 1868), this does not reflect the timing of the community's research and understanding of their characteristics. For example, the concept of source directivity, introduced by BEN-MENAHEM and ROSENMAN (1972) in the wake of the 1964 Alaskan tsunami, predated the identification of the 1700 Cascadia earthquake by SATAKE *et al.* (1996).

In addition, the last section of this paper critically analyzes the response of the warning centers and of the communities at risk during the nine significant tsunamis which have occurred since the 2004 Sumatra–Andaman disaster. It points out an alarming diversity of performance, including both false alarms and missed warnings, as well as both successful evacuations and tragic death tolls. This clearly indicates that a continued effort is required, in particular, regarding the education of populations at risk.

2. Cascadia, 26 January 1700—Danger in America's Backyard

Upon the advent of plate tectonics, it became clear that the Western US and Canadian margin, from Cape Mendocino, California to Vancouver Island, British Columbia, constitutes a subduction zone where the small Juan de Fuca plate, a remnant of the larger Farallon plate (ATWATER 1970), is consumed under North America. While typical attributes of subduction zones such as active arc volcanism and deeper than usual seismicity (albeit extending only to 73 km) are present in Cascadia, the area is notably deprived of large interplate thrust earthquakes expressing the subduction. Indeed, the CMT catalog, now extending over 34 years, lists no such event of

[1] Department of Geological Sciences, Northwestern University, Evanston, IL 60208, USA. E-mail: emile@earth.northwestern.edu

moment $>10^{25}$ dyn*cm. This relative quiescence had suggested that the subduction zone is unlocked, accommodating the convergence through aseismic creep (ANDO and BALAZS, 1979).

However, SAVAGE et al. (1981) interpreted geodetic profiles in the Seattle area as suggesting that the plate boundary was actually locked. HEATON and KANAMORI (1984) argued that Cascadia was, after all, not so different in its tectonic properties from other locations where giant earthquakes are known, such as Southwest Japan or Colombia, although decades later, the 2004 Sumatra earthquake was to prove that tectonic parameters alone are a poor predictor of the maximum earthquake along a subduction zone (STEIN and OKAL, 2007). Later, ATWATER (1987) located buried vegetated soils in intertidal basins, which he interpreted as tsunami deposits.

Any large Cascadia events would have to feature extended recurrences times, so that the last one would predate the dawn of available historical records (essentially going back to Lewis and Clark's expedition in 1805), but would then be expected to recur in the future, casting a new and somewhat ominous light on the question of seismic risk in the Pacific Northwest of the United States (HEATON and HARTZELL, 1987).

In this framework, NELSON et al. (1995) used ^{14}C dating of earthquake-killed vegetation to show that a major earthquake with a fault length of 900 km had taken place between the late 1600s and early 1800s. Finally, SATAKE et al. (1996) identified the "orphan" tsunami of 26 January 1700, whose records in Japan could not be associated with any known large Pacific earthquake, as having originated in Cascadia, and later provided a quantitative modeling of the far-field (tsunami) and local (subsidence) data to infer a most probable value of 5×10^{29} dyn*cm for the seismic moment of the proposed earthquake (SATAKE et al., 2003). The precise year was also confirmed from tree-ring evidence (JACOBY et al., 1997).

Later work by OBERMEIER and DICKENSON (2000) on liquefaction evidence identified a previous event around 1100 A.D., but yielded deficient accelerations for the 1700 earthquake, which would require some level of source slowness in order to be reconciled with the SATAKE et al. (2003) moment value. NELSON et al. (2006) have further documented in the stratigraphic record a series of predecessors, whose exact sizes show identifiable fluctuations, as reported in many other provinces, since the pioneering work of ANDO (1975).

The following are important lessons to be heeded from the 1700 earthquake, most of which will be common themes in the present study:

- The U.S. is at risk from a potentially catastrophic near-field tsunami for which warning times could be as short as 15 min.
- Mega-earthquakes ($M_0 \geq 10^{29}$ dyn*cm) can occur in areas where incomplete understanding of the tectonic framework has made them hitherto unexpected.
- Many mega-earthquakes feature source slowness, resulting in accelerations (in particular felt by humans) which can be deceptive as a warning of an impending tsunami.

3. Lisbon, 01 November 1755—Europe's Deadliest Natural Disaster

With a death toll approaching 100,000 (CHESTER, 2001), the All Saints Day earthquake and tsunami represent the largest natural disaster to affect Europe in modern times. The tsunami is also remarkable in that waves of up to 4–5 m amplitude were reported in the Caribbean, which constitutes one of only two known cases of damage in the far field across the Atlantic Basin.[1] Following numerous attempts by many authors (e.g., THIÉBOT and GUTSCHER, 2006) to interpret the earthquake and its tsunami in the context of the regional plate tectonics framework, BARKAN et al. (2009) recently used numerical hydrodynamic simulations to forward model a large number of possible scenarios; they narrowed down the most probable source to being a thrust fault section of the Azores-Gibraltar segment of the Eurasia-Africa plate boundary, located at 36.5°N and 13°W in the Horseshoe abyssal plain, and striking ~ 345°N. They suggested a large moment, of about 10^{29} dyn*cm, but

---

[1] The other known transatlantic tsunami took place on 31 March 1761; its source may have been an aftershock of the 1755 earthquake (O'LOUGHLIN and LANDER, 2003).

any surficial expression of their proposed source of the 1755 earthquake remains to be documented in the local bathymetry.

BARKAN *et al.* (2009) showed that only their model can explain the most remarkable variation of the tsunami reports along the Western shore of the Atlantic, namely damaging in the Caribbean and notable in Newfoundland, but conspicuously absent along the Eastern seaboard of the United States, despite the existence of many settlements there in 1755. In this respect, the distribution of tsunami amplitudes in the far field is a subtle combination of classical source directivity (BEN-MENAHEM and ROSENMAN, 1972) and focusing by irregular bathymetry (WOODS and OKAL, 1987; SATAKE, 1988).

The most important lesson from the Lisbon tsunami is the vulnerability of the Eastern coast of the Americas, from Newfoundland to the Caribbean, to transatlantic tsunamis. However, the variability in location and focal mechanism of the major earthquakes along the Azores-Gibraltar seismic belt (evidenced by the 1755, (1761?), 1941, 1969 and 1975 earthquakes), suggests that the next earthquake with potential transatlantic hazard may not duplicate the 1755 event. Even a minor change in fault orientation and/or in source location could significantly affect directivity and focusing, resulting in an altered distribution of tsunami amplitudes. In particular, there is no reason to believe that the somewhat miraculous protection of coastal North America in 1755 would be repeated under a future scenario.

4. Southern Peru, 13 August 1868—A True Giant which Scoffs at Barriers

This event was the last mega-earthquake to rupture the whole coast of southern Peru and to generate a basin-wide tsunami from that province. The tsunami ran up locally to as high as 18 m, and is perhaps best known for the anecdote of the *Watery*, a US Navy steamer which was visiting the port of Arica (then in Peru, now in Chile). The vessel was swept ashore and deposited against the cliff of El Morro, 3 km inland, only to be returned to the vicinity of the shoreline during the next tsunami, on 09 May 1877 (BILLINGS, 1915). In the far field, the tsunami was particularly intense in New Zealand, with heights of 7–8 m, and reached all the way to Japan and the Philippines. There is some suggestion that it may have unseasonably calved large icebergs off the coast of Antarctica (SOLOV'EV and GO, 1984).

An intriguing aspect of this tsunami is that it caused complete destruction at Pisco, in central Peru, only 200 km southeast of Lima, suggesting that the 1868 earthquake could not be just a repeat of the previous large Southern Peru earthquake, on 23 November 1604, during which the tsunami had been more moderate. In attempting to model the effect of the 1868 tsunami in Pisco, OKAL *et al.* (2006a) showed that it was necessary to extend the seismic rupture northwest some 300 km; this requires the fault to extend across the Nazca Ridge. In this context, the ridge cannot be regarded as a natural barrier acting to bound the rupture of large earthquakes, as it probably had done during the 1604 event (DORBATH *et al.*, 1990). Thus, the a priori identification of the size of a future large earthquake along a given subduction province cannot be guided by our perception of natural barriers which may be jumped during exceptional events. Indeed, the tsunamigenic earthquake of 01 April 2007 in the Solomon Islands is another example in which the rupture propagated across a major tectonic feature—in this instance the triple junction between the Pacific, Australian and Woodlark plates (TAYLOR *et al.*, 2008).

5. Sanriku, Japan, 15 June 1896—The First Identified "Tsunami Earthquake"

With a death toll of over 27,000, this event is the deadliest recorded tsunami in the history of Japan. It represents the first known "tsunami earthquake", whose tsunami was much larger than expected from the amplitude of its seismic waves. As summarized by KANAMORI (1972), the earthquake was felt only mildly along the Sanriku coast, but the tsunami featured catastrophic proportions, with run-up reaching 30 m in the near field, up to 5 m in Hawaii, and damage reported in Santa Cruz, California. The anomalous character of the seismic source spectrum of the great 1896 "Meiji Sanriku" earthquake was asserted by KANAMORI (1972) from a slower-than-normal decay of seismic intensities with distance, which argues for a lower-frequency seismic spectrum, and from the deficiency in high-frequency P waves with respect to a more regular local earthquake as recorded on a nearby short-period seismometer.

One hundred years after the event, TANIOKA and SATAKE (1996) showed that local maregraph records of the tsunami could be modeled using a source rupturing in the sedimentary wedge overlying the interplate contact in the vicinity of the Sanriku trench, with a seismic moment of 1.2×10^{28} dyn*cm, about double the value obtained by KANAMORI (1972) at a period of 20 s, and 60 times that inferred from 4-s S waves, thus upholding the concept of an anomalously slow rupture.

The geometry proposed by TANIOKA and SATAKE (1996) is also in agreement with FUKAO'S (1979) model for the "tsunami earthquakes" of 20 October 1963 and 10 June 1975 in the Kurile Islands. However, those events occurred as aftershocks of larger earthquakes with regular rupture properties, whereas the 1896 Sanriku earthquake did not.

6. Kamchatka, 03 February 1923—The First Warning in the Far Field

This event represents, to our knowledge, the first case of a realistic, if unheeded, tsunami warning in the far field, based on the interpretation of seismic waves from the parent earthquake. The details of this remarkable episode are given by JAGGAR (1930), even though he persistently describes the earthquake as located in the Aleutian Islands.

Thomas Jaggar was, at the time, Director of the Volcano Observatory located on the rim of Kilauea caldera, on the "Big" Island of Hawaii, where he had deployed Omori seismometers with the purpose of monitoring locally generated volcanic tremors. The Kamchatka earthquake occurred at 16:01 GMT, and its seismic waves were recorded in Hawaii (whose time zone was then GMT-10:30) around 05:40 local time. Upon reaching his laboratory on the morning of Saturday, 03 February, Jaggar noticed the recording of a very large earthquake. With only one station, he was unable to precisely locate the event, but he could estimate a distance, probably from the S–P delay, inferring that something "big and far" had just

happened somewhere in the Pacific Basin. Just three months earlier, on 11 November 1922, Hawaii had been affected by the tsunami from the South Atacama Chilean earthquake, which had run up to 2.1 m in Hilo, and whose arrival time provided an average speed of tsunami waves on the high seas. Epicentral distance was all Jaggar needed to predict the arrival of a tsunami later that morning. He then notified the local authorities in Hilo, who unfortunately regarded his warning as nothing more than the fantasy of a gentleman scientist perched on "his" volcano, and simply ignored it. The tsunami arrived at 12:20 p.m. local time, inflicting more than 1.5 million 1923-dollars worth of damage on the islands, and killing one person.

The next tsunami alert in Hawaii came on 02 March 1933 following the Showa Sanriku earthquake. By a repeated stroke of luck, the event occurred at about the same time, leading to a remarkably similar timeline of measurements and warning by Jaggar. This time, however, the civil defense authorities in Hilo took it seriously, and evacuated people from critical areas. The tsunami was damaging but no lives were lost.

Unfortunately, as will be described in Sect. 7, the situation was different on 01 April 1946, during the Aleutian tsunami, which remains to this day the deadliest in the recorded history of Hawaii. The timing of the source (12:29 GMT), the anomalously slow character of the event (KANAMORI, 1972; LÓPEZ and OKAL, 2006) and Jaggar's retirement in 1940, combined to provoke a total surprise upon the arrival of the waves, which had a disastrous impact on Hilo (see Sect. 7).

Several lessons are to be learned from this story and remain pertinent to this day. First is the value of permanent, grass roots observation of seismic waves. Nowadays, this function has been delegated to computers, which can superbly locate earthquakes in real time and usually provide an adequate estimate of seismic moment. However, it takes the human mind to properly assess a new, unforeseen, observation. In addition, this episode illustrates the delicate interaction between the scientist and the civil defense decision-makers. The example of the 2006 Java tsunami (see Sect. 18) serves proof that progress is still needed in this respect.

Finally, it is worth noting that Jaggar issued an appropriate tsunami warning without much command of theoretical fluid dynamics [as transpires from a critical reading of JAGGAR (1930)], and above all without the correct location of the source. It is unclear whether he had formulated an estimate of the epicenter before issuing the warning, or was simply relying on "big and far". In the former case, his estimate would have been wrong, since 7 years later he still believed that the 1923 earthquake was off-shore from Unimak, 2,300 km from its true location. Yet, his warning was proved correct since the tsunami caused significant damage and death, even though the relevant error in epicentral distance would have amounted to an error of 2 h in arrival time, which, under today's standards, would most probably have resulted in the perception of a false alarm and consequently in an untimely "all clear". However, in the context of this 1923 episode, it may not be irrelevant to reflect on the possibly subtle value added to the usefulness of a far-field warning by elaborate real-time refinements of earthquake source parameters.

The 1923 Kamchatka tsunami is also remarkable in that it was followed on 13 April 1923 by a particularly destructive tsunami at Ust' Kamchatsk during an otherwise moderate aftershock (SOLOV'EV and FERCHEV, 1961). That event could constitute the first example of a "tsunami earthquake" reported in the aftermath of a larger shock, although the tsunami could also be due to underwater slumping off the mouth of the Kamchatka River.

7. Aleutian Islands, 01 April 1946—First and Still Deadliest Tsunami Disaster in U.S. History

With 159 deaths in Hawaii and 5 on Unimak, the 1946 Aleutian tsunami remains the deadliest to hit the U.S. and its possessions in the twentieth century, and is also the first major "tsunami earthquake" for which a quantitative analysis of its source characteristics is possible from historical seismograms (LÓPEZ and OKAL, 2006). The 1946 disaster resulted in the creation of the Tsunami Warning Center [later Pacific Tsunami Warning Center] at the Honolulu Geomagnetic Observatory in 1949.

The earthquake took place at 12:29 GMT, i.e., in the middle of the night at the epicenter. Its source slowness is reflected in the modest conventional magnitude ($M = 7.4$) assessed by GUTENBERG and RICHTER (1954), in the absence of hydroacoustic T waves (OKAL et al., 2003a), and in that its moderate aftershock (27 mn later) had been felt more strongly by the watchstanders at Scotch Cap lighthouse who would meet their deaths in the tsunami a few minutes later (SANFORD, 1946). The event generated a Pacific-wide tsunami which reached Hawaii in the early morning (06:54 local time or 17:24 GMT). It destroyed the coastal infrastructure in Hilo and did significant damage in the Marquesas, Easter Island, and as far South as Antarctica (FUCHS, 1982). In the near field, the tsunami eradicated the lighthouse at Scotch Cap, which had been built of reinforced concrete only 6 years earlier, with a local run-up reaching 42 m as measured later by OKAL et al. (2003b). Total losses from the tsunami in Hawaii were estimated at 25 million 1946-dollars (SHEPARD et al., 1950).

The disparity between the size of the seismic source (at least as measured from conventional waves) and the catastrophic nature of the tsunami led KANAMORI (1972) to introduce the concept of "tsunami earthquake", i.e., of an event whose tsunami is stronger than expected from the size of its seismic waves. Later work (FUKAO, 1979; NEWMAN and OKAL, 1998; POLET and KANAMORI, 2000) has shown that such earthquakes are characterized by a deficiency in rupture velocity along the fault plane, leading to destructive interference for all but the longest-period components of the seismic source, and resulting in an underestimation of its long-period or static level moment (responsible for tsunami excitation) when assessed from conventional seismic waves. Indeed, a very-long period investigation of the source of the 1946 earthquake has suggested a moment as large as 8.5×10^{28} dyn*cm and a slowness parameter $\Theta = -7.0$, making it one of the 10 largest events ever recorded, and the slowest one ever analyzed (LÓPEZ and OKAL, 2006).

Between 1999 and 2002, OKAL et al. (2002, 2003b) were able to reconstruct a database of run-up and inundation in both the near and far fields, based on the testimony of elderly witnesses. These datasets, comparable to those resulting from modern-day post-tsunami surveys, revealed two fundamental results. In the far field, run-up amplitudes exhibit a very strong directivity effect, which is the trademark of a dislocation source, and they can be successfully modeled using LÓPEZ and OKAL'S (2006) seismic source (OKAL and HÉBERT, 2007). However, in the near field, both the exceptional amplitude of run-up and its concentration along a short segment of the coast of Unimak Island cannot be reconciled with generation by any dislocation compatible with seismic observations, even at the longest available periods; this requires an alternate source for the local tsunami, most probably a large landslide triggered by the seismic event, and for which OKAL et al. (2003b) proposed a model with a volume of 200 km^3, allowing a satisfactory match to the surveyed run-up amplitudes. While anecdotal evidence exists, reported by elderly fishermen, to support the landslide hypothesis, a definitive identification is still lacking in the local bathymetry, and would require a modern mapping effort in this respect. Note, finally, that because of its much shorter wavelengths and extremely slow source process, any landslide source fails to propagate efficiently to the far field, where it has little effect on the distribution of run-up at distant receiving shores.

The reassessment of the seismic source of the 1946 event by LÓPEZ and OKAL (2006) raises interesting questions in the local seismotectonic context. First, it requires a bilateral rupture of approximately 200 km along the Eastern Aleutian arc, which eliminates the so-called "Unimak gap" between the presumed Eastern extent of the 1957 Andreanof rupture, and the previously recognized fault area of the 1946 earthquake. To the East, the fault zone of the 1946 earthquake does not necessarily extend over the Shumagin gap. The latter remains a potential zone for a future large earthquake, although such an event may not necessarily duplicate the catastrophic earthquakes of 1788 in the Shumagin–Kodiak segment of the trench (SOLOV'EV, 1968), given the known variability in rupture length among large events of a given subduction zone (ANDO, 1975).

The same variability would suggest that not all large earthquakes along the Unimak segment—past and future—share the characteristics of size and slowness of the 1946 event. This may help explain

the apparent discrepancy between the large size of the 1946 earthquake and the lack of evidence from geodetic data for a locked contact along its rupture zone in what could be the very early stages of a long interseismic cycle (MANN and FREYMUELLER, 2003).

8. Kamchatka, 04 November 1952—The Cloaked Killer

With a moment estimated at 3.5×10^{29} dyn*cm (KANAMORI, 1976), the 1952 Kamchatka earthquake was, at the time, the largest seismic event recorded instrumentally, and remains to this day the fourth largest. With significant progress (BENIOFF, 1935) in long-period instrumentation in the 1930s, BENIOFF (1958) was, indeed, able to propose the first detection of the Earth's fundamental free oscillation, $_0S_2$, on a Pasadena strainmeter record of the event, a claim later validated (not without certain qualifications) by KANAMORI (1976). A strong tsunami was generated, causing close to one million 1952-dollars in damage in Hawaii, but fortunately no deaths.

Because of the absence of casualties in the far field, this event was often perceived as involving a deceptive tsunami, as no reports were available from the near field. The 1952 Kamchatka tsunami was, in fact, a closely guarded state secret in the then-USSR, especially since we now know that it had eradicated the sensitive naval base at Severo-Kuril'sk. After the fall of the Soviet Union in 1991, information started to slowly trickle out in the form either of dissemination abroad of existing reports (e.g., SAVARENSKIY et al., 1958), or of studies resulting from new research into this matter (KAISTRENKO and SEDAEVA, 2001). Among the latter, SMYSHLYAEV (2003) reported 7,802 civilian deaths in the Northern Kurils, and estimated that the total death toll in the city of Severo-Kuril'sk, including military casualties, must have reached 10,000 and perhaps as high as 17,000, making the event by far the deadliest tsunami in the twentieth century.

9. Chile, 22 May 1960—Still in a Class by Itself

With a moment estimated anywhere from 2 to 5 times 10^{30} dyn*cm, the 1960 Chilean earthquake remains the largest seismic event recorded instrumentally and studied quantitatively (CIFUENTES and SILVER, 1989). It is also the last one whose tsunami exported destruction and death across the entire Pacific Basin, all the way to Japan, where it claimed 142 lives.

In Hawaii, the tsunami totally destroyed the waterfront district of the city of Hilo, inflicting 20 million 1960-dollars worth of damage, and causing 61 deaths. A most unfortunate aspect of this episode is that the combination of reports from the epicentral area and an assessment by scientists at the Honolulu Geomagnetic Observatory and the Hawaii Volcano Observatory, had led to a warning at 18:47 local time (9.5 h after origin time), resulting in a call for evacuation at 20:30 for an expected arrival time around midnight local time. As detailed by EATON et al. (1961), after the first wave reached Hilo around 00:13 (local time; 23 May) with a benign run-up on the order of 1.5 m, the alarm was not maintained, and the much larger third wave ran up 12 m and penetrated 1 km in land at 01:05 on 23 May, devastating the waterfront area.

The lesson to be learned from the Hilo disaster in 1960 is that the maximum wave during a distant tsunami is rarely the first one. The very long periods of the phenomenon (typically 40 mn or longer) can give a sense of security to residents—and to civil defense authorities who will be tempted to sound an all clear—even though the worst is yet to come. This situation was to be dramatically repeated in Crescent City, California, four years later during the Good Friday Alaskan tsunami.

The exceptional size of the 1960 Chilean earthquake led to a paradox, first outlined by KANAMORI (1977a), as the combination of the slip released during the event (at least 20 m), and the perceived recurrence rate of catastrophic earthquakes along the Central Chilean subduction zone (125 years) leads to a rate of seismic release (16 cm/year) greater than inverted from global kinematic models of plate motions (11 cm/year) or, in other words, to a seismic efficiency along the plate boundary >100%. This inconsistency was eventually resolved from paleotsunami studies (CISTERNAS et al., 2005) which showed that most predecessors of the 1960 earthquake were actually of smaller size, and could not be considered as equivalent instances in the seismic cycle, illustrating once again the ANDO (1975) model of randomness in the sequences of earthquake ruptures at subduction zones.

10. Alaska, 28 March 1964—The Concept of Directivity

This earthquake (which occurred on Good Friday, 27 March at its epicenter) is the largest ever to hit the United States. Its moment, assessed at 8.2×10^{29} dyn*cm by KANAMORI (1970) using 250-s surface waves, may feature a longer component to its source (NETTLES et al., 2005), and is essentially in a tie with the 2004 Sumatra earthquake for second-largest seismic moment ever measured. It generated a tsunami which killed 124 people (as opposed to only 15 from the earthquake). The event resulted in the creation of the Alaska/West Coast Tsunami Warning Center in 1967.

In the near field, the detailed effects of the tsunami were enhanced by a number of local landslides (HAEUSSLER et al., 2007). In the far field, the tsunami did considerable damage and caused 12 deaths in Crescent City, California. Even though a warning had been issued and an evacuation ordered, the residents acquired a sense of safety after the first two waves, and several returned to their houses to start the process of clean-up. The third wave, running up to 7 m in the middle of the night (1:40 a.m. local time), caused more destruction and killed the majority of the victims. By contrast, no victims were to be claimed in Hawaii, where the tsunami did cause some flooding.

The earthquake also gave rise to significant seiches in estuaries along the Gulf of Mexico (DONN, 1964), which McGARR (1965) modeled theoretically as locally excited by Love and Rayleigh waves of exceptional amplitudes but of conventional periods. Such oscillations are, however, unrelated to the tsunami, since similar effects have been observed in the far field for continental earthquakes (KVALE, 1955; BARBEROPOULOU et al., 2006).

The onslaught of the tsunami in the far field (towards the North American coastline from British Columbia to California) featured a geographic distribution different from that of the 1946 event, which was aimed at the Central Pacific. In a landmark contribution, BEN-MENAHEM and ROSENMAN (1972) showed that this could be explained by directivity resulting from the spatial extent of the source. Using the formalism introduced by BEN-MENAHEM (1961) to explain the directivity pattern of seismic surface waves, and the 600-km fault line suggested by KANAMORI (1970), but allowing for the slow phase velocities of tsunamis (at most 220 m/s) relative to the rupture velocities along fault lines [typically 3 km/s, and at least 1 km/s for even the slowest ruptures (POLET and KANAMORI, 2000)], BEN-MENA-HEM and ROSENMAN (1972) explained that tsunamis are of maximum amplitude in the direction perpendicular to the fault strike (the only one for which the interference between the various source segments along the fault can be constructive). This, of course, was different in 1946 and 1964, due to the curvature of the Alaska–Aleutian arc. OKAL and TALANDIER (1991) later showed that the width of the directivity lobe decreases with increasing earthquake size.

This concept of source directivity, first introduced in the wake of the 1964 Good Friday tsunami, is crucial to understanding the long range propagation of tsunamis. For example, it readily explains the extreme amplitudes of the 2004 Sumatra tsunami in Somalia, as opposed to Southern Africa (and of course Australia), and suggests that a future large Mentawai tsunami would not share the directivity pattern of 2004, with the results that different far-field shores would find themselves at maximum risk (OKAL and SYNOLAKIS, 2008).

11. Petatlan, Mexico, 14 March 1979; Gulf of Alaska, 30 November 1987 and 06 March 1988

On the Long Road to DART Sensors

The 1979 Petatlan event was a relatively moderate subduction earthquake ($M_0 = 1.7 \times 10^{27}$ dyn*cm) which generated a minor tsunami with a run-up of 1.3 m in Acapulco. What makes it remarkable is that it produced the first ever recording of a tsunami in deep water, on a pressure sensor deployed on the ocean floor 981 km away from the epicenter, at the

entrance to the Gulf of California, during a seafloor magnetotelluric experiment (FILLOUX, 1982). This observation led to the development of ocean-bottom pressure recorders specifically engineered as tsunami detectors (BERNARD and MILBURN, 1985), which, coupled with real-time communications, later resulted in the Deep-Ocean Assessment and Reporting of Tsunamis (DART) network.

The first detections by long-term DART prototypes were obtained off the Alaska peninsula from tsunamis generated by the Gulf of Alaska intraplate earthquakes of 1987 and 1988 (GONZÁLEZ et al., 1991). Despite the low seismic moment of these events (8×10^{26} and 4×10^{27} dyn*cm, respectively), their tsunamis were recorded in deep water with equivalent surface amplitudes of 1–3 cm, on the same order of magnitude as suggested by preliminary numerical simulations using the SWAN code (MADER, 1998). These successful detections and interpretations of tsunami signals motivated the later development of the full DART real-time algorithm (GONZÁLEZ et al., 1998).

In retrospect, an additional interesting aspect of the detection of the tsunamis generated by the 1987–1988 Alaska Bight earthquakes is that these had strike-slip mechanisms. Conventional wisdom suggests that this geometry produces no vertical displacement of the ocean floor and hence should not generate tsunamis. However, when investigated under WARD'S (1980, 1981) application of normal mode theory, strike-slip geometries are found to be relatively efficient tsunami generators. OKAL (2008) has explained this paradox by noting that a strike-slip fault contributes to static vertical ground motion through zones of deformation located at the tips of the fault. Other strike-slip events having generated detectable tsunamis include the Macquarie earthquake of 23 December 2004 (OKAL and MACAYEAL, 2006).

12. Nicaragua, 02 September 1992

First Digital Age "Tsunami Earthquake" and the Initiation of Systematic Surveys

This event represents the first "tsunami earthquake" for which digital data allows a modern investigation of its seismic source. The earthquake was characterized by an exceptional discrepancy between its body-wave magnitude, $m_b = 5.3$, and its conventional surface-wave magnitude, $M_s = 7.2$, with a Harvard CMT of $M_0 = 3.4 \times 10^{27}$ dyn*cm. As a result of this deficiency in high-frequency body waves, the earthquake was not felt in many sections of the Nicaraguan coast, thus depriving the population of any natural tsunami warning. The tsunami arrived 40 min later, running up to 9.9 m, causing considerable damage, and killing more than 160 persons.

This tragedy renewed interest in the so-called "tsunami earthquakes", defined by KANAMORI (1972) as events whose tsunamis are stronger than would be expected from their conventional seismic magnitudes. The availability of high-quality data from digital networks allowed detailed studies of the seismic source, which documented extremely slow rupture velocities leading to destructive interference in the high-frequency part of the source spectrum (KANAMORI and KIKUCHI, 1993; VELASCO et al., 1994), and later interpreted as expressing an irregular rupture over a jagged plate interface resulting from sediment starvation (TANIOKA et al., 1997; POLET and KANAMORI, 2000).

In the wake of this event (and of similar "tsunami earthquakes" in 1994 in Java, and in 1996 at Chimbote, Peru), NEWMAN and OKAL (1998) introduced a slowness parameter, $\Theta = -\log_{10} E^E/M_0$, comparing the estimated energy E^E carried by high-frequency seismic body waves, to the seismic moment M_0 measured on long-period surface waves. This parameter, inspired by BOATWRIGHT and CHOY'S (1986) quantification of seismic energy, is expected to be an invariant for earthquakes whose sources follow seismic scaling laws; on the other hand, typical "tsunami earthquakes" feature deficiencies in Θ of 1–2 logarithmic units. The slowness parameter can be computed in real-time using robust algorithms which have been implemented at the warning centers (WEINSTEIN and OKAL, 2005). The 1992 Nicaragua earthquake was also remarkable for its deficient T phases, which similarly led OKAL et al. (2003a) to define a discriminant quantifying the ratio of their energy flux to seismic moment.

The substantial low-frequency component of the 1992 Nicaragua earthquake was noted on its seismograms in the form of an ultra-long period oscillation taking place between P and Rayleigh waves by KANAMORI (1993), who identified it as energy multiply reflected in the upper mantle, and hence baptized it "W" phase, by analogy with whistling radioelectric modes in the atmosphere. Despite early investigations (OKAL, 1993), it would not be until the 2004 Sumatra earthquake that the potential of the W phase would be realized for providing an early estimate of the size of seismic sources at the longest seismic periods (KANAMORI and RIVERA, 2008).

The 1992 Nicaragua tsunami also inaugurated the era of systematic surveying in the wake of major tsunamis (SYNOLAKIS and OKAL, 2005), in order to build comprehensive, homogeneous databases of horizontal and vertical inundation, which can be later used for numerical modeling. The Nicaragua survey documented substantial values of run-up (8–10 m) along a 290-km stretch of coastline (ABE et al., 1993), which turned out to be impossible to model using the then-standard simulation algorithms, which consisted of stopping the calculation at a shallow, but arbitrary, water depth (typically 5–10 m), and of considering the coastline as a fully reflecting boundary (IMAMURA et al., 1993). In such computations, the tsunami waves were as much as one order of magnitude smaller than the surveyed values. This discrepancy pointed out the crucial effect of the interaction of the tsunami with the shore, and motivated the development of a prototype computational algorithm, modeling the penetration by the wave over initially dry land, which was able to successfully reproduce the surveyed values (TITOV and SYNOLAKIS, 1993), and which later matured into the MOST code (TITOV and SYNOLAKIS, 1998).

13. Mexico, 09 October 1995—Validating the Leading Depression Wave

This earthquake remains moderate by the standards of mega-earthquakes ($M_0 = 1.15 \times 10^{28}$ dyn*cm), but it generated the largest tsunami along the Mexican coast since the 1932 series, along essentially the same stretch of shore. Run-up was surveyed in the 5-m range along a 200-km stretch of coastline, with a splash on a cliff locally reaching a height of 10.9 m (BORRERO et al., 1997).

The field survey was remarkable in that it documented for the first time (with evidence recorded in the form of a photograph) the systematic initial withdrawal of the sea at a local beach upon arrival of the tsunami. Such a "leading depression" wave had been predicted theoretically by TADEPALLI and SYNOLAKIS (1994, 1996), and challenged the paradigm of a soliton model, in the expected geometry of an interplate thrust fault. Beyond providing a welcome experimental validation to the theory, this observation predicts that in the most widely expected geometry of an inter-plate thrust fault, the local beach will benefit from a natural warning to the population at risk in the form of an initial down-draw, which should be inherently benign to individuals on the shore.

Note, however, that the characteristic of tsunami waves in this framework, fortunate from the standpoint of warning and mitigation, suffers from several significant limitations: (1) it obviously does not apply in the far-field where the polarities of the wave are expected to be inverted; (2) an initial down-draw may be dangerous at sea, e.g., boats in harbors may be slammed against the bottom, and water intake activities, crucial, for example, to the safety of nuclear plants, may face starvation; and (3) not all tsunamigenic earthquakes are interplate thrusts, even in subduction provinces. In the case of outer rise normal faults, the polarity of the tsunami would obviously be reversed, as was the case, for example, during the 1933 Showa Sanriku earthquake.

14. Papua New Guinea, 17 July 1998—Landslides on Front Stage

This moderate earthquake ($M_0 = 3.7 \times 10^{26}$ dyn*cm) took place along the subduction zone separating the Australian plate and the Caroline fragment of the Pacific plate. It generated a locally catastrophic tsunami which eradicated several villages in the vicinity of Sissano Lagoon, with a death toll of 2,300. Field work in the area (SYNOLAKIS et al., 2002)

revealed a number of singular properties: (1) the run-up on the shore (at this location a perfectly linear coastline) reached 15 m, an excessive value given the slip on the fault, suggested to be around 1 m by seismic scaling laws; (2) the large run-up values were concentrated on a stretch of coastline not exceeding 25 km, and fell quickly to benign values outside that segment; (3) the tsunami was locally lethal but recorded only at decimetric amplitudes in Japan. All these observations suggested a break-down of the scaling laws governing the excitation of tsunamis by seismic sources, as expressed later theoretically by OKAL and SYNOLAKIS (2004), and thus required a different mechanism for the generation of the tsunami.

The case was cracked by witness reports of a delay in the arrival of the wave, which ruled out generation of the tsunami by the main seismic shock. Examination of hydroacoustic records at a number of hydrophone and seismic stations in the Pacific Basin identified an event occurring 13 min after the mainshock with an epicenter located inside an underwater amphitheater (OKAL, 2003), which was interpreted as a 4-km^3 landslide triggered (with a slight delay) by the main shock. Although they could obviously not be dated to this precision, fresh landslide debris were identified during oceanographic cruises (SWEET and SILVER, 2003), using both seismic reflection and direct visualization from a remotely operated vehicle. Finally, numerical hydrodynamic modeling of the tsunami using the landslide source provided a good fit to the surveyed run-up (HEINRICH et al., 2000; SYNOLAKIS et al., 2002).

This identification of a landslide as the source of a locally catastrophic tsunami, triggered by a moderate earthquake, acted to sensitize the tsunami community to the hazard posed by these specific sources. They present a particular challenge since the Papua New Guinea case showed that landslides can be triggered by relatively small earthquakes, which are not limited to large subduction zones, but could occur in a wide spectrum of tectonic environments. In particular, in Southern California, a number of offshore faults have a history of hosting earthquakes with $M = 6–7$, accounting for as much as 20% of the shear between the North American and Pacific plates (DEMETS and DIXON, 1999). In addition to having, themselves, the potential for a locally damaging tsunami, the largest events among them could be responsible for triggering the large landslides documented in the bathymetry (EDWARDS et al., 1993; LEGG and KAMERLING, 2003; LOCAT et al., 2004), whose recurrence could generate tsunamis running up to as much as 15 m on nearby coasts (BORRERO et al., 2001).

15. Vanuatu, 26 November 1999—Education Works!

This relatively moderate earthquake ($M_0 = 1.7 \times 10^{27}$ dyn*cm) shook the central islands of Vanuatu and was accompanied by a number of sub-aerial and underwater landslides; it generated a local tsunami, which was damaging on the islands of Pentecost and Ambryn (PELLETIER et al., 2000).

What makes the event noteworthy is the history of the village of Baie Martelli on the southern coast of Pentecost (CAMINADE et al., 2000). Following the 1998 Papua New Guinea disaster, a video program had been shown in the local language on battery-operated television sets, explaining the natural origin of tsunamis, and stressing the need to immediately self-evacuate low-lying areas upon feeling strong earthquake tremors, especially if accompanied by a recess of the sea. Just a few months later, the earthquake struck in the middle of the night, and a villager reported a down-draw. The village chief then ordered an immediate full evacuation. The tsunami completely destroyed the village, but fortunately, of the 300 residents, only three lost their lives: two elderly invalids who could not be evacuated and a drunken man, who refused to leave.

The lesson from this event is simple: Education works!

16. Aleutian Islands, 17 November 2003

First Operational Use of DART Sensor in Real Time

This event represents the first successful operational use of DART buoys in real time. The seismic epicenter (51.14°N, 177.86°E) was only 450 km west of that of 07 May 1986 (51.33°N, 175.43°W), an event which had triggered a false alarm at the Pacific Tsunami Warning Center, resulting in the evacuation of the Waikiki beaches and district in Honolulu, at an estimated cost to the local economy of 40 million 1986-dollars (BERNARD et al., 2006). The 2003 event was, however of smaller seismic moment ($M_0 = 5.3 \times 10^{27}$ dyn*cm as opposed to 1.04×10^{28} dyn*cm).

At the time of the 2003 event, the algorithm later described by TITOV et al. (2005) was operational at PMEL. After the earthquake occurred at 06:43 GMT, a tsunami advisory was issued by PTWC and a regional warning for the Aleutian Islands by ATWC, at 07:09. The tsunami was received at the recently deployed DART buoy Number D-171 at 07:50 with an equivalent amplitude of 2 cm. Based on pre-computed far-field tsunami amplitudes for a database of sources in the Aleutians, expected wave heights were then estimated for the Hawaiian Islands, including a benign value of only 11 cm at Hilo. On this basis, the tsunami warning was cancelled at 08:12 (MCCREERY, 2005). The tsunami reached Hilo at 12:00 GMT with a maximum amplitude of 17 cm, only slightly higher than the simulation performed 4 h earlier.

Because the tsunami was, in the end, benign in Hawaii, and no evacuation had been mandated, its successful quantitative prediction did not attract much publicity among the general public. Nevertheless, based on the experience in 1986, and allowing for inflation, it is estimated that the cancellation of what would have become a false alarm saved 67 million 2003-dollars. In this respect, it can be stated that the whole DART program, as it existed in 2003, paid for itself during this one event. The coordinated performance of PMEL and PTWC on that occasion must be regarded as an astounding success. It remains to be hoped that it will be as seamless, and will lead to saving lives through a successful evacuation, when the next dangerous transpacific tsunami strikes in the future.

17. Sumatra–Andaman, 26 December 2004— Deadliest in Recorded History

With a death toll generally estimated between 250,000 and 300,000, the 2004 Sumatra earthquake unleashed the deadliest tsunami in recorded history and probably in the whole history of mankind. Among its many aspects, which have been described in detail in countless publications, we will retain the following, which have arguably changed the outlook of the community on both the scientific and operational aspects of tsunami mitigation.

17.1. The Earthquake Occurred Where It Was Not Expected

Prior to the 2004 earthquake, our perception of the largest earthquake possible on any subduction zone was governed by a seminal model proposed by RUFF and KANAMORI (1980). These authors had argued that a combination of age of subducted lithosphere and rate of convergence at the boundary adequately predicts the maximum earthquake observed in the seismic or historical record at individual subduction zones. The rationale behind their model was that an increased lithospheric age would make the subducting plate colder, and hence heavier, thereby helping subduction and decreasing the coupling at the interface, while on the other hand, an increase in convergence rate would enhance coupling. Based on a compilation of events recorded at 21 subduction zones, they claimed an impressive 80% correlation between observed maximum magnitudes and those predicted by their model.

According to RUFF and KANAMORI's (1980) model, the northern Sumatra subduction zone should have featured a maximum magnitude of 8.2, corresponding to a moment of 2.5×10^{28} dyn*cm. The 2004 earthquake was about 40 times larger. Furthermore, STEIN and OKAL (2007) showed that, over 25 years, progress in estimates of convergence rates, lithospheric ages and moments of historical earthquakes, actually decreased the correlation between maximum earthquakes observed and predicted by Ruff and Kanamori's model to about 35%, a value which becomes statistically insignificant (essentially, there are more subduction zones violating the paradigm than there are following it).

In this respect, the 2004 Sumatra event is a lesson in humility: we must accept that we cannot rule out mega-earthquakes at a subduction zone simply on the basis of its most easily observable physical properties. Alternatively, RUFF (1989) had suggested that sedimentary cover could play a role in sealing the plate contact and enhancing plate coupling, thus favoring large earthquakes. This idea, recently revived by SCHOLL et al. (2007), has merit, but suffers from significant exceptions, e.g., Southern Peru and Northern Chile (STEIN and OKAL, 2007). Thus, the precautionary conclusion is that the maximum earthquake size on any given subduction zone may be constrained only by the maximum length over which a coherent fault rupture may develop. As discussed above (Sect. 4), the determination of that maximum length may itself be far from trivial.

17.2. However, Predecessors Existed

The largest events known prior to 2004 along the Northern Sumatra–Andaman boundary were the Car Nicobar earthquake of 31 December 1881, and the Andaman event of 26 June 1941. ORTíz and BILHAM (2003) reassessed the seismic moment of the former as $M_0 = 9 \times 10^{27}$ dyn*cm based on Indian maregraph records. The latter was assigned a very high magnitude, $M = 8.7$, by GUTENBERG and RICHTER (1954), certainly an excessive figure given BRUNE and ENGEN's (1969) later study of its 100-s Love waves, for which they proposed $M_{100} = 8.0$, which KANAMORI (1977b) later expressed as a much smaller $M_w = 7.6$. A reassessment of this event based on inversion of mantle waves at four stations in the $100 - 200$ s period range, using the PDFM method (OKAL and REYMOND, 2003) yields $M_0 \approx 3 \times 10^{28}$ dyn*cm. Thus, the only quantified large events in that province were clearly much smaller than the 2004 earthquake.

By contrast, and further South, ZACHARIASEN et al. (1999) had documented the exceptional size ($M_0 = 6 \times 10^{29}$ dyn*cm) of the 1833 Central Sumatra event, based on the inversion of coral uplift data in the Mentawai Islands. However, their results were limited to the central section of Sumatra, and in the absence of a similar study to the North of Mentawai, the potential for a mega-earthquake in the Northern Sumatra–Andaman province was not realized before 2004. In retrospect, the newly quantified 1833 event was one more example of a violation of RUFF and KANAMORI's (1980) paradigm.

In the aftermath of the 2004 disaster, paleoseismic data from the Andaman Islands and the Eastern coast of India suggested the identification of predecessors with a recurrence time on the order of 1,000 years (RAJENDRAN *et al.*, 2007). More recently, JANKAEW *et al.* (2008) and MONECKE *et al.* (2008) used tsunami deposits from excavations in marshy swales in Southern Thailand and Northern Sumatra to date the last two predecessors of the 2004 event at about 600 and 1,100 years B.P.

This discussion illustrates, if need be, the incomplete character of our command of the seismic record concerning mega-earthquakes in provinces featuring recurrence times greater than a few centuries, but also the significant promise of paleotsunami studies in this respect. There remains the practical fact that the incentive to initiate such valuable research projects will often come only after a destructive tsunami. While Cascadia (see Sect. 2 above) constitutes a remarkable exception to the trend, sedimentologists will know where to start digging only in the aftermath of a major disaster.

17.3. The Failure to Warn was a Failure of Communication More than of Science

While a considerable death toll was reported in Sumatra, which was hit as little as 20 min after the initiation of rupture (H_0), the numbers were catastrophic in Thailand (reached at $H_0 + 01:30$; 5,000 deaths), Sri Lanka ($H_0 + 02:00$; 31,000 deaths), India ($H_0 + 02: 30$; 16,000 deaths) and Somalia ($H_0 + 07:30$; 300 deaths). Even Tanzania ($H_0 + 09:30$; at least 20 deaths) and South Africa ($H_0 + 11:30$; 2 deaths) suffered casualties. Such travel times should have allowed the issuance of warnings and, in turn, the protection of the populations at risk through evacuation. In this context, it is worth retracing why no warning was issued.

The initial estimates of the moment M_0 of the earthquake were deficient, and expectedly so. The first estimates, obtained at ($H_0 + 00:15$), were in the range of 1.2×10^{28} dyn*cm, revised around ($H_0 + 01:00$) to about 7×10^{28} dyn*cm. The value listed in the global CMT catalogue (3.95×10^{29} dyn*cm) required a customized processing at longer periods (300 s) than the routine algorithm then allowed, and

was available at ($H_0 + 04:20$). The final seismic estimates of the moment ($\sim 10^{30}$ dyn*cm) required the analysis of the Earth's free oscillations and were obtained one month after the event (STEIN and OKAL, 2005); a composite, authoritative and customized multiple source inversion at very long periods was finalized in the Spring of 2005 (TSAI *et al.*, 2005). Such delays in the assessment of the long-period characteristics of the earthquake source are expected for mega-earthquakes when only conventional methods are used in real time to retrieve its seismic moment, since source finiteness has long been known to result in primarily destructive interference for all types of standard seismic waves (BEN-MENAHEM, 1961; GELLER, 1976).

The use of alternate strategies to infer the low-frequency or static value of M_0, such as duration of high-frequency P waves (NI *et al.*, 2005), W phases (KANAMORI and RIVERA, 2008), or even possibly geodetic data (BLEWITT *et al.*, 2009), may significantly improve warning times. However, one must keep in mind that mega-earthquakes are expected from scaling laws to feature extremely long sources (in practice 600 s for the 2004 Sumatra event). It is clear that when the duration of the earthquake becomes comparable to, or even conceivably greater than, the travel time of the tsunami to the nearest beach, accurate predictions in the near field are inherently impossible. Once again, near-field mitigation must rely on direct evacuation by personally motivated, and therefore educated, individuals.

But the point remains that the estimate available 1 h after H_0, $M_0 = 7 \times 10^{28}$ dyn*cm (incidentally, the largest moment ever computed at the warning centers), was already sufficient to have triggered a basin-wide tsunami alarm, had it involved the Pacific Basin, for which an algorithm was in place at the Pacific Tsunami Warning Center (PTWC). Such an alarm would certainly have helped mitigate the human disaster in Sri Lanka and beyond, and possibly even in Thailand.

It is worth repeating that there existed at the time no tsunami warning system in the Indian Ocean, and that PTWC was not, in 2004, charged with the issuance of warnings for that ocean. The center had no client to whom to send a warning, especially since it was Christmas Day in Honolulu, and Sunday,

Boxing Day, in the Indian Ocean. In short, this was the wrong time for what amounted to leafing through the yellow pages in search of an adequate contact. There can be no room for improvisation in an emergency situation. This absence of established communication protocol at the time of the event remains the major reason for the failure to provide a useful warning in the far field.

17.4. Some People Escaped, but Tsunami Exposure is a Worldwide Threat

Notwithstanding the horrible death toll, it is worth mentioning here several cases of successful evacuation during the Sumatra tsunami. First, there were no reported casualties among the Sentinelese people of the Andaman Islands, who live essentially in the Stone Age. Apparently alone among the residents of the epicentral areas, they spontaneously evacuated to higher ground upon feeling the earthquake. Perhaps because their culture had not been displaced by outside influences resulting from the explosion of information technology, they were able to keep the ancestral memory of tsunamis for at least 20 generations, in practice long enough to span what we now know to be the exceptionally long recurrence time of mega-earthquakes along the Northern Sumatra Subduction zone (JANKAEW et al., 2008).

The story of Tilly Smith, the 10-year old British school girl vacationing in Phuket, Thailand, who identified the impending tsunami and triggered an evacuation which probably saved 100 lives, based on a geography class she had been taught at school only two weeks before, has been publicized all over the world press. A significant ingredient in her story is the presence of a Japanese person in the hotel staff who relayed the warning, and who was himself culturally educated about tsunamis.

Finally, one of the most remarkable stories is that of our colleague Professor Chris Chapman, a specialist in theoretical seismology, who was at the time staying as a tourist at a beachfront hotel in Ahangulla, Sri Lanka (CHAPMAN, 2005). Intrigued by the first (and small) positive wave, he correctly deduced that it had to have been generated by an earthquake, and together with his wife, warned the hotel manager of impending danger. When the much larger recess of

the sea took place 20 min later, the hotel staff, again warned by the Chapmans, ordered vertical evacuation of the beach area before the onslaught of the second wave, another 20 min later. Despite a few close calls, no lives were lost among guests or staff of the hotel.

These three stories, among many others, exemplify once again the value of education, and illustrate that it can take diverse forms: ancestral, schooling, and professional.

Another lesson learned from the 2004 tsunami is that, in a world where vacationers travel vast distances away from their homeland, geological hazards such as tsunamis are not the exclusive concern of countries located in zones at risk: Sweden, for example, lost 428 people (mostly tourists) to the 2004 disaster, or about one in 21,000 of its citizens, a figure strikingly similar to the world-wide statistic (250,000 victims for a 5.5-billion population of the planet). This remark stresses that tsunami education knows no frontiers and must be a world-wide effort, especially in developed countries where long-reach travel is common for business or vacation.

17.5. A Tsunami is a Global Physical Phenomenon Involving the Whole Earth as a System

The 2004 Sumatra tsunami was so big that it was recorded by many instruments which had not been designed for that purpose. Such apparently anecdotal situations were often the result of a subtle coupling between the ocean, in which the tsunami is developed, and other media such as the atmosphere and the solid Earth. As such, they point to interesting physical concepts which may bear some promise in terms of the potential use of unsuspected technologies in the context of tsunami warning. In other instances, the tsunami was recorded outside of its classical technical domain, underlying some known but hitherto undetected properties. We itemize the following observations:

17.5.1 Satellite Altimetry

The 2004 Sumatra tsunami was recorded by a number of satellite altimeters, most notably Jason-1 (GOWER, 2005). While OKAL et al. (1999) had reported a similar recording of the 1992 Nicaragua tsunami by the ERS-1 satellite, its amplitude, a mere 8 cm on the high seas, was at the limit of the noise level. The amplitude of the 2004 Jason-1 signal, 70 cm zero-to-peak, and its sharpness provide irrefutable evidence of the concept. This measurement is crucial because it matches the numerical simulations in the far field (e.g., TITOV et al., 2005) and thus validates them for the first time against a direct observation of the deformation of the surface of the ocean, rather than through the convoluted, if legitimate, detection by sea–floor pressure sensors (GONZÁLEZ et al., 1998), until then the only available measurement of a tsunami on the high seas.

Unfortunately, satellite altimetry bears little promise of useful contribution to future tsunami warning systems, as it requires intensive and time-consuming data processing, and above all, the presence of a satellite at the right place at the right time. In this respect, the availability of altimeter satellites over the Bay of Bengal in the hours following the Sumatra event was nothing short of a lucky coincidence.

17.5.2 IMS Hydrophones

The Sumatra tsunami was recorded by hydrophones of the International Monitoring System (IMS) of the Comprehensive Nuclear-Test Ban Treaty Organization (CTBTO), notably at Diego Garcia (HANSON and BOWMAN, 2005). These instruments are pressure detectors floating in the SOFAR channel and tethered through the ocean bottom to a nearby shore station (OKAL, 2001). Since they were designed to detect underwater explosions, they include a hard-wired high-pass filter with a corner frequency of 10 Hz, and it is remarkable that they recorded conventional tsunami waves traveling under the shallow-water approximation (SWA) with periods of $\sim 1,800$ s. More importantly, they provided the first record in the far field of the full tsunami branch, dispersed outside the SWA, down to periods of ~ 70 s. OKAL et al. (2007) showed that the corresponding spectral amplitudes around 10 mHz could be modeled quantitatively using the formalism describing a tsunami as a special branch of spheroidal free oscillations of the Earth (WARD, 1980). The conventional frequencies, while observed, could not be modeled quantitatively,

as the response of the instrumental filter had lessened their signal to less than one digital unit (OKAL et al. 2007).

This first modeling of the high-frequency components of the tsunami is important because surveys on the Western shore of the Indian Ocean Basin have revealed that in several ports (Le Port, Réunion; Toamasina, Madagascar; Salalah, Oman; and tentatively Dar-es-Salaam, Tanzania), strong currents developed (with large ships breaking their moorings and damaging or threatening infrastructure), several hours after the passage of the conventional tsunami (OKAL et al., 2006b, c, d, 2009). Preliminary modeling for Toamasina has shown that the phenomenon results from the harbor being set in resonance at a period of 105 s, precisely upon arrival of the relevant component of the tsunami, delayed by its dispersion outside the SWA (PANČOŠKOVÁ et al., 2006). The successful modeling of 10-mHz energy on the Diego Garcia hydrophone record shows that one can predict quantitatively the timing and amplitude of the resonant component threatening a distant port, paving the way for realistic simulation models in advance of future tsunamis.

17.5.3 Ionospheric Detection

Shortly before the Sumatra tsunami, ARTRU et al. (2005) had shown, notably in the case of the 2001 Peru tsunami, that there exists an ionospheric signal accompanying tsunami propagation in the far field. The idea behind this phenomenon, suggested nearly 40 years ago by HINES (1972) and detailed by PELTIER and HINES (1976), is that the tsunami wave is prolonged into the atmosphere at the ocean surface, which is not a "free" boundary with a vacuum, but merely one between two fluids, the upper one simply having a considerably lesser density. Because of the rapid rarefaction of the atmosphere with height, the amplitude of the particle motion of the tsunami's continuation in the atmosphere can actually grow with altitude, to the extent that a 10-cm tsunami on the ocean could induce kilometric oscillations of the bottom of the ionosphere, at 150 km altitude. The latter can be detected and mapped using perturbations in GPS signals traversing the ionosphere, and recorded at dense arrays, such as the Japanese GEONET (Artru et al., 2005).

Ionospheric detection was repeated during the 2004 Sumatra tsunami (Liu et al., 2006) and Occhipinti et al. (2006) successfully modeled the variation in Total Electron Content observed around 300 km of altitude, by using a numerical simulation of the tsunami at the surface of the ocean as an initial condition for the generation of gravity waves in the atmosphere.

Such observations could bear some promise in terms of application to warning, through the use of techniques such as Over-The-Horizon (OTH) radar, which allow a fully land-based probing of the ionosphere. Furthermore, the approach of Lognonné et al. (1998), which considers a single wave spanning the ocean and its adjoining media (atmosphere and solid Earth), should allow an efficient direct quantification of the relationship between earthquake source, tsunami amplitude and ionospheric oscillations.

17.5.4 Tsunami Shadows

Prior to the 1990s, there existed a number of anecdotal reports of people "sighting" tsunami waves from elevated positions, e.g., lighthouses or flying aircraft (Dudley and Lee, 1998; p. 5), upon their arrival near a shore. Walker (1996) gave them credence by publishing frames from a video made by an amateur standing on a beach in Northern Oahu during the 1994 Kuriles tsunami. Later, Godin (2004) suggested that the phenomenon could be explained through a combination of hydrodynamics and atmospheric physics. Specifically, a shoaling tsunami wave may increase the slope of the ocean surface to the extent that the boundary conditions for atmospheric circulation are modified and can result, in the presence of an appropriate wind, in the development of a turbulent regime in the lowermost layers of the atmosphere. In turn, the turbulence would affect the reflective properties of light rays at the sea surface, making it appear darker and creating the "tsunami shadow".

Following the 2004 tsunami, Godin et al. (2009) studied the amplitude of the signal reflected by the Jason-1 altimeter (see above), and were indeed able to confirm the detection of a "tsunami shadow" in two separate frequency bands.

Godin et al.'s (2009) space-based observation bears little promise for tsunami warning because of the difficulties inherent in sparse spacecraft coverage, as discussed above regarding detection by satellite altimetry. However, land-based techniques such as OTH radar might be used in the future to probe distant ocean surfaces for tsunami shadows.

17.5.5 Infrasound

Le Pichon et al. (2005) reported the observation, on the infrasound array of the IMS/CTBTO at Diego Garcia, of a deep infrasound signal (0.05–0.1 Hz) whose origin they traced to the Southern coast of Myanmar at the time of arrival of the tsunami at that shoreline. It is intriguing that this powerful signal emanated from a location where the amplitude of the tsunami was moderate (maximum run-up: 3 m), and its damage relatively contained (61 reported casualties) (Swe et al., 2006). While no modeling of the generation of the infrasound signal has been proposed to date, these effects may be related to the interaction of the tsunami with the extended continental shelf present offshore of Myanmar.

17.5.6 Tsunami Recorded by Onland Seismometers

Following the Sumatra earthquake, Yuan et al. (2005) made the remarkable observation that the arrival of the tsunami was clearly recorded on horizontal seismograms at island (or coastal continental) stations of the Indian Ocean, filtered in the 0.1–10 mHz band, with amplitudes on the order of a few mm of ground displacement. These results were confirmed by Hanson and Bowman (2005). Okal (2007a) conducted a systematic search of such signals, and showed that they could be recorded worldwide, as long as the receiver was within ~35 km (i.e., 1/10 of a typical tsunami wave length) of an abyssal plain. He further showed that the recording could be interpreted quantitatively by making the radical assumption that the seismometer sat on the ocean floor and recorded not only the small horizontal component of the prolongation of the tsunami eigenfunction into the solid Earth, but also its associated components of tilt and gravity potential (GILBERT, 1980). He further showed that such signals could be detected at a smaller amplitude on vertical seismometers, and also identified during smaller tsunamis.

Such observations open the way, at least in principle, for the use of existing seismic stations as in situ detectors of tsunamis propagating in ocean basins, complementing, in essence, the network of bottom pressure sensors. As described in OKAL (2007a), such recordings are directly representative of the properties of the tsunami on the high seas, as opposed to a maregraphic record which is affected by harbor response. In addition, the deployment and maintenance of seismic stations come at much lower costs than that of DART stations; they require, however, an island environment, and thus can only serve in a complementary role.

Finally, we note that a similar observation had been made at Apia by ANGENHEISTER (1920), following the 1918 Kuriles tsunami. While we recently confirmed the existence of the signal on a copy of the original record, its quantification remains elusive, due to instrumental non-linearity in the relevant seismogram.

17.5.7 Tsunami Recorded by Seismometers on Icebergs

As part of a project investigating the origin of high-frequency tremor in tabular icebergs, OKAL and MACAYEAL (2006) operated portable seismometers during the austral Summer 2004–2005 on two icebergs parked in the Ross Sea, and on a fragment of the Ross Ice Shelf expected to calve in the next few years (Station "Nascent"). These three stations recorded the arrival of the Sumatra tsunami 16 h after the earthquake. OKAL and MACAYEAL (2006) showed that the amplitude of the signal (14 cm peak-to-peak at Nascent) was in agreement with the iceberg just floating like a raft on the ocean surface and thus directly recording the deformation η of the surface upon the passage of the tsunami. What makes this observation remarkable is that the recording was three-dimensional, i.e., that the seismometer caught the horizontal displacement of the iceberg (and hence of the water) as well (133 cm peak-to-peak on the north–south component at Nascent), with the aspect ratio (9.5) of the particle motion in good agreement with the theoretical value predicted in the Shallow-Water Approximation $\left[u_x/u_z = (1/\omega)\sqrt{g/h} \right]$. To our knowledge, this constitutes the first detection of the horizontal motion of a tsunami on the high seas. Since this number is much larger than 1, this observation opens up, at least in principle, the possibility of detecting a tsunami on the high seas in real time by recording (e.g., by GPS) the horizontal drifting of a floating observatory, which could take the form of a DART-type buoy, or simply of a ship in transit whose trajectory could be slightly affected by the passage of the tsunami.

18. Tsunamis Since Sumatra—Have We Become Wiser?

In the aftermath of the 2004 Indian Ocean disaster, "tsunami" has become a household word, and this in itself constitutes a positive development, since it raises worldwide awareness of this form of natural hazard. However, at least nine large tsunamis have followed since 2004, with alarmingly disparate results in terms of the behavior (and eventual death toll) of the populations at risk, of the performance of the warning algorithms, which included both extremes (false alarm and failure to warn), and of the implementation of actual alerts following the issuance of warnings, at least one of which remained unheeded.

We present here a brief report card on these events, aimed at analyzing what constituted a satisfactory, life-saving response or, on the other hand, a clear functional or behavioral failure with a tragic ending. This sort of "wisdom index" is not meant to be quantitative and, in particular, does not simply express the death toll inflicted by the tsunami. Rather, it assesses, in an admittedly subjective way, the performance of both the populations at risk and the decision-makers responsible for issuing and carrying out an alert in mitigation of the tsunami hazard. The events studied are listed in order of decreasing success.

- We award a "Gold" mark to the Bengkulu earthquake of 12 September 2007 (BORRERO *et al.*, 2009). This event featured what was then the third largest solution in the CMT catalog (6.7×10^{28} dyn*cm), and generated a significant local tsunami which caused damage over a 300-km stretch of coastline. Yet, no deaths or injuries were attributed directly to the tsunami. The field survey revealed that the population had correctly self-evacuated upon feeling the earthquake. This happy outcome (probably helped by the timing of the event, 18:10 local time) is an illustration of a successful scenario, proving once again the value of awareness and education among coastal populations. Incidentally, the 2007 event was not the mega-earthquake largely expected to occur in the not-too-distant future in the prolongation of the 2004 and 2005 ruptures (and neither was the tragic Padang intermediate-depth event of 30 September 2009, which did not generate a tsunami). Hence, the Mentawai segment is still ripe for a mega-earthquake which will occur in the future, albeit at an unpredictable date. When it does, it is imperative that the population respond as well as in 2007. Only continued awareness fueled by regular education will achieve this goal.

- We give a bright "Green" mark to the Solomon Islands earthquake of 01 April 2007. This major event ($M_0 = 1.6 \times 10^{28}$ dyn*cm) is remarkable in that its rupture jumped the triple junction between the Pacific, Australia, and Woodlark plates (TAYLOR *et al.*, 2008), re-emphasizing the difficulty of predicting maximum rupture lengths of future large events. It triggered a strong local tsunami which affected more than 300 coastal communities in the Western Solomon Islands. As detailed by FRITZ and KALLIGERIS (2008), only 52 people were killed by the tsunami, despite the destruction of more than 6,000 houses, thanks to spontaneous self-evacuation of the low-lying areas in the minutes following the shaking. This fortunate reflex led to fatality ratios among the population at risk as low as in the case of Baie Martelli, Vanuatu (1999; see Sect. 15). It was motivated by the fresh memory of the 2004 Sumatra disaster, and by ancestral heritage, with the last regional tsunami (17 August 1959) still present in the memory of the village elders. Remarkably, the smaller event of 03 January 2010 ($M_0 = 5.3 \times 10^{26}$ dyn*cm)

generated a tsunami which similarly caused no casualties, despite running up to 5 m on Rendova Island (FRITZ and KALLIGERIS, 2010), once again thanks to self-evacuation by the local population. These tsunamis illustrate the significance of awareness and education in mitigating local tsunami risks.

- We give an "Olive" card to the Nias event of 28 March 2005. This tint, intermediate between green and yellow, reflects positive aspects in the near field, where no victims were attributed to the tsunami, but also the panic generated, in the far field, by a warning which turned out to be a false alarm.

We recall that this earthquake was indeed gigantic ($M_0 = 1.05 \times 10^{29}$ dyn*cm), and took 600 lives in Nias and 100 in Simueleu. Its tsunami was weaker than expected, since a significant fraction of the deformation in the source area involved those large islands ("the earthquake moved a large amount of rock and not much water"). Nevertheless, the local impact of the tsunami was important, but no deaths were definitively attributed to it, largely because of awareness rooted in ancestral tradition, and of the fact that most inhabitants had been relocated away from the beaches in the wake of the 2004 disaster (McADOO *et al.*, 2006).

In the far field, the tsunami was recorded instrumentally, but was too small to be reported by witnesses. This effect was explained by its generation in shallow seas (OKAL and SYNOLAKIS, 2008), and constituted a perfect illustration of GREEN's (1837) law. However, because of the large seismic moment of the Nias earthquake, a tsunami warning had been issued for the entire Indian Ocean Basin, and resulted in a false alarm. In itself, this should not be considered *prima facie* as a failure of the warning process, given the value of precaution and the specific circumstances; after all, the Nias earthquake would have been the largest one in 40 years, but for the 2004 Sumatra event. More ominous was the reaction of distant populations, sensitized to tsunami hazards by the Sumatra disaster only 3 months earlier, who responded to the warning in a chaotic fashion. Six people were killed in traffic accidents that night in Toamasina, Madagascar, during an episode of panic cruising through its streets (OKAL et al., 2006c).

- We give a "Yellow" card to the Kuril Islands tsunami of 15 November 2006. This very large earthquake ($M_0 = 3.5 \times 10^{28}$ dyn*cm; seventh largest in the Global CMT catalogue) expectedly generated a substantial tsunami, which went largely unreported because of the remoteness of the local shores. It took nine months for a surveying party to reach the uninhabited Central Kuril Islands and to document run-up reaching 21 m on Matua Island (MACINNES et al., 2009). As there were no casualties, and no infrastructure to be destroyed, the tsunami was largely ignored by the scientific community. Yet, it attacked Crescent City, California 8.5 h after origin time, and caused significant damage to floating docks and to several boats, another 2.5 h later (DENGLER et al., 2009). Initial estimates of the damage in Crescent City ranged around $700,000, but a full assessment later documented structural damage to the pilings of the floating docks; their reconstruction may cost up to $9 million (DENGLER et al., 2009). Flooding was also reported at several locations in Hawaii.

The performance of the warning centers during the 2006 Kuril tsunami was mediocre: In Hawaii, PTWC cancelled the tsunami warning 2.5 h before the arrival of the wave, the latter causing some local damage, with one swimmer having a very close call. Similarly, WCATWC repeatedly issued statements of "no warning" or "no watch" for California, several hours before the onslaught on Crescent City harbor. Yet, numerical simulation of the tsunami (DENGLER et al., 2008) reproduces the marigram eventually recorded at Crescent City and, in particular, the evolution with time of the amplitude of the wave. The failure to warn may have been influenced by the late character of the seismic source. In a way reminiscent of the 2001 Peru earthquake (WEINSTEIN and OKAL, 2005), the initial rupture corresponds to a smaller source, and the full extent of moment release occurs only 50 s into the

rupture. We describe such sources as "late" or "delayed", as opposed to "slow", since their spectra are not anomalous, and in contrast to truly slow events (e.g., "tsunami earthquakes"), they do not exhibit deficient energy-to-moment ratios when the full extent of their source is analyzed (OKAL, 2007b). It is clear that the recognition of delayed events in real time is a challenge since algorithms analyzing only a fraction of the P waveforms will fail to catch their true size.

In addition, this event points to the lack of awareness in the community at risk (Crescent City) of the singularities in the response of the harbor and, in particular, of the delays in the arrival of the most destructive wavetrains, which may reflect maximum amplitudes or maximum current velocities.

- The tsunami of 15 August 2007 in Peru also gets a "Yellow" card, despite a moderate death toll (only three fatalities attributed to the tsunami). With a moment of 1.1×10^{28} dyn*cm, this earthquake was among the weaker tsunamigenic events in central Peru, being smaller than the 1974 earthquake, and certainly no match for the catastrophic events of 1687 and 1746 (DORBATH et al., 1990; OKAL et al., 2006a). The earthquake caused widespread destruction in the city of Pisco, resulting in more than 500 fatalities. It generated a significant tsunami, which ran up to a maximum of 10 m South of the Paracas Peninsula, with sustained values in the 5–7 m range along a 40-km segment of coastline (FRITZ et al., 2008). Despite such high values, most shoreline villages were successfully evacuated based on a network of Coast Guard sergeants triggering the evacuation upon feeling the earthquake and directing people to pre-arranged shelters, none of which were reached by the tsunami. This episode illustrates the success of an evacuation featuring awareness of the population and a well designed and rehearsed plan originating at the community level, an important point since most local communications had been knocked down by the earthquake.

On the other hand, no evacuation was conducted at the village of Lagunilla, which had no Coast Guard outpost, and where three people lost their lives to the tsunami. This gap in an otherwise well designed and well executed evacuation plan is both regrettable and unexplained.

- The recent Maule, Chile tsunami of 27 February 2010 also earns a "Yellow" card, on account of the alarming diversity of response in both the near and far fields. With a moment of 1.8×10^{29} dyn*cm, this earthquake was the second largest in 46 years, surpassed only by the 2004 Sumatra event, and the first one since 1960 to generate run-up amplitudes of 80 cm in Japan across the whole extent of the Pacific Ocean. Yet, the death toll, probably definitive at the time of writing, is contained to a total of about 500, of which <300 are attributable to the tsunami. No casualties are known outside Chile.

In the near field, a higher death toll was avoided through a reflex of self-evacuation by the local population, thanks to proper education of the coastal community, and despite the night-time occurrence of the disaster. Tragically, the majority of the tsunami victims in coastal Chile were campers trapped with little if any means of escape on Orrego Island in the estuary of the Maule River in Constitución, many of them vacationers from the hinterland with little awareness of tsunami danger (PETROFF, 2010).

By contrast to a largely successful, individually triggered evacuation, the response at the National government level was nothing short of abysmal. The official warning unit of the Chilean Navy failed to issue a tsunami alert, and the President herself dismissed the possibility of the generation of a tsunami in the minutes following the earthquake. In a country with a long history of local tsunamis, common sense should have dictated (as it did to the coastal populations) that a clearly major earthquake of particularly long duration, inflicting significant damage to countless buildings and a total black-out in the capital city of Santiago, had the potential for a dangerous tsunami.

This failure to warn was particularly tragic in the case of the Juan Fernández Islands, located 700 km offshore of central Chile, for which a useful warning could have been issued before the tsunami reached them a little less than 1 h after origin time; its onslaught was catastrophic with run-up reaching 15 m (FRITZ, 2010) and about 30 deaths.

In the far field, warning centers had the luxury of time, allowing the computation of simulated forecasts which correctly predicted that the lobe of tsunami energy would be focused south of Hawaii, where inundation would be minimal and run-up heights less than metric; the coastal areas of Hawaii were nonetheless evacuated. Further south, an evacuation was ordered for the coastal areas of the 68 populated islands of French Polynesia. As a result, and despite run-up reaching 4 m in the Marquesas Islands, no victims were reported, and only one fishing boat was lost, his owner having refused to take it out to sea (REYMOND et al., 2010).

Response in California, where the tsunami did at least $10 million damage, was rather chaotic, with some beaches being evacuated and others not. Perhaps more importantly, it demonstrated a lack of sophistication, with the coastal community not prepared to wait long enough for individual harbor responses, characterized by strong and potentially treacherous currents, to develop during the arrival of higher frequency components traveling outside the Shallow-Water Approximation [C. Synolakis, pers. comm., 2010]. In this respect, it is worth sensitizing the population to the fact that tsunami arrival times broadcast by the warning centers represent the expected initiation of the phenomenon, which can last many hours thereafter.

In conclusion, the 2010 Maule tsunami points out to the need to further educate decision-makers, both in the near and far field.

- The Samoan event of 29 September 2009 earns an "Orange" star. Its tsunami was very destructive locally (OKAL et al. 2010), causing more than $200 million of damage, principally on the islands of Tutuila (American Samoa; where it ran up to 17 m at Poloa), Upolu (Samoa) and Niuatoputapu (Tonga). In particular, the downtown area in Pago Pago was heavily damaged as a result of the amplification of the waves in its narrow bay, as were the cities of Leone (Utuila), and Lepa (Upolu). Under the circumstances, the total death toll, 189, would appear reasonably contained, as a result of the population having generally self-evacuated the shoreline upon either feeling the earthquake, or more often, noticing a recess of the ocean.

In this respect, one can generally credit the local inhabitants on Tutuila with awareness of tsunami danger, which may have been enhanced by a comprehensive signage project, under which standard, blue "tsunami hazard zone" signs had been erected along the shore, although to be precise, those do not suggest *whither* to evacuate. A strong element of community bonding, notably on the part of local elected officials, resulted in a grassroots warning and evacuation, which probably helped keep the death toll on Tutuila at 34. While, of course, regrettable, this figure means hundreds, perhaps thousands, of lives saved thanks to the evacuation, which stemmed from a certain level of education of the population.

Unfortunately, the situation was to be different on Upolu, where 143 people lost their lives, even though the tsunami spared the more populated northern shore, devastating mostly the southeastern corner of the island (OKAL *et al.*, 2010). While many inhabitants knew to evacuate after the earthquake, and scores successfully did so, a significant number became victims of entrapment in vehicles, either stuck in traffic jams, or proceeding parallel to the shore. The general lack of preparedness was also reflected by the absence of signage of hazard zones, the alleged emphasis on the capital city, Apia located on the northern shore, during tsunami drills, and the erroneous perception of automobiles as being a great help—if not an outright panacea—in mitigating tsunamis, notably in the immediate aftermath of the "road switch" to left-hand driving, which took place 22 days prior to the tsunami.

The orange card given to this event reflects the contrast between what amounts to a reasonably

successful evacuation on Tutuila, and significant deficiencies in preparedness and execution on Upolu. It stresses once again the value of education and stepped up awareness of the populations at risk for the eventual reduction in loss of life from near-field tsunamis.

- The tragic event of 17 July 2006 in Java earns a "Red" star. This "tsunami earthquake" was strongly reminiscent of the 1994 East Java tsunami, whose lessons should have remained vivid just 12 years later and only 600 km away along the coast of Java. While the slow character of the event resulted in minimal felt intensities along the coast, the long-period moment (4.6×10^{27} dyn*cm) was assessed at a sufficient level for the Japan Meteorological Agency to issue a warning 27 min after the earthquake. This delay was relatively long, but the warning might still have been useful, had it been heeded. By contrast, PTWC issued a statement of no warning 17 min after the event. Possibly because of these conflicting statements, and probably on account of the wrongful perception of a benign event based on felt reports, no official evacuation was mandated. Forty minutes after the earthquake, the tsunami inflicted severe damage, and a death toll of about 700, on a 200-km section of coastline centered on Pangandaran, with run-up reaching 21 m (FRITZ *et al.*, 2007). This represents an unfortunate instance of insufficient and contradictory warnings, mismanagement of the existing one, and lack of preparedness on an island which had lived through an essentially similar disaster 12 years earlier. It also reaffirms the particular challenge posed by "tsunami earthquakes", which must be detected in real time. The pair of Java events (1994, 2006) strongly suggests that there is a regional character to their occurrence, an idea already hinted at by OKAL and NEWMAN (2001), but which clearly warrants more research.

19. Conclusion

The review of 27 tsunamis generated by earthquakes over the past 310 years outlines a number of common conclusions. From the seismological standpoint, we must accept that we still lack a reliable understanding of the conditions controlling the occurrence of mega-earthquakes with the potential for transoceanic tsunamis. In the wake of the 2004 Sumatra event, we have had to abandon the paradigm of a "maximum earthquake" predictable from simple tectonic parameters (RUFF and KANAMORI, 1980), and a growing number of studies have reaffirmed the ANDO (1975) concept of an element of randomness in the exact size (determined for example through the analysis of paleotsunami deposits) of large events which might otherwise qualify as repeating instances in the earthquake cycle (CISTERNAS et al., 2005; KELSEY et al., 2005; OKAL et al., 2006a). Similarly, we lack a full understanding of the environments prone to hosting the treacherous "tsunami earthquakes" which still pose a formidable challenge to the warning community.

Our ability to produce in real time, and occasionally before tsunamis reach distant shores, reliable simulations of their detailed inundation characteristics expresses our good command of the fundamental aspects of the generation of tsunamis by earthquakes. Yet, some events clearly violate this pattern, with wave amplitudes either too large or too small. The former could arise from the triggering of underwater landslides as in the case of Papua New Guinea (Sect. 14), and the latter from shallow bathymetry and/or the presence of islands at the source, as in the case of the 2005 Nias event. Such situations emphasize the challenges faced when attempting to automate the process of tsunami warning in real time.

The study of the most recent, post-Sumatra, tsunamis reveals a disturbing diversity, both in the performance of the warning centers, and in the response of the communities at risk. It is somewhat discomforting to retrace the 2006 Java debacle (and to a lesser extent, the damage suffered in the far field at Crescent City following the 2006 Kuril event), while at the same time realizing that a successful evacuation had taken place 73 years earlier in Hilo, following T. Jaggar's warning of the 1933 Sanriku tsunami. A common conclusion of the close examination of both successes and failures during recent tsunamis remains the value of education, either in a traditional, ancestral form deeply rooted in the local culture, or in formal programs such as schooling and drills. This is particularly critical in the near field where there can be no substitute for self-evacuation, which inherently requires awareness and preparedness of the populations involved.

In summary, this review documents how individual tsunamis have resulted in critical progress in our understanding of the intricate mechanism by which large earthquakes can (but occasionally, do not) trigger dangerous tsunamis, and in our efforts in mitigating their effects. Such incremental steps remind us of the great French poet Victor Hugo, who once wrote "Science is the asymptote of Truth" (HUGO, 1864). While the converse might have been more proper mathematically, we can expect that future catastrophic tsunamis will keep bringing us closer to a sense of perfection in knowledge, and through an appropriate application to societal needs, to the mitigation of their disastrous effects. Yet, an asymptote is never reached, and there will always come the intriguing tsunami with an unforeseen property, which will seed further research and, we hope, generate improved mitigation; the latter will always require an enhanced educational effort.

Acknowledgments

I am grateful to my many collaborators in the tsunami community for helping me shape many of the ideas contained in this work. They are too numerous to list individually, but a special acknowledgment goes to Costas Synolakis for sharing so many personal moments, in the field and the lab. I thank Phil Cummins for inviting me to give a presentation on this subject at the AOGS meeting in August 2009 in Singapore. The paper was improved by the comments of two reviewers.

REFERENCES

ABE, KU., ABE, KA., TSUJI, Y., IMAMURA, F., KATAO, H., IIO, Y., SATAKE, K., BOURGEOIS, J., NOGUERA, E., and ESTRADA, F. (1993), *Field survey of the Nicaragua earthquake and tsunami of September 2, 1992*, Bull. Earthq. Res. Inst. Tokyo Univ. *68*, 23–70.
ANDO, M. (1975), *Source mechanism and tectonic significance of historical earthquakes along the Nankai Trough, Japan*, Tectonophysics, *27*, 119–140.

ANDO M., and BALAZS E.I. (1979), *Geodetic evidence for aseismic subduction of the Juan de Fuca plate*, J. Geophys. Res. *84*, 3023–3028.

ANGENHEISTER, G. (1920), *Vier Erdbeben und Flutwellen im Pazifischen Ozean, beobachtet am Samoa-Observatorium, 1917-1919*, Nachr. K. Gesellsch. Wissensch. Göttingen, pp. 201–204.

ARTRU, J., DUČIĆ, V., KANAMORI, H., LOGNONNÉ, P., and MURAKAMI, M. (2005), *Ionospheric detection of gravity waves induced by tsunamis*, Geophys. J. Intl. *160*, 840–848.

ATWATER, B.F. (1987) *Evidence for great Holocene earthquakes along the outer coast of Washington state*, Science *236*, 942–944.

ATWATER, T. (1970), *Implications of plate tectonics for the Cenozoic tectonic evolution of western North America*, Geol. Soc. Am. Bull. *81*, 3513–3536.

BARBEROPOULOU, A., QAMAR, A., PRATT, T.L., and STEELE, W.P. (2006), *Long-period effects of the Denali earthquake on water bodies in the Puget Lowland: Observations and modeling*, Bull. Seismol. Soc. Amer. *96*, 519–535.

BARKAN, R., TEN BRINK, U.S., and LIN, J. (2009), *Far-field tsunami simulations of the 1755 Lisbon earthquake: Implications for tsunami hazard to the U.S. East Coast and the Caribbean*, Mar. Geol. *264*, 109–122.

BENIOFF, H. (1935), *A linear strain seismograph*, Bull. Seismol. Soc. Amer., *25*, 283–309.

BENIOFF, H. (1958), *Long waves observed in the Kamchatka earthquake of November 4, 1952*, J. Geophys. Res. *63*, 589–593.

BEN-MENAHEM, A. (1961), *Radiation of seismic surface-waves from finite moving sources*, Bull. Seismol. Soc. Amer., *51*, 401–435.

BEN-MENAHEM, A., and ROSENMAN, M. (1972), *Amplitude patterns of tsunami waves from submarine earthquakes*, J. Geophys. Res. *77*, 3097–3128.

BERNARD, E.N., and MILBURN, H.B. (1985) *Long-wave observations near the Galápagos Islands*, J. Geophys. Res. *90*, 3361–3366.

BERNARD, E.N., MOFJELD, H.O., TITOV, V.V., SYNOLAKIS, C.E., and GONZÁLEZ, F.I. (2006), *Tsunami: scientific frontiers, mitigation, forecasting and policy implications*, Phil. Trans. Roy. Soc. *364A*, 1989–2007.

BILLINGS, L.G. (1915), *Some personal experiences with earthquakes*, Nat. Geographic Mag. *27*, *(1)*, 57–71.

BLEWITT, G., HAMMOND, W.C., KREEMER, C., PLAG, H.-P., STEIN, S., and OKAL, E.A. (2009), *GPS for real-time earthquake source determination and tsunami warning systems*, J. Geodesy *83*, 335–343.

BOATWRIGHT, J., and CHOY, G.L. (1986), *Teleseismic estimates of the energy radiated by shallow earthquakes*, J. Geophys. Res. *91*, 2095–2112.

BORRERO, J.C., ORTÍZ, M., TITOV, V.V., and SYNOLAKIS, C.E. (1997), *Field survey of Mexican tsunami produces new data, unusual photos*, Eos, Trans. Amer. Geophys. Un. *78*, 85 and 87–88.

BORRERO, J.C., DOLAN, J.F., and SYNOLAKIS, C.E. (2001), *Tsunamis within the Eastern Santa Barbara Channel*, Geophys. Res. Letts. *28*, 643–646.

BORRERO, J.C., WEISS, R., OKAL, E.A., HIDAYAT, R., SURANTO, ARCAS, D., and TITOV, V.V. (2009), *The tsunami of 12 September 2007, Bengkulu Province, Sumatra, Indonesia: Post-tsunami survey and numerical modeling*, Geophys. J. Intl. *178*, 180–194.

BRUNE, J.N., and ENGEN G.R. (1969), *Excitation of mantle Love waves and definition of mantle wave magnitude*, Bull. Seismol. Soc. Amer. *59*, 923–933.

CAMINADE, J.-P., D. CHARLIE, U. KÂNOĞLU, S. KOSHIMURA, H. MATSUTOMI, A. MOORE, C. RUSCHER, C. SYNOLAKIS, and T.

TAKAHASHI (2000), *Vanuatu earthquake and tsunami cause much damage, few casualties*, Eos, Trans. Amer. Geophys. Un. *81*, 641 and 646–647.

CHAPMAN, C. (2005), *The Asian tsunami in Sri Lanka: a personal experience*, Eos, Trans. Amer. Un. *86*, *(2)*, 13–14.

CHESTER, D.K. (2001), *The 1755 Lisbon earthquake*, Prog. Phys. Geogr. *25*, 363–383.

CIFUENTES, I.L., and SILVER, P.G., (1989), *Low-frequency source characteristics of the great 1960 Chilean earthquake*, J. Geophys. Res. *94*, 643–663.

CISTERNAS, M., ATWATER, B.F., TORREJÓN, F. , SAWAI, Y., MACHUCA, G., LAGOS, M., EIPERT, A.,YOULTON, C., SALGADO, I. KAMATAKI, T., SHISHIKURA, M., RAJENDRAN, C.P., MALIK, J.K., and HUSNI M. (2005), *Predecessors of the giant 1960 Chile earthquake*, Nature, *437*, 404–407.

DEMETS, D.C., and DIXON, T.H. (1999), *New kinematic models for Pacific-North America motion from 3 Ma to present: 1. Evidence for steady motion and biases in the NUVEL-1A model*, Geophys. Res. Letts. *26*, 1921–1924.

DENGLER, L., USLU, B., BARBEROPOULOU, A., BORRERO, J., and SYNOLAKIS, C. (2008), *The vulnerability of Crescent City, California to tsunamis generated in the Kuril Islands region of the Northwestern Pacific*, Seismol. Res. Letts. *79*, 608–619.

DENGLER, L., USLU, B., BARBEROPOULOU, A., YIM, S.C., and KELLY, A. (2009), *The November 15, 2006 Kuril Islands-generated tsunami in Crescent City, California*, Pure Appl. Geophys. *166*, 37–53.

DONN, W.L. (1964), *Alaskan earthquake of 27 March 1964: Remote seiche excitation*, Science *145*, 261–262.

DORBATH, L., CISTERNAS, A., and DORBATH, C. (1990) *Assessment of the size of large and great historical earthquakes in Peru*, Bull. Seismol. Soc. Amer. *80*, 551–576.

DUDLEY, W.C., and LEE, M. (1998), *Tsunami!,* (2nd ed.), Univ. Hawaii Press, p. 5, Honolulu.

EATON, J.P., RICHTER, D.H., and AULT, W.U. (1961), *The tsunami of May 23, 1960 on the island of Hawaii*, Bull. Seismol. Soc. Amer. *51*, 135–157.

EDWARDS, B.D., LEE, H.J., and FIELD, M.J. (1993), *Seismically induced mudflow in Santa Barbara Basin*, U.S. Geol. Survey Bull. Rept., B 2002, ed. by W.C. SCHWAB, H.J., LEE, and D.C. TWICHELL, pp. 167–173.

FILLOUX, J.H. (1982), *Tsunami recorded on the open ocean floor*, Geophys. Res. Letts. *9*, 25–28.

FRITZ, H.M. (2010), *Field survey of the 2010 tsunami in Chile*, Proc. Amer. Geophys. Un. Chapman Conf. on Giant Earthquakes and their Tusnamis, Valparaiso, 16–24 May 2010, p. 8, 2010 [abstract].

FRITZ, H.M., and KALLIGERIS, N. (2008), *Ancestral heritage saves tribes during 1 April 2007 Solomon Islands tsunami*, Geophys. Res. Letts. *35*, *(1)*, L01607, 5 pp.

FRITZ, H.M., and KALLIGERIS, N. (2010), *Field survey report of the Solomon Islands tsunami of 03 January 2010*, Geophys. Res. abstracts, *12*, submitted, 2010 [abstract].

FRITZ H. M., KONGKO, W., MOORE, A., MCADOO, B., GOFF, J., HARBITZ, C., USLU, B., KALLIGERIS, N., SUTEJA, D., KALSUM, K., TITOV, V., GUSMAN, A., LATIEF, H., SANTOSO, E., SUJOKO, S., DJULKARNAEN, D., SUNENDAR, H., and SYNOLAKIS, C. (2007), *Extreme runup from the 17 July 2006 Java tsunami*, Geophys. Res. Letts. *34*, *(12)*, L12602, 5 pp.

FRITZ, H.M., KALLIGERIS, N., BORRERO, J.C., BRONCANO, P., and ORTEGA, E. (2008), *The 15 August 2007 Peru tsunami: run-up observations and modeling*, Geophys. Res. Letts. *35, (10)*, L10604, 5 pp.

FUCHS, SIR V.(1982), *Of Ice and Men: The story of the British Antarctic Survey, 1943-73,* Anthony Nelson, Oswestry, 383 pp.

FUKAO, Y. (1979), *Tsunami earthquakes and subduction processes near deep-sea trenches*, J. Geophys. Res. *84*, 2303–2314.

GELLER, R.J. (1976), *Scaling relations for earthquake source parameters and magnitudes*, Bull. Seismol. Soc. Amer. *66*, 1501–1523.

GILBERT, F. (1980), *An introduction to low-frequency seismology*, in: *Proc. Intl. School Phys. "Enrico Fermi", 78*, ed. by A.M. DZIEWONSKI and E. BOSCHI, pp. 41–81, North Holland, Amsterdam.

GODIN, O.A. (2004), *Air-sea interaction and feasibility of tsunami detection in the open ocean*, J. Geophys. Res. *104, (C5)*, C05002, 20 pp.

GODIN, O.A., IRISOV, V.G., LEBEN, R.R., HAMLINGTON, B.D., and WICK, G.A. (2009), *Variations in sea surface roughness induced by the 2004 Sumatra-Andaman tsunami*, Nat. Haz. Earth System Sci. *9*, 1135–1147.

GONZÁLEZ, F.I., MADER, C.L., EBLE, M.C., and BERNARD, E.N. (1991) *The 1987-88 Alaskan Bight tsunamis: Deep ocean data and model comparisons*, Natural Hazards *4*, 119–139.

GONZÁLEZ, F.I., MILBURN, H.M., BERNARD, E.N., and NEWMAN, J. (1998), *Deep-ocean assessment and reporting of tsunamis (DART): Brief overview and status report*, Proc. Intl. Workshop Tsunami Disaster Mitigation, pp. 118–129, Tokyo, Japan, 1998.

GOWER, J. (2005), *Jason-1 detects the 26 December 2004 tsunami*, Eos, Trans. Amer. Geophys. Un. *86*, 37–38.

GREEN, G. (1837), *On the motion of waves in a canal of variable depth*, Cambridge Phil. Trans. *6*, 457–462.

GUTENBERG, B., and RICHTER, C.F. (1954) *Seismicity of the Earth and associated phenomena*, 310 pp., Princeton Univ. Press.

HANSON, J.A., and BOWMAN, J.R. (2005) *Dispersive and reflected tsunami signals from the 2004 Indian Ocean tsunami observed on hydrophone and seismic stations*, Geophys. Res. Letts.*32, (17)*, L17606, 5 pp.

HAEUSSLER, P.J., LEE, H.J., RYAN, H.F., KAYAN, R.E., HAMPTON, M.A., and SULEIMANI, E. (2007), *Submarine slope failures near Seward, Alaska, during the M = 9.2 1964 earthquake*, Adv. Natur. Technol. Haz. Res. *27*, 269–278.

HEATON, T.H., and HARTZELL, S.H. (1987), *Earthquake hazards on the Cascadia subduction zone*, Science, *236*, 162–168.

HEATON, T.H., and KANAMORI, H. (1984), *Seismic potential associated with subduction in the Northwestern United States*, Bull. Seismol. Soc. Amer. *74*, 933–941.

HEINRICH, P., PIATANESI, A., OKAL, E.A., and HÉBERT, H. (2000), *Near-field modeling of the July 17, 1998 tsunami in Papua New Guinea*, Geophys. Res. Letts. *27*, 3037–3040.

HINES, C.O. (1972), *Gravity waves in the atmosphere*, Nature *239*, 73–78.

HUGO, V. (1864), *William Shakespeare,* 572 pp., Librairie Internationale, Paris

IMAMURA, F., SHUTO, N., IDE, S., YOSHIDA, Y., and ABE, K. (1993) *Estimate of the tsunami source of the 1992 Nicaraguan earthquake from tsunami data*, Geophys. Res. Letts. *20*, 1515–1518.

JACOBY, G.C., BURKER, D.E., and BENSON, B.E. (1997), *Tree-ring evidence for an A.D. 1700 Cascadia earthquake in Washington and northern Oregon*, Geology *25*, 999–1002.

JAGGAR, T. (1930), The Volcano Letter *274*, 1–4.

JANKAEW, K., ATWATER, B.F., SAWAI, Y., CHOOWONG, M., CHAROENTITIRAT, T., MARTIN, M.E., and PRENDERGAST, A. (2008),

Medieval forewarning of the 2004 Indian Ocean tsunami in Thailand, Nature *455*, 1228–1231.

KAISTRENKO, V., and SEDAEVA, V. (2001), 1952 North Kuril tsunami: new data from archives, In: *Tsunami research at the end of a critical decade,* ed. by G.T. HEBENSTREIT, Adv. Natur. Technol. Res. *18*, pp. 91–102, Kluver, Dordrecht, 2001.

KANAMORI, H. (1970), *The Alaska earthquake of 1964: Radiation of long-period surface waves and source mechanism*, J. Geophys. Res. *75*, 5029–5040.

KANAMORI, H. (1972), *Mechanism of tsunami earthquakes*, Phys. Earth Planet. Inter. *6*, 346–359.

KANAMORI, H. (1976), *Re-examination of the Earth's free oscillations excited by the Kamchatka earthquake of November 4, 1952*, Phys. Earth Planet. Inter. *11*, 216–226.

KANAMORI, H. (1977a), Seismic and aseismic slip along subduction zones and their tectonic implications, **in**: *Island arcs, Deep-sea trenches and Back-arc basins,* ed. by M. TALWANI and W.C. PITMAN III, Amer. Geophys. Un. Maurice Ewing Ser. *1*, 163–174.

KANAMORI, H. (1997b), *The energy release in great earthquakes*, J. Geophys. Res. *82*, 2981–2987.

KANAMORI, H. (1993) *W phase*, Geophys. Res. Letts. *20*, 1691–1694.

KANAMORI, H., and KIKUCHI, M. (1993), *The 1992 Nicaragua earthquake: a slow tsunami earthquake associated with subducted sediments*, Nature *361*, 714–716.

KANAMORI, H., and RIVERA, L. (2008), *Source inversion of W phase: speeding up tsunami warning*, Geophys. J. Intl. *175*, 222–238.

KELSEY, H.M.,NELSON, A.R., HEMPHILL-HALEY, E., and WITTER, R.C. (2005), *Tsunami history of an Oregon coastal lake reveals a 4000-yr. record of great earthquakes on the Cascadia subduction zone*, Geol. Soc. Amer. Bull. *117*, 1009–1032.

KVALE, A. (1955), *Seismic seiches in Norway and England during the Assam earthquake of August 15, 1950*, Bull. Seismol. Soc. Amer. *45*, 93–113.

LEGG, M.R., and KAMERLING, M.J. (2003), *Large-scale basement-involved landslides, California continental borderland*, Pure Appl. Geophys. *160*, 2033–2051.

LE PICHON, A., HERRY, P., MIALLE, P., VERGOZ, J., BRACHET, N., GARCÉS, M., DROB, D., and CERANNA, L. (2005), *Infrasound associated with 2004-2005 large Sumatra earthquakes and tsunami*, Geophys. Res. Letts. *32, (19)*, L19802, 5 pp.

LIU, J.Y., TSAI, Y.B., CHEN, S.W., LEE, C.P., CHEN, Y.C., YEN, H.Y., CHANG, W.Y., and LIU, C. (2006), *Giant ionospheric disturbances excited by the M = 9.3 Sumatra earthquake of 26 December 2004*, Geophys. Res. Letts. *33, (2)*, L02103, 3 pp.

LOCAT, J., LEE, H., LOCAT, P., and IMRAM, J. (2004), *Numerical analysis of the mobility of the Palos Verdes debris avalanche, California, and its application for the generation of tsunamis*, Mar. Geol. *203*, 269–280.

LOGNONNÉ, P., CLÉVÉDÉ, E., and KANAMORI, H. (1998), *Computations of seismograms and atmospheric oscillations by normal mode summation for a spherical Earth model with a realistic atmosphere*, Geophys. J. Intl. *135*, 388–406.

LÓPEZ, A.M., and OKAL, E.A. (2006), *A seismological reassessment of the source of the 1946 Aleutian "tsunami" earthquake*, Geophys. J. Intl. *165*, 835–849.

MACINNES, B.T., PINEGINA, T.K., BOURGEOIS, J. , RAZHIGAEVA, N.G., KAISTRENKO, V.M., KRAVCHUNOVSKAYA,, E.A. (2009), *Field survey and geological effects of the 15 November 2006 Kuril Tsunami in the Middle Kuril Islands*, Pure Appl. Geophys. *166*, 9–36.

MADER, C.L. (1988) *Numerical modeling of water waves,* 206 pp., Univ. Calif. Press, Berkeley.

MANN, D., and FREYMUELLER, J. (2003), *Volcanic and tectonic deformation on Unimak Island in the Aleutian Arc, Alaska,* J. Geophys. Res. *108, (B2),* 2108, 12 pp.

MCADOO, B.G., DENGLER, L., PRASETYA, G., and TITOV, V., (2006), SOMG: *How an oral history saved thousands on Indonesia's Simeulue Island during the December 2004 and March 2005 tsunamis,* Earthquake Spectra *22,* S661–S669.

MCCREERY, C.S. (2005), *Impact of the National Tsunami Hazard Mitigation program on operations of the Richard H. Hagemeyer Pcaific tsunami Warning Center,* Natural Hazards *35,* 73–88.

MCGARR, A. (1965), *Excitation of seiches in channels by seismic waves,* J. Geophys. Res. *70,* 847–854.

MONECKE, K., FINGER, W., KLARER, D., KONGKO, W., MCADOO, B.G., MOORE, A.L., and SUDRAJAT, S.U. (2008), *A 1,000-year sediment record of tsunami recurrence in Northern Sumatra,* Nature *455,* 1232–1234.

NELSON, A.R., ATWATER, B.F., BOBROWSKY, P.T., BRADLEY, L.-A., CLAGUE, J.J., CARVER, G.A., DARLENZO, M.E., GRANT, W.C., KRUEGER, H.W., SPARKS, R., STAFFORD, T.W., JR., and STULVER, M. (1995), *Radiocarbon evidence for extensive plate-boundary rupture about 300 years ago at the Cascadia subduction zone,* Nature *378,* 371–374.

NELSON, A.R., KELSEY, H.M., and WITTER, R.C. (2006), *Great earthquakes of variable magnitude at the Cascadia subduction zone,* Quatern. Res. *65,* 354–365.

NETTLES, M., EKSTRÖM, G., DZIEWOŃSKI, A.M., and MATERNOVSKAYA, N. (2005), *Source characteristics of the great Sumatra earthquake and its aftershocks,* Eos, Trans. Amer. Geophys. Un. *86, (18),* U43A-01, 2005 [abstract].

NEWMAN, A.V., and OKAL, E.A. (1998), *Teleseismic estimates of radiated seismic energy: The E/M$_0$ discriminant for tsunami earthquakes,* J. Geophys. Res. *103,* 26885–26898.

NI, S., KANAMORI, H., and HELMBERGER, D.V. (2005), *Energy radiation from the Sumatra earthquake,* Nature *434,* 582.

O'LOUGHLIN, K.F., and LANDER, J.F. (2003), *Caribbean tsunamis, A 500-year history from 1498 to 1998,* Adv. Natur. Tech. Haz. Res. *23,* Kluwer, Dordrecht, 263 pp.

OBERMEIER, S.F., and DICKENSON, S.E. (2000), *Liquefaction evidence for the strength of ground motions resulting from Late Holocene Cascadia subduction earthquakes, with emphasis on the event of 1700 A.D.,* Bull. Seismol. Soc. Amer. *90,* 876–896.

OCCHIPINTI, G., LOGNONNÉ, P. KHERANI, E.A., and HÉBERT, H. (2006), *Three-dimensional wave form modeling of ionospheric signature induced by the 2004 Sumatra tsunami,* Geophys. Res. Letts. *33, (20),* L20104, 5 pp.

OKAL, E.A. (1993), *WM$_m$: An extension of the concept of mantle magnitude to the W phase, with application to real-time assessment of the ultra-long component of the seismic source,* Eos, Trans. Amer. Geophys. Un. *74,* (43), 344 [abstract].

OKAL, E.A. (2001), *T-phase stations for the International Monitoring System of the Comprehensive Nuclear-Test Ban Treaty: A global perspective,* Seismol. Res. Letts. *72,* 186–196.

OKAL, E.A. (2003), *T waves from the 1998 Papua New Guinea earthquake and its aftershocks: Timing the tsunamigenic slump,* Pure Appl. Geophys. *160,* 1843–1863.

OKAL, E.A. (2007a), *Seismic records of the 2004 Sumatra and other tsunamis: A quantitative study,* Pure Appl. Geophys. *164,* 325–353.

OKAL, E.A. (2007b), *Performance of robust source estimators for last year's large earthquakes,* Eos, Trans. Amer. Geophys. Un. *88, (52),* S44A-01 [abstract].

OKAL, E.A. (2008), The excitation of tsunamis by earthquakes, In: *The Sea: Ideas and observations on progress in the study of the seas,* 15, Edited by E.N. BERNARD and A.R. ROBINSON, pp. 137-177, Harvard Univ. Press, Cambridge.

OKAL, E.A., and HÉBERT, H. (2007), *Far-field modeling of the 1946 Aleutian tsunami,* Geophys. J. Intl. *169,* 1229–1238.

OKAL, E.A., and MACAYEAL, D.R. (2006), *Seismic recording on drifting icebergs: Catching seismic waves, tsunamis and storms from Sumatra and elsewhere,* Seismol. Res. Letts. *77,* 659–671.

OKAL, E.A., and NEWMAN, A.V. (2001), *Tsunami earthquakes: The quest for a regional signal,* Phys. Earth Planet. Inter. *124,* 45–70.

OKAL, E.A., and REYMOND, D. (2003), *The mechanism of the great Banda Sea earthquake of 01 February 1938: Applying the method of Preliminary Determination of Focal Mechanism to a historical event,* Earth Planet. Sci. Letts. *216,* 1–15.

OKAL, E.A., and SYNOLAKIS, C.E. (2004), *Source discriminants for near-field tsunamis,* Geophys. J. Intl. *158,* 899–912.

OKAL, E.A., and SYNOLAKIS, C.E. (2008), *Far-field tsunami hazard from mega-thrust earthquakes in the Indian Ocean,* Geophys. J. Intl. *172,* 995–1015.

OKAL, E.A., and TALANDIER, J. (1991) *Single-station estimates of the seismic moment of the 1960 Chilean and 1964 Alaskan earthquakes, using the mantle magnitude M$_m$,* Pure Appl. Geophys. *136,* 103–126.

OKAL, E.A., PIATANESI, A., and HEINRICH, P. (1999), *Tsunami detection by satellite altimetry,* J. Geophys. Res. *104,* 599–615.

OKAL, E.A., SYNOLAKIS, C.E., FRYER, G.J., HEINRICH, P., BORRERO, J.C., RUSCHER, C. ARCAS, D., GUILLE, G., and ROUSSEAU, D. (2002), *A field survey of the 1946 Aleutian tsunami in the far field,* Seismol. Res. Letts. *73,* 490–503.

OKAL, E.A., ALASSET, P.-J., HYVERNAUD, O., and SCHINDELÉ, F. (2003a), *The deficient T waves of tsunami earthquakes,* Geophys. J. Intl. *152,* 416–432.

OKAL, E.A., PLAFKER, G., SYNOLAKIS, C.E., and BORRERO, J.C. (2003b), *Near-field survey of the 1946 Aleutian tsunami on Unimak and Sanak Islands,* Bull. Seismol. Soc. Amer. *93,* 1226–1234.

OKAL, E.A., BORRERO, J.C., and SYNOLAKIS, C.E. (2006a), *Evaluation of tsunami risk from regional earthquakes at Pisco, Peru,* Bull. Seismol. Soc. Amer. *96,* 1634–1648.

OKAL, E.A., SLADEN, A., and OKAL, E.A.-S. (2006b), *Rodrigues, Mauritius and Réunion Islands field survey after the December 2004 Indian Ocean tsunami,* Earthquake Spectra *22,* S241–S261.

OKAL, E.A., FRITZ, H.M., RAVELOSON, R., JOELSON, G., PANČOŠKOVÁ, P., and RAMBOLAMANANA, G. (2006c), *Madagascar field survey after the December 2004 Indian Ocean tsunami,* Earthquake Spectra, *22,* S263–S283.

OKAL, E.A., FRITZ, H.M., RAAD, P.E., SYNOLAKIS, C.E., AL-SHIJBI, Y., and AL-SAIFI, M. (2006d), *Oman field survey after the December 2004 Indian Ocean tsunami,* Earthquake Spectra *22,* S203–S218.

OKAL, E.A., TALANDIER, J., and REYMOND, D. (2007), *Quantification of hydrophone records of the 2004 Sumatra tsunami,* Pure Appl. Geophys. *164,* 309–323.

OKAL, E.A., FRITZ, H.M., and SLADEN, A. (2009), *2004 Sumatra tsunami surveys in the Comoro Islands and Tanzania and regional tsunami hazard from future Sumatra events,* South Afr. J. Geol. *112,* 343–358.

OKAL, E.A., FRITZ, H.M., SYNOLAKIS, C.E., BORRERO, J.C., WEISS, R., LYNETT, P.J., TITOV, V.V., FOTEINIS, S., JAFFE, B.E., LIU, P.L.-F., and CHAN, I. (2010) *Field Survey of the Samoa Tsunami of 29 September 2009,* Seismol. Res. Letts. *81,* 577–591.

ORTÍZ, M., and BILHAM, R. (2003), *Source area and rupture parameters of the 31 December 1881 ($M_w = 7. 9$) Car Nicobar earthquake estimated from tsunamis recorded in the Bay of Bengal*, J. Geophys. Res. *108, (B4)*, 2215, 16 pp.

PANČOŠKOVÁ, P., OKAL, E.A., MACAYEAL, D.R., and RAVELOSON, R. (2006), *Delayed response of far-field harbors to the 2004 Sumatra tsunami: the role of high-frequency components*, Eos, Trans. Amer. Geophys. Un., *87, (52)*, U53A-0021 [abstract].

PELLETIER, B., RÉGNIER, M., CALMANT, S., PILLET, R., CABIOCH, G., LAGABRIELLE, Y., BORE, J.-M., CAMINADE, J.-P., LEBELLEGARD, P., CHRISTOPHER, I., and TEKAMON, S. (2000), *Le séisme d'Ambryn-Pentecôte du 26 novembre 1999 ($M_w = 7,5$): données préliminaires sur la séismicité, le tsunami et les déplacements associés*, C.R. Acad. Sci., Sér. 2 *331*, 21–28.

PELTIER, W.R., and HINES, C.O. (1976), *On the possible detection of tsunamis by a monitoring of the atmosphere*, J. Geophys. Res. *81*, 1995–2000.

PETROFF, C. (2010), *Rapid reconnaissance survey of the February 27, 2010 Chile tsunami: Constitución to Colcura, Quidico to Mehuin*, Proc. Amer. Geophys. Un. Chapman Conf. on Giant Earthquakes and their Tusnamis, Valparaiso, 16–24 May 2010, p. 8 [abstract].

POLET, J., and KANAMORI, H. (2000), *Shallow subduction zone earthquakes and their tsunamigenic potential*, Geophys. J. Intl. *142*, 684–702.

RAJENDRAN, C.P., RAJENDRAN, K., ANU, R., EARNEST, A., MACHADO, T., MOHAN, P.M., and FREYMUELLER, J. (2007), *Crustal deformation and seismic history associated with the 2004 Indian Ocean earthquake: a perspective from the Andaman-Nicobar Islands*, Bull. Seismol. Soc. Amer. *97*, S174–S191.

REYMOND, D., HYVERNAUD, O., OKAL, E.A., ALLGEYER, S., JAMELOT, A., and HÉBERT, H. (2010), *Field survey and preliminary modeling of the 2010 Chilean tsunami in the Marquesas Islands, French Polynesia*, Proc. Eur. Geophys. Un. Gen. Assemb., Vienna, 02–07 May 2010, Paper 15707 [abstract].

RUFF, L.J. (1989), *Do trench sediments affect great earthquake occurrence in subduction zones?*, Pure Appl. Geophys. *129*, 263–282.

RUFF, L.J., and KANAMORI, H. (1980), *Seismicity and the subduction process*, Phys. Earth Planet. Inter. *23*, 240–252.

SANFORD, H.B. (1946), *Log of Coast Guard Unit Number 368, Scotch Cap DF station, relating the Scotch Cap Light station tragedy of 1946*, U.S. Coast Guard, Washington, DC, 11 pp.

SATAKE, K. (1988), *Effects of bathymetry on tsunami propagation: Application of ray tracing to tsunamis*, Pure Appl. Geophys. *126*, 27–36.

SATAKE, K., SHIMAZAKI, K., TSUJI, Y., and UEDA, K. (1996), *Time and size of a giant earthquake in Cascadia inferred from Japanese tsunami records of January 1700*, Nature *379*, 246–249.

SATAKE, K., WANG, K., and ATWATER, B.F. (2003), *Fault slip and seismic moment of the 1700 Cascadia earthquake inferred from Japanese tsunami descriptions*, J. Geophys. Res. *108, (B11)*, **ESE_7**, 17 pp.

SAVAGE, J.C., LISOSWSKI, M., and PRESCOTT, W.H. (1981), *Geodetic strain measurements in Washington*, J. Geophys. Res. *86*, 4929–4940.

SAVARENSKIY, E.F., TISHCHENKO, V.G., SVYATLOVSKIY, A.E., DOBROVOL'SKIY, A.D., and ZHIVAGO, A.V. (1958), *Tsunami 4-5 noyabrya 1952 g.*, Byulleten' sovieta po seismologii *4*, 63 pp., Izdat. Akad. Nauk SSSR, Moskva [in Russian].

SCHOLL, D.W., KIRBY, S.H., KERANEN, K.M., WELLS, R.E., BLAKELY, R.J., MICHAEL, F., and VON HUENE, R. (2007), *Megathrust slip and the care and feeding of the subduction channel through which the seismogenic zone runs*, Eos, Trans. Amer. Geophys. Un. *8, (52)*, T51E-06 [abstract].

SHEPARD, F.P., MACDONALD, G.A., and COX, D.C. (1950), *The tsunami of April 1, 1946*, Bull. Scripps Instit. Oceanog. *5*, 391–528.

SMYSHLYAEV, A.A. (2003), *Noch' okeana*, In: *Vremya krasnoy ryby*, pp. 249-320, Novaya Kniga, Petropavlovsk-Kamchatskiy [in Russian].

SOLOV'EV, S.L. (1968), *Sanakh-Kad'yakskoye tsunami 1788 g.*, In: *Problema Tsunami*, ed. by M.A. SADOVSKIY and A.A. TRESKOV, AKAD. NAUK SSSR, MOSKVA, pp. 232–237 [in Russian].

SOLOV'EV, S.L., and FERCHEV, M.D. (1961), *Summary of data on tsunamis in the USSR*, Bull. Council Seismol. Acad. Sci. USSR *9*, 23–55.

SOLOV'EV, S.L., and GO, CH. N. (1984), *Catalogue of tsunamis on the Eastern shore of the Pacific Ocean*, Can. Transl. Fish. Aquat. Sci *5078*, 293 pp.

STEIN, S., and OKAL, E.A. (2005), *Size and speed of the Sumatra earthquake*, Nature *434*, 581–582.

STEIN, S., and OKAL, E.A. (2007), *Ultra-long period seismic study of the December 2004 Indian Ocean earthquake and implications for regional tectonics and the subduction process*, Bull. Seismol. Soc. Amer. *97*, S279–S295.

SWE, T.L., SATAKE, K., AUNG, T.T., SAWAI, Y., OKAMURA, Y., WIN, K.S., SWE, W., SWE, C., TUN, S.T., SOE, M.M., OO, T., and ZAW, S.H. (2006), *Myanmar Coastal Area Field Survey after the December 2004 Indian Ocean Tsunami*, Earthquake Spectra *22*, S285–S294.

SWEET, S., and SILVER, E.A. (2003), *Tectonics and Slumping in the Source Region of the 1998 Papua New Guinea Tsunami from Seismic Reflection Images*, Pure Appl. Geophys. *160*, 1945–1968.

SYNOLAKIS, C.E., and OKAL, E.A. (1992–2002), *Perspective on a decade of post-tsunami surveys*, In: *Tsunamis: Case studies and recent developments*, ed. by K. SATAKE, Adv. Natur. Technol. Hazards, *23*, pp. 1–30.

SYNOLAKIS, C.E., BARDET, J.-P., BORRERO, J.C., DAVIES, H.L., OKAL, E.A., SILVER, E.A., SWEET, S., and TAPPIN, D.R. (2002), *The slump origin of the 1998 Papua New Guinea tsunami*, Proc. Roy. Soc. (London), Ser. A *458*, 763–789.

TADEPALLI, S., and SYNOLAKIS, C.E. (1994), *The runup of N-waves*, Proc. Roy. Soc. London, Ser. A *445*, 99–112.

TADEPALLI, S., and SYNOLAKIS, C.E. (1996), *Model for the leading waves of tsunamis*, Phys. Rev. Letts. *77*, 2141–2145.

TANIOKA, Y., and SATAKE, K. (1996), *Fault parameters of the 1896 Sanriku tsunami earthquake estimated from tsunami numerical modeling*, Geophys. Res. Letts. *23*, 1549–1552.

TANIOKA, Y., RUFF, L.J., and SATAKE, K. (1997), *What controls the lateral variation of large earthquake occurrence along the Japan trench?* Island Arc *6*, 261–266.

TAYLOR, F.W., BRIGGS, R.W., FROHLICH, C., BROWN, A., HORNBACH, M., PAPABATU, A.K., MELTZNER, A.J., and BILLY, D. (2008), *Rupture across arc segment and plate boundaries in the 1 April 2007 Solomons earthquake*, Nature Geosci. *1*, 253–257.

THIÉBOT, E., and GUTSCHER, M.-A. (2006), *The Gibraltar arc seismogenic zone (part 1): Constraints on a shallow east-dipping fault plane source for the 1755 Lisbon earthquake provided by seismic data, gravity and thermal modeling*, Tectonophysics *426*, 135–152.

TITOV, V.V., and SYNOLAKIS, C.E. (1993), *A numerical study of wave runup of the September 2, 1992 Nicaraguan tsunami*, Proc.

Intl. Un. Geol. Geophys. Tsunami Symp., ed. by Y. TSUCHIYA and N. SHUTO, Japan Soc. Civil Eng., pp. 627–635, Wakayama, Japan.

TITOV, V.V., and SYNOLAKIS, C.E. (1998), *Numerical modeling of tidal wave runup*, J. Wtrwy. Port Coast. Engng. *B124*, 157–171.

TITOV, V.V., RABINOVICH, A.B., MOFJELD, H.O., THOMSON, R.E., and GONZÁLEZ, F.J. (2005), *The global reach of the 26 December 2004 Sumatra tsunami*, Science *309*, 2045–2048.

TSAI, V.C., NETTLES, M., EKSTRÖM, G., and DZIEWOŃSKI, A.M. (2005), *Multiple CMT source analysis of the 2004 Sumatra earthquake*, Geophys. Res. Letts. *32, (17)*, 17304, 4 pp.

VELASCO, A., AMMON, C.J., LAY, T., and ZHANG, J. (1994), *Imaging a slow bilateral rupture with broadband seismic waves: The September 2, 1992 Nicaraguan tsunami earthquake*, Geophys. Res. Letts. *21*, 2629–2632.

WALKER, D.A. (1996), *Observations of tsunami "shadows": A new technique for assessing tsunami wave heights*, Sci. Tsunami Haz. *14*, 3–11.

WARD, S.N. (1980), *Relationships of tsunami generation and an earthquake source*, J. Phys. Earth *28*, 441–474.

WARD, S.N. (1981), *On tsunami nucleation: I. A point source*, J. Geophys. Res. *86*, 7895–7900.

WEINSTEIN, S.A., and OKAL, E.A. (2005), *The mantle wave magnitude M_m and the slowness parameter Θ: Five years of real-time use in the context of tsunami warning*, Bull. Seismol. Soc. Amer. *95*, 779–799.

WOODS, M.T., and OKAL, E.A. (1987), *Effect of variable bathymetry on the amplitude of teleseismic tsunamis: a ray-tracing experiment*, Geophys. Res. Letts. *14*, 765–768.

YUAN, X., KIND, R., and PEDERSEN, H. (2005), *Seismic monitoring of the Indian Ocean tsunami*, Geophys. Res. Letts. *32, (15)*, L15308, 4 pp.

ZACHARIASEN, J., SIEH, K., TAYLOR, F.W., EDWARDS, R.L., and HANTORO, W.S. (1999), *Submergence and uplift associated with the giant 1833 Sumatran subduction earthquake: Evidence from coral microatolls*, J. Geophys. Res. *104*, 895–919.

(Received January 31, 2010, revised June 15, 2010, accepted June 17, 2010, Published online November 30, 2010)

Reprinted from the journal

Pure Appl. Geophys. 168 (2011), 997–1014
© 2010 Springer Basel AG
DOI 10.1007/s00024-010-0227-5

Geological and Hydrodynamical Examination of the Bathyal Tsunamigenic Origin of Miocene Conglomerates in Chita Peninsula, Central Japan

Toru Tachibana[1] and Yoshinobu Tsuji[2]

Abstract—A conglomerate appears on a rocky coast called "Tsubutega-ura Coast", located on the southwestern coast near the southern tip of the Chita Peninsula, Aichi Prefecture, central Japan. The conglomerate belongs to Miocene sedimentary rocks termed the Morozaki Group. The conglomerate includes meter-scale boulders, indicating that it was formed by an extraordinary event. In the geological investigation, we observed that the conglomerate shows alternate changes of paleocurrent directions between seaward and landward. This feature is supposed to be formed by tsunami currents. In the hydrodynamical investigation, we obtained following results: (1) the lowest limit of a current velocity to move a boulder of about 3 m in diameter would be about 2–3 m/s, (2) the speed of tsunami currents reproduced by tsunami simulation exceeds 3 m/s at 300 m in depth when the tsunami is generated by a gigantic earthquake with magnitude 9.0 or more, (3) the transport distance of the boulder would be several hundred meters to several kilometers by one tsunami event caused by a gigantic earthquake. We conclude that tsunamis best explain the formation of the conglomerate deposited in upper bathyal environments about 200–400 m depth, both from geological and hydrodynamical viewpoints.

Key words: Tsunami, conglomerate, numerical simulation, critical current velocity, transported distance, upper bathyal.

1. Introduction

Tsunamis can leave lasting geological traces in onshore and lagoonal environments (Sugawara *et al.*, 2008; Bourgeois, 2009). By contrast, tsunami deposits formed in offshore areas have been much less studied than those in onshore to nearshore areas (Dawson and Stewart, 2007, 2008; Smit *et al.*, 2007). There are still only a small number of examples of studies on

tsunamis by using offshore deposits, even if they have gradually increased in the recent years (e.g., Le Roux *et al.*, 2004; Cantalamessa and Di Celma, 2005; Fujiwara and Kamataki, 2007; Noda *et al.*, 2007; Le Roux *et al.*, 2008). Dawson and Stewart (2007, 2008) states that the mechanisms of formation of offshore tsunami deposits are still not always clear. Tsunami deposits in offshore areas can contain evidence of paleotsunamis, so that researches on these deposits should also be pursued.

In such research on tsunami deposits, deciding whether given deposits show evidence of tsunami origin or not is a fundamental problem. However, it is often difficult to distinguish whether the deposits were formed by tsunamis or by other events, for example, storm surges, sea bottom slumping. The deposits formed by storm surges can resemble tsunami deposits in onshore to nearshore areas (Dawson *et al.*, 1991; Dawson and Shi, 2000; Williams and Hall, 2004). In deep sea areas, the deposits formed by gravity currents can also resemble those formed by tsunamis (e.g., Brookfield *et al.*, 2006; Le Roux *et al.*, 2008). Despite such difficulties, researchers on tsunami deposits have developed the criteria to distinguish tsunami deposits from other deposits (e.g., Goff *et al.*, 2004; Morton *et al.*, 2007). In common with other research on tsunami deposits, it is necessary also in the present study to assume that the deposits were formed by tsunamis.

In the present study, we focus on a conglomerate formed on the deep sea bottom in the early Miocene Epoch. The conglomerate includes meter-scale boulders and displays a peculiar appearance in comparison with the surrounding deep sea sedimentary rocks. Meter-scale boulders are not commonly contained in deep sea sedimentary rocks. In the case that such large boulders are contained in these rocks, they

[1] Soil Engineering Corporation, 195 Toyota, Higashi-ku, Okayama 704-8162, Japan. E-mail: t-tachibana@sand.ocn.ne.jp

[2] Earthquake Research Institute, University of Tokyo, 1-1-1 Yayoi, Bunkyo-ku, Tokyo 113-0032, Japan. E-mail: tsuji@eri.u-tokyo.ac.jp

are likely to have been transported by some extraordinary events such as tsunamis (SHIKI and YAMAZAKI, 1996), rock falls (PICKERING, 1984), and debris flows (SOHN, 2000). The conglomerate was interpreted as tsunami deposits by SHIKI and YAMAZAKI (1996) based on cluster bedforms which are interpreted to be formed by traction currents. However, from a hydrodynamical viewpoint, the tsunami origin of conglomerates in deep sea environments was doubted (e.g. PICKERING et al., 1991). The purpose of the present study is to verify that the conglomerate is that of tsunami deposits by using numerical simulations of tsunamis.

We investigate the formation of the conglomerate both from the geological and hydrodynamical viewpoints. In Sect. 3, we discuss the geological investigation; our observations and description of the conglomerate and related deposits in the study area. In Sects. 4, 5, 6 we theoretically examined the possibility that large boulders could have been moved and transported by tsunamis.

The results of the geological investigation show that the conglomerate was formed by currents with alternate changes of direction, landward and seaward. We theoretically show that the lowest limit of a current velocity to move the largest boulder in the conglomerate (3 m in diameter) is about 2–3 m/s. Our tsunami simulations show that the boulder can be moved by tsunamis caused by a gigantic (M9.0 class) earthquake if the boulder is laid on the sea bottom shallower than 300 m depth. We theoretically show that the boulder would be transported seaward for several hundred meters to several kilometers by one tsunami event induced by a gigantic earthquake. Therefore, we can conclude that tsunamis give the best explanation of formation of the conglomerate in upper bathyal environments about 200–400 m depth.

2. Geological Background

The conglomerate discussed in the present study appears on a rocky coast, the "Tsubutega-ura Coast", located on the southwestern coast near the southern tip of the Chita Peninsula, Aichi Prefecture, central Japan (Fig. 1). The conglomerate is included in Miocene sedimentary rocks known as the Morozaki Group.

The Morozaki Group is distributed in the southern part of the Chita Peninsula, and partly covered by the late Miocene to Pleistocene Tokai Group. The Morozaki Group is about 1,000 m thick, and mainly composed of mudstone and a mudstone-dominated mud-sand alternation (KONDO and KIMURA, 1987; SHIBATA, 1988). Layers of tuffaceous sand or thick sandstones also occasionally appear in this sequence. The Morozaki Group dips at about 10–30° towards the northeast. This group is divided into four formations: the Himaka, Toyohama, Yamami, and the Utsumi Formation, in ascending order. The conglomerate belongs to the Yamami Formation (KONDO and KIMURA, 1987; Fig. 1a).

The Morozaki Group was deposited in deep sea environments (a few to several 100 m depth) excluding the lowermost Himaka Formation formed in a shallow marine condition (several tens of meters) (SHIBATA and ITOIGAWA, 1989). The Morozaki Group yields fossils of bivalves, fishes, and sea urchins. These fossils indicate that the upper three formations, in which the conglomerate is included, were deposited in upper bathyal environments (SHIBATA, 1977; THE TOKAI FOSSIL SOCIETY, 1993).

The age of the Morozaki Group is early to middle Miocene on the basis of fission-track dating and foraminiferal assemblages (ITOIGAWA and SHIBATA, 1992). Taking the stratigraphic position of the conglomerate in the Morozaki Group into account, the conglomerate formed about 17 million years ago (17 Ma).

Early to middle Miocene sedimentary rocks correlated to the Morozaki Group, the Ichishi, Mizunami, and the Shitara Group are widely distributed around the Chita Peninsula (Fig. 1b). These Miocene sedimentary rocks were deposited in various environments, terrestrial to deep sea. Reconstructed early to middle Miocene coastline by SHIBATA and ITOIGAWA (1989) and ITOIGAWA and SHIBATA (1992) is shown in Fig. 1b.

The Pacific Plate was directly subducted below the Eurasian Plate at about 17 Ma, while the Philippine Sea Plate is subducted at present. (YAMAJI and YOSHIDA, 1998). The study area was located north of the trough or trench, where the Pacific Plate was being subducted below the Eurasian Plate during the early to middle Miocene (SHIKI et al., 2002). This subduction zone would be a probable source area of

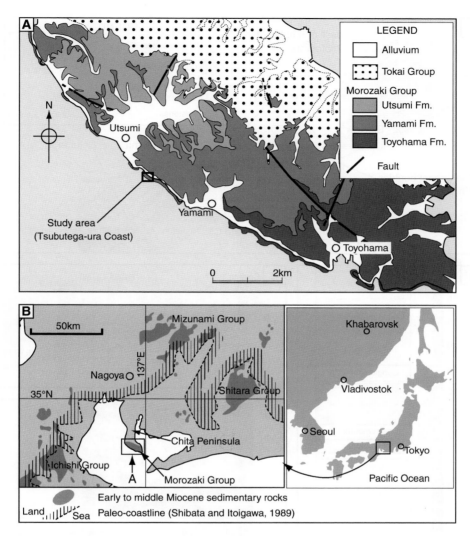

Figure 1
Index map. **a** Location of the Tsubutega-ura Coast and the distribution of the Morozaki Group. **b** Distribution of early to middle Miocene sedimentary rocks around the study area and the estimated paleocoastline in early Miocene. Modified from KONDO and KIMURA (1987), SHIBATA (1988), SHIBATA and ITOIGAWA (1989)

tsunamis, though the precise location of this zone is unclear.

3. Geological Field Survey

3.1. Sedimentary Features of the Miocene Rocks on the Tsubutega-ura Coast

The Miocene sequence of the Tsubutega-ura Coast is about 20 m thick, and is composed of bioturbated mudstones, medium-grained to gravelly sandstones, and conglomerates (Fig. 2a). Many small-scale faults are observed on the outcrop (Fig. 2a). Fault F1 is the largest one in this area, and divides the outcrop into two parts. In the present study, we call the northwestern part "Block A" and the southeastern part "Block B".

Bioturbated mudstones are the predominant sedimentary rocks in this area. Trace fossils suggest that the mudstones formed under a low-energy and small-sediment supply condition without extraordinary events such as tsunamis or storm surges (STOW et al., 1996). Thin layers of white-colored very

37

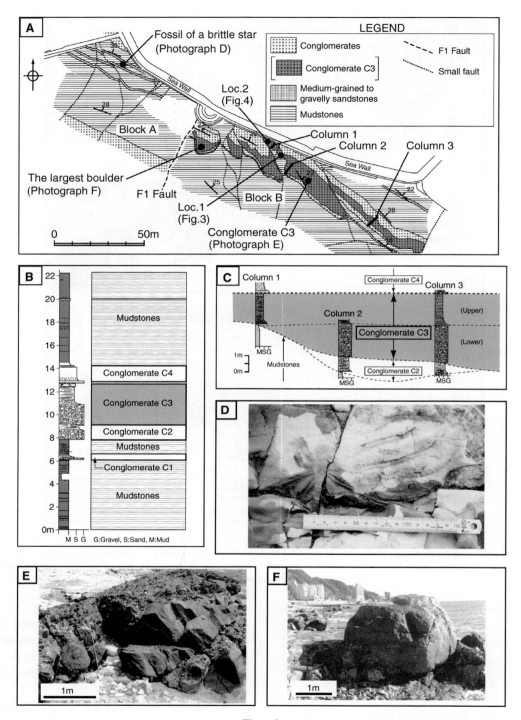

Figure 2
Summary of geological field survey in the Tsubutega-ura Coast. **a** Geological map of the study area. The outcrop is divided into two *blocks* by *F1 Fault*. **b** Columnar section of the Miocene sequence in the *Block B*. Four conglomerates are present in this *block*. **c** The correlation of Column 1–3. The conglomerate C3 was deposited as shallow channel-fill conglomerate and overlying *sheet-like* sandstone. **d** Photograph showing a fossil *brittle star*. **e** Photograph showing a typical example of the *lower part* of the conglomerate C3. Many angular boulders are present. **f** Photograph showing the largest boulder in the study area (3 m in diameter). This boulder has *spherical shape*

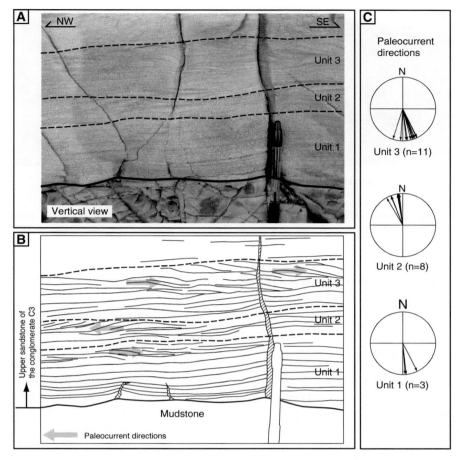

Figure 3
Paleocurrent directions inferred from laminae in the *upper* sandstones in the conglomerate C3 (Loc. 1). **a** Photograph showing the sandstone part of the conglomerate C3. Ripple cross-laminae are present in abundant parallel-laminae. **b** *Line* drawing of laminae in the sandstone. *Arrows* show paleocurrent directions. **c** Diagrams showing paleocurrent directions reconstructed from ripple cross-laminae

fine-grained sand are rarely interbedded in these mudstones. These sandstones are interpreted as distal turbidites, which could have formed under conditions of storm surges (SHIKI *et al.*, 2002).

Medium-grained to gravelly sandstones appear in the upper part in Block A and Block B. These sandstones are yellow–brown-colored and have an erosional base. They are several centimeters in thickness, and often exhibit deformation structures such as load casts. Gravels included in these sandstones are granule to pebble sized.

Conglomerates appear in the lower and uppermost part of Block A and in the middle part of Block B (Fig. 2a). These conglomerates are very poorly sorted, and erosionally cover the underlying deposits.

The conglomerates are clast-supported and grade into sandstones. Two beds of conglomerate appear in Block A, and four in Block B.

The medium-grained to gravelly sandstones and the conglomerates clearly contrast with the background sediments in grain size. These coarse sediments may have been formed in some extraordinary event.

Fossil of a brittle star (*Brisingella* sp.) appears in Block A (Fig. 2a, d). This fossil is present in mudstone. Because the fossil appears in background deposits, probably it was not transported by an event flow. Therefore, the fossil indicates the sedimentary environment which was an upper bathyal sea bottom. This environment is consistent with that mentioned in SHIBATA and ITOIGAWA (1989). YAMAZAKI *et al.* (1989)

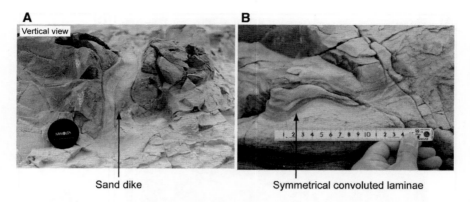

Figure 4
Soft-sediment deformation structures in *upper* sandstone of the conglomerate C3. **a** Photograph showing a sand dike. The dike was formed by intrusion of fluidized sand. **b** Photograph showing symmetrical convolute laminae. These structures are present in Loc. 2

estimate that the depositional depth of sedimentary rocks in the Tsubutega-ura Coast was about 200–400 m depth.

3.2. Sedimentary Features of the Conglomerate C3

We term four conglomerates in Block B as C1 to C4, in ascending order (Fig. 2b). These conglomerates are composed of a set of lower conglomerate and upper sandstone. The conglomerate C3 is the thickest one and includes the largest boulder in the study area. The lower conglomeratic part of the conglomerate C3 is up to 3 m thick, and pinches out toward the northwest (Fig. 2c). The upper sandstone part is about 2 m thick, and laterally continues throughout Block B.

Most of gravels in the conglomerate are fragments of gneiss ranging mainly between pebble to boulder in size. Most of the gravels are angular to subangular, ranging up to 2.5 m in the long axis (Fig. 2e). Rip-up mud clasts ranging from a few centimeters to 1 m in diameter are common and wood fragments are rare in the conglomerate. The matrix of the conglomerate mainly consists of medium- to very coarse-grained sand and granules, and shows normal grading. The matrix of the upper part of conglomeratic part predominantly consists of medium- to coarse-grained sand, which continuously changes into the upper sandstone part of the conglomerate C3. This feature shows that the lower conglomeratic part and upper sandstone part were continuously deposited.

Therefore, the conglomerate C3 is interpreted as deposits by one event.

A remarkably large boulder up to 3 m in diameter is present in the conglomerate C3 (Fig. 2f) and is spherical in shape. The sphericity is about 0.9 in the classification of LINDHOLM (1987). The roundness is "rounded" in the classification by LINDHOLM (1987). The shape of the boulder shows that it came from a very shallow water area in which the boulder was rounded by waves or currents.

The upper sandstone, in which parallel laminae are commonly observed, consists of fine- to very coarse-grained sand and shows normal grading. The lower part of the sandstone is characterized by ripple cross-stratification. The ripple cross-stratification of Unit 1, and those of Unit 3, show the south- to southeastward (i.e., seaward) paleocurrent direction (Fig. 3). In contrast, north- to northwestward (i.e., landward) paleocurrent direction is recognized in ripple cross-stratification in Unit 2. A part of the cross-stratification of this unit shows a rounded crest and slightly symmetrical shape. This feature possibly means combined flow origin. These three units show reversal of paleocurrent directions. Such reversal is observed at a few sites of the conglomerate C3 in the study area.

Sand dikes and symmetrical convoluted laminae are present in this sandstone (Fig. 4). These deformed structures can be formed by intense ground shaking by earthquakes (e.g., SCOTT and PRICE, 1988; OBERMEIER, 1996). Considering tectonic settings and sedimentary environments of the study area, ground shaking is the probable cause for these structures.

4. Critical Current Velocity Required to Move the Boulders

4.1. Estimation of the Critical Current Velocity to Move the Boulders

In this section, a critical current velocity to move a meter-scale boulder in water flow is estimated. Though the amount of research on the transportation of meter-scale boulders by water current is still small, some researchers have discussed the movement of large boulders by tsunamis (e.g., Noтт, 1997; Mastronuzzi and Sansò, 2000; Noтт, 2003; Noormets et al., 2002).

In the present study, we adopted a theoretical route, "pivoting analysis" (Komar and Li, 1986), to estimate the critical current velocity to move a boulder. This analysis focuses on a clastic particle and examines the rotational momenta acting on it. Because our interest is in a single boulder which is much larger than other gravels, pivoting analysis is suitable for the present study.

4.2. Formulating the Model to Estimate a Critical Current Velocity

We use a spheroid boulder in our model, because the largest boulder in the conglomerate C3 is approximately spherical. A spheroid boulder is set on a gently dipping bottom of the angle ξ in a flow of current velocity u (Fig. 5). The bottom is assumed to consist of spheres of d_0 in diameter. The boulder receives gravity, buoyancy, and hydrodynamic drag and lift force. We assume that these forces work in the gravitational center. The boulder is moved as rolling when the current velocity is larger than a specific one. We call the specific velocity to move the bounder as the critical current velocity. When the current velocity is the critical one, rotational momenta of the forces, which are gravity, buoyancy, drag force, and lift force, are balanced at the center of the rotation (Point A; see Fig. 5). We can estimate the critical velocity from the balance of rotational momenta acting on the boulder.

The balance of rotational momenta at Point A is represented in the following form:

$$F_D \frac{d}{2}\cos\theta + F_L \frac{d}{2}\sin\theta - F_G \frac{d}{2}\sin(\theta - \xi) = 0 \quad (1)$$

where F_D is the drag force acting on the boulder by a flow, F_L is the lift force, and F_G is gravity with buoyancy. In Eq. 1, d is the diameter of the boulder; ξ is the dip angle of the sea bottom, and θ is the angle formed by the Line GA and vertical line (Fig. 5a).

The forces, F_D, F_L, and F_G, are represented by the following Eq. 2a–2c.

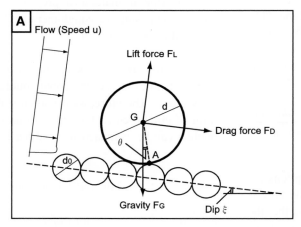
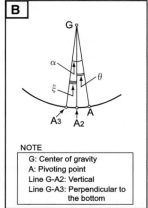

Figure 5
Diagram of the pivoting analysis for a boulder. **a** Schematic figure of a *spheroid boulder* on the sea bottom arranged by relatively small gravels in water flow, and of forces acting on the boulder. **b** Definition of the angle α, and the relationship between the angles ξ, θ, α

$$F_D = \frac{1}{2}\rho_w \left(\frac{\pi d^2}{4}\right) u^2 C_D \varepsilon \qquad (2a)$$

$$F_L = \frac{1}{2}\rho_w \left(\frac{\pi d^2}{4}\right) u^2 C_L \varepsilon \qquad (2b)$$

$$F_G = (\rho - \rho_w)\left(\frac{\pi d^3}{6}\right) g \qquad (2c)$$

where ρ is the density of boulders, ρ_w is the density of sea water, C_D is the drag coefficient, C_L is the lift coefficient, u is the current velocity, ε is the shading coefficient, and g is the gravitational acceleration (about 9.8 m/s).

Substituting Eq. 2a–2c into Eq. 1, the critical current velocity to move the boulder is obtained in the following form:

$$u_c = \sqrt{\frac{4}{3}\left(\frac{\rho}{\rho_w} - 1\right)\frac{gd}{C_D\varepsilon} \cdot \frac{\sin\theta}{\cos(\theta + \xi) + k_L \sin(\theta + \xi)}}$$
$$(3)$$

where k_L is the ratio of lift force to drag force, C_L/C_D.

When the boulder is lying on the bottom consisting of gravels of d_0 in diameter, the following relationships are satisfied geometrically (Fig. 5b);

$$\theta + \xi = \alpha \qquad (4)$$

$$\sin\alpha = \frac{d_0}{d + d_0} \qquad (5a)$$

$$\cos\alpha = \frac{\sqrt{d^2 + 2dd_0}}{d + d_0} \qquad (5b)$$

where α is the angle formed between Line GA$_3$ (perpendicular to the bottom) and Line GA. Substituting Eq. 4, 5a and 5b into Eq. 3, the critical current velocity to move the boulder of d in diameter is represented as a following form.

$$u_c = \sqrt{\frac{4}{3}\left(\frac{\rho}{\rho_w} - 1\right)\frac{gd}{C_D\varepsilon} \cdot \frac{d_0 \cos\xi - \sqrt{d^2 + 2dd_0}\sin\xi}{\sqrt{d^2 + 2dd_0} + k_L d_0}}$$
$$(6)$$

In the formulation of Eq. 6, two assumptions are required about the flow. The first is that the flow is uniform along the vertical axis. The other is that the effects of viscosity are negligible. These assumptions are approximately satisfied for the flow of tsunami-induced currents in an offshore area by following

reasons: (i) Based on the linear long wave theory, motion of a water particle is approximated to the uniform harmonic oscillation parallel to the sea bottom at any depth, (ii) Thickness of boundary layers are estimated at $\sqrt{\pi/(Tv)}$ (SHUTO, 1981), where T is a cycle of a tsunami and v is a coefficient of kinetic viscosity of water. In tsunamis the thickness is up to several centimeters, which is relatively thin compared with meter-scale boulders. This means that the vertical component of current velocity is negligible and the velocity is uniform in the vertical. In this way, we can treat the flow around the boulder as uniform.

4.3. Deriving the Critical Current Velocity to Move the Largest Boulder in the Conglomerate C3

The critical current velocity to move the boulder (diameter 3 m) is derived from Eq. 6. The values of parameters, coefficients, or constants in this equation are as follows;

$$\rho = 2.7 \times 10^3 \,(\text{kg/m}^3), \rho_w = 1.0 \times 10^3 \,(\text{kg/m}^3),$$
$$d = 3.0(\text{m}), g = 9.8 \,(\text{m/s}^2),$$
$$C_D = 0.20, C_L = 0.18, \varepsilon = 1, \xi = 2.0(\text{degree})$$

where ξ is assumed considering the present seafloor dip of shelf and continental slope.

We can obtain the relationship between d_0 and u_c as shown in Fig. 6, where d_0 is the diameter of the bottom materials and u_c is the critical current velocity. Bottom material is presumed to be gravels mainly composing the conglomerarte C3. Then, d_0 is assumed to be 0.1–0.3 m.

In the present study, we need the lower limit of the critical current velocity, because we examine hydrodynamical possibility about boulder movements by tsunamis. Therefore, we can assume that the lower limit of critical current velocity to move the largest boulder can be estimated to be about 2–3 m/s.

5. Tsunami Simulations

5.1. Numerical Simulations of Tsunamis

In this section we intend to verify hydrodynamically whether the conglomerate C3 could have been

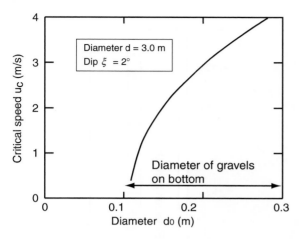

Figure 6

The relationship between diameter of bottom material (d_0) and critical speed (u_c). The diameter of the boulder is 3 m (i.e. $d = 3$ m). The dip of the slope on which the boulder rests is set at 2°. Viewing this figure, we can see that the lower limit of critical speed of currents is about 2–3 m/s

formed by tsunamis or not. The purpose is to estimate what degree of tsunami currents can be induced by assumed earthquakes of various magnitudes with considering the conditions of plate dynamics in this region. We examined the maximum speed of sea water current in the layer just above the sea bed of several 100 m depth.

In order to estimate the tsunami-induced current speed in the open sea at about 200–400 m depth, we conducted numerical simulations of tsunamis for the three cases of great to gigantic earthquakes, which can occur along plate boundaries. The first one is of M8.0 class. An example of such earthquakes is the 1944 Tonankai Earthquake. The second one is of M8.5 class, which is the nearly same magnitude as the 1707 Hoei Earthquake, one of the largest earthquakes recorded in Japanese history. The third one is of M9.0 class, which is equivalent to the 2004 Sumatra–Andaman Earthquake in Indonesia.

When we conduct numerical calculations of tsunamis, the initial displacement of the water surface is given by assuming that it takes the same form as the sea bottom displacement, which can be computed by the method of MANSINHA and SMYLIE (1971), giving a set of fault parameters for each case. In our tsunami simulations, we replaced the sea depth as 100 m for the grid mesh having depth less than

100 m to avoid numerical disturbance in the shallower sea area. As the depositional area of the conglomerate is about 200–400 m depth, the replacement of the depth in the shallower region has little effect to the results. We neglect the effects of the rotation of the Earth, viscosity effects of sea water, and non-linearity. In addition, we assume total reflection at the coastline.

5.2. The Topography of the Numerically Calculated Sea Region and the Source Area of Earthquakes

We assume the shape and bathymetry of the present sea bottom with the paleocoastline of the early Miocene period (Fig. 7), which was reconstructed by SHIBATA and ITOIGAWA (1989) and ITOIGAWA and SHIBATA (1992). These authors estimated features of topography on the basis of geological data such as sediment properties and fossils. The dislocated planes of the earthquakes are assumed to be situated on the subduction zone between the Pacific and the Eurasian Plates, which is noted as the "Paleotrench" in Fig. 7. Because the topography is assumed based on the present one, there is the possibility that the source area of tsunamis in the actual topography was far or near from the study area compared with that in the assumed one.

5.3. Fault Parameters and Initial Conditions

The initial sea surface displacement is arrived at by calculating the sea bottom crustal deformations using fault parameters. These parameters consist of eight elements; locality of the end point of the upper side of the fault plane (latitude, longitude, and the depth), length, width, strike (from north to clockwise), dip, rake, and the amount of slip.

Magnitudes of earthquakes are affected by the amounts of fault slip and fault-rupture length. To set these parameters for assumed earthquakes, we use the method of WELLS and COPPERSMITH (1994). We made the figures showing the relationship between the magnitude of earthquakes and the maximum fault slip and fault-rupture length based on MENKE et al. (2006) and the earthquake catalog of Japan (SATO et al., 1989) (Fig. 8). Figure 8a shows the relationship

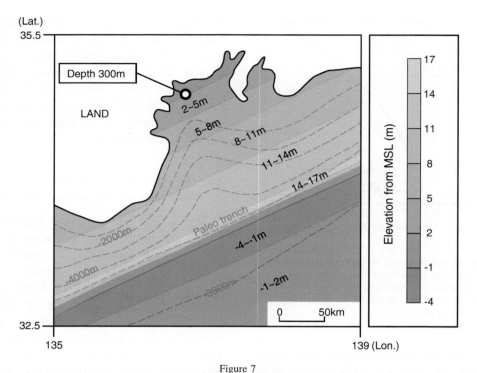

Figure 7

The topography of the numerically calculated sea region and initial sea surface displacement computed with the fault parameters of a gigantic earthquake (M9.0 class). "Paleotrench" corresponds to the rupture zone of assumed earthquakes in the present tsunami simulation

between the magnitude of earthquakes and the maximum slip. This figure shows that a gigantic earthquake (M9.0 class) like the 2004 Sumatra–Andaman Earthquake (M9.1–9.3) has the maximum slip at about 20–40 m. A great to gigantic earthquake (M8.5 class) like the 1707 Hoei Earthquake (M8.6) has the maximum slip at 10–20 m. A great earthquake (M8.0 class) has the maximum slip at 4–8 m, in general. Figure 8b shows the relationship between the magnitude of earthquakes and their fault length. This figure shows that fault-rupture lengths of the 2004 Sumatra–Andaman Earthquake, the 1707 Hoei Earthquake, and the 1944 Tonankai Earthquake are about 1,200, 600, and 200 km, respectively. We carried out numerical tsunami simulations for these three classes. The fault parameters of each class are shown in Table 1. The initial sea surface displacement of M9.0 class is shown in Fig. 7.

5.4. Propagation of Tsunamis

In our simulations we neglect the rotation of the Earth, the curvature of the sea surface, the viscosity

of sea water, and the bottom friction. We can neglect the effect of dispersion in the case that the propagation distance does not exceed a 1,000 km. The vertically integrated governing equations are as follows:

$$\frac{\partial \eta}{\partial t} = -\left(\frac{\partial q_x}{\partial x} + \frac{\partial q_y}{\partial y}\right) \tag{7a}$$

$$\frac{\partial q_x}{\partial t} = -gD\frac{\partial \eta}{\partial x} \tag{7b}$$

$$\frac{\partial q_y}{\partial t} = -gD\frac{\partial \eta}{\partial y} \tag{7c}$$

where η is the vertical displacement of the water surface above the still water level, q_x and q_y are discharge fluxes of x axis and y axis, D is the still water depth, and g is the gravitational acceleration.

Tsunami waves have a small ratio of water depth to wave length. A vertical water-particle velocity is negligible and a horizontal water-particle velocity is approximately uniform in the vertical direction. Therefore, the x and y axes components of the

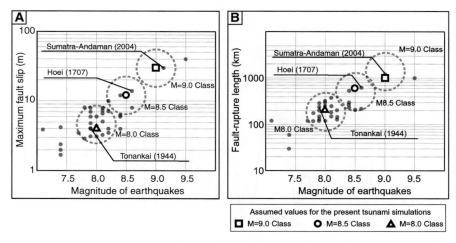

Figure 8

The relationship between the maximum fault slip and the magnitude of earthquakes (**a**), and between the fault-rupture length and the magnitude of earthquakes (**b**). The *dotted circles* show the approximate range of the maximum slip for each class. Assumed values for the present tsunami simulation are also shown in these figures. The data on the maximum fault slip, the fault-rupture length, and magnitude of earthquakes are based on Sato *et al.* (1989) and Menke *et al.* (2006)

Table 1

Fault parameters of the earthquakes for the present tsunami simulation

Parameters	M9.0 class	M8.5 class	M8.0 class
End point (latitude)	35	35	34
End point (longitude)	143	140	138
Depth (km)	3	3	3
Length (km)	1,000	600	200
Width (km)	200	150	100
Strike (°)	246	246	246
Dip (°)	30	30	30
Rake (°)	90	90	90
Slip (m)	30	12	4

horizontal water-particle velocity V_x and V_y are derived from q_x and q_y, respectively as follows:

$$V_x = \frac{1}{D} \int_{SeaBottom}^{SeaSurface} v_x(z)dz \approx \frac{q_x}{D} \qquad (8a)$$

$$V_y = \frac{1}{D} \int_{SeaBottom}^{SeaSurface} v_y(z)dz \approx \frac{q_x}{D} \qquad (8b)$$

The water-particle speed is given by the following Eq. 9

$$|V| = \sqrt{V_x^2 + V_y^2} = \frac{\sqrt{q_x^2 + q_y^2}}{D} \qquad (9)$$

5.5. Results of the Tsunami Simulation

The results of the tsunami simulation were output at six points at depths of 100, 200, 300, 400, 500, and 600 m. These selected points are placed along a line nearly normal to the estimated coastline. The output of our tsunami simulation consists of the following results at each selected point;

1. Time history of speed of currents, which was computed by the Eq. 9.
2. Time history of vertical displacement of water surface above the still water level.
3. Time history of current direction (seaward or landward). The direction is decided from the velocity of tsunami currents normal to an estimated local coastline.

5.5.1 M9.0 Class Earthquake

Time histories of the current speed, the vertical displacement of the water surface, and the direction of the tsunami current of an M9.0 class earthquake at the selected point which is 300 m below the surface are illustrated in Fig. 9a.

The current speed shows a first peak of 1.7 m/s at time $t = t_1$ (about 20 min), whose direction is landward. The first peak of the displacement of the

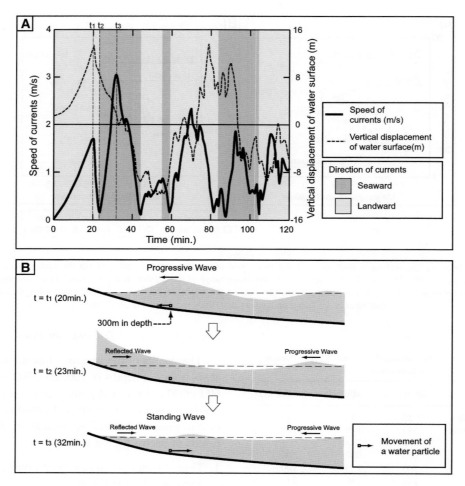

Figure 9
Results of the tsunami simulation at 300 m depth, a gigantic earthquake (M9.0 class). **a** Time history of the speed of current (*the solid line*) and of the vertical displacement of water surface (*the broken line*). The direction of currents is also shown; *dark grey* interval denotes seaward, and *light gray* landward. **b** Schematic figure of wave forms and bottom currents at 300 m depth during the initial stage of a tsunami. The first wave of the tsunami arrives at time $t = t_1$, about 20 min. The wave progresses landward and reflects at the coastline at time $t = t_2$, about 23 min. The reflected wave and following progressive wave take the form of a standing wave. The speed of the tsunami current is at a maximum at time $t = t_3$, about 32 min. At this time, this point corresponds to a nodal point of the standing wave

water surface coincides with the first peak of the current speed, which shows that the wave takes a form of a progressive wave.

Just after the first peak ($t = t_1$) the current speed decreases, and at time $t = t_2$ (about 23 min) the current speed becomes nearly equal to zero. At that time ($t = t_2$) the current direction reverses from landward to seaward.

At time $t = t_3$ (about 32 min) the current speed shows the second peak. The current speed takes the largest one whose value is about 3.0 m/s. The current direction is seaward. We note that the current speed

at time $t = t_3$ (3.0 m/s) is about twice that at $t = t_1$ (1.7 m/s). We also point out that it is theoretically known that the current speed of a standing wave at a nodal point reaches twice that of the progressive wave. At that time, the vertical displacement of the water surface has returned to zero, which shows that the selected point corresponds to a nodal point of a standing wave, which is formed by overlaying of the incident and reflected waves (Fig. 9b).

We also output current speeds at the points of 100, 200, 400, 500, and 600 m depth. The relationship between the maximum seaward current speed to the

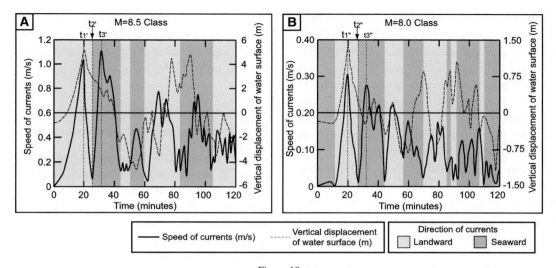

Figure 10
Time history of speed of tsunami currents (*the solid line*) and of the vertical displacement of the water surface (*the broken line*) at 300 m depth. The direction of currents is also shown; *dark grey* interval seaward, *light gray* landward. **a** The results of an M8.5 class earthquake, **b** M8.0 class

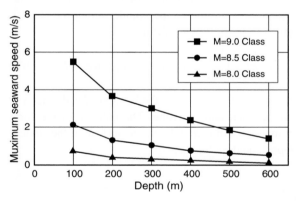

Figure 11
The maximum seaward speed of tsunami currents calculated by the present tsunami simulation at the selected points. As the depth of the selected point becomes shallower, the speed increases

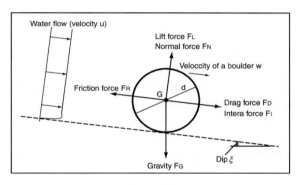

Figure 12
Schematic diagram of forces acting on a boulder moving along a gentle slope. Gravitational force F_G, drag force F_D, intra force F_I, lift force F_L, friction force F_R, and normal force F_N are assumed to act at the gravitational center of the boulder. The velocity of the boulder is represented as w, and that of water as u

depth is shown in Fig. 11. It was possible to move the largest boulder in the conglomerate C3 if the boulder was on the sea bottom of 300 m depth or shallower.

5.5.2 M8.5 Class and M8.0 Class Earthquakes

Results of the tsunami simulations for M8.5 and M8.0 class earthquakes at the point of 300 m depth are illustrated in Fig. 10a and b, respectively. These figures also show the time history of the current speed, the vertical displacement of the water surface, and the current direction in the same way as Fig. 9a.

The time history of the current speed shows the first peak at time $t = t_1'$ (about 20 min), and its speed is about 1.0 m/s. The second peak appears at time $t = t_3'$ (about 32 min), its speed is 1.1 m/s. We should note that the value of the second peak is not twice that of the first peak, but about the same as that of the first peak, which shows the second peak is not the nodal point of a standing wave. Moreover, we can also recognize this fact by noticing that at time $t = t_3$ the surface displacement (broken line) does not return to zero. We can interpret this as meaning that, even if

47

the second peak of current speed takes the largest value as in the case of M9.0 class, the wave is not composed of a perfect standing wave. The absolute value of the maximum current speed is only 1.1 m/s at 300 m depth. The current speed is therefore insufficient to move the largest boulder in the conglomerate C3 (Fig. 11).

The time history of the current speed with an M8.0 class earthquake is shown in Fig. 9b. Unlike an M9.0 class, the absolute value of the current speed is even less sufficient to move the largest boulder in the conglomerate around its depositional area (Fig. 11).

6. Transported Distance of Boulders by Tsunamis Along a Submarine Slope

6.1. Estimation of Transported Distance of Boulders by Tsunamis Along a Submarine Slope

In this section, we theoretically estimate transported distance of a boulder by tsunamis along sea bottom. We assume that a boulder is situated along a gently-dipping submarine slope in tsunami currents by using one-dimensional model.

Some researchers have studied gravel transportation on coastal area by tsunamis on hydrodynamical viewpoints (e.g., IMAMURA et al. 2008; GOTO et al.,

2010). They suggested a numerical model for transportation of a cubic boulder by tsunami currents. We apply representation of external forces acting on a boulder proposed by IMAMURA et al. (2008).

6.2. Formulation of a Model to Estimate Transported Distance of Boulders by Tsunami Currents

In our model, we consider a spheroid boulder which is moving with a velocity w along a gently dipping slope of the angle ξ in a flow of current velocity u. The boulder receives following forces; gravitational force and buoyancy (F_G) in vertical direction, hydrodynamic drag force (F_D), intera force (F_I), and a bottom frictional force (F_R) along the slope, a hydrodynamic lift force (F_L) and a normal force (F_N) in perpendicular to surface of the slope (Fig. 12). We assume that these forces work at the gravitational center of the boulder. Along the slope, equation of motion of the boulder along the slope is given in the following form;

$$\rho \frac{4}{3}\pi \left(\frac{d}{2}\right)^3 \frac{dw}{dt} = F_D + F_I + F_G \sin \xi + F_R \quad (10a)$$

where ρ is the density of the boulder, d is diameter of the boulder, and t is time. The balance of the force components in perpendicular to surface of the slope is represented as follow;

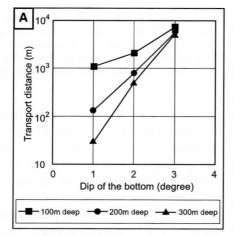

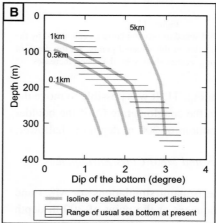

Figure 13

The transported distance calculated with results of the present tsunami simulations at 100–300 m depth. **a** The relationship between the transported distance and the slope dip at each depth of an initial point. **b** Diagram showing *isolines* of transported distance and range of usual sea bottom at present

$$F_L + F_N - F_G \cos \xi = 0 \qquad (10b)$$

These forces are expressed in the following forms;

$$F_G = (\rho - \rho_w) \frac{4}{3} \pi \left(\frac{d}{2}\right)^3 g \qquad (11a)$$

$$F_D = \frac{1}{2} \rho_w \pi \left(\frac{d}{2}\right)^2 C_D (u - w)|u - w| \qquad (11b)$$

$$F_I = \rho_w \frac{4}{3} \pi \left(\frac{d}{2}\right)^3 C_M \frac{du}{dt} - \rho_w \frac{4}{3} \pi \left(\frac{d}{2}\right)^3 (C_M - 1) \frac{dw}{dt}$$
$$(11c)$$

$$F_R = -\frac{w}{|w|} \mu_r F_N \qquad (11d)$$

$$F_L = \frac{1}{2} \rho_w \pi \left(\frac{d}{2}\right)^2 C_L (u - w)^2 \qquad (11e)$$

where ρ_w is the density of sea water, C_D is the drag coefficient, C_M is the mass coefficient, C_L is the lift coefficient, μ_r is the coefficient of rolling friction, and g is the gravitational acceleration.

Substituting Eq. 10b into Eq. 11d, the frictional forces F_R takes the form as follow;

$$F_R = \frac{w}{|w|} \mu_r F_L - \frac{w}{|w|} \mu_r F_G \cos \xi \qquad (12)$$

Substituting Eqs. 11a–11e, and Eq. 12 into Eq. 10a, the acceleration of the boulder dw/dt is represented as follow;

$$\frac{dw}{dt} = \frac{3}{4} \frac{\rho_w}{\rho + \rho_w (C_M + 1)} \frac{C_D}{d} (u - w)|u - w|$$
$$+ \frac{\rho_w C_M}{\rho + \rho_w (C_M + 1)} \frac{du}{dt}$$
$$+ \frac{3}{4} \frac{w}{|w|} \mu_r \frac{\rho_w}{\rho + \rho_w (C_M + 1)} \frac{C_L}{d} (u - w)^2$$
$$- \frac{\rho - \rho_w}{\rho + \rho_w (C_M + 1)} g \left\{ \frac{w}{|w|} \mu_r \cos \xi - \sin \xi \right\}.$$
$$(13)$$

Equation 13 is an ordinary differential equation governing the velocity of the boulder w. We numerically calculated the velocity by using the Runge–Kutta method. We estimated the transported distance of the boulder by numerical integration of the velocity.

We showed in Sect. 4 that the critical velocity to move the boulder is 2–3 m/s. We also showed in Sect. 5 that tsunami currents exceed 3 m/s in the case of a gigantic earthquake (M9.0 class). We adopted the results of the current velocity u for the case of tsunami currents induced by a gigantic earthquake. When the current velocity u reaches 3 m/s at the depths of 100, 200, and 300 m, we set $t = 0$ and $w = 0$ as the initial condition of the Eq. 13.

6.3. Estimated Results of the Transported Distance

We adopted some coefficients in the Eq. 13 as the same as in Sect. 4. In addition, we assumed to be fixed $C_M = 1.5$ and $\mu_r = 0.04$. The coefficient of rolling friction μ_r is corresponding to that of a tire on a rough road (SOCIETY OF AUTOMOTIVE ENGINEERS OF JAPAN, 1970). The dip of the slope ξ is assumed as 1–3°, which is corresponding to that of the shelf to continental slope at present.

We calculated the transported distance of the boulder for the cases that the boulder was set on the bottom of 100, 200, and 300 m in depth as initial points. The results of the calculation are shown in Fig. 13a. The transported distance increase with increase of the dip of the slope. In the case that the dip of the slope is 1°, calculated transported distance from the point of 100 m in depth is about 1 km, and that from the point of 300 m in depth is about 30 m. For the case that the dip is 3°, transported distance from the point of 100 m in depth is about 7 km, and that from the point of 300 m in depth is about 5 km. These results show that transported distance strongly depends on the dip of slope.

7. Discussion

In general, in the case that we find sedimentary structures in submarine conglomerates which are formed by sea water currents, we can classify their causes into three categories: tsunamis, storm surges, and submarine debris flows. At the Tsubutega-ura Coast, the conglomerate C3, which is composed of upper sandstone and lower conglomeratic parts, can be recognized as deposits formed by currents in one event. This conglomerate C3 was deposited at sea bed of 200–400 m depth. Moreover, we can recognize alternate reversal of paleocurrent direction in the sandstone. WEISS and BAHLBURG (2006) shows that storm surge currents cannot affect the deep sea bottom deeper than about 65 m in depth. Therefore, it is absolutely impossible to consider the cause of forming it as storm surges. Submarine debris flows cannot make alternative reversal of paleocurrent direction during a single event, and therefore submarine debris flows are also impossible. Hence we can conclude that the cause of forming of the conglomerate C3 is best explained by tsunami currents though the gravity possibly had an effect on transportation of clasts in the conglomerate.

Sand dikes and symmetrical convoluted laminae in the conglomerate C3 (Fig. 4) suggest that they were formed by ground motion due to an earthquake (ROSSETTI et al., 2000; PRATT, 2002; MONTENAT et al., 2007). There is no evidence that shows volcanic activity in the conglomerate, in which most gravels are fragments of gneiss. Repeated deposition of conglomerates will negate the possibility that they were formed by bolide impacts. The tectonic setting in this study area is consistent with tsunamis of seismic origin. Tsunamis induced by earthquakes can be best explained as forming the conglomerate.

The lower limit of critical speed of currents to move the boulder of 3 m in diameter (the largest boulder in the conglomerate) is about 2–3 m/s. As we proved in Sect. 5, the seaward current speed reaches 3.0 m/s at 300 m depth in the case that the tsunami is caused by a gigantic earthquake whose magnitude is M9.0 or more. This result indicates that tsunami currents can move even the largest boulder on the sea bottom near the depositional area of the conglomerate (Fig. 11). On the other hand, currents of tsunamis induced by earthquakes whose magnitude is not greater than M8.5 class cannot move the boulders in the conglomerate C3. Tsunamis induced by earthquakes of such magnitude cannot move the boulder even if it is set on the bottom in 100 m depth.

We clarified in Sect. 6 that transported distance of the largest boulder in the conglomerate C3 is several 100 m to several kilometers in the case that the dip of sea bottom is 1–3° (Fig. 13b). The transported distance seems to be short compared with the distance between the coastal area and the depositional area (200–400 m depth). Therefore, it is suggested that a few tsunami events would be required to transport boulders from coastal area to the depositional area.

8. Conclusions

The conglomerate, which includes a boulder of 3 m in diameter and grades from conglomerate to sandstone, appears in Miocene upper bathyal (about 200–400 m depth) sedimentary rocks in the Tsubut-ega-ura Coast. It is considered to be formed by the tsunami accompanied with a gigantic earthquake of magnitude M9.0 or more. In the present study, our conclusions are as follows; (1) The trace of alternating paleocurrent directions in the upper sandstone part of the conglomerate shows that it was formed by tsunami currents, (2) Our tsunami simulation shows that only such a gigantic earthquake (M9.0 class) can move the largest boulder on a sea bed of about 300 m depth, (3) Transported distance of the largest boulder is estimated to be several 100 m to several kilometers by one tsunami event.

Acknowledgments

We thank Dr. Tsunemasa Shiki for enhancing this paper, Dr. Teiji Yamazaki for discussions on the field work, and Dr. Yuichi Namegaya for helpful assistance with the tsunami simulation. We also thank two referees, Dr. Osamu Fujiwara and Dr. Brian F. Atwater, and the editor, Kenji Satake, for thoughtful comments. This work was supported financially by a Scientific Grant-in-Aid (20310102) from the Ministry of Education, Sports, Science and Culture (Monbukagakusho) of Japan.

REFERENCES

BOURGEOIS, J. (2009) Geological effects and records of tsunamis, In BERNARD, E.N. and ROBINSON, A.R. (eds.), The Sea, Volume 15, 55-91, Harvard Univ. Press, Cambridge.

BROOKFIELD, M.E., BLECHSCHMIDT, I., HANNIGAN, R., CONIGLIO, M., SIMONSON, B., and WILSON, G. (2006) Sedimentology and geochemistry of extensive very coarse deepwater submarine fan sediments in the Middle Jurassic of Oman, emplaced by giant tsunami triggered by submarine mass flows, Sedimentary Geology, 192, 75-98, doi:10.1016/j.sedgeo.2006.03.026.

CANTALAMESSA, G. and DI CELMA, C. (2005) *Sedimentary features of tsunami backwash deposits in a shallow marine Miocene setting, Mejillones Peninsula, northern Chile*, Sedimentary Geology, 178, 259-273, doi:10.1016/j.sedgeo.2005.05.007.

DAWSON, A.G., FOSTER, I.D.L., SHI, S., SMITH, D.E., and LONG, D. (1991) *The identification of tsunami deposits in coastal sediment sequences*, Science of Tsunami Hazards, 9, 73-82.

DAWSON, A.G. and SHI, S. (2000) *Tsunami deposits*, Pure Appl. Geophys., 157, 875-897.

DAWSON, A.G. and STEWART, I (2007) *Tsunami deposits in the geological record*, Sedimentary Geology, 200, 166-183, doi: 10.1016/j.sedgeo.2007.01.002.

DAWSON, A.G. and STEWART, I (2008) Offshore tractive current deposition: The forgotten tsunami sedimentation process, In SHIKI, T. et al. (eds.), Tsunamiites –Features and Implications–, 153-161, Elsevier B.V., Amsterdam,. doi:10.1016/B978-0-444-51552-0.00010-2.

FUJIWARA, O. and KAMATAKI, T. (2007) *Identification of tsunami deposits considering the tsunami waveform: An example of subaqueous tsunami deposits in Holocene shallow bay on southern Boso Peninsula, Central Japan*, Sedimentary Geology, 200, 295-313, doi:10.1016/j.sedgeo.2007.01.009.

GOFF, J., MCFADGEN, B.G., and CHAGUÈ-GOFF, C. (2004) *Sedimentary differences between the 2002 Easter storm and the 15th-century Okoropunga tsunami, southeastern North Island, New Zealand*, Marine Geology, 204, 235-250, doi:10.1016/S0025-3227(03)00352-9.

GOTO, K., OKADA, K., and IMAMURA, F. (2010) *Numerical analysis of boulder transport by the 2004 Indian Ocean tsunami at Pakarang Cape, Thailand*, Marine Geology, 268, 97-105, doi:10.1016/j.margeo.2009.10.023.

IMAMURA, F., GOTO, K., and OHKUBO, S. (2008) *A numerical model for the transport of a boulder by tsunami*, J. Geophys. Res., 113, C01008, doi:10.1029/2007JC004170.

ITOIGAWA, J. and SHIBATA, H. (1992) The *Miocene paleogeography of the Setouchi distinct (Revised)*, Bull. Mizunami Fossil Museum, 19, 1-12 (in Japanese with English abstract).

KOMAR, P.D. and LI, Z. (1986) *Pivoting analyses of the selective entrainment of sediments by shape and size with application to gravel threshold*, Sedimentology, 33, 425-436.

KONDO, Y. and KIMURA, I. (1987) *Geology of the Morozaki distinct. With Geological Sheet Map at 1:50,000*, Geol. Surv. Japan (in Japanese with English abstract).

LE ROUX, J. P., GÓMEZ, C., FENNER, J., and MIDDLETON, H. (2004) *Sedimentological processes in a scarp-controlled rocky shoreline to upper continental slope environment, as revealed by unusual sedimentary features in the Neogene Coquimbo Formation, north-central Chile*, Sedimentary Geology, 165, 67-92, doi:10.1016/j.sedgeo.2003.11.006.

LE ROUX, J. P., NIELSEN, S.N., KEMNITZ, H., and HENRIQUEZ, Á. (2008) *A Pliocene mega-tsunami deposit and associated features in the Ranquil Formation, southern Chile*, Sedimentary Geology, 203, 164-180, doi:10.1016/j.sedgeo.2007.12.002.

LINDHOLM, R., (1987) A practical approach to sedimentology, Allen & Unwin, Winchester, 276p.

MANSINHA, L. and SMYLIE, D. (1971) *The displacement fields of inclined faults*, Bull. Seismol. Soc. Am., 61, 1433-1440.

MASTRONUZZI, G. and SANSÒ, P. (2000) *Boulders transport by catastrophic waves along the Ionian coast of Apulia (southern Italy)*, Marine Geology, 170, 93-103.

MENKE, W., ABEND, H., BACH, D., NEWMAN, K., and LEVIN, V. (2006) *Review of the source chatacteristics of the Great Sumatra-Andaman Island earthquake of 2004*, Surv. Geophys., 27, 603-613, doi:10.1007/s10712-006-9013-4.

MONTENAT, C., BARRIER, P., OTT D'ESTEVOU, P., and HIBSCH, C. (2007) *Seismites: An attempt at critical analysis and classification*, Sedimentary Geology, 196, 5-30, doi:10.1016/j.sedgeo.2006.08.004.

MORTON, R.A., GELFENBAUM, G., and JAFFE, B.E. (2007) *Physical criteria for distinguishing sandy tsunami and storm deposits using modern examples*, Sedimentary Geology, 200, 184-207, doi:10.1016/j.sedgeo.2007.01.003.

NODA, A., KATAYAMA, H., SAGAYAMA, T., SUGA, K., UCHIDA, Y., SATAKE, K., ABE, K., and OKAMURA, Y. (2007) *Evaluation of tsunami impacts on shallow marine sediments: An example from the tsunami caused by the 2003 Tokachi-oki earthquake, northern Japan*, Sedimentary Geology, 200, 314-327, doi:10.1016/j.sedgeo.2007.01.010.

NOORMETS, R., FELTON, E.A., and CROOK, K.A.W. (2002) *Sedimentology of rocky shorelines: 2: Shoreline megaclasts on the north shore of Oahu, Hawaii - origins and history*, Sedimentary Geology, 150, 31-45.

NOTT, J. (1997) *Extremely high-energy wave deposits inside the Great Barrier Reef, Australia: determining the cause–tsunami or tropical cyclone*, Marine Geology, 141, 193-207.

NOTT, J. (2003) *Waves, coastal boulder deposits and the importance of the pre-transport setting*, Earth Planet. Sci. Lett., 210, 269-276, doi:10.1016/S0012-821X(03)00104-3.

OBERMEIER, S.F. (1996) *Use of liquefaction-induced features for paleoseismic analysis—An overview of how seismic liquefaction features can be distinguished from other features and how their regional distribution and properties of source sediment can be used to infer the location and strength of Holocene paleo-earthquakes*, Engineering Geology, 44, 1-76.

PICKERING, K.T. (1984) *The Upper Jurassic 'Boulder Beds' and related deposits: a fault-controlled submarine slope, NE Scotland*, Journal of Geological Society of London, 141, 357-374.

PICKERING, K.T., SOH, W. and TAIRA, A. (1991) *Scale of tsunami-generated sedimentary structures in deep water*, Journal of Geological Society of London, 148, 211-214.

PRATT, B.R. (2002) *Storms versus tsunamis: Dynamic interplay of sedimentary, diagenetic, and tectonic processes in the Cambrian of Montana*, Geology, 30, 423-426.

ROSSETTI, D.F., GOÈS, A.M., TRUCKENBRODT, W. and ANAISSE, J. (2000) *Tsunami-induced large-scale scour-and-fill structures in Late Albian to Cenomanian deposits of the Grajaù Basin, northern Brazil*, Sedimentology, 47, 309-323.

SATO, R., ABE, K., OKADA, Y., SHIMAZAKI, K., and SUZUKI, Y. (1989) The handbook of parameters of the earthquake faults in Japan, Kashima-Syuppankai, 390p. (in Japanese).

SCOTT, B. and PRICE, S. (1988) *Earthquake-induced structures in young sediments*, Tectonophysics, 147, 165-170.

SHIBATA, H. (1977) *Miocene mollusks from the southern part of Chita Peninsula, central Honshu*, Bull. Mizunami Fossil Museum, 4, 45-53.

SHIBATA, H. (1988) The Morozaki Group, In Editorial Committee of CHUBU II (ed.), Regional geology of Japan Part 5 Chubu II, 125-126, Kyoritu Shuppan, Tokyo (in Japanese).

SHIBATA, H. and Itoigawa, J. (1989) The Setouchi distinct and the old Setouchi Sea, Urban Kubota, 28, 2-9, Kubota Corporation (in Japanese).

Reprinted from the journal

SHIKI, T. and YAMAZAKI, T. (1996) *Tsunami-induced conglomerates in Miocene upper bathyal deposits, Chita Peninsula, central Japan*, Sedimentary Geology, 104, 175-188.

SHIKI, T., YAMAZAKI, T., and TACHIBANA, T. (2002) *The Tsubute-gaura tsunamiite and the rotation of the southwest Japan Island Arc in Miocene epoch*, Gekkan-Chikyu (Chikyu Monthly), 24, 718-723 (in Japanese).

SHUTO, N. (1981) Hodrology of oceanic waves (Giho-do, Tokyo) 217 pp. (in Japanese).

SMIT, J., FORTUIN, A.R., ZIJP, M., KLEIPOOL, L., MEIJER, L., MEULE-NAARS, K, and MONTANARI, A. (2007) *Marine tsunami deposits: New examples from Messinian offshore sediments*, Geol. Soc. Am. Abstracts with Programs, 39, 159.

SOCIETY OF AUTOMOTIVE ENGINEERS OF JAPAN (1970) Automotive engineers' hand book, Tosho Shuppan Sha, Tokyo (in Japanese).

SOHN, Y.K. (2000) *Depositional processes of submarine debris flows in the Miocene fan deltas, Pohang Basin, SE Korea with special reference to flow transformation*, J. Sediment. Res., 70, 491-503.

STOW, D.A.V., READING, H.G., and COLLINSON, J.D. (1996) Deep Seas, In Reading, H.G. (ed.) Sedimentary Environments: Processes, Facies, and Stratigraphy, 395-453, Blackwell Science, Malden.

SUGAWARA, D., MINOURA, K., and IMAMURA, F. (2008) Tsunami and tsunami sedimentology, In Shiki, T. et al. (eds.), Tsunamiites –

Features and Implications–, 9-49, Elsevier B.V., Amsterdam,. doi:10.1016/B978-0-444-51552-0.00003-5.

THE TOKAI FOSSIL SOCIETY (1993) Fossils from the Miocene Morozaki Group, Bisaisha, Tokyo, 297p. (in Japanese with English abstract).

WELLS, D.L. and COPPERSMITH, K.J. (1994) *New empirical relationships among magnitude, rupture length, rupture width, rupture area, and surface displacement*, Bull. Seismol. Soc. Am., 84, 974-1002.

WEISS, R. and BAHLBURG, H. (2006) *A note on the preservation of offshore tsunami deposits*, J. Sediment. Res., 76, 1267-1273, doi: 10.2110/jsr.2006.110.

WILLIAMS, D.M. and HALL, A.M. (2004) *Cliff-top megaclast deposits of Ireland, a record of extreme waves in the North Atlantic - storms or tsunamis?*, Marine Geology, 206, 101-117, doi:10.1016/j.margeo.2004.02.002.

YAMAJI.,A. and YOSHIDA,T. (1998) *Multiple tectonic events in the Miocene Japan arc: The Heike microplate hypothesis*, Jour. Miner. Petrol. Econ. Geol., 93, 389-408, doi:10.2465/ganko. 93.389.

YAMAZAKI, T., YAMAOKA, M. and SHIKI, T. (1989) Miocene offshore tractive current-worked conglomerates -Tsubutegaura, Chita Peninsula, central Japan-, In Taira, A. and Masuda, F. (eds.), Sedimentary Facies in the Active Plate Margin, 483-494, Terra Scientific Pub. Co, Tokyo.

(Received December 1, 2009, revised April 15, 2010, accepted May 31, 2010, Published online November 12, 2010)

Pure Appl. Geophys. 168 (2011), 1015–1031
© 2010 Springer Basel AG
DOI 10.1007/s00024-010-0216-8

❚ Pure and Applied Geophysics

The Transoceanic 1755 Lisbon Tsunami in Martinique

J. Roger,[1,2] M. A. Baptista,[1] A. Sahal,[3] F. Accary,[2,3] S. Allgeyer,[4] and H. Hébert[4]

Abstract—On 1 November 1755, a major earthquake of estimated M_w=8.5/9.0 destroyed Lisbon (Portugal) and was felt in the whole of western Europe. It generated a huge transoceanic tsunami that ravaged the coasts of Morocco, Portugal and Spain. Local extreme run-up heights were reported in some places such as Cape St Vincent (Portugal). Great waves were reported in the Madeira Islands, the Azores and as far as the Antilles (Caribbean Islands). An accurate search for historical data allowed us to find new (unpublished) information concerning the tsunami arrival and its consequences in several islands of the Lesser Antilles Arc. In some places, especially Martinique and the Guadeloupe islands, 3 m wave heights, inundation of low lands, and destruction of buildings and boats were reported (in some specific locations probably more enclined to wave amplification). In this study, we present the results of tsunami modeling for the 1755 event on the French island of Martinique, located in the Lesser Antilles Arc. High resolution bathymetric grids were prepared, including topographic data for the first tens of meters from the coastline, in order to model inundations on several sites of Martinique Island. In order to reproduce as well as possible the wave coastal propagation and amplification, the final grid was prepared taking into account the main coastal features and harbour structures. Model results are checked against historical data in terms of wave arrival, polarity, amplitude and period and they correlate well for Martinique. This study is a contribution to the evaluation of the tele-tsunami impact in the Caribbean Islands due to a source located offshore of Iberia and shows that an 8.5 magnitude earthquake located in the northeastern Atlantic is able to generate a tsunami that could impact the Caribbean Islands. This fact must be taken into account in hazard and risk studies for this area.

Key words: Tsunami, earthquake, Caribbean, far-field, wave amplification, run-up.

1. Introduction

Martinique Island is part of a subduction volcanic arc of 850 km length, resulting from the convergence of the Atlantic Plate under the Caribbean Plate at an average rate of 2 cm/year (Stein *et al.*, 1982) (Fig. 1). This subduction is the cause of shallow earthquakes, some of them with magnitude greater than 7, as was the case of the 5 April 1690, 8 February 1843 (Feuillet *et al.*, 2002) the 18 November 1867 Virgin Island $M_w = 7.5$ earthquake (Zahibo *et al.*, 2003a, b) and the 21 November 2004 $M_w = 6.3$ earthquake of Les Saintes (Zahibo *et al.*, 2005). Important seismic activity is also associated with magmatic activity. The volcanic activity itself can generate pyroclastic flows or lahars that are able to reach the sea and create tsunamis (De Lange *et al.*, 2001; Waythomas and Watts, 2003).

Tsunamis observed in the area result from strong magnitude earthquakes ($M \geq 7$), namely the 1867 Virgin Islands $M_w = 7.5$ earthquake (O'Loughlin and Lander, 2003; Zahibo *et al.*, 2003a, b), or from submarine mass failures (for example, see Lopez-Venegas *et al.*, 2008) as the 14 January 1907 Jamaica landslide (O'Loughlin and Lander, 2003), or the potential landslide on the flank of the Kick'em Jenny underwater volcano (Smith and Shepherd, 1996). Such a landslide could be very large in the Lesser Antilles (Deplus *et al.*, 2001; Le Friant *et al.*, 2009).

According to Pelinovsky *et al.* (2004), volcanic eruptions in the area may also cause tsunamis, as was the case of the July 2003 eruption in Montserrat. For Martinique Island, tsunami waves were observed at least in April 1767 following an earthquake SE of Barbados, and in 1902 due to the volcanic eruption and explosion of Mount Pelée (O'Loughlin and Lander, 2003). Lander *et al.* (2002) collected data from around 30 tsunamis for the Caribbean region

---
[1] Centro de Geofisica da Universidade de Lisboa, Rua Ernesto de Vasconcelos, Faculdade de Ciências, Ed. C8, 6°, 1700 Lisbon, Portugal. E-mail: jeanrog@hotmail.fr
[2] Ecole Normale Supérieure, Laboratoire de Géologie, UMR 8538, 24, rue Lhomond, 75231 Paris Cedex 5, France.
[3] Université Paris 1 Panthéon-Sorbonne, Laboratoire de Géographie Physique, UMR 8591, 1 place Aristide Briand, 92195 Meudon Cedex, France.
[4] CEA, DAM, DIF, 91297 Arpajon, France.

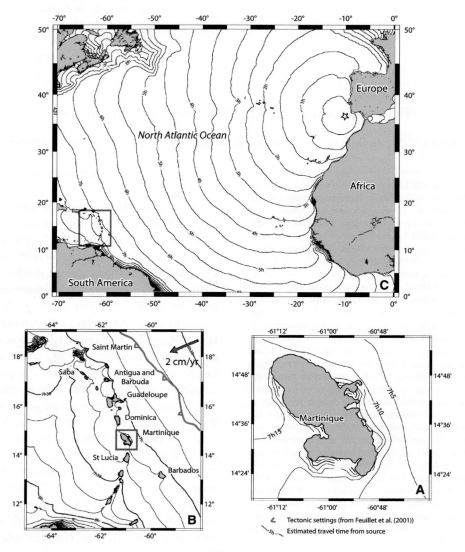

Figure 1
Geographic map locating Martinique Island (**a**) within the Lesser Antilles Arc (**b**) and in the North Atlantic Ocean (**c**). The tsunami travel times (*TTT*), based on a point source (*white star*) close to the source of Baptista *et al.* (2003), are represented by *continuous black curves*

including local sources (source distance <200 km), regional events (<1,000 km) and transoceanic events (>1,000 km). Among them, reliable sources report observations for the 1755 Lisbon tsunami.

The tsunami observed in the Antilles at that time has been associated with the great Lisbon earthquake of November 1, 1755. This event was observed all along the eastern Atlantic shores from Morocco to the United Kingdom, and caused many casualties and damage (BAPTISTA *et al.*, 1998b, 2009a). In addition,

numerous coeval reports indicate important abnormal waves in the Antilles.

Recent results of tsunami modeling show that an earthquake with magnitude up to 8.0/8.5 with an epicenter located offshore the Iberian Peninsula is indeed able to produce significant wave heights in the western Atlantic (BARKAN *et al.*, 2009), and more particularly in the coastal areas of Guadeloupe Island (ROGER *et al.*, 2010), 7 h 30 min of tsunami propagation after the main shock (see tsunami travel times on Fig. 1).

In order to shed some light on the event observed in the French Antilles on 1 November 1755, we made a detailed search for historical documents on these islands and we present here a compilation of those observations with focus on Martinique Island.

The main objective of this study is to test the impact of a tsunami generated by a seismic source proposed for the 1755 event using numerical modeling and high resolution bathymetric data near the coast. We investigate the tsunami far field propagation and the coastal wave amplification close to Martinique Island. The results of numerical modeling correlate well with the available historical data in some selected sites in Martinique Island.

2. The 1755 Event

On 1 November 1755, a great earthquake of estimated magnitude $M = 8.5 \pm 0.3$ (SOLARES and ARROYO, 2004) destroyed the town of Lisbon and was felt in the whole of western Europe, as far east as Hamburg (Germany). Compilations of historical data concerning the earthquake are presented by SOUSA (1919), MACHADO (1966), SOLARES and ARROYO (2004), while compilations on tsunami data are presented in ROMERO (1992), BAPTISTA et al., (1998a, 2003), KAABOUBEN et al. (2009) and BARKAN et al. (2009).

Several authors investigated the source of the Lisbon earthquake, using either macroseismic data (MACHADO, 1966; MARTÍNEZ SOLARES et al., 1979; LEVRET, 1991; SOLARES et al., 2004), average tsunami amplitudes (ABE, 1979), or scale comparisons with the 28 February 1969 event (JOHNSTON, 1996). A different approach was considered by BAPTISTA (1998) and BAPTISTA et al. (1998a, b) throughout the systematic study of the historical records of the 1755 tsunami wave heights observed along the Iberian and Morocco coasts. These authors proposed a source location, based on tsunami hydrodynamics modeling, located close to the southwest Portuguese continental margin. ZITELLINI et al. (1999) identified a very large active, compressive, tectonic structure located 100 km offshore SW Cape St Vincent (Marques de Pombal thrust fault) which was proposed as a good candidate for the generation of the 1755 event, although its dimensions cannot justify the seismic moment of the 1755 earthquake. Later, BAPTISTA et al. (2003) used this structure to build a composite source and checked its reliability against the NE Atlantic tsunami data.

An alternative solution was proposed by GUTSCHER et al. (2002) as an active accretionary wedge overlying an eastward dipping basement and connected to a steep, east dipping slab of cold, oceanic lithosphere beneath Gibraltar. Tsunami simulation results, using this source geometry, are presented in GUTSCHER et al. (2006). VILANOVA et al. (2003) considered an event triggered in the Lower Tagus Valley as the source of most of the damage observed close to Lisbon, and even of some "tsunami like" phenomena described in Oeiras and along the estuary of the Tagus River (BAPTISTA and MIRANDA, 2009b). Recently, a new source based on historical data in the NW Atlantic and far-field tsunami modeling was proposed with an orientation perpendicular to previously suggested trending features (BARKAN et al., 2009).

2.1. Historical Data

2.1.1 Data Sources and Descriptions

The results of the research of historical data concerning the observation of the 1755 tsunami in the Caribbean are summarized in Table 1, showing that the tsunami was observed on several islands, including the French Antilles.

Most of these reports have been quoted in later documents such as the *Procès-Verbal des Séances de l'Académie des Sciences* of 1756 (ANONYMOUS, 1755; LETTÉE, 1755), or the supplement to the Gentleman's Magazine (URBAN, 1755). Most of the reports provide information on the location of historical observations (Table 1). Indeed, at this time, Martinique Island was among the most important trade center, especially Fort-de-France's Bay, attended by experienced sailors.

The accurate reading of these documents allows us to conclude that there are only three distinct sources of information: the first one is the letter read by Duhamel concerning an anonymous witness (ANONYMOUS, 1755); the second one is the letter of LETTÉE (1755); and the third one is the document

Table 1

Historical observed tsunami data in the Lesser Antilles for 1 November 1755 event

Place	Lon. (°W)	Lat. (°N)	Run-up (m)	Maximum inundation distance (MID) (m)	Withdrawal depth (m)	Withdrawal distance (MWD) (m)	Source
Martinique							
La Trinité	60.96	14.74	0.6 (3), 0.9 (2), 1.2ᵃ (4, 5), 9.0 (1)	66 (2)	9.0 (1)	6ᵇ (2), 66 (4, 5)	(1) ANONYMOUS (1755), (2) LETTÉE (1755), (3) DANEY (1846), (4) BRUNET (1850), (5) BALLET (1896)
Le Galion	60.92	14.73	Minor effects				BRUNET (1850), BALLET (1896)
Le Robert	60.94	14.68	*Nothing observed*				*BRUNET (1850), BALLET (1896)*
Sainte-Marie	60.99	14.78					*BRUNET (1850), BALLET (1896)*
Saint-François (actual Le François)	60.89	14.62	Just mentioned				ANONYMOUS (1755)
Lamentin's river	61.01	14.60	The sea rise up in the rivers				BRUNET (1850), BALLET (1896)
Fort Royal's river (actual Fort-de-France)	61.06	14.60	circa 0.9 m more than normal				BRUNET (1850), BALLET (1896)
Epinette's river	60.96	14.735					DANEY (1846), BRUNET (1850), BALLET (1896)
Martinique	61.00	14.60	Just mentioned				AFFLECK (1756)
Guadeloupe							
Saint-Anne	61.38	16.22	3.2*	220*		600*	BALLET (1896)
Barbados							
Carlisle Bay Barbados	59.01	13.08					AFFLECK (1756)
Barbados	59.55	13.16	3.8 (6)				(6) AFFLECK (1756), (7) URBAN (1755), (8) ANONYMOUS (1756)
Antigua	61.80	17.07	1.2 (7)–3.8 (6)		1.8		(6) AFFLECK (1756), (7) URBAN (1755)
Sabia	63.23	17.63	6.3				AFFLECK (1756)
St. Martin	63.05	18.05			4.5ᶜ		AFFLECK (1756)

The italisized entries indicate the places where nothing was observed. The conversion between the historical measures French *Pas du Roy* and meters is 1 pas du Roy = 15/16 English foot = 0.324 m. The numbers within brackets refer to the information source

* Indicates values measured in situ and deduced on maps according to historical observations (this concerns only Guadeloupe)

ᵃ Value given above the high tides

ᵇ This value from LETTÉE, 1755 could be both the withdrawal distance or the withdrawal depth

ᶜ Report of a boat moored at 4.5 m of water that falls on the side: the withdrawal depth could be more or less important

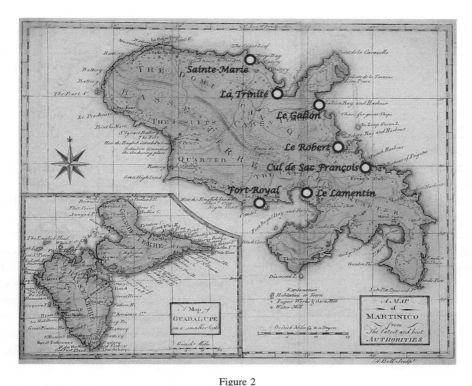

Figure 2
Geographical location of the historical observations and studied sites on Martinique Island on an historical map of Martinique and Guadeloupe Islands (BELL, 1759, *Courtesy of* J. Bodington.)

certainly used by DANEY (1846), BRUNET (1850) and BALLET (1896).

However, this third document is by far the richest one with respect to the tsunami. It is a very precise description of the hydrological phenomenon, focusing especially on La Trinité Bay, describing the various oscillations of the sea level: the succession of flows and withdrawals, amplitudes, periods, etc. In most records, the arrival of several waves is mentioned (actually flow and withdrawal), the first one not always being the strongest. The same document also informs us about the observation or the non-observation of these same wave-trains around the island: limited at Le Galion Bay, nothing at either Le Robert or in St Marie, an "unusual deposit" by the sea in the Epinette River, and specific responses of the Lamentin and the Fort-Royal Rivers (west coast) are also mentioned. These locations are indicated on a British marine map of this period (Fig. 2).

The letter read by Duhamel (ANONYMOUS, 1755) indicates that the sea reached about 9 m (30 ft, in the original) above its usual level four times. The

phenomenon was observed from La Trinité Bay to the François Cul-de-sac. LETTÉE (1755) indicates that the phenomenon started at 4 p.m. at La Trinité Bay, beginning with a 6-meter drop of the sea level (20 ft, in the original), flooding the shore 60 m inland (200 ft, in the original), damaging houses up to 1 m from the ground. It took 30 min for the sea level to return to normal.

Concerning the other islands of the Antilles (Barbados, Guadeloupe, Saba and St Martin, located on Fig. 1), we can find some information about the inundation of docks in harbors, streets, houses and other.

We tried to read/interpret all this information in terms of tsunami parameters. All details concerning the number of waves, the period, and the height are summarized in Table 1.

2.2. Studied Sites in Martinique

The studied sites are presented in Fig. 2. These are La Trinité Bay, located on the east coast of the

Table 2

Parameters of the two source segments used for tsunami modeling

Source		Lon. (°)	Lat. (°)	Depth of center of fault plane (km)	Average slip (m)	Strike (°)	Dip (°)	Rake/slip angle (°)	Length (km)	Width (km)	Rigidity (N m^2)	Mo (N m)
BAPTISTA et al.	GB	−8.7	36.1	20.5	20	250	45	90	105	55	30.0 10^9	3.46 10^{21}
(2003)	MPTF	−10	36.8	20.5	20	21.7	24	90	96	55	30.0 10^9	3.17 10^{21}

island, and Fort-de-France Bay, on the west coast of the island, presenting a special focus on the harbor (already here in 1755) and the international airport of Le Lamentin.

A few other sites, mentioned in the historical reports, are also analyzed: Ste-Marie, Le Galion Bay, Le Robert, St-François. These sites are presented in Fig. 2.

3. Tsunami Modeling

3.1. The Model Earthquake

The model earthquake used in this study for the 1755 earthquake is the double segment source proposed by BAPTISTA et al. (2003), that includes the Marques de Pombal thrust fault (MPTF) identified by ZITELLINI et al. (1999), and a second thrust fault oriented along the Guadalquivir Bank (GB).

They are included in Fig. 1 (as a point source) and their parameters, presented in Table 2, account for a M_w 8.5 earthquake with a seismic moment of $M_o = 6.63 \times 10^{21}$ N m.

The selection of this model earthquake was based upon two facts: (1) GUTSCHER et al. (2002)'s proposed source produces late tsunami arrivals in the near field (GUTSCHER et al., 2006); (2) BARKAN et al. (2009)'s source is not a tectonic based source and its direction cuts the most prominent structures in the area, although it is able to radiate energy towards the Caribbean.

3.2. Numerical Method

The numerical model used in this study is based on the non linear shallow water wave theory. It allows us to compute tsunami generation and propagation associated with an earthquake and has been used for years in order to study tsunami hazards for various exposed regions, from French Polynesia (SLADEN et al., 2007) to the Mediterranean Sea (ALASSET et al., 2006; ROGER and HÉBERT, 2008; YELLES-CHAOUCHE et al., 2009; SAHAL et al., 2009).

Our method assumes instantaneous displacement of the sea surface, identical to the vertical sea-bottom deformation, transmitted without losses to the entire water column; the vertical sea-bottom deformation is computed using the elastic dislocation model of OKADA (1985). Given the initial free surface elevation, the model solves the hydrodynamical equations of continuity (1) and momentum (2). Non linear terms are taken into account, and the resolution is carried out using a finite difference method centred in time and using an upwind scheme in space.

The inundation is calculated based on the methodology presented by KOWALIK and MURTY (1993), relying on an extrapolation of the fluxes calculated in wet cells and in dry meshes:

$$\frac{\partial(\eta + h)}{\partial t} + \nabla[v(\eta + h)] = 0 \qquad (1)$$

$$\frac{\partial v}{\partial t} + (v\nabla)v = -g\nabla\eta \qquad (2)$$

η corresponds to the water elevation, h to the water depth, v to the horizontal velocity vector, g to the gravity acceleration.

3.3. Bathymetric Grids

The wave propagation is calculated from the epicenter area offshore of the Iberian Peninsula (southern Portugal and Spain to the east) across the Atlantic Ocean on six levels of imbricated grids of increasing resolution, approaching the Lesser Antilles including Martinique Island with special focus on La Trinité Bay and Fort-de-France Bay. The largest grid (grid 0, level 1), corresponding to the geographical coordinates of Fig. 1a, is built from GEBCO World Bathymetric Grid 1′ (IOC, IHO and BODC, 2003) and is just a resampling of this grid at a space step of 5′ (∼9,250 m). The grid resolution increases close to the studied site in order to account for a correct description of shorter wavelengths. Indeed, the wave celerity is expressed by $c = \sqrt{gh}$ (in shallow water non dispersive assumption), and thus decreases when h decreases near the coast, implying wave shortening. The time step used to solve the equations decreases when the grid step decreases, and respects for each grid level the Courant-Friedrichs-Lewy (CFL) criterion to ensure the numerical stability. The resolution for the levels 2 (grid 1), 3 (grid 2), 4 (grid 3), 5 (grid 4) and 6 (grid 5 and 6) are, respectively, 1′ (1,850 m), 500, 150, 40 and 20 m. The highest resolution grids (levels 5 and 6), 40 and 20 m, correspond to the zooms on La Trinité Bay and the northern part of Fort-de-France Bay including the harbor and

Lamentin International Airport. The bathymetric dataset was obtained through the merging of GEBCO 1′ data, high resolution multi-beam and resampled bathymetric data from the French Hydrographic Service (SHOM). The intermediate grids (1–4) have been included for numerical stability reasons and correct wavelength sampling during the imbrication. In order to compute tsunami propagation on land, topographic data were manually digitized from topographic maps published by IGN (2006a, b, c).

4. Modeling Results and Comparison with Historical Data

Figure 3 displays the maximum water heights computed across the Atlantic Ocean after 9 h 30 min of propagation. It shows three main energy paths: the strongest towards South America (Brazil), a second

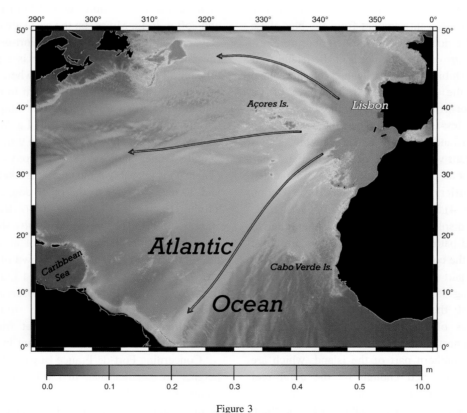

Figure 3
Maximum wave heights over the Atlantic Ocean after 9 h 30 min of tsunami propagation, calculated with the combined source of Baptista *et al.* (2003). The *arrows* highlight the three main tsunami energy paths. The two segments of the source are represented by the *black* and *white rectangles*

towards Newfoundland and the weakest towards the USA (Florida). This radiation pattern is due to the geometrical shape of the source and its azimuth, and to the most relevant submarine features (submarine basins, ridges and transform faults, for example) along the oceanic path that will act as waveguides during tsunami propagation as noted by SATAKE (1988), HÉBERT et al. (2001) and TITOV et al. (2005). It is worth noting that the Caribbean area is not among the most impacted areas for this computed tele-tsunami on this large-scale grid.

In Fig. 4, we present the maximum wave heights along Martinique Island (grid 2, resolution 500 m and grid 3, resolution 150 m) obtained after 9 h 30 min of tsunami propagation. It clearly shows that only a few sites are prone to wave amplification around the island. This corresponds to sites either directly exposed to long wave arrival coming from the Iberian Peninsula or also located on the other side of the island, in the Caribbean Sea. The wave heights observed along the coast of Martinique vary between 1 and 2 m. The coastal segment from the bay of La Trinité and the north coast of the neighboring *Presqu'île de la Caravelle* to the north of the island near Le Lorrain exhibits maximum values of more than 2 m. Along the southeast coast, the bays of Le Galion, Le Robert and Le François, the wave heights are generally less significant. Then the southeastern coast of the island, offshore of Le Vauclun, shows again significant wave heights of more than 1.5 m.

The potential protective role of the fragmented coral reef barrier from Le Vauclun to Le Galion (shown in Fig. 4) against long wave arrivals has to be stressed. The display of the maximum tsunami height with a shaded bathymetric gradient shows a relative protection of the coastal sites by the coral reef, on the southeastern part of the island. This residual coral reef (appearing as a line on the right) leads to an attenuation of the tsunami effect for the thus-protected bays of Le Galion, Le Robert and Le François. The northeastern (La Trinité, Ste Marie, Le Lorrain) and southern part of the island, which are probably not protected enough by the coral reef which is too deep (5–10 m under sea level), shows again some significant wave heights, at the northern part of the island, from La Trinité to Le Lorrain and farther north.

The surfing spots indicated in Fig. 4 highlight the coastal areas not protected by a sufficient coral reef barrier against classic wind long waves.

Figure 5 (grid 5 and 6) present a focus on the specific site of La Trinité Bay and Fort-de-France Bay and neighboring areas after 9 h 30 min of tsunami propagation. It shows the maximum water height reached by the sea level and the flow depth (maximum wave height minus topography) on land.

The high resolution (20 and 40 m) grids of La Trinité and Fort-de-France Bays (Fig. 5) are able to reproduce the segments of this coral reef barrier, the harbour morphology and coastal shapes as well as the shallow bathymetric features that could affect significantly tsunami propagation near the coast and might contribute to wave trapping and amplifications, potentially associated with resonance phenomena (ROGER et al., 2010).

We can clearly see that several places are inundated in both grids, sometimes until several hundreds of meters from the shore: until 100 m in La Trinité and 250 m in La Moïse, on the east side of La Trinité Bay; and until more than 1 km in Fort-de France Bay (near the airport). This inundation is especially significant all around La Trinité Bay where we can find flow depth values of more than 2 m in the town but also in other urban areas such as La Clique and Anse Cosmy (north of La Trinité) and La Moïse, on the eastern side of the bay (Fig. 5). The 9 m (30 ft) wave height value indicated in ANONYMOUS (1755) (Table 1) is probably a mistake; it is likely between 3 and 30 ft if we refer to the other descriptions at La Trinité (LETTÉE, 1755; DANEY, 1846; BRUNET, 1850; BALLET, 1896). The presented results show a maximum inundation distance (MID) of about 100 m in the southern part of the bay (the town of La Trinité), and 250 m in the northeastern area (Anse Cosmy); thus, longer than the historical observations. However, this computed inundation limit may be overestimated due to the fact that friction is not considered and this may be important in urban areas.

Concerning Fort-de-France Bay (grid 6), the wave heights are smaller than in La Trinité (by about a factor of 3), but they can reach 1.5 m offshore of Fort St-Louis and in the inlet of Château Lézards, deep inside of the bay, south of the airport of Le Lamentin. In addition, several places exhibit inundation, in the

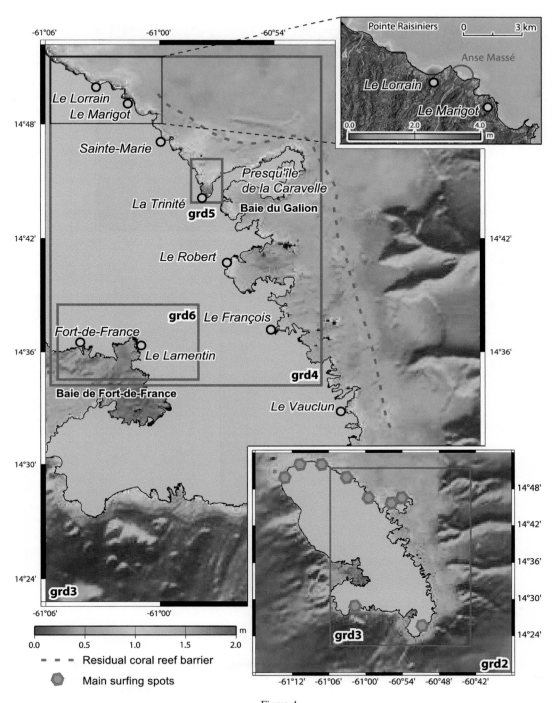

Figure 4
Maximum wave heights illuminated by a bathymetric gradient on Martinique Island on grid 2 and 3 after 9 h 30 min of tsunami propagation using Baptista *et al.* (2003)'s seismic source. The *yellow dots* are the places mentioned in the text. The *red rectangles* show the location of the different imbricated grids. A focus (*black rectangle* on grid 3) shows evidence of wave amplification offshore of a lagoon domain (Anse Massé) southwestward to Le Lorrain. The residual coral reef barrier is indicated with dashed pink curve (from Battistini, 1978). The main *surfing spots* are indicated by *green hexagons* (from http://www.wannasurf.com)

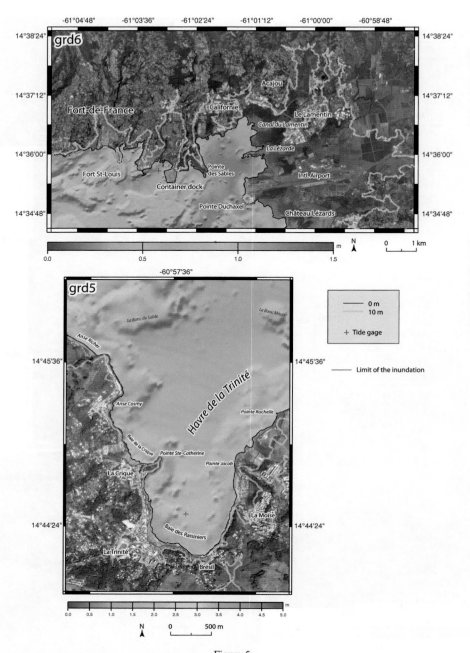

Figure 5
Maximum wave heights illuminated by a bathymetric gradient at sea and maximum water depth on land in high resolution grids 5 and 6 after
9 h 30 min of *tsunami* propagation. The *red line* underlines the inundation limit. The *red crosses* represent the synthetic tide gauges location.
The altitude limits of 0 and 10 m are indicated, respectively, by *black* and *yellow lines*

Fort-de-France town center, which is very low and in the area of the container dock, but also the areas close to the canal of Le Lamentin and the Lézarde River, close to the airport, which are partially inundated. All these inundations in Fort-de-France Bay happen in low lands and mostly in swamps with maximum wave heights of no more than 50 cm. This is in good agreement with the historical data indicating that the Lamentin River, located north of the Airport, was subject to an abnormal phenomenon on 1 November

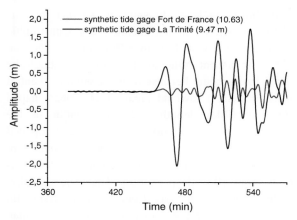

Figure 6
Synthetic maregrams obtained after 9 h 30 min of tsunami propagation for two synthetic tide gauges located in the bays of La Trinité and Fort-de-France. Their positions are given in Fig. 4. The water depth at the gauge location is indicated

1755 with the sea rising up in the rivers 3 feet (∼90 cm) more than normal (BALLET, 1896).

Synthetic tide gauges have been positioned (Fig. 5) in order to obtain information concerning principally tsunami arrival, wave polarities, amplitude and periods at specific locations in both bays.

Figure 6 represents the synthetic signal recorded by two synthetic tide gauges located on both sides of the island, one in La Trinité Bay and one in Fort-de-France Bay. It shows that the effects of the tsunami would be less dramatic in Fort-de-France Bay than they would be in La Trinité Bay at approximately the same water depth (∼10 m). Then it indicates that the first tsunami wave arrives in La Trinité Bay within a travel time of about 7 h 30 min. This is in agreement with the time announced in the available historical documents.

Concerning La Trinité, the computed polarity and the relative amplitudes are in agreement with the reported historical facts: there is a small sea elevation of 70 cm (reported to be 60 cm above the maximum tide level) followed by an significant withdrawal in about 10 min (reported to occur in 4 min) and then a significant inundation of the docks and the streets. The time between the first two waves has been estimated to be 15 min. The computed time between these two waves is around 20 min. According to BALLET (1896)'s accurate description of the phenomenon in

La Trinité, we are globally in good agreement concerning periods and relative amplitude between each wave, except for the position of the most significant and destructive wave: it is reported to be the fourth one (BALLET, 1896) but the results of computation show that it is the fifth (Fig. 6).

5. Discussion

The effects of the tide and friction have not been considered in this study.

The historical tide prediction (done using the actual mean sea level with data from 1980–1985 for Le Robert and data from 2005–2008 for Fort-de-France) on 1 November 1755 for Le Robert indicate that, despite the fact that the amplitude of tide was only of about 40 cm crest to trough, the sea was up or at the beginning of withdrawal at 2 p.m., the hour of arrival of the tsunami according to the historical documents. For data concerning Fort-de-France, the amplitude of tide has been estimated to be less than 20 cm crest to trough. In both cases, this tide amplitude certainly could have had an additional effect on the tsunami coastal amplification and inundation, even a negligible effect regarding the tsunami height of more than 3 m in La Trinité Bay.

The simulations have been done without taking into account the friction effects. Even though DOTS-ENKO (1998) shows that the dissipation due to friction effects is negligible offshore (open-sea and shelf areas), DAO and TKALICH (2007) show that the roughness parameter is important in wave-shore interaction including shallow water and inundation friction. This is something important to be noted because it means that, in our case, the friction term is equal to 0 and, thus, the run-up limits presented in the following are certainly overestimated regarding the computed scenarios. In fact, if the friction is important due to the presence of lots of buildings or dense vegetation, for example, so the propagation on land will be slowed down more quickly than without buildings (YANAGASIWA et al., 2009). According to HÉBERT et al. (2009) the non consideration of friction could correspond to an overestimation of wave heights of about 30%.

5.1. Role of Coastal Features

It is important to try to reproduce as well as possible the coastal and bathymetric features in low water depth, i.e. in the area of wave shoaling and refraction processes around seafloor topographic highs, because the particular characteristics of the coastline (coastal geo-morphology, e.g. the geometry of bays, harbours, slope of beaches), or the presence of submarine canyons or coral reef barriers, will have direct consequences on the wave behavior and amplification factor and on the inundation or run-up (CHATENOUX and PEDUZZI, 2005, 2007; COCHARD et al., 2008; DUONG et al., 2008).

In the same way, as underlined by ROGER and HÉBERT (2008) for the Balearic Islands in the Mediterranean Sea, the knowledge of the location of submarine canyons is important to assess the tsunami hazard along the coasts because of the focusing role they can play on long wavelengths. Thus, the impact on long waves of the submarine canyons located a few kilometers from the shore in the southeastern part of the island (Fig. 3) should be determined in the future, especially if the coral reef, actually acting as a shield, is going to disappear.

Thus, La Trinité is a U-shaped bay (or funnel-shaped bay), with a maximum length of about 1.2 km and a maximum width of about 1.0 km, oriented N–S and opened northward with a mean depth of 4 m and a very low bathymetric slope (0.33°). This shape is particularly interesting to consider in the case of tsunami wave amplification studies and hazard assessment. In fact, this apparently protected bay with a narrow inlet can amplify the tsunami, and thus its destructive power, presenting a funnel-shape for the arrival waves to travel through (MONSERRAT et al., 2006). This could explain the observed and modeled wave amplification at this specific location. In addition, it is important to mention that the coral reef barrier in front of this bay could be qualified as residual, i.e. not able to protect the bay against long wave arrival because it is too deep and cut. This situation is emphasized by the high touristic frequentation all year long, especially for this location.

Fort-de-France is located eastward of swamplands, lowlands bordering the Lamentin River, and is constantly inundated with a mean altitude of less than 1 m above sea level. In spite of the fact that the historical reports do not mention any catastrophic wave arrival in Fort-de-France Bay in these places in 1755, the present vulnerability of the area should be taken into account because of its economical central role, located in lowland areas. This omega-shaped (Ω) bay (9 km length and 3 km width in the narrowest place) is oriented E–W and opened westward. Its maximum water depth is about 30 m in the boats channel to the harbor but elsewhere it is only about 10 m deep at most. The general bathymetric slope of the bay from the east (Lamentin Airport) to the west (entrance of the bay) is less than 0.1°.

Several authors have referred to the effects of the presence of coral reef barriers close to the coast, such as the increase in the propagation time, and the reduction of the amplitude (BABA et al., 2009). But on the other side, COCHARD et al. (2008) indicate that when fragmented, waves are able to accelerate through so-created channels.

For Martinique Island, Fig. 4 shows that the coral reef barrier could be qualified as residual; only a line of 25 km length between the presqu'île de la Caravelle and Le Vauclin is visible. The progressive disappearance of the coral reef in Martinique is due to geological reasons such as fast subsidence or volcanic eruptions (BATTISTINI, 1978), and to human stresses such as the pollution or the overfishing in these rich areas (BOUCHON et al., 2008; LEGRAND et al., 2008).

This happens in particular offshore of the northeast coast where the reef does not protect from the assault of normal waves because it is generally underwater at 5–10 m depth (BATTISTINI, 1978) as shown in Fig. 4 with the location of surfing spots. In fact, only the southeastern part of the reef remains, partially protecting the coast from classical waves, with a width sprawl of about 1–2 km; three of the sites discussed in this paper are affected: the bays of Le Galion, Le Robert and Le François. In 1755, according to the historical documents, we know that nothing was observed in Le Robert and just a little in Le Galion (BALLET, 1896). Despite the fact that we have not tested the real effect of this coral barrier, the general results obtained with maximum wave heights in the case of the 1755 event are in favor of this.

Le François is only mentioned in one document (ANONYMOUS, 1755), but in view of this supposed important protection by the different coral reef parts at this time, we could easily suppose that it was too protected to receive anything or that there was simply nobody able to report something there, or was at mean significant damage/impact in 1755. Thus, numerical modeling results of maximum wave heights of about 0.5–1.0 m inside this bay (Fig. 4) could mean that the used bathymetry on the coral reef has changed in 250 years in agreement with the previous remark concerning the coral disappearance.

On the contrary, Sainte-Marie, located north of La Trinité, shows a good exposure to long wave arrival and thus the tsunami modeling (Fig. 3) indicates significant wave heights (more than 1.5 m) in this location in spite of the fact that historical reports clearly mention that nothing was observed here on 1 November 1755 (BALLET, 1896).

The lack of historical information concerning wave arrival near the urban coastal areas of Sainte-Marie, Le Marigot or Le Lorrain in the north and Le Vauclain in the south, where numerical modeling indicates wave heights of more than 2 m (Fig. 4), could be explained by the lack of population here in 1755, according to the available historical maps of 1753 (LE ROUGE, 1753) and 1759 (BELL, 1759), or simply the lack of educated people able to write a report of the phenomenon. A search for tsunami deposits in some typical lagoon areas on La Martinique Coast as behind the Anse Massé with the Lorrain River or the Capot River at the Pointe des Raisiniers (Fig. 4) could provide additional information about this tsunami of 1755.

5.2. Discussion on Vulnerability and Hazard Map Purposes

The results shown in Fig. 5 could be considered as a contribution to the tsunami (hazard) vulnerability map of La Martinique Island. The use of satellite views reveals the location of populated areas and economic interests in general, correlated with a water elevation map (sea and land) on these high resolution grids (Fig. 5).

The maximum wave heights are well correlated with the surfing spots as in the case of Guadeloupe Island (ROGER et al., 2010), i.e. the places of high touristic frequentation (Fig. 4).

At the time of the 1755 tsunami, the population of the French Antilles is not known exactly, but in Martinique, it corresponds to about 100,000 inhabitants, including 84,000 slaves. The shore inhabitants were mainly fishermen and sailors. Although it was populated, the vast majority of the population lived quite far from the shore working in sugar cane activity. Historical synthesis reports that most of them were illiterates (about 95% of the whole population of the French Antilles).

Nowadays, the situation is quite different; the French Antilles count 810,000 inhabitants, including about 400,000 inhabitants for Martinique, with an important influx of tourists estimated to reach about 1 million people per year, resulting in highly frequented beaches, especially during high season. Also, the main economic activities are located along the shore with an estimated income of about 278 million euros in 2007 (Comité Martiniquais du Tourisme, 2008): the development of the tourism industry and the lack of a coastal management policy has furthermore increased this exposure, leading to a concentration of 90% of the population along the shores, in places less than 20 m high (SCHLEUPNER, 2007), which is to say 343,000 inhabitants in 1999 (INSEE, 1999). This population is highly exposed to coastal inundation hazards.

In addition, our study also clearly shows that some vital exchange areas (economic, touristic, and above all, for emergency aid) such as Lamentin International Airport or the container's dock (Fort-de-France harbor) are prone to tsunami inundation due to the wave arrival from the eastern Atlantic Margin, despite its orientation towards the west (especially the low lands of no more than one meter altitude (and particularly the airport runway).

6. Final Conclusion and Perspectives

This study shows that the historical observations of 1 November 1755 tsunami in Martinique Island can be reproduced using a tsunami source located offshore of Iberia. The predicted inundation parameters are in agreement with the historical reports at La Trinité and Fort-de-France Bay.

It also indicates that some places along the coast seem to be partially protected from tsunami impact by the residual coral reef barrier. This point deserves further in situ investigations.

Martinique is presently a highly populated island offering some of the most popular tourist beaches in the Caribbean. There could be considerable human casualties in the case of a tsunami event. In fact, this part of the world is well-prepared for hurricane hazards, but is relatively unprepared for the suddenness of a tsunami-like event, especially coming from the eastern part of the Atlantic Ocean.

The tsunami risk in Martinique is not quite existent in people's minds, as meteorological events (storms, cyclones) occur more frequently. Local administrations are not much prepared for tsunamis and rescue units vulnerable to earthquakes and inundations from the sea. For example, they would be destroyed if a like earthquake like the one in 1839 (which destroyed Fort-de-France) occurred (COURTEAU, 2007). The increasing exposure of the Martinique population to tsunami hazards, combined with a functional and economic vulnerability, including tourism pressure, makes Martinique highly exposed to tsunami risks. The occurrence of an event comparable to the one of 1755 would, nowadays, have a much more important impact on the life in the island.

This study represents the initial stage for the production of a vulnerability map concerning the tsunami hazard, using far-field sources. Further investigation of tsunami hazards in the area should consider the impact of potential local sources.

Another aspect that should be further investigated concerns the tsunami deposits. For example, a special focus on the region of Le Lorrain is presented in Fig. 4; it allows us to indicate that the wave amplification could have been sufficient here to inundate the lowlands of the river of Le Lorrain. The estuary of this river presents a kind of lagoon system, with lowlands potentially floodplain protected partially by a rocky dune; this could have stopped some of the water from the tsunami in 1755. Thus, it is a potential site to look for tsunami deposits. A second site qualified for tsunami deposits is located north of Le Lorrain and corresponds to the alluvial fan of the Capot River (Pointe des Raisiniers), presenting a lagoon profile too. Further study should model the tsunami inundation capabilities in this area, depending mainly on the dune height.

Acknowledgments

The authors would like to thank the SHOM (France) for providing the high resolution bathymetric dataset for Guadeloupe; Paul Louis Blanc (IRSN) for sending some original reports from Martinique and for discussions; João Catalão (University of Lisbon) for bathymetry digitizing and preparation of the bathymetric grid; Ronan Créach (SHOM) for his expertise on oceanic tides; Suzanne Débardat (Paris Observatory) for the understanding of historical time zones; Alain Rabaute (GeoSubSight company) for technical advices. They would like to thank Uri ten Brink (USGS) and an anonymous referee for their constructive comments for the improvement of the manuscript. This study has been funded by the project MAREMOTI from the French ANR (Agence Nationale de la Recherche), under the contract ANR-08-RISKNAT-05-01c.

REFERENCES

ABE, K. (1979), *Size of great earthquakes of 1873–1974 inferred from tsunami data*. J. Geophys. Res. 84, 1561–1568.

AFFLECK, B. (1755), *An account of the agitation of the sea at Antigua, Nov. 1, 1755. By Capt. Affleck of the Advice Man of War. Communicated by Charles Gray, E/q; F.R.S in a Letter to William Watson, F.R.S.*

ALASSET, P.-J., HÉBERT, H., MAOUCHE, S., CALBINI, V., MEGHRAOUI, M. (2006), *The tsunami induced by the 2003 Zemmouri earthquake ($M_w = 6.9$, Algeria): modelling and results*. Geophys. J. Int. 166, 213–226.

ANONYMOUS (1755), *Lettre de Martinique du 15 décembre 1755, lue par Duhamel le 24 mars 1756*. P.V. Séances Acad. Sci. Paris, 75, p. 145.

ANONYMOUS (1756), Journal Historique sur les Matières du tems, juin 1756. Suite des Tremblements de Terre. pp. 462–464.

BABA, T., MLECZKO, R., BURBIDGE, D., CUMMINS, P.R., THIO, H.K. (2009), *The Effect of the Great Barrier Reef on the Propagation of the 2007 Solomon Islands Tsunami Recorded in Northeastern Australia*. Pure Appl. Geophys. 165, 2003–2018.

BALLET, J. (1896), *La Guadeloupe. Renseignements sur l'histoire, la flore, la faune, la géologie, la minéralogie, l'agriculture, le commerce, l'industrie, la législation, l'administration. Tome IIe – 1715–1774*. Basse-Terre, Imprimerie du Gouvernement.

BAPTISTA, M.A. (1998), *Génese propagação e impacte de tsunamis nas costas portuguesas*. PHD Thesis, University of Lisbon, Portugal (in Portuguese).

BAPTISTA, M.A., MIRANDA, J.M. (2009a), *Revision of the Portuguese catalog of tsunamis*, Nat. Hazards Earth Syst. Sci. 9, 25–42. http://www.nat-hazards-earth-syst-sci.net/9/25/2009/nhess-9-25-2009.html

BAPTISTA, M.A., MIRANDA, J.M. (2009b), *Evaluation of the 1755 Earthquake Source Using Tsunami Modeling*, in Geotechnical, Geological and Earthquake Engineering, Book Series, Vol. 7, 425–423: The 1755 Lisbon Earthquake Revisited. Springer, Netherlands. ISBN:978-1-4020-8608-3.

BAPTISTA, M.A., HEITOR, S., MIRANDA, J.M., MIRANDA, P., and MENDES-VICTOR, L. (1998a), *The 1755 Lisbon tsunami; evaluation of the tsunami parameters*, J. Geodyn. 25, 143–157.

BAPTISTA, M.A., MIRANDA, P.M.A., MIRANDA, J.M., MENDES-VICTOR, L. (1998b), *Constrains on the source of the 1755 Lisbon tsunami inferred from numerical modelling of historical data on the source of the 1755 Lisbon tsunami*. J. Geodyn. 25(1–2), 159–174.

BAPTISTA, M.A., MIRANDA, J.M., CHIERICI, F., ZITELLINI, N. (2003), *New Study of the 1755 Earthquake Source Based on Multichannel Seismic Survey Data and Tsunami Modeling*, Nat. Hazards and Earth Syst. Sci. 3, 333–340.

BARKAN, R., BRINK, T. U., LIN, J. (2009), *Far field tsunami simulations of the 1755 Lisbon earthquake: implications for tsunami hazard to the U.S. East Coast and the Caribbean*. Mar. Geol. 264, 109–122.

BATTISTINI, R. (1978), *Les récifs coralliens de la Martinique. Comparaison avec ceux au sud-ouest de l'Océan Indien*. Cah. O.R.S.T.O.M., sér. Océanogr. Vol. XVI (2), 157–177.

BELL, A. (1759), *Map of Martinico for the latest and best authorities. Map of Guadalupe on a smaller scale*. Scots Magazine. Available at http://evo.bio.psu.edu/caribmap/lesser/bodington.htm

BOUCHON, C., PORTILLO, P., BOUCHON-NAVARO, Y., LOUIS, M., HOETJES, P., DE MEYER, K., MACRAE, D., ARMSTRONG, H., DATADIN, V., HARDING, S., MALLELA, J., PARKINSON, R., VAN BOCHOVE, J.-W., WYNNE, S., LIRMAN, D., HERLAN, J., BAKER, A., COLLADO, L., NIMROD, S., MITCHELL, J., MORRALL, C., ISAAC, C. (2008), *Status of Coral Reefs of the Lesser Antilles: The French West Indies, The Netherlands Antilles, Anguilla, Antigua, Grenada, Trinidad and Tobago*. In: Wilkinson, C et al. (eds) Status of coral reefs of the world. Vol. 3, 265–280. Australian Institute of Marine Sciences, Australia.

BRUNET, P. (attribué à -) (1850), *"Journal d'un vieil habitant de Sainte-Marie (1745–1765)" ou "Ephémérides d'un vieil habitant de Sainte-Marie")*. Annexe *in* Rufz de Lavison, Etienne (Dr), 1850. Etudes historiques et Statistiques sur la Population de la Martinique. St. Pierre. p. 394.

CHATENOUX, B., PEDUZZI, P. (2005), *Analysis on the role of bathymetry and other environmental parameters in the impacts from the 2004 Indian Ocean Tsunami*. A Scientific Report for the UNEP Asian Tsunami Disaster Task Force. UNEP/GRID-Europe. http://www.grid.unep.ch/product/publication/download/environment_impacts_tsunami.pdf.

CHATENOUX, B., PEDUZZI, P. (2007), *Impacts from the 2004 Indian Ocean Tsunami: analyzing the potential protecting role of environmental features*. Nat. Hazards. 40, 289–304. doi:10.1007/s11069-006-0015-9.

COCHARD, R., RANAMUKHAARACHCHI, S.L., SHIVAKOTI, G.P., SHIPIN, O.V., EDWARDS, P.J., SEELAND, K.T., (2008), *The 2004 tsunami in Aceh and Southern Thailand: A review on coastal ecosystems,*

wave hazards and vulnerability. Perspectives in Plant Ecology, Evolution and Systematics. 10, 3–40.

COMITÉ MARTINIQUAIS DU TOURISME (2008), *Bilan Grand Public*. 9 p.

COURTEAU, R. (2007), *Rapport sur l'évaluation et la prévention du risque du tsunami sur les côtes françaises en métropole et outremer*. Office parlementaire d'évaluation des choix scientifiques et technologiques, 168 p.

DANEY, S. (1846), *Histoire de la Martinique depuis la colonisation jusqu'en 1815*; Par M. Sidney Daney, Membre du conseil colonial de la Martinique, Tome III. Fort-Royal, E. Ruelle, Imprimeur du Gouvernement. pp. 237–238.

DAO, M.H., TKALICH, P., (2007), *Tsunami propagation modelling—a sensitivity study*. Nat. Hazards Earth Syst. Sci. 7, 741–754.

DE LANGE, W.P., PRASETYA, G.S., HEALY, T.R. (2001), *Modelling of tsunamis generated by pyroclastic flows (ignimbrites)*. Natural Hazards, 24(3), 251–266. doi:10.1023/A:1012056920155.

DEPLUS, C., LE FRIANT, A., BOUDON, G., KOMOROWSKI, J.-C., VILLEMANT, B., HARFORD, C., SÉGOUFIN, J., CHEMINÉE, J.-L. (2001), *Submarine evidence for large-scale debris avalanches in the Lesser Antilles Arc*. Earth Planet. Sci. Lett. 192, 145–157.

DOTSENKO, S.F. (1998), *Numerical modelling of the propagation of tsunami waves in the Crimean Peninsula shelf zone*. Phys. Oceanogr. 9(5), 323–331.

DUONG, N.A., KIMATA, F., MEILANO, I. (2008), *Assessment of Bathymetry Effects on Tsunami Propagation in Viet Nam*. Adv. Nat. Sci. 9(6).

FEUILLET, N., MANIGHETTI, I., TAPPONNIER, P., JACQUES, E. (2002), *Arc parallel extension and localization of volcanic complexes in Guadeloupe, Lesser Antilles*. J. Geophys. Res. 107(B12), 2331. doi:10.1029/2001JB000308.

GUTSCHER, M.A., MALOD, J., REHAULT, J.P., CONTRUCCI, I., KLINGELHOEFER, F., MENDES-VICTOR, L.A., SPAKMAN, W. (2002), *Evidence for active subduction beneath Gibraltar*. Geology 30, 1071–1074.

GUTSCHER, M.-A., BAPTISTA, M.A., MIRANDA, J.M. (2006), *The Gibraltar Arc seismogenic zone (part 2): Constraints on a shallow east dipping fault plane source for the 1755 Lisbon earthquake provided by tsunami modeling and seismic intensity*. Tectonophysics 426, 153–166.

HÉBERT, H., SCHINDELÉ, F., HEINRICH, P. (2001), *Tsunami risk assessment in the Marquesas Islands (French Polynesia) through numerical modeling of generic far-field events*. Nat. Hazards Earth Syst. Sci. 1, 233–242.

HÉBERT, H., REYMOND, D., KRIEN, Y., VERGOZ, J., SCHINDELÉ, F., ROGER J., LOEVENBRUCK, A. (2009), *The 15 August 2007 Peru earthquake and tsunami: influence of the source characteristics on the tsunami heights*. Pure Appl. Geophys. 166, 1–22.

INSEE (2009), *Population et logements par commune depuis le recensement de 1962 (1961 pour les Dom)*. Available on http://www.insee.fr/fr/themes/detail.asp?reg_id=99&ref_id=poplogcom.

INSTITUT GÉOGRAPHIQUE NATIONAL (2006a), *Fort-de-France, Montagne Pelée, PNR de la Martinique*. Carte de Randonnée, 4501 MT, édition 2, 1: 25000.

INSTITUT GÉOGRAPHIQUE NATIONAL (2006b), *Le Lamentin, presqu'île de la Caravelle, PNR de la Martinique*. Carte de Randonnée, 4502 MT, édition 2, 1: 25000.

INSTITUT GÉOGRAPHIQUE NATIONAL (2006c), *Le Marin, presqu'île des trois îlets, PNR de la Martinique*. Carte de Randonnée, 4503 MT, édition 2, 1: 25000.

IOC, IHO and BODC (2003), *Centenary Edition of the GEBCO Digital Atlas, published on CD-ROM on behalf of the Intergovernmental Oceanographic Commission and the International Hydrographic Organization as part of the General Bathymetric Chart of the Oceans*. British Oceanographic Data Centre, Liverpool, UK.

JOHNSTON, A. (1996), *Seismic moment assessment of earthquakes in stable continental regions. III. New Madrid, 1811–1812, Charleston 1886 and Lisbon 1755*. Geophys. J. Int. 126, 314–344.

KAABOUBEN, F., BAPTISTA, M.A., IBEN BRAHIM, A., EL MOURAOUAH, A., TOTO, A. (2009), *On the moroccan tsunami catalogue*, Nat. Hazards Earth Syst. Sci. 9, 1227–1236.

KOWALIK, Z., MURTY, T.S. (1993), *Numerical simulation of two-dimensional tsunami run-up*. Marine Geodesy. 16, 87–100.

LANDER, J.F., WHITESIDE, L.S., LOCKRIDGE, P.A. (2002), *A brief history of tsunami in the Caribbean Sea*. Sci Tsunami Hazards 20, 57–94.

LE FRIANT, A., BOUDON, G., ARNULF, A., ROBERTSON, R.E.A. (2009), *Debris avalanche deposits offshore St. Vincent (West Indies): Impact of flank-collapse events on the morphological evolution of the island*. J. V. Geotherm. Res. 179(1–2), 1–10.

LE ROUGE, G.-L. (1753), *La Martinique une des Antilles Françoises de l'Amérique*. Available at http://evo.bio.psu.edu/caribmap/lesser/bodington.htm.

LEGRAND H., ROUSSEAU Y., PÉRÈS C., and MARÉCHAL J.-P. (2008), *Suivi écologique des récifs coralliens des stations IFRECOR en Martinique de 2001 à 2006*. Revue d'Ecologie. 63(1–2), 67–84.

LETTÉE (MR) (1755), *Lettre de Martinique du 5 novembre 1755, lue par Réaumur le 28 janvier 1756*. P.V. Séances Acad. Sci. Paris, 75, pp. 48–49.

LEVRET, A. (1991), *The effects of the November 1, 1755 "Lisbon" earthquake in Morocco*. Tectonophysics 193, 83–94.

LOPEZ-VENEGAS, A.M., TEN BRINK, U.S., GEIST, E.L. (2008), *Submarine landslide as the source for the October 11, 1918 Mona Passage tsunami: observations and modeling*. Marine Geol. 254(1–2), 35–46.

MACHADO, F. (1966), *Contribuiçao para o estudo do terramoto de 1 de Novembro de 1755*, Rev. Fac. Ciencias de Lisboa, 2ª Serie-C, 14(1), 19–31.

MARTÍNEZ SOLARES, J. M., LÓPEZ ARROYO, A., MEZCUA, J. (1979), *Isoseismal map of the 1755 Lisbon earthquake obtained from Spanish data*. Tectonophysics 53, 301–313.

MONSERRAT, S., VILIBIC, I. AND RABINOVICH, A.B. (2006), *Meteotsunamis: atmospherically induced destructive ocean waves in the tsunami frequency band*. Nat. Hazards Earth Syst. Sci. 6, 1035–1051.

O'LOUGHLIN, K.F., LANDER, J.F. (2003), *Caribbean tsunamis: a 500-year history from 1498–1998*. Advances in Natural and Technological Hazards Research, Kluwer Academic Pulishers, Boston, 263 pp.

OKADA, Y. (1985), *Surface deformation due to shear and tensile faults in a half-space*. Bull. Seismol. Soc. Am. 75, 1135–1154.

PELINOVSKY, E., ZAHIBO, N., DUNKLEY, P., EDMONDS, M., HERD, R., TALIPOVA, T., KOZELKOV, A., NIKOLKINA, I. (2004), *Tsunami generated by the volcano eruption on July 12-13, 2003 at Montserrat, Lesser Antilles*. Sci. Tsunami Hazards, 22(1), 44–57.

ROGER, J., HÉBERT, H. (2008), *The 1856 Djijelli (Algeria) earthquake: implications for tsunami hazard in Balearic Islands*. Nat. Hazards Earth Syst. Sci. 8, 721–731.

ROGER, J., ALLGEYER, S., HÉBERT, H., BAPTISTA, M.A., LOEVENBRUCK, A., SCHINDELÉ, F. (2010), *The 1755 Lisbon tsunami in Guadeloupe Archipelago: contribution of numerical modelling*. Open Oceanogr. J. 4, 58–70.

ROMERO, M.L.C. (1992), *El riesgo de Tsunamis en España. Analisis y valoracion geográfica*. 209 pp, Insituto Geografico Nacional, Madrid. ISBN:84-7819-041-4, in Spanish

SAHAL, A., ROGER, J., ALLGEYER, S., LEMAIRE, B., HÉBERT, H., SCHINDELÉ, F., LAVIGNE, F. (2009), *The tsunami triggered by the 21 May 2003 Boumerdes-Zemmouri (Algeria) earthquake: field investigations on the French Mediterranean coast and tsunami modeling*. Nat. Hazards Earth Syst. Sci. 9, 1823–1834.

SATAKE, K. (1988), *Effects of bathymetry on tsunami propagation: application of ray tracing to tsunamis*. Pure Appl. Geophys. 126(1), 27–36.

SCHLEUPNER, C. (2007), *Spatial assessment of sea level rise on Martinique's coastal zone and analysis of planning frameworks for adaptation*. J. Coast. Conserv. 11, 91–103.

SLADEN, A., HÉBERT, H., SCHINDELÉ, F., REYMOND, D. (2007), *Evaluation of far-field tsunami hazard in French Polynesia based on historical data and numerical simulations*. Nat. Hazards Earth Syst. Sci. 7, 195–206.

SMITH, M.S., SHEPHERD, J.B. (1996), *Tsunami waves generated by volcanic landslides: an assessment of the hazard associated with Kick'em Jenny*. Geological Society, London, Special Publications, 110, 115–123.

SOLARES, J.M.M., ARROYO, A.L. (2004), *The great historical 1755 earthquake. Effects and damage in Spain*. J. Seismol. 8, 275–294.

SOUSA, F.L.P. (1919), *O Terremoto do 1° de Novembro de 1755 em Portugal*. In: Um estudo demográfico Vol. I, Serviços Geológicos de Portugal e II.

STEIN, S., J.F. ENGELN, D.A. WIENS, K. FUJITA, R.C. (1982), *Speed, Subduction seismicity and tectonics in the Lesser Antilles arc*. J. Geophys. Res. 87, B10, 8642–8644.

TITOV, V., RABINOVICH, A.B., MOFJELD, H.O., THOMSON, R.E., GONZALEZ, F.I. (2005), *The global reach of the 26 December 2004 Sumatra Tsunami*. Science. 309, 2045. doi:10.1126/science.1114576.

URBAN, S. (1755), Supplement to the Gentleman's Magazine for the year 1755, printed by: Henry, D. and Cave, R., St. John' Gate, London, 587–591.

VILANOVA, S.P., NUNES, C.F., FONSECA, J.F.B.D. (2003), *Lisbon 1755: a case of triggered onshore rupture?* Bull. Seismol. Soc. Am. 93(5), 2056–2068.

WAYTHOMAS, C.F., WATTS, P. (2003), *Numerical simulation of tsunami generation by pyroclastic flow at Aniakchak Volcano*, Alaska. Geophysical Res. Lett. 30(14), 51–54.

YANAGASIWA, H., KOSHIMURA, S., GOTO, K., MIYAGI, T., IMAMURA, F., RUANGRASSAMEE, A., TANAVUD, C. (2009), *The reduction effects of mangrove forest on a tsunami based on field surveys at Pakarang Cape, Thailand and numerical analysis*. Estuar. Coastal Shelf Sci. 81, 27–37.

YELLES-CHAOUCHE, A.K., ROGER, J., DÉVERCHÈRE, J., BRACENE, R., DOMZIG, A., HEBERT, H., KHERROUBI, A. (2009), *The Tsunami of Djidjelli (eastern Algeria) of August 21-22nd, 1856: Seismotectonic context, Modelling and implications for the Algerian coast*. Pure Appl. Geophys. Topical Volume. doi:10.1007/s00024-008-0433-6.

ZAHIBO, N., PELINOVSKY, E., YALÇINER, A., KURKIN, A., KOSELKOV, A., ZAITSEV, A. (2003a), *The 1867 Virgin Island tsunami: observations and modeling*. Oceanol. Acta 26(5–6), 609–621.

ZAHIBO, N., PELINOVSKY, E., YALÇINER, A., KURKIN, A., KOSELKOV, A., ZAITSEV, A. (2003b), *The 1867 Virgin Island tsunami*. Nat. Hazards Earth Syst. Sci. 3, 367–376.

ZAHIBO, N., PLINOVSKY, E., OKAL, E., YALÇINER, A., KHARIF, C., TALIPOVA, T., KOZELKOV, A. (2005), *The earthquake and tsunami of November 21, 2004 at Les Saintes, Guadeloupe, Lesser Antilles*. Sci. Tsunami Hazards 23(1), 25–39.

ZITELLINI, N., CHIERICI, F., SARTORI, R., TORELLI, L. (1999), *The tectonic source of the 1755 Lisbon earthquake and tsunami*. Annali di Geofisica. 42, 49–55.

(Received December 31, 2009, revised May 3, 2010, accepted June 7, 2010, Published online November 13, 2010)

Pure Appl. Geophys. 168 (2011), 1033–1043
© 2010 Springer Basel AG
DOI 10.1007/s00024-010-0217-7

Evaluating Tsunami Impact on the Gulf of Cadiz Coast (Northeast Atlantic)

R. OMIRA,[1,3] M. A. BAPTISTA,[1,2] and J. M. MIRANDA[1]

Abstract—The Gulf of Cadiz coasts are exposed to tsunamis. Emergency planning tools are now taking into account this fact, especially because a series of historical occurrences were strikingly significant, having left strong evidence behind, in the mareographic records, the geological evidence or simply the memory of the populations. The study area is a strip along the Algarve coast, south Portugal, an area known to have been heavily impacted by the 1 November 1755 event. In this study we use two different tsunami scenarios generated by the rupture of two thrust faults identified in the area, corresponding to 8.1–8.3 magnitude earthquakes. Tsunami propagation and inundation computation is performed using a non-linear shallow water code with bottom friction. Numerical modeling results are presented in terms of flow depth and current velocity with maximum values of 7 m and 8 m/s for inundation depth and flow speed, respectively. These results constitute a valuable tool for local authorities, emergency and decision planners to define the priority zones where tsunami mitigation measures must be implemented and to develop tsunami-resilient communities.

Key words: Tsunami, Gulf of Cadiz, inundation maps, current velocity.

1. Introduction

Tsunamis originated from different triggering mechanisms are reported along the Atlantic coasts of Europe since prehistoric times. The Storegga submarine slide circa 8,000 years ago (BONDEVIK *et al.*, 2003, 2005) in the Norwegian Sea is the oldest well-established event, whereas for the Gulf of Cadiz, Northeast Atlantic, the oldest described paleo-tsunami is dated 7000 BP (LUQUE *et al.*, 2001). The largest tsunami event eye-witnessed in the area is the one associated with the Lisbon 1755 earthquake (BAPTISTA *et al.*, 1998a, b, 2003). It struck the Iberian and the North African coasts, severely damaging coastal communities, as described by a large number of historical documents that testify the impact of the tsunami waves. These littoral areas are now the location of vital sectors of the economy and tourism, are intensely populated, and the damage from a 1755-like event could be much greater.

Previous paleotsunami (LUQUE *et al.*, 2001, 2002) and historical (BAPTISTA and MIRANDA, 2009) studies focused on the Gulf of Cadiz region show that there is enough evidence to support the existence of events similar to the 1 November 1755 tsunami in Lisbon in the historical period. LUQUE *et al.* (2001) identified three tsunami-generated deposits and also deduced an average interval of about 2,000 years between two consecutive events. In light of these results, the likely tsunami recurrence period for 1755-like events is considered quite large. In the twentieth century three tsunamis impacted the area caused by earthquakes of magnitudes close to 8 (BAPTISTA and MIRANDA, 2009): 25 November 1941 ($M = 8$) (BUFORN *et al.*, 1988) and 28 February 1969 ($M_s = 7.9$) (FUKAO, 1973); these and the 26 May 1975 ($M_s = 7.9$) (KAABOUBEN *et al.*, 2008) events testify that the tsunami is a real menace in the Gulf of Cadiz, and thus the protection of the coastal areas of the region should be a priority.

To protect coastal communities against the tsunami threat, beside a reliable tsunami warning system, evacuation planning in the vulnerable areas is of crucial importance. Such plans require the availability of inundation maps that provide estimates of the expected damage-prone areas, the spatial distribution of flow depth and the current velocity within the flooded zone. The deterministic tsunami hazard approach based on particular source scenarios is the

---

[1] Instituto Dom Luiz (IDL), University of Lisbon, Lisbon, Portugal. E-mail: omirarachid10@yahoo.fr; mavbaptista@gmail.com; jmmiranda@fc.ul.pt
[2] Instituto Superior de Engenharia de Lisboa, Lisbon, Portugal.
[3] University Ibn Tofail, Kenitra, Morocco.

well-established tool to derive such inundation maps (TINTI and ARMIGLIATO, 2003).

In this study we employ the most credible tsunamigenic scenario approach together with numerical modeling to assess the tsunami hazard and impact along the Algarve coastal region in southern Portugal.

The study area corresponds to a 15-km strip along the coast (cf. Fig. 1a, b for locations), which includes the towns of Lagos and Portimão with 30,000 and 50,000 inhabitants, respectively. The area is characterized by sandy beaches that are crowed during the high tourist season, when the population can easily double. The tide gauge data recorded during the 28 February 1969 (BAPTISTA et al., 1992; HEINRICH et al., 1994; GJEVIK et al., 1997) and the simulation results of the 1755 event (BAPTISTA et al., 1998b) show that this area is the first to be struck by tsunamis generated in the Gulf of Cadiz. Moreover this was one of the most devastated areas by the tsunami of 1 November 1755 (CASTRO, 1768). The effects of the 1755 tsunami in the area are described in detail by BAPTISTA et al. (2008), BAPTISTA and MIRANDA (2009), and PEDROSA and GONÇALVES (2008).

Tsunami impact is presented in terms of maximum wave heights (MWHs) and high-resolution inundation and current velocity maps. Both linear and non-linear approximations of shallow water equations were adopted to simulate the deep-ocean tsunami propagation and the near-shore inundation, respectively. Moreover, a sensitivity study related to the influence of the bottom friction on the variation of the maximum flow depths and the current velocities was carried out using three different values of Manning's coefficient.

Results show that both scenarios produce a dramatic tsunami impact along the whole study area. Major variations in the maximum flow depth, inundation limits and current velocity have been observed when the bottom friction coefficient is changed.

2. Tsunami Scenarios

To investigate the impact of tsunami events in the Gulf of Cadiz it is necessary to define the seismic scenarios able to generate tsunamis in the area. In this study we employ the concept of typical fault to infer the Maximum Credible Earthquake Scenarios (MCE). Typical faults are defined from all positively identified submarine structures in the Gulf of Cadiz large enough to generate tsunamigenic earthquakes, adding the following additional criteria: (1) having been identified by seismo-stratigraphic research, (2) providing clear identification of quaternary activity and (3) having been deduced from instrumental seismic data (MIRANDA et al., 2008; OMIRA et al., 2009a).

Recent studies focused on tsunami impact in selected areas in the Gulf of Cadiz, Casablanca in Morocco (OMIRA et al., 2009b) and Huelva in Spain (LIMA et al., 2010), considered a set of five different typical faults. In this study we focus on two typical faults, both thrusts, that we consider the most relevant candidate sources: the Marques de Pombal fault (MPF) and Horseshoe fault (HSF) [cf. Fig. 2 and discussion in OMIRA et al. (2009a) and LIMA et al. (2010)]. The fault characteristics and the computed earthquake magnitudes are specified in Table 1. The scaling relationship of SCHOLZ (1982) that is based on fault lengths and length/width relations was used to fix the slip magnitude. The magnitude shown in Table 1 is obtained from the dimensions and slip of the fault following the seismic moment definition of AKI (1966) and the M_o-M_w relation defined by KANAMORI and ANDERSON (1977). For tsunami modeling, the geometry of the candidate sources is simplified to a rectangle (cf. Fig. 2 for locations) for the computation of seafloor initial deformation.

3. Modeling Inundation and Current Velocity

Tsunami hydrodynamic modeling was done with a slightly modified version of the LIU et al. (1998) COMCOT code (OMIRA et al., 2009a, b) that uses an explicit leap-frog finite difference scheme to solve linear and non-linear shallow water equations on a dynamically coupled system of nested grids. The Coriolis effect is not considered in this study given the relatively small computation region in which the earth rotation effect is not prominent. Nested grids have resolutions of 800, 200 and 50 m, respectively, in order to assure a good description of bathymetric and topographic features in the area. The finer grid is focused along the Lagos-Portimão south Portuguese

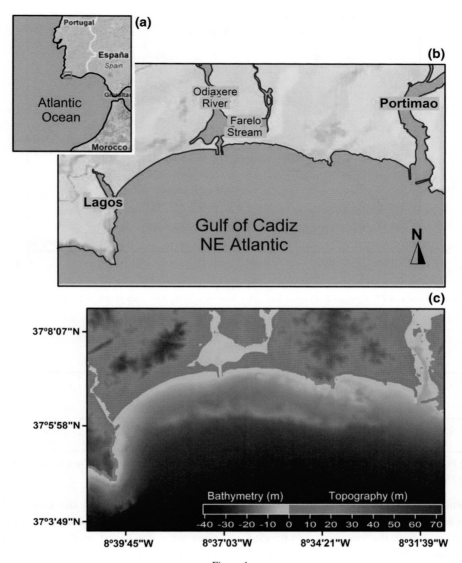

Figure 1
Location of the study area. **a** Regional overview of the SW Iberian margin. **b** Localities referred to in the *text*. **c** Bathymetric and topographic data used in the numerical modeling. All coordinates correspond to the UTM system, Zone 29, and are expressed in meters

coast. The digital terrain model (DTM) (bathymetry/topography) of the Lagos-Portimão area (Fig. 1c) was generated from a compilation of multisource height/depth data from multibeam surveys, digitized bathymetric charts and digital cartographic data. The final data set is referenced to the mean sea level, and all grids are in Cartesian coordinates (UTM 29), which are sufficiently accurate, given the size of the study area. The coupling between a sub-grid and their parent grid follows the requirements of WANG and LIU

(2007) and LIU *et al.* (1998). In the outer grid an open boundary radiation condition is used.

The static vertical displacement of the ocean floor due to the submarine earthquake scenario is modeled using the MANSINHA and SMYLIE (1971) homogenous elastic half space approach, as implemented in the Mirone suite (LUIS, 2007). Slip in the source is considered non-homogeneous, following the smooth closure condition of GEIST and DMOWSKA (1999). For run-up and inundation computations, a moving

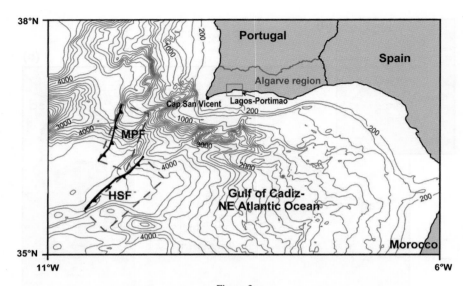

Figure 2
Typical faults used in the study. *MPF* Marques de Pombal fault; *HSF* Horsehoe fault. As a background the bathymetric data are plotted every 200 m

Table 1

Fault parameters of the simulated tsunamigenic scenarios in the Gulf of Cadiz region

Scenarios name	L (km)	W (km)	Epicenter coordinates		D (km)	Slip (m)	Strike (°)	Dip (°)	Rake (°)	μ (Pa)	M_w
			Lon (W)	Lat (N)							
MPF	129	70	9°53′24″	36°34′26″	4.0	8.0	20.0	35	90	3.0×10^{10}	8.1
HSF	165	70	9°54′47″	35°47′45″	4.0	10.7	42.1	35	90	3.0×10^{10}	8.3

MPF Marques de Pombal fault, *HSF* Horseshoe fault, L the fault length in kilometers, W the fault width in kilometers, D the depth from the sea bottom to the top of the fault in kilometers; μ the shear modulus and M_w the moment magnitude

boundary scheme to track the moving shoreline (LIU *et al.*, 1995) is adopted. To parameterize the effect of the bottom friction in both shallow water and flooded areas, the Manning coefficient, which varies with the bottom roughness, is used in the numerical model.

The impact of tsunamis generated in the Gulf of Cadiz is analyzed along the coastal areas of south Portugal using the computed MWH, maximum flow depth and current velocities.

4. Results and Discussion

Tsunami modeling results were processed to obtain the spatial distribution of MWH as well as the inland maximum flow depths and flow velocities for the Lagos-Portimão region. MWHs were computed in the parent grid to show the large-scale tsunami

energy direction toward the Gulf of Cadiz coasts. However, inundation and current velocity computations were conducted in the high-resolution grid to evaluate the local tsunami impact.

4.1. Maximum Wave Height

The results of MWH computations for MPF and HSF are presented in Figs. 3a and 4a, respectively. Examination of these results shows that both scenarios steer tsunami energy toward the coastal areas of the Algarve region. The MPF generates large waves of 2–7-m amplitude along the southern Portuguese coast. However, the impact of the HSF in this area, compared to the one of MPF, is less with a MWH of 4 m. It is clear that the fault strike constrains the tsunami energy distribution. At first order, the tsunami amplitude is maximal in the direction perpendicular to the fault strike, but when the wave reaches the near-shore, the bathymetry affects the wave form and the shallow water amplifies the wave amplitude. For such reasons, the results of the spatial distribution of MWH indicate a concentration of the maximal tsunami energy in the Algarve coastal region for MPF and a radiation of the maximal tsunami energy toward northwest Morocco for the HSF. Also, the shallower depths SW of Cap San Vicent (Fig. 2) act to guide tsunami energy from the northern area of the MPF fault to the Algarve coast (Fig. 3), whereas the orientation and more southerly location of the HSF fault (Fig. 4) does not allow this to happen, or at least to a much less extent.

It must be added that in spite of the scenarios' relatively modest (~ 8) magnitude (Table 1), the initial sea surface displacements resulting from the proposed earthquake mechanisms reach 7 m. This is primarily due to two main reasons: (1) the shallow rupture mechanism and (2) the spatially varying slip distribution. GEIST and DMOWSKA (1999) show that the distributed slip affects the initial wave profile, giving wave amplitude that is greater than that for a uniform slip distribution, and it therefore affects the tsunami wave field away from the source region. Such effects

are particularly important for local tsunamis, as is the case in the Gulf of Cadiz, where the resulting tsunami run-up is significantly affected by the initial wave profile (GEIST and DMOWSKA, 1999).

4.2. Mapping Inundation: Effect of Bottom Friction

Figures 3b and 4b show the spatial distribution of inundation and flow depths overland in the Lagos-Portimão area for the two proposed earthquake scenarios considering different bottom friction conditions. These results do not take into account the tide. Both scenarios produce large inundations within the study area. Clearly, the threat posed by the MPF scenario is greater than the one posed by the HSF scenario with respect to the Manning coefficient used. As expected, the changing of the bottom condition affects the maximum flow depth considerably. Figures 3b.1–3 and 4b.1–3 illustrate the variation of the flow depth with different Manning coefficients ($n = 0.000$; 0.015 and 0.030). The case with no bottom friction ($n = 0.000$) represents the worst case of flooding in terms of flow depth and inundation limits for each tested scenario (Figs. 3b.1, 4b.1). In this case, tsunami flow depths vary from 1 to 7 m and from 0.5 to 5 m at the Lagos-Portimão site for MPF

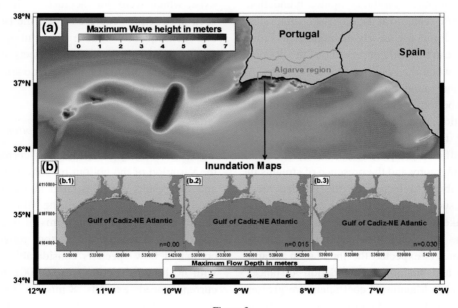

Figure 3
Results of the propagation and run-up modeling for the Marques de Pombal fault

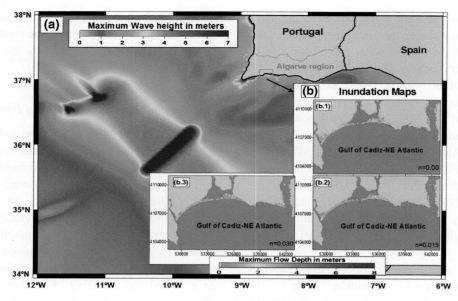

Figure 4
Results of the propagation and run-up modeling for the Horseshoe fault

and HSF, respectively. These values decrease considerably and vary from 0.5 to 4.5 m and from 0.2 to 3 m for MPF and HSF, respectively, when a large bottom friction is considered ($n = 0.030$) (Figs. 3b.3, 4b.3).

In Fig. 5, we also present the effect of the variation of the bottom roughness on the computed inundation limits for the MPF scenario at the Lagos-Portimão site. The inundation limits are clearly distinguished. From these results, it can be easily observed that the flooded area decreases when the bottom friction increases. A maximum inland inundation distance of 1.10 km is reached for no bottom roughness; on the other hand, at the same location, distances of 1.0 and 0.80 km are computed for the values of 0.015 and 0.030 of Manning's coefficient, respectively.

The flat topography and the presence of streams in the area contribute to increasing the flooded area. Other factors, such as the earthquake source parameters, earthquake location and near-shore bathymetry, also control the variation in flow depth in the Lagos-Portimão sector. As expected the inundation parameters (run-up and maximum inundation distance) obtained with zero Manning's coefficient are greater than those obtained with Manning's coefficients of 0.015 and 0.030.

The use of $n = 0.000$ for Manning's coefficient may overestimate the inundation parameters in the area for a tsunami scenario corresponding to an 8.1–8.3 earthquake, but it can also be considered as an approximation to the worst case scenario. However, various natural and man-made obstructions exist, which were not included in the DTM model; such obstructions could dissipate the tsunami energy and consequently reduce the run-up (WIJETUNGE, 2009). The inclusion of the effects of vegetation, buildings and other structures in modeling inundation remains difficult.

4.3. Current Velocity: Effect of Bottom Friction

The sensitivity of the overland current velocity to the variation of the bottom roughness is investigated, and the results are illustrated in the Fig. 6. These results present the impact of the MPF scenario at the site of Lagos-Portimão in terms of overland current speed. The effect of the bottom roughness on the computed flow speed is considerable. For the case with no bottom friction ($n = 0.000$), the maximum current speed exceeds 8 m/s at some locations (Fig. 6a). This value of overland flood velocity decreases and reaches 6 and 3 m/s for Manning's

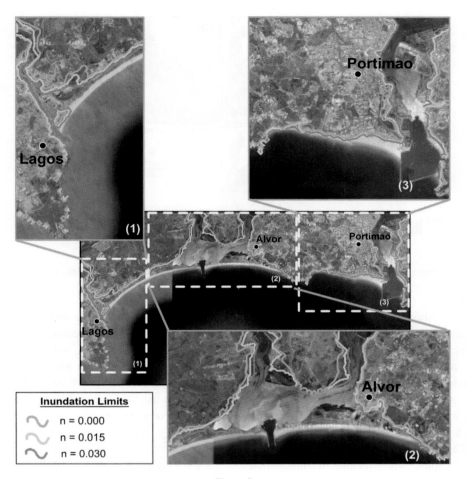

Figure 5
Comparison of inundation areas computed for three different values of the Manning coefficient ($n = 0.000$, 0.015 and 0.030) for the MPF scenario

coefficients of 0.015 and 0.030, respectively (Fig. 6b, c). Waves of such velocities could have devastating consequences on coastal communities and buildings.

According to an experimental study by TAKAHASHI (2005), at locations where the flow depth exceeds 0.5 m, generally people cannot remain standing if the current velocity exceeds 1.5 m/s. Current velocity computation results obtained for different bottom friction conditions (Fig. 6a–c) show values much larger than 1.5 m/s at most locations in the studied area, thus indicating that the Lagos-Portimão communities are exposed to a major tsunami threat. We note here that the computed flow speed may be overestimated due to the fact that the numerical simulations were done over bare land with a uniform

distribution of the bottom friction, and both natural and man-made obstacles were not included. On the other hand, the presence of buildings within the flooded area could channel the flow and consequently increase the flow velocities locally, as occurred during the Sumatra event of 2004.

4.4. Comparison with Historical Data

The comparison of the model results with the reported historical data for the 1755 event must consider the fact that: (1) the tsunami scenarios used in this study correspond to earthquakes of 8.1 and 8.3 magnitudes, which are smaller than the estimated magnitude for the 1755 event, and (2) the land and

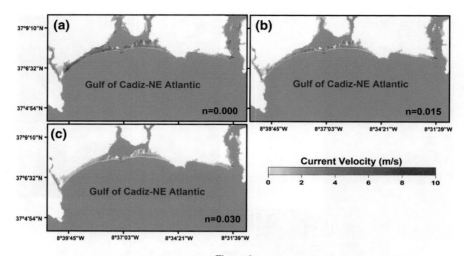

Figure 6
Results of the water current velocity computed for three different values of the Manning coefficient ($n = 0.000$, 0.015 and 0.030) for the MPF scenario

waters near the shoreline and the harbor have undergone significant changes since the late eighteenth century, including dredging and construction of the harbor, marinas and breakwaters.

Given these two points, we compared the inundation results corresponding to the MPF scenario (for $n = 0.00$) with the historical reports, only to check the likelihood of our results (see Figs. 7, 8). The analysis of Fig. 7 shows that the highest flow depths and maximum inundation distance (MID) values occurred in the Alvor and Portimão areas.

Examination of Fig. 8a indicates that in the area west of the Lagos town center, the mean inundation distance reaches 500 m, with a local maximum inundation depth of 6 m. MDJF (1756 in BAPTISTA and MIRANDA, 2009) described the 1755 event at the Lagos site as: "(…) the sea entered onshore 7 poles high; the very strong city walls suffered this misfortune(…);" another report from an eyewitness described "the sea rising up till 13 and a half palms (~7 m) high" (BAPTISTA and MIRANDA, 2009). These reports correlate well with the computed results, if we consider that the quoted value of ~7 m corresponds

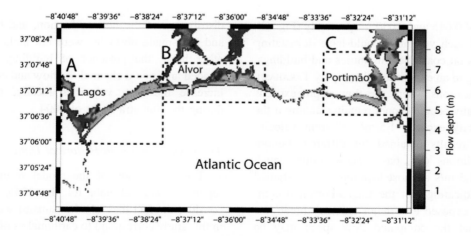

Figure 7
Inundation map for the study area resulting from the MPF earthquake scenario with a $n = 0.000$ Manning's coefficient; flow depth scale in meters

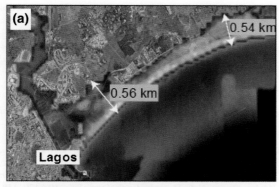

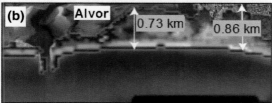

Figure 8

Flooding maps and computed inundation distances for the MPF earthquake scenario with a $n = 0.000$ Manning's coefficient. *Insets* for Lagos (**a**), Alvor (**b**) and Portimão (**c**)

to the maximum flow depth observed for the 1755 event.

Figure 8b shows that the computed MID values at Alvor reach 700 and 860 m, and the local maximum flow depth is 7.3 m. These results are in agreement with reported inundation distances for the 1755 event indicating a value of 600 m (LOPES, 1841; PEDROSA and GONÇALVES, 2008).

For the area of Portimão (Fig. 8c) the maximum flow depth value of 8 m is computed at a distance of circa 100 m from the shoreline. In this area the rivers and the streams act as wave channels causing the flooding of the river/stream banks within 3 km from the shoreline. A similar phenomenon is reported by CASTRO (1768) for the 1755 event: "In the town of

Portimão (...) alarming/formidable waves run upstream more than one league."

5. Conclusion

We simulated the coastal inundation and the overland current velocity for two tsunamigenic scenarios. Both scenarios produce significant flow depths and current velocities. The areas where the small Algarve rivers reach the ocean, due to their morphological characteristics, with relatively large shallow areas, will sustain most of the inundation and damage.

We investigated the sensitivity of the inundation limit and the flow speed with respect to the bottom friction coefficients used ($n = 0.000, 0.015$ and 0.030 in this study). As expected, both the flow depth and speed decrease when the bottom friction increases, but in all cases the inundated area is significant. When compared to the historical descriptions of the 1755 event, our numerical model shows values somehow lower than the maxima described in historical documents; this is in agreement with the fact that our target magnitude was 8.1–8.3, while the 1755 event is supposed to have been generated by a 8.5–8.7 earthquake.

As noted previously by LIMA *et al.* (2010) the tide level in the area is relevant, 3–4 m, thus affecting the flooding distances, flow depths and run-up. This fact should be taken into account in tsunami risk studies, although we know that the probability of simultaneous occurrence of a high tide and tsunami worst case scenario is very low. The Lagos-Portimão coastal segment is the location of some of the more popular beaches, which are crowded during the summer, and this study clearly shows that these will be inundated, up to 7 m in height, with flow velocities in the range of 3–8 m/s. These results together with the very short tsunami travel time to the coast must be taken into account by emergency planners in the design of evacuation routes.

Acknowledgments

This work was funded by NEAREST and TRANSFER 6FP European Union projects, and by the

Portuguese authority for civil protection, ANPC. The authors wish to thank the anonymous reviewers for their valuable and constructive comments.

REFERENCES

AKI, K. (1966), *Earthquake mechanism*, Tectonophysics 13(1–4), 423–432.

BAPTISTA, M.A., MIRANDA, P.M.A., MENDES-VICTOR, L. (1992), *Maximum entropy analysis of Portuguese tsunamis: The tsunamis of 28/02/1969 and 26/05/1975*, Sci. Tsunami Hazards, 10(1), 9–20.

BAPTISTA, M.A., HEITOR, S., MIRANDA, J.M., MIRANDA, P., and MENDES-VICTOR, L. (1998a), *The 1755 Lisbon tsunami; evaluation of the tsunami parameters*, J. Geodynamics 25, 143–157.

BAPTISTA, M.A., MIRANDA, P.M.A., MIRANDA, J.M., and MENDES-VICTOR, L. (1998b), *Constraints on the source of the 1755 Lisbon tsunami inferred from numerical modeling of historical data on the source of the 1755 Lisbon tsunami*, J. Geodynamics 25, 159–174.

BAPTISTA, M.A., MIRANDA, J.M., CHIRERICCI, F., and ZITELLINI, N. (2003), *New Study of the 1755 Earthquake Source Based on Multi-channel Seismic Survey Data and Tsunami Modeling*, Nat. Hazards Earth Syst. Sci. 3, 333–340. http://www.nat-hazards-earth-syst-sci.net/3/333/2003/nhess-3-333-2003.html.

BAPTISTA, M.A., MIRANDA, J.M., LIMA, V., CATALÃO, J., and ROQUETE, P. (2008), *Technical Report: Estudo do Risco Sísmico e de Tsunamis no Algarve*. Contract research to ANPC – Autoridade Nacional de Protecção Civil, Portugal. (in Portuguese).

BAPTISTA, M.A., and MIRANDA, J.M. (2009), *Revision of the Portuguese catalog of tsunamis*, Nat. Hazards Earth Syst. Sci. 9, 25–42. http://www.nat-hazards-earth-syst-sci.net/9/25/2009/nhess-9-25-2009.html

BONDEVIK, S., MANGERUD, J., DAWSON, S., DAWSON, A.G., and LOHNE, O. (2003), *Record-breaking height for 8000 years-old tsunami in the North Atlantic*. EOS, 84: 289–300.

BONDEVIK, S., LØVHOLT, F., HARBITZ, C., MANGERUD, J., DAWSON, A., and SVENDSEN, J.I. (2005), *The Storegga slide tsunami – Comparing field observations with numerical simulations*. Marine and Petroleum Geology 22,195–208.

BUFORN, E., UDIAS, A., and COLOMBAS, M. (1988), *Seismicity, source mechanisms and tectonics of the Azores – Gibraltar plate-boundary*, Tectonophysics 152, 89–118.

CASTRO, D.L.F. (1768). *História Geral de Portugal e suas conquistas (offerecida à Sacra Real e Augusta Magestade da Fidelíssima Raynha D. Maria I, Nossa Senhor)*, Livro 1, Cap. IV, 21–36. Manuscript 691 of the database of Fundo Antigo da Academia de Ciências de Lisboa. (in Portuguese).

FUKAO, Y. (1973), *Thrust faulting at a lithosphere plate boundary. The Portugal earthquake of 1969*, Earth Planet Sci. Lett. 18, 205–216.

GEIST, E.L., and DMOWSKA, R. (1999), *Local tsunamis and distributed slip at the source*, Pure Appl. Geophys. 154, 485–512.

GJEVIK, B., PEDERSEN, G., DYBESLAND, E., HARBITZ, C.B., MIRANDA, P.M.A., BAPTISTA, M.A., MENDES-VICTOR, L., HEINRICH, Ph., ROCHE, R., and GUESIMA, M. (1997), *Modeling tsunamis from earthquake sources near Gorringe Bank southwest of Portugal*, J. Geophys. Res. 102(C13), 27931–27949.

HEINRICH, Ph., BAPTISTA, M.A., MIRANDA, P.M.A. (1994). Numerical *Simulation of the 1969 Tsunami along the Portuguese Coasts. Preliminary Results*, Sci. Tsunami Hazards 12(1), 3–23.

KAABOUBEN, F., BRAHIM, A.I., TOTO, E.A., BAPTISTA, M.A., MIRANDA, J.M., SOARES, P., and LUIS, J.F. (2008), *On the focal mechanism of the 26.05.1975 North Atlantic event contribution from tsunami modeling*, J. Seismology, doi:10.1007/s10950-008-9110-6.

KANAMORI, H., and ANDERSON, D.L. (1977), *Importance of physical dispersion in surface-wave and free oscillation problems—review*, Rev. Geophys. 15(1), 105–112.

LIMA, V.V., MIRANDA, J.M., BAPTISTA, M.A., CATALÃO, J.C., GONZALEZ, M., OTERO, L., OLABARRIETA, M., ÁLVAREZ-GÓMEZ, J.A., and CARREÑO, E. (2010), *Impact of a 1755 like tsunami in Huelva Spain*, Nat. Hazards Earth Syst. Sci. 10, 139–148. http://www.nat-hazards-earth-syst-sci.net/10/139/2010/nhess-10-139-2010.html.

LIU, P.L.-F., CHO, Y.-S., BRIGGS, M. J., SYNOLAKIS, C.E., and KANOGLU, U. (1995), *Run-up of solitary waves on a circular island*, J. Fluid Mech. 302, 259–285.

LIU, P. L.-F., WOO, S-B., and CHO, Y-S. (1998), *Computer programs for tsunami propagation and inundation*, Technical report, Cornell University.

LOPES, J.B.S. (1841), *Corografia ou memória económica do reino do Algarve*, Ed. Academia de Ciências Lisboa, 169 pp. (in Portuguese).

LUIS, J.F. (2007), *Mirone: A multi-purpose tool for exploring grid data*, Computers and Geosciences 33, 31–41.

LUQUE, L., LARIO, J., ZAZO, C., GOY, J.L., DABRIO, C.J., and SILVA, P.G. (2001), *Tsunami deposits as paleoseismic inidcators: examples from the Spanish coast*, Acta Geologica Hispanica 36(3–4), 197–211.

LUQUE, L., LARIO, J., CIVIC, J., SILVA, P.G., ZAZO, C., GOY, J.L., and DABRIO, C.J. (2002), *Sedimentary record of a tsunami during Roman times, Bay of Cadiz, Spain*, Journal of Quaternary Science 17(5–6), 623–631.

MANSINHA, L., and SMYLIE, D.E. (1971), *The displacement field of inclined faults*, Bull. Seismol. Soc. Am. 61(5), 1433–1440.

MIRANDA, J.M., BAPTISTA, M.A., TERRINHA, P., and MATIAS, L. (2008), *Tsunamigenic source areas for Portugal mainland, Iberia, Oral Communication*, Session on Tsunami Early Warning Systems and Tsunami Risk Mitigation in the European-Mediterranean Region, 31st General Assembly of the European Seismological Commission, Crete, Greece.

OMIRA, R., BAPTISTA, M.A., MATIAS, L., MIRANDA, J.M., CATITA, C., CARRILHO, F., and TOTO, E. (2009a), *Design of a Sea-level Tsunami Detection Network for the Gulf of Cadiz*, Nat. Hazards Earth Syst. Sci. 9, 1327–1338. http://www.nat-hazards-earth-syst-sci.net/9/1327/2009/nhess-9-1327-2009.html.

OMIRA, R., BAPTISTA, M.A., MIRANDA, J.M., TOTO, E., CATITA, C., and CATALÃO, J. (2009b), *Tsunami vulnerability assessment of Casablanca-Morocco using numerical modelling and GIS tools*, Natural Hazards, doi:10.1007/s11069-009-9454-4.

PEDROSA, F.T., and GONÇALVES, J. (2008), *The 1755 earthquake in the Algarve (South of Portugal): what would happen nowadays?* Adv. Geosci. 14, 59–63.

SCHOLZ, C.H. (1982), *Scaling laws for large earthquakes: consequences for physical models*, Bull. Seismol. Soc. Am. 72, 1–14.

TAKAHASHI, S. (2005), *Tsunami disasters and their prevention in Japan—Toward the performance design of coastal defences*,

Proceedings of the International Symposium on Disaster Reduction on Coasts, Melbourne, Australia, 2005.

TINTI, S., and ARMIGLIATO, A. (2003), *The use of scenarios to evaluate the tsunami impact in southern Italy*, Marine Geology 199, 221–243.

WANG, X., and LIU, P.L-F. (2007), *COMCOT user manual-version 1.6*. School of Civil and Environmental Engineering, Cornell University Ithaca, NY 14853, USA. http://ceeserver.cee.cornell.edu/pll-group/doc/comcot_user_manual_v1_6.pdf

WIJETUNGE, J.J. (2009), *Numerical simulation and field survey of inundation due to 2004 Indian Ocean tsunami in Trincomalee, Sri Lanka*, Natural Hazards, doi:10.1007/s11069-009-9459-z.

(Received January 5, 2010, revised April 22, 2010, accepted April 28, 2010, Published online November 13, 2010)

Reprinted from the journal

Pure Appl. Geophys. 168 (2011), 1045–1052
© 2010 Springer Basel AG
DOI 10.1007/s00024-010-0219-5

Slip Distribution of the 1963 Great Kurile Earthquake Estimated from Tsunami Waveforms

KEI IOKI[1] and YUICHIRO TANIOKA[1]

Abstract—The 1963 great Kurile earthquake was an underthrust earthquake occurred in the Kurile–Kamchatka subduction zone. The slip distribution of the 1963 earthquake was estimated using 21 tsunami waveforms recorded at tide gauges along the Pacific and Okhotsk Sea coasts. The extended rupture area was divided into 24 subfaults, and the slip on each subfault was determined by the tsunami waveform inversion. The result shows that the largest slip amount of 2.8 m was found at the shallow part and intermediate depth of the rupture area. Large slip amounts were found at the shallow part of the rupture area. The total seismic moment was estimated to be 3.9×10^{21} Nm (M_w 8.3). The 2006 Kurile earthquake occurred right next to the location of the 1963 earthquake, and no seismic gap exists between the source areas of the 1963 and 2006 earthquakes.

Key words: Tsunami simulation, 1963 great Kurile earthquake, slip distribution.

1. Introduction

On 13 October 1963, a great earthquake occurred off the Kurile Islands (Fig. 1). The origin time, location, and focal depth of the earthquake given by United States Coast and Geodetic Survey (USCGS) are 05 h 17 m 57 s, 44.8°N, 149.5°E, and 60 km, respectively. This event was an underthrust earthquake due to the subduction of the Pacific plate beneath the Kurile Islands. KANAMORI (1970) estimated fault parameters, strike = 223°, dip = 22°, rake = 90°, and seismic moment = 7.5×10^{21} Nm (M_w = 8.5) from long-period surface wave analysis. He also estimated the fault length of 250 km and width of 150 km from aftershock distribution. The same fault length was also estimated using Rayleigh waves by FURUMOTO (1979) and using Love and

Rayleigh waves by BEN-MENAHEM and ROSENMAN (1972). Detailed moment release of the earthquake along the rupture area was determined using teleseismic body waves by several previous studies (RUFF and KANAMORI, 1983; BECK and RUFF, 1987; KIKUCHI and FUKAO, 1987; SCHWARTZ and RUFF 1987). The results from RUFF and KANAMORI (1983), BECK and RUFF (1987), and SCHWARTZ and RUFF, (1987) indicated that the earthquake ruptured three asperities.

The tsunami generated by the 1963 earthquake propagated through the Pacific Ocean and Okhotsk Sea. Maximum double amplitudes of the observed tsunami were 2 m at Yuzhno Kurilsk (Kunashiri Island) and 1.3 m at Hanasaki (Hokkaido). The source area was estimated from arrival times of tsunami observed at Russian tide gauges (SOLOV'EV, 1965; HATORI, 1971), and that was larger than the source area estimated by the above seismological analyses (Fig. 1). The largest aftershock, occurred on October 20, generated extensive tsunami waves but relatively weak seismic waves, and it was classified as a tsunami earthquake (FUKAO, 1979).

The Pacific plate subducts under the Kurile Islands about 8 cm per year (APEL, 2006), and many great underthrust earthquakes occurred along the Kurile–Kamchatka subduction zone. The most recent great underthrust earthquake in this subduction zone was the 2006 Kurile earthquake occurred about 350 km northeast from the epicenter of the 1963 earthquake (Fig. 1). The slip distribution of the 2006 earthquake was estimated by tsunami waveform analysis (FUJII and SATAKE, 2008). The result indicates that the source dimension is 200×100 km as shown in Fig. 1.

In this paper, slip distribution of the 1963 earthquake is estimated using tsunami waveform inversion to investigate source processes of the earthquake. We compare the source area of the 1963 earthquake estimated in this study and that of the 2006 earthquake

[1] Institute of Seismology and Volcanology, Hokkaido University, N10W8 Kitaku, Sapporo 060-0810, Japan. E-mail: iokikei@mail.sci.hokudai.ac.jp

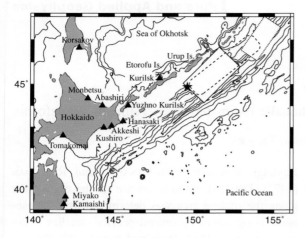

Figure 1

A map near the source area of the 1963 Kurile earthquake. A *star* shows the epicenter of the 1963 earthquake. A *solid rectangle* shows the rupture area of the earthquake estimated by KANAMORI (1970). A *rounded-vertex rectangle* shows the source area of the earthquake estimated from arrival times of observed tsunami (SOLOV'EV, 1965). A *dotted rectangle* shows the tsunami source area of the 2006 Kurile earthquake (FUJII and SATAKE, 2008). *Triangles* show the tide gauge stations near Japan used in the tsunami waveform inversion. The depth contour interval is 1,000 m

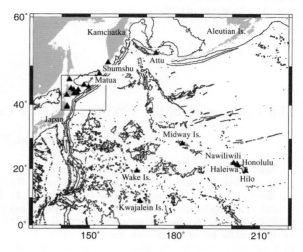

Figure 2

The tsunami computed area. A *star* shows the epicenter of the 1963 Kurile earthquake. *Triangles* show the tide gauge stations used in the tsunami waveform inversion. A *rectangle* shows the area of Fig. 1. The depth contour interval is 3,000 m

estimated by previous studies to answer a key question: does a seismic gap exist between the rupture areas of the two great earthquakes?

2. Tsunami waveform data and fault model

We used 21 tsunami waveforms observed at eight tide gauges in Japan, Monbetsu, Abashiri, Hanasaki, Akkeshi, Kushiro, Tomakomai, Miyako, and Kamaishi, obtained from the Tsunami Chart Data along the coast of Japan (1899–1969) published by Japan Weather Association, four tide gauges in Russia, Korsakov, Kurilsk, Matua, and Shumshu, published by SOLOV'EV (1965), and 9 tide gauges in Attu, Midway Island, Hawaiian Islands, Kwajalein Island, Wake Island, and Yuzhno Kurilsk, obtained from the National Geophysical Data Center at the National Oceanic and Atmospheric Administration (NGDC-NOAA). Locations of those tide gauge stations are shown in Figs. 1 and 2. For the tsunami waveform analysis, the tsunami signals needed to be separated from the tide signals. First, tide signals are estimated by calculating moving average of 3 h from original

data. Second, the estimated tide signals are removed from the original data, to get the tsunami signals only.

We used the fault parameters estimated by KANAMORI (1970), length = 250 km, width = 150 km, the shallowest depth = 4 km, strike = 223°, dip = 22°, and rake = 90°. The fault area estimated by KANAMORI (1970) was divided into 15 subfaults with a size of 50 × 50 km. Furthermore, three subfaults (subfault 1, 9, 17) were added at west side and six subfaults (subfault 7, 8, 15, 16, 23, 24) were added at east side as shown in Fig. 3 to investigate the size of the source area of the 1963 earthquake because the source area estimated from arrival times of observed tsunami (SOLOV'EV, 1965; HATORI, 1971) was longer than that estimated from long-period surface wave analysis (KANAMORI, 1970). The fault models used in this study are shown in Fig. 1 and Table 1. The epicenter is located in subfault 2, at the western part of the rupture area.

3. Tsunami numerical simulation

In order to compute tsunami propagation, the ocean bottom deformation of each subfault was calculated using Okada's equations (OKADA, 1985). The ocean surface deformation, the initial condition of tsunami, is assumed to be the same as the ocean

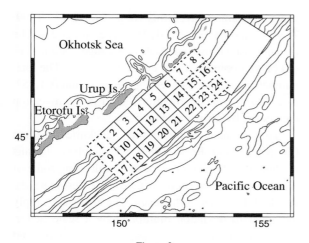

Figure 3

A map showing location of subfaults used for the tsunami waveform inversion. *Solid small rectangles* show the 15 subfaults that subdivide the rupture area estimated by KANAMORI (1970). *Dotted small rectangles* show the added nine subfaults to investigate the size of source area of the 1963 Kurile earthquake. A *solid large rectangle* shows the tsunami source area of the 2006 Kurile earthquake (FUJII and SATAKE, 2008). The depth contour interval is 1,000 m

bottom deformation due to faulting of a large earthquake, because the wavelength of the ocean bottom deformation is much larger than the ocean depth. Then, linear long-wave equations were solved to compute the synthetic tsunami waveforms. A finite-difference scheme with a staggered grid system was used to solve the equations (see SATAKE, 2007). The Coriolis term is small, but the effect is not negligible when the propagation time is long. In this paper, the Coriolis term is included since some of the tide gauge stations are far from the source and the data of tsunami waveform used in the inversion extend to about 460 min from the earthquake origin time. In general, for a staggered grid system, 1' grid (the GEBCO One Minute Grid, 2003) was used to calculate tsunami waveforms. Near Kurile Islands, 1' digital bathymetry from GUSIAKOV and LANDER (1998) was used. Around Japan, 20" grid bathymetry was created using digital contour data, M7000 series (2007) and digital grid data, MIRC-JTOPO30 (2003). We also digitized NAUTCAL CHARTS around Attu, Hawaiian

Table 1

The location of each subfault and result of the tsunami waveform inversion

Subfault number	Longitude (°E)	Latitude (°E)	Depth (m)	Slip (m)	Error (m)
1	149°52'	44°41'	34.9	0.4	0.47
2	150°18'	44°58'	34.9	0.0	0.49
3	150°44'	45°15'	34.9	2.3	0.67
4	151°11'	45°33'	34.9	0.0	0.29
5	151°37'	45°50'	34.9	0.0	0.08
6	152°03'	46°08'	34.9	1.0	0.40
7	152°26'	46°26'	34.9	0.3	0.22
8	152°56'	46°55'	34.9	0.4	0.41
9	150°13'	44°23'	19.5	0.3	0.29
10	150°40'	44°41'	19.5	1.5	0.39
11	151°07'	44°59'	19.5	1.2	0.45
12	151°33'	45°16'	19.5	1.4	0.56
13	152°00'	45°34'	19.5	1.6	0.39
14	152°26'	45°52'	19.5	2.8	0.49
15	152°52'	46°10'	19.5	0.6	0.13
16	153°22'	46°39'	19.5	0.2	0.29
17	150°35'	44°05'	4.0	0.4	0.26
18	151°02'	44°23'	4.0	0.7	0.33
19	151°29'	44°41'	4.0	1.7	0.44
20	151°56'	44°59'	4.0	2.8	0.53
21	152°23'	45°17'	4.0	2.0	0.46
22	152°50'	45°35'	4.0	1.2	0.39
23	153°17'	45°53'	4.0	1.4	0.16
24	153°47'	46°22'	4.0	0.0	0.24

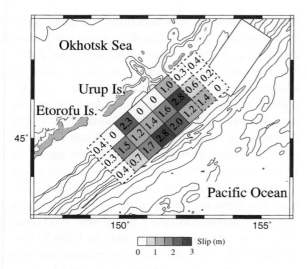

Figure 4
The slip distribution of the 1963 Kurile earthquake estimated from the tsunami waveform inversion using 24 subfaults. A *large rectangle* shows the tsunami source area of the 2006 Kurile earthquake (FUJII and SATAKE, 2008). The depth contour interval is 1,000 m

Islands, Kwajalein Island, Midway Island, and Yuzhno Kurilsk to create 20″ grid data. The 20″ grid size is finer than the grid sizes used by previous tsunami waveform inversion studies (e.g., JOHNSON *et al.*, 1996; HIRATA *et al.*, 2003; FUJII and SATAKE, 2008). Tsunami computation was made every 1 s to satisfy a stability condition. The rise time of tsunami initial wave was assumed to be 70 s. It means that 1/70 of the co-seismic deformation calculated from the fault model was added to the ocean surface deformation at each time step until 70 s after the origin time.

Tsunami waveforms were numerically computed from each subfault with a unit amount of slip, and used as the Green's function for the inversion. Then, slip amount on each subfault were estimated using the tsunami waveforms inversion. This technique of the tsunami waveform inversion is basically the same as that of SATAKE (2007). But the difference is that positive constraints are assigned for the slip estimates. As data for the inversion, first few pulses of tsunami waves at each tide gauge were used because later phases should be influenced by larger non-linear coastal effect and reliability of the computed tsunami waveforms decreases with time. This data selection is similar to the previous earthquake source studies

using tsunami waveforms (e.g., JOHNSON, 1999; TANIOKA and SATAKE, 2001; HIRATA et al., 2003). The tsunami waveforms for each tide gauge station consist of data points with an interval of 1 min. The total number of data points used for the inversion is 1,157. The data of tsunami waveform used in the inversion are shown by arrows in Fig. 5.

To estimate errors, the jackknife method (TICHELAAR and RUFF, 1989) was applied. In this method, the inversion is repeated by deleting some of the data randomly from all the data to estimate the standard deviation of the result. The errors are simply the standard deviation multiplied by a scale factor, K (see equation (5) in the paper by TICHELAAR and RUFF, 1989). K is defined as

$$K = \sqrt{\frac{(n - j - p + 1)}{j}} \qquad (1)$$

where n is the total number of data points, j is the number of dropped data points, p is the number of the model parameters which is the number of subfaults in this paper.

In this study, we inverted the tsunami waveforms 50 times by randomly dropping 500 data points out of 1,157 data points to estimate the errors. The scale factor, K, is 1.13.

4. *Results and discussions*

The result of the tsunami waveform inversion is shown in Fig. 4 and Table 1. The estimated slip distribution shows that the largest slip amount of 2.8 m was found at east of the rupture area in subfault 14 and south edge of the rupture area in subfault 20. And large slip amounts were found at the intermediate depth and in the shallow part of the rupture area. Another large slip amount of 2.3 m was found in the deep part of the rupture area in subfault 3. This slip distribution indicates three asperities of deep, and intermediate depth and in the shallow part of the rupture area in subfault 3, 14 and 20. This result agrees with previous studies that found at least three asperities for the 1963 earthquake (RUFF and KANAMORI, 1983; BECK and RUFF, 1987; SCHWARTZ and RUFF 1987). Since there are little slip amounts on

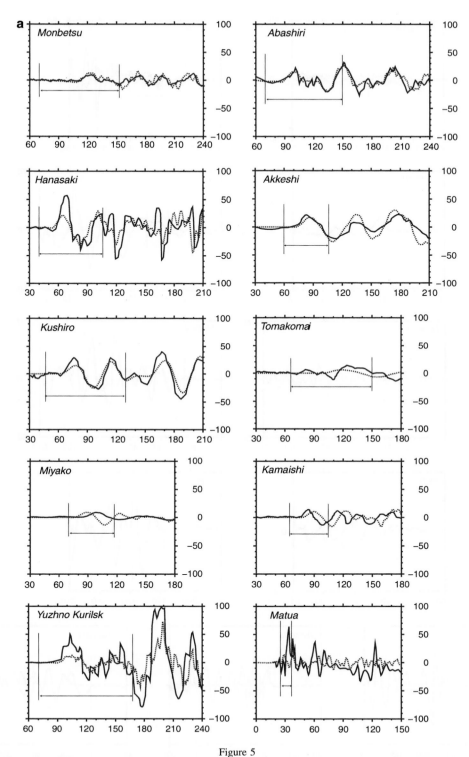

Figure 5
Comparison of observed (*solid line*) and synthetic (*dotted line*) tsunami waveforms at each station used in the inversion. Horizontal axis is time (min) from the origin time of the earthquake and vertical axis is amplitude (cm). *Arrows* show the data of tsunami waveform used for the inversion

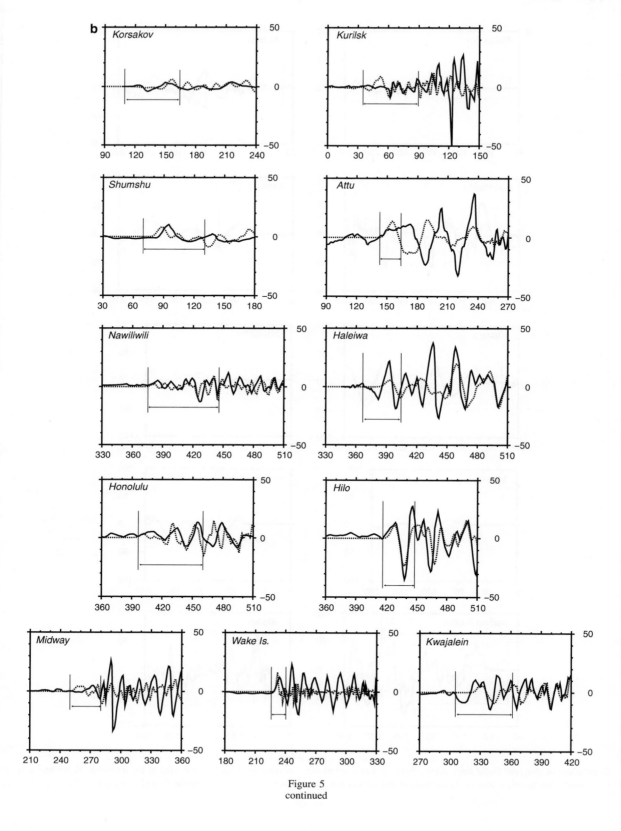

Figure 5
continued

the western edge of the fault model in subfault 1, 9, and 19 and on the eastern edge of the fault model in subfault 8, 16 and 24, the rupture length was estimated about 300 km. The rupture length of 300 km estimated from the slip distribution is longer than that of 250 km estimated by KANAMORI (1970). But the length coincides with that estimated by KIKUCHI and FUKAO (1987). Also the length is slightly smaller than that estimated from arrival times of observed tsunami (SOLOV'EV, 1965; HATORI, 1971). A main slip area, where a large slip amount of more than 1.5 m was estimated, is almost the same as the source area estimated by KANAMORI (1970). The source area of the 1963 earthquake is very close to that of the 2006 Kurile earthquake, but doesn't overlap the 2006 source area (Fig. 4).

Comparisons of observed and computed tsunami waveforms are shown in Fig. 5. Overall, computed tsunami waveforms fit well the observed ones. Especially, tsunami waveforms observed at Japanese tide gauge stations are well explained by the computed ones. However, computed tsunami waveforms at Attu and Midway Island don't match so well. We think the bathymetries near the two tide gauges are not good enough to compute tsunami accurately. For example, at Midway Island, near the tide gauge station one can find a large shallow water region with corals.

The seismic moment was calculated to be 3.9×10^{21} Nm ($M_w = 8.3$) by assuming that the rigidity is 7×10^{10} N/m^2. This result is smaller than the seismic moment of 7.5×10^{21} Nm ($M_w = 8.5$) by KANAMORI (1970). The moment magnitude is also slightly smaller than the tsunami magnitude, $M_t = 8.4$, estimated by ABE (1979).

5. Conclusions

We estimated the source area and the detailed slip distribution of the 1963 Kurile earthquake using tsunami waveforms observed at coastal tide gauge stations along the Pacific and Okhotsk Sea. The estimated slip distribution indicates that large slip amounts were found at the intermediate depth and in the shallow part of the rupture area. Also there are three asperities at deep, intermediate

depth as well as in the shallow part of the rupture area. We estimated that the fault length is about 300 km and the width is about 150 km. The source area was longer to northeast side than that estimated by KANAMORI (1970) but not longer than that estimated by SOLOV'EV (1965) and HATORI (1971). The total seismic moment estimated from the tsunami waveforms inversion was 3.9×10^{21} Nm ($M_w = 8.3$). The 2006 Kurile earthquake occurred just next to the 1963 earthquake. The 2006 earthquake didn't rupture the source area of the 1963 earthquake, and no seismic gap exists between the source areas of the 1963 and 2006 earthquakes.

Acknowledgments

We would like to thank two anonymous referees and Prof. Stefano Tinti for their helpful comments and suggestions.

REFERENCES

ABE, K. (1979), *Size of great earthquakes of 1837-1974 inferred from tsunami data*, J. Geophys. Res., *84*, 1561–1568.

APEL, E. V. (2006), *Independent active microplate tectonics of northeast Asia from GPS velocities and block modeling*, Geophys. Res. Lett., *33*, L11303, doi:10.1029/2006GL026077.

BECK, S. L. and RUFF, L. J. (1987), *Source process of the 1963 Kurile Islands earthquake*, J. Geophys. Res., *92*, 14123–14138.

BEN-MENAHEM, A. and ROSENMAN, M. (1972), *Amplitude patterns of tsunami Waves from submarine earthquakes*, J. Geophys. Res., *77*, 3097–3128.

FUKAO, Y. (1979), *Tsunami earthquakes and subduction processes near deep-sea trenches*, J. Geophys. Res., *84*, 2303–2314.

FUJII, Y. and SATAKE, K. (2008), *Tsunami source of the November 2006 and January 2007 great Kurile earthquakes*, Bull. Seism. Soc. Am., *98*(3), 1559–1571.

FURUMOTO, M. (1979), *Initial phase analysis of R waves from great earthquakes*, J. Geophys. Res., *84*, 6867–6874.

GUSIAKOV, V. and LANDER, J. (1998), International workshop on bathymetry and coastal topography data managemen, Seattle, 20–21 March 1998

HATORI, T. (1971), *Tsunami source in Hokkaido and Southern Kurile Regions*, Bull. Earthquake Res. Inst. Tokyo Univ., *43*, 103–109.

HIRATA, K., GEIST, E., SATAKE, K., TANIOKA, Y. and YAMAKI, S. (2003), *Slip distribution of the 1952 Tokachi-Oki earthquake (M 8.1) along the Kurile Trench deduced from tsunami waveform inversion*, J. Geophys. Res., *108*, B4, 2196, doi:10.1029/2002JB001976.

JEAN M. JOHNSON, SATAKE, K., HOLDAHL S. R. and SAUBER J. (1996), *The 1964 Prince William Sound earthquake: Joint inversion of tsunami and geodetic data*, J. Geophys. Res., *101*, 523–532.

JEAN M. JOHNSON (1999), *Heterogeneous coupling along Alaska-Aleutians as inferred from tsunami, seismic, and geodetic inversions*, Advances in Geophysics, *39*, 1–116.

KANAMORI, H. (1970), *Synthesis of long-period surface waves and its application to earthquake source studies—Kurile Islands Earthquake of October 13*, J. Geophys. Res., *75*, 5011–5027.

KIKUCHI, M. and FUKAO, Y. (1987), *Inversion of long-period P waves from great earthquakes along subduction zones*, Tectonophysics, *144*, 231–247.

MIRC-JTOPO30 (2003), 30 seconds grid data of depth in near Japan, (http://www.mirc.jha.or.jp/products/JTOPO30/), M7000 series (2007), digital contour data, CD-R.

OKADA, Y. (1985), *Surface deformation due to shear and tensile faults in a half-space*, Bull. Seism. Soc. Am., *75*, 1135–1154.

RUFF, L. J. and KANAMORI, H. (1983), *The rupture process and asperity distribution of three great earthquakes from long-period differenced P-waves*, Phys. Earth Planet. Inter., *31*, 202–230.

SATAKE, K. (2007), *Tsunamis*, in *"Treatise on Geophysics Volume 4: Earthquake Seismology"*, ed. by H. KANAMORI, Elsevier Science, Amsterdam, 483–512.

SCHWARTZ, S. and RUFF, L. J. (1987), *Asperity distribution and earthquake occurrence in the southern Kurile Arc*, Phys. Earth Planet. Inter., *49*, 54–77.

SOLOV'EV, S. L. (1965), *The Urup earthquake and associated tsunami of 1963*, Bull. Earthquake Res. Inst. Tokyo Univ., *43*, 103–109.

TANIOKA Y. and SATAKE K. (2001), *Coseismic slip distribution of the 1946 Nankai earthquake and aseismic slips caused by the earthquake*, Earth Planets Space, *53*, 235–241.

The GEBCO One Minute Grid (2003), (https://www.bodc.ac.uk/data/online_delivery/gebco/info1/#bugs).

TICHELAAR, B. W. and RUFF, L. J. (1989), *How good are our best model? Jackknifing, bootstrapping, and earthquake depth*, EOS, *70*, 593, 605–606.

(Received December 15, 2009, revised May 5, 2010, accepted May 13, 2010, Published online November 9, 2010)

Pure Appl. Geophys. 168 (2011), 1053–1074
© 2010 Springer Basel AG
DOI 10.1007/s00024-010-0228-4

Combined Effects of Tectonic and Landslide-Generated Tsunami Runup at Seward, Alaska During the M_W 9.2 1964 Earthquake

ELENA SULEIMANI,[1] DMITRY J. NICOLSKY,[1] PETER J. HAEUSSLER,[2] and ROGER HANSEN[1]

Abstract—We apply a recently developed and validated numerical model of tsunami propagation and runup to study the inundation of Resurrection Bay and the town of Seward by the 1964 Alaska tsunami. Seward was hit by both tectonic and landslide-generated tsunami waves during the M_W 9.2 1964 megathrust earthquake. The earthquake triggered a series of submarine mass failures around the fjord, which resulted in landsliding of part of the coastline into the water, along with the loss of the port facilities. These submarine mass failures generated local waves in the bay within 5 min of the beginning of strong ground motion. Recent studies estimate the total volume of underwater slide material that moved in Resurrection Bay to be about 211 million m^3 (Haeussler et al. in Submarine mass movements and their consequences, pp 269–278, 2007). The first tectonic tsunami wave arrived in Resurrection Bay about 30 min after the main shock and was about the same height as the local landslide-generated waves. Our previous numerical study, which focused only on the local landslide-generated waves in Resurrection Bay, demonstrated that they were produced by a number of different slope failures, and estimated relative contributions of different submarine slide complexes into tsunami amplitudes (Suleimani et al. in Pure Appl Geophys 166:131–152, 2009). This work extends the previous study by calculating tsunami inundation in Resurrection Bay caused by the combined impact of landslide-generated waves and the tectonic tsunami, and comparing the composite inundation area with observations. To simulate landslide tsunami runup in Seward, we use a viscous slide model of Jiang and LeBlond (J Phys Oceanogr 24(3):559–572, 1994) coupled with nonlinear shallow water equations. The input data set includes a high resolution multibeam bathymetry and LIDAR topography grid of Resurrection Bay, and an initial thickness of slide material based on pre- and post-earthquake bathymetry difference maps. For simulation of tectonic tsunami runup, we derive the 1964 coseismic deformations from detailed slip distribution in the rupture area, and use them as an initial condition for propagation of the tectonic tsunami. The numerical model employs nonlinear shallow water equations formulated for depth-averaged water fluxes, and calculates a temporal position of the shoreline using a free-surface moving boundary

algorithm. We find that the calculated tsunami runup in Seward caused first by local submarine landslide-generated waves, and later by a tectonic tsunami, is in good agreement with observations of the inundation zone. The analysis of inundation caused by two different tsunami sources improves our understanding of their relative contributions, and supports tsunami risk mitigation in south-central Alaska. The record of the 1964 earthquake, tsunami, and submarine landslides, combined with the high-resolution topography and bathymetry of Resurrection Bay make it an ideal location for studying tectonic tsunamis in coastal regions susceptible to underwater landslides.

Key words: Tsunami, runup, inundation, numerical modeling, 1964 Alaska Earthquake, submarine landslides, Resurrection Bay, Seward.

1. Introduction

The Prince William Sound tsunami of March 27, 1964 was generated by the M_W 9.2 Alaskan earthquake, the largest instrumentally recorded earthquake in North America. It ruptured an 800-km long section of the Aleutian megathrust, producing vertical displacements over an area of about 285,000 km^2 in south-central Alaska (PLAFKER, 1969). The area of coseismic subsidence (CS) included Kodiak Island, Kenai Peninsula, Cook Inlet and part of the northern Prince William Sound (Fig. 1). The major zone of uplift was seaward of the subsidence zone, in Prince William Sound and in the Gulf of Alaska (PLAFKER, 1969). Although the ground shaking was long and violent, 92% of fatalities directly associated with this earthquake were caused by tsunami waves (LANDER, 1996). The impact of coseismic crustal deformations on the ocean surface and on numerous water bodies in south-central Alaska was very complex. The vertical sea floor displacement generated a major tectonic tsunami that caused fatalities and great damage in

---
[1] Geophysical Institute, University of Alaska Fairbanks, 903 Koyukuk Dr., Fairbanks, AK 99775-7320, USA. E-mail: elena@gi.alaska.edu
[2] USGS, Alaska Science Center, 4200 University Dr., Anchorage, AK 99508-4626, USA.

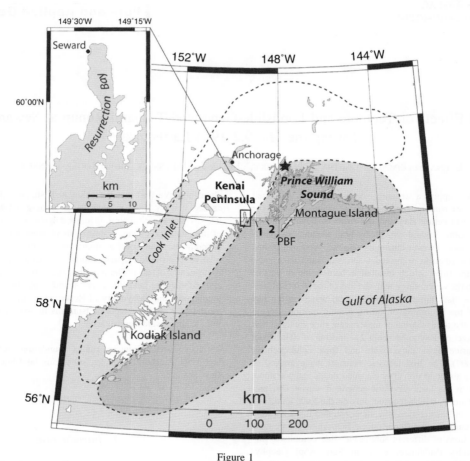

Figure 1

Map of south-central Alaska with the rupture zone of the M_W 9.2 1964 Great Alaska earthquake. The *star* indicates the earthquake epicenter. The *dashed contour* delineates regions of coseismic uplift (*shaded*) and subsidence of the 1964 rupture area (PLAFKER, 1969). The *inset* map includes Resurrection Bay, which is shown in detail in Fig. 2. Notations: *1*—Whidbey Bay, *2*—Puget Bay, *PBF*—Patton Bay fault

Alaska, Hawaii, the west coast of the United States and Canada, and was recorded on tide gauges as far as Australia and New Zealand (SPAETH and BERKMAN, 1972). In addition to the major tectonic wave, about 20 local tsunamis were generated by submarine mass failures from the steep fjord walls in a number of bays in south-central Alaska (LANDER, 1996).

The village of Seward in Resurrection Bay (Fig. 1) was the only community that suffered from the combined effects of local landslide-generated waves and the tectonic tsunami during the 1964 earthquake (HAEUSSLER *et al.*, 2007). Strong ground shaking triggered several underwater slides in Resurrection Bay within seconds of the beginning of the earthquake, and locally generated waves flooded the town 1 min later. The first tectonic wave, which was as destructive as the earlier local waves, arrived from the Gulf of Alaska

about 30 min after the main shock. Seward has the northeasternmost near-field observations of the tectonic tsunami. The effects of the 1964 earthquake and tsunami waves in Resurrection Bay, including wave amplitudes and extent of inundation, were documented by several investigators (WILSON and TØRUM, 1968; LEMKE, 1967; PLAFKER, 1969), and will be used in this work to verify results of numerical modeling.

The work described in this paper is part of an effort by the Alaska Earthquake Information Center to conduct tsunami inundation modeling and mapping for coastal communities in Alaska. The goal is to improve tsunami hazard assessment and mitigation in communities that are at risk for future tsunamis. To ensure that coastal communities are provided with tsunami inundation maps produced with scientifically solid and tested methodology (SYNOLAKIS *et al.*

(2008), we validate and verify our numerical models of tsunami propagation and runup. The model that we use in this study (NICOLSKY et al., 2010) was tested in a comprehensive set of analytical and field benchmarks suggested by NOAA with the purpose of establishing quality standards for tsunami inundation products (SYNOLAKIS et al., 2007). The work by NICOLSKY et al. (2010) describes the numerical algorithm and summarizes results of analytical, laboratory, and field benchmarking. The purpose of this study is to improve our understanding of the different nature of submarine landslide tsunami compared to that of a tectonic tsunami, and to demonstrate that the near-field tectonic and landslide tsunami hazard can be assessed as it relates to south-central Alaska.

This paper presents the first complete numerical modeling study of tectonic and landslide-generated tsunami waves in Resurrection Bay, Alaska, during the 1964 Great Alaska Earthquake. Because the 1964 tsunami waves at Seward are relatively well documented, this case provides a unique opportunity to study the integrated effects of tectonic and landslide-generated tsunami runup. The previous numerical study by SULEIMANI et al. (2009) focused only on local landslide-generated tsunami in Resurrection Bay. It tested the hypothesis that the waves were produced by a number of different slope failures, and showed that three slides in the upper bay were the major contributors of tsunami amplitudes at Seward and other fan deltas in the upper bay. We extend our previous work by first calculating tsunami inundation at Seward and around Resurrection Bay by local landslide-generated waves. Then we model propagation and runup of tectonic tsunami waves that were generated by coseismic deformation of a large segment of the continental shelf in the Gulf of Alaska (Fig. 1). The tectonic tsunami timing, which is relatively well known, can be an additional constraint on the source of the near-field tectonic tsunami. LEMKE (1967) reported that, except for some minor secondary slumping, the trigger for local landslide-generated waves in Resurrection Bay ceased at the end of ground shaking, which was about 25 min before the arrival of the tectonic tsunami. Although it is possible that individual slides were triggered at different times after the initial ground shaking, there is no independent evidence to support this hypothesis. Therefore, we assume that we can separate the tectonic and landslide tsunami sources, and that they are independent and can be modeled separately. After we characterize the tectonic and landslide tsunami hazard of south-central Alaska, we describe numerical models that we use to simulate tsunami waves in Resurrection Bay caused by the tectonic and landslide sources (Sect. 3). Section 4 outlines different source mechanisms, and we describe the numerical modeling results in Sect. 5. We complete the analysis by comparing the union of inundation areas computed independently for tectonic and landslide-generated waves with the observed composite inundation pattern, and analyze calculated and observed tsunami time series (Sect. 6). We demonstrate that our modeling approach can be used in tsunami inundation mapping of coastal communities located in seismically active regions, where tectonic tsunami hazard is combined with susceptibility of the fjord environment to underwater slope failures and locally generated waves.

2. Tsunami Hazard in South-Central Alaska

Coastal Alaska has a long record of tsunami waves generated by a variety of geologic sources, which include subduction zone earthquakes, active volcanoes, and submarine and subaerial landslides (LANDER, 1996). Tectonic tsunamis originating off Alaska can travel across the Pacific and impact coastal areas hours after they were generated. However, the same waves are a near-field hazard for Alaska, and can reach coastal communities within minutes of the earthquake. Tsunami hazard varies substantially along the Alaska coastline, and includes the full spectrum of events from far-field tectonic tsunamis with relatively low impact on the Alaska coast, to the dangerous combination of near-field tectonic and landslide-generated tsunami waves. The focus of this paper is on south-central Alaska (Fig. 1), whose coastline is exposed to both local tectonic and landslide tsunami potential.

2.1. Tectonic Tsunami Hazard

The seismic and tsunami hazards in Alaska are controlled by processes along the Aleutian subduction zone, a seismically active plate boundary. Almost the entire length of the subduction zone ruptured in the past century in a series of large and great earthquakes (CARVER and PLAFKER, 2008). The megathrust earthquakes of 1938, 1946, 1957, 1964, and 1965 generated Pacific-wide tsunamis that resulted in widespread damage and loss of life along the Pacific coast of Alaska and other exposed locations around the Pacific Ocean (LANDER, 1996). The area of this study in south-central Alaska is characterized by very high rates of seismicity. Tectonic activity in the region is dominated by the convergence of the Pacific and North American Plates, which interact along the Aleutian megathrust (PAGE et al., 1991). Resurrection Bay is close to the northeast end of the Aleutian megathrust, where it is strongly coupled and has a shallow dip of 3–4°. This zone has the potential to produce some of the largest earthquakes and tsunamis in the world, as demonstrated by the M_W 9.2 Great Alaska earthquake of 1964. The 1964 rupture area extended from Prince William Sound (PWS) to the southern end of Kodiak Island (KI) (Fig. 1). The major long period trans-Pacific tsunami was generated by the uplift of the continental shelf in the Gulf of Alaska that resulted from slip on the megathrust, although the highest and the most destructive waves in the near-field were probably generated by vertical displacements on megathrust splay faults (PLAFKER, 2006). There were two areas of high moment release, representing the two major asperities of the 1964 rupture zone: the PWS asperity and the KI asperity (CHRISTENSEN and BECK, 1994). This result was very similar to those derived from several studies that involved joint inversion of different combinations of seismic, tsunami and geodetic data sets (HOLDAHL and SAUBER, 1994; JOHNSON et al., 1996; ICHINOSE et al., 2007). Analysis of historical earthquake data in PWS and KI regions (NISHENKO and JACOB, 1990) showed that the KI asperity produced both large and great earthquakes more frequently and also independently of the PWS asperity.

The eastern part of the Aleutian megathrust is the only section of the subduction zone for which information on great historic earthquakes is available: nine paleosubduction earthquakes in the past ~5000 years are recognized from paleoseismic evidence of sudden land changes and tsunami deposits (CARVER and PLAFKER, 2008). Although the 1964 tsunami was the most destructive event experienced in Alaska in recorded history, a recent paleoseismic study (SHENNAN et al., 2009) showed that earthquakes about 1500 and 900 years BP ruptured a larger area than that of the 1964 earthquake. The rupture area was calculated to be 23,000 km^2 greater than that of the 1964 earthquake, with a 15% increase in seismic moment. The authors concluded that the larger extent and the amount of deformation of the penultimate earthquake also contributed to greater tsunamigenic potential. Therefore, it is possible that the worst-case tsunami scenario for coastal communities in the Gulf of Alaska could exceed the 1964 event in magnitude.

2.2. Landslide Tsunami Hazard

Tsunamis caused by slope failures are a significant hazard in the fjords of coastal Alaska and other high-latitude fjord coastlines. KULIKOV et al. (1998) analyzed tsunami catalog data for the north Pacific coast and showed that this region has a long record of tsunami waves generated by submarine and subaerial landslides, avalanches and rockfalls. Those authors also found that, in the majority of cases, tectonic tsunamis that arrive in bays and fjords from the open ocean have relatively small amplitudes, but a great number of local landslide-generated tsunamis have much larger wave amplitudes. For example, as a result of the 1964 earthquake, about 20 local submarine and subaerial landslide tsunamis were generated in Alaska (LANDER, 1996), which accounted for 76% of the tsunami fatalities. KULIKOV et al. (1998) noted that, due to the sparse population of the area, the actual number of historical landslide tsunami events is unknown, and probably much greater than the number of events observed or recorded.

The coast of south-central Alaska has numerous fjords (Fig. 1). In a fjord setting, rivers and streams emanate from the glacier that initially eroded the valley, forming a fjord-head delta and depositing sediment that easily loses strength during an earthquake. LEE et al. (2002) studied different regions of the US Exclusive Economic Zone and found that Alaskan fjords are likely the most susceptible environment to slope failures. MASSON *et al.* (2006) divide all factors that contribute to initiation of submarine landslides into two groups: the factors related to geological properties of landslide material (e.g. overpressure due to rapid deposition), and those associated with external events (e.g. earthquakes or sea level change), noting that usually more than one factor may contribute to a single landslide event. HAMPTON *et al.* (1996) note that in a fjord environment, where the deltaic sediment is deposited rapidly, the sediment builds up pore-water pressures and could liquefy under extreme low tide conditions or ground shaking during an earthquake, due to low static shear strength. While ground shaking is one of the most common triggering mechanisms for submarine slope failures, the close relationship has been demonstrated between coastal landslides and extreme low tides (THOMSON *et al.*, 2001; KULIKOV *et al.*, 1998). Human activities can also trigger submarine landslides (MASSON *et al.*, 2006; THOMSON *et al.*, 2001; BORNHOLD *et al.*, 2001). Because of these diverse mechanisms, assessment of landslide-generated tsunami hazard is a challenging task. For the Alaska tsunami inundation mapping project, we use the approach for estimating long-term landslide tsunami hazard developed by BORNHOLD *et al.* (2001). The approach consists of two steps: analysis of historical events and verification of model results with runup observations at the site; and numerical simulation of hypothetical tsunami scenarios. In this study we contribute to the first step by modeling inundation of Seward caused by locally generated tsunami waves on March 27, 1964.

2.3. 1964 Tsunami in Resurrection Bay: History and Observations

The town of Seward is near the northwest corner of Resurrection Bay, about 200 km south of Anchorage (Fig. 1). The entire head of Resurrection Bay is a fjord-head delta that was built by the Resurrection River. Lowell Point, Tonsina Point, and Fourth of July Creek are locations of other alluvial fans that extend into the bay as fan deltas (Fig. 2). The flat floor of the bay extends north to south, with its deepest part approximately 300 m below sea level. The bay is separated from the Gulf of Alaska by a

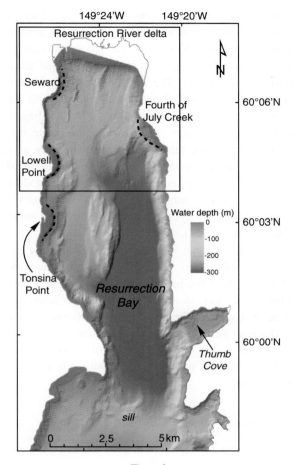

Figure 2

Multibeam bathymetric image of Resurrection Bay. The *dashed black lines* indicate bounds of the major fan deltas. The area of the upper Resurrection Bay outlined by the *black rectangle* is shown in Fig. 6

sill, which inhibits sediment transport by tidal currents to the southern part of the bay (HAEUSSLER *et al.*, 2007).

The town of Seward is built mostly on the Lowell Creek alluvial fan (the Lowell Creek fan is different than the Lowell Point fan, which lies to the south). In years before the earthquake, additional land for waterfront facilities was created by artificial fill of loose sand and gravel along the shoreline. The 1964 earthquake at Seward was characterized by strong ground motion that lasted about 3–4 min (LEMKE, 1967). Ground shaking triggered a series of slope failures within the fjord that resulted in landsliding of part of the Seward waterfront into the bay, along with the loss of the port facilities (WILSON and TØRUM,

1968; HAEUSSLER et al., 2007). The slope failures generated an initial drawdown of water at the Seward waterfront about 30 s after the ground started to shake, when the water level suddenly dropped about 6 m (LEMKE, 1967). The highest locally generated wave at Seward was about 6–8 m high and hit the waterfront about 1.5–2.0 min after the shaking began, causing much damage. The Seward tide gauge was located on a dock that collapsed into the bay as a result of the submarine failures. Although the tidal record was lost, the sequence of waves generated by the slope failures was reconstructed from observations provided by eyewitnesses (WILSON and TØRUM, 1968; LEMKE, 1967).

The first tectonic tsunami wave came into the bay about 30 min after the earthquake, impacting the entire width of the bay (WILSON and TØRUM, 1968). This wave was as high as the initial landslide-generated waves. The wave extended further inland in the river delta at the head of the bay, than any of the local waves. According to observations, the waves continued to arrive for about 10 h after the earthquake.

2.4. Previous Studies

A number of engineering, geologic and geophysical papers related to landslides and tsunami waves in Resurrection Bay were published in the years following the 1964 earthquake. The investigations conducted in the Resurrection Bay area right after the earthquake by LEMKE (1967), WILSON and TØRUM (1968), and SHANNON and HILTS (1973) confirmed that strong ground motion during the earthquake caused several submarine slope failures along the Seward waterfront and in other areas within the upper bay. There is a consensus among all the investigators that the large waves observed during ground shaking were generated by the underwater slope failures.

WILSON and TØRUM (1968) compiled the chronological sequence of waves in Seward and other locations in Resurrection Bay during and after the earthquake, and interpreted the eyewitnesses accounts in the form of inferred marigram. The authors acknowledged though that "at best this marigram can convey only a crude picture of the true state of affairs", due to uncertainty of the eyewitnesses' accounts. The authors investigated oscillating properties of Resurrection Bay and gave a comprehensive overview of tsunami damage at Seward.

Lemke (1967) summarized results of geologic investigations that were conducted in the Resurrection Bay area right after the earthquake, and compiled the maximum observed tsunami runup in downtown Seward and at the head of Resurrection Bay, which is shown by the yellow dashed line in Figs. 3 and 4, respectively. The observed maximum inundation line at Seward represents the combined effects from both local landslide-generated tsunami and the major tectonic tsunami, whereas the observations of maximum run-up at the head of the bay delineate the area that was flooded mostly by seismically generated waves. LEMKE (1967) also described the geologic setting of Seward and other nearby fan deltas, analyzed triggering mechanism of the submarine landslides, and provided the sequence and interpretation of waves in the bay. He concluded that the major factors that contributed to the total volume and aerial extent of the slide material were the long duration of ground motion, the configuration of underwater slopes, and the type of sediment forming these slopes—unconsolidated and fine-grained materials. He noted that the stability of the sediment was also decreased by the low tidal level at the time of the earthquake, and by the rapid drawdown of water due to the initial slope failure, which prevented the pore water from draining from the sediment quickly enough to maintain hydrostatic conditions.

SHANNON and HILTS (1973) conducted a subsurface geotechnical investigation of materials that failed in Resurrection Bay during the 1964 earthquake. They found that failures consisted of loose alluvial sand and gravel, marine silts and fine sands. It was shown that high artesian pressures within aquifers of the Resurrection River delta combined with the extra load caused by waterfront artificial fill and the shoreline development also contributed to the slope failures. The authors inferred that large masses of sediment might have been transported over great distances into the deep part of Resurrection Bay. Both LEMKE (1967) and SHANNON and HILTS (1973) concluded that underwater slope failures have not improved slope stability of the Seward waterfront,

Figure 3
Observed 1964 inundation line at Seward, shown by the dashed yellow contour [from LEMKE (1967)], and inundation limits calculated for different tectonic tsunami sources and the landslide source. Orthophoto image *courtesy* of National Resources Conservation Service, USDA, 1996

and thus the same slopes could be expected to fail again during the next large earthquake in the same manner as they did during the 1964 earthquake.

The most recent geologic studies by LEE *et al.* (2006) and HAEUSSLER *et al.* (2007) utilized a 2001 NOAA high-resolution multibeam bathymetry survey of Resurrection Bay (LABAY and HAEUSSLER, 2008) to study the morphology and depth changes of the fjord bottom. This high quality data set helped to visualize a variety of seafloor features related to these

submarine slides for the first time. LEE *et al.* (2006) identified remains of the Seward waterfront that failed in 1964 as a result of strong ground shaking, and debris flows that correspond to failures of the Resurrection River delta. Their analysis showed that the 1964 earthquake could potentially have triggered different failure types simultaneously. HAEUSSLER *et al.* (2007) provided analysis of bathymetric data and high resolution subbottom profiles of Resurrection Bay and showed convincing evidence of massive

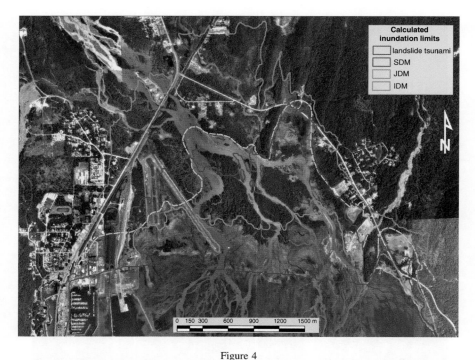

Figure 4
Observed 1964 inundation line at the head of Resurrection Bay, shown by the *dashed yellow contour* [from LEMKE (1967)], and inundation limits calculated for different tectonic tsunami sources and the landslide source. Orthophoto image *courtesy* of National Resources Conservation Service, USDA, 1996

submarine slope failure. The location and extent of submarine mass failures were estimated based on analysis of pre- and post-earthquake bathymetry. HAEUSSLER *et al.* (2007) created a bathymetric difference grid that shows depth changes in the bay after the 1964 earthquake. They concluded that several failures initiated along the fjord walls at relatively shallow depths, and the mass flows produced by these failures transported most of the material as far as 6–13 km into the deepest part of the fjord, covering the entire basin with a flow deposit. The total volume of slide material was estimated at 211 million m^3. The authors derived a map of the slide material thickness from the bathymetric difference grid, identified 10 different landslide areas and calculated their volumes.

In the first numerical modeling study of local tsunamis in Resurrection Bay, SULEIMANI *et al.* (2009) utilized the findings of HAEUSSLER *et al.* (2007) to investigate the contribution of individual slide complexes to the observed tsunami amplitudes at Seward and other locations around the bay. SULEIMANI *et al.* (2009) used the viscous slide model of JIANG and

LEBLOND (1994) coupled with nonlinear shallow water equations to test the hypothesis that the local tsunami waves in Resurrection Bay were produced by a number of different slope failures. The distribution of the slide material from HAEUSSLER *et al.* (2007) served as an initial condition for simulation of the slide motion and the surface water waves that it generated. The numerical models confirm that the waves observed at the Seward waterfront and in several other locations in Resurrection Bay were caused by multiple submarine slope failures. The models indicate that three slides in the northern part of the bay were the major contributors to the tsunami amplitudes at Seward, and that the contribution from other slide complexes was negligible.

While these most recent studies described above do provide analysis of causes and effects of the submarine landslides and locally generated tsunami waves in Resurrection Bay, they give much less attention to the tectonically generated wave. According to observations (LEMKE, 1967; WILSON and TØRUM, 1968), this wave was as high and destructive as local waves, but penetrated much further inland at the head of the bay. This study is an attempt to make the analysis complete by modeling the integrated effects of tsunami runup at Seward caused by both tectonic and landslide-generated waves.

3. Methodology

In this section we describe numerical tools and data used to simulate tsunami waves from the 1964 earthquake and landslides in Resurrection Bay. There are three major components in the numerical algorithm: the nonlinear shallow water model for tsunami propagation, a moving boundary scheme that tracks the temporal position of the shoreline for calculation of inundation, and a viscous slide model coupled with shallow water equations for simulation of landslide tsunamis.

3.1. Model Description

We simulate tsunami propagation and inundation with a nonlinear shallow water model that is formulated for depth-averaged water fluxes in both spherical and rectangular coordinates. Here we give a brief overview of the model and describe its major features, while the work by NICOLSKY et al. (2010) provides the full description of the model, including its mathematical formulation and numerical implementation. In a problem of tsunami runup, the shallow water equations are solved in a water domain that changes its geometry in time due to variable position of the shoreline. Our model employs the fictitious domain method, in which the water domain is embedded into a larger domain that is fixed in time (MARCHUK et al., 1986). The advantage of this method is in using the same governing equations for both dry and wet domains that allows for all variables to be continuously extended through the boundary between the domains. Other methods commonly used in solving the numerical problem of tsunami runup are discussed in NICOLSKY et al. (2010). In order to calculate the extent of water domain at every time step, we use a free-surface moving boundary algorithm, which determines the position of the shoreline based on the direction of the water flux between the adjacent grid cells. The shallow water equations, which are approximated by finite

differences on a staggered grid, solved semi-implicitly in time using a first order scheme. We efficiently parallelized the algorithm using the domain decomposition technique. The finite difference scheme is coded in FORTRAN using the Portable Extensible Toolkit for Scientific computation (PETSc). The model uses ocean surface displacement due to an underwater earthquake as an initial condition. NOAA recently published a technical memorandum that outlines major requirements for numerical models used in inundation mapping and tsunami forecasting, and describes a procedure for model evaluation (SYNOLAKIS et al., 2007). Using NOAA's procedure as a guideline, NICOLSKY et al. (2010) validated the tsunami model that is used in this study through a comprehensive set of analytical benchmarks, and tested it against laboratory and field data.

To simulate tsunami runup produced by landslide-generated waves, we use a numerical model of a viscous underwater slide with an arbitrary shape, which deforms in three dimensions. The model assumes full interactions between the deforming slide and the water waves that it generates. This type of viscous or Newtonian model was initially proposed by JIANG and LEBLOND (1994), and it is adequate for describing landslides made of fine-grained water-saturated deformable sediments. Submarine sediments in different coastal areas may have different rheological behavior due to grain size distribution and chemical composition (JIANG and LEBLOND, 1993). Another model used for characterization of underwater slides is a Bingham visco-plastic model, in which a finite yield stress has to be applied to the fluid for deformation to occur (MEI and LIU, 1987; LIU and MEI, 1989; JIANG and LEBLOND, 1993). The Bingham model is most applicable to dynamics of concentrated cohesive mud, a mixture of water and very fine particles of clay minerals (MEI and LIU, 1987). The results of a subsurface geotechnical investigation described in Sect. 4 indicate that the viscous slide model by JIANG and LEBLOND (1994) is adequate for description of underwater slides in Resurrection Bay. FINE et al. (1998) further improved the model by including realistic bathymetry, and also by correcting errors in the governing equations. We apply here the corrected version of the model presented in THOMSON et al. (2001). The model assumptions as well as its applicability to simulate underwater landslides are discussed by Jiang and LeBlond in their formulation of the viscous slide model (JIANG and LEBLOND, 1992, 1994), and also by RABINOVICH et al. (2003) and THOMSON et al. (2001). Other depth-integrated numerical models of landslide-generated waves are summarized in SULEIMANI et al. (2009).

The physical system consists of two layers—the upper one is water, and the lower layer is slide material. The slide is assumed to be an incompressible viscous fluid. We assume a sharp interface between the layers, with no mixing allowed between water and sediments. The disturbance of the water surface is produced by the motion of the deforming slide, which is driven only by the force of gravity. The equations for the slide were initially derived under the assumption that it rapidly reaches a steady state regime, and horizontal velocities have a parabolic vertical profile (JIANG and LEBLOND, 1994). In this model, the slide and the surface waves are fully coupled, meaning that not only does the motion of the slide affect the water surface, but a change in water surface pressure influences the slide thickness. The variable that couples the two systems is the total water depth above the slide. TITOV and GONZALEZ (2001) applied the model for source determination study of the 1998 Papua New Guinea tsunami. The model was successfully applied to simulate tsunami waves in Skagway Harbor, Alaska, generated by the collapse of a dock on November 3, 1994 (FINE et al., 1998; THOMSON et al., 2001). The results of numerical simulations were in good agreement with the tide gauge record in Skagway Harbor, which is one of numerous fjords in southeastern Alaska. RABINOVICH et al. (2003) simulated potential underwater landslides in British Columbia fjords, in geologic settings similar to Resurrection Bay, and they used the model for tsunami hazard assessment. Most recently, this model was applied by SULEIMANI et al. (2009) to simulate multiple submarine slope failures in Resurrection Bay, Alaska, during the Great Alaska earthquake of 1964, and to study the contribution of individual slide complexes to the observed tsunami amplitudes at Seward and other locations around the bay. In this work, we made the model more robust by implementing the moving boundary algorithm, which allows for calculation of runup on the shore, as well as for the "wetting" and "drying" of the slide surface.

3.2. Data and Numerical Grids

To simulate the 1964 tectonic tsunami waves, which were generated by coseismic bottom deformation of the continental shelf of south-central Alaska, we used five nested telescoping grids, or digital elevation models, as input data for the tsunami modeling. These nested grids allow us to propagate waves from the deep waters of the tsunami source region in the Gulf of Alaska to shallow coastal areas of Resurrection Bay. The external grid spans the entire north Pacific with the grid step of 2 arc-minutes, which corresponds to 1.85×3.7 km at latitude 60°N. The intermediate grids have resolution of 24, 8 and 3 arc-seconds (370×741 m, 123×247 m, and 48×97 m, respectively). Bathymetry data for low and intermediate resolution grids come from the ETOPO2 data set (http://www.ngdc.noaa.gov/mgg/global/etopo2.html) and NOAA's National Ocean Service surveys (http://www.ngdc.noaa.gov/mgg/bathymetry/hydro.html). The computational time step is different for each grid and is calculated according to the Courant–Friedrichs–Levy (CFL) stability criterion. The numerical simulation used a constant Manning's roughness of $0.03 \, \text{s} \, \text{m}^{-1/3}$.

The highest resolution grid covers northern Resurrection Bay, including Seward, Lowell Point and Fourth of July Point (Fig. 2), with the grid step of $\Delta x = \Delta y = 15$ m. LABAY and HAEUSSLER (2008) developed this grid using the best available high-resolution topography and multibeam bathymetry from the following data sets: (1) low-altitude LIDAR topography collected for the Kenai Watershed Forum in 2006, (2) U.S. Army Corps of Engineers harbor soundings for the Seward City Marina and surroundings collected in 2006, and (3) multibeam bathymetric surveys of Resurrection Bay, conducted by NOAA's National Ocean Service in 2001 (LABAY and HAEUSSLER, 2008). In this grid, the combined bathymetric and topographic data allow for application of the moving boundary condition for calculation of runup heights and the extent of tsunami inundation.

One of the challenges in near-field earthquake-triggered tsunami modeling is to account for coseismic and post-seismic tectonic land changes, and also to account for a difference between the datum of the numerical grid and the tide stage at the time of the earthquake. The high-resolution numerical grid of combined bathymetry and topography data for Resurrection Bay by LABAY and HAEUSSLER (2008) was referenced to the tidal datum of mean high water (MHW) (LABAY and HAEUSSLER, 2008). Tide was low at the time of the main shock, which was one of the major factors contributed to the large scale of landsliding (LEMKE, 1967). However, the low tide also helped to lessen the amount of damage from the first tectonic wave. According to the NOAA tide calculator (http://tidesandcurrents.noaa.gov), the first tectonic wave arrived at the local tide minimum, which corresponds to 0.175 m below mean lower low water (MLLW).

Vertical tectonic land changes at Seward are demonstrated in Fig. 5. The landmass in the Seward area experienced coseismic subsidence (CS) of about 1.15 m (LEMKE, 1967); as a result, many areas that were above sea level before the earthquake, became submerged after the earthquake. LARSEN *et al.* (2003) analyzed relative sea level changes from tide gauge records at 15 sites along the coast of south-central Alaska to determine vertical crustal motions in the period from 1937 to 2001. From their analysis, the total postseismic uplift (PU) at Seward was estimated

to be about 20 cm. The following equation, therefore, provides the relationship between the water depth in Resurrection Bay at the time of the earthquake, H_1, and the present water depth, H_2, which was measured in 2001 by the NOAA multibeam bathymetry survey:

$$H_1 = H_2 - CS + PU - \Delta H,$$

where $\Delta H (> 0)$ is a difference between the present MHW datum and sea level at the time of the earthquake. By using the adjusted vertical datum in the bathymetry grid, the numerical model reproduces the effects of tsunami inundation occurring at Seward under conditions close to those that were present in the 1964 earthquake. The value of ΔH is different for the cases of tectonic and landslide tsunami calculations, due to a slight difference in the stage of tide between the times when underwater slope failures were triggered, and when the tectonic wave arrived.

4. Tsunami Sources

4.1. Justification of Separation of Source Mechanisms

In his interpretation of types and origin of waves observed in Resurrection Bay on March 27, 1964, Lemke (1967) noted that sliding terminated at the end of ground shaking, which means that all local waves were generated within the first 2–3 min of the beginning of the earthquake. From results of

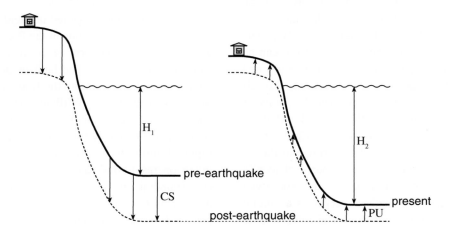

Figure 5
A diagram that shows vertical tectonic land changes during and after the 1964 earthquake. H_1 is the bathymetry before the earthquake, H_2 is the present day bathymetry, CS is coseismic subsidence, PU is postseismic uplift. Note that the diagram is not to scale

numerical simulations, SULEIMANI *et al.* (2009) estimated that it took the slide masses about half an hour to get transported from the steep fjord slopes to the deepest part of the fjord. The slide motion was subcritical with Froude number $Fr < 1$ (PELINOVSKY and POPLAVSKY, 1996; FINE *et al.*, 2003), and was characterized by leading crests that rapidly propagated offshore ahead of the moving slides (SULEIMANI *et al.*, 2009). Since the initial stages of slide motion are most important for wave generation (HARBITZ *et al.*, 2006), it is reasonable to assume that the motion of the slides after the termination of ground shaking did not produce any significant wave activity. The first tectonic wave arrived about 25 min after shaking stopped, when the locally generated waves had subsided (LEMKE, 1967); therefore, we assume that these events are independent and can be modeled separately. Our focus is on simulating tectonic and landslide tsunami waves at Seward to demonstrate that the inundation zone was a product of two tsunami events. We will compare the integrated effects of landslide and tectonic tsunami inundation with the observed inundation pattern.

4.2. Landslide Tsunami Sources

The numerical study of landslide-generated waves in Resurrection Bay by SULEIMANI *et al.* (2009) derived the conclusion that slides initiated in the upper bay were the major contributors of tsunami wave energy there during the period of ground shaking. The study demonstrated that waves in the bay were generated by 10 different slides that moved during the earthquake, but the highest locally generated wave observed at the Seward waterfront can be reproduced by the superposition of waves generated by slides offshore of downtown Seward, Lowell Point, and Fourth of July Creek. The locations of these three slides and their thickness distribution, which was derived by HAEUSSLER *et al.* (2007) from the bathymetric difference grid, are shown in Fig. 6. We use these slide complexes as a source of locally generated waves in our numerical study. The given distribution of the slide material serves as an initial condition for tsunami simulation. The total volume for these slides was estimated at approximately 80 million m^3 (HAEUSSLER *et al.*, 2007).

4.3. Tectonic Tsunami Sources

There are several existing models of coseismic deformation of the 1964 Great Alaska earthquake that yield the asperity and slip distribution patterns of the rupture area. HOLDAHL and SAUBER (1994) inverted geodetic and geologic measurements of the surface deformation for the slip distribution of the 1964 rupture, using a priori slip estimates from tsunami modeling on the oceanic part of the fault plane. The models by JOHNSON *et al.* (1996) and ICHINOSE *et al.* (2007) are based on joint inversion methods, each of them using different combinations of seismic, geodetic and tsunami data sets. The model by SANTINI *et al.* (2003) employs the Monte Carlo method to generate different slip distribution patterns, and the most recent study by SUITO and FREYMUELLER (2009) presents the coseismic deformation model developed jointly with the afterslip model in order to describe the postseismic deformations caused by the 1964 earthquake. In this paper we consider three coseismic deformation models of the 1964 earthquake to determine the initial condition for simulation of tectonic tsunami waves in Resurrection Bay. We refer to the deformation models by abbreviations of the primary authors last names: JDM, the model by JOHNSON *et al.* (1996); IDM, the model by ICHINOSE *et al.* (2007); and SDM, the model by SUITO and FREYMUELLER (2009).

A detailed analysis of the 1964 rupture zone was presented by JOHNSON *et al.* (1996) through joint inversion of tsunami and geodetic data. To derive a slip distribution, they inverted far-field tsunami wave forms from 23 tidal stations in the Pacific Ocean, and geodetic data in the form of vertical displacements and horizontal vectors. The fault model consisted of eight subfaults representing the Kodiak asperity, nine subfaults in the Prince William Sound asperity, and one subfault representing the Patton Bay fault (Fig. 1), one of the two megathrust splay faults that ruptured during the earthquake (PLAFKER, 1967). The inversion results indicated two regions of high slip corresponding to areas of high moment release derived by CHRISTENSEN and BECK (1994) from long period P-wave seismograms: the Prince William Sound asperity with an average slip of 18 m, and the Kodiak asperity with an average slip of 10 m.

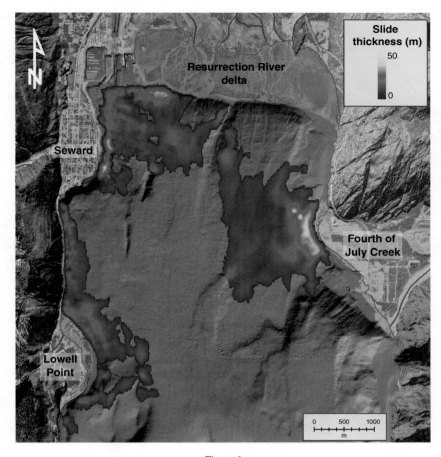

Figure 6
Reconstructed thicknesses and initial extent of the three major slide complexes in the upper Resurrection Bay. Orthophoto image *courtesy* of National Resources Conservation Service, USDA, 1996

ICHINOSE *et al.* (2007) estimated the spatial and temporal distribution of slip for the 1964 earthquake from joint inversion of teleseismic P-waves, far-field tsunami records from nine tidal stations, and geodetic leveling survey observations. The fault model consisted of 85 subfaults on the megathrust and 10 subfaults along the Patton Bay fault. The inversion results indicated three areas of major seismic moment release, where slip was more than twice the average. The contribution of tsunami Green's functions was improved in this model compared to that in JDM by introducing higher resolution grids surrounding the tide gauge stations and by using nonlinear hydrodynamic wave equations with a moving boundary condition.

SUITO and FREYMUELLER (2009) introduced a new coseismic deformation model of the 1964 earthquake, which was developed jointly with the afterslip model.

SDM uses a realistic geometry with an elastic slab of very low dip angle. Coseismic displacements and postseismic deformations are calculated using a finite element method on a high resolution 3-D mesh. The main difference between SDM and other models is in prediction of slightly higher slip near the down-dip end of the rupture. Also, SDM assumes that the Patton Bay splay fault extended much farther to the southwest than it did in JDM and IDM, in order to explain subsidence along the southern coast of the Kenai Peninsula (Fig. 1).

We used the equations of OKADA (1985) to calculate vertical coseismic displacements for each of the three deformation models described above (Fig. 7). We simulated tsunami waves generated by these three source functions and compared the results in the far- and near-field regions. The tsunami wave

103

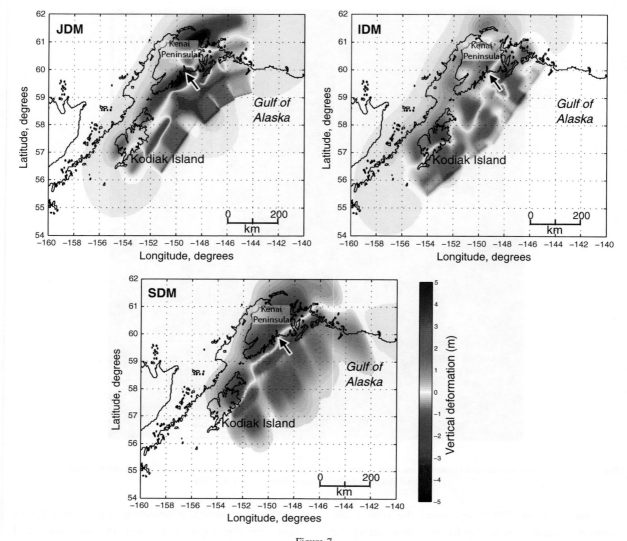

Figure 7
Vertical coseismic displacements calculated from the deformation models of JOHNSON *et al.* (1996) (JDM), ICHINOSE *et al.* (2007) (IDM), and SUITO and FREYMUELLER (2009) (SDM). The *arrow* points at the entrance to Resurrection Bay

forms, arrival times and amplitudes were almost identical for all three deformation models in the far-field, but the same sources produced very different results in the near-field (SULEIMANI *et al.*, 2008). These findings agree with the conclusions of GEIST (2002) who investigated effects of rupture complexity on local tsunami amplitudes. He demonstrated that for shallow subduction zone earthquakes, such as the 1964 earthquake, changes in slip distribution result in significant variations in the local tsunami wave field, suggesting that the near-field tsunami runup is highly

sensitive to variability of slip along the rupture area. All coseismic deformation models of the 1964 tsunami have one limitation in common: they are not constrained by observations of tsunami in the near-field (PLAFKER *et al.*, 1969; PLAFKER, 1969). The preliminary numerical study by (SULEIMANI *et al.*, 2008) confirmed the conclusion derived by PLAFKER (2006) that local splay faults played crucial role in generating large tsunami amplitudes observed along the coastlines of the Kenai Peninsula, Kodiak Island, and Montague Island (Fig. 1).

5. Numerical Simulations

We performed runup calculations using a high-resolution grid of combined bathymetric and topographic data for the upper Resurrection Bay (Fig. 6). This data set reflects the most recent configuration of the Seward waterfront and the position of the shoreline. The boat harbor in the northeastern corner of the bay, the breakwaters, and the cruise ship terminal (Fig. 3) did not exist in 1964. In order to recreate the conditions at the time of the earthquake, we digitally removed the breakwaters and all other constructions in the harbor area by replacing the corresponding data points with the pre-1964 bathymetric soundings. Then, we adjusted the bathymetry of the landslide source and deposition areas in order to define the pre-earthquake depths in Resurrection Bay. In the numerical simulation of landslide-generated waves, the slide material moved down from the offshore slopes into the deepest part of the fjord, filling the north-south depression with sediment (Fig. 2). Because we assume that the tectonic wave arrived to the bay after the slide motion had terminated, we used the new modified bathymetry of Resurrection Bay with the slide material redistributed on the fjord bottom for simulation of the tectonic tsunami. We did not modify the land topography around the bay to match it to the pre-earthquake topography, because the pre-1964 elevation data in Alaska are of very poor quality, especially in the coastal zone. Instead, we used the high-quality topographic LIDAR data (LABAY and HAEUSSLER, 2008).

5.1. Inundation of Resurrection Bay by Landslide-Generated Waves

We extend the previous work of SULEIMANI et al. (2009) by calculating runup of local waves caused by submarine slope failures in Resurrection Bay during the 1964 earthquake. The computational domain is shown in Fig. 6. This area is covered by a continuous bathymetry-topography grid with horizontal resolution of 15 m (LABAY and HAEUSSLER, 2008). The distribution of the slide material serves as an initial condition for tsunami simulation. At the southern open boundary of the grid, we specify the radiation boundary condition for the water waves. The boundary condition for the slide mass allows the slide to leave the computational domain without reflection. The moving boundary condition at the shore line and at the slide-water interface allows for wetting and drying of land as described in NICOLSKY et al. (2010). We assume that the slides were initially at rest, then triggered by ground shaking at $t = 0$, and moved afterwards only under the force of gravity. In our model all slides started moving at the same time, because there is no independent evidence of slides being triggered at different times. Following THOMSON et al. (2001), we ran the numerical simulation with a time step $\Delta t = 0.01$ s, which is at least an order of magnitude smaller than the value required by the CFL stability criterion for water waves.

The maximum observed extent of inundation at Seward and at the head of the bay is shown in Figs. 3 and 4, respectively, by the yellow dashed line. The inundation line at Seward was digitized from the U.S. Army Corps of Engineers aerial photo of Seward that was taken one day after the earthquake, and the maximum observed extent of inundation at the head of the bay was digitized from the geologic map (LEMKE, 1967). The observed inundation line represents the maximum runup reached by one or more waves, of both local and tectonic origin, and therefore delineates the composite inundation zone. The blue line in Figs. 3 and 4 outlines the area inundated by simulated landslide-generated waves at Seward and at the head of the bay, respectively. At the Seward waterfront (Fig. 3), the calculated inundation area is not significantly different from the observed one, while in the area adjacent to the modern harbor and Seward highway the observed and calculated extents of inundation are far apart. The calculated inundation caused by landslide-generated waves in this area follows the 1964 shoreline, and the observed inundation extends beyond the lagoon, which is to the west from the Seward highway. This result agrees with observations (LEMKE, 1967) that locally generated waves did not reach the highway, and people were able to drive out of the town on this road across the lagoon after the ground shaking ceased. This road was completely blocked by houses, boats, and other debris brought later by the tectonically generated waves. In 1964, the lagoon extended to both sides of the highway, while the eastern part of it is now covered with artificial fill and is home to a new business district, harbor and port facilities. We did not modify elevations in this area to match them to the 1964 topography, and that probably explains why the inundation line did not extend further inland.

The results of runup simulation at the Resurrection River delta (Fig. 4) show that the inundation area caused by landslide-generated waves is much smaller than the observed composite inundation area. This result also agrees with observations that the tectonic wave extended much further inland at the head of the bay than any of the locally generated waves (LEMKE, 1967). This is explained by the fact that tectonically generated waves had much larger wavelengths and therefore carried more energy than the landslide-generated waves. Also, the locally generated wave that did the greatest damage in downtown Seward arrived from the Fourth of July Creek slide (Fig. 6). This wave approached Seward from the southeast, and therefore did not inundate far inland in the northwestern part of the town, in the lagoon area. Numerical results show that the same wave dissipated quickly when it reached the intertidal zone at the head of the bay.

There is no documented inundation line at Lowell Point and Fourth of July Creek. The blue contour in Figs. 8 and 9 outlines the calculated inundation areas. According to several eyewitness accounts (LEMKE, 1967; WILSON and TØRUM, 1968), the first wave hit Lowell Point at the northeast corner of the fan when ground was still shaking. It penetrated inland several hundred feet, which corresponds to the position of the calculated inundation line in the northern part of the fan delta. The timing of the wave and its direction indicate that this wave was generated by the slide offshore the Seward waterfront. From observations of debris position and scars on trees (LEMKE, 1967), it was concluded that another wave came to Lowell Point from the east and overran the shore moving to the west. The largest wave, which hit Lowell Point about 30 min after the first one, came from the south and did most of the damage at Lowell Point. Because of its arrival time and amplitude, it was most probably the tectonically generated wave.

According to LEMKE (1967), it was difficult to reconstruct the number of waves and their directivity

patterns at Fourth of July Creek (Fig. 9). The extent of the inundation in some areas was marked by a debris line several hundred feet or more inland. WILSON and TØRUM, (1968) cited an account of one witness who reported the wave "running inland about a quarter of a mile" (1320 ft, 402 m). The distance from the westernmost tip of the fan delta to the calculated inundation line for landslide-generated waves is about 260 m (850 ft).

5.2. Inundation of Resurrection Bay by a Tectonic Tsunami

We performed numerical simulations of tectonic tsunami runup in northern Resurrection Bay using the three source functions discussed in Sect. 3. Coseismic deformations calculated from JDM, IDM, and SDM (Fig. 7) served as initial conditions for water surface. Because relatively large waves kept arriving at Seward until about 11:30 pm on March 27, 1964, we ran computer simulations for 8 h of physical time. We evaluate coseismic deformations for each of the source models by analyzing the tsunami arrival time, phase of the first wave, and extent of the inundation zone.

The arrival time of the first tectonic wave at Seward is a critical constraint on tectonic source models. The wave was observed to be large with a positive first motion (arriving as a crest) that came to Seward about 25 min after the shaking stopped, or about 30 min after the beginning of the earthquake. Also, arrival times of the same tectonic wave to Whidbey Bay and Puget Bay (Fig. 1) were about 19 and 20 min after the shaking started (PLAFKER, 1969), and the reported first motion was also positive. We calculated time series of the tectonic tsunami at the Seward waterfront for each of the source functions (Fig. 10). We show the series for the first 3 h after the earthquake to clearly illustrate the arrival of the first wave. The wave modeled with the SDM initial condition best matches observations. It has the right polarity, and the arrival time of 35 min after the beginning of the earthquake is very close to observations. The wave modeled with the JDM has a negative phase, and the wave corresponding to IDM has small amplitude and late arrival.

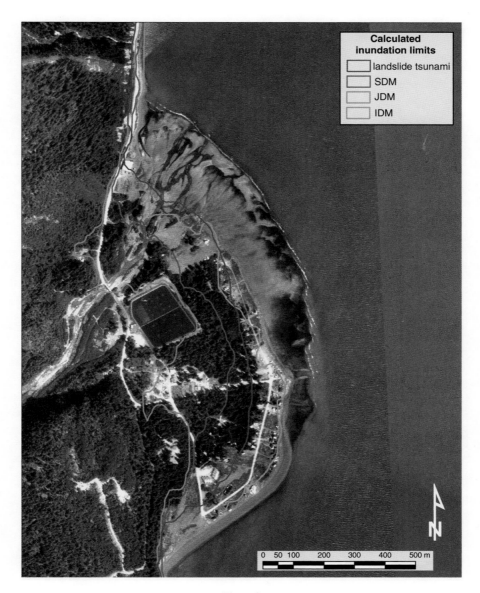

Figure 8
Inundation limits calculated for different tectonic tsunami sources and the landslide source at Lowell Point. Orthophoto image *courtesy* of National Resources Conservation Service, USDA, 1996

The modeled inundation at the head of the bay shows critical differences between the three models (Fig. 4). The tectonic wave corresponding to JDM penetrated deeper inland and completely inundated the airport. These results vastly overestimate inundation of the airport area (the wave was reported to flood the airstrip only partially) and the rest of the river delta. The wave simulated with the IDM

deformations produced little inundation in the delta and did not flood the airstrip. The wave associated with SDM produced an inundation zone that matches observations better than inundation zones corresponding to the IDM and JDM waves. The observed inundation line (yellow dashed line) has two pronounced lobes in the Resurrection River delta. The SDM line matches the right lobe very well. The

Reprinted from the journal

Figure 9
Inundation limits calculated for different tectonic tsunami sources and the landslide source at Fourth of July Creek. Orthophoto image *courtesy* of National Resources Conservation Service, USDA, 1996

discrepancy between the lines in the area of the left lobe could be explained by natural and anthropogenic changes in the topography of the river delta due to redirection of the multiple river channels.

Numerical simulations of the three source models produce similar results in downtown Seward, but differ significantly in the region north of town near the boat harbor (Fig. 3). The inundation line associated with SDM is the closest to the observed line. Modeling results agree with observations of the tectonic wave in the area of modern harbor, that the wave crashed into the lagoon, and debris completely blocked the Seward highway (LEMKE, 1967). The inundation line produced with the IDM deformations greatly underestimates the flooded area, whereas the JDM line extends further inland than the observed inundation line. The landslide-generated waves inundated further inland in the

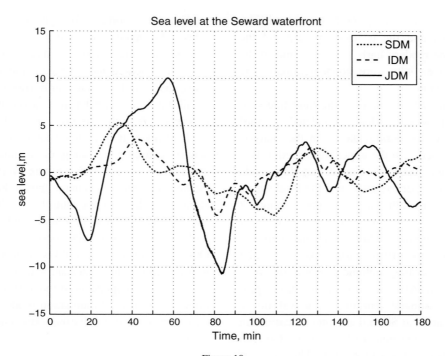

Figure 10
Simulated tectonic tsunami waveforms at Seward waterfront for three different source functions. Time $t = 0$ corresponds to the 1964 earthquake's origin time

downtown area than the SDM tectonic waves did. We note that at the southern end of the Seward fan the inundation lines corresponding to SDM and to the landslides, circle around the Alaska SeaLife Center. During the recent construction of this facility, the waterfront area was raised up substantially with respect to its elevation at the time of the earthquake, which explains the discrepancy with the observed inundation line. Overall, the union of inundation areas computed for landslide-generated waves and for the SDM-produced tectonic waves, is in good agreement with the observed composite inundation zone.

The results of numerical simulation of tectonic scenarios at Lowell Point and Fourth of July Creek (Figs. 8 and 9) show that tectonic waves corresponding to the SDM and JDM scenarios produced greater inundation than that of the landslide-generated waves. These results can not be tested against observations of debris lines, because of the lack of eyewitness accounts of the wave sequence. The debris line was about 30 and 25 feet above MLLW at Lowell Point and Fourth of July Creek,

respectively, which roughly corresponds to tsunami runup of the JDM-produced tsunami waves.

6. Conclusions

The numerical simulations of tectonic and landslide-generated tsunami runup in Resurrection Bay generated by the 1964 earthquake are consistent with observations of the tsunami wave sequence. The town of Seward was flooded within 5 min of the beginning of the strong ground shaking by local waves generated by multiple submarine mass failures. The tectonic tsunami wave arrived at Seward about 25–30 min after shaking stopped, when the locally generated waves had subsided, which allowed for separation of the tsunami source mechanisms in the numerical model. Our numerical results agree with the interpretation given by LEMKE (1967) of the observed maximum tsunami runup at Seward and at the head of the bay as a composite inundation area. We demonstrated that the runup zone is a product of two events: the maximum runup at the Seward waterfront was produced by both local landslide-generated waves and the tectonic waves, and the areas next to the modern harbor, lagoon, and in the Resurrection River delta were flooded primarily by the tectonic tsunami.

We determined the source of the landslide-generated tsunami waves, which inundated Seward immediately after the earthquake, from the analysis of tsunami time series in the upper Resurrection Bay (SULEIMANI et al., 2009). We found that three slide complexes in the upper bay generated the local waves that were the major contributors to tsunami runup at Seward. To define a source for tectonic tsunami waves, we used outputs of three coseismic deformation models of the 1964 earthquake as initial conditions for modeling tectonic tsunami runup in Resurrection Bay. All three source functions produced different tsunami amplitudes, arrival times, and inundation areas at Seward and other locations in the upper bay, and the model of SUITO and FREYMUELLER (2009) fits the observations well. The model of JOHNSON et al. (1996) overestimates tsunami runup, and the model of ICHINOSE et al. (2007) tends to underestimate tsunami runup. The presented results suggest that initial tsunami wave amplitudes in the source area of the 1964 earthquake, which are product of coseismic displacements, are crucial for the near-field tsunami modeling, and that the inundation results are sensitive to the fine structure of slip distribution. The combination of inundation areas produced by local waves from the three major slides in the upper bay, and the tectonic waves simulated with the source function of SUITO and FREYMUELLER (2009), produced a good match with observations.

When analyzing results of numerical modeling and comparing them with observations, we take into account several limitations of the model. One of them, and probably the most important, is the decoupling of tides and tsunamis. The last seismic wave at Seward was reported about 11 h after the earthquake. During this time, tidal level made a full cycle changing from its minimum at the time of the earthquake, then to the maximum at midnight, and then back to minimum at the time when the last wave was observed. The waves that came on the rising tide could have been amplified due to interactions of tsunami waves with tides. MYERS and BAPTISTA (2001)

studied the importance of dynamic superposition of tides and tsunami waves and concluded that nonlinear tsunami-tide interactions could be important and need to be included in local tsunami inundation studies. Also, the model simulates only free seiches induced by tilting of a water basin as a result of coseismic deformations in the rupture area, and those initiated by landslides. It does not take into account forced seiches caused by passing of seismic waves (BARBEROPOULOU et al., 2006). Future work will include the development of a tsunami model that dynamically simulates tides and accounts for nonlinear tsunami-tide interactions, and simulates seiches in bays and harbors due to horizontal motion of the side walls. Our future study of the 1964 tsunami source function will determine the important source parameters and the essential components of the numerical model that affect the near-field inundation modeling of tsunami waves generated by earthquakes on the Aleutian megathrust.

Acknowledgments

This study was supported by NOAA grants 27-014d and 06-028a through Cooperative Institute for Arctic Research. We thank Prof. Efim Pelinovsky and one anonymous reviewer for helpful suggestions that improved this manuscript. Dr. Alexander Rabinovich gave us a number of critical comments and valuable recommendations that we greatly appreciate. The authors also thank Eric Geist and Jason Chaytor for their thorough and constructive reviews. We are grateful to Prof. Jeff Freymueller for valuable discussions, and to Dr. Hisashi Suito for providing us with parameters of his model. Numerical calculations for this work are supported by a grant of High Performance Computing resources from the Arctic Region Supercomputing Center at the University of Alaska Fairbanks as part of the US Department of Defense HPC Modernization Program.

REFERENCES

BARBEROPOULOU A, QAMAR A, PRATT T, STEELE W (2006) Longperiod effects of the Denali earthquake on water bodies in the Puget Lowland: observations and modeling. Bull Seism Soc Am 96(2):519–535, doi:10.1785/0120050090

BORNHOLD B, THOMSON R, RABINOVICH A, KULIKOV E, FINE I (2001) *Risk of landslide-generated tsunamis for the coast of British Columbia and Alaska.* In: 2001 An Earth Odyssey. Proceedings of the Canadian Geotechnical Conference, pp 1450–1454

CARVER G, PLAFKER G (2008) *Paloseismicity and neotectonics of the Aleutian subduction zone—an overview.* In: Freymueller J, Haeussler P, Wesson R, Ekström G (eds) Acive tectonics and seismic potential of Alaska, AGU, Washington, DC, Geophysical Monograph Series 179, pp 43–63

CHRISTENSEN D, BECK S (1994) *The rupture process and tectonic implications of the Great 1964 Prince William Sound earthquake.* Pure Appl Geophys 142(1):29–53

FINE I, RABINOVICH A, KULIKOV E, THOMSON R, BORNHOLD B (1998) *Numerical modelling of landslide-generated tsunamis with application to the Skagway Harbor tsunami of November 3, 1994.* In: Proc. Int. Conf. on Tsunamis, Paris, pp 211–223

FINE I, RABINOVICH A, THOMSON R, KULIKOV E (2003) *Numerical modeling of tsunami generation by submarine and subaerial landslides.* In: YALCINER A, PELINOVSKY E, OKAL E, SYNOLAKIS C (eds) Submarine Landslides and Tsunamis, Kluwer, pp 69–88

GEIST E (2002) *Complex earthquake rupture and local tsunamis.* J Geophys Res 107(B5):1–16

HAEUSSLER P, LEE H, RYAN H, LABAY K, KAYEN R, HAMPTON M, SULEIMANI E (2007) *Submarine slope failures near Seward, Alaska, during the M9.2 1964 earthquake.* In: LYKOUSIS V, SAKELLARIOU D, LOCAT J (eds) Submarine Mass Movements and their consequences, pp 269–278

HAMPTON M, LEE H, LOCAT J (1996) *Submarine landslides.* Rev Geophys 34:33–59

HARBITZ C, LØVHOLT F, PEDERSEN G, MASSON D (2006) *Mechanisms of tsunami generation by submarine landslides: a short review.* Norwegian Journal of Geology 86:255–264

HOLDAHL S, SAUBER J (1994) *Coseismic slip in the 1964 Prince William sound earthquake: A new geodetic inversion.* Pure Appl Geophys 142:55–82

ICHINOSE G, SOMERVILLE P, THIO H, GRAVES R, O'CONNELL D (2007) *Rupture process of the 1964 Prince William sound, Alaska, earthquake from the combined inversion of seismic, tsunami, and geodetic data.* J Geophys Res 112(B07306)

JIANG L, LEBLOND P (1992) *The coupling of a submarine slide and the surface waves which it generates.* J Geophys Res 97(C8):12731–12744

JIANG L, LEBLOND P (1993) *Numerical modeling of an underwater Bingham plastic mudslide and the waves which it generates.* J Geophys Res 98(C6):10303–10317

JIANG L, LEBLOND P (1994) *Three-dimensional modeling of tsunami generation due to a submarine mudslide.* J Phys Oceanogr 24(3):559–572

JOHNSON J, SATAKE K, HOLDAHL SR, SAUBER J (1996) *The 1964 Prince William sound earthquake: Joint inversion of tsunami and geodetic data.* J Geophys Res 101:523–532

KULIKOV E, RABINOVICH A, FINE I, BORNHOLD B, THOMSON R (1998) *Tsunami generation by landslides at the Pacific coast of North America and the role of tides.* Oceanology 38(3):361–367

LABAY K, HAEUSSLER P (2008) *Combined high-resolution LIDAR topography and multibeam bathymetry for upper Resurrection Bay, Seward, Alaska.* U.S. Geological Survey Digital Data Series 374, http://pubs.usgs.gov/ds/374/

LANDER J (1996) *Tsunamis affecting Alaska. 1737–1996.* No. 31 in NGDC Key to Geophysical Research, National Geophysical Data Center, Boulder, Colo.

LARSEN C, ECHELMEYER K, FREYMUELLER J, MOTYKA R (2003) *Tide gauge records of uplift along the northern pacific-north american plate boundary, 1937 to 2001.* J Geophys Res 108(B4):2216, doi:10.1029/2001JB001685

LEE H, SCHWAB W, BOOTH J (2002) *Submarine landslides: an introduction.* In: Schwab W, Lee H, Twichell D (eds) Submarine Landslides: Selected Studies in the US Exclusive Economic Zone, US Geological Survey Bulletin, pp 1–13

LEE H, RYAN R, KAYEN R, HAEUSSLER P, DARTNELL P, HAMPTON M (2006) *Varieties of submarine failure morphologies of seismically-induced landslides in Alaska fjords.* Norwegian Journal of Geology 86:221–230

LEMKE R (1967) *Effects of the Earthquake of March 27, 1964, at Seward, Alaska.* U.S. Geological Survey Professional Paper 542-E, 48 pp.

LIU K, MEI C (1989) *Slow spreading of a sheet of Bingham fluid on an inclined plane.* J Fluid Mech 207:505–529

MARCHUK GI, KUZNETSOV YA, MATSOKIN AM (1986) *Fictitious domain and domain decomposition methods.* Sov J Numer Anal Math Modelling 1:3–35

MASSON D, HARBITZ C, WYNN R, PEDERSEN G, LØVHOLT F (2006) *Submarine landslides: processes, triggers and hazard prediction.* Phil Trans R Soc A 364:2009–2039, doi:10.1098/rsta.2006.1810

MEI C, LIU K (1987) *A Bingham-plastic model for a muddy seabed under long waves.* J Geophys Res 92(C13):14581–14594

MYERS E, BAPTISTA A (2001) *Analysis of factors influencing simulations of the 1993 Hokkaido Nansei-Oki and 1964 Alaska tsunamis.* Nat Hazards 23:1–28

NICOLSKY D, SULEIMANI E, HANSEN R (2010) *Validation and verification of a numerical model for tsunami propagation and runup.* Pure Appl Geophys. doi:10.1007/s00024-010-0231-9

NISHENKO S, JACOB K (1990) *Seismic potential of the Queen Charlotte-Alaska-Aleutian seismic zone.* J Geophys Res 95(B3): 2511–2532

OKADA Y (1985) *Surface deformation due to shear and tensile faults in a half-space.* Bull Seism Soc Am 75:1135–1154

PAGE R, BISWAS N, LAHR J, PULPAN H (1991) *Seismicity of continental Alaska.* In: SLEMMONS D, ENGDAHL E, ZOBACK M, BLACKWELL D (eds) Neotectonics of North America, Boulder, Colorado, Geol. Soc. Am., Decade Map V. 1, pp 47–68

PELINOVSKY E, POPLAVSKY A (1996) *Simplified model of tsunami generation by submarine landslides.* Phys Chem Earth 21(12):13–17

PLAFKER G (1967) *Surface faults on Montague Island associated with the 1964 Alaska Earthquake.* U.S. Geological Survey Professional Paper 543-G, 42 pp.

PLAFKER G (1969) *Tectonics of the March 27, 1964 Alaska Earthquake.* U.S. Geological Survey Professional Paper 543-I, 74 pp.

PLAFKER G (2006) *The great 1964 Alaska Earthquake as a model for tsunami generation during megathrust earthquakes with examples form Chile and Sumatra.* Abstracts of the AGU Chapman Conference on the Active Tectonics and Seismic Potential of Alaska

PLAFKER G, KACHADOORIAN R, ECKEL E, MAYO L (1969) *Effects of the Earthquake of March 27, 1964 on various communities.* U.S. Geological Survey Professional Paper 542-G, 50 pp.

RABINOVICH AB, THOMSON RE, BORNHOLD BD, FINE IV, KULIKOV EA (2003) *Numerical modelling of tsunamis generated by hypothetical landslides in the Strait of Georgia, British Columbia.* Pure Appl Geophys 160(7):1273–1313

Reprinted from the journal

SANTINI S, DRAGONI M, SPADA G (2003) *Asperity distribution of the 1964 Great Alaska earthquake and its relation to subsequent seismicity in the region.* Tectonophysics *367*:219–233, doi: 10.1016/S0040-1951(03)00130-6

SHANNON W, HILTS D (1973) *Submarine landslide at Seward.* In: The Great Alaska Earthquake of 1964. Engineering, National Academy of Sciences, Washington, D.C., pp 144–156

SHENNAN I, BRUHN R, PLAFKER G (2009) *Multi-segment earthquakes and tsunami potential of the Aleuatian megathrust.* Quaternary Science Reviews *28*:7–13

SPAETH M, BERKMAN S (1972) *Tsunami of March 28, 1964, as recorded at tide stations and the Seismic Sea Waves Warning System.* In: The Great Alaska Earthquake of 1964. Oceanography and Coastal Engineering, National Academy of Sciences, Washington, D.C., pp 38–100

SUITO H, FREYMUELLER J (2009) *A viscoelastic and afterslip postseismic deformation model for the 1964 Alaska earthquake.* J Geophys Res *114*(B11404), doi:10.1029/2008JB005954

SULEIMANI E, RUPPERT N, FISHER M, WEST D, HANSEN R (2008) *The contribution of coseismic displacements due to spaly faults into the local wavefiled of the 1964 Alaska tsunami.* In: Eos Trans. AGU, Fall Meet. Suppl., vol *89*(53), abstract OS43D-1334

SULEIMANI E, HANSEN R, HAEUSSLER P (2009) *Numerical study of tsunami generated by multiple submarine slope failures in Resurrection Bay, Alaska, during the M9.2 1964 earthquake.* Pure Appl Geophys *166*:131–152, doi:10.1007/s00024-004-0430-3

SYNOLAKIS C, BERNARD E, TITOV V, KÂNOĞLU U, GONZÁLEZ F (2007) *Standards, criteria, and procedures for noaa evaluation of tsunami numerical models.* NOAA Tech. Memo. OAR PMEL-135, NTIS: PB2007-109601, NOAA/Pacific Marine Environmental Laboratory, Seattle, WA, 55 pp.

SYNOLAKIS C, BERNARD E, TITOV V, KÂNOĞLU U, GONZÁLEZ F (2008) *Validation and verification of tsunami numerical models.* Pure Appl Geophys *165*:2197–2228

THOMSON RE, RABINOVICH AB, KULIKOV EA, FINE IV, BORNHOLD BD (2001) *On numerical simulation of the landslide-generated tsunami of November 3, 1994 in Skagway Harbor, Alaska.* In: HEBENSTREIT GT (ed) Tsunami Research at the End of a Critical Decade, Kluwer, pp 243–282

TITOV V, GONZALEZ F (2001) *Numerical study of the source of the July 17, 1998 PNG tsunami.* In: Hebenstreit GT (ed) Tsunami Research at the End of a Critical Decade, Kluwer, pp 197–207

WILSON B, TØRUM A (1968) *The tsunami of the Alaskan Earthquake, 1964: Engineering evaluation.* U.S. Army Corps of Engineers, Technical memorandum No. 25, 401 p.

(Received January 1, 2010, revised April 12, 2010, accepted April 21, 2010, Published online November 30, 2010)

Pure Appl. Geophys. 168 (2011), 1075–1088
© 2010 Springer Basel AG
DOI 10.1007/s00024-010-0218-6

Field Survey of the March 28, 2005 Nias-Simeulue Earthquake and Tsunami

Jose C. Borrero,[1,2] Brian McAdoo,[3] Bruce Jaffe,[4] Lori Dengler,[5] Guy Gelfenbaum,[4] Bretwood Higman,[6] Rahman Hidayat,[7,8,14] Andrew Moore,[9] Widjo Kongko,[7] Lukijanto,[7] Robert Peters,[4] Gegar Prasetya,[7,10] Vasily Titov,[11,12] and Eko Yulianto[13]

Abstract—On the evening of March 28, 2005 at 11:09 p.m. local time (16:09 UTC), a large earthquake occurred offshore of West Sumatra, Indonesia. With a moment magnitude (M_w) of 8.6, the event caused substantial shaking damage and land level changes between Simeulue Island in the north and the Batu Islands in the south. The earthquake also generated a tsunami, which was observed throughout the source region as well as on distant tide gauges. While the tsunami was not as extreme as the tsunami of December 26th, 2004, it did cause significant flooding and damage at some locations. The spatial and temporal proximity of the two events led to a unique set of observational data from the earthquake and tsunami as well as insights relevant to tsunami hazard planning and education efforts.

Key words: Tsunami, earthquake, Sumatra, subduction zone, natural hazards, hazard mitigation.

[1] ASR Limited, Marine Consulting and Research, Raglan 3225, New Zealand. E-mail: jborrero@usc.edu

[2] Tsunami Research Center, University of Southern California, Los Angeles, CA 90089-2531, USA.

[3] Department of Earth Science and Geography, Vassar College, Poughkeepsie, NY 12604-0735, USA.

[4] US Geological Survey, Pacific Sciences Center, Santa Cruz, CA 95060, USA.

[5] Department of Geology, Humboldt State University, Arcata, CA, USA.

[6] Department of Earth Science, University of Washington, Seattle, WA, USA.

[7] Coastal Engineering Laboratory-BPPT, Jl. Grafika 2, Yogyakarta 55281, Indonesia.

[8] *Present Address*: Meguro Laboratory, Institute of Industrial Science, The University of Tokyo, Komaba 4-6-1, Meguro-ku, Tokyo 153-8505, Japan.

[9] Department of Geology, Kent State University, Kent, OH, USA.

[10] *Present Address*: New Zealand Institute of Geological and Nuclear Sciences, Lower Hutt, New Zealand.

[11] NOAA Center for Tsunami Research, 7600 Sand Point Way, Seattle, WA 98195, USA.

[12] Joint Institute for the Study of the Atmosphere and Ocean, University of Washington, Seattle, WA 98195, USA.

[13] Indonesian Institute of Science, Jakarta, Indonesia.

[14] Institute for Sustainability and Peace-United Nations University (UNU-ISP), Shibuya-ku, Tokyo 150-8925, Japan.

1. Introduction

Just 3 months after producing the second largest instrumentally recorded earthquake in human history (Stein and Okal, 2005) and an associated tsunami responsible for the deaths of over 230,000 people worldwide (Synolakis and Kong, 2006, Geist et al., 2006a), the Sumatra Subduction Zone (SSZ) produced another large earthquake. On March 28, 2005 at 11:09 p.m. local time (16:09 UTC), an earthquake with moment magnitude (M_w) 8.6 occurred just a few hundred kilometers south of the most tsunami-devastated regions of Sumatra. The earthquake epicenter was located at approximately 2.07° N, 97.01° E (USGS) (Fig. 1). With the regional population already at a heightened sense of anxiety due to the extreme effects of the December event, this earthquake served to send the people into outright panic. Various news stories in the popular media reported such scenes in countries affected by the December 26th, 2004 event.

1.1. Post-Event Survey

When the March 28th earthquake occurred, an international team of researchers was in Jakarta preparing to begin a research cruise from Padang in Sumatra, through the islands west of Sumatra, north to Banda Aceh. The aim of the cruise was to collect tsunami field data related to the December 26th event from offshore islands and otherwise inaccessible

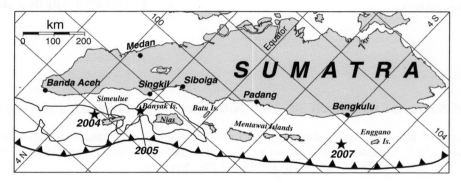

Figure 1
A location map for Sumatra. The stars indicate the epicenters of the 2004, 2005 and 2007 earthquakes. The thin irregular black lines represent the rupture areas of the December 2004 and March 2005 earthquakes; slip was >1 m inside the lines (MELTZNER *et al.*, 2006, BRIGGS *et al.*, 2006). The barbed line is the seafloor trace of the Sunda megathrust, which dips beneath Sumatra

areas of the Sumatran mainland between Padang and Banda Aceh (JAFFE *et al.*, 2006). The timing of the March 28th earthquake provided a unique opportunity to collect relevant tsunami field data from two events simultaneously. This paper will publish, for the first time, the complete data set recorded by the survey team for the March 28th event.

2. Observations of Tsunami and Earthquake Effects

The effects of the March 28th earthquake and tsunami overlapped with areas affected by the December 26th event—most notably on Simeulue Island. Because the tsunami was observed mostly in the immediate source area, runup, flow depth and inundation distances have to be considered relative to land level changes that happened as the tsunami was generated and immediately prior to its arrival on land. The tsunami runup data presented here has been corrected for tide and is presented in Tables 1, 2, 3.

The March 28th earthquake occurred in the late evening, when most people were indoors or asleep. Because the local population was very aware of tsunami hazards due to the publicity associated with the December tragedy, many people wisely evacuated to higher ground where a direct observation of the event was not possible. As a result, eyewitness accounts were not common and much of our data is derived from watermarks and tsunami traces.

The survey started in the southern Batu Islands and continued northward stopping in Nias, the mainland port of Singkil, the Banyak Islands and Simeulue Island. Data were collected using standard field techniques to survey runup elevations relative to sea level at the time of the earthquake (UNESCO, 1998; SYNOLAKIS and OKAL, 2005). Land level changes were estimated based on preserved high-tide lines, locations of dead corals, and stressed coastal vegetation in the swash zone. Position information was recorded using hand held GPS units.

After departing from Padang on 31 March 2005, the team first stopped at Teluk Bendara on Tanahbala Island, Hayaui Island and Simuk Island in the Batu Island group, south of Nias (Fig. 2). The earthquake was widely felt; however, there was no damage related to ground shaking nor was any tsunami observed from the March 28th event. At Teluk Bendara, coastal erosion left palm trees stranded in the surf zone, giving the impression of subsidence; however, residents stated that those particular trees were in that state prior to the earthquake. On Simuk, however, dying intertidal pools with desiccated algae suggested 10−20 cm of uplift.

There were, however, some interesting eyewitness accounts related to the December 26, 2004 event. Residents of Tanahbala reported that on December 26th, within an hour of the main shock (approximately 9 a.m. locally), they noticed small-scale water level fluctuations at the shoreline. These oscillations continued throughout the day but did not exceed the normal high tide levels. However, at approximately 3 pm, the height of the surges increased and culminated in a surge that flooded approximately 100 m

Table 1

Tsunami data collected for Nias and vicinity

Site (number)	Lat (°N)	Long (°E)	Distance from shore (m)	Tsunami flow depth (m)	Tsunami elevation (m)	Uplift (+) subsidence (−) (m)	Comments
Nias							
Lagundri Bay	0.57171	97.74588	150			0.7–0.8	
Lagundri Bay	0.57483	97.72488	255	1.14	3.5		Hiliamaetaniha area, significant damage to structures from earthquake and tsunami
Lagundri Bay	0.57605	97.72959	574		3.3	0.2	Limit of inundation, back of rice fields
Lagundri Bay	0.58167	97.73746	225		2.2		Inundation to mosque
Lagundri Bay	0.58167	97.73746		1.5	3.6		
Lagundri Bay	0.58285	97.73726	163	1.14	3.3	0.2	Scratches on building used for flow mark
Lagundri Bay	0.58298	97.73723	179	0.67	2.5	0.2	Flow mark on walls of building.
Lagundri Bay	0.58420	97.73723	255		2.0	0.2	Limit of inundation–debris line in front of mosque
Humanga Beach	1.48433	97.34718	30		2.0	Uplift	
Humanga Beach	1.48436	97.34708	69	0.7	1.8	0.9	Limit of inundation–locals report both tsunamis reached same distance inland–just over berm. Difficult to distinguish December 2004 from March 2005
Labuhan Aceh	1.40695	97.08376				∼3	
Afulu						1.7	
Asu							
Pulau Asu	0.90430	97.28008	14	0.2		1.6	Wells dry from uplift
Pulau Asu	0.90544	97.26982	94		3.4	1.2	West side of island, limit of inundation, wrack line
Sarangbuang							
Pulau Sarangbuang	1.69570	97.44872	64			−1.7	Wrack line in village
Pulau Sarangbuang	1.70486	97.44499	88		0.5	−1.7	Wrack line, back side of island
Pulau Sarangbuang	1.70533	97.44478	4		0.9	−1.7	Berm, high point on profile

inland with a flow depth of 0.7 m and a total runup of 1.3 m.

Residents from nearby Simuk Island also reported a late-arriving large wave on December 26th that caused approximately 200 m of inundation. We were not able, however, to confirm this with additional witnesses from the local harbor where the report originated. A similar phenomenon was also reported at Lagundri Bay on Nias Island (discussed in the next section). It is interesting to note that similar observations related to the arrival time of the December 26th tsunami were also reported by residents of Muara Maras, located on the Sumatra mainland south of Bengkulu (see Fig. 1). These reports were recorded during a survey of the September 2007 Bengkulu earthquake and tsunami (BORRERO *et al.*, 2009). The exact cause of the late arrival of the largest waves has never been specifically addressed in the open literature.

2.1. Nias and Vicinity

Continuing north, the team visited Lagundri Bay on the southwest corner of Nias Island (Fig. 3). The earthquake was felt very strongly at Lagundri Bay and ground shaking was responsible for several collapsed buildings, especially in the popular tourist area of Sorake Beach on the west side of the bay. The earthquake was followed by the tsunami, which arrived just minutes after the earthquake. A maximum tsunami runup of 3.2 m and horizontal inundation distance of up to 300 m was recorded based on watermarks and eyewitness accounts. According to one resident, however, there was, "No tsunami"– noting that after the earthquake stopped, the sea rose up and came inland then receded, but "nothing like what happened in Aceh" (paraphrased from the translation.)

Table 2

Banyak Islands and Singkil

Site	Lat (°N)	Long (°E)	Distance from shore (m)	Tsunami flow depth (m)	Tsunami elevation (m)	Uplift (+) subsidence (−) (m)	Comments
Banyak islands							
Palau Tuangku, Teluk Mariabah (1)	2.05595	97.33350			3.3	0	
Bangkaru	2.09046	97.09753	69		3.5	0.6	Ridge, high point along profile. Too dense for GPS position from shoreline
Bangkaru	2.09046	97.09753	69	0.5	3.5	0.6	Sand plastered on vegetation and tree trunks. Too dense for GPS position from shoreline
Bangkaru	2.09046	97.09753	85		3.05	0.6	Wrack line, impenetrable jungle, too dense for GPS position from shoreline
Bangkaru	2.09696	97.09616		0.5	~1	0.4	
Banyak island	2.10597	97.27027	60	2	2.6		
Tuangku	2.06118	97.33074	28		>1.3	0	Wrack line in thick jungle, Inundation beyond wrack line into impenetrable jungle
Tuangku	2.10617	97.27018	30		3		
Tuangku	2.10623	97.27077	34	2.5	>2.5	0	Wrack line in thick jungle, broken vegetation and debris, Inundation beyond wrack line into impenetrable jungle
Tuangku	2.12939	97.26230	51	0.9	0.1	0	Wrack line in jungle
Tuangku	2.12968	97.26210	34		2.5	−0.5	
Singkil							
Singkil	2.26663	97.80968			1.5		One wave, 10 min. after quake, drained slowly for 1 h
Singkil	2.26925	97.81042	21	1.5	2.3	−0.8	Water marks on buildings

There was ample evidence of characteristic tsunami damage, including destroyed walls parallel to the shore while perpendicular walls of the same structures remained intact (Fig. 4). Tsunami induced scour and erosion were observed, especially in the Sorake Beach section. Fortunately, there were no fatalities in Lagundri; this may be because the peak tourist season had not yet begun, so many of the collapsed buildings used for tourist accommodation were not occupied. We estimated coseismic uplift to be between 0.2 and 0.8 m based on exposed reefs and desiccated algae, which was still somewhat green, 5 days after the earthquake. Uplift at Hiliamataniha Village, on the east side of Lagundri Bay, was 0.5–0.55 m based on the elevation difference between high-tide marks.

From Lagundri, the survey moved to the Hinako Island group located off the central west coast of Nias

(Fig. 3). Here, the local residents reported only negligible tsunami effects. On Asu Island, we measured 1.2–1.6 m of coseismic uplift from the March 28th earthquake. This was based on observed changes in the local high tide line, exposed nearshore reefs and a stand of mangroves raised above the high-tide line. Residents of the island were left without water as the wells were uplifted above the water table. The residents on the eastern side of the island did not report any surges from the March 28th tsunami exceeding the high tide level and there was no evidence of a tsunami. However, there was evidence on the western side of the island of tsunami runup of 3.4 m.

The survey continued on to the northwestern corner of Nias. This region experienced significant uplift as a result of the March 28th earthquake. Uplift was estimated at 1.7 m near Afulu, 0.5–1.0 m at

Table 3

Babi, Simeulue and mainland Sumatra

Site	Lat (°N)	Long (°E)	Inundation distance (m)	Flow depth (m)	Tsunami height (m)	Uplift (+) subsidence (−) (m)	Comments
Babi							
Babi	2.09400	96.61582	140	1.4	2.0	0.8	Berm—high point on profile. Broken branches 2 m above ground level near top of berm. Reef uplifted—exposed for 123 m. Mangroves too dense for GPS, position from current shoreline
Babi	2.09400	96.61582	179	0.5	2.3	0.8	Edge of uplifted mangrove swamp. Mangrove snapped off at ∼2.3 m above ground level
Babi	2.09400	96.61582	295	0.7		0.8	Limit of inundation in mangroves. Mangroves too dense for GPS, position from shoreline
Babi	2.09437	96.61618			2.0	0.8	
Simeulue							
Busung Bay	2.38517	96.33547	131		3.3	1.1	3/28 tsunami deposits overlie 12/26 tsunami deposit
Busung Bay	2.39127	96.33382			4.2	1.4	
Busung Bay	2.39177	96.33286	100	0.5–0.8	4.2	1.4	Uplift from present to previous high tide lines; flow depth at 3 m elevation in yard at surf camp
Busung Bay					2.6	1.2	
Kariya Bakti	2.63815	95.80393	37		1.7		High elevation on profile. Lat Long from shoreline
Kariya Bakti	2.63815	95.80393	64		1.5		Buildings in village, destroyed by 12/26, rebuilt, then damaged by 3/28. 3/28 wrack line not evident in village or beyond, though recent damage evident
Langi	2.82444	95.75753			1		High water mark on beach, debris, eye witness
Labuhan Bakti	2.39911	96.4678	300		2.5	+1.4	
Sumatra							
Kuala Meurisi	4.61084	95.62215	200		2.4		Possible deposit from both events
Lhok Leum Pang	4.68754	95.53168			1		Location from shore most waypoint

Humanga Bay. At Labuhan Aceh, between the two, uplift was on the order of 3 m based on differences in the high tide lines. Because the tsunami occurred at night and the village at Afulu is located several hundred meters from shore, there were no eyewitnesses to the tsunami. There was, however, evidence of tsunami debris in the vegetation between the beach and the village. We assume that this was from the March 28th event; however, we cannot be certain that it was not produced by a previous storm high tide or the December 26th tsunami. At Humanga Bay there was a clear indication of a debris line inland of any possible high tide mark, which we interpret to have been deposited by the March 28th tsunami. On an uninhabited section of the northern shore of Nias,

evidence suggested a 1 m high tsunami, which we assume was caused by the March 28th earthquake.

Northeast of Nias on Saranbaung Island, the local residents did not observe a tsunami on either December 26th or March 28th. However, the March 28th earthquake caused subsidence on the order of 1.7 m. This estimate was based on a small dock, which had been previously used to offload boats and was now completely submerged. Further evidence of subsidence was seen in the increase in well-water levels in the village. Water in wells was no longer potable due to salt intrusion resulting from being dropped below the island's thin freshwater lens.

At Singkil, a provincial port town located on the mainland of Sumatra (Fig. 1), the most obvious effect

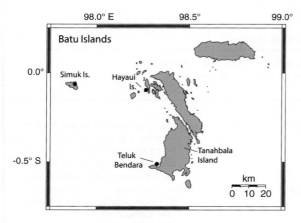

Figure 2
Locations surveyed in the Batu Islands

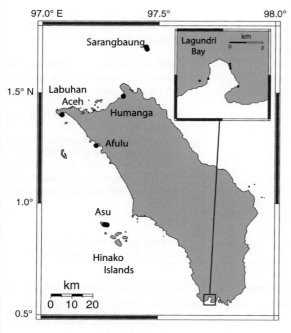

Figure 3
Sites surveyed on and around Nias Island and Lagundri Bay

the area remained flooded as the water slowly drained off to its current level. The tsunami reached a maximum runup of 2.3 m. A charter boat captain working in the area informed us that the wharf at Singkil had been recently upgraded; however, it suffered significant damage as a result of the earthquake. Throughout the area, there was ample evidence of liquefaction and lateral spreading as well as uneven settlement of structures (Fig. 6).

The Banyak Islands lie immediately adjacent to the epicenter of the March 28th earthquake (Fig. 7). The Banyak group consists of two main islands, the larger Tuangku and the smaller Bangkaru. Because these islands are sparsely inhabited, we did not encounter any eyewitnesses to the March 28th event.

Despite being separated by only a few kilometers, the earthquake and tsunami effects on the two islands were quite different. On Bangakaru Island, exposed corals and trapped fish in tide pools indicated approximately 0.6 m of uplift. However the sites surveyed on Tuangku had clearly subsided on the order of 0.5 m. Tsunami traces at each of our survey locations in the Banyak Islands consisted of flattened vegetation not yet dead from salt water exposure as well as large logs deposited in the jungle and debris hanging from trees. Tsunami heights were measured at 3.0–3.5 m on Bangkaru and 1.0–3.0 m on Tuangku.

The survey continued northward from the Banyak Islands towards Simeulue Island (Fig. 7). The first stop along the way was the uninhabited Babi Island. On Babi there was clear evidence of approximately 0.8 m of tectonic uplift associated with the March 28th earthquake in the form of newly exposed nearshore reefs. There was also evidence of tsunami overwash and debris deposited in the forest. The tsunami runup height was estimated at 2.0–2.3 m with inundation extending 140–295 m inland.

Babi Island very clearly displayed the stages of tectonic evolution typical to the islands west of Sumatra (Fig. 8). Dead trees near shore due to saltwater intrusion indicate the gradual subsidence of the islands during the interseismic period when the plates are locked. After the earthquake these trees are now located 10s to 100s of meters inland and surrounded by a newly exposed section of uplifted nearshore reef.

of the March 28th earthquake was the widespread coastal subsidence and subsequent flooding of the nearshore area. We estimated coseismic subsidence of 0.5–0.8 m, which left the nearshore area permanently flooded, including oil storage facilities and several kilometers of shorefront businesses (Fig. 5). A tsunami was also observed at Singkil; eyewitnesses reported one large surge arriving approximately 10 min after the earthquake. After the initial wave,

Figure 4
Houses located on the eastern side of Lagundri Bay damaged by the March 28th tsunami. The flow direction in the upper photo was towards the camera. Shore perpendicular walls are still intact, while those oriented shore parallel (perpendicular to the flow direction) have been destroyed. In the lower photo, the flow direction was roughly from left to right, also indicated by flow-parallel walls that are still partially intact

Moving on to Simeulue, our understanding of the March 28th tsunami was complicated by overlapping effects from December 26th. In southwestern Simeulue at Busung Bay (Fig. 8), the December earthquake caused 0.3–0.5 m of subsidence (MELTZNER et al., 2006) and a non-destructive 2.3 m tsunami that inundated approximately 120 m inland. The December tsunami flowed over the road and into a rice paddy where it left a clear debris line still evident during our survey. On March 28th, however, this area was uplifted by approximately 1.4 m. We deduced this value by comparing the high tide debris lines on the beach. The tsunami on March 28th caused runup of between 2.6 and 4.2 m in Busung Bay and inundated up to 80 m (Fig. 9).

119

Figure 5
Shoreline subsidence at Singkil caused by the March 28th earthquake (*top*) and subsidence at an oil storage facility located near the port (*bottom*). Note the uneven settlement of the oil storage tank

Tsunami deposits from both events were evident in the sediments at Busung Bay. Grass had grown and sent roots into the December 26th tsunami deposit in the 3 months before the March 28th tsunami arrived. The March 28th deposit was identified by sand devoid of roots overlying the rooted sand of the December 26th deposit. The contact between the deposits was sharp, indicating erosion of the uppermost portion of the December 26th deposit. Similarly,

the base of the December 26th deposit had sharp erosional contact with the underlying soil.

Labuhan Bakti near the southeastern tip of Simeulue Island experienced approximately 1.4 m of uplift and was affected by a damaging tsunami on the order of 2.5 m high inundating approximately 300 m inland. Up to 50% of the buildings in Labuhan Bakti were destroyed by the 2005 tsunami, although there was no loss of life due in large part to the local oral history of

Figure 6

Top Subsidence at Singkil. This image shows three things: (1) uneven settling, possibly due to liquefaction induced subsidence during ground shaking, (2) permanent coseismic subsidence evidenced by the standing seawater, and (3) the horizontal mud line (indicated by the *black arrows*) implies that the tsunami inundation occurred after the house settled. *Bottom* An earthquake and tsunami disaster relief station set up after the 2004 event that was subsequently damaged by the 2005 event

the tsunami that devastated the island in 1907 (McAdoo *et al.*, 2006). At Labuhan Bakti there was clear evidence of the 2004 tsunami overlapping the 2005 tsunami (Fig. 10). Continuing to the east, the wave heights rapidly dropped off behind an extensive mangrove swamp where the debris field suggests a wave only a few centimeters high.

At the fishing village of Kariya Bakti on the NW shore of Simuelue, the March 28th tsunami overtopped a 3.2 m high berm, but did not damage the village. In contrast, the 26th December tsunami was larger and more energetic with a surge approximately 2 m high that flowed through the village, and completely destroyed all buildings. The village,

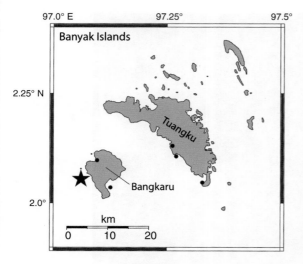

Figure 7
Locations surveyed in the Banyak Islands. The *star* indicates the USGS epicenter of the March 28th earthquake. Bangkaru Island was uplifted while Tuangku Island subsided

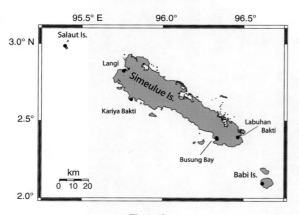

Figure 8
Simeulue Island and vicinity

evidence of uplift or subsidence in this area during the March 28th earthquake.

Langi at the northern tip of Simeulue was also affected by both tsunami events; however, the December 26th event was significantly more destructive. Tsunami heights were on the order of 10–15 m on December 26th (YALCINER et al., 2005) and on the order of 1 m on March 28th. At Langi we learned of the importance of education and oral tradition in hazard mitigation. The local population was affected by a deadly tsunami in 1907 and had, therefore, learned the association between strong earthquakes and the tsunami that might follow. As a result of the stories of the 'smong' passed down through generations, the locals knew to evacuate to higher ground after the earthquake stopped on December 26th. As a result, most of the population survived, in stark contrast to villages on the western coast of the Sumatran mainland where most people were caught unaware and killed (McADOO et al., 2006).

North of Simeulue, the team surveyed a few locations on the small, and uninhabited Salaut Island. This island shows the traces of a very large tsunami, which we believe to have been caused by the December 26th event. Because the high tide debris line was intact around the island, we believe the March 28th tsunami did not exceed this level nor overtop the nearshore berm and was, therefore, less than 2 m in height.

3. Comparison to Other Recent Tsunamis

As expected, the runup produced by the March 28th event was generally much smaller than that recorded for the December 26th (JAFFE et al., 2006)

which is approximately 20 km south of the northern tip of Simeulue Island, had already been rebuilt by the time of the March 28th tsunami. There was no

Figure 9
The stages of tectonic evolution on Babi Island. The dead trees on the left are caused by saltwater intrusion as the island slowly subsided during the previous inter-seismic period. During the March 28th earthquake, the area was uplifted exposing the nearshore reefs on the right

Figure 10
Labuhan Bakti. This image shows the complexity of unraveling two events spaced closely in time and space. The 26 December 2004 tsunami was measured at this location to be 2 m above mean sea level with associated coseismic subsidence of 0.5 m (YALCINER *et al.*, 2005). During the March 28th event, 1.4 m of uplift followed by a tsunami of 2.5 m height left a water-mark below that of the 2004 event, making it appear that the 2005 tsunami was smaller than the 2004 event, yet it was 50 cm higher. This highlights the challenges in deciphering the March 28th tsunami due to temporal and spatial proximity to the December 26, 2004 event

event. Runup heights from the March 28th event were comparable to the December 26, 2004 tsunami only in southern Simeulue where the two events overlapped (Fig. 11).

Although the tsunami effects extended over a longer coastal area, the runup heights from the March 28th tsunami are generally equal to or smaller than those measured after the September 12, 2007 Bengkulu earthquake ($M_w = 8.5$), which occurred ~ 500 km to the south (BORRERO *et al.*, 2009). The larger runup from the smaller 2007 earthquake can be explained by differences in the location of the largest seafloor deformation. In 2005, a large fraction of the coseismic uplift occurred under northern Nias and southern Simeulue Islands (BRIGGS *et al.*, 2006) and did not contribute to tsunami generation (KAJIURA, 1981; GEIST *et al.*, 2006b), whereas in 2007, the uplift occurred underwater, along the bathymetric rise extending southeast from the Mentawai group towards Enggano Island (JI, 2007; FUJII and SATAKE, 2008; LORITO *et al.*, 2008; KONCA *et al.*, 2008). That both events had a relatively small far field signature can be

explained by the reasoning above for 2005 and by the overall smaller magnitude ($M_o = 0.5 \times 10^{29}$ vs. 1.1×10^{29} dyn-cm) of the 2007 event with the largest coseismic deformation occurring under relatively shallow (200–500 m depth) water.

The measured tsunami runup from the March 28th earthquake also gives insight into the details of the coseismic deformation. Early estimates of the seafloor deformation pattern (JI, 2007; GEIST *et al.*, 2006b), despite agreeing qualitatively with observed uplift and subsidence patterns, do not seem to sufficiently explain all of the observed runup heights, particularly the high values recorded at Lagundri on the southern tip of Nias Island. Deformation models constrained with uplift data (i.e. BRIGGS *et al.*, 2006, KONCA *et al.*, 2007) suggest the existence of a secondary slip patch to the south of Nias beneath Simuk Island, which is consistent with our observations of uplift there. It is conceivable that this portion of the slip patch provided the source of the observed tsunami at Lagundri. However, a detailed numerical modeling study would be necessary to fully evaluate each of these scenarios.

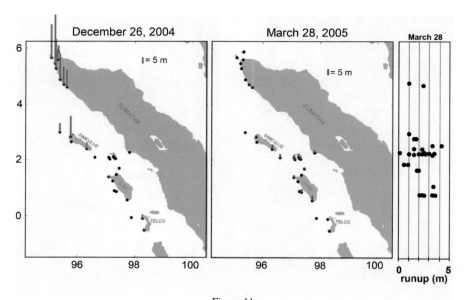

Figure 11

Comparison between runup values measured by this survey team, the December 26th tsunami (*left*) and the March 28th tsunami (*right*). Tsunami heights are comparable between the two events only at the southern end of Simeulue Island. Runup heights for the March 28th event are plotted versus latitude in the far *right panel*

4. *Summary and Conclusions*

The earthquake of March 28, 2005 caused a damaging tsunami affecting approximately 500 km of the Sumatra coast and offshore islands. The tsunami caused runup of up to 4 m with the largest and most damaging effects observed on southern Nias and Simeulue Islands. Besides compiling a detailed database of runup and inundation, the survey of the March 28th event also highlighted a number of tsunami hazard mitigation issues relevant to tsunami preparedness in the region and throughout the Indian Ocean.

Of primary importance is the effectiveness of oral history and community education in reducing tsunami casualties. This was clearly demonstrated during the December 2004 tsunami by the residents of Simeulue and was based on the community experience from a tsunami in 1907 (McAdoo *et al.*, 2006). The community of Baie Martile also demonstrated this learned response to great effect during the 1999 Vanuatu tsunami that destroyed their village but caused only three deaths (Caminade *et al.*, 2000).

Interestingly, while conducting interviews of the local populations in areas affected by the March 28th earthquake, we found that many residents claimed

that there "was no tsunami" but rather that the sea level merely rose up, flooded their land and knocked down some houses. It was evident that the extreme nature of the December 26th tsunami had skewed even the local population's perception of the definition of a tsunami. This distortion of reality was also evident in the coverage of the event by the global media who ignored the March 28th tsunami story despite repeatedly being told that there was indeed a damaging tsunami.

Coseismic uplift and subsidence produced challenges for those living in the coastal zone. Hand-dug water wells were, in some cases, uplifted clear above the water table, and new wells had to be dug to secure a water supply. In some areas of subsidence, the potability of well water was compromised due to salt intrusion from the underlying salt-water wedge. Unlike salinization from wells simply overtopped by a tsunami, this damage is long lasting (decadal), and pumping will do nothing to remediate the wells. Coseismic uplift also caused significant damage to offshore coral reefs, which affects local fishermen due to the loss of habitat. The changes in the reefs also have had an effect on the local, economically important, surfing tourism industry. Several renowned surfing breaks were altered by the earthquake, some for the worse when previously submerged reefs were pushed out of the water, while others, such as the legendary right hander in Lagundri Bay, Nias, may have actually been improved, becoming fractionally shallower, resulting in a more intense and fast moving breaker.

Finally, the March 28th event had a significant amount of its deformation occur under land, which diminished the tsunami's effect. This is a particularly important consideration for assessing tsunami hazards along the Mentawai segment of the Sumatra Subduction Zone since a significant portion of the uplift from those events may occur under the relatively large islands of the Mentawai archipelago (BORRERO et al., 2006). Thus the most potentially destructive portion of the SSZ in terms of the local and far-field tsunami would lie to the south of the Mentawai islands.

Acknowledgments

The authors would like to acknowledge Captain Lee Clarke, First Mate Darren Stockwell and the crew of the M.V. Seimoa for their efforts in making the voyage safe and successful. Anthony Marcotti and Jordan Heuer of Saraina Koat Mentawai Surf Charters were instrumental in organizing the trip's complicated logistics. The University of Southern California, the National Science Foundation, USAID Office of Foreign Disaster Assistance, the US Geological Survey and Vassar College provided funding for this study. Etienne Kingsley assisted in the field data collection effort. JCB would like to thank Dunstan and Trish Hogan for providing a tranquil location in St. Francis Beach, South Africa where significant progress in the preparation of this report for publication was made.

REFERENCES

BORRERO, J., SIEH, K., CHLIEH, M., and SYNOLAKIS, C.E. (2006), *Tsunami Inundation Modeling for Western Sumatra*, Proc. Nat. Acad. Sci. USA., 103, 19673–19677.

BORRERO, J., WEISS, R., OKAL, E., HIDAYAT, R., SURANTO, ARCAS, D., and TITOV, V. (2009), *The tsunami of September 12, 2007, Bengkulu province, Sumatra, Indonesia: Post-Tsunami Field Survey and Numerical Modeling*, Geophys. J. Int., 178, 180–194.

BRIGGS, R., SIEH, K., MELTZENER, A., NATAWIDJAJA, D., GALETZKA, J., SUWARGADI, B., HSU, Y.-J., SIMONS, M., HANANTO, N., SUPRIHANTO, I., PRAYUDI, D., AVOUAC, J.-P., PRAWIRODIRJO, L., and BOCK, Y. (2006), *Deformation and slip along the Sunda Megathrust in the great 2005 Nias–Simeulue earthquake*, Science, 311, 1897–1901.

CAMINADE, J., CHARLIE, D., KANOGLU, U., KOSHIMURA, S., MATSUTOMI, H., MOORE, A., RUSCHER, C., SYNOLAKIS, C., and TAKAHASHI, T. (2000), *Vanuatu earthquake and tsunami cause much damage, few casualties*, Eos, Trans. Amer. Geophys. Un., 81, 641, 646–647.

FUJII, Y., and SATAKE, K. (2008), *Tsunami waveform inversion of the 2007 Bengkulu, southern Sumatra, earthquake*, Earth Planets and Space, 60, 993–998.

GEIST, E., TITOV, V., and SYNOLAKIS C. (2006a), *Tsunami: wave of change*, Sci. Am., 294, 56–63.

GEIST, E., BILEK, S., ARCAS, D., and TITOV, V. (2006b), *Differences in tsunami generation between the December 26th, 2004 and March 28, 2005 Sumatra earthquakes*, Earth Planets and Space, 58, 185–193.

JAFFE, B., BORRERO, J., PRASETYA, G., DENGLER, L., GELFENBAUM, G., HIDAYAT, R., HIGMAN, B., KINGSLEY, E. LUKIYANTO, McADOO, B., MOORE, A., MORTON, R., PETERS, R., RUGGIERO, P., TITOV, V., KONGKO, W. and YULIANTO, E., (2006), *The December 26, 2004 Indian Ocean Tsunami in Northwest Sumatra and Offshore Islands*, Earthquake Spectra, 22, S3, S105–S136.

JI, C. (2007), Preliminary result of the Sep 12, 2007 Sumatra earthquake, http://earthquake.usgs.gov/eqcenter/eqinthenews/2007/us2007hear/finite_fault.php.

KAJIURA, K. (1981), *Tsunami energy in relation to parameters of the earthquake fault model*, Bull. Earthquake Res. Inst. (Japan), 56, 415–440.

KONCA, O, VALA, H., TEH-RU, A., AVOUAC, J.-P., HELMBERGER, D., JI, C., SIEH, K., BRIGGS, R., MELTZNER A. (2007), *Rupture kinematics of the 2005, M_w 8.6, Nias—Simeulue earthquake from the joint inversion of seismic and geodetic data*, Bull. Seism. Soc. Am., 97, S307–S322.

KONCA, A., AVOUAC, J.-P., SLADEN, A., MELTZNER, A.J., SIEH, K., PENG, F., LI, Z., GALETZKA, J., GENRICH, J., CHLIEH, M., NATAWIDJAJA, D., BOCK, Y., FIELDING, E.J., JI, C., and HELMBERGER, D. (2008), *Partial rupture of a locked patch of the Sumatra megathrust during the 2007 earthquake sequence*, Nature, 456, 631–635.

LORITO, S., ROMANO, F., PIATANESI, A., and BOSCHI E. (2008) *Source process of the September 12, 2007, M_w 8.4 southern Sumatra earthquake from tsunami tide gauge record inversion*, Geophys. Res. Lett., 35, L02310.

McADOO, B., DENGLER, L., TITOV, V. and PRASETYA, G. (2006), *Smong: How an oral history saved thousands on Indonesia's Simeulue Island*, Earthquake Spectra, 22, S3, S661–S669.

MELTZNER, A., SIEH, K., ABRAMS, M, AGNEW, D., HUDNUT, K, AVOUAC, J.-P., and NATAWIDJAJA, D. (2006), *Uplift and subsidence associated with the great Aceh-Andaman earthquake of 2004*, J. Geophys. Res., 111, B02407.

STEIN, S., and OKAL, E. (2005), *Size and speed of the Sumatra earthquake*, Nature, 434, 581–582.

Synolakis, C., and Kong, L. (2006), *Runup Measurements of the December 2004 Indian Ocean Tsunami*, Spectra, 22, S3, S67–S91.

SYNOLAKIS, C., and OKAL, E.A. (2005), 1992–2002: perspective on a decade of post-tsunami surveys, in: Tsunamis: case studies and recent developments, ed. by SATAKE, K., Adv. Natur. Technol. Hazards, 23, pp 1–30.

UNESCO, Intergovernmental Oceanographic Commission, Post-Tsunami Survey Field Guide, IOC Manuals and Guides, no. 37.

YALCINER, A., PERINCEK, D., ERSOY, S., PRASETYA, G., HIDAYAT, R. and MCADOO, B. (2005), *December 26, 2004 Indian Ocean tsunami field survey (Jan. 21–31, 2005) at north of Sumatra Island, UNESCO IOC Report*.

(Received November 30, 2009, revised June 21, 2010, accepted June 21, 2010, Published online November 12, 2010)

Pure Appl. Geophys. 168 (2011), 1089–1100
© 2010 The Author(s)
This article is published with open access at Springerlink.com
DOI 10.1007/s00024-010-0220-z

▌Pure and Applied Geophysics

Observation and Modeling of the January 2009 West Papua, Indonesia Tsunami

Yushiro Fujii,[1] Kenji Satake,[2] and Yuji Nishimae[3]

Abstract—We modeled a tsunami from the West Papua, Indonesia earthquakes on January 3, 2009 ($M_w = 7.7$). After the first earthquake, tsunami alerts were issued in Indonesia and Japan. The tsunami was recorded at many stations located in and around the Pacific Ocean. In particular, at Kushimoto on Kii Peninsula, the maximum amplitude was 43 cm, larger than that at Manokwari on New Guinea Island, near the epicenter. The tsunami was recorded on near-shore wave gauges, offshore GPS sensors and deep-sea bottom pressure sensors. We have collected more than 150 records and used 72 stations' data with clear tsunami signals for the tsunami source modeling. We assumed two fault models (single fault and five subfaults) which are located to cover the aftershock area. The estimated average slip on the single fault model (80×40 km) is 0.64 m, which yields a seismic moment of 1.02×10^{20} Nm ($M_w = 7.3$). The observed tsunami waveforms at most stations are well explained by this model.

Key words: West Papua, Indonesia 2009 earthquake, tide gauge, wave gauge, GPS buoy, ocean bottom tsunami sensor, tsunami simulation.

1. Introduction

A large earthquake occurred on the north coast of Doberai Peninsula, West Papua, Indonesia (0.408°S, 132.886°E, $M_w = 7.7$ at 19:43:50 UTC according to USGS) on January 3, 2009. This earthquake was followed by the second event (0.707°S, 133.361°E, $M_w = 7.4$ at, 22:33:40 UTC, according to USGS) 3 h later at about 60 km southeast. Focal mechanisms of thrust type by USGS's CMT solutions and the shallow depth of about 20 km indicate that these events

occurred on the plate boundary along the Manokwari Trench (e.g. Okal, 1999) where the Pacific Plate is subducting beneath the Australian Plate (Fig. 1).

After the first event, Meteorological, Climatological and Geophysical Agency, Indonesia (BMKG) issued an alert for a local tsunami potential near the source region. According to the field survey of the coastal area, northern West Papua, near the sources (Muhari et al., 2009), the run-up heights were up to 1.97 m. The tsunami did not cause much damage to houses or fisheries facilities, and there were no casualties.

Far from the West Papua coast, the Japan Meteorological Agency (JMA) issued a Tsunami Advisory to the Izu-Bonin Islands, the southwestern coasts of Honshu and Shikoku Islands facing to Pacific Ocean, eastern coast of Kyushu Island, and Satsunan Islands (Fig. 2). The observed tsunamis at tide gauges along the Japanese coast range from a few to several tens of centimeters. The maximum tsunami amplitude of 43 cm was recorded at Kushimoto.

Around New Guinea Island, many earthquakes have occurred in the past. The earthquakes in 1996, 1998, September and October 2002, which generated tsunamis are noted with their labels in Fig. 1. The 1996, 2002 September and October tsunamis reached coasts in Japan, and were observed at some tide gauges. For the 1996 and September 2002 events, maximum tsunami heights of 1.04 m at Chichijima and 0.20 m at Naze were recorded, respectively (JMA, 2002, 2009).

The 2009 tsunamis were recorded not only at highly dense coastal tide gauges and near shore wave gauges but also at GPS buoys and ocean bottom tsunami sensors (OBTS) recently installed. For example, JMA's OBTS system in Tonankai was just started in November 2008 to monitor oceanographic phenomena such as tides, wind waves or tsunamis.

[1] Building Research Institute (BRI), International Institute of Seismology and Earthquake Engineering (IISEE), 1-3 Tachihara, Tsukuba, Ibaraki 305-0802, Japan. E-mail: fujii@kenken.go.jp
[2] Earthquake Research Institute (ERI), University of Tokyo, 1-1-1 Yayoi, Bunkyo-ku, Tokyo 113-0032, Japan.
[3] Japan Meteorological Agency (JMA), 1-3-4 Otemachi, Chiyoda-ku, Tokyo 100-8122, Japan.

In this paper, we describe the observed tsunami heights and waveforms, and model the tsunami to estimate the tsunami source using those data.

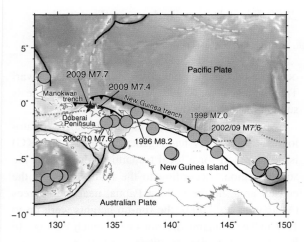

Figure 1

Epicenters of the January 2009 West Papua, Indonesia earthquakes (*black star* first event, *white star* second event). *Gray circles* indicate the previous earthquakes whose magnitudes are greater than seven, of which the events with labels are tsunamigenic earthquakes

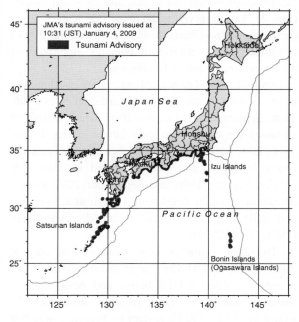

Figure 2

Coastal areas of Japan, where tsunami advisories were issued by JMA for the January 2009 West Papua, Indonesia earthquakes

2. Observed Tsunamis

Tsunamis from the 2009 West Papua, Indonesia earthquakes were recorded on many coastal tide gauges in and around the Pacific Ocean (Fig. 3), as well as near-shore wave gauges, off-shore GPS buoys, and cabled OBTS (pressure gauges) off the Japanese coasts (Fig. 4). We have collected 105 tide gauge waveforms including tsunami signals from Indonesia's National Coordination Agency for Surveys and Mapping (BAKOSURTANAL), JMA, Japan Coastal Guard (JCG), Japan's Geographical Survey Institute (GSI), and USA's West Coast/Alaska Tsunami Warning Center (WCATWC). The tsunamis were also recorded at 29 near-shore wave gauges and eight offshore GPS buoys operated by Japan's Nationwide Ocean Wave information network for Ports and HArbourS (NOW-PHAS). Tsunami sensors installed on the ocean bottom by JMA and the Japan Agency for Marine-Earth Science and Technology (JAMSTEC), 11 sensors in total (Boso 1, one of JMA's OBTS, malfunctioned), successfully recorded tsunami signals as well as seismic signals. Among these data, we selected 50 tide gauges, 10 wave gauges, 3 GPS buoys and 9 OBTS, which clearly recorded tsunami signals to be used for tsunami modeling. The locations of these selected stations, 72 in total, are listed in Table 1.

Figures 3b and 4b show the maximum tsunami heights (positive values of zero-to-peak in tsunami waveforms after the data processing which will be described later) at the observation stations. The tsunami heights are larger along the Izu-Bonin ridge system and the southern coasts of Japan, because of the waveguide effect (trapped wave energy in shallow ridge region) as pointed out by SATAKE and KANAMORI (1991) and SATAKE et al. (1992).

The tide gauge, wave gauge, GPS buoy and OBTS records usually include low frequency ocean tides and high frequency waves such as seismic waves or wind waves. We filter these records to retrieve the tsunami signals in the following way. First, we approximate the tidal component as a polynomial function, and remove the tides from the original records. Then, we apply a moving average with a box-car function which has a band width of three sampling points to reduce the high frequency noises. Figure 5 shows the processed records as examples of

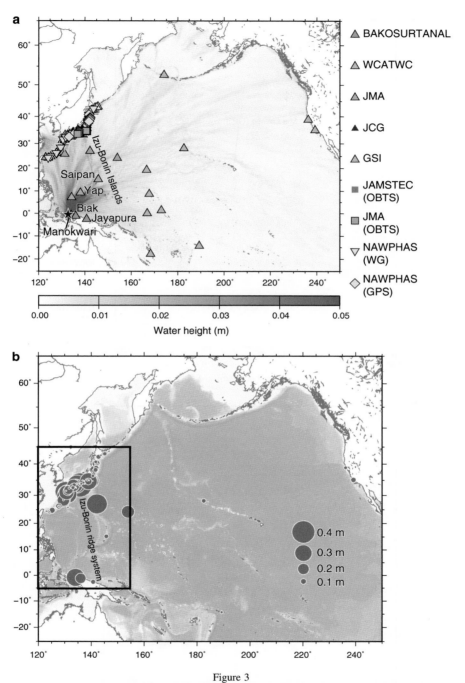

Figure 3

a Locations of stations which recorded the 2009 West Papua, Indonesia tsunami, overlaid on the distribution of the simulated maximum tsunami height. *Triangles*, *squares*, *inverted triangles* and *diamonds* indicate the tide gauges, ocean bottom tsunami sensors (*OBTS*), wave gauges (*WG*) and GPS buoys, respectively. Epicenter of the first event (*black star*) is also shown. **b** Maximum heights (absolute values of zero-to-peak or zero-to-trough) of the observed tsunamis. *Rectangular* shows the computation area for tsunami simulations

a wave gauge at Shionomisaki, a GPS buoy off Mie Owase, and an OBTS of MPG2 off Shikoku (see Fig. 4a for the locations).

The observed tsunami waveforms indicate that the tsunami amplitudes range from a few to 40 cm at the tide gauges, a few to 10 cm at the wave gauges, up to

129

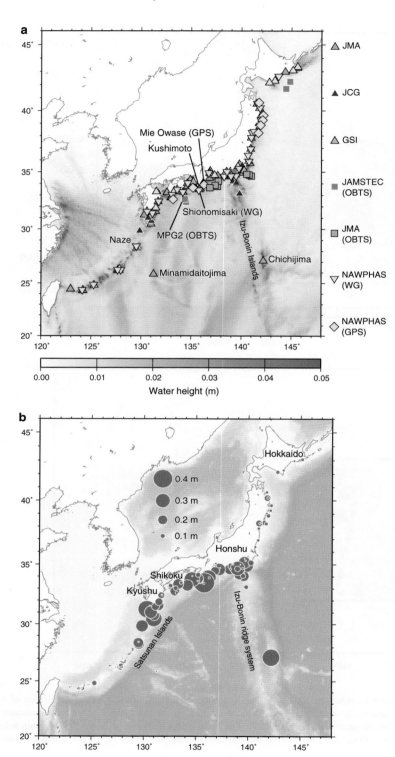

Figure 4

a Same as Fig. 3a, but for the region around Japan. The sources of the 2009 West Papua, Indonesia earthquakes are far south of this map (see Fig. 3a). **b** Same as Fig. 2b, but for the region around Japan

Table 1

List of tide gauges, wave gauges, GPS buoys and OBTS

Station*	Latitude (deg:min:s)	Longitude (deg:min:s)	Water depth (m)	Record sampling	MTH (m)**	Agencies***
Manokwari	0:51:25S	134:04:38E		1 min	0.32	BAKO
Biak	1:10:40S	136:03:21E		3 min	0.19	BAKO
Jayapura	2:32:42S	140:42:46E		1 min	0.088	BAKO
Yap	9:18:18N	138:04:37E		1 min	0.014	UH
Saipan	15:13:36N	145:44:31E		1 min	0.083	UH
Chichijima	27:06N	142:12E		15 s	**0.36**	JMA
Hachijojima	33:07:36N	139:48:28E		30 s	0.094	JCG
Miyakejima	34:03N	139:33E		15 s	**0.22**	JMA
Kozushima	34:12:18N	139:08:12E		30 s	**0.23**	JCG
Soma	37:50N	140:58E		30 s	0.094	GSI
Katsuura	35:08N	140:15E		30 s	0.12	GSI
Mera	34:55N	139:50E		15 s	**0.28**	JMA
Boso 2 (OBTS)	34:44:57N	140:45:29E	2,098	1 s	0.0087	JMA
Boso 3 (OBTS)	34:47:58N	140:30:42E	1,912	1 s	0.012	JMA
Yokosuka	35:17:05N	139:39:17E		30 s	0.084	JCG
Aburatsubo	35:10N	139:37E		30 s	**0.25**	GSI
HPG1 (OBTS)	35:00:11N	139:13:29E	1,176	1 s	0.017	JAMS
Ito	34:53N	139:08E		30 s	0.043	GSI
Shimoda	34:41N	138:58E		0.5 s	0.30	NAW
Shimoda (WG)	34:38:48N	138:57:11E	51.1	0.5 s	0.12	NAW
Irozaki	34:37N	138:51E		15 s	0.092	JMA
Tago	34:48N	138:46E		30 s	0.035	GSI
Uchiura	35:01N	138:53E		15 s	0.098	JMA
Shimizuminato	35:01N	138:31E		15 s	0.044	JMA
Yaizu	34:52N	138:20E		30 s	0.13	GSI
Omaezaki (WG)	34:37:17N	138:15:33E	22.8	0.5 s	0.045	NAW
Tokai (OBTS)	33:45:54N	137:35:23E	2,202	1 s	0.013	JMA
Tonankai 1 (OBTS)	33:39:15N	136:50:26E	2,050	1 s	0.0079	JMA
Tonankai 2 (OBTS)	33:51:28N	137:21:34E	1,120	1 s	0.013	JMA
Tonankai 3 (OBTS)	34:13:02N	137:41:31E	1,103	1 s	0.0098	JMA
Maisaka	34:41N	137:37E		15 s	0.060	JMA
Owase	34:05N	136:12E		15 s	**0.20**	JMA
Kumano	33:56N	136:10E		15 s	**0.32**	JMA
Mie owase (GPS)	33:54:08N	136:15:34E	210	1 s	0.049	NAW
Uragami	33:34N	135:54E		15 s	**0.23**	JMA
Kushimoto	33:29N	135:46E		15 s	**0.43**	JMA
Shionomisaki (WG)	33:25:59N	135:44:50E	54.7	0.5 s	0.044	NAW
Shirahama	33:41N	135:23E		15 s	0.13	JMA
Gobo	33:51N	135:10E		15 s	**0.23**	JMA
Wakayama	34:13N	135:09E		15 s	0.067	JMA
Wakayama SW (GPS)	33:38:32N	135:09:24E	201	1 s	0.033	NAW
Komatsushima	34:01N	134:35E		15 s	0.097	JMA
Awayuki	33:46N	134:36E		15 s	**0.32**	JMA
Murotomisaki	33:16N	134:10E		15 s	**0.24**	JMA
MPG1 (OBTS)	32:23:27N	134:28:31E	2,308	1 s	0.0095	JAMS
MPG2 (OBTS)	32:38:35N	134:21:53E	1,507	1 s	0.013	JAMS
Kochi	33:30N	133:34E		15 s	0.12	JMA
Kochi (WG)	33:28:57N	133:35:13E	24.1	0.5 s	0.071	NAW
Susaki	33:23N	133:18E		0.5 s	**0.22**	NAW
Kure	33:20N	133:15E		30 s	0.16	GSI
Kamikawaguchi (WG)	33:01:54N	133:03:29E	27.9	0.5 s	0.10	NAW
Tosashimizu	32:47N	132:58E		15 s	**0.20**	JMA
Kochi W (GPS)	32:37:52N	133:09:21E	309	1 s	0.064	NAW
Hosojima	32:26N	131:40E		30 s	0.14	GSI
Hosojima (WG)	32:26:36N	131:43:42E	48.3	0.5 s	0.040	NAW

Table 1 *continued*

Station*	Latitude (deg:min:s)	Longitude (deg:min:s)	Water depth (m)	Record sampling	MTH (m)**	Agencies***
Aburatsu	31:35N	131:25E		15 s	**0.21**	JMA
Shibushi	31:29N	131:07E		0.5 s	0.16	NAW
Odomari	31:01:12N	130:41:29E		30 s	**0.26**	JCG
Nishinoomote	30:43:53N	130:59:40E		30 s	**0.21**	JCG
Tanegashima	30:28N	130:58E		15 s	**0.33**	JMA
Naze (WG)	28:27:07N	129:31:18E	54.6	0.5 s	0.031	NAW
Amami	28:19N	129:32E		15 s	**0.24**	JMA
Nakagusu	26:20N	127:50E		0.5 s	0.11	NAW
Nakagusu (WG)	26:14:32N	127:57:55E	39.6	0.5 s	0.052	NAW
Okinawa	26:11N	127:49E		30 s	0.10	GSI
Naha	26:13N	127:40E		15 s	0.085	JMA
Naha (WG)	26:15:28N	127:38:52E	51.0	0.5 s	0.033	NAW
Taira	24:49N	125:17E		0.5 s	0.11	NAW
Ishigaki	24:20N	124:10E		15 s	0.080	JMA
Ishigakioki (WG)	24:21:55N	124:06:10E	34.8	0.5 s	0.036	NAW
Yonaguni	24:27N	122:57E		15 s	0.037	JMA
Minamidaitojima	25:52N	131:14E		15 s	0.039	JMA

Values written in bold are from JMA (2009), the others are read in this study

WG wave gauge, *GPS* GPS buoy, *OBTS* ocean bottom tsunami sensor, *JMA* Japan Meteorological Agency, *UH* University of Hawaii, Sea Level Center, *BAKO* National Coordination Agency for Surveys and Mapping, Indonesia (BAKOSURTANAL), *JCG* Japan coastal guard, *GSI* Geographical Survey Institute, *NAW* Nationwide Ocean Wave information network for Ports and HArbourS (NOWPHAS), *JAMS* Japan Agency for Marine-Earth Science and Technology (JAMSTEC)

* Station names with the sensor types in parentheses. Tide gauges are listed without parentheses

** Maximum tsunami height (positive value of zero-to-peak of the observed tsunami waveform)

*** Agencies or networks which are responsible for the tsunami waveforms data

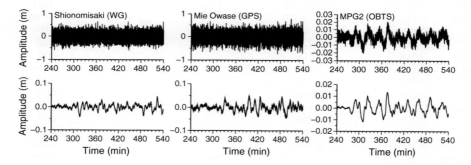

Figure 5
Tsunamis recorded on near-shore wave gauge (*left*), offshore GPS buoy (*middle*) and ocean bottom tsunami sensor (*right*). At each station (the locations are shown in Fig. 4a) the upper trace shows the de-tided records including short-period components, and the *bottom traces* are the tsunami signals by filtering out the short-period components

5 cm at the GPS buoys, and up to 1.5 cm at the OBTS, respectively. These differences of the tsunami amplitude are basically due to the differences in water depth at the observation point. The tide gauges are installed along coastal areas at depths of a few to several meters, wave gauges at depths of about 10 to 50 m, GPS buoys at depths of about 200 m, and OBTS at depths of about 1,000–4,000 m. The tsunami with maximum amplitude of 36 cm was observed at Chichijima located on Izu-Bonin ridge, which is comparable to that observed at Manokwari, the nearest tide gauge to the sources.

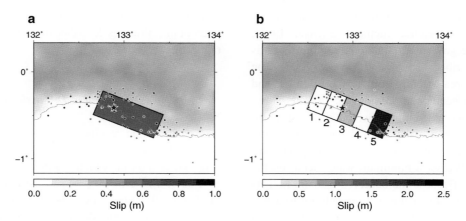

Figure 6

Slip distributions estimated by tsunami waveform inversions adopting different fault models (**a** single fault, **b** five subfaults) with subfault numbers. *Black star* shows the mainshock epicenter. *Circles in black* indicate aftershocks within about 3 h after the mainshock (before the second event). The second event and following aftershocks within 1 day after that event are also shown in *gray symbols*

3. Tsunami Modeling

3.1. Bathymetry Data

Since phase velocities of shallow-water (tsunami) waves depend on water depth, accurate bathymetric data are essential for tsunami numerical computations. For the global ocean, a gridded bathymetry dataset is available from GEBCO (British Oceanographic Data Centre, 1997). The GEBCO data was newly updated with 30 arc-second grid resolution (GEBCO_08). We use this bathymetry data for calculating tsunami waveforms or Green functions.

3.2. Fault Models

We first assume a single fault for the first event and estimate the average slip on the fault. Then, in order to estimate the extent of the tsunami source and its slip distribution, we divide the tsunami source into five subfaults to cover the area of aftershocks that occurred during 3 h after the first event but before the second event (Fig. 6). A fault model for the second event is not considered, because the tsunami from the second event overlapped with the later phases of the first event's tsunami, which made it difficult to distinguish the arrival of the second event's tsunami from the observed records.

We perform two sets of inversion to estimate the tsunami source using the single fault model and five-

Table 2

Slip distributions estimated by tsunami waveform inversions with different fault models

No.	Latitude (°S)	Longitude (°E)	Slip and error (m)	
			Single fault	Five subfaults
1	0.15	132.6	–	0.00 ± 0.14
2	0.21777	132.76661	0.64 ± 0.32	0.00 ± 0.00
3	0.28553	132.93323		0.70 ± 0.34
4	0.35330	133.09984		0.00 ± 0.17
5	0.42106	133.26597		2.07 ± 1.10

Location (latitude and longitude) indicates the northwest corner of each fault or subfault

subfault model. The size of the fault is 80 × 40 km for the single fault model. For the five subfault model, each subfault is 20 × 40 km (Fig. 6 and Table 2). The focal mechanism of strike 112°, dip 36°, slip angle 77°, from the USGS CMT solution of the first event, and the top depths of 10 km, are adopted for all the fault models. We assume an instantaneous rupture for the two fault models, because the tsunami propagation velocity is 0.1 km/s for the water depth of 1,000 m, much smaller than the typical rupture velocity of a few km/s. The epicenter is located between subfaults 2 and 3.

3.3. Finite-Difference Computation

In order to calculate tsunami propagation from each fault to the stations, the linear shallow-water, or long-wave, equations were numerically solved by using a finite-difference method (SATAKE, 1995). Details of the governing equations without Coriolis force are described in FUJII and SATAKE (2007). The computation area extends from 120°E to 155°E and 5°S to 45°N (rectangular area in Fig. 3a. The bathymetric grid interval is uniformly 30″ (30 arc-seconds, about 0.9 km), hence there are 4,200 × 6,000 grid points along the longitude and latitude directions, respectively. We set a minimum water depth on the coasts to 2 m. Because the observed tsunami heights of the West Papua tsunami were mostly up to a few tens of centimeters at the tide gauges, the small amplitude assumption in linear shallow-water long-wave equations is valid. We made the computations of 9 h for tsunami propagation. A time step of 1 s is used to satisfy the stability condition for the finite-difference method.

As an initial condition for the tsunami numerical computation, static deformation of the seafloor is calculated for a rectangular fault model (OKADA, 1985) and used assuming that the initial water height distribution is the same as that of seafloor. We also consider the effects of coseismic horizontal displacement in regions of steep bathymetric slope (TANIOKA and SATAKE, 1996). We assumed a constant rise time (or slip duration) of 30 s for the single fault model and each subfault. Waveforms at the observed stations were computed and used as Green functions for the inversion.

3.4. Tsunami Waveform Inversions

We used the non-negative least square method (LAWSON and HANSON, 1974) and delete-half jackknife method (TICHELAAR and RUFF, 1989) to estimate slips and errors, respectively. The observed tsunami waveforms were resampled at 1 min intervals, hence synthetic waveforms are also computed at 1 min interval. We used the first cycles of the tsunami waveforms for the inversions, because the limited resolution of bathymetry data near coastal tide gauges and near-shore wave gauges may prevent accurate modeling of later phases such as reflected waves. The total number of data points used for the inversions is 641. We weight the OBTS data ten times, GPS buoy data five times, and wave gauge data three times greater than the other tide gauge data, because the amplitudes

of near-shore or offshore records are smaller, by an order of magnitude as described in Sect.2, than those of tide gauge records.

4. Results and Discussions

The inversion results are shown in Table 2 and Fig. 6. The estimated slip on the single fault model (Fig. 6a) is 0.64 m, which yields a seismic moment of 1.02×10^{20} Nm ($M_w = 7.3$) assuming a rigidity of 5.0×10^{10} N/m^2. For the five-subfault model (Fig. 6b), a moderate slip of 0.70 m was estimated near the epicenter (subfault 3) and a large slip of 2.07 m was located on the eastern end of the source (subfault 5). The amount of largest slips at the eastern end of the source region in the five-subfault models may not be well resolved because of the large error (1.10 m; see Table 2). The total seismic moment is calculated as 1.11×10^{20} Nm ($M_w = 7.3$) for the five-subfault model, assuming the same rigidities of 5.0×10^{10} N/m^2 for all the subfaults. Regardless of the fault models, the estimated moment magnitude is smaller than that inferred from seismic data (cf. $M_w = 7.6$ from USGS CMT solution). Before the inversions, we performed a forward modeling referring the source model of $M_w = 7.6$ and found that the first-wave amplitudes of synthetic waveforms at some stations of OBTS (off Tokai, Tonankai and Shikoku) were overestimated for the observed amplitudes. Since the Green functions of such OBTS installed in deep sea, which were used for the inversions, must be calculated more accurately than the ones of tide gauges or wave gauges located near coasts, the moment magnitude of 7.6 might be slightly overestimated for the tsunami generation. The source process of the 2009 West Papua earthquake has been inferred from teleseismic body waves by HAYES (2009) and POIATA et al. (2010). Their results show a single asperity around the epicenter. The large slip on subfault 3 in the five-subfault model may correspond to their single asperities.

Comparison of the observed tsunami waveforms and the synthetic ones from the single fault model is shown in Fig. 7. The calculated tsunami waveforms from the five-subfault model are not shown, because the differences in synthetic waveforms from the two

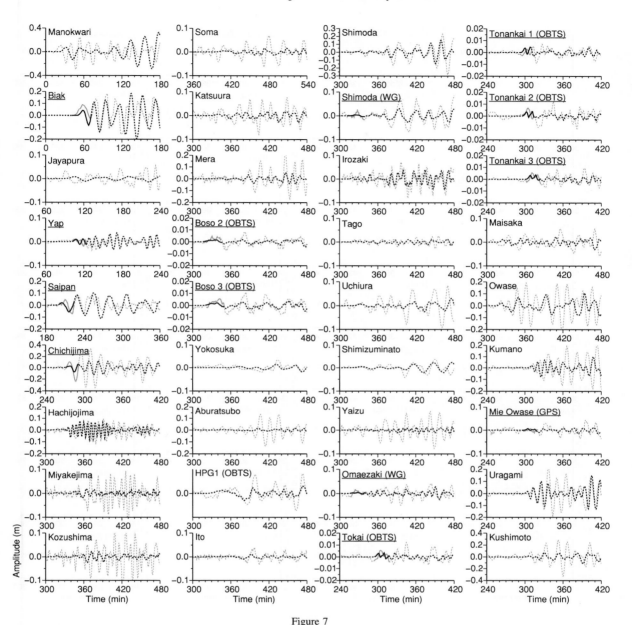

Figure 7

a Comparisons of the observed (*gray lines*) and synthetic (*black lines*) tsunami waveforms computed from the estimated slip by adopting the single model. Time ranges shown by solid curves are used for the inversions; the dashed parts are not used for the inversions, but shown for comparison. Out of 36 waveforms shown here, we used parts of 13 records (*underlined stations*) for the inversions. **b** (cont'd) Out of 36 waveforms shown here, we used parts of 13 records (*underlined stations*) for the inversions. (Submitted January 3, 2010, Revised June 15, 2010, Accepted July 1, 2010)

fault models are much smaller than the differences between the observed and synthetic waveforms. We used most of the observed tsunami waveforms at wave gauges, GPS buoys, and OBTS around Japan for the inversions. On the other hand, we used the observed tsunami waveforms at five tide gauges on

the small islands (Biak, Yap, Saipan, Chichijima, Minamidaitojima) which are located on the tsunami's way from the source to the offshore or near-shore stations of the Japanese main islands. Some stations' data were not used for the inversions, because the first arrivals of the observed waveforms do not match the

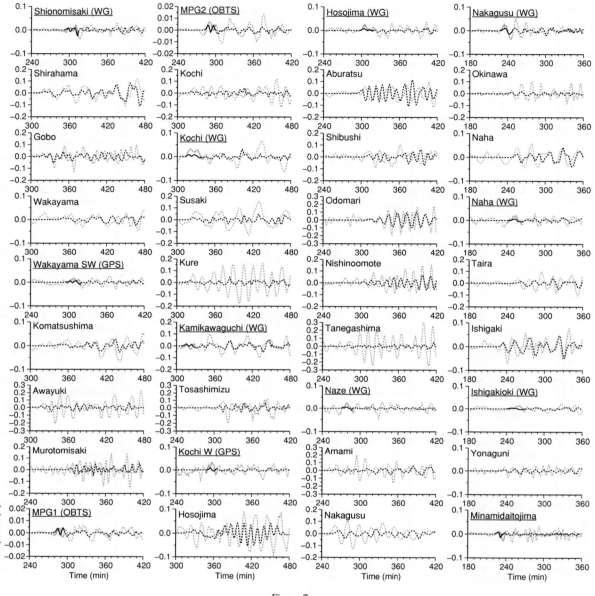

Figure 7
continued

synthetic ones (e.g. Manokwari, Jayapura, HPG1 (OBTS)), although the tide gauges are located close to the source. The synthetic waveforms generally agree with the observed phases at most stations, however, the calculated tsunami amplitudes are consistently underestimated. At some stations (e.g. Biak, Saipan, Shimoda (WG)), the synthetic waveforms are well reproduced not only for the first cycles of tsunami waveforms (inversion time windows) but also for the later phases which were not used in the inversions. It is difficult to judge which of the single fault and five-subfault model is the best model, because the differences of the synthetic waveforms among the both fault models are very small. This may indicate the limitation due to the poor station coverage to resolve the extent of the tsunami source; in this case we mainly used far field data located in the direction perpendicular to the fault strike.

5. Conclusions

The tsunamis generated by the January 2009 West Papua, Indonesia earthquakes were recorded not only at many coastal tide gauges located in and around the Pacific Ocean but also at near-shore wave gauges, off-shore GPS buoys and OBTS off the Japanese coasts. Using the observed tsunami waveforms, we modeled the tsunami from the first event to estimate the tsunami source and found that the tsunami data observed at tide gauges, wave gauges, GPS buoys and OBTS were well reproduced. The recently updated bathymetry data of GEBCO_08, 30 arc-second grid data was used in the tsunami simulations. The average slip of 0.64 m was estimated on the single fault of 80×40 km. The calculated seismic moment is 1.01×10^{20} Nm ($M_w = 7.3$), slightly less than the magnitude inferred from seismic data ($M_w = 7.7$).

Acknowledgments

We thank the National Coordination Agency for Surveys and Mapping (BAKOSURTANAL), Japan Coastal Guard (JCG), Geographical Survey Institute (GSI), and West Coast/Alaska Tsunami Warning Center (WCATWC) for providing us tide gauge data. We also thank Ports and Harbors Bureau (PHB) under the Ministry of Land, Infrastructure, Transport and Tourism (MLIT) and Port and Airport Research Institute (PARI) for providing us with tide gauge, wave gauge and GPS buoy data. The data of ocean bottom tsunami sensors of the Japan Agency for Marine-Earth Science and Technology (JAMSTEC) were downloaded from their web site. We thank Efim Pelinovsky and an anonymous reviewer for their valuable comments which have improved our manuscript. Most of the figures were generated using the Generic Mapping Tools (WESSEL AND SMITH, 1998).

This research was partially supported by Grants-in-Aid for Scientific Research (B) (No. 21310113), Ministry of Education, Culture, Sports, Science and Technology (MEXT), and Science and Technology Research Partnership for Sustainable Development (SATREPS) from Japan Science and Technology Agency (JST), Japan International Cooperation Agency (JICA), State Ministry of Research and Technology of Indonesia (RISTEK) and Indonesian Institute of Science (LIPI).

REFERENCES

British Oceanographic Data Centre (1997). The centenary edition of the GEBCO digital atlas (CD-ROM).

FUJII, Y., and SATAKE, K. (2007). Tsunami source of the 2004 Sumatra–Andaman earthquake inferred from tide gauge and satellite data, *Bull. Seism. Soc. Am.*, *97*, S192–S207.

HAYES, G. (2009). Preliminary result of the Jan 3, 2009 M_w 7.6 Papua Earthquake, http://earthquake.usgs.gov/eqcenter/eqinthenews/2009/us2009bjbn/finite_fault.php.

JMA (2002). Monthly report on earthquakes and volcanoes in Japan, September, 2002 (in Japanese).

JMA (2009). Monthly report on earthquakes and volcanoes in Japan, January, 2009 (in Japanese).

LAWSON, C. L., and HANSON, R. J. (1974). *Solving least squares problems*, 340 pp., Prentice-Hall, Inc., Englewood Cliffs, NJ.

MUHARI, A., KISMAN, M., WANMA, B., and WANMA, F. (2009). The 'Doublet' earthquake at Papua, Indonesia January 3rd, 2009, *Survey Report and Preliminary Model Analysis, Sub Directorate for Coastal Disaster Mitigation Ministry of Marine Affairs and Fisheries*.

OKADA, Y. (1985). Surface deformation due to shear and tensile faults in a half-space, *Bull. Seismol. Soc. Am.*, *75*, 1135–1154.

OKAL, E. A. (1999). Historical seismicity and seismotectonic context of the great 1979 Yapen and 1996 Biak, Irian Jaya earthquakes, *Pure. Appl. Geophys.*, *154*, 633–675.

POIATA, N., KOKETSU, K., and MIYAKE, H. (2010). Source processes of the 2009 Irian Jaya, Indonesia, earthquake doublet, *Earth Planets Space*, *62*, 475–481.

SATAKE, K. (1995). Linear and nonlinear computations of the 1992 Nicaragua earthquake tsunami, *Pure. Appl. Geophys.*, *144*, 455–470.

SATAKE, K., and KANAMORI, H. (1991). Abnormal tsunamis caused by the June 13, 1984, Torishima, Japan, earthquake, *J. Geophys. Res. Solid Earth*, *96*, 19933–19939.

SATAKE, K., YOSHIDA, Y., and ABE, K. (1992). Tsunami from the Mariana earthquake of April 5, 1990–Its abnormal propagation and implications for tsunami potential from outer-rise earthquakes, *Geophys. Res. Lett.*, *19*, 301–304.

Tanioka, Y., and Satake, K. (1996). Tsunami generation by horizontal displacement of ocean bottom, *Geophys. Res. Lett.*, *23*, 861–864.

Tichelaar, B. W., and Ruff, L. J. (1989). How good are our best models? Jackknifing, bootstrapping, and earthquake depth, *Eos Trans. AGU*, *70*, 593, 605–606.

Wessel, P., and Smith, W. H. F. (1998). New, improved version of the generic mapping tools released, *EOS Trans. AGU*, *79*, 579.

(Received January 3, 2010, revised June 15, 2010, accepted July 1, 2010, Published online December 14, 2010)

Pure Appl. Geophys. 168 (2011), 1101–1112
© 2011 Springer Basel AG
DOI 10.1007/s00024-010-0222-x

Synthesis of a Tsunami Spectrum in a Semi-Enclosed Basin Using Its Background Spectrum

Kuniaki Abe[1]

Abstract—We explained spectra of distant tsunamis observed in enclosed basins by applying the synthesis method based on joint analysis of tsunami and background spectra from a number of stations. This method is the generalization of the method proposed by Rabinovich (J. Geopys. Res. 102, 12663-12676, 1997) to separate source and topography effects in recorded tsunami waves. The source function is extracted by inversion of the tsunami/ background spectra averaged from many observational sites. The method is applied to the 2009 Papua tsunami observed at the Owase tide station in southwest Japan, a region with complicated topography and numerous bays and inlets. The synthesized spectrum explains the observed spectral amplitudes for each frequency component. It is shown that averaging of tsunami and background from various tide gauge stations in semi-enclosed basins is an efficient approach to extract the source function.

Key words: 2009 Papua tsunami, tide gauge records, synthesis of tsunami spectra, background oscillations, semi-enclosed basin, linear response.

1. Introduction

Tsunamis are ocean waves arising from vertical displacement of the sea bottom, which is mainly caused by fault ruptures associated with submarine earthquakes. A driven vertical displacement over a wide area generates a long wave. Such waves can propagate over long distances with little decrease in amplitude. Since the fault horizontal extension is finite, the generated wave normally has a wavelength matching this length. The corresponding period is related to the time for the wave to cross the source area. Yamashita and Sato (1974) suggested an analytical expression for · tsunami frequency spectra. According to this expression, the tsunami has a broadband spectrum with a peak value associated with the fault length or width and wave speed, c, determined by the water depth H in the source area, $c = \sqrt{gH}$, where g is the acceleration of gravity. The wide spectral range suggests the possibility that the tsunami resonates within bays in a wide range of periods.

Tsunami waves arriving from the open ocean are observed at tide gauge stations. The superposition of reflected and incident waves, as well as the shoaling effect, cause significant amplification of tsunami waves at the coast. The reflected waves, being trapped in semi-enclosed basins such as bays or harbors, produce seiche oscillations. This is the origin of local eigen-oscillations excited by tsunamis. Takahashi and Aida (1963) showed that particular periods at each station dominate the observed spectra for various tsunamis. Following this study, Miller (1972) proposed an idea of the universal tide gauge response to different tsunamis. Recently, Rabinovich (1997), using linear response theory, developed this idea and suggested that source and topography effects can be separated in the observed tsunami spectra. To estimate the tsunami source function, he used recorded tsunami oscillations and background oscillations observed at the station before tsunami arrival. Afterwards, Rabinovich *et al.* (1998, 2004, 2006, 2008) and Vich and Monserrat (2009) successfully used this method to isolate source functions for various tsunami events. A similar idea was also used by Monserrat *et al.* (1998) to estimate the source function for atmospherically generated seiches. Abe (2005a) indicated for tsunami research that it is important to study ordinary background oscillations in semi-enclosed basins, and examined such oscillations at many bays and harbors in northeast Japan. Then, he explained tsunami amplification in terms of bay resonances on respective dominant modes. Since

---

[1] Junior College at Niigata, Nippon Dental University, Hamauracho 1-8, Chuouku, Niigata 951-8580, Japan. E-mail: abeku@ngt.ndu.ac.jp

the amplitudes are larger at the heads of bays and harbors, he estimated mode amplitudes specifically at these locations. The observed spectra depend mainly on local topographic properties and are almost uniform in time. In the case of tide stations located near bay heads, it is possible to use them to estimate the transfer functions of the corresponding bays. The effectiveness of this "synthesis" method can be examined by applying it to distant tsunamis simultaneously recorded at tide gauge stations in various bays, because tsunami oscillations recorded at numerous tide stations would be excited by almost the same incident wave. As an example, the 2009 Papua tsunami is used in the present study to demonstrate the effectiveness of this approach.

2. The 2009 Papua Tsunami

The 2009 Papua tsunami was generated near the northern coast of West Papua, Indonesia, on 3 January 2009 at 19:44 (UTC). The earthquake, $M_w = 7.6$ (USGS), had focal depth of 17 km. Within about 5 h after the main shock, the tsunami reached southwest Japan and was observed at numerous tide gauge stations facing the Pacific Ocean (Fig. 1). We selected 13 coastal tide gauge stations with best quality records to examine tsunami properties. An open-ocean station PG1 located off the Murotomisaki tide gauge station was used to evaluate specific effects of the synthesis method; the tsunami dominant period observed at this station was compared with the period obtained from the inversion of the source function computed from coastal tide gauges. The pressure gauge PG1 was installed by the Japan Agency for Marine-Earth Science and Technology (JAMSTEC) at depth of 2,308 m at location with coordinates 32.3907°N and 134.4753°E (Fig. 1). The following tide gauges were used for the inversion method: Shimoda ($n = 1$), Omaezaki ($n = 2$), Kumano ($n = 3$), Uragami ($n = 4$), Kushimoto ($n = 5$), Awayuki ($n = 6$), Murotomisaki ($n = 7$), Susaki ($n = 8$), Kure ($n = 9$), Tosashimizu ($n = 10$), Hosojima ($n = 11$), Miyazaki ($n = 12$), and Aburatsu ($n = 13$). The tide gauge station used for the synthesis was located at Owase ($k = 1$).

It is well known that each tide gauge with a well and a connecting pipe has specific response characteristics. To estimate real sea level oscillations, in particular amplitude correction and recovery time, we used the method of SATAKE et al. (1988). If we could not estimate the recovery time, we assumed this time to be $t_r = 269$ s (based on results of ABE, 2003). After the correction, the sea levels at tide gauge stations were restored with 1-min sampling interval for 6-h segments starting 1 h before tsunami arrival. The waveforms are shown in Fig. 2. Spectra for these waveforms were calculated by the Goertzel method with 6-h Hanning window, then the spectra were smoothed by averaging of five points, similarly as was done by ABE (2005a). The 14 spectra including the spectrum at Owase tide station are shown in Fig. 3a, b.

3. Dominant Periods of Background Spectra

The background spectra are the spectra of ordinary sea level oscillations observed in the absence of major events such as tsunamis. These spectra were estimated by ABE (2005b, 2006, 2009) for the same basins where tide gauges that recorded the 2009 tsunami were located. The original data were 6-h sea level oscillations with sampling interval of 1 min recorded by pressure gauges at the heads of the respective bays and harbors. The background spectra were calculated in the same manner as the tsunami spectra; both types of spectra are shown in Fig. 3. The observational sites for both tide gauges and temporal pressure gauges are shown in Fig. 4. At all sites except four, the pressure gauges were located at distances of less than 0.5 km from the tide gauges.

Based on particular spectral features shown in Fig. 3 we were able to classify all spectra into three representative types associated with different types of bays or harbors: (1) narrow, long inlets, such as Uragami and Susaki, having similar structure of tsunami and background spectra with less short-period components; (2) wide and moderately long bays, such as Owase, Kushimoto, and Awayuki, which indicted blue-shift of the dominant tidal peak relative to the background peak (i.e., shift to shorter periods); and (3) harbors surrounded by breakwaters, such as

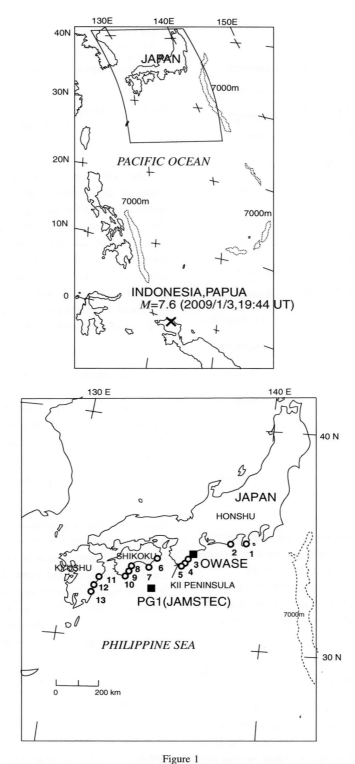

Figure 1
Location of the epicenter of the 2009 Papua Earthquake (*cross*), the pressure gauge PG1, and Owase tide station (*solid rectangles*) and the tide stations used for averaging (*open circles*)

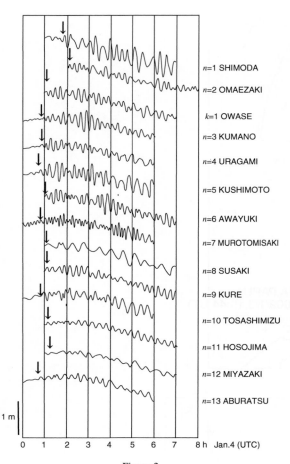

Figure 3 ▶
Power spectra of the 2009 Papua tsunami observed at tide stations (*solid line*) and background oscillations observed at the coast nearest to the tide stations (*dotted line*). The solid triangles given for the background oscillations indicate the most dominant periods

Figure 2
Time histories of the 2009 Papua tsunami used in the spectral analysis. *Arrows* indicate arrival times

fundamental bay mode, T_f, corresponds to two round-trips between the head and mouth, we have

$$T_f = 4t. \tag{2}$$

The periods estimated by Eq. 2 were found to be close to the dominant periods of the background spectra, as shown in Fig. 6. However, they differ from the observed dominant periods for bays with double-mouth structures; for example, Hosojima Bay has a neck inside the bay, as shown in Fig. 5. As a result, the nodal line shifts from the mouth to the neck. Except such specific cases, the bays have dominant observed periods approximately equivalent to those of the fundamental mode (Fig. 6).

4. Method of Inversion and Synthesis

In the framework of the linear theory, a tsunami spectrum $Y_{t,n}(f)$ observed at the nth coastal tide gauge station as a function of frequency f may be represented as

$$Y_{t,n}(f) = W_n(f)X_t(f), \tag{3}$$

where $W_n(f) = \phi_n^2(f)$, $\phi_n(f)$ is the transfer function describing the topographic transformation of the wave approaching the coast, and $X_t(f)$ is the tsunami source spectrum, which is assumed to be the same for all stations. In the present case, we can assume that the tsunami source spectrum is the spectrum of tsunami waves on the boundary between the continental slope and the deep-sea area. Similarly, the background spectrum $Y_{s,n}(f)$ at the nth coastal station is

$$Y_{s,n}(f) = W_n(f)X_s(f), \tag{4}$$

where $X_s(f)$ is the background open-sea spectrum. The transfer function, $\phi_n(f) = \sqrt{W_n(f)}$, is assumed to be the same for both the tsunami and background spectra, but to be different for each station (cf. Rabinovich, 1997). Individual coastal stations ($n = 1$,

Omaezaki and Murotomisaki, which demonstrated significant amplification of short-period components in both the tsunami and background spectra.

The propagation time of the long wave, t, from the mouth to the head in each bay and harbor was estimated assuming stepwise sea depth variations (Fig. 5):

$$t = \sum_i^n \frac{\Delta x}{\sqrt{gh_i}}, \tag{1}$$

where $\Delta x = 0.5$ km is the grid interval of the wave propagation track and h_i is the mean sea depth at the ith grid step. Multiple reflections between the head and mouth synchronized to the incident waves and formed standing waves. Since the period of the

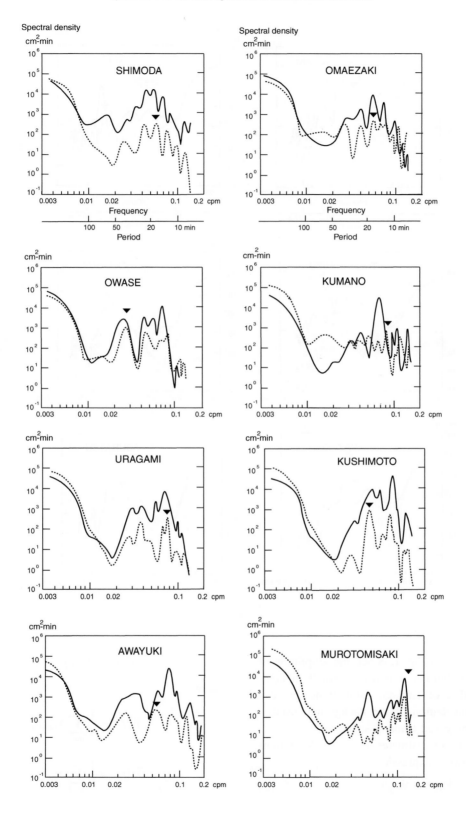

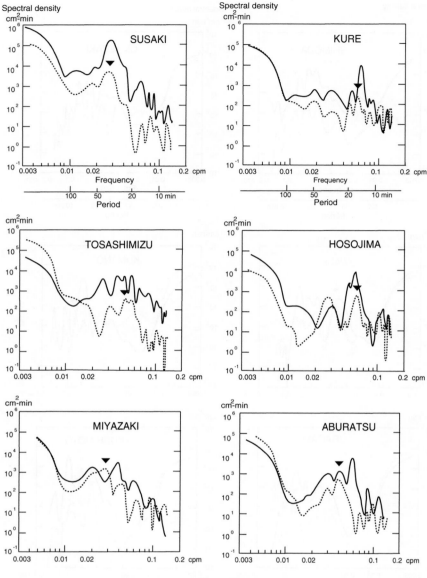

Figure 3
continued

..., N) are shown in Fig. 1. Since the amplitude of background oscillations is normally small in comparison with that of tsunami oscillations, we can neglect the contribution of the background oscillations into the observed tsunami spectrum.

Averaging these estimates over all N stations yields the following expressions:

$$\overline{Y_t}(f) = \overline{W}(f)X_t(f), \tag{5}$$

$$\overline{Y_s}(f) = \overline{W}(f)X_s(f), \tag{6}$$

where

$$\overline{Y_t}(f) = \frac{1}{N}\sum_{n=1}^{N} Y_{t,n}(f), \tag{7}$$

$$\overline{Y_s}(f) = \frac{1}{N}\sum_{n=1}^{N} Y_{s,n}(f), \tag{8}$$

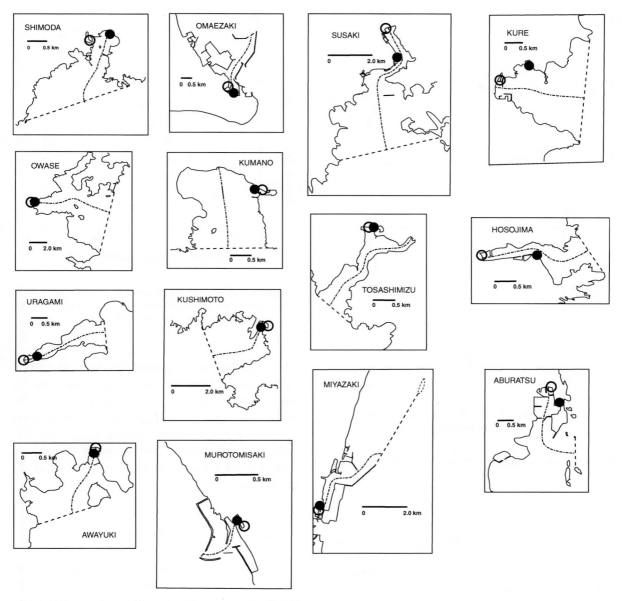

Figure 4
Location of the tide stations (*solid circles*) and points observing the background (*open circles*). The *dotted lines* are the assumed *base lines* corresponding to the bay mouths. The *dash-dotted lines* are the propagation paths used for the travel time

$$\overline{W}(f) = \frac{1}{N} \sum_{n=1}^{N} W_n(f). \qquad (9)$$

Eliminating $\overline{W}(f)$ from 5 and 6, we obtain

$$S(f) = \frac{X_t(f)}{X_s(f)} = \frac{\overline{Y}_t(f)}{\overline{Y}_s(f)}. \qquad (10)$$

Thus, using the observed tsunami and background spectra averaged over N stations, we obtain the relative source spectrum $S(f)$. This method enables us to estimate the relative tsunami source spectrum for the waves arriving at the continental slope from the source region.

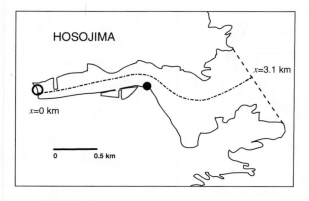

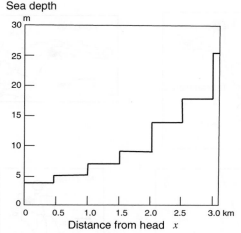

Figure 5
Map of Hosojima Bay and the profile of the sea depth applied to the propagation path

5. Synthesis

Based on the relative source spectrum, we can synthesize the expected tsunami spectrum at any given coastal station. For the kth station, we replace n in Eqs. 3 and 4 with k, so that

$$Y_{t,k}(f) = \frac{X_t(f)}{X_s(f)} Y_{s,k}(f). \tag{11}$$

This means that the transfer function $\phi_k(f)$ is replaced by $[Y_{s,k}(f)/X_s(f)]^{1/2}$. The kth station is an independent station not included in the first N stations. Finally, we obtain an expression for the synthesized spectrum at the kth station by substituting $X_t(f)/X_s(f)$ from 10 into 11:

$$Y_{t,k}(f) = Y_{s,k}(f)\frac{\overline{Y}_t(f)}{\overline{Y}_s(f)}, \tag{12}$$

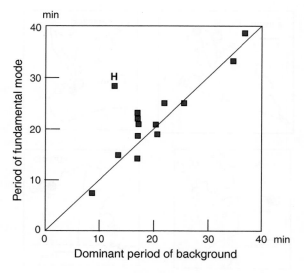

Figure 6
Correlation between a dominant period of the background oscillation and a period of fundamental mode for each bay or harbor. *H* indicates the case of Hosojima

where $Y_{s,k}(f)$ is the background spectrum estimated at the kth station. Thus, the tsunami spectrum at the kth tide station $Y_{t,k}(f)$ is derived as the product of the relative spectrum, $\overline{Y}_t(f)/\overline{Y}_s(f)$, and the background spectrum at the kth coastal station, $Y_{s,k}(f)$. This formula does not include any unknown factors and enables us to estimate the tsunami spectrum at the specific site.

6. Results

The mean tsunami and background spectra were obtained by averaging the respective individual spectra at 13 coastal stations (Fig. 7). The mean tsunami spectrum has a dominant period of 17 min ($f = 0.059$ cpm), while the mean background spectrum has a peak period at 36 min ($f = 0.028$ cpm); at shorter periods the background spectral energy decreases gradually with frequency. Following expression 12, the tsunami spectra at each station were estimated and compared with the observed spectra. An unexpected shape of the mean background spectrum resulted from the averaging of individual spectra at each site that suppressed peculiar peaks associated with local seiche oscillations.

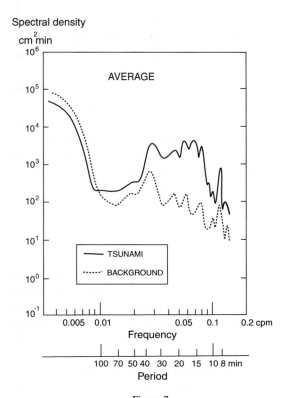

Figure 7

Spectra averaged for tide stations in the 2009 Papua tsunami and points observing the background oscillations except for the case of Owase

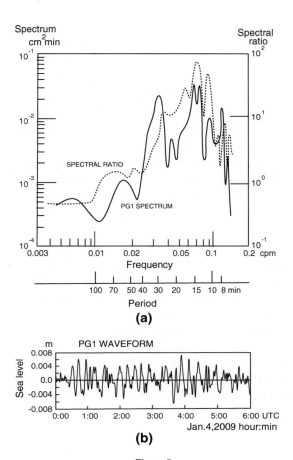

Figure 8

a Spectral ratio of the averaged tsunami spectrum to the averaged background spectrum (*dotted line*) and spectrum of PG1 (*solid line*). **b** The waveform observed by the PG1 pressure gauge

By calculating ratio 10 we obtained the relative source spectrum (Fig. 8a). In comparison with the mean tsunami spectrum (Fig. 7), the prevailing period in the relative spectrum shifted from 17 min to 15 min, while the peak with period of 33 min almost disappeared. These results were compared with the spectrum at the PG1 open-ocean station (Fig. 8b). The 6-h PG1 record with 1-min sampling beginning at 00:00 (UTC) of 4 January 2009 was low-pass filtered (Fig. 8b); the PG1 spectrum was constructed in the same way as for the coastal stations (see ABE, 2005a).

It is seen that the dominant period (15 min) of the inverted spectrum is also observed in the open-ocean spectrum of PG1 (Fig. 8a). This fact suggests this period is related to the tsunami source properties. The spectral component of 33 min (0.03 cpm) was also observed at PG1 station and even had a larger amplitude. The waves reflected from the continental shelf affect the PG1 spectrum, apparently being responsible for this component. The dominant oscillations at PG1 appear to be produced by the multiple reflections of waves on the shelf. The relative source spectrum in Fig. 8a is nondimensional, while the deep-sea PG1 spectrum has dimension of power density. As indicated by expression 10, $S(f)$ is not the spectrum of incident tsunami waves, $X_t(f)$, but the ratio of incident waves and background oscillations $S(f) = X_t(f)/X_s(f)$. However, $X_s(f)$ has a frequency dependence of f^{-2}. This means that the estimated relative spectrum $S(f)$ is the modulation of $X_t(f)$ by f^2. This is the reason why the respective peak in the $S(f)$ spectrum is attenuated, while in the spectrum of $X_t(f)$ it is evident. Therefore, we may conclude that the main properties of the arriving tsunami waves are reproduced in the relative spectrum.

Then, we applied the relative spectrum to the Owase tide station ($k = 1$) and synthesized the tsunami spectrum according to expression 12. To estimate the background spectrum at Owase, we used sea level oscillations observed in the neighborhood of the tide gauge station by ABE (2005b). The vicinity of Owase and locations of the observational sites are shown in Fig. 4a. The observed tsunami and background spectra at Owase are shown in Fig. 3. Figure 9 presents the synthesized and observed tsunami spectra, which are in good agreement. The general spectral structure of high-frequency components, 0.04–0.09 cpm (11–25 min), are particularly well reproduced by the synthesized spectrum. The tsunami spectrum observed at Owase had not been used to estimate the source spectrum of the tsunami waves arriving at the continental shelf. Accordingly, we can check the validity of the synthesis by comparing the observed and synthesized spectra. Thus, the two spectra in Fig. 9 are independent and their matching indicates the validity of the synthesis. Using the same source function and the respective background spectrum, we can synthesize the tsunami

spectrum for any other tide gauge station shown in Fig. 1. In this way we synthesized tsunami spectra for Awayuki and Tosashimizu stations. The agreement with the observed spectra is reasonable but not as good as for Owase. For both Awayuki and Tosashimizu stations the dominant tsunami periods were explained, but long-period components remained unexplained; for example, there is a defect in explanation of 36-min component at Tosashimizu attributed to the defect of this component in the background spectrum, as shown in Fig. 3.

7. Discussion

RABINOVICH (1997) assumed that the topographic transfer function is constructed by three independent components associated with: (1) open-ocean transmission, (2) continental shelf, and (3) bay/harbor resonance. In this study, we do not start from the tsunami source but from the deep sea and integrate the effects of the two latter components. Therefore, our transfer function expresses a unified effect of the continental shelf and bay/harbor. The effect of the continental shelf appears to be responsible for the spectral peak of 33 min observed in both the mean background and mean tsunami spectra (averaged over 13 observational sites). This observed period almost coincides with the theoretical resonance period of the continental shelf resonance (32 min) derived using Merian's formula for shelf width of 15 km and uniform depth of 100 m. Such a one-step model is a good approximation of the continental shelf off Kii Peninsula, Honshu Island, Japan. Generally speaking, the continental shelf in southwestern Japan, including the Kii Peninsula, is narrow. That is why the fundamental resonant period of the shelf is comparatively small. Because this 33-min peak is common to both the tsunami and background spectra, and related to the resonant influence of topography, it is absent in the relative source spectrum (Fig. 8a), which is related to the source properties.

ALLEN and GREENSLADE (2009) determined the topographic admittance function for the spectra observed at coastal tide gauge stations as an amplification indicator of arriving waves. The resulting function is similar to our transfer function. They

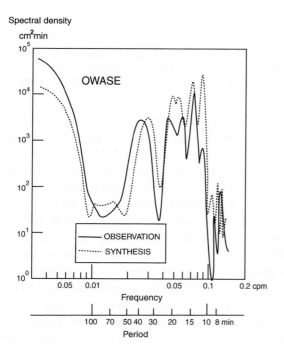

Figure 9
Spectra of the 2009 Papua tsunami observed and synthesized at Owase Bay

obtained the frequency dependence as inversely proportional to the square of the frequency. This means that $X_s(f)$ is proportional to f^{-2}. Their result was obtained based on a 3-month observational series. Our background spectra were estimated from time series of only 6 h. Therefore, it is difficult to discriminate some universal properties from our background spectra. For this reason, we left the frequency dependence as unknown, but it should be noted that this unknown parameter does not affect the synthesis results.

Finally, in regard to the background spectra, we used only those estimated by Abe (2005b, 2006, 2009). The background spectra are not deterministic but probabilistic. Our result is extracted from a single observation and is shown without weighting. However, it is considered that the reproducibility is partly expressed in the spectral amplitude, because the amplitude is a result of frequent appearance of a particular period or frequency during a limited time. For example, a dominant period of 36 min as seen in the background of Susaki Bay is expected to be observed in a high probability from the amplitude and the isolated appearance.

8. Conclusions

This study proposed a method of synthesizing spectra of distant tsunamis observed in a semi-enclosed basin. This method was applied to the 2009 Papua tsunami observed in southwest Japan, and to synthesize a tsunami spectrum for Owase Bay. The results proved that this approach works well and that the reconstructed synthesized spectrum is a good approximation of the observed tsunami spectrum at Owase tide station. Based on tsunami and background observations at 13 coastal tide gauge stations located in the vicinity of Owase, the relative tsunami source spectrum was constructed. This source spectrum was compared with the open-ocean spectrum from PG1 deep-sea station and found to be in reasonable agreement.

Topographic transfer functions extracted from background spectra at selected sites were found to approximate well the fundamental modes of the respective bays, except double-necked bays.

Acknowledgments

The author is grateful to Dr. Baba for preparing the deep-sea record PG1 and to the Japan Meteorological Agency, Geographical Survey Institute, and Chubu Regional Bureau of Japan for providing the tide gauge records.

References

ABE, K. (2003), *Source model of a small tsunami accompanying a volcanic earthquake at Kouzu-shima on July 1, 2000*, Zisin 2 (56), 181–187 (in Japanese).

ABE, K. (2005a), *Tsunami resonance curve on dominant periods observed at bays*. In: SATAKE K. (Ed.), *Tsunamis: case studies and recent developments*, Springer Publishing, Dordrecht, The Netherlands, 97–113.

ABE, K. (2005b), *Observations of dominant periods in bays on the Kii Peninsula and the tsunami response*, Zisin 2 (58), 83–89 (in Japanese).

ABE, K. (2006), *Resonance curve of the 1946 Nankai Tsunami on the Pacific coast of Shikoku district*. Zisin 2 (59), 39–48 (in Japanese).

ABE, K. (2009), *Spectra of seiches observed at Kanto and Tokai Coastal Districts and the dominant periods*. Report of Disaster Control Research Center, Tohoku University, 26, 17–26 (in Japanese).

ALLEN, S.C.R., and GREENSLADE, D.J.M. (2009), *A spectral climatology of Australian and South-West Pacific tide gauges*, CAWCR Technical Report No.011, 1–52.

MILLER, G.R. (1972), *Relative spectra of tsunami*. Hawaii Inst. Geophys., Univ. Hawaii, 72(8), 1–6.

MONSERRAT, S., RABINOVICH, A.B., and CASAS, B. (1998), *On the reconstruction of the transfer function for atmospherically generated seiches*, Geophys. Res. Lett. 12, 2197–2200.

RABINOVICH, A.B. (1997), *Spectral analysis of tsunami waves: Separation of source and topography effects*, J. Geopys. Res. 102, 12663–12676.

RABINOVICH, A.B., and STEPHENSON, F.E. (2004), *Longwave measurements for the coast of British Colombia and improvements to the tsunami warning capability*, Nat. Hazards 32, 313–343.

RABINOVICH, A.B., STEPHENSON F.E., and THOMSON, R.E. (2006), *The California tsunami of 15 June 2005 along the coast of North America*, Atmosphere-Ocean 44, 415–427.

RABINOVICH, A.B., MIRANDA, P., and BAPTISTA, M.A. (1998), *Analysis of the 1969 and 1975 Tsunamis at the Atlantic coast of Portugal and Spain*, Oceanology, 38, 463–469.

RABINOVICH, A.B., THOMSON, R.E., TITOV, V.V., STEPHENSON, F.E., and ROGERS, G.C. (2008), *Locally generated tsunamis recorded on the coast of British Colombia*, Atmosphere-Ocean 46, 343–360.

SATAKE, K., OKADA, M., and ABE, K. (1988), *Tide gauge response to tsunamis: Measurements at 40 tide stations in Japan*. J. Mar. Res. 46, 557–571.

TAKAHASHI, R., and AIDA, I. (1963), *Spectra of several tsunamis observed on the coast of Japan*. Bull. Earthq. Res. Inst., Tokyo Univ. 41, 299–314 (in Japanese).

Reprinted from the journal

VICH, M., and MONSERRAT, S. (2009), *The source spectrum for the Algerian tsunami of 21 May 2003 estimated from coastal tide gauge data*, Geophys. Res. Lett. 36, L20610.

YAMASHITA, T., and SATO, R. (1974), *Generation of tsunami by fault model*, J. Phys. Earth 22, 415–440.

(Received November 11, 2009, revised May 31, 2010, accepted June 26, 2010, Published online March 17, 2011)

Pure Appl. Geophys. 168 (2011), 1113–1123
© 2010 Springer Basel AG
DOI 10.1007/s00024-010-0221-y

The 29 September 2009 Samoa Islands Tsunami: Simulations Based on the First Focal Mechanism Solutions and Implications on Tsunami Early Warning Strategies

Roberto Tonini,[1] Alberto Armigliato,[1] and Stefano Tinti[1]

Abstract—The tsunamigenic earthquake (Mw = 8.1) that occurred on 29 September 2009 at 17:48 UTC offshore of the Samoa archipelago east of the Tonga trench represents an example of the so-called "outer-rise" earthquakes. The areas most affected were the south coasts of Western and American Samoa, where almost 200 people were killed and run-up heights were measured in excess of 5 m at several locations along the coast. Moreover, tide gauge records showed a maximum peak-to-peak height of about 3.5 m near Pago Pago (American Samoa) and of 1.5 m offshore of Apia (Western Samoa). In this work, different fault models based on the focal mechanism solutions proposed by Global CMT and by USGS immediately after the 2009 Samoan earthquake are tested by comparing the near-field recorded signals (three offshore DART buoys and two coastal tide gauges) and the synthetic signals provided by the numerical simulations. The analysis points out that there are lights and shadows, in the sense that none of the computed tsunamis agrees satisfactorily with all the considered signals, although some of them reproduce some of the records quite well. This "partial agreement" and "partial disagreement" are analysed in the perspective of tsunami forecast and of Tsunami Early Warning System strategy.

Key words: Tsunami, Samoa, tsunami early warning systems, outer-rise earthquakes, tsunami forecast, tsunami modelling.

1. Introduction

At 6:48 AM local time (17:48 UTC time), a strong earthquake of magnitude Mw = 8.1 occurred <200 km south of the Samoa Islands (Western Samoa and American Samoa), triggering a tsunami that was detected by several tide gauges and offshore buoys located all around the source area. The main characteristic of this event is that it belongs to a special category of earthquakes called "outer-rise"

earthquakes. These events are unusual tsunami sources, and they can be generated close to ocean trenches due to the mainly extensional tectonic stress driven by the main subduction mechanism and acting on the portion of the crust which is not yet part of the subducting plate. The outer-rise earthquakes are characterized by a prevailing normal fault mechanism with the tension axis being almost parallel to the direction of subduction, as opposed to the almost pure thrust mechanism expected for earthquakes generated along the subduction zone. The 26 June 1917 earthquake (Fig. 1) is another example of a tsunamigenic outer-rise event that occurred almost in the same area, north of the Tonga trench (see OKAL and BORRERO, 2004). Other historical examples of such events in other areas occurred on 19 August 1977 in Sumba (Indonesia) (Mw = 8.3, see GUSMAN et al., 2009), on 2 March 1933 at Sanriku (Japan, Mw = 8.4, see KANAMORI, 1971) and on 13 January 2007 at Kurile Islands (Russia, Mw = 8.0, see TANIOKA et al., 2008).

The analysis presented here uses the example of the Samoa event to launch a discussion about possible discrepancies between tsunami simulations and tsunami observations and about the consequent implication on the performance of the tsunami forecast models and of the Tsunami Early Warning Systems.

In the following we examine five different source models for the Samoa earthquake: four of them are homogeneous one-segment sources; whereas, the fifth is the heterogeneous slip model proposed by USGS and posted on the web shortly after the event.

The numerical simulations are computed by means of the UBO-TSUFD code, developed and maintained by the Tsunami Research Team of the University of Bologna, Italy. The code solves the linear and non-linear shallow water equations through

---
[1] Department of Physics, Sector of Geophysics, University of Bologna, Bologna, Italy. E-mail: roberto.tonini2@unibo.it; stefano.tinti@unibo.it

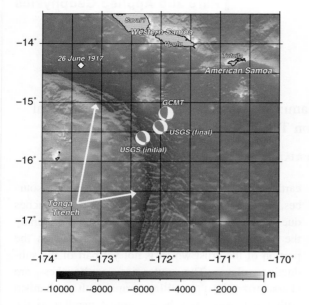

Figure 1
Bathymetry of the source area of the 29 September 2009 earthquake (GEBCO_08). The epicentral (USGS) and centroid (GCMT) locations provided by different seismological institutions and published on the web are plotted through the *beach balls* representation. The relocated epicenter position of the tsunamigenic outer-rise earthquake of 26 June 1917 is also shown (OKAL and BORRERO, 2004)

a finite-difference technique and can compute inundation inland in the non-linear version. Furthermore, the computational domain can be split into grids of different space resolution in order to have more detailed results in specific areas.

The results of the tsunami simulations are then compared with the signals recorded by three different DART buoys and with the tide gauge signals recorded in Apia (Western Samoa) and Pago Pago (American Samoa).

2. Tectonic Background and First Source Model Solutions

The 29 September 2009 Samoa earthquake occurred very close to the point where the Tonga trench changes its direction from northward to westward. Here the Pacific plate moves westward beneath the Australia plate, determining a subduction zone along the north-oriented segment of the trench, and a transform zone along the west-oriented

segment. Most of tsunamis are triggered by shallow-dip, thrust-mechanism earthquakes occurring along the subduction zone. The Samoan earthquake was caused by the stresses on the crust induced by the bending of the subducting plate. This flexing movement of the plate uplifts the sea-bottom which can break with a normal mechanism almost parallel to the oceanic trench. These earthquakes are called "outer-rise" events.

The epicenter location in this complex tectonic frame makes identifying the fault mechanism responsible for the tsunami generation a non-trivial task. For this earthquake, different hypocentral locations are available, and here we take into account the ones by USGS (http://earthquake.usgs.gov) and by Global CMT (http://www.globalcmt.org). The locations vary to some extent, which may be relevant to tsunami generation and propagation. Moreover, the solution coming from a given provider varied with the time after the earthquake; for example, in the case of USGS, the location varied from $(-172.300°, -15.600°)$ a few minutes after the earthquake to $(-172.034°, -15.509°)$ some hours later (Fig. 1). Even trickier is the focal mechanism, having best double couple estimates that are different to an extent that may be "negligible" from a seismological point of view, but significant from the tsunami generation perspective. An additional source of uncertainty is represented by the estimate of the source dimensions and of the slip distribution to be used in the computation of the tsunami initial condition.

Here, five seismic source models have been considered. Four cases, referred to as GCMT-1, GCMT-2, USGS-1, and USGS-2 in the following, are derived from the first Global CMT (Mw = 8.1) and USGS (Mw = 8.0) moment tensor solutions after the quake. These models have a simple rectangular shape and differ in the position (with the centroid supposed to coincide with the midpoint of the upper edge of the fault) and in the focal mechanism. The differences are significant, suggesting that the actual source mechanism is not easily recognizable. The fault dimensions and the slip, assumed for simplicity to be uniform on the fault plane, are retrieved from the regression formulas by WELLS AND COPPERSMITH (1994) valid for normal faults. All the seismic parameters for these four cases are shown in Table 1.

The fifth case (Mw = 8.0) considered here, denoted as USGS-432 hereafter, is the finite fault model proposed by USGS some time after the shock: it consists in a 432 sub-faults system characterized by a highly heterogeneous slip distribution (see http://earthquake.usgs.gov/earthquakes/eqinthenews/2009/us2009mdbi/finite_fault.php).

The coseismic vertical displacement of the sea-floor has been computed by means of the set of formulas proposed by OKADA (1992) on the basis of the elastic theory, and the initial water level movement is considered to be equal to the corresponding vertical sea-bottom displacement. In Fig. 2 the tsunami initial condition together with the fault geometry for each of the considered cases are shown.

3. Tsunami simulations

All simulations have been performed by means of the linear version of the code UBO-TSUFD (University of Bologna—Tsunami Finite Difference), solving both linear and non-linear shallow water equations for tsunami propagation through the finite-difference method. The model is based on a leap-frog numerical technique using a staggered grid scheme. A moving boundary algorithm has been implemented in order to investigate run-up and inundation processes on the coast, as well as a nested grids system that allows one to study the computational domain with different space resolution. The UBO-TSUFD model was successfully benchmarked in the framework of the European Community (EC) funded project TRANSFER against the so-called Catilina

Island 2004 benchmark set (see e.g., LIU et al., 2008) and it was also used to perform inundation maps for the Messina Straits and eastern Sicily, Italy, in the frame, respectively, of the EC projects TRANSFER (http://www.transferproject.eu/) and SCHEMA (http://www.schemaproject.org/). A set of three nested computational grids has been considered. The coarsest grid is formed by square cells with a resolution of 3 km and covers the domain shown in Fig. 3, including the source area, the Samoa Islands and the three closest DART buoys. Through an intermediate grid with resolution of 600 m (white rectangle in Fig. 3), we arrive to the smallest 200-m grid step, covering the Samoa Island (both Western and American Samoa) and including the two tide gauges of Apia and Pago Pago (Fig. 4). Topography and bathymetry data interpolated using the freely available 30-s resolution GEBCO dataset (the GEBCO_08 Grid, version 20090202, http://www.gebco.net). This resolution can be considered enough offshore, but it is insufficient close to the coasts, where very detailed information on the bathymetry and the topography is needed and is recognized to be a crucial factor affecting the way the tsunami waves attack the coasts. This point will be further stressed later on, when the comparison between the computed signals and the Apia and Pago Pago records will be discussed.

Maximum elevation fields computed during a 3-h propagation interval are shown in Fig. 5. The wave propagations differ considerably, especially as regards the impact on the Samoa Islands. The GCMT-2 and USGS-432 exhibit the most pronounced directivity effects. In the GCMT-2 case, the strike of the fault is responsible for the beam of maximum tsunami energy

Table 1

Seismic parameters of the fault models based on the first centroid solutions calculated after the shock

	USGS-1	USGS-2	GCMT-1	GCMT-2
L (km)	134.9	134.9	154.9	154.9
W (km)	46.5	46.5	51.2	51.2
Strike	345°	124°	129°	7°
Dip	52°	46°	31°	72°
Rake	299°	240°	216°	296°
Slip (m)	4	4	4,8	4,8
Position	−172.034°, −15.509°	−172.034°, −15.509°	−171.91°, −15.19°	−171.91°, −15.19°
Depth (km)	5	5	5	5

The "position" and "depth" parameters refer to the mid-point of the upper edge of each rectangular fault model

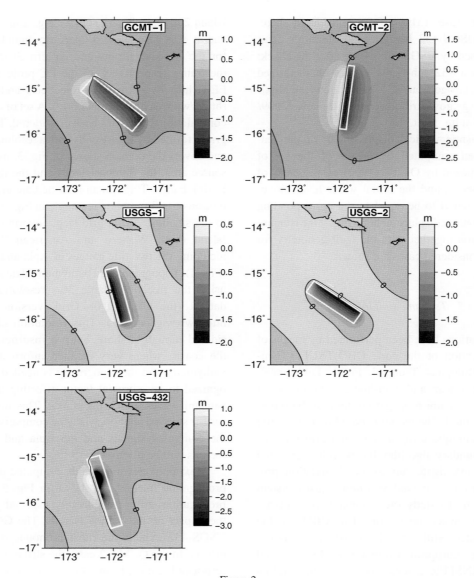

Figure 2

Coseismic vertical displacement (coinciding with the tsunami initial conditions) computed for the source models GCMT-1, GCMT-2, USGS-1, USGS-2, and USGS-432. The zero-level contour line (*black*) is plotted to distinguish better the passage from positive to negative heights in a gray-scale palette. The maximum negative and maximum positive displacements in the different cases are (−1.81, 0.55) m for GCMT-1, (−2.11, 1.04) m for GCMT-2, (−1.93, 0.36) m for USGS-1, (−1.93, 0.25) m for USGS-2, (−5.86, 1.06) m for USGS-432. The *white rectangles* represent the projection of the fault plane on the seafloor while the *white solid line* represents the intersection of the plane containing the fault rectangle with the seafloor itself

that almost bypasses the Samoa Islands. Instead, for GCMT-1 and USGS-2 the tsunami energy is more focused towards both Western and American Samoa, which may suggest a better representation of what happened. USGS-1 tsunami path attacks with more energy the American Samoa, but it seems saving the Western Samoa coasts. The heterogeneous slip fault

model USGS-432 concentrates its maximum elevations close to the source and towards American Samoa.

By these first considerations, it is already possible to suggest that one of the source model solutions (GCMT-2) could be rejected on the basis of the impact data collected by the post tsunami surveys

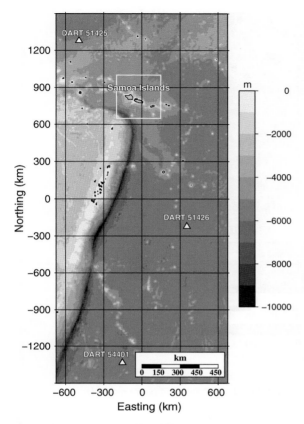

Figure 3

Geographical domain extension of the 3-km resolution grid. The 600-m intermediate grid external boundary is represented by the *white rectangle*. The position of the three DART buoys 51425, 51426 and 54401 is shown

in turn a much more detailed bathymetric dataset. The 200-m grid resolution is not enough to describe the complex morphology of the topo-bathymetry of the coastal areas, and, moreover, it must be remarked that this grid has been obtained by interpolating the 30-s GEBCO dataset, which in Cartesian coordinates corresponds to about 800–900 m.

4. Observed Data and Simulation Results

In the previous section we tried a preliminary source selection by observing tsunami energy paths obtained from the simulations, but it was not possible to discriminate the source models without high-resolution information on the bathymetry and the topography, which could permit a more detailed evaluation of the maximum elevation distribution along the coasts. We could only suggest that GCMT-2 source is quite far from being the candidate for the 2009 Samoan earthquake, based on the tsunami energy pattern.

The best way to understand tsunami propagation is by observing tsunami signals recorded by offshore buoys or by stations located close to the coasts. Tide gauge records are very important to support the investigation of the source mechanism. The 2009 Samoa event was recorded by several stations. In this section we compare our results with the tsunami signal recorded by offshore buoys and coastal stations in the near field.

Figure 6 shows the computed time-histories versus the tsunami records taken by the three DART buoys that are the closest to the source. If we consider the DART buoys 51426 and 54401 that are both south of the Samoa Islands, we have a curious result. All sources lead to arrival times that are reasonably correct, though they seem to be slightly delayed by about 200 s. Even the wave amplitude is not far from the observed one. But the polarity of the first wave is reversed: positive in the record and negative in the computations. Since the used tsunami model is linear, inversion of the polarity of the source would lead to an inversion of the polarity of the computed tsunami and consequently to a much better matching between numerical results and offshore signals, but this would be unacceptable from the seismological point of view. The analysis of the signal of the DART buoy

(see, for example, the compilation of web links at the NOAA web page: http://nctr.pmel.noaa.gov/samoa 20090929-weblink.html; also see the quite detailed report contributed by the International Tsunami Survey Team that also includes one of the authors of the present paper, Various Authors, 2009). These surveys have reported very severe damages and measured run-up heights exceeding 10 m in the south-western area of American Samoa, and more than 5 m in many areas to south-east of Upolu (Western Samoa).

One possible way to discriminate sources against observations would be to compare the extreme tsunami elevations obtained at the Samoa Islands coasts with the run-up heights measured by the post-event surveys. But such a comparison would be unfair for the present study, since it would have required a much finer resolution of the computational grids and

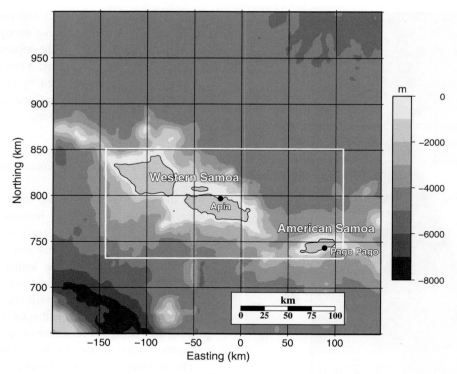

Figure 4
Six hundred meter grid domain. Apia and Pago Pago are located inside the 200-m grid (*white rectangle*)

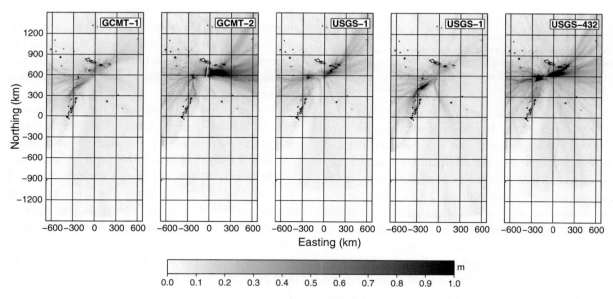

Figure 5
Maximum tsunami elevation fields computed for the different source models

51425 that is located north-west of the Samoa Islands is slightly different. The signal is quite low and noisy and the tsunami is not well recognizable. Probably one can identify the first tsunami arrival in a negative wave with minimum elevation touched around 4,000 s in the graph of Fig. 6. If this is true, then all calculated tsunamis produce an anticipated arrival. As regards the amplitude of the first wave, it is reasonably acceptable for GCMT-1 and USGS-2, but not for cases GCMT-2, USGS-1, and USGS-432 that are significantly stronger than the observed one. The polarity of the first wave is reversed for the CMT sources and probably acceptable for all USGS sources.

In Fig. 7 the numerical results are compared with the signals recorded by the tide gauge stations of Apia and Pago Pago. These results have a generally better accordance with the observed data. Concerning arrival times, there must be a preliminary consideration about Pago Pago. Here, the simulated tsunamis of all models anticipate by 300 s or more the recorded signal. As mentioned in previous sections, detailed bathymetry and topography are fundamentally close to the coasts in tsunami simulations. The dataset used here is not detailed enough, and in the case of Pago Pago, this fact results in a quite great discrepancy between the real coast shape and the coastline used for the calculations. Pago Pago lies on a shallow and narrow bay that in the computational grid does not exist. Tsunami waves move very slowly in shallow waters and the missing path inside the bay could explain the computed signal being earlier than the observed one. The same does not hold for Apia, where one model (GCMT-2) produces an earlier (circa 400 s) arrival, two models (USGS-2 and USGS-432) produce a late (about 200 s) arrival and

the other two models give a perfectly matching arrival for the tsunami. Further, the agreement is good considering both amplitude and polarity of the first arrivals.

From the comparison of all the graphs of Fig. 7, it results that GCMT-1 source model gives the best agreement. The first peak-to-peak signal in the computed marigram at Apia is almost equal to the recorded signal and, neglecting the bathymetry-caused first arrival shift, the first negative-positive arrival at Pago Pago is very close to the observed data. As for the USGS-2 model, we can state that it leads to results similar to the GCMT-1 for the Pago Pago station and that it also shows a good accordance with amplitude and polarity of the Apia observed signal, but it is about 200 s late. Further, it is interesting to analyse the USGS-432 model which is the only source with a heterogeneous slip distribution considered here. The Apia computed signal is a little delayed with respect to the observed one, but at Pago Pago the time shift is smaller than the one of the GCMT-1 model, and polarity and amplitude of the first wave are acceptably good, as for the other models.

5. Conclusions and Implications on Tsunami Forecast and on TEWS Strategy

The 29 September 2009 earthquake-induced tsunami is quite interesting from different points of

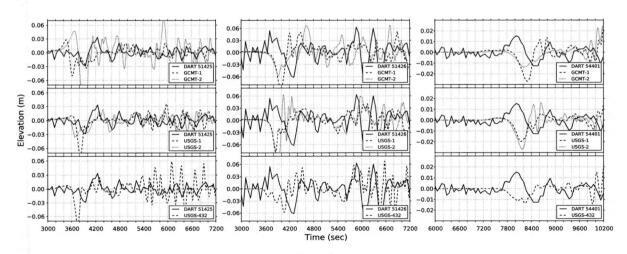

Figure 6
Offshore DART buoys tsunami signal against simulated records

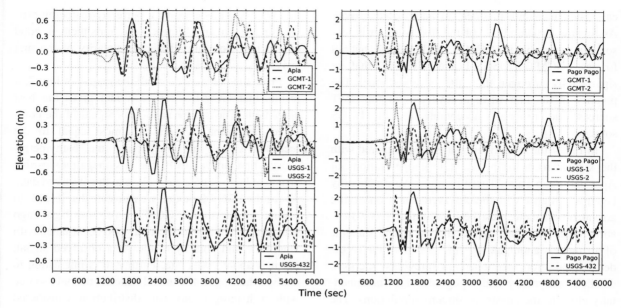

Figure 7
Apia and Pago Pago tsunami signal against computed records

view. In the first place, the fact that the tsunami source was an outer-rise earthquake suggests an immediate consideration concerning the efficiency of the forecast models. The operational tsunami forecast models, like the one routinely used by NOAA (GICA, 2008), are based on pre-computed databases of tsunami propagation models, which in turn are based on pre-defined unit sources placed along known and potential earthquake zones. Typically, these zones are the main subduction zones all over the world oceans. Operational forecast models could be efficient and effective when a tsunamigenic earthquake actually occurs along the pre-defined source regions. But so far the models do not include the outer-rise earthquakes as possible sources for tsunamis. Therefore, for the Samoa earthquake as well as for earthquakes of the same category, the forecast models cannot work properly, since these sources are not contained in the pre-computed database and disagreement between forecasts and observations has to be expected. The main recommendation is that the outer-rise earthquakes should be incorporated into the set of potential tsunami sources and the corresponding tsunami scenarios be added to the dataset of the pre-computed solutions for operational tsunami forecasting. This in turn imposes the identification of

such sources on a global scale, i.e., in all interested ocean basins, which is not a simple task to complete and is certainly more controversial than the identification of the tsunami sources along the subduction zones.

A second series of useful considerations can be drawn from the analysis of the results we obtained using five different source models for the Samoa earthquake. The analysis was mainly based on comparison between computed and observed tsunami time histories. Computed signals compared to the offshore DART buoys records show that there is a relevant discrepancy for all the fault models considered here. Otherwise the signals computed at Apia (Western Samoa) and Pago Pago (American Samoa), located where the tsunami caused the worst damages and most fatalities, have a better agreement with the recorded ones, especially for the GCMT-1 source model.

A conclusion that can be drawn is that none of the tsunamis computed from the examined source models match satisfactorily all the near-field records. The discrepancy deserves some comments. As usual, one can argue that the main reason resides in the inadequacy either of the source models or of the tsunami propagation model, or both. Let us consider the tsunami model first. The tsunami simulation code UBO-TSUFD used in this work solves the linear non-dispersive shallow-water equations with initial tsunami conditions given by a null velocity field and an initial elevation equaling the vertical displacement of the sea-floor induced by the earthquake and corrected by topography effects. Let us split the analysis into two parts: one concerning the equations and one concerning their numerical implementation. Linear shallow-water models are quite reliable and can be tested against a large number of theoretical solutions, which was the case for the code UBO-TSUFD. Therefore, discrepancy cannot be attributed to weakness or artifacts of the numerical code. As to the equations, the purpose of the shallow-water approximation and of the linear approximation to compute offshore and tide-gauge records cannot be questioned, since tsunamis induced by large earthquakes (and, hence, with sources of large horizontal extent) are certainly long waves, and, moreover, non-linear terms are basically important solely in very shallow coastal waters and probably only for flooding computations. The only objection that can have some ground is that dispersive terms have been omitted in the present computations. They are relevant only when the propagation path is much longer than the dominant tsunami wavelength, which was not the case in this investigation that was restricted to the near-field. However, omitting dispersion terms may have some effect on the leading wave size and polarity. The conclusion is that the observed discrepancy is not, or is only very mildly, to be attributed to the tsunami propagation model.

On the other hand, the seismic source models, though differing from each other, have some coherence and all agree on the basic normal focal mechanism of the parent shock that identifies this earthquake as one belonging to the category of the so-called outer-rise earthquakes. Seismologists have applied their inversion methods routinely for very many years and have accumulated a huge amount of focal solutions that have been used in a multiplicity of applications (some of which may be considered independent testing methods), and, hence, it is hard to state that discrepancy is due to uncertainties in the seismic inversion process.

This ambiguity, therefore, seems to lead to an irresolvable dead end, and may constitute a problem for tsunami science. One possible way out is to attribute the discrepancy to the inadequate representation of the tsunami generation process (we took the initial sea surface elevation to be equal to the vertical coseismic displacement of the seafloor), and to suggest that probably the tsunami generation process is more complicated and the assumptions that the water is an incompressible fluid and the pressure profile is essentially hydrostatic should be removed to compute the tsunami in the area close to the source. Exploring this possibility seems an interesting field of future research.

We are interested, however, to regard this misfit of the computations in the perspective of a Tsunami Early Warning System; that is, the question to address is "Does the uncertainty in the tsunami result affect the tsunami forecast and the alert messages to issue to the affected coastal communities, and if yes, by how much?". In order to address this problem, first we notice that in actual practice, the informative elements that are distributed to the communities through watch and warning messages by the Tsunami Centers (e.g., the PTWC in the Pacific Ocean and national centers with regional responsibilities in the Indian Ocean) are the estimated tsunami arrival times (ETA) and the arrival and amplitude of the recorded tsunami, when observations are available. Other tsunami centers (see, for example, JMA for Japan, and the BMKG, the center of the InaTEWS, for Indonesia) provide also the estimated tsunami height (ETH), though discretized in a few classes (e.g., 0.1–0.5 m, 0.5–3.0 m, >3 m). The discrepancy we have found in the computation regards more the polarity of the leading wave rather than the arrival times and the tsunami size. The polarity was found to be wrong for the offshore buoys. However, arrival times seem to be incorrect at most for some 5–10 min, which is not dramatic for a warning system. Surprisingly, and most importantly, the size of the tsunami is satisfactorily correct and the amplification of the signal from offshore to the coastal waters is appreciably well taken (from a few centimeters offshore, the computed wave reaches about 1 m in Apia and more than 2 m in Pago Pago). A consequence is that, if one had used anyone of the tsunami sources examined here and a linear tsunami simulation model to make estimates of the tsunami, the forecast would have been correct, or at least adequate to the today's standards for the content of the tsunami bulletins.

This reassuring observation, however, cannot prevent us from also considering the other side of the coin. On comparing the observed and computed signals (Figs. 6, 7), one can see that the misfit tends to grow with time, and that only the first waves (if not only the first wave or the first half-wave) are reproduced satisfactorily. Therefore, the discrepancy between computations and records is even more severe than the one underlined so far. This means that today's modeling (altogether seismic + tsunami modeling) is able to provide correctly only some rough features of the tsunami (such as tsunami wave pattern, first arrival times, wave height), but not the complete tsunami waveforms. The consequence is that it is useless for a TEWS to disseminate tsunami forecast information more detailed than the ones that are distributed today. In general, the constrained factor for disseminating results over a very extended area is considered today the bandwidth of the communication link, i.e., more a problem of available financial resources than of available technology. What is stressed here is that the Samoa case shows that the real limiting factor is our inability to compute adequate tsunami evolution, which is more dramatic, since we do not know which elements can produce real progress: generically we can state that by improving the seismic and sea-level monitoring system, the bathymetry and topographic dataset, the modeling, we would obtain better results. But since we do not know at present what is the crucial element, and if it resides in the field of technology or research or both, the solution is not in the immediate future.

Our considerations, though stemming from the 29 September Samoa tsunami, are quite general. We neglect here the fact that the seismic solutions were available soon, but too late to be used by the PTWS, and that the first tsunami bulletin was actually issued by the PTWC almost at the same time the tsunami made contact with the Samoa Islands. The fact that the tsunami forecast in the TEWS real-time practice has to rely on even less information than the ones used here (essentially the epicenter location and some estimate of the focal mechanism based on the regional tectonics, rather than on seismic inversion, since usually it takes too much time to compute focal mechanism solutions) has the effect of increasing the uncertainties related to the forecast and reinforces the point we sustain here.

We note further that an important implication deriving from the discussed limitations of forecast models, which is from the impossibility to rely fully on pre-computed tsunami databases in order to forecast the potential tsunami impact, is that it appears vital to get direct observations of tsunami waves; indeed, a dense network of real-time tsunami recorders (offshore and coastal) adequately covering at least the near-field region of potential tsunami sources could provide very good constraints to tsunami forecast models, and help to reduce the aforementioned uncertainties and gaps between observations and synthetic data.

The final conclusion is that real progress in tsunami forecast in the TEWS can be achieved only by improving our basic knowledge of the tsunami process and only if adequate investments are made in technology and in applied research.

Acknowledgments

This work has been financed by the European projects DEWS (2007-2010) and SCHEMA (2007–2010). The authors are indebted to the organizations that made the dataset of the tsunami records available on the web soon after the event.

REFERENCES

GICA, E., SPILLANE M., TITOV V. V., CHAMBERLIN C., and NEWMAN J.C. (2008): Development of the forecast propagation database for NOAA's Short-term Inundation Forecast for Tsunamis (SIFT). NOAA Tech. Memo. OAR PMEL-139, 89 pp.

GUSMAN, A. R., TANIOKA, Y., MATSUMOTO, H., and IWASAKI S. (2009), Analysis of the tsunami generated by the great 1977 Sumba earthquake that occurred in Indonesia. Bull. Seism. Soc. Am., 99, 2169–2179.

KANAMORI, H. (1971), Seismological evidence for a lithospheric normal faulting—The Sanriku earthquake of 1933, Phys. Earth Planet. Inter., 4, 289–300.

LIU P. L. F., YEH H. and SYNOLAKIS C.E. (2008), Benchmark problems, in "Advanced Numerical Models for Simulating Tsunami Waves and Run-up" (Eds. LIU P.L.F., YEH H., SYNOLAKIS C.E.), Vol.10 of "Advances in Coastal and Ocean Engineering", World Scientific Publishing, Singapore, 223–230.

OKADA (1992), Internal deformation due to shear and tensile faults in a half-space. Bull. Seism. Soc. Am., 82, 1018–1040.

OKAL, E., BORRERO, J., and SYNOLAKIS C.E. (2004), The earthquake and tsunami of 1865 November 17: evidence for far-field tsunami hazard from Tonga, Geophys. J. Int., 157, 164–174.

TANIOKA, Y., HASEGAWA, Y. and KUWAYAMA, T. (2008), Tsunami waveform analyses of the 2006 underthrust and 2007 outer-rise Kurile earthquakes. Adv. Geosci., 14, 129–134.

Various Authors (2009), UNESCO-IOC International Tsunami Survey Team, Samoa (ITST Samoa)—Interim Report of Field Survey 14th–21st October 2009 (eds. D. DOMINEY-HOWES, R. THAMAN, J. GOFF), Australian Tsunami Research Centre Miscellaneous Report No. 2, pp. 190.

WELLS, D. L., and COPPERSMITH, K. J. (1994), New empirical relationships among magnitude, rupture length, rupture width, rupture area, and surface displacement. Bull. Seism. Soc. Am., 84, 974–1002.

(Received January 4, 2010, revised April 1, 2010, accepted April 3, 2010, Published online January 11, 2011)

Reprinted from the journal

Pure Appl. Geophys. 168 (2011), 1125–1136
© 2010 Springer Basel AG
DOI 10.1007/s00024-010-0223-9

Tsunami Forecasting and Monitoring in New Zealand

WILLIAM POWER[1] and NORA GALE[1]

Abstract—New Zealand is exposed to tsunami threats from several sources that vary significantly in their potential impact and travel time. One route for reducing the risk from these tsunami sources is to provide advance warning based on forecasting and monitoring of events in progress. In this paper the National Tsunami Warning System framework, including the responsibilities of key organisations and the procedures that they follow in the event of a tsunami threatening New Zealand, are summarised. A method for forecasting threat-levels based on tsunami models is presented, similar in many respects to that developed for Australia by Allen and Greenslade (Nat Hazards 46:35–52, 2008), and a simple system for easy access to the threat-level forecasts using a clickable pdf file is presented. Once a tsunami enters or initiates within New Zealand waters, its progress and evolution can be monitored in real-time using a newly established network of online tsunami gauge sensors placed at strategic locations around the New Zealand coasts and offshore islands. Information from these gauges can be used to validate and revise forecasts, and assist in making the all-clear decision.

Key words: Tsunami, forecasting, monitoring, warning system, tide gauge network, New Zealand.

1. Introduction

The written historical record of tsunami in New Zealand contains 51 well-identified events in the period since European settlement (post-1840). Of these, 21 are from distant sources, 11 are from regional sources and 19 are from local sources (DOWNES, *pers comm*). Three of these events had run-ups exceeding 10 m and eight had run-ups exceeding 4 m. Of the distant source events the most notable and damaging events are those caused by earthquakes in South America in 1868, 1877 and 1960 (POWER *et al.*, 2007). Notable local-source tsunami include those caused by the 1855 Wairarapa Fault earthquake

(GRAPES and DOWNES, 1997) and those caused by tsunami-earthquakes (KANAMORI, 1972) near Gisborne in March and May 1947 (DOWNES *et al.*, 2001; BELL *et al.*, 2010).

In addition to the written historical record there are a number of events that could be interpreted as tsunami in the legends and oral history of the Maori, New Zealand's indigenous population (MCFADGEN, 2007). Paleotsunami studies (e.g. COCHRAN *et al.*, 2005; GOFF *et al.*, 2000; NICHOL *et al.*, 2003) have also identified a number of large inundation events in the pre-historic period. In the case of both oral history and paleotsunami analysis it is often difficult to determine either a precise date or source. What is clear is that New Zealand has a significant tsunami hazard that the shortness of the historical record may not adequately represent.

In recent years improved communication systems and scientific monitoring have alerted authorities to potentially threatening events, some of which may not have been previously recorded in the historical record. Since 2001 there have been, on average, two tsunamigenic events per year that were identified as potential threats to New Zealand (Table 1).

The main islands of New Zealand are located in the southwest Pacific between 34° and 48° south and 166° and 179° east. The country is located on the Pacific 'Ring-of-Fire', which is formed along the boundary between the Pacific oceanic plate and the adjacent continental plates. In the case of New Zealand the boundary is with the Australian plate (Fig. 1), and the relative motion of these plates leads to subduction, in the northeast and south of the country, and strike-slip motion along the Alpine Fault. Subduction zones are associated with tsunami-causing earthquakes, and subduction earthquakes were responsible for the tsunami in March and May 1947, and the Fiordland tsunami in 2003 and 2009.

[1] GNS Science, 1 Fairway Drive, Avalon, PO Box 30368, Lower Hutt, New Zealand. E-mail: w.power@gns.cri.nz

Reprinted from the journal

Table 1

Potential threats to New Zealand from tsunamigenic earthquakes since 2001

Year	Location	Magnitude
2001	Peru	8.4
2003	Fiordland	7.2
2004	Puysegur	7.1
2004	Macquarie Ridge	8.1
2004	Sumatra	9–9.3
2006	Tonga	8.0
2006	Kuril Islands	8.3
2007	Kuril Islands	8.1
2007	Peru	8.0
2007	Solomon Islands	8.1
2007	Auckland Islands	7.4
2009	Fiordland	7.8
2009	Samoa	8.0
2009	Vanuatu	7.6
2010	Chile	8.8

The predominantly strike-slip Wairarapa Fault earthquake of 1855 was also tsunamigenic; it caused substantial vertical motion of the seafloor in Cook Strait. This crustal fault lies within the area of transition between subduction and strike-slip motion on the nearby continental plate interface.

The location of New Zealand also exposes it to tsunami hazards from sources in the Southwest Pacific region and from distant parts of the Pacific Rim. Within the southwest Pacific it would at first appear that there are relatively few subduction zones that are well oriented to send tsunami energy towards New Zealand. However, the three major ridges, the Lord Howe Rise, the Norfolk Ridge and the Three Kings Ridge, that extend to the north and west of the country act as strong tsunami waveguides that increase the wave energy that gets directed towards New Zealand. Regarding the distant sources in the wider Pacific, it is generally those that are to the east and northeast of New Zealand that pose the greatest threat based on computer modelling and the historical record; most of these sources have tsunami travel times to New Zealand greater than 12 h. Tsunami energy from the northwest Pacific is partly prevented from propagating directly towards New Zealand by reflection and refraction from the chain of island arcs between Papua New Guinea and Samoa.

The information that can be inferred from past events, and the setting of New Zealand within the Ring-of-Fire, both suggest that there is a significant tsunami hazard. Mitigation of this hazard can be achieved in several ways: through education, by land-use planning and engineering, and through the dissemination of warnings. The remainder of this article focuses on the tools and procedures that have been developed to assist in producing advice that results in timely and effective warning and cancellation messages, though it is important that warnings are not viewed in isolation but as part of a holistic approach to tsunami hazard mitigation.

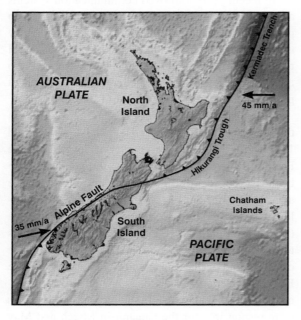

Figure 1
Tectonic setting of New Zealand

2. National Tsunami Warning System Framework

Tsunami threat evaluation and message dissemination in New Zealand is a tiered system that is handled by multiple organisations within the National Tsunami Warning System framework (Fig. 2; MCDEM, 2008). Here, the roles of the key organisations, which include the Pacific Tsunami Warning Center (PTWC), the Ministry of Civil Defence and Emergency Management (MCDEM), GNS Science, and Civil Defence and Emergency Management (CDEM) groups, are discussed.

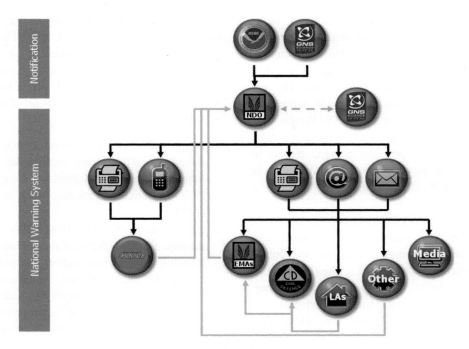

Figure 2

Flow chart of tsunami threat notification, evaluation and national advisory process. The National Disaster Office (*NDO*) of MCDEM is notified of tsunami threats via NOAA's PTWC or GNS Science's GeoNet Duty Team. Following notification, the NDO will seek scientific advice from the GeoNet Duty Officer and/or Tsunami Experts Panel. This advice will be relayed to Emergency Management Authorities (*EMAs*), Civil Defence (*CD*), Local Authorities (*LAs*), the media and the police

The PTWC, which is located in Hawaii, serves as the operational headquarters for the Pacific Tsunami Warning System (US IoTWS 2007). The PTWC monitors an expansive seismic and sea level network in the Pacific. Tsunami messages are issued in accordance with predefined threshold criteria that use the location, magnitude and depth of earthquakes as the initial determinants. The messages are issued under the following categories: Tsunami Information Bulletin, Tsunami Information Statement, Tsunami Advisory, Tsunami Watch and Tsunami Warning. Within New Zealand, these messages are disseminated directly to both MCDEM and GNS Science. The PTWC message categories are not applied directly in New Zealand; instead MCDEM uses the PTWC messages as one of several considerations when initiating official national advisories and warnings.

MCDEM is responsible for the dissemination of national official tsunami notifications in New Zealand. With technical support from GNS Science, MCDEM assesses all messages received from the PTWC to determine the threat for New Zealand.

Official tsunami notifications for New Zealand are disseminated by MCDEM via the National Warning System on a 24/7 basis. These notifications fall into one of the following categories:

- National Advisory: Tsunami—No Threat to New Zealand,
- National Advisory: Tsunami—Potential Threat to New Zealand,
- National Warning: Tsunami—Threat to New Zealand,
- National Advisory: Tsunami—Threat to New Zealand Cancellation, or
- National Warning: Tsunami—Threat to New Zealand Cancellation.

A National Advisory or Warning will be followed by hourly (or more frequent) messages until a cancellation is issued. MCDEM has a memorandum of understanding with the media such that they can request public radio and television stations to broadcast national advisories and warnings.

GNS Science maintains a national geological hazard monitoring system called GeoNet, which monitors and collects data on the nation's earthquakes, tsunami, volcanoes, and landslides. In this capacity, GNS Science acts as the national technical adviser to MCDEM for these geological hazards. GNS Science has an on-call Duty Team who are available on a 24/7 basis to provide advice to MCDEM within 20 min of an event. The Wellington-based GeoNet Duty Officer is responsible for notifying MCDEM of any potential tsunami threats to New Zealand and providing scientific advice via consultation with the Tsunami Experts Panel (GALE et al., 2009).

CDEM Groups and CDEM Group members are responsible for the planning, development and maintenance of local tsunami response and public alerting systems. In the advent of a tsunami threat to New Zealand, CDEM Groups and CDEM Group members will receive national tsunami advisories and warnings directly from MCDEM. This information will be used in conjunction with local threat assessments to decide on the appropriate level of public alerting. CDEM Groups may also include local broadcasters in their public alerting systems.

2.1. GNS Science Response Procedures

The GNS Science procedures for advising MCDEM on a tsunami threat vary in accordance with the tsunami travel time from the source to the nearest New Zealand coast. Local source tsunami (travel time of less than 1 h) offer very little time to implement official warning procedures as most local source tsunami are less than 30 min travel time from the nearest New Zealand coast. For this reason, MCDEM is promoting public awareness to be able to recognise and individually respond to natural warning signs. Regional source tsunami (travel time of 1–3 h) do not give much time before national advisories or warnings need to be issued and initial advice is likely to be given based on rule of thumb thresholds related to the earthquake parameters. Distant source tsunami (travel time of more than 3 h) give adequate time for national advisories and warnings to be issued that include predicted travel times, regional threat levels and coastal water height estimates.

The procedures outlining the provision of technical advice from GNS Science to MCDEM upon the

acknowledgment of a potential tsunami threat are listed below. The level of response will be dictated by the available time from tsunami initiation to its arrival on the New Zealand coasts. Consequently, in the case of local and regional source tsunami, there will only be time for an initial subset of procedures to be followed.

1. If applicable, check Tsunami Watch or Warning issued by PTWC and earthquake information issued by the United States Geological Survey (USGS) National Earthquake Information Center (NEIC).

2. Give preliminary advice to MCDEM on the likely tsunami threat to New Zealand based on PTWC tsunami information and/or GeoNet or USGS earthquake characteristics. Predefined thresholds levels for magnitude, depth and location will be used to determine the appropriate MCDEM national tsunami notification category.

3. Advise GNS Science management of the situation. If the Duty Officer is likely to be busy solely with the earthquake response, discuss delegation of tasks including activation of the Tsunami Experts Panel, providing technical advice to MCDEM and answering media enquires.

4. *If time allows*, arrange for a Liaison Officer to go to the National Crisis Management Centre at MCDEM. This can be either a member of the Tsunami Experts Panel or the Duty Officer. This person will take over the primary responsibility for conveying technical advice to MCDEM on the tsunami threat.

5. *If time allows*, activate the Tsunami Experts Panel. The first meeting will usually be held by telephone conference.

6. Advise MCDEM on threats to regions of New Zealand, by referring to the tsunami threat level pdf, and expected arrival times at key localities on the New Zealand coast, by utilising Tsunami Travel Time (WESSEL, 2009) software.

7. Provide the first detailed advice from the Tsunami Experts Panel to MCDEM within 1 h. The panel should assess all current seismic and sea-level data (from both DART buoys and tide gauges, using internationally shared data where appropriate) against available tsunami forecast models (e.g.

travel time, wave height and threat level models) as well as historical tsunami data to provide advice to MCDEM on the likelihood of tsunami generation and, if applicable, the impact to New Zealand.

Hourly updates will be provided to MCDEM even if there is no new information and after each new message from PTWC. Advising of an 'all clear' is reliant on tsunami propagation models to determine the travel times of the latest potentially destructive waves to the New Zealand coasts and confirming the modelled latest arrivals with the tsunami gauge data.

3. Forecasting

One useful form of advice that can inform tsunami warnings comes from numerical modelling. Tsunami modelling software has advanced to the stage where all stages of the tsunami process, initiation, propagation and impact, can be simulated. This has the potential to provide a forecast of tsunami impacts ahead of the tsunami arrival, but while in some situations it may be possible to model these processes faster than real-time, it is very challenging to do this reliably. For this reason the initial approach adopted in New Zealand is to develop a database of pre-computed scenarios which can be referred to in order to find close analogues to an actual event without the need for real-time modelling. Tools such as SIFT (Gica et al., 2008) and webSIFT (Merati et al., 2010) seek to solve some of the challenges associated with real-time forecasting and may be adopted in future. The Tsunami Assessment Modeling System (Annunziato, 2007; http://www.gdacs.org/tsunami) uses a mixed approach with both pre-calculated scenarios and real-time modelling.

The initial development of the forecast database was focussed on providing forecasts for events with first-arrival travel times to New Zealand exceeding 3 h. This includes some of the more distant southwest Pacific sources, as well as all those in all the other regions of the Pacific Rim. Subsequent and currently ongoing work is acting to fill in the database with models from closer regional sources; the 3 h cutoff was chosen as the minimum time required to

guarantee dissemination of a formal warning until other aspects of the warning system could be improved. For local sources it is envisaged that the primary means of hazard mitigation is through education in the natural signs of tsunami and the appropriate response to them. A forecast database may still be useful in this situation as a means to provide estimates to emergency services on the likely scale of response required post-event.

3.1. Creation of the Scenario Database

For all potentially significant subduction zones of the Pacific Rim with >3 h travel time to New Zealand, a set of source models at magnitudes M_w 8.7, 9.0 and 9.3 were developed (Figs. 3, 4, 5). For all sources except those in South America, the source models were created using the NOAA FACTS server (Borrero et al., 2004). For the South American sources the models developed by Power et al. (2007) were used. These sources were designed to be approximately contiguous (i.e. the end of one source rupture is the start of the next).

For each source model the FACTS server, or a MOST (Titov and González, 1997; Titov and Synolakis, 1998) propagation model in the case of South American sources, was used to produce time-series boundary conditions for the water height and currents around New Zealand, specifically the area from 165°E to 180°E and 49°S to 33°S.

Each set of boundary conditions were applied to a MOST model of New Zealand covering the area from 165.6°E to 179.5°E and 48.5°S to 33.5°S on a one arc minute grid up to a minimum depth of 10 m. This allows some of the non-linear shallow-water physics to be captured and the effects of bathymetry features on scales down to a few km to be taken into account.

The results from each MOST model were processed to find the maximum water level reached at each point within the New Zealand grid. The coast was divided into predefined zones and the maximum water level within each zone identified. This value was then used to set the hazard-level for the zone in the specific scenario.

The results of the scenario modelling were compared against observations of historical events,

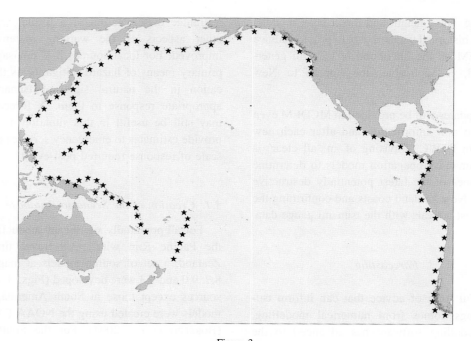

Figure 3
Epicentre locations for the M_w 8.7 scenario models. Locations on the Kermadec arc and southern New Hebrides are provisional locations for regional source models

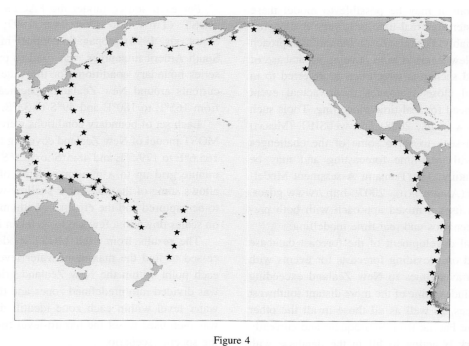

Figure 4
Epicentre locations for the M_w 9.0 scenario models. Locations on the Kermadec arc and southern New Hebrides are provisional locations for regional source models

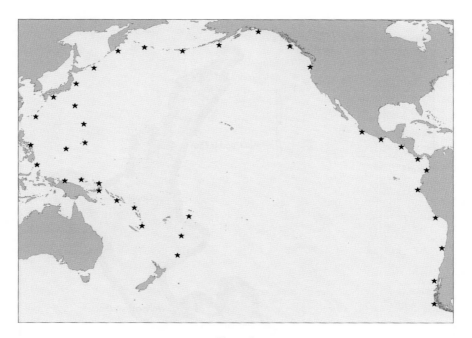

Figure 5
Epicentre locations for the M_w 9.3 scenario models. Locations on the Kermadec arc and southern New Hebrides are provisional locations for regional source models

including the 1868 Peru (Fig. 6), 1960 Peru and 1964 Alaska tsunami. Given the substantial uncertainties in interpreting maximum water levels from historical accounts and the uncertainties in the source parameters of these events, the results demonstrated an acceptable level of agreement (POWER *et al.*, 2010).

To provide easy access to the forecast database an indexed plot of the coastal threat levels for each scenario was created in the form of a pdf file. The pdf has been designed to be used interactively, using clickable maps and tables to find the threat level figure for any particular scenario, but a system of page numbering is also available so that the document can be also be used in printed form (Fig. 7).

4. Monitoring

The New Zealand Tsunami Monitoring Network measures tsunami waves arriving on the offshore islands and the two main islands of New Zealand (Fig. 8). When completed in 2010, the network will consist of 19 monitoring stations. Five stations located on offshore islands, including the New Zealand stations on Raoul Island (at Boat Cove and Fishing Rock)

and Chatham Island, and the Australian stations on Norfolk Island and Macquarie Island, will monitor incoming regional and distant events en route to the main islands of New Zealand. Seven stations positioned along at-risk coasts, comprising North Cape, Manukau, Great Barrier Island, East Cape, Castlepoint, Kaikoura and Puysegur, will detect the first landfall of tsunami waves on the main islands. A further seven stations installed at centres of population that are vulnerable to tsunami, comprising Auckland, Tauranga, Gisborne, Napier, Wellington, Christchurch and Dunedin, will be used to issue an 'all clear' after an event. During an event, the data from the network will be useful for determining actual first arrival times at the stations and monitoring the variability in wave height at these locations throughout the event.

At each of the New Zealand tsunami monitoring stations wave height is measured by two pressure sensors submerged in the ocean. The sensors are either attached to a vertical structure, such as a wharf, or bolted to the seafloor. The sensors are connected to data logging equipment that records relative sea level, sampling ten times per second. An equipment cabinet houses the data logger, communications gear and batteries. Accurate timing is achieved via an external

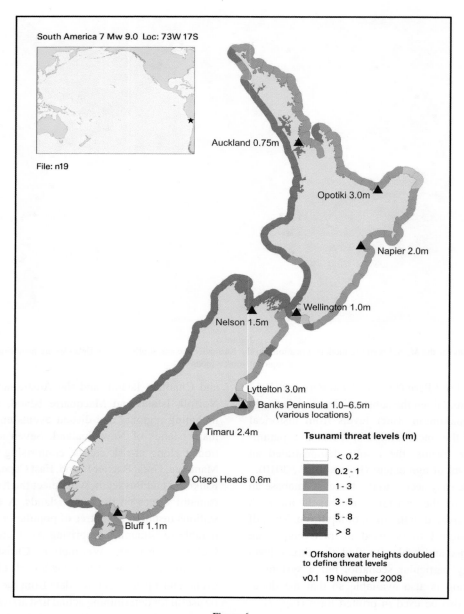

South America 7 Mw 9.0 Loc: 73W 17S

File: n19

Auckland 0.75m

Opotiki 3.0m

Napier 2.0m

Wellington 1.0m

Nelson 1.5m

Lyttelton 3.0m
Banks Peninsula 1.0–6.5m
(various locations)

Timaru 2.4m

Otago Heads 0.6m

Bluff 1.1m

Tsunami threat levels (m)

	< 0.2
	0.2 - 1
	1 - 3
	3 - 5
	5 - 8
	> 8

* Offshore water heights doubled
to define threat levels

v0.1 19 November 2008

Figure 6

Model results for a M_w 9.0 earthquake in the approximate location of the 1868 Peru earthquake. Superimposed triangles show the estimated maximum water-levels from historical observations of the 1868 tsunami at key locations

GPS unit. Telemetry equipment, and in some cases solar panels, are also installed.

The tsunami data are transmitted in near real-time to the GeoNet Data Management Centre in Lower Hutt where they are disseminated for use by national and international tsunami advisers. Raw and de-tided data from the tsunami monitoring stations are displayed on the GeoNet website. An example of tsunami data from the 30 September 2009 Samoa Tsunami is shown in Fig. 9. The tsunami data assist in emergency response and is freely available for research via the GeoNet website: http://www.geonet.org.nz. The tsunami monitoring network contributes towards an international collaboration to collect and share tsunami data in the Pacific.

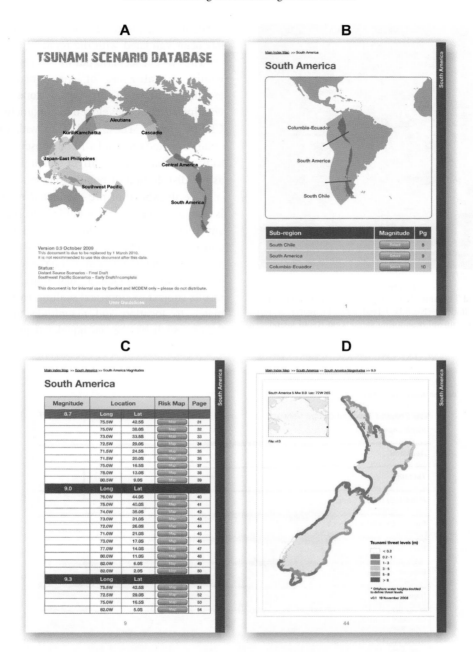

Figure 7
Example pages from the clickable pdf of pre-calculated threat-level scenarios. **a** Cover page and regional index, **b** sub-region index, **c** magnitude and location index, **d** threat-level map

5. Future Plans

The current scenario database is being expanded to include a more comprehensive set of models for regional events, in particular at lower magnitude levels. A revised set of bathymetric grids is also being developed for this work with a resolution of ten arc seconds in the near-shore area for the entire coast. Within these refined grids modelling will take place to the shoreline, removing the need for the amplification parameter currently used to scale offshore water-levels. The distant source scenarios will also be

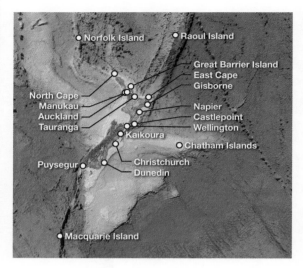

Figure 8
The New Zealand Tsunami Monitoring Network and complementary Australian Stations (Norfolk Island and Macquarie Island). There are two tsunami monitoring stations on Raoul Island

recalculated using these finer grids once the process has been validated with the regional sources.

The current scenario pdf illustrates the threat level within coastal zones of approximately 40 km in length. A new set of coastal zones for tsunami warnings is being developed in conjunction with local CDEM groups. These will align with existing governance boundaries and will be chosen with reference to natural features that affect tsunami impact as well as the distribution of population density.

One drawback of pre-calculated model scenarios is that any actual event is unlikely to precisely match any one scenario. The location will in general not correspond exactly to one of the scenarios, and in most cases the magnitude will have to be rounded up to the nearest modelled magnitude, or the model results subject to empirical scaling. Even with a close match to location and magnitude there are other factors, such as the earthquake depth and detailed

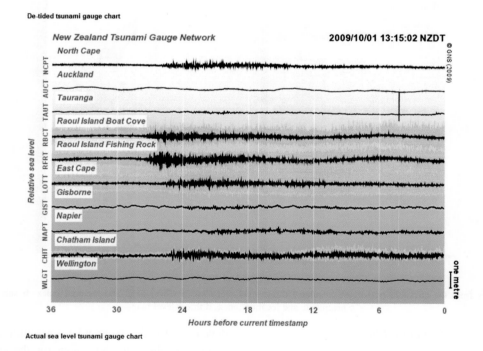

Figure 9
De-tided tsunami gauge data as displayed on the GeoNet website during the 30 September 2009 Samoa Tsunami. The timestamp shown at the *top right* is the time when the image was created. The previous 36 h of sea level variations from all operational sites are displayed, oldest to most recent from *left* to *right*. Within the sampling period of 1 min, the *dark part* of the trace shows the average sea level height, whilst the *grey part* shows the maximum and minimum values. The vertical line in the Tauranga data at ~4 h before the timestamp is attributed to a faulty sensor

slip-distribution, that affect the scale of the tsunami generated. Ideally the tsunami source should be inferred from direct measurements of the tsunami, such as from DART buoys (GONZÁLEZ et al., 2005). Systems such as SIFT (GICA et al., 2008) or web-SIFT (MERATI et al., 2010), in development at NOAA, are designed to operate in this way enabling a fast determination of the tsunami source and forward modelling to its likely impact. It is anticipated that New Zealand will adopt a scheme such as one of these at some stage in the future.

A historical database of tsunami and their impacts in New Zealand has been in development for several years and is nearly complete. The data from this database will be made available to the GeoNet Duty Team and the Tsunami Experts Panel to be used in the event of a tsunami to find historical analogues that can help constrain tsunami forecasts.

The east coast of the North Island has experienced two tsunami-earthquakes in 1947, and a possible earlier tsunami-earthquake in 1880 (BELL et al., 2010). These events are especially problematic because of the low felt intensities that make self-evacuation of nearby residents unlikely. The low rupture speeds also make it difficult to quickly and accurately determine the earthquake moment magnitude. The possibility of using real-time GPS streaming from continuous stations on the coast near the areas of suspect tsunami-earthquake activity is being investigated. This could potentially assist early identification of tsunami-earthquakes through their ground deformation effects. Producing an effective warning even with this information is still very challenging due to the short travel times.

6. Conclusions

The historical and pre-historical records of tsunami in New Zealand demonstrate a clear risk to people and infrastructure. One aspect of mitigating this risk is to provide warnings of impending tsunami to local emergency management groups who are able to coordinate evacuations and other preventative measures.

A set of procedures has been put in place to be followed by emergency management authorities in the event of a potential tsunami threat. Advice of a potential threat may come from the PTWC or the GeoNet Duty Team and is passed to the National Disaster Office who may seek further scientific guidance before disseminating warnings to the local organisations able to organise a response. In the first instance scientific advice is provided by an on-call Duty Officer from GeoNet, and if time permits an expert panel is convened to provide more detailed advice.

A database of pre-computed tsunami models has been compiled that can be referred to in order to provide an initial forecast of likely tsunami impacts and the consequent appropriate level of response. Currently this database incorporates models for distant tsunami sources at an appropriate range of magnitudes and locations. An easily referenced pdf file has been compiled showing the level of threat for each part of the New Zealand coastline as inferred from the database scenario. Scenarios from this database have been compared with historical events, and it is believed that the level of threat inferred from the models provides more appropriate guidance than can be derived purely from magnitude and distance from source alone.

Monitoring of a tsunami when it reaches the coast is achieved through a network of online real-time gauges that are publicly accessible through the GeoNet website. At completion the network will consist of 19 stations; at the time of the 30 September 2009 Samoa tsunami 10 of these stations were operational. Some stations are located on the extremities of New Zealand and on offshore islands in order to provide information on incoming waves, while others are positioned at major population centres with a view to providing 'all-clear' information.

Future work will see expansion of the scenario database to cover more regional scenarios and the implementation of improved techniques for using real-time water level information to provide more accurate forecasts.

Acknowledgments

All data from the New Zealand Tsunami Monitoring Network is made available free of charge through the New Zealand GeoNet project (http://www.geonet.

org.nz) to facilitate research into hazards and assessment of risk. We acknowledge the GeoNet project and its sponsors: the New Zealand Earthquake Commission (EQC), GNS Science and Land Information New Zealand (LINZ). We also acknowledge support from the Ministry for Civil Defence and Emergency Management (MCDEM) and from the Foundation for Research, Science and Technology (FRST). We thank Diana Greenslade, Vasily Titov and Gaye Downes for many helpful discussions, and NOAA Pacific Marine Environmental Laboratory for assistance with the MOST code and use of the FACTS server.

REFERENCES

ALLEN, S.C.R. and GREENSLADE, D.J.M. (2008), *Developing tsunami warnings from numerical model output*, Natural Hazards 46, 35–52.

ANNUNZIATO, A. (2007), *The Tsunami Assessment Modelling System by the Joint Research Centre*, Science of Tsunami Hazards, 26(2), 70–92.

BELL, R., WANG, X., POWER, W., DOWNES, G., and HOLDEN, C. (2010), *Hikurangi margin tsunami-earthquake generated by slip over a subducted seamount*, in preparation.

BORRERO, J.C., GONZÁLEZ, F.I., TITOV, V.V., NEWMAN, J.C., VENTURATO, A.J., and LEGG, G. (2004), *Application of FACTS as a tool for modeling, archiving and sharing tsunami simulation results*, Eos Trans. AGU, 85(47), Fall Meet Suppl., Abstract OS23D-1362.

COCHRAN, U..A., BERRYMAN, K.R., MILDENHALL, D.C., HAYWARD, B.W., SOUTHALL, K., and HOLLIS C.J. (2005), *Towards a record of Holocene tsunami and storms for northern Hawke's Bay, New Zealand*, New Zealand Journal of Geology and Geophysics 48, 507–515.

DOWNES, G., WEBB, T., MCSAVENEY, M., DARBY, D., DOSER, D., CHAGUÉ-GOFF, C. and BARNETT, A., *The 26 March and 17 May 1947 Gisborne earthquakes and tsunami: implications for tsunami hazard for the east coast, North Island, New Zealand*, In Tsunami Risk Assessment Beyond 2000: Theory, Practice and Plans, (GUSIAKOV, V.K., LEVIN, B.W. and YAKOVENKO, O.I., 2001) 55–67.

GALE, N.H. *Tsunami Duty Training Manual*, GNS Science Report (2009/67).

GICA, E., SPILLANE, M. C., TITOV, V.V., CHAMBERLIN, C. D., NEWMAN, J. C. (2008) *Development of the forecast propagation database for NOAA's Short-term Inundation Forecast for Tsunami (SIFT)*, NOAA Technical Memorandum OAR PMEL-139.

GOFF, J.R., ROUSE, H.L., JONES, S.L., HAYWARD, B.W., COCHRAN, U., MCLEA, W., DICKINSON, W.W. and MORLEY, M.S. (2000), *Evidence for an earthquake and tsunami about 3100-3400 yr ago, and other catastrophic saltwater inundations recorded in a coastal lagoon, New Zealand*, Marine Geology 170, 231–249.

GONZÁLEZ, F.I., BERNARD, E.N., MEINIG, C., EBLE, M., MOFJELD, H.O. and STALIN, S. (2005) *The NTHMP tsunameter network*. Natural Hazards 35 (1), Special Issue, U.S. National Tsunami Hazard Mitigation Program, 25–39.

GRAPES, R. and DOWNES, G. (1997) *The 1855 Wairarapa, New Zealand, earthquake: analysis of historical data*, Bulletin of the New Zealand National Society for Earthquake Engineering 30(4), 271–368.

KANAMORI, H. (1972) *Mechanism of Tsunami Earthquakes*, Physics of the Earth and Planetary Interiors 6, 346–359.

MCFADGEN, B.G. (2007) *Hostile shores: catastrophic events in prehistoric New Zealand and their impacts on Maori coastal communities*, Auckland University Press, Auckland.

MERATI, N., CHAMBERLIN, C., MOORE, C., TITOV, V.V. and VANCE, T.C. (2010) *Integration of Tsunami Analysis Tools into a GIS Workspace – Research, Modelling, and Hazard Mitigation efforts Within NOAA's Center for Tsunami Research*, in Geospatial Techniques in Urban Hazard and Disaster Analysis, Pamela S. Showalter and Yongmei Lu, Springer, Netherlands.

MINISTRY OF CIVIL DEFENCE AND EMERGENCY MANAGEMENT (MCDEM, June 2008) *National Tsunami Advisory and Warning Plan*.

NICHOL, S.L., LIAN, O.B., and CARTER, C.H. (2003) *Sheet-gravel evidence for a late Holocene tsunami run-up on beach dunes, Great Barrier Island, New Zealand*, Sedimentary Geology 155, 129–145.

POWER, W., DOWNES, G. and STIRLING, M. (2007) *Estimation of tsunami hazard in New Zealand due to South American earthquakes*, Pure and Applied Geophysics 164, 547–564.

POWER, W., GALE, N., LUKOVIC, B., GLEDHILL, K., CLITHEROE, G., BERRYMAN, K. PRASETYA, G. *Use of numerical models to inform distant-source tsunami warnings*, GNS Science Report 2010/11.

TITOV, V.V., and GONZÁLEZ, F.I. (1997) *Implementation and testing of the method of splitting tsunami (MOST) model*, NOAA Technical Memorandum ERL PMEL-112.

TITOV, V.V. and SYNOLAKIS, C.E. (1998) *Numerical modeling of tidal wave runup*, Journal of Waterway, Port, Coastal, and Ocean Engineering-Asce 124, 157–171.

U. S. INDIAN OCEAN TSUNAMI WARNING SYSTEM PROGRAM (US I-OTWS). Tsunami Warning Centre Reference Guide supported by the United States Agency for International Development and partners, Bangkok, Thailand, (2007), 331 p.

WESSEL, P. (2009) *Analysis of Observed and Predicted Tsunami Travel Times for the Pacific and Indian Oceans*, Pure and Applied Geophysics 166, 301–324.

(Received December 18, 2009, revised March 17, 2010, accepted March 22, 2010, Published online November 12, 2010)

Pure Appl. Geophys. 168 (2011), 1137–1151
© 2010 Springer Basel AG
DOI 10.1007/s00024-010-0229-3

An Evaluation of Tsunami Forecasts from the T2 Scenario Database

Diana J. M. Greenslade,[1] Stewart C. R. Allen,[1] and M. Arthur Simanjuntak[1]

Abstract—A tsunami scenario database (T2) has recently been developed for use within the Joint Australian Tsunami Warning Centre (JATWC). This scenario database has proven to be a very useful tool for forecast guidance, issuing of tsunami warnings and general event analysis. In this paper, the T2 scenarios are described, and evaluated by comparing them with observations of sea level from tsunameters for a number of recent tsunami events. In general, the T2 scenario database performs very well in terms of predicting the arrival time of the tsunami and the wave amplitudes at tsunameter locations.

Key words: Tsunami, tsunami forecast, tsunameters.

1. Introduction

The T2 scenario database (Greenslade *et al.*, 2009) has been developed to support the tsunami warning service of the Joint Australian Tsunami Warning Centre (JATWC). This scenario database is a replacement for the original, first-generation scenario database, T1 (Greenslade *et al.*, 2007), which was developed rapidly and used operationally by the JATWC from 2007 to 2009. These scenario databases are used as the basis for the issuing of tsunami warnings in the Australian region.

Previous evaluations of the T2 scenarios have been performed, but there is a need for ongoing assessment as tsunami events occur. The JATWC warnings provide a broad method for evaluating the T2 scenario database; for example, it is possible to assess whether tsunami warnings based on the predicted sea level from T2 were appropriate given the resulting impacts. However, there have been very few occasions for which tsunami warnings were actually required for the Australian coastline, and while it is somewhat useful to be able to confirm that warnings were not issued when they were not necessary, there is a need to be able to evaluate the sea level predictions from the T2 scenarios more quantitatively.

The T2 scenarios cover the deep ocean up to a depth of 20 m with spatial resolution of 4 arcmin. This means that it is not possible to use tide gauge data directly for quantitative evaluation, because a large portion of the variability seen at a tide gauge is due to the local, small-scale bathymetry and coastal topography, which is not resolved by deep-ocean scenarios. Similarly, T2 does not incorporate any inundation aspects, so observed inundation levels for events cannot be used as a comparison. One way to address this is to nest an inundation model for a particular region within the deep-water scenarios, as was done in Greenslade and Titov (2008). Here, we concentrate on verifying the deep-ocean model output directly against deep-ocean tsunameter observations. The global tsunameter network has expanded considerably since the Indian Ocean event of 2004, and so it is now quite feasible to use these observations for evaluation of tsunami model output.

Section 2 of this paper describes some general features of the T2 scenario database. Section 3 presents the evaluation of the scenarios for a number of tsunami events. We also include comparisons with the first-generation scenario database, T1, where possible. These results are discussed further in Sect. 4, and Sect. 5 includes a summary and some indications of further work.

2. The T2 Scenario Database

Only a few relevant details of the T2 scenario database are described here; further details can be

---
[1] Centre for Australian Weather and Climate Research, Bureau of Meteorology, Melbourne, Australia. E-mail: d.greenslade@bom.gov.au

found in GREENSLADE *et al.* (2009). The basis for the source locations within T2 is the set of subduction zones as defined by BIRD (2003). All subduction zones within the Indian and Pacific Oceans are included in T2. This incorporates subduction zones such as the Makran subduction zone south of Pakistan and the "Ring of Fire" around the Pacific Ocean rim. In addition, several source locations that are not designated as subduction zones by BIRD (2003) are included. These non-subduction-zone sources are located:

- Along the Timor Trench to the north of Australia
- To the north of Timor
- In the Manus region (north of Papua New Guinea)
- Between the Cascadia Fault and Alaska
- Along the Hjort Trench, near Macquarie Island (MECKEL *et al.*, 2003)
- And the Sunda Arc is extended northwards, according to CUMMINS (2007).

The South Sandwich subduction zone in the South Atlantic Ocean is also included. This results in a total of 521 source locations for T2. These are all shown in Fig. 1.

The T2 scenario database includes four earthquake magnitudes of $M_w = 7.5$, 8.0, 8.5 and 9.0 at each source location. The ruptures for large earthquakes are represented as the sum of a number of smaller 100-km-long rupture elements, each of which

has its strike closely aligned with the local subduction zone. For example, for a $M_w = 8.0$ scenario, two adjacent rupture elements are combined to create one rupture with length of approximately 200 km (this will not be exact due to the curvature of the subduction zone), width of 65 km and slip of 2.2 m. Details of the rupture dimensions for each magnitude are shown in Table 1. These have been derived from the relationship between magnitude and rupture dimensions as follows. The magnitude (M_w) is related to seismic moment (M_o) as

$$M_w = \frac{2}{3}(\log_{10} M_o - 9.1), \quad (1)$$

and seismic moment is related to the rupture characteristics of the earthquake as

$$M_o = \mu L W u_o, \quad (2)$$

where μ is the shear modulus and L, W and u_o are the length, width and slip of the rupture, respectively (in metres). Here we take μ to be 4.5×10^{10} N m^{-2}.

Note that the rupture elements are not identical for each magnitude, i.e. this is not a unit source technique as used in as the National Oceanic and Atmospheric Administration (NOAA)'s short-term inundation forecasting for tsunamis (SIFT) system (GICA *et al.*, 2008), as the width and slip of the ruptures are different for each magnitude. Note also that the details of the $M_w = 9.0$ event on the South

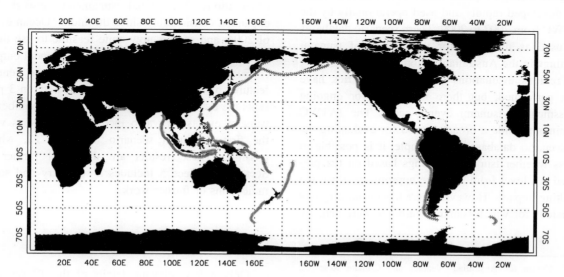

Figure 1
Source locations included in the T2 scenario database

Table 1

Details of the initial conditions used for the scenarios in the T2 scenario database

Magnitude (M_w)	Seismic moment M_o (Nm)	Width (W) (km)	Number of rupture elements	Length (approximate) (L) (km)	Slip (u_o) (m)
7.5	2.24×10^{20}	50	1	100	1
8.0	1.26×10^{21}	65	2	200	2.2
8.5	7.2×10^{21}	80	4	400	5
9.0	4.0×10^{22}	100	10	1,000	8.8
9.0 (Sandwich only)	4.0×10^{22}	100	8	800	11

Sandwich subduction zone (Fig. 1) are slightly different from all other $M_w = 9.0$ events in the database. This is due to the fact that this subduction zone is not long enough to support an event of length 1,000 km. An example of a $M_w = 9.0$ rupture, i.e. the initial conditions imposed on the ocean surface, is shown in Fig. 2.

A result of the T2 multiple rupture element technique is that the source location for each T2 scenario can be provided as a set of locations, rather than as an individual source location. This has some advantages when the rupture direction is not known in real time, as a set of possible scenarios, rather than a single scenario, can be selected to provide warning guidance. Figure 3 shows the locations of the centroid of each rupture element that contributes to scenarios 43a, 43b, 43c and 43d. Note that the location of the $M_w = 7.5$ rupture element is staggered relative to the rupture elements of the other magnitude scenarios. This was specified so that the midpoint of the top edges of the ruptures would be colocated for all scenarios of any magnitude at

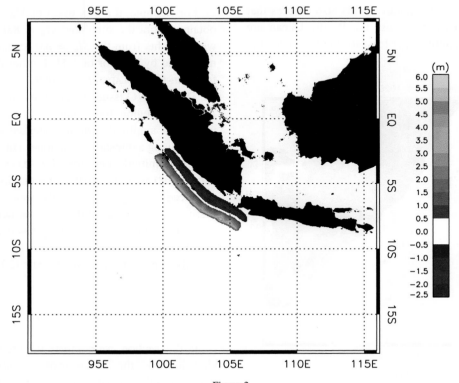

Figure 2

Initial conditions for scenario 45d from the T2 scenario database

177

a particular mid-point. Mid-points are spaced 100 km along the strike of the fault. When all four magnitude scenarios are included, this results in a total of 1,865 individual scenarios in the T2 scenario database.

Recent research (D. BURBIDGE, personal communication) has provided improved estimates of the value of the dip for global subduction zones, and this information is incorporated into the T2 scenario database. These values are shown in Fig. 4, where it can be seen that the dip values range from a shallow 8° along the Makran Fault, to almost 70° along the Hjort Trench. In the locations where a dip rate has not been established (for example, the Manus region) a standard dip value of 25° is used. The underlying bathymetry dataset used in T2 is the same 4 arcmin dataset as was used in the first version of the scenario database (T1) and is described in GREENSLADE et al. (2007). All of the T2 scenarios have the same rake (90°) and depth (top of rupture = 10 km) of the hypocentre.

The method of splitting tsunamis (MOST) model (TITOV and SYNOLAKIS, 1998) is used to generate the scenarios. The model run-time for each scenario is 24 h to ensure that reflections off underwater features or distant coasts are captured. This also ensures that tsunamis propagating across the Pacific Ocean are appropriately simulated at least for the first arrival at the Australian coast. The horizontal grid spacing for T2 is 4 arcmin, and through the Courant–Friedrichs–Lewy (CFL) criterion, this imposes a limit of 12 s on the time step. The maximum tsunami amplitude for each scenario is calculated at each time step, ensuring that all peaks are accurately captured in the maximum amplitude maps. Only positive amplitudes are considered in the determination of maximum tsunami amplitude.

Intermediate magnitude earthquakes, i.e. those with magnitudes other than 7.5, 8.0, 8.5 and 9.0, are derived from the pre-computed scenarios by applying a scaling factor to the sea level elevation. This provides guidance for earthquakes with magnitudes ranging from 7.3 to 9.2 at 0.1 magnitude intervals. The scaling is derived by assuming that the only difference between the rupture of the pre-computed scenario (with magnitude, say, M_1) and the rupture of the new earthquake (with magnitude, say, M_2) is the slip. The scaling factor, F_s, can therefore be derived from Eqs. 1 and 2 as

$$F_s = 10^{\frac{3}{2}(M_2 - M_1)}. \tag{3}$$

For example, if a new event of $M_w = 8.1$ is to be obtained from the simulated $M_w = 8.0$ scenario, the wave heights from the $M_w = 8.0$ scenario should be multiplied by a factor of 1.41. Further details can be found in GREENSLADE et al. (2009).

The JATWC issues tsunami warnings within the Australian region by examining the values of the maximum amplitude within specified coastal zones and applying a threshold technique. This is based on a technique initially described by ALLEN and GREENSLADE (2008) as applied to the T1 scenario database. An enhanced technique has recently been developed that firstly addresses some of the issues associated with the previous technique and secondly has been developed specifically for the T2 scenarios. This technique is described in ALLEN and GREENSLADE (2010).

3. Evaluation

In this section, we compare the predicted surface elevation from the T2 scenarios with observations of sea level in the open ocean for several recent tsunami events. Due to the rapid increase in the number of

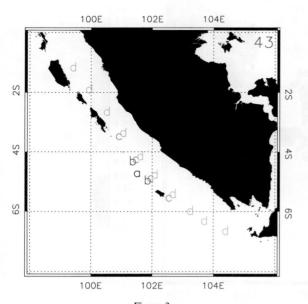

Figure 3
Locations of the centroid of each rupture element that contributes to scenarios 43a, 43b, 43c and 43d

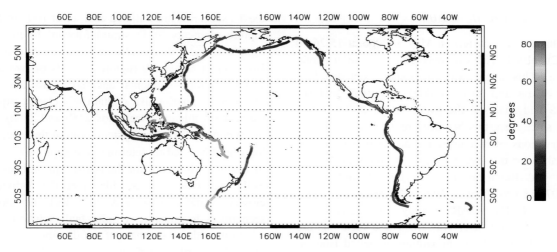

Figure 4
Value of the dip for subduction zones in the Indian and Pacific Oceans

Table 2

Details of the tsunami events used for evaluation

Region	Lon/lat	Date/time (UTC)	Magnitude (M_w)
Tonga 2006	185.84°E, 20.13°S	15:26 3rd May 2006	8.0
Sumatra 2007	101.37°E, 4.52°S	11:10 12th September 2007	8.4
Kuril Islands 2009	155.16°E, 46.86°N	17:49 15th January 2009	7.4
Tonga 2009	185.33°E, 23.05°S	18:18 19th March 2009	7.6

tsunameters deployed in the global oceans over the past few years, there are an increasing number of tsunami events that are well observed. In this paper, it is not possible to evaluate every event that has been observed by a tsunameter. We consider two events that have previously been considered in GREENSLADE and TITOV (2008) with respect to the T1 scenario database, and also include two recent events from 2009. In total, four events are considered here and they are listed in Table 2.

All earthquake details are taken from the US Geological Survey (USGS) historical earthquakes information.[1] Note that these are sometimes different from the magnitudes that the JATWC uses in real time. For the purposes of this work, we are not assessing the operational forecasts, but the accuracy of the sea level in hindsight, given the "true" earthquake magnitude. So we use the best available post-processed magnitudes, in this case, the USGS historical estimates.

The tsunameter observations used for verification of the T2 sea level forecasts need processing before they can be used directly as comparison with the T2 scenarios. In particular, the tidal signal and other low-frequency variability needs to be removed from the sea level signal. The observed tsunameter time series during a tsunami event typically consists of a number of sections with different sampling rates: 15-s frequency during the arrival of the Rayleigh waves, 1-min frequency covering the arrival time of the tsunami, and then a return to the standard 15-min frequency non-event mode reporting. For the first two events examined here, processed data was provided by NOAA's Pacific Marine Environmental Laboratory (PMEL). For the two events of 2009, cubic spline interpolation was used to produce a 1-min time series, and a Kaiser–Bessel high-pass filter was then applied to the data. The filter has 300 weights and a cut-off period of 180 min.

---

[1] http://earthquake.usgs.gov/earthquakes/world/historical.php.

3.1. Tonga 2006, $M_w = 8.0$

This event occurred on May 3, 2006 at 15:26:40 (UTC) about 160 km northeast of Nuku'Alofa, Tonga. This event was previously considered in GREENSLADE and TITOV (2008). For that analysis, USGS had analysed the event as $M_w = 7.9$. However, since then, this has been revised to $M_w = 8.0$. Observations of sea level in the deep ocean were available for this event from a Deep-ocean Assessment and Reporting of Tsunamis (DART) buoy (51407) at (203.493°E, 19.634°N) and an easy-to-deploy (ETD) DART buoy at (201.887°E, 20.5095°N), both near Hawaii. These locations are shown, along with the maximum modelled tsunami amplitude from T2, in Fig. 5. It can be seen that the locations of the tsunameters are quite distant from the main tsunami signal. Nevertheless, the tsunami was observed by these buoys with a maximum amplitude of approximately 1 cm.

In order to obtain the forecast sea level from the T2 scenario database, we need to find the closest (in space) $M_w = 8.0$ scenario. As mentioned in Sect. 2,

the T2 scenarios are initiated as a set of 100-km-long rupture elements. It is straightforward to find the rupture element that is closest to the event (Fig. 6). However, a $M_w = 8.0$ rupture consists of two individual rupture elements and so there are two $M_w = 8.0$ scenarios that contain this closest rupture element (in this case scenarios 245b and 246b). For the operational warning system, both of these scenarios would be used to determine the appropriate level of warning. However, for the post-event analysis and evaluation here, we consider just the individual closest scenario. One way to select the closest scenario is to consider a finite fault solution. This would provide an estimate of the distribution of slip over the Earth's surface, which could then be compared with the initial conditions from the relevant scenarios. In this case, a finite fault solution was not available, but a comparison of the sea level time series from the two potential scenarios with the observations shows that the most appropriate T2 scenario is 246b.

The time series of surface elevation from the tsunameters and from the scenario database is shown

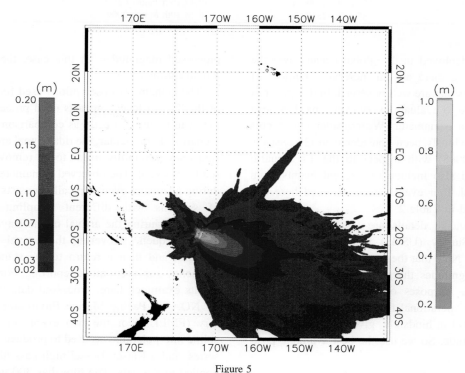

Figure 5
Maximum tsunami amplitude from T2 during the May 3rd, 2006 Tonga event. The locations of the tsunameters are shown here by the *orange circles* near Hawaii

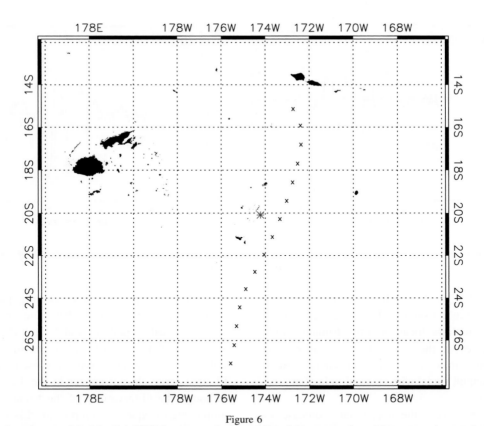

Figure 6

Map showing the epicentre of the May 3rd, 2006 Tonga event (*red asterisk*) and the centre points of the rupture elements in the region that contribute to scenarios in the T2 scenario database (*black crosses*). The closest rupture element to the event is designated by a cross that is slightly bolder than the others

in Fig. 7. Time series from the closest T1 scenario are also shown here (reproduced from GREENSLADE and TITOV, 2008). For the DART II (Fig. 7a) it can be seen that there is not much difference between the T1 and T2 scenarios; both predicted the arrival time and amplitude of the first wave and the overall frequency of the wave reasonably well. However, there are a number of peaks that are missed by both scenarios. One explanation for this may be that the later strong arrivals seen in the observations are due to reflections from features that are not captured by the coarse resolution model.

A more significant difference between the two scenario databases can be seen at the ETD location shown in Fig. 7b. While the arrival time and first few wave amplitudes are again captured reasonably well by both scenarios, T2 does a considerably better job at capturing the maximum positive peak, while T1 misses it completely. This suggests that this peak is

probably due to reflection or scattering of the wave from a bathymetric feature outside the T1 domain. While there are a number of improvements that have been incorporated in T2, the aspect most likely to have had a positive impact here is the expansion of the domain to cover the entire Pacific Ocean. This is discussed further in GREENSLADE et al. (2009).

3.2. Sumatra 2007, $M_w = 8.4$

This event occurred on September 12, 2007 at 11:10:26 (UTC) off southern Sumatra. This event had some significant impacts with 25 fatalities and numerous people injured. According to USGS, this event was $M_w = 8.4$ and occurred at (101.374°E, 4.52°S) at a depth of 34 km. During this event, a DART II buoy deployed in the Indian Ocean by the Thailand Meteorological Department observed the tsunami. The tsunameter is located to the west-northwest of Phuket

181

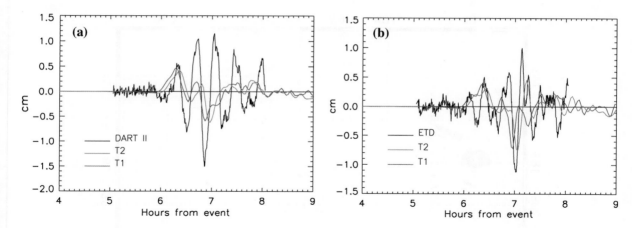

Figure 7

a Comparison of observed and modelled (scenario 246b) sea level at the DART II for the $M_w = 8.0$ Tonga event of 3rd May, 2006. **b** Same as (**a**) but for the ETD

at (88.54°E, 8.9°N). Figure 8 shows the maximum modelled amplitude from the closest T2 scenario (see below) along with the location of this tsunameter. As for the Tonga event, the tsunameter observation is not located in the main beam of the tsunami energy, but did register a tsunami signal with an amplitude of approximately 2 cm.

In order to obtain the appropriate forecast sea level from the T2 scenario database, we need to find the closest $M_w = 8.5$ scenario and multiply it by a factor of 0.71 to derive the amplitudes for a $M_w = 8.4$ event. For this event, there are four $M_w = 8.5$ scenarios that contain the closest rupture element to the earthquake. As for the Tonga event, we want to consider only the individual closest scenario. Examination of the time series from each of the four "closest" scenarios, in conjunction with the observations, indicates that scenario 43c is the most appropriate.

Figure 9 shows a comparison of the observed sea level from the tsunameter and the output from the T2 scenario database. Sea level from the closest T1 scenario is also shown here (reproduced from GREENSLADE and TITOV, 2008). It can be seen that both T1 and T2 do a good job of forecasting the tsunami arrival time, with T2 arriving slightly early and T1 slightly late. The amplitudes of both the crest and trough components of the first wave are captured very well by T2, but underestimated by T1, and T1 also misses the location of the trough. This first crest is where the maximum amplitudes occur, and so it is

an important input into the warning process (see ALLEN and GREENSLADE, 2010). The second small crest is missed by both T1 and T2, but the third peak is well predicted by T1 and overestimated by T2. Note also that the high-frequency oscillations in the T1 time series do not appear in the T2 time series. Although the observations of the tsunami contain a similar high-frequency component, this is not likely to be a physical aspect of the tsunami wave, because these oscillations also occur in the observed sea level before the tsunami arrives at the tsunameter. Overall, given that the first wave from T2 is so well predicted, we conclude that the T2 scenario provides a significant improvement over the T1 scenario for this event.

3.3. Kuril Islands 2009, $M_w = 7.4$

This earthquake occurred on January 15th, 2009 at 17:49 (UTC). USGS has analysed the event as $M_w = 7.4$ at 36 km depth and located at (155.156°E, 46.862°N). Observations of sea level in the deep ocean were available for this event from three nearby tsunameters. In order to obtain the forecast sea level from the T2 scenario database, we need to find the closest $M_w = 7.5$ scenario and multiply the sea level by a factor of 0.71. The $M_w = 7.5$ scenarios consist of only one rupture element, so in this case the closest scenario is 324a. The maximum amplitude from this scenario (appropriately scaled) is shown in Fig. 10 along with the locations of the tsunameters.

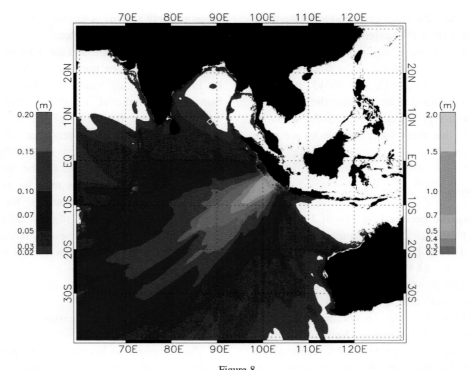

Figure 8
Maximum tsunami amplitude from T2 during the September 12th 2007 Sumatra event. The Thai DART II buoy is designated by a white diamond

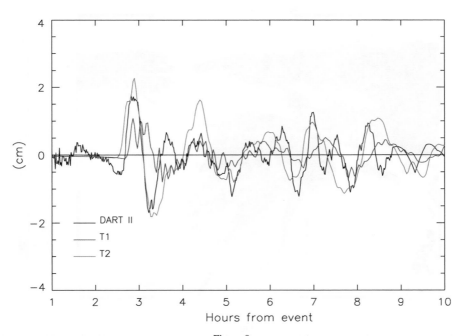

Figure 9
Comparison of observed and modelled sea level for the $M_\text{w} = 8.4$ event of 12th September 2007

The time series of surface elevation from the three tsunameters and from the scaled scenario are shown in Fig. 11. In each case, the model predicted the arrival time and the amplitude of the first peak very well. For tsunameters 21413 and 46413, however, there are some peaks that arrive after the first wave that are not well reproduced by the model scenario. Note, however, that these wave amplitudes are quite small—<0.5 cm.

3.4. Tonga 2009, $M_w = 7.6$

This earthquake occurred on March 19, 2009 at 18:18 (UTC) about 220 km south-southeast of Nuku'Alofa, Tonga. USGS has analysed the event as $M_w = 7.6$ at 34 km depth and located at (185.33°E, 23.05°S). Observations of the tsunami were available for this event from the nearby tsunameter 51426. In order to obtain the forecast sea level from the T2 scenario database, we multiply the sea level from the closest $M_w = 7.5$ scenario by a factor of 1.41. In this case, the closest scenario is 243a. The maximum amplitude from this scenario

(appropriately scaled) is shown in Fig. 12 along with the location of the tsunameter.

The time series of surface elevation from the tsunameter and from the scaled scenario is shown in Fig. 13. In this case, the first wave of the tsunami is predicted extremely well, with the arrival time and frequency of the wave very well reproduced. It can be seen that the maximum amplitude of the first crest is slightly underestimated, while the amplitude of the first trough is slightly overestimated. This may be an artefact of the processing of the observations; for example, if the mean were calculated slightly differently, then this would reduce both of these differences. Despite this, overall this event is represented very well by the T2 scenario.

4. Discussion

The comparisons here have been performed in a qualitative rather than a quantitative manner. The main features that we wish to predict from the model

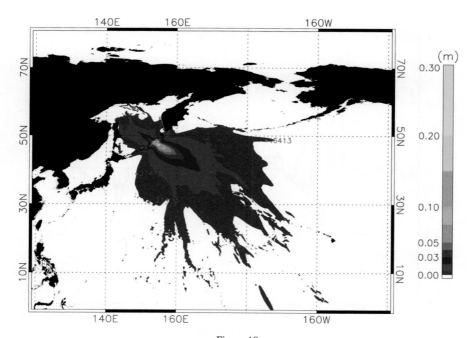

Figure 10
Maximum amplitude map for the 15th January Kuril Islands event. Locations of tsunameters 21413, 21418 and 46413 are indicated by *orange circles*

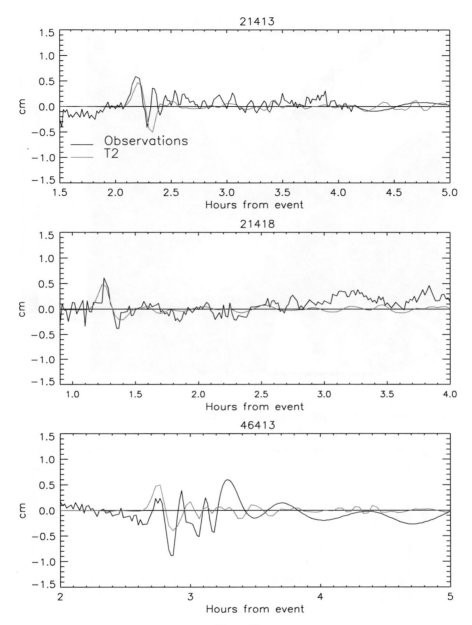

Figure 11
Comparison of observed and modelled sea level for the $M_w = 7.4$ Kuril Islands event of 15th January 2009

are the arrival time, the maximum amplitude and the frequency of the tsunami. Given the assumptions inherent in the scenario database and the complexity of the physical system, only these broad features of the tsunami are expected to be predictable. These can be assessed by visual inspection of the time series, as has been done here. Any quantitative assessments would need to take account of the potentially different spatial and temporal scales of variability between the model and observations. For example, in the cases examined here, the modelled time series are at 2-min frequency, while the observations are at 1 min. Further issues could arise from small phase errors, which could lead to adjacent model grid points being more

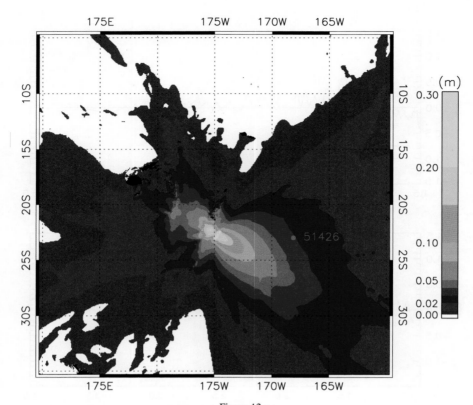

Figure 12
Maximum amplitude map for the 19th March 2009 Tonga event. The location of tsunameter 51426 is indicated by the *orange circle*

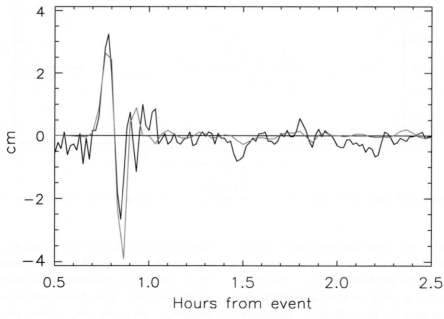

Figure 13
Comparison of observed and modelled sea level for the $M_w = 7.6$ Tonga event of 19th March 2009

appropriate locations for comparison with the observations.

The previous section has shown that, in almost all cases, the closest T2 scenario for each event provides a very good prediction of most aspects of the ensuing tsunami wave. In particular, the arrival time is predicted very well in each case and the maximum amplitudes are also predicted reasonably well. The cases where the sea level variability is not well reproduced (e.g. at tsunameters 21413 and 46413 during the Kuril Islands event) are typically smaller-amplitude events.

The JATWC warning strategy is based on the maximum amplitudes from the T2 scenarios within coastal regions (ALLEN and GREENSLADE, 2010) so it is most important, from a warning perspective, to get those correct. The four cases considered here have shown that we can have confidence in the tsunami amplitudes from T2, which in turn gives us confidence in the tsunami warnings based on T2. By re-examining the events evaluated in GREENSLADE and TITOV (2008), we can also be confident that the T2 scenario database provides improved sea level predictions over the T1 database.

Care has been taken in the processing of the tsunameter sea level observations, but results from the Tonga 2009 event suggest that some of the differences seen between the model and observations may be due to the processing of the observations, rather than deficiencies in the model. Developing an appropriate technique for processing tsunameter observations is challenging. Further issues relating to processing of the observations occur if the tsunameter is located close to the source (say, to provide adequate time for detection and warning). In this case, the observations of a tsunami may be aliased with Rayleigh waves. Since the Rayleigh waves are higher in frequency than the tsunami, they can often be removed by applying a band-pass filter instead of a high-pass filter. This has not been necessary here, but it will be an issue for the Australian tsunameters located close to the Puysegur subduction zone (south of New Zealand) and a number of tsunameters that have been deployed in the Indian Ocean.

Selection of the closest scenario for events with long ruptures has been done here by examining the time series from all possible "closest" scenarios and comparing them with the observed time series at the tsunameter(s). By considering the arrival times, this provides an indication of which scenario is closest to the event. This can in turn provide some insight into the actual rupture—in particular, if the arrival time from the scenario compares well to the observations, then it is likely that the slip distribution matches that in the scenario database.

5. Further Work

This report has described the T2 scenario database that is used operationally within the JATWC to provide guidance for tsunami warnings in the Australian region. Evaluations against tsunameter observations have shown that the scenario database provides accurate deep-water sea level predictions during a tsunami event. However, this evaluation has shown that, in some respects, there is scope for further improvement in the sea level predictions. Future work will involve development of a more quantitative assessment technique and investigation of the cases where the model forecasts are seen to have deficiencies. Additional validation studies will be undertaken as more tsunami events are observed by the expanding tsunameter network.

There are several other aspects to the work which are currently undergoing development, or that require further research. For example, predicted arrival times are an important component of tsunami warnings and can also be used to assess the warning characteristics of an observing network (e.g. see WARNE and GREENSLADE, 2008). The JATWC currently determines arrival times using the tsunami travel time (TTT) software (GEOWARE, 2007). It should be possible to determine accurate arrival times (of both the first wave and the maximum wave) directly from the T2 scenarios, and this might be expected to produce more accurate arrival times, given that the T2 ruptures are more physically realistic than the point sources typically used in the TTT calculations.

One current area of active research involves the development of a tsunami data assimilation scheme. The initial aim of such a scheme is to use observations of sea level from deep-ocean tsunameters to modify the T2 scenarios during an event and provide improved estimates of coastal sea level as a basis for the issuing of tsunami warnings. Preliminary results of this research have been encouraging.

Further improvements that could be made to the scenario database involve the development of more appropriate boundary conditions for the southern boundary, i.e. at the Antarctic ice-edge, and the incorporation of improved global or regional bathymetric data sets when they become available. As subduction zone science develops, for example, as knowledge of the dip of a particular subduction zone improves, this could also be incorporated into the scenario database. It may be that, in the cases of the most distant subduction zones, tsunami waves might be expected to arrive beyond the 24-h limit. This will be addressed in the future by inspecting these extreme cases and extending the run-time if necessary.

The T2 scenario database is currently being enhanced by the addition of further scenarios. The highest priority for these is the addition of a full series of $M_w = 7.0$ scenarios, focussing first on the Indian Ocean. In addition, a number of higher-magnitude scenarios will be generated to provide appropriate guidance for events of $M_w = 9.3$ and above. The precise magnitude of these large scenarios will need to be considered. For example, if they are generated for $M_w = 9.5$ events, then this allows scaling up to $M_w = 9.7$ and it is not clear whether this would really be necessary. It may be more appropriate to generate scenarios for $M_w = 9.3$ earthquakes, providing guidance for events up to $M_w = 9.5$.

Eventually, it is envisaged that, when a potentially tsunamigenic earthquake occurs, the deep-water component of the tsunami model will be run in real time on the Bureau of Meteorology's supercomputing facilities, initialised using event-specific rupture details obtained from seismic data and incorporating a sophisticated data assimilation scheme for sea level observations. Detailed inundation models could then be run for areas identified to be at risk, using boundary conditions from the real-time deep-water forecast. As an intermediate alternative, high-resolution grids could be nested within the pre-computed scenarios. Tsunami warnings could be refined based on the output of the inundation models. In addition to

the need for high-resolution coastal bathymetry and topography data, significant computational resources would be required for this sort of system, and research into optimising the MOST code for real-time integration would be necessary. This could incorporate a nested grid scheme, variable spatial resolution, or some alternative techniques to reduce the computational time.

Acknowledgments

David Burbidge (Geoscience Australia) is acknowledged for providing details of the dip values for global subduction zones. NOAA/PMEL is thanked for providing the processed ETD and DART data for the Tonga 2006 and Sumatra 2007 events. Useful comments on the manuscript were provided by Paul Whitmore, Oscar Alves, Tony Leggett and one anonymous reviewer.

REFERENCES

ALLEN, S.C.R. and GREENSLADE, D.J.M. (2008), *Developing Tsunami Warnings from Numerical Model Output*, Nat. Hazards, 46(1), 35–52, doi:10.1007/s11069-007-9180-8.

ALLEN, S.C.R. and GREENSLADE, D.J.M. (2010), *Model-based tsunami warnings derived from observed impacts*, Nat. Hazards Earth Syst. Sci. (accepted).

BIRD, P. (2003), *An updated digital model of plate boundaries*, Geochemistry Geophysics Geosystems, 4(3), 1027, doi:10.1029/2001GC000252.

CUMMINS, P.R. (2007), *The potential for giant tsunamigenic earthquakes in the northern Bay of Bengal*, Letters to Nature, 449, doi:10.1038/nature06088.

GEOWARE (2007), *TTT - A tsunami travel time calculator*.

GICA, E., SPILLANE, M.C., TITOV, V.V., CHAMBERLIN, C.D. and NEWMAN, J.C. (2008), *Development of the Forecast Propagation Database for NOAA's Short-Term Inundation Forecast for Tsunamis (SIFT)*, NOAA Technical Memorandum, OAR PMEL-139, 89 PP.

GREENSLADE, D.J.M. and V.V. TITOV (2008), *A Comparison Study of Two Numerical Tsunami Forecasting Systems*, Pure Appl. Geophys. Topical Volume, 165(11/12), doi:10.1007/s00024-008-0413-x.

GREENSLADE, D.J.M, SIMANJUNTAK, M.A., CHITTLEBOROUGH, J. and BURBIDGE, D. (2007), *A first-generation real-time tsunami forecasting system for the Australian region*, BMRC Research Report No. 126, Bur. Met., Australia.

GREENSLADE, D.J.M, SIMANJUNTAK, M.A., and ALLEN, S.C.R. (2009), *An Enhanced Tsunami Scenario Database:T2*, CAWCR Technical Report No. 14, Bur. Met., Australia.

MECKEL, T.A., COFFIN, M.F., MOSHER, S., SYMONDS, P., BERNADEL, G. and MANN, P. (2003), *Underthrusting at the Hjort Trench,*

Australian-Pacific plate boundary: Incipient subduction?, Geochem. Geophys. Geosyst., 4(12*)*, doi:10.1029/2002GC000498.

TITOV, V.V. and SYNOLAKIS, C.E. (1998), *Numerical Modeling of Tidal Wave Runup*, J. Waterw. Port Coast. Ocean Eng, 124(4), pp 157–171.

WARNE, J. and GREENSLADE, D.J.M. (2008) *Tsunami Network Design and Review – How do you know the tsunami will be observed by your network?* Proceedings of the International Conference on Tsunami Warning, Bali, Indonesia, November, 2008.

(Received December 18, 2009, revised March 17, 2010, accepted March 23, 2010, Published online November 12, 2010)

Pure Appl. Geophys. 168 (2011), 1153–1173
© 2010 Springer Basel AG
DOI 10.1007/s00024-010-0230-x

▌Pure and Applied Geophysics

Tsunami Simulations for Regional Sources in the South China and Adjoining Seas

EMILE A. OKAL,[1] COSTAS E. SYNOLAKIS,[2,3,4] and NIKOS KALLIGERIS[3,4]

Abstract—We present 14 scenarios of potential tsunamis in the South China Sea and its adjoining basins, the Sulu and Sulawezi Seas. The sources consist of earthquake dislocations inspired by the the study of historical events, either recorded (since 1900) or described in historical documents going back to 1604. We consider worst-case scenarios, where the size of the earthquake is not limited by the largest known event, but merely by the dimension of the basin over which a coherent fault may propagate. While such scenarios are arguably improbable, they may not be impossible, and as such must be examined. For each scenario, we present a simulation of the tsunami's propagation in the marine basin, exclusive of its interaction with the coastline. Our results show that the South China, Sulu and Sulawezi Seas make up three largely independent basins where tsunamis generated in one basin do not leak into another. Similarly, the Sunda arc provides an efficient barrier to tsunamis originating in the Indian Ocean. Furthermore, the shallow continental shelves in the Java Sea, the Gulf of Thailand and the western part of the South China Sea significantly dampen the amplitude of the waves. The eastern shores of the Malay Peninsula are threatened only by the greatest—and most improbable—of our sources, a mega-earthquake rupturing all of the Luzon Trench. We also consider two models of underwater landslides (which can be triggered by smaller events, even in an intraplate setting). These sources, for which there is both historical and geological evidence, could pose a significant threat to all shorelines in the region, including the Malay Peninsula.

Key words: Tsunami, South China Sea, focal mechanism, numerical simulation.

1. Introduction

We consider in this study a number of tsunami scenarios in the South China Sea and its adjoining basins. As shown in Fig. 1, the South China Sea constitutes an essentially enclosed basin, which communicates with the Indian and Pacific Oceans only through a number of narrow straits whose widths vary from 250 km (Luzon Straits) to only a few km (Malacca Straits). In addition, the island of Borneo is separated from the Philippines by the Sulu and Sulawezi Seas, and from Java and the other Sunda arc islands by the Java Sea, which themselves are basically enclosed basins. We do not include in the present study the Flores, Banda, and Molucca Seas. The geological nature of the South China and adjoining seas is variable, as the eastern half of the South China Sea and the Sulu and Sulawezi Seas are oceanic basins with depths in excess of 4,000 m, while the western South China Sea and the Java Sea are continental shelves not exceeding 200 m in depth.

This region is bordered by some of the most active subduction systems on Earth, notably the Sumatra and Java arcs to the west and south. To the east, the boundary with the Philippine plate is broken up along a number of segments involving the Taiwan, Luzon, East Philippine, Moro, Sangihe and Mindanao subduction zones. As HAMILTON (1979) summarized in a landmark contribution, the extreme complexity of this tectonic pattern is a result of the ongoing collision between the Australian plate to the south and Eurasia to the north, with the added influence of the eastward push of the Chinese block into the Pacific, due to the Himalayan collision.

In this context, and in the wake of the 2004 Sumatra–Andaman disaster, it is important to assess the tsunami hazard which may threaten the South China Sea and its adjoining basins, especially since its shores host a number of mega-cities, as shown in Fig. 1. Our approach in the present paper follows in the general steps of a previous contribution in which we had modeled a number of scenarios for far-field

---
[1] Department of Earth and Planetary Sciences, Northwestern University, Evanston, IL 60201, USA. E-mail: emile@earth.northwestern.edu

[2] Department of Civil Engineering, University of Southern California, Los Angeles, CA 90089, USA.

[3] Department of Environmental Engineering, Technical University of Crete, 73100 Chania, Greece.

[4] Institute of Applied and Computational Mathematics, P.O. Box 1385, 71110 Heraklion, Greece.

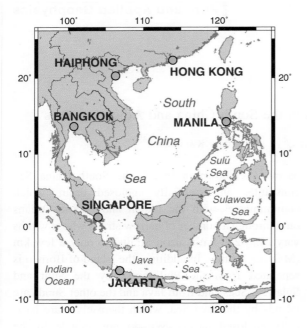

Figure 1

Location map of the study area. The South China Sea and its adjoining basins are labeled, as are some of the major ports located on shores facing their respective basins, or immediately up relevant estuaries

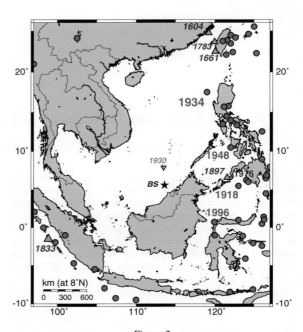

Figure 2

Background seismicity of the study area. The *dots* denote earthquakes from the instrumented era (1900–2007) with at least one magnitude $M \geq 7.5$; events discussed in the text are labeled in *bold*. *Upward triangles* (with date in *italics*) identify pre-instrumental earthquakes with a tsunami reported as damaging, and used as a potential scenario in the text. The star identifies the Brunei Slide (*BS*) discussed in Sect. 8, and the inverted triangle the nearby intraplate earthquake of 21 July 1930

tsunami risk in the Indian Ocean (OKAL and SYN-OLAKIS, 2008; hereafter Paper I), and whose general methodology we will follow. In particular, we will consider worst-case scenarios for each of the seismic regions with the potential of generating a tsunami in the South China Sea; however, the emphasis will be on regional sources, since we will show in Sect. 7 that tsunamis originating outside of the basins cannot substantially penetrate them. In addition, we will discuss a few scenarios of landslide-generated tsunamis.

2. Methodology

Figure 2 shows a map of background shallow seismicity in the study area, with individual dots showing earthquakes from the instrumental era (post-1900) for which at least one published magnitude exceeds 7.5. Also shown, as triangles, are pre-instrumental earthquakes documented to have generated locally damaging tsunamis. This map can be used to identify seismic zones where earthquakes

could generate tsunamis potentially damaging in the South China Sea.

In each of these regions, and following the approach in Paper I, we examine documented earthquakes having generated tsunamis and, when necessary, conduct a full seismological study of their source based on historical seismograms. We then discuss whether larger events could take place along similar fault systems. We are motivated in this respect by the documented variability of the mode of strain release along a regional plate boundary. In lay language, even large events along a given subduction zone are not necessarily repeats of each other; they can vary in size, and the last (and obviously best-documented) large earthquake may not represent the potential maximum event along the boundary. This point was first illustrated by ANDO (1975) in the case of the Nankai Trough, and similar conclusions were reached in a growing number of provinces, e.g., central Chile (CISTERNAS *et al.*, 2005), southern Peru

Table 1

Parameters of dislocation sources used in this study

Number of scenario	Description	Figure	Moment M_0 (10^{28} dyn cm)	Length L (km)	Width W (km)	Slip Δu (m)	Focal mechanism			Depth to top of fault (km)
							ϕ (°)	δ (°)	λ (°)	
1	Mindanao 1976	Fig. 3	1.9	150	75	3.5	327	22	69	10
2	Mindanao 1918	Fig. 5	3.0	200	75	4.1	327	22	69	10
3	Sulawezi 1996	Fig. 6	0.8	90	60	3.0	53	7	66	10
4	Hypothetical North Sulawezi	Fig. 7	4.4	250	70	5	100	20	93	10
5	Sulu Islands 1897	Fig. 8	4.5	300	60	5	45	30	90	10
5a	Sulu Islands variant		10	500	60	7	45	30	90	10
6	Hypothetical West of Panay	Fig. 9	1.5	120	60	3.5	349	12	83	10
7a	West of Luzon 1934	Fig. 11	0.22	67	33	2	338	46	53	10
8	Hypothetical Luzon Straits	Fig. 12	10	400	90	6	355	35	57	10
9	Hypothetical Luzon Trench	Fig. 13	10	400	90	6	355	24	72	10
10	Taiwan Straits inspired by 1604	Fig. 14	1.0	111	56	4.5	50	45	90	10
11	Taiwan Straits inspired by 1782	Fig. 15	1.0	111	56	4.5	50	45	90	10
12	Taiwan Straits inspired by 1661	Fig. 16	1.5	127	63	5.1	107	59	−73	10
13	Hypothetical South of Java	Fig. 17	36	500	150	10	290	10	102	10

(OKAL *et al.*, 2006), southern Kuriles (NANAYAMA *et al.*, 2003) and Cascadia (NELSON *et al.*, 2006). In practice, this means that the size of a potential earthquake along a given subduction zone could be limited only by the length along which a coherent rupture could take place.

Once we obtain a model of a potential earthquake, we proceed to simulate the tsunami in the regional field by first using scaling laws (GELLER, 1976) to derive values of the earthquake source parameters (fault length L, fault width W and seismic slip Δu; see Table 1), which allow the computation of the static field of surface vertical displacement in the source area, using the algorithm of MANSINHA and SMYLIE (1971)). In turn, this field of displacement is taken as the initial wave height of the tsunami, $\eta(x, y; t = 0_+)$, with the additional condition of zero initial velocity. The validity of this classical approximation stems from the generally short nature of the source of an earthquake-generated tsunami, the velocity of rupture along the fault being always hypersonic with respect to the phase velocity of the tsunami. The simulation then proceeds using the MOST code (TITOV and SYNOLAKIS, 1998; SYNOLAKIS, 2003), which solves the non-linear shallow water approximation of the equations of hydrodynamics using a finite difference algorithm and the method of fractional steps (GODUNOV, 1959). The MOST code has been validated and verified as outlined by SYNOLAKIS *et al.* (2008). The

computation is carried out on a 4-min grid extending from 10°S to 26°N, and from 95°E to 127°E. We do not simulate the interaction of the wave with initially dry land, and the computation is thus stopped at the last marine point in the grid in front of each coastline. The detailed simulation of run-up at individual locations would require a much finer resolution of bathymetry and topography and is beyond the scope of the present paper. Our results are interpreted using maps of the maximum value over time of the wave height $\eta(x, y)$ at each point in the basins.

3. The Sea of Sulawezi

3.1. Scenario 1: The 1976 Mindanao Earthquake

The Mindanao earthquake and tsunami of 16 August 1976 was one of the most devastating events of the twentieth century in the Philippines, and involved subduction of the floor of the Sulawezi Sea under the Island of Mindanao. A detailed seismological study was published by STEWART and COHN (1979) who proposed a moment $M_0 = 1.9 \times 10^{28}$ dyn cm. EKSTRÖM and NETTLES (1997) later obtained a CMT solution based on a restricted digital dataset, with a significantly lower moment (1.1×10^{28} dyn cm). A detailed field survey was carried out by WALLACE *et al.* (1977) who reported run-up

193

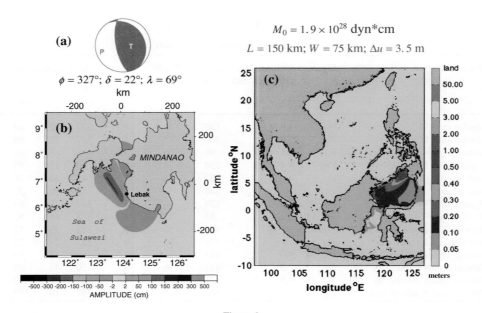

Figure 3
Simulation of *Scenario 1* (Mindanao 1976). **a** Focal mechanism used in simulation. **b** Field of initial displacements computed from MANSINHA and SMYLIE'S (1971) algorithm and used as the initial condition of the hydrodynamic simulation. **c** Maximum simulated wave height reached in the study area. Note that the tsunami is essentially contained in the Sea of Sulawezi

reaching 5 m; the death toll was estimated as high as 8,000, with most casualties reportedly due to the tsunami (SOLOV'EV *et al.*, 1986), making the event the second deadliest tsunami worldwide in the twentieth century.

For the purpose of simulation, we use STEWART and COHN'S (1979) model, since the dataset used for the CMT solution was fragmentary. All relevant parameters are listed in Table 1. Figure 3 regroups the static displacement field used as the initial condition of the simulation and the field of maximum wave amplitude computed over the whole basin. The maximum amplitudes (about 1.5 m before run-up on the beaches) are found on the eastern side of the Gulf of Moro and generally compatible with reports of maximum run-up in the area of Lebak (SOLOV'EV *et al.*, 1986). Furthermore, our results show that the tsunami remains essentially contained inside the Sea of Sulawezi, with only minimal penetration of the straits of Makassar to the southwest and of Talaud to the east.

3.2. Scenario 2: The 1918 Mindanao Earthquake

The Moro subduction system, along which the 1976 earthquake took place, was also the site of a

major event on 15 August 1918, for which data is obviously more scant. This earthquake was given magnitudes of $M = 8\frac{1}{4}$ by GUTENBERG and RICHTER (1954) and $M_s = 8.0$ by GELLER and KANAMORI (1977). It generated a devastating tsunami whose run-up reached 8 m along the southwestern coast of Mindanao (MASÓ, 1918), even though a definitive death toll was never compiled. As compared with the 1976 event, field descriptions suggest a more powerful tsunami, and a greater impact farther to the southeast along the southwestern coast of Mindanao (SOLOV'EV and GO, 1984). This would indicate that the seismic source of the 1918 event was stronger than in 1976, and in turn that the latter does not represent a worst case scenario along the relevant subduction zone.

In this framework, we conducted a separate seismological study of the 1918 event. Using 26 travel times listed in the International Seismological Summary (ISS), and the algorithm of WYSESSION *et al.* (1991), we relocated the event at 5.58°N, 123.63°E (Fig. 4). This solution is in excellent agreement with STEWART and COHN'S (1979) (5.7°N; 123.5°E), even though we keep in our dataset stations with larger residuals. We estimate the quality of our solution by a

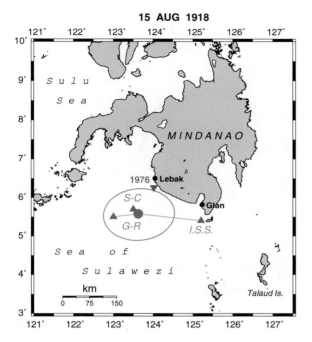

15 AUG 1918

Figure 4

Relocation of the 1918 Mindanao earthquake. The *dot* is our relocated epicenter with Monte Carlo ellipse ($\sigma_G = 10$ s), the *triangles* are epicenters proposed by the ISS, GUTENBERG and RICHTER (1954) (*G-R*) and STEWART and COHN (1979) (*S-C*), respectively. For reference, the *inverted triangle* shows the 1976 epicenter

Monte Carlo procedure injecting Gaussian noise with $\sigma_G = 10$ s, adequate for the 1910s. Our confidence ellipse is much larger than the precision of 15 km claimed by STEWART and COHN (1979); it does encompass GUTENBERG and RICHTER'S (1954) epicenter, but the ISS epicenter, more than 150 km to the east, is incompatible. The conclusion of this relocation is that the 1918 earthquake originated in the general same section of the Moro subduction system as the 1976 event.

We were further able to assess the moment of the 1918 earthquake from a record of its Love wave at Riverview, Australia (RIV). Assuming the same focal geometry as in 1976, we obtain an average of $M_0 = 3 \times 10^{28}$ dyn cm in the 64–256 s period range. This suggests that the 1918 event was indeed somewhat larger than the 1976 shock, and that the apparently stronger tsunami damage in 1918 in the southern section of coastline, between Lebak and Glan, could reflect a fault line extending farther to the southeast than in 1976.

In this context, we model the 1918 earthquake using a longer fault ($L = 200$ km), and greater slip ($\Delta u = 4.1$ m) than in 1976. Results, shown in Fig. 5, show once again that the tsunami remains contained

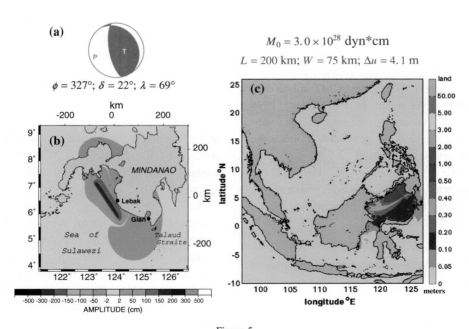

Figure 5

Same as Fig. 3 for *Scenario 2* (Mindanao 1918). Note that the tsunami remains essentially contained in the Sea of Sulawezi

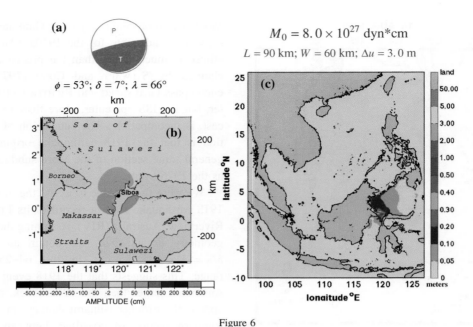

(a)

$$M_0 = 8.0 \times 10^{27} \text{ dyn*cm}$$

$$L = 90 \text{ km}; \ W = 60 \text{ km}; \ \Delta u = 3.0 \text{ m}$$

$\phi = 53°; \ \delta = 7°; \ \lambda = 66°$

Figure 6

Same as Fig. 3 for *Scenario 3* (Sulawezi 1996). Note that the tsunami remains essentially contained in the Sea of Sulawezi, with the exception of a small leak into the Makassar Straits

inside the Sea of Sulawezi. The larger moment of the 1918 earthquake is not sufficient to export substantial waves outside its basin.

3.3. Scenario 3: The 1996 Sulawezi Event

The southern shore of the Sea of Sulawezi is the locus of a small subduction system where its oceanic crust sinks under the curving Minahassa peninsula of the Island of Sulawezi. The largest CMT solution in the area is the Siboa event of 01 January 1996 ($M_0 = 7.8 \times 10^{27}$ dyn cm), expressing oblique subduction under the island. It generated a moderate tsunami, with run-up reaching 3.5 m and nine confirmed deaths (PELINOVSKY *et al.*, 1997). These results are supported by our simulation, which shows the tsunami largely confined to the northern section of the Makassar Straits (Fig. 6).

3.4. Scenario 4: A Potential Large Event in Northern Sulawezi

To the east of the 1996 epicenter, ten CMT solutions with thrusting mechanisms are available, notably between 122°E and 124°E, in the range of

10^{25}–3.3×10^{27} dyn cm. While such earthquakes were apparently too small to generate reportable tsunamis, they indicate that active subduction is taking place at this margin, and raise the possibility of larger events. Indeed, four historical earthquakes are documented in the area with magnitudes assigned by GUTENBERG and RICHTER (1954) in the 7.0–8.4 range, although none of them generated reported tsunamis, and the latter (22 January 1905) cannot be associated definitely with the North Sulawezi subduction. In this framework, we consider as a plausible, although undocumented, scenario an underthrusting event rupturing the 250-km segment covered by the 10 recent (CMT) subduction earthquakes. Scaling laws suggest that it would reach $M_0 = 4.4 \times 10^{28}$ dyn cm.

Results shown in Fig. 7 show a tsunami largely contained in the Sulawezi Sea, In addition to the obvious threat to the Minahassa Peninsula, the stronger moment results in deep-water offshore amplitudes reaching 1 m off the western peninsula of Mindanao. Also, the tsunami exits the Sulawezi Sea at the Talaud Straits into the Caroline Sea, which, however, is outside the area of the present study. The weak propagation into the Molucca Sea, to the south

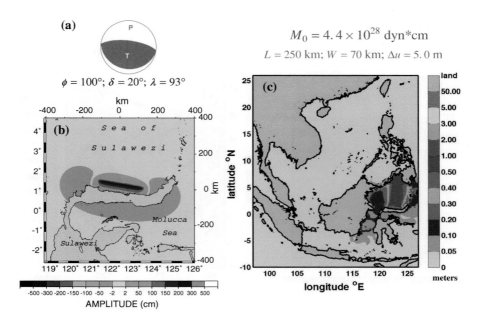

(a)

$M_0 = 4.4 \times 10^{28}$ dyn*cm

$L = 250$ km; $W = 70$ km; $\Delta u = 5.0$ m

$\phi = 100°$; $\delta = 20°$; $\lambda = 93°$

Figure 7

Same as Fig. 3 for a hypothetical large event along the north coast of Sulawezi (*Scenario 4*). Note the penetration of the straits of Makassar and Talaud

of the Minahassa peninsula expresses the extension of the field of subsidence of the earthquake south of that narrow land mass. Finally, the tsunami affects the whole coast of East Borneo, as it propagates into the Makassar Straits. However, it fails to reach the Sunda Arc across the Java Sea.

4. The Sulu Sea

4.1. Scenario 5: The 1897 Zamboanga earthquake(s)

The western peninsula of Mindanao (with its capital city, Zamboanga) and the Sulu Island chain which extends to the east of Borneo, were the site of two large earthquakes, 10 h apart, on 20 and 21 September 1897. Historical documents (CORONAS, 1899) describe a tsunami affecting the northwestern coast of Mindanao, the Sulu islands of Basilan and Jolo, and Cuyo in the north of the Sulu Sea. The tsunami killed at least 20 people, and ran up to 7 m on Basilan. Despite some confusion in timing, the tsunami can be definitely attributed to the second, stronger shock. The earthquakes were accompanied by the emergence of a small island, possibly a mud

volcano, near Labuán off the northern coast of Borneo, 700 km from the presumed epicenter; the mechanism of this ancillary phenomenon remains intriguing, especially since the earthquake was not reported as having been felt in Labuán. CORONAS (1899) also reports the emergence of another new islet near Kúdat, at the northernmost tip of Borneo, possibly associated with the *first* earthquake. In addition, SOLOV'EV and GO (1984) transcribe a report by FIGEE (1898) of the observation of a tsunami at Kúdat, and most remarkably of a "flood wave" on the east coast of Sumatra, for which, unfortunately, no further details, such as exact location and timing, are provided in the original report by FIGEE (1898).

It is all the more remarkable that these events occurred in the vicinity of the Sulu Islands, where no major earthquakes are known in the twentieth century (Fig. 2). Indeed, the largest CMT solution in the area has a moment of only 2.4×10^{24} dyn cm. GUTENBERG and RICHTER (1954) assigned magnitudes of 8.6 and 8.7 to the 1897 events. These are probably overestimated, since the absence of catastrophic reports in the southwestern Sulu Islands (Tapul group) suggests that the rupture did not extend along the full Sulu arc. In this context, we model the main

197

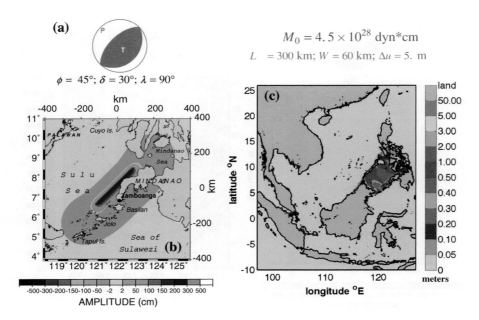

(a)

$M_0 = 4.5 \times 10^{28}$ dyn*cm

$L = 300$ km; $W = 60$ km; $\Delta u = 5.$ m

$\phi = 45°; \delta = 30°; \lambda = 90°$

AMPLITUDE (cm)

Figure 8

Same as Fig. 3 for a large event in the Sulu Sea, modeled after the 1897 earthquake (*Scenario 5*). Note that the tsunami remains confined to the Sulu Sea and the interior seas east of it. It penetrates neither the Sea of Sulawezi, nor the South China Sea

event as a 300-km rupture involving a slip of 5 m, corresponding to $M_0 = 4.5 \times 10^{28}$ dyn cm (Fig. 8). Our focal geometry is adapted from a local CMT solution (14 June 1978) by rotating the fault to conform with the orientation of the Sulu arc.

Simulation results shown in Fig. 8 indicate maximum tsunami amplitudes along the Zamboanga peninsula of Mindanao, and the eastern Sulu archipelago (Jolo, Basilan), as well as across the Sulu Sea towards Cuyo Island. The tsunami does penetrate the complex system of inner seas of the Philippine archipelago to the east of the Sulu Sea (the Mindanao Sea to the southeast and the Sibuyan Sea to the north of Panay), but does not leak into the Sea of Sulawezi south of the Sulu arc. To the north, it leaks marginally into the Balabac Straits between Palawan and Borneo, but fails to develop into the South China Sea. This model would explain the observation of a wave at Kúdat, near the Balabac Straits, but not FIGEE's (1898) reports on the east coast of Sumatra.

In this context, we considered a worst-case variant (Scenario 5a), where the fault length is extended to 500 km (and the slip accordingly scaled up to 7 m), thus rupturing the entire southern boundary of the Sulu Sea. We emphasize that this model violates the reports (CORONAS, 1899) of a felt intensity fast decreasing to the SW in the Tapul Islands. Even so, we have verified that this model, involving the largest source that can be fit inside the Sulu Basin, cannot explain the phenomenon reported on Sumatra. In the absence of detailed information about the latter's precise location and timing, we speculate that it could represent seiching of an estuary triggered by seismic surface waves, as widely observed at comparable or even greater distances from large, or even significantly smaller, events (e.g., KVALE, 1955; CASSIDY and ROGERS, 2004; BARBEROPOULOU et al., 2006).

4.2. Scenario 6: Inspired by the Iloilo, Panay Earthquake of 24 January 1948

The event of 24 January 1948 on Panay Island was assigned a magnitude $M = 8.3$ by GUTENBERG and RICHTER (1954), and is therefore often described as the strongest earthquake in the Philippines in the twentieth century. However, based on a single Pasadena record, OKAL (1992) suggested that this value was overestimated. The earthquake caused considerable damage over the island of Panay, and

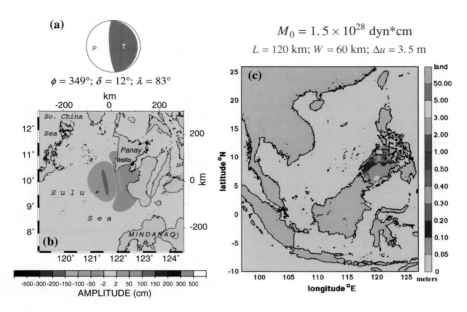

$$M_0 = 1.5 \times 10^{28} \text{ dyn*cm}$$

$L = 120$ km; $W = 60$ km; $\Delta u = 3.5$ m

Figure 9

Same as Fig. 3 for *Scenario 6*. The tsunami remains contained in the Sulu Sea

triggered a small tsunami near Iloilo, with two deaths attributed to the tsunami (IRVING and TEVES, 1948).

We inverted the moment tensor of the source using long-period mantle waves recorded at Paris, Tucson, Huancayo and San Juan, through the PDFM algorithm introduced by REYMOND and OKAL (2000). This method inverts only the spectral amplitude and discards the phase information; it is especially suited to historical seismograms for which timing uncertainties could affect spectral phases (OKAL and REYMOND, 2003). The inherent indeterminacy of $\pm 180°$ on both the strike and slip angles (ROMANOWICZ and SUÁREZ, 1983) can be lifted through the use of first motion polarities at critical stations. The resulting focal mechanism, shown in Fig. 9, expresses thrust faulting ($\lambda = 83°$) on a plane striking $\phi = 13°$, and dipping $\delta = 26°$ to the east. The inverted seismic moment, $M_0 = 6 \times 10^{27}$ dyn cm, is in general agreement with OKAL's (1992) estimate, and difficult to reconcile with the published $M = 8.3$.

We consider as Scenario 6 an event of moment $M_0 = 1.5 \times 10^{28}$ dyn cm, rupturing 120 km along the trench running west of Panay Island, from Mindoro to Mindanao. This fault system has supported a much smaller earthquake of moment 1.1 × 10^{25} dyn cm, (05 January 1983), whose focal geometry is used for Scenario 6.

As shown in Fig. 9, our simulation yields a tsunami confined to the Sulu Sea, which fails to penetrate the South China Sea.

5. *The Luzon Trench*

The western shore of Luzon is generally regarded as an active subduction zone, where the Sunda plate, bearing the South China Sea, subducts under the Philippine Sea plate. This system is expressed in the bathymetry as the Luzon Trench, extending from Taiwan in the north to the Palawan Islands off Mindoro in the south (a distance of 1,200 km) and reaching a depth of 4,500 m. This interpretation is also supported by the presence of an active volcanic arc including Pinatubo and Taal Volcanoes. However, no large subduction earthquakes are known along the Luzon Trench from Taiwan to Mindoro. The largest thrust solutions in the CMT catalog are the events of 01 June 2008 near the Batan Islands at the extreme north of the system ($M_0 = 3.9 \times 10^{25}$ dyn cm) and of 29 August 1977 off northern

Luzon ($M_0 = 3.3 \times 10^{25}$ dyn cm). Such small earthquakes cannot contribute significantly to releasing the local convergence, expected to total 10 cm/year between the Sunda and Philippine plates (SELLA et al., 2002).

This raises the possibility of larger subduction events along the Luzon Trench, especially given the relatively young age of the South China lithosphere off Luzon [25 Ma at 17°N (MÜLLER et al., 2008)]. Indeed, catalogues of historical seismicity document a significantly larger earthquake on 14 February 1934, assigned $M = 7.9$ by GUTENBERG and RICHTER (1954), and which we examine in detail as Scenario 7. In turn, this leaves open the possibility of even larger seismic sources along the Luzon trench. No such earthquakes are documented in the instrumental seismological record of the past 100 years, nor does REPETTI's (1946) authoritative catalogue going back to the sixteenth century A.D. reveal any catastrophic tsunami on the western shore of Luzon. In this context, the occurrence of any such event remains improbable, but we do not regard it as *impossible*, and therefore consider two such mega-earthquakes as Scenarios 8 and 9.

5.1. Scenario 7: The Western Luzon Earthquake of 14 February 1934

This event took place in the vicinity of the 1977 epicenter, and generated a small tsunami on the nearby coast of Luzon, notably at San Esteban (SOLOV'EV et al., 1984); unfortunately, quantified reports of its run-up are not available. The published magnitude estimate, $M = 7.9$, suggests that the event was much larger than any of the CMT solutions from the digital era. Thus, it is important to determine its exact size, focal solution, and to investigate the source of its tsunami. We will show that this event consists of an earthquake of moment $M_0 = 2.2 \times 10^{27}$ dyn cm, accompanied by an underwater landslide.

Focusing first on the seismological data, we relocated the event using the arrival times published by the ISS and the method of WYSESSION et al. (1991). The solution converges to 17.47°N, 119.09°W on a dataset of 138 stations, with a standard deviation of only $\sigma = 2.9$ s; the Monte Carlo ellipse ($_G = 6$ s) is less than 50 km in major axis (Fig. 10a).

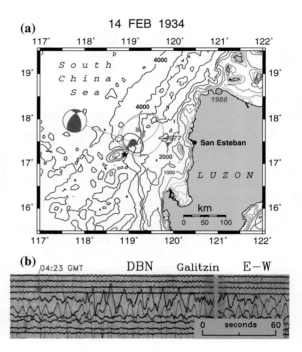

Figure 10

a Map of the epicentral area of the 1934 earthquake. The *large dot* is the relocated epicenter, with its Monte Carlo ellipse; the *triangle* is the ISS location. The *faint-toned squares* (with ellipses) show the relocated aftershocks of 14 February (17:14 GMT) and 25 February 1934. Note the seamount topping at 500 m b.s.l. about 40 km SW of the epicenter. The *star* shows the proposed location of the landslide on the flank of the seamount. The *beachball* at *left* shows the mechanism obtained by the PDFM inversion. The *inverted triangle* locates the largest CMT solution in the area (29 August 1977). The event of 24 June 1988 in northern Luzon is also shown. **b** Close-up of the *S* wavetrain recorded on the East–West Galitzin instrument at De Bilt. Note the long-period oscillation lasting approximately 1.5 min after the *SKS–S–ScS* arrivals, which at $\Delta = 90.1°$, should all be contained within 25 s

We then proceeded to invert the moment tensor of the source using long-period mantle waves recorded at De Bilt, Tucson and San Juan, through the PDFM algorithm. The resulting focal mechanism, shown in Fig. 10, can be interpreted as an oblique thrust ($\lambda = 53°$) on a plane striking $\phi = 338°$, and dipping $\delta = 46°$ to the northeast. This mechanism also agrees well with an extensive set of first motions compiled by REPETTI (1934). The inverted seismic moment, $M_0 = 2.2 \times 10^{27}$ dyn cm, is more than 5 times the largest published CMT in the area, but fails to characterize the event as a great subduction zone earthquake. The seismic character of the event is also confirmed by its abundant aftershocks, both locally

Table 2

Observation and modeling of low-frequency phase during the Luzon event of 14 February 1934

Station		Distance (°)	Azimuth (°)	Back-Azimuth (°)	Modeled radiation patterns			Low-frequency wave
Code	Name				$\lvert R^P \rvert$	$\lvert R^{SV} \rvert$	$\lvert R^{SH} \rvert$	
HKC	Hong Kong	6.68	316.9	135.2	0.99	0.07	0.10	Present on P phase
PLV	Phu-Lien, Vietnam	12.23	287.8	103.6	0.88	0.31	0.37	Present on P phase
ZKW	Zi-ka-wei, China	13.84	8.4	189.4	0.50	0.23	0.84	Present on S phase
KOC	Kochi, Japan	22.15	32.7	219.2	0.01	0.10	1.00	Present on S phase
PEK	Chiufeng (Beijing), China	22.67	354.2	172.8	0.47	0.55	0.69	Absent
DBN[a]	De Bilt, The Netherlands	90.13	325.7	60.6	0.25	0.93	0.27	Present on S phase (EW)

[a] This study

detected as reported by REPETTI (1934) (36 shocks over 3 days), and teleseismically recorded (2 shocks over 12 days).

However, evidence clearly points to the triggering of a landslide by this earthquake. Most significantly, the event resulted in the rupture of telegraphic cables in the South China Sea; upon their repair, significant changes were documented in the seafloor topography (REPETTI, 1934), which is the clear mark of an underwater landslide, as documented in the case of similar ruptures off the Grand Banks of Newfoundland (18 November 1929), the northern coast of Algeria (9 September 1954, 10 October 1980 and presumably 21 May 2003), and the southern coast of Fiji (14 September 1953) (HEEZEN and EWING, 1952, 1955; HOUTZ, 1962; EL-ROBRINI et al., 1985; BOUHADAD et al., 2004).

In addition, REPETTI (1934) describes, unfortunately without figures, a long-period (13–22 s) wave, of an "unknown exact nature", lasting about 1 min and appearing shortly after the P wave on seismograms at Hong Kong and Phu-Lien, and at the time of the S arrival (or shortly thereafter) at Zi-ka Wei and Kochi. He further mentions that seismograms at Chiufeng (Beijing) are "normal", i.e., do not feature this long-period wave, but does not comment on its observation (or absence) at greater distances. Among the seismograms available to us, we were able to document a particularly long-lasting S wavetrain on the East–West component at De Bilt (Fig. 10b) which would appear to share the characteristics of REPETTI's (1934) observations in terms of period and duration.

The records of these long-period wave trains, summarized in Table 2, can be interpreted as the P and S waves of an ancillary source, namely a landslide essentially coeval with the earthquake. In Fig. 10a, we note that the earthquake relocates to the immediate vicinity (40 km) of a major seamount with relatively steep slopes, which the seismic dislocation could have destabilized. We propose that a landslide was initiated on the eastern side of the seamount, and generated a turbidity current which broke the nearby Manila–Shanghai cable, as reported by REPETTI (1934). In Table 2, we further use the formalism of Equation (1) of KANAMORI et al. (1984) to compute the relevant radiation pattern coefficients of the P and S waves of the landslide source, modeled as a sub-horizontal force ($\delta = 4°$) in the azimuth $\phi_f = 130°$. Apart from Chiufeng, the agreement is excellent: those stations (HKC and PLV; at short distance and in the azimuth of the force) where the "long" wave appears with the P phase are precisely those where the landslide P wave is expected to be strongest and the S wave minimal, and conversely at ZKW, KOC, DBN (at large distance or at right angle to the force). At DBN, we verify that the S arrival is prominent on the EW component, approaching SV polarization.

We conduct two separate simulations of the tsunami generated by the 1934 earthquake. In Scenario 7a, we use the dislocation source; in Scenario 7b, we consider a landslide source, using a dipolar initial deformation of the sea surface consisting of a 19-m deep trough and a 16-m high hump, separated y a 22-km lever. The size of the poles is inspired from those used to model the 1998 Papua New Guinea tsunami (SYNOLAKIS et al., 2002), but the lever is lengthened since the Papua New Guinea slide took place in a confined amphitheater. In the absence of

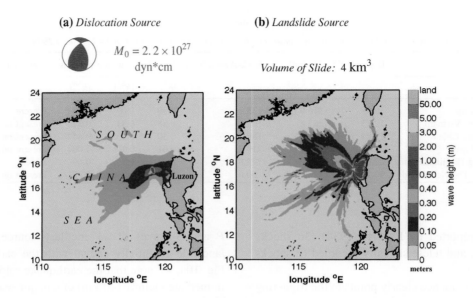

(a) *Dislocation Source*

$M_0 = 2.2 \times 10^{27}$ dyn*cm

(b) *Landslide Source*

Volume of Slide: 4 km^3

Figure 11

Simulations for *Scenarios 7* (West Luzon earthquake of 14 February 1934), using **a** the dislocation source inverted in this study (see Fig. 10), and **b** a landslide source inspired by the 1998 Papua New Guinea event. The *scale* is common to both *frames*

details on the geometry of the landslide, we regard this model as a compromise between the need for a substantial slide detected teleseismically, and the relatively minor tsunami described qualitatively by REPETTI (1934). Our simulations shown in Fig. 11 show that the tsunami from the dislocation source reaches the Luzon shore with deep-water amplitudes of ~0.1 m, while the landslide simulation is not much larger; neither of them threatens distant shores in the South China Sea.

The possibility of even moderate earthquakes along the northwestern coast of the Philippines generating tsunamis through the triggering of landslides is further suggested by the small earthquake of 24 June 1988 in Bangui, northern Luzon ($m_b = 5.4$; $M_0 = 3.7 \times 10^{24}$ dyn cm), which generated the largest tsunami wave recorded in Hong Kong (1 m). We note the steepness of the bathymetry in its epicentral area, which could suggest the triggering of a significantly larger landslide than in 1934.

5.2. Scenarios 8 and 9: Catastrophic Earthquakes at the Luzon Trench

We consider in this section the possibility that the Luzon Trench could support mega-earthquakes with a moment reaching 10^{29} dyn cm. We wish to re-emphasize that no such earthquakes are documented in the seismological record (including historical reports) available to us. However, we cannot entirely forgo the possibility that they could actually take place, with an extremely long recurrence time. A similar paradigm existed in Cascadia prior to the identification of the 1700 earthquake (SATAKE *et al.*, 1996), or to a large extent along the Andaman-Nicobar segment of the Sumatra Trench prior to 2004. Further research on paleo-tsunamis using sedimentological techniques could confirm or infirm this hypothesis in the case of the Luzon Trench.

It is in this context that we consider in Scenario 8 an event rupturing the full 400 km of the Luzon Straits from the southern tip of Taiwan to the northern tip of Luzon, and in Scenario 9 an event of similar size rupturing along the western shore of Luzon. Source parameters for these events are derived from scaling laws with geometries inspired by the local tectonics. All relevant parameters are listed in Table 1, with results shown in Figs. 12 and 13. Our source for Scenario 9 is smaller than that considered by MEGAWATI *et al.* (2009), since we restrict ourselves to a reasonably linear fault zone.

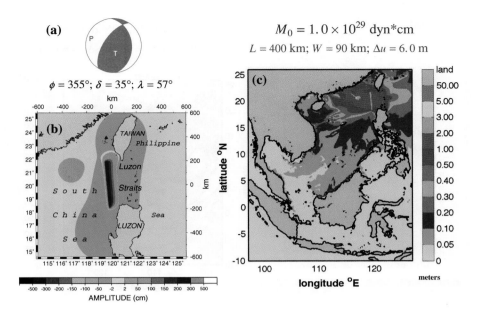

Figure 12
Same as Fig. 3 for hypothetical *Scenario 8*, a catastrophic earthquake rupturing the full length of the Luzon Straits. Note that the tsunami has very high amplitudes over all of the South China Sea (with the exception of the Gulf of Thailand) and leaks into the Philippine Sea, but does not penetrate the Sulu Sea or the interior seas of the Philippine archipelago

As expected, the size of the events results in catastrophic levels of hazards. Under Scenario 8, all shores of the South China Sea are threatened. Metric deep-water amplitudes are predicted for the southern coast of China around Hong Kong. Expectedly, the tsunami leaks through the Luzon Straits into the Philippine Sea, affecting the eastern coast of Taiwan and the Ryukyu archipelago, and even the eastern coast of Luzon. It keeps at most centrimetric amplitudes in the Gulf of Thailand, but could become noticeable along the northern shore of the Malay Peninsula. Under Scenario 9, results are generally similar, but the western coast of Luzon obviously bears the onslaught of the tsunami, while source directivity and focusing by bathymetric features combine to displace the brunt of the attack from southern China to Vietnam and, albeit more moderately, to the northern coast of Borneo. In addition, the Malay peninsula is clearly threatened at the latitude of the Narathiwat and Pattani provinces of southern Thailand (Fig. 13).

However, a remarkable result of our simulations is that, even for those catastrophic, and perhaps unrealistic sources, the tsunami does not penetrate the Sulu Sea, except for very minor leaks at the Mindoro

and Balabac Straits. Similarly, under Scenario 9, the Luzon Straits remain, by and large, an effective barrier.

6. Taiwan Straits Events

Historical records document a number of catastrophic events in the Taiwan Straits which generated locally severe tsunamis. While no record exists (to our knowledge) of the propagation of these tsunamis into the South China Sea, it is legitimate to examine and simulate these sources in order to assess their potential threat to our study area. We base our discussion on the review by MA and LEE (1997).

6.1. Scenario 10: The Hsinchu Event of 29 December 1604

This major intraplate earthquake took place in Fujian Province and caused considerable destruction over a 700-km section of coastline, from Shanngyu in the north to Zhangpu in the south. ZHOU and ADAMS (1988) indicate that a tsunami affected the mainland, but to our knowledge, no such reports exist for

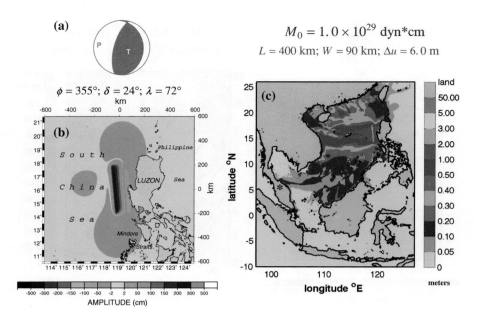

Figure 13

Same as Fig. 3 for hypothetical *Scenario 9*, a catastrophic earthquake at the Luzon Trench, off the western shore of the island. The results are generally similar to those of *Scenario 8*, with the exception of stronger effects on the coast of Borneo, higher amplitudes in Narathiwat and Pattani provinces in Thailand (*asterisk*), but no penetration of the Philippine Sea

Taiwan. Isoseismals compiled by YE *et al.* (1993) suggest a fault line of ~150 km, which B.S Huang (pers. com, 2003) has interpreted in terms of a moment of ~3×10^{27} dyn cm. As a worst-case scenario, we use in our simulation $M_0 = 10^{28}$ dyn cm, with a pure 45°-thrust geometry along the general strike of the straits ($\phi = 50°$). Our results (Fig. 14) do predict significant wave heights off the mainland coast and to a lesser extent Taiwan, but the tsunami fails to penetrate either the East or South China Seas.

6.2. Scenario 11: The Fo-kien earthquake of 22 May (or October?) 1782

Reports from travelers describe a catastrophic tsunami causing up to 40,000 deaths in Taiwan and destroying the forts of Zelandia (presently Tainan) and Pingkchingi (GAZETTE DE FRANCE, 1783), although claims of the island being "nearly entirely covered" (by water) are clearly fanciful. There is some discrepancy on the date of the event which may also have been accompanied—or triggered—by a volcanic eruption. In the absence of more definitive information on the earthquake (incidentally, absent from MA and LEE's (1997) compilation), we simply

move the source of Scenario 10 across the straits, off the coast of Taiwan. Since it is probable that the 1782 earthquake took place in the general area of the Taiwan Straits, Scenarios 10 and 11 can represent geographic endmembers for potential sources in the straits. Our results, shown in Fig. 15, are essentially unchanged, i.e., the tsunami does not propagate significantly outside the straits.

6.3. Scenario 12: The Tainan earthquake of 08 January 1661

This catastrophic event was described in detail by SCHOUTEN (1725), suggesting a destructive tsunami in the Fort Zelandia (Tainan) area, with run-up probably greater than the 1–2 m suggested by HSU (1996) and modeled by MA and LEE (1997), perhaps as a consequence of triggered submarine landslides.

Following MA and LEE (1997), we place the source of the event used in our simulation in the seismically active belt around 22°N, 119°E, but give it the normal faulting mechanism of the largest CMT in the area (16 September 1994). Under a worst-case scenario, we boost the moment to 1.5×10^{28} dyn cm, with a fault length (127 km)

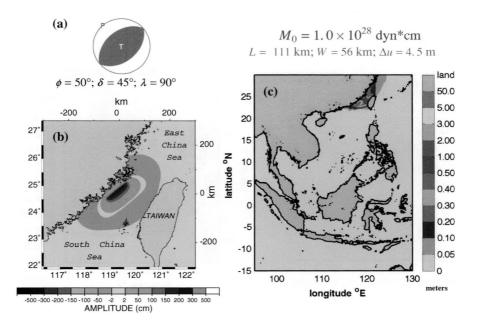

Figure 14
Same as Fig. 3 for *Scenario 10*, a major earthquake along the mainland coast of the Taiwan Straits, inspired by the 1604 Hsinchu earthquake. Note that the tsunami remains contained in the straits

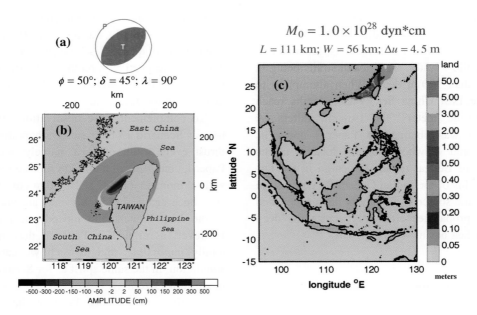

Figure 15
Same as Fig. 14 for *Scenario 11*, where the earthquake is displaced towards the coast of Taiwan, as inspired by reports of the 1782 event. The far-field effects of the tsunami are unchanged

representative of the local extent of seismicity. Our results show very strong amplitudes along the southwestern coast of Taiwan, in the area of Tainan, and in the mainland coastal region, as far south as Hong Kong and Hainan. Significantly, the tsunami also extends into the East China Sea, and affects the northern coast of Luzon, the Palawan Islands and possibly the central coast of Vietnam (Fig. 16).

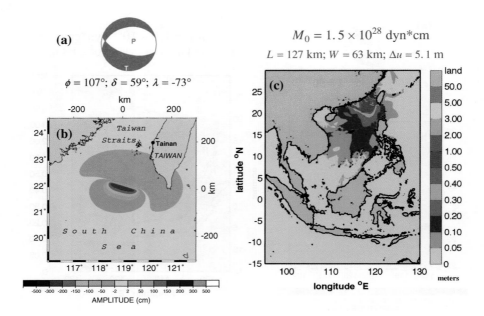

Figure 16

Same as Fig. 14 for Scenario 12, inspired by the 1661 event. As the earthquake is moved to a deep-water environment, the tsunami is able to expand into the South China Sea, and threatens the coasts of Hainan, Vietnam and Palawan

This difference in behavior, relative to Scenarios 10 and 11, is a classical illustration of GREEN's (1837) law. In the latter two, the tsunami is generated in extremely shallow water, the Taiwan straits being in general less than 100 m deep. When attempting to penetrate the East China Sea, where depths reach several thousand meters, the tsunami falters. A similar result was obtained in Paper I under its Scenarios 3 and 4, whose sources located in the shallow Bay of Bengal remained benign in the far-field deep basins of the Indian Ocean. By contrast, in Scenario 12, the source is already in deep water, and the tsunami propagates efficiently across the deep South China Sea basin.

7. Danger from the Indian Ocean?

In this section, we examine the possibility of a significant tsunami penetrating into the South China Sea and its adjoining basins from outside, and focus on possible sources located in the Indian Ocean.

During the 2004 Sumatra–Andaman earthquake, no significant tsunami was reported inside our study area, expressing the convoluted and inefficient path such waves would have had to take through the straits of Malacca. Similarly, during the 1994 and 2006 Java "tsunami earthquakes", whose run-ups reached 14 m and 21 m, respectively, on the southern coast of Java (TSUJI et al., 1995; FRITZ et al., 2007), no tsunami was detected in the Java Sea.

To complement these observations, we examine here as Scenario 13 the case of a hypothetical mega-thrust event south of Java, namely Scenario 8 of Paper I, consisting of a 500-km rupture south of Java, with a moment of 3.6×10^{29} dyn cm. We emphasize, once again, that such events are undocumented in the Java Trench, and indeed, most improbable. However, as argued in Paper I, they may not be totally *impossible*, and as such we carry out this simulation, in the same spirit as for Scenarios 8 and 9 in western Luzon.

Results shown in Fig. 17 show that the tsunami fails to propagate significantly into the Java Sea. It features only a small leak through the Straits of Bali and Lombok, and essentially none at the Sunda Straits. Given the documented absence of penetration in 2004, and the shelter provided by the island of Sumatra for tsunamis generated along its central and southern segments [e.g., in the geometry of the 1833

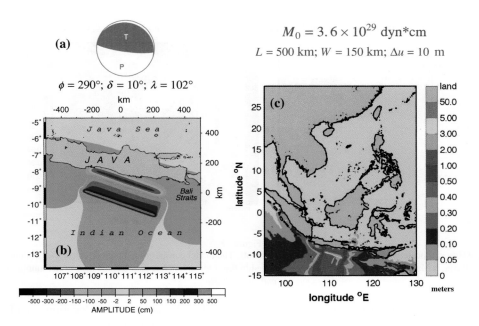

Figure 17

Same as Fig. 3 for Scenario 13 (hypothetical mega-thrust event south of Java). Note that the tsunami hardly penetrates into the Java Sea at the Bali Straits

Mentawai earthquake (ZACHARIASEN *et al.*, 1999)], we conclude that Indian Ocean tsunamis cannot significantly affect the South China Sea and its adjoining basins.

Finally, the largest transpacific tsunamis (Peru, 1868; Chile, 1960) were observed at decimetric amplitudes in the Philippines, without, however, reaching damaging levels. No mega-earthquakes are known at a regional distance in the Pacific Basin (e.g., Ryukyus; East Luzon); while their possibility cannot be totally discounted, they remain improbable and transcend the scope of this paper.

8. The Case of the Brunei Slide

Finally, we investigate in this section the scenario of a catastrophic landslide occurring inside the South China Sea Basin. We are motivated by the work of GEE *et al.* (2007), who used 3-dimensional seismic imaging to document the presence of such a structure off the coast of Brunei, at the delta of the Baram River (Fig. 2). Its estimated volume, 1,200 km³, makes it one of the largest underwater slides in the world, comparable to the Saharan and Hinlopen

slides (EMBLEY, 1976; VANNESTE *et al.*, 2006), and as much as one-third the volume of the record Storrega slide (BUGGE *et al.*, 1988). However, the Brunei Slide is unique in being "thicker", i.e., differing in aspect ratio from the other mega-slides, and in occurring in an environment with abundant sediment flux from the Baram River. The age of the Brunei slide is debated, but it could be as recent as Holocene, while deeper structures in the seismic stratigraphy suggest repeated episodes of sliding (GEE *et al.*, 2007). In this context, the Brunei slide might be reactivated in the future, and should be included as a source of tsunami hazard in the South China Sea.

We consider in Scenario 14 a model of the Brunei Slide using a dipolar source with a 90-m trough and a 60-m hump, separated by an 80-km lever. These numbers are obtained by scaling the Papua New Guinea dipole (SYNOLAKIS *et al.*, 2002) to the expected thickness and movement of the Brunei slide, while constraining the length of the lever to its mapped extent. Results, shown in Fig. 18, show deep-water amplitudes reaching 5 m on the nearby coast of Borneo (which would lead to complete devastation) and approaching 1 m along the coast of Vietnam. Although, as expected from its shorter

207

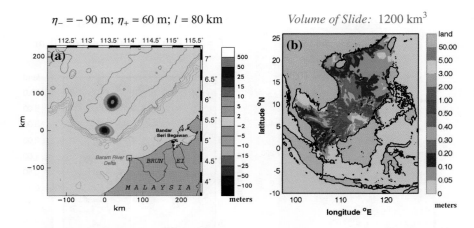

$$\eta_- = -90 \text{ m}; \ \eta_+ = 60 \text{ m}; \ l = 80 \text{ km} \qquad \textit{Volume of Slide:} \ 1200 \text{ km}^3$$

Figure 18

Simulation of the Brunei monster slide. **a** Field of initial displacements. The model consists of a dipole oriented N15°E along the slope of the South China Sea Basin. **b** Maximum simulated wave height reached in the study area. Note catastrophic deep-water amplitudes in the central part of the basin

wavelengths, the tsunami disperses quickly in the far field, amplitudes in deep water off Luzon, the southern coast of China and southern Taiwan remain decimetric, and could lead to damage upon run-up. Significant inundation is expected along the Palawan Islands, but the tsunami leaks only moderately into the Sulu Sea along the Malaysian coast of Borneo. It remains decimetric as it approaches the northern coast of the Malay peninsula, with the potential for damage along most of its shores. However, the tsunami does not reach the Java Sea.

The mechanism of triggering of the Brunei slide remains unknown; GEE *et al.*, (2007) have suggested as possible agents intraplate earthquake activity, anticline collapse or the destabilization of gas hydrates, as suggested for example by BOURIAK *et al.*, (2000) at the Storrega site in the context of the Fennoscandian deglaciation. We note the occurrence on 21 July 1930 of an earthquake assigned $M = 6$ by GUTENBERG and RICHTER (1954), in the center of the South China Sea basin, which we relocated to 7.92° and 113.48°E (Fig. 2), in a deep portion of the South China Basin, and approximately 120 km north of the toe of the Brunei Slide. While the earthquake is too small to be successfully studied on the basis of historical seismograms, the magnitude proposed by GUTENBERG and RICHTER (1954) could be sufficient, especially given its intraplate character, to create accelerations inducing landslides along ridge structures located 50 km to the southeast. A larger

earthquake at the same location could conceivably trigger the motion of a precarious structure in the general area of the Brunei slide. In addition, we note that other river systems provide sedimentary fluxes into the South China Basin along the north coast of Borneo. Thus, the risk of a Brunei-type slide may be present along all of the northern half of the coast of Borneo, where the South China Sea features a deep oceanic basin.

9. Discussion and Conclusion

The principal results from this study can be summarized as follows:

- With the exception of the complex system of interior seas of the western shores of the Philippines, our simulated scenarios generally result in containment of the tsunamis to their original individual basin. The Palawan–Calamian system on the one hand, and the Sulu archipelago on the other, make up effective barriers preventing the propagation of tsunamis from one basin to the next. The Luzon straits separating Taiwan from the Philippines, and the Talaud straits joining the Sulawezi Basin with the Philippine Sea, are expectedly less effective, and allow some leakage of energy. The Makassar Straits also damp considerably the amplitude of waves crossing them.

These results, largely documented from historical tsunamis, remain robust when worst-case scenarios featuring improbable, but perhaps not impossible, seismic moments, are considered in the simulations. By the same token, Indian Ocean tsunamis cannot penetrate into the South China Sea, through the narrow Bali and Sunda Straits.

- In addition, the extensive very shallow bathymetry comprising the western part of the South China Basin and the Java Sea acts to dampen regional tsunamis propagating from the deeper basins in the eastern South China Sea and across the Straits of Makassar, with the result that the relevant shorelines in the Gulf of Thailand, and the eastern shores of Sumatra, the western and southern coasts of Borneo, and the north coast of Java are not inundated under most of our tectonic scenarios. Only for the improbable mega-thrust event off western Luzon (Scenario 9) and for the catastrophic Brunei slide (Scenario 14) are the northern shores of the Malay Peninsula threatened. A comparison of Figs. 13 and 18 reveals that in both cases the largest amplitudes are found offshore from the southernmost provinces of Narathiwat and Pattani in Thailand. This is probably due to the focusing effect of a domain of extremely shallow bathymetry directly offshore of these locations, where we have verified that the 50-m isobath extends more than 150 km into the Gulf of Thailand.

On the other hand, the intriguing report by FIGEE (1898) of a flood wave in Sumatra during the 1897 Sulu event could not be explained under any acceptable scenario for its source, and we speculate that it may have resulted from a seiche in an estuary, triggered by seismic surface waves of large amplitude.

- The modern seismological record clearly underestimates the tsunami potential in the region. No significant recent earthquake is known along the Sulu arc, in the epicentral area of the 1897 shock. Modern analyses of historical seismograms show that the events of 1918 in the Moro Gulf and 1934 off Luzon are significantly larger than their modern counterparts. Historical chronicles in Taiwan and mainland China also provide convincing evidence of earthquakes much larger than instrumentally recorded, and accompanied by damaging tsunamis.

Such events will be repeated, even if we presently do not understand their recurrence times.

- In this respect, and by contrast with the smaller adjoining seas, the South China Sea Basin is large enough that it can accommodate the fault line of a mega earthquake, such as envisioned in Scenarios 8 and 9, and propagate its tsunamis over at least 1,500 km, a distance beyond the reach of felt seismic waves, even from the largest earthquakes, and as such often taken as separating near-field and far-field tsunamis for the purpose of warning and mitigation. In short, some shores of the South China Sea, most notably the southern Chinese mainland from the Taiwan straits to Hainan and the Gulf of Tonkin, Vietnam, and northern Borneo may feature far-field tsunami risk under Scenarios 8, 9, and 12, which are certainly most improbable, but should not be considered impossible.

- Significant tsunami risk from underwater landslides exists in the South China Sea Basin, as documented both in modern and geological history. The recent example of the 1998 Papua New Guinea disaster (SYNOLAKIS et al., 2002) should re-emphasize that even moderate earthquakes (typically around magnitude 6), can trigger submarine slides creating locally catastrophic tsunamis. Such earthquakes are documented even along apparently passive margins, e.g., the 1930 shock shown in Fig. 2, in an area where the monstrous Brunei Slide points out to a geological environment generally favoring the accumulation of precarious sediment masses.

- Notwithstanding the worst-case scenarios that we have studied systematically, the most probable form of tsunami hazard along the shorelines of the South China Sea and its adjoining basins remains a large earthquake ($\approx 10^{28}$ dyn cm), rupturing one of the many active shorter fault systems in this extremely complex region. As exemplified by Scenario 1, such sources have the potential for a tsunami of disastrous dimension, especially in view of the ever-growing population along the relevant shorelines. Because of the general effectiveness of the barriers separating the various basins, such a tsunami will be mostly of near-field character; the populations at risk having little if any time to get out of harm's way. In this context, self-evacuation will be the only practical form of mitigation, and it remains an absolute priority to emphasize awareness and education, which have proven repeatedly to be the key to reducing human losses in the near field (CAMINADE *et al.*, 2000; FRITZ and KALLIGERIS, 2008; OKAL *et al.*, 2010).

Acknowledgments

This research was partially supported by the National Science Foundation under grant CMMI 09-28905 to CES. We are grateful to James Dewey, Steve Kirby, Bernard Dost and Phil Cummins for access to historical seismogram collections at the USGS (Golden), the Royal Netherlands Meteorological Institute, and Geoscience Australia. The paper was improved through the comments of Hermann Fritz, another reviewer and Editor Utku Kânoğlu. Maps were drawn using the GMT software (WESSEL and SMITH, 1991).

REFERENCES

ANDO, M., *Source mechanism and tectonic significance of historical earthquakes along the Nankai Trough, Japan*, Tectonophysics, 27, 119–140, 1975.

BARBEROPOULOU, A., A. QAMAR, T.L. PRATT, and W.P. STEELE, *Long-period effects of the Denali earthquake on water bodies in the Puget Lowland: Observations and modeling*, Bull. Seismol. Soc. Amer., 96, 519–535, 2006.

BOUHADAD, Y., A. NOUR, A. SLIMANI, N. LAOUAMI, and D. BELHAI, *The Boumerdes (Algeria) earthquake of May 21, 2003 (M_w = 6.8): Ground deformation and intensity*, J. Seismol., 8, 497–506, 2004.

BOURIAK, S., M. VANNESTE, and A. SAOUTKINE, *Inferred gas hydrates and clay diapirs near the Storrega Slide on the Southern edge of the Vøring Plateau, offshore Norway*, Mar. Geol., 163, 125–148, 2000.

BUGGE, T., R.H. BELDERSON, and N.H. KENYON, *The Storrega slide*, Phil. Trans. Roy. Soc. (*London*), 325, 357–388, 1988.

CAMINADE, J.-P., D. CHARLIE, U. KÂNOĞLU, S. KOSHIMURA, H. MATSUTOMI, A. MOORE, C. RUSCHER, C.E. SYNOLAKIS, and T. TAKAHASHI, *Vanuatu earthquake and tsunami cause much damage, few casualties*, Eos, Trans. Amer. Geophys. Un., 81, 641 and 646–647, 2000.

CASSIDY, J. F., and G. C. ROGERS, *The M_w = 7.9 Alaska earthquake of 3 November 2002: Felt reports and unusual effects across western Canada*, Bull. Seismol. Soc. Amer., 94, S53–S58, 2004.

CISTERNAS, M., B.F. ATWATER, F. TORREJÓN, Y. SAWAI, G. MACHUCA, M. LAGOS, A. EIPERT, C. YOULTON, I. SALGADO, T. KAMATAKI, M. SHISHIKURA, C.P. RAJENDRAN, J.K. MALIK, Y. RIZAL, and M. HUSNI, *Predecessors of the giant 1960 Chile earthquake*, Nature, 437, 404–407, 2005.

CORONAS, J., *La actividad seîsmica en el archipélago Filipino durante el año 1897*, Observatorio de Manila, 129 pp., Manila, 1899.

EKSTRÖM, G., and M. NETTLES, *Calibration of the HGLP seismograph network and centroid-moment tensor analysis of significant earthquakes of 1976*, Phys. Earth Planet. Inter., 101, 219–243, 1997.

EL-ROBRINI, M., M. GENNESSEAUX, and A. MAUFFRET, *Consequences of the El-Asnam earthquakes: Turbidity currents and slumps on the Algerian margin (Western Mediterranean)*, Geo-Marine Letts., 5, 171–176, 1985.

EMBLEY, *New evidence for the occurrence of debris flow deposits in the deep sea*, Geology, 4, 371–374, 1976.

FIGEE, S., *Vulkanische verschijnselen en aardbevingen in den O.I. Archipel waargenomen gedurende het jaar 1897*, Natuurkunding Tijdschrift voor Nederlandsch-Indië, 58, 137–162, 1898.

FRITZ, H.M., and N. KALLIGERIS, *Ancestral heritage saves tribes during 1 April 2007 Solomon Islands tsunami*, Geophys. Res. Letts., 35, (*1*), L01607, 5 pp., 2008.

FRITZ, H.M., W. KONGKO, A. MOORE, B. MCADOO, J. GOFF, C. HARBITZ, B. USLU, N. KALLIGERIS, D. SUTEJA, K. KALSUM, V.V. TITOV, A. GUSMAN, H. LATIEF, E. SANTOSO, S. SUJOKO, D. DJULKARNAEN, H. SUNENDAR, and C.E. SYNOLAKIS, *Extreme run-up from the 17 July 2006 Java, Tsunami*, Geophys. Res. Letts., 34, (*12*), L12602, 4 pp., 2007.

GAZETTE DE FRANCE, *Organe officiel du Gouvernement Royal*, Paris, 12 août 1783.

GEE, M.J.R., H.S. UY, J. WARREN, C.K. MORLEY, and J.J. LAMBIASE, *The Brunei Slide: A giant marine slide on the Northwest Borneo Margin revealed by 3-D seismic data*, Mar. Geol., 246, 9–23, 2007.

GELLER, R.J., and H. KANAMORI, *Magnitudes of great shallow earthquakes from 1904 to 1952*, Bull. Seismol. Soc. Amer., 67, 587–598, 1977.

GELLER, R.J., *Scaling relations for earthquake source parameters and magnitudes*, Bull. Seismol. Soc. Amer., 66, 1501–1523, 1976.

GODUNOV, S.K., *Finite difference methods for numerical computations of discontinuous solutions of the equations of fluid dynamics*, Matemat. Sbornik, 47, 271–295, 1959.

GREEN, G., *On the motion of waves in a variable canal of small depth*, Cambridge Phil. Trans., 6, 457–462, 1837.

GUTENBERG, B., and C.F. RICHTER, *Seismicity of the Earth and associated phenomena* (Princeton University Press. 1954), 310 pp

HAMILTON, W., *Tectonics of the Indonesian region*, U.S. Geol. Surv. Prof. Paper, 1078, 345 pp., 1979.

HEEZEN, B.C., and W.M. EWING, *Turbidity currents and submarine slumps, and the 1929 Grand Banks earthquake*, Amer. J. Sci., 250, 849–878, 1952.

HEEZEN, B.C., and W.M. EWING, *Orléansville earthquake and turbidity currents*, Bull. Amer. Soc. Petrol. Geol., 39, 2505–2514, 1955.

HOUTZ, R.E., *The 1953 Suva earthquake and tsunami*, Bull. Seismol. Soc. Amer., 52, 1–12, 1962.

HSU, M.K., *Tsunamis in Taiwan and its near-by regions*, Acta Oceanogr. Taiwanica, 35, 1–16, 1996 (in Chinese).

IRVING, E.M., and J.S. TEVES, *The Iloilo earthquake of January 25, 1948, Panay Island, P.I.*, Philippine Geologist, 2, (*2*), 6–17, 1948.

KANAMORI, H., J.W. GIVEN, and T. LAY, *Analysis of body waves excited by the Mount St. Helens eruption of May 18, 1980*, J. Geophys. Res., 89, 1856–1866, 1984.

KVALE, A., *Seismic seiches in Norway and England during the Assam earthquake of August 15, 1950*, Bull. Seismol. Soc. Amer., 45, 93–113, 1955.

MA, K.-F., and M.-F. LEE, *Simulation of historical tsunamis in the Taiwan region*, TAO, *8*, 13–30, 1997.

MANSINHA, L., and D. E. SMYLIE, *The displacement fields of inclined faults*, Bull. Seismol. Soc. Amer., *61*, 1433–1440, 1971.

MASÓ, M.S., *Great earthquake and tidal wave in Southern Mindanao, P.I.*, Bull. Seismol. Soc. Amer., *8*, 125–126, 1918.

MEGAWATI, K., F. SHAW, K. SIEH, Z. HUANG, T.-R. WU, Y. LIN, S.K. TAN, and T.-C. PAN, *Tsunami hazard from the subduction megathrust of the South China Sea: Part I. Source characterization and the resulting tsunami*, J. Asian Earth Sci., *36*, 13–20, 2009.

MÜLLER, R.D., M. SDROLIAS, C. GAINA, and W.R. ROEST, *Age, spreading rates, and spreading asymmetry of the world's ocean crust*, Geochem. Geophys. Geosyst., *9*, *(4)*, Q04006, 19 pp., 2008.

NANAYAMA, F., K. SATAKE, R. FURUKAWA, K. SHIMOKAWA, K. SHIGENO, and B.F. ATWATER, *Unusually large earthquakes inferred from tsunami deposits along the Kuril Trench*, Nature, *424*, 660–663, 2003.

NELSON, A.R., H.M. KELSEY, AND R.C. WITTER, *Great earthquakes of variable magnitude at the Cascadia subduction zone*, Quatern. Res., *65*, 354–365, 2006.

OKAL, E.A., and C.E. SYNOLAKIS, *Far-field tsunami hazard from mega-thrust earthquakes in the Indian Ocean*, Geophys. J. Intl., *172*, 995–1015, 2008.

OKAL, E.A., and D. REYMOND, *The mechanism of the great Banda Sea earthquake of 01 February 1938: Applying the method of Preliminary Determination of Focal Mechanism to a historical event*, Earth Planet. Sci. Letts., *216*, 1–15, 2003.

OKAL, E.A., H.M. FRITZ, C.E. SYNOLAKIS, J.C. BORRERO, R. WEISS, P.J. LYNETT, V.V. TITOV, S. FOTEINIS, B.E. JAFFE, P.L.-F. LIU, and I. CHAN, *Field Survey of the Samoa Tsunami of 29 September 2009*, Seismol. Res. Letts., *81*, 577–591, 2010.

OKAL, E.A., J.C. BORRERO, and C.E. SYNOLAKIS, *Evaluation of tsunami risk from regional earthquakes at Pisco, Peru*, Bull. Seismol. Soc. Amer., *96*, 1634–1648, 2006.

OKAL, E.A., *Use of the mantle magnitude M_m for the reassessment of the seismic moment of historical earthquakes. I: Shallow events*, Pure Appl. Geophys., *139*, 17–57, 1992.

PELINOVSKY, E., D. YULIADI, G. PRASETYA, and R. HIDAYAT, *The 1996 Sulawesi tsunami*, Natural Hazards, *16*, 29–38, 1997.

REPETTI, W.C., *Catalogue of Philippine earthquakes, 1589–1899*, Bull. Seismol. Soc. Amer., *36*, 133–322, 1946.

REPETTI, W.C., *The China Sea earthquake of February 14th, 1934*, **in:** *Seismological Bulletin for 1934 January-June*, Dept. Agriculture & Commerce, Govt. of the Philippine Is., pp. 22–29, Manila, 1934.

REYMOND, D., and E.A. OKAL, *Preliminary determination of focal mechanisms from the inversion of spectral amplitudes of mantle waves*, Phys. Earth Planet. Inter., *121*, 249–271, 2000.

ROMANOWICZ, B. and G. SUÁREZ, *An improved method to obtain the moment tensor of earthquakes from the amplitude spectrum of Rayleigh waves*, Bull. Seism. Soc. Amer., *73*, 1513–1526, 1983.

SATAKE, K., K. SHIMAZAKI, Y. TSUJI, and K. UEDA, *Time and size of a giant earthquake in Cascadia inferred from Japanese tsunami records of January 1700*, Nature, *379*, 246–249, 1996.

SCHOUTEN, G., *Voyage de Gauthier Schouten aux Indes Orientales, commencé l'an 1658 et fini l'an 1665*, Vol. 1, pp. 322–323, Pierre Cailloué, Rouen, 1725.

SELLA, G., T.F. DIXON, and A. MAO, *REVEL: A model for recent plate velocities from space geodesy*, J. Geophys. Res., *107*, *(B4)*, ETG_11, 32 pp., 2002.

SOLOV'EV, S.L., and Ch.N. GO, *A catalogue of tsunamis on the Western shore of the Pacific Ocean*, Can. Transl. Fisheries Aquat. Sci., *5077*, 439 pp., Ottawa, 1984.

SOLOV'EV. S.L., Ch.N. GO, and Kh.S. KIM, 1986 *Katalog tsunami v Tikhom Okeane, 1969–1982 gg.*, Akad. Nauk SSSR, 164 pp., 1986 (in Russian).

STEWART, G.S., and S.N. COHN, *The 1976 August 16, Mindanao, Philippines, earthquake ($M_s = 7.8$)—evidence for a subduction zone South of Mindanao*, Geophys. J. Roy. astr. Soc., *57*, 51–63, 1979.

SYNOLAKIS, C.E., Tsunami and seiche, in: *Earthquake Engineering Handbook*, ed. by W.-F. Chen and C. Scawthron, pp. 9_1–9_90, CRC Press, Boca Raton, 2003.

SYNOLAKIS, C.E., E.N. BERNARD, V.V. TITOV, U. KÂNOĞLU, and F.I. GONZÁLEZ, *Validation and verification of tsunami numerical models*, Pure Appl. Geophys., *165*, 2197–2228, 2008.

SYNOLAKIS, C.E., J.-P. BARDET, J.C. BORRERO, H.L. DAVIES, E.A. OKAL, E.A. SILVER, S. SWEET, and D.R. TAPPIN, *The slump origin of the 1998 Papua New Guinea tsunami*, Proc. Roy. Soc. (London), Ser. A, *458*, 763–789, 2002.

TITOV, V.V., and C.E. SYNOLAKIS, *Numerical modeling of tidal wave runup*, J. Waterw. Port, Coastal & Ocean Eng., *124*, 157–171, 1998.

TSUJI, Y., F. IMAMURA, H. MATSUTOMI, C.E. SYNOLAKIS, P.T. NANAG, JUMADI, S. HARADA, S.S. HAN, K. ARAI, and B. COOK, *Field survey of the East Java earthquake and tsunami of June 3, 1994*, Pure Appl. Geophys., *144*, 839–854, 1995.

VANNESTE, M., J. MIENERT, and S. BUNZ, *The Hinlopen slide: a giant submarine slope failure on the Northern Svalbard margin*, Arctic Ocean. Earth Planet. Sci., *245*, 373–388, 2006.

WALLACE, R.E., G. PARARAS-CARAYANNIS, R. VALENZUELA, and J.N. TAGGART, *Earthquake and tsunamis of August 16, 1976, Mindanao, Philippines*, Geol. Soc. Amer. Abst. Prog., *9*, 523, 1977 (abstract).

WESSEL, P., and W.H.F. SMITH, *Free software helps map and display data*, Eos, Trans. Amer. Un., *72*, 441 and 445–446, 1991.

WYSESSION, M.E., E.A. OKAL, and K.L. MILLER, *Intraplate seismicity of the Pacific Basin, 1913–1988*, Pure Appl. Geophys., *135*, 261–359, 1991.

YE, L., X. WANG, and C. BAO, *Tsunami in the China seas and its warning service*, Proc. IUGG/IOC Intl. Symposium, 23–27 Aug. 1993, pp. 771–778, 1993.

ZACHARIASEN, J., K. SIEH, F.W. TAYLOR, R.L. EDWARDS, AND W.S. HANTORO, 1999 *Submergence and uplift associated with the giant 1833 Sumatran subduction earthquake atoll: Evidence from coral microatolls*, J. Geophys. Res., *104*, 895–919, 1999.

ZHOU, Q., and W.M. ADAMS, *Tsunami risk analysis for China*, Natural Hazards, *1*, 181–195, 1988.

(Received October 31, 2009, revised June 11, 2010, accepted June 11, 2010, Published online November 23, 2010)

Pure Appl. Geophys. 168 (2011), 1175–1185
© 2010 Springer Basel AG
DOI 10.1007/s00024-010-0224-8

Effects of Harbor Modification on Crescent City, California's Tsunami Vulnerability

Lori Dengler[1] and Burak Uslu[2,3]

Abstract—More damaging tsunamis have impacted Crescent City, California in historic times than any other location on the West Coast of the USA. Crescent City's harbor has undergone significant modification since the early 20th century, including construction of several breakwaters, dredging, and a 200 × 300 m² small boat basin. In 2006, a M_w 8.3 earthquake in the Kuril Islands generated a moderate Pacific-wide tsunami. Crescent City recorded the highest amplitudes of any tide gauge in the Pacific and was the only location to experience structural damage. Strong currents damaged docks and boats within the small boat basin, causing more than US $20 million in damage and replacement costs. We examine how modifications to Crescent City's harbor may have affected its vulnerability to moderate tsunamis such as the 2006 event. A bathymetric grid of the basin was constructed based on US Army Corps of Engineers soundings in 1964 and 1965 before the construction of the small boat basin. The method of splitting tsunamis was used to estimate tsunami water heights and current velocities at several locations in the harbor using both the 1964–1965 grid and the 2006 bathymetric grid for the 2006 Kuril event and a similar-sized source along the Sanriku coast of Japan. Model velocity outputs are compared for the two different bathymetries at the tide gauge location and at six additional computational sites in the harbor. The largest difference between the two grids is at the small boat basin entrance, where the 2006 bathymetry produces currents over three times the strength of the currents produced by the 1965 bathymetry. Peak currents from a Sanriku event are comparable to those produced by the 2006 event, and within the boat basin may have been higher. The modifications of the harbor, and in particular the addition of the small boat basin, appear to have contributed to the high current velocities and resulting damage in 2006 and help to explain why the 1933 M_w 8.4–8.7 Sanriku tsunami caused no damage at Crescent City.

Key words: Tsunami, Crescent City, California, 2006 Kuril Islands, natural hazards, hazard mitigation.

Submitted to: Pure and Applied Geophysics (PAGEOPGH) Topical Issue on Tsunami, 30 December 2009.

[1] Geology Department, Humboldt State University, #1 Harpst St, Arcata, CA 95521, USA. E-mail: lori.dengler@humboldt.edu

[2] Joint Institute for the Study of Ocean and Atmosphere, University of Washington, Seattle, WA 98105, USA. E-mail: Burak.Uslu@noaa.gov

[3] Pacific Marine Environmental Laboratory, NOAA, 7600 Sand Point Way NE, Seattle, WA 98115, USA.

1. Introduction

Crescent City, located on the California coast about 460 km north of San Francisco (Fig. 1), has suffered greater damage from tsunamis in historic times than any other community on the West Coast of North America. Thirty-three tsunamis have been observed at Crescent City since a tide gauge was established in 1933, including 11 with maximum peak-to-trough wave range exceeding 1 m and 4 that caused damage [National Geophysical Data Center (NGDC) 2009]. Crescent City's tsunami vulnerability has been recognized since the March 28, 1964 tsunami caused by the M_w 9.2 Alaskan earthquake produced more damage than anywhere outside of Alaska, killing 11, flooding 29 city blocks, and causing an estimated 15 million 1964-US dollars in losses (Lander et al., 1993; Dengler and Magoon, 2006). The most recent tsunami to cause damage was in November 2006, when the M_w 8.3 Kuril Islands earthquake generated a moderate Pacific-wide tsunami. Crescent City was the only area in the Pacific to experience significant damage, and repair/replacement costs were estimated at over US $20 million (Kelly et al., 2006; Dengler et al., 2008, 2009).

A number of researchers have examined the factors that contribute to Crescent City's tsunami vulnerability, including both far-field travel path effects and near-shore resonance (Wiegel, 1965; Wilson and Torum, 1968, 1972; Keulegan et al., 1969; Roberts and Kauper, 1964; Kowalik et al., 2008; Horrillo et al., 2008). In this paper, we take a different perspective and examine how modifications to the harbor may have contributed to Crescent City's tsunami vulnerability, particularly to moderate events such as the 2006 Kuril tsunami.

Figure 1

Crescent City Harbor. **a** The earliest known depiction of Crescent City Harbor shows an open crescent-shaped harbor with shallow shorelines. Lithograph published in Ballou's magazine, 1857. *Star* on inset map shows Crescent City's location. **b** October 1962 air photo collage, courtesy Orville Magoon. **c** 2009 Google Earth image

2. Crescent City's Tsunami and Harbor History

Northernmost coastal California and the Crescent City area was the home of the Tolowa people for at least 1,000 years prior to Euro-American contact. The natural crescent-shaped harbor (Fig. 1) was open to the west and south and experienced flooding from large storm and high-tide events and occasional tsunamis from both near and far sources. Oral history recorded by University of California Berkeley anthropologist P. Goddard in the early 20th century (GODDARD *et al.*, 1992) and stories still told today by the Tolowa people describe a great local earthquake and ensuing tsunami. This event is now regarded most likely as the 1700 earthquake documented by SATAKE *et al.* (1996). Jedidiah Smith was the first documented Euro-American to visit the Crescent City area, in 1828, and development began around 1850. Numerous rocks and shoals made entry to Crescent Harbor treacherous, and the US Army Corps of

Engineers began construction on the outer breakwater in 1928. The 1,000-m structure was completed in 1930, and dredging of the outer harbor to depths of near 7 m was completed in 1936. A 370-m inner breakwater was added in 1946, dividing the harbor into an inner and outer area. Until the construction of the small boat basin, commercial and recreational vessels were anchored within the inner harbor (Fig. 2a). As part of post-1964-tsunami reconstruction efforts, a 137-m dogleg extension to the inner breakwater was added, and in 1972 a 200×300 m² small boat basin was carved into the northeastern shore of the harbor (Fig. 2b, c).

A tide gauge was established in Crescent Harbor in 1933, a little over a month after the 1933 Sanriku tsunami, and moved to Citizens Dock when it was completed in 1950. Modest tsunamis were recorded in 1946, 1952, and 1957. The 1960 tsunami originating in southern Chile flooded the downtown area to 2nd Street, capsized several boats, and caused at

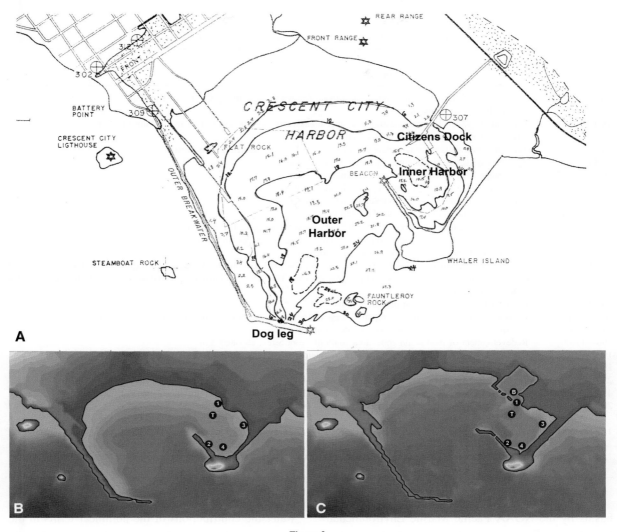

Figure 2

Bathymetric grids and model output locations. **a** 1965 numerical model developed from US Army Corp navigation charts. **b** The modeled 1965 numerical grid with synthetic tide gauge locations. **c** The 2006 grid with synthetic tide gauge locations

least US $30,000 in damage. The worst historic tsunami event occurred 4 years later when the 1964 Alaska tsunami flooded 29 city blocks, killed 10, and caused at least 15 million 1964-US dollars in damages. A summary of Crescent City's tsunami history and harbor modifications is given in Table 1.

3. Methods

The method of splitting tsunamis (MOST) model (TITOV and GONZALEZ, 1997; TITOV and SYNOLAKIS, 1998) and National Oceanic and Atmospheric Administration (NOAA)'s Tsunami Propagation Database (GICA et al., 2008; TANG et al., 2009, 2010) have been used in far-field tsunami modeling. The model, which has been validated through a series of laboratory experiments and benchmarked with numerous field surveys, uses nonlinear shallow-water equations to propagate long waves away from a generating source. The numerical codes conform to the standards and procedures outlined by SYNOLAKIS et al. (2008). A precomputed propagation database consisting of water level and flow velocities over all basin grid points and based on potential seismic unit sources has been developed for the world ocean

Table 1

Crescent City: a chronology of significant tsunami events and harbor development

	Tsunami events Harbor modifications and developments
26 January 1700	$M \sim 9.0$ Cascadia earthquake tsunami destroyed Tolowa villages in the Crescent City area
1857	Battery Point Lighthouse built
18 July 1929	US Army Corps of Engineers authorizes outer breakwater construction from Battery Point to Fauntleroy, and Rock Breakwater from shore to Whaler Island
1930	1,000-m outer breakwater completed using 20+ ton boulders quarried from Preston Island
2 March 1933	M_w 8.4 Sanriku, Japan tsunami; not noted at Crescent City
10 April 1933	Tide gauge established in Crescent City Harbor
1936	Outer harbor basin dredging to 7 m completed, except in rock
1946	370 m inner breakwater from Whaler Island completed
1 April 1946	0.9 m tsunami observed from Aleutians earthquake
1948–1949	330-m main breakwater extension initiated but quickly damaged; crest elevation raised and concrete cap constructed
1950	Citizens Dock completed with two piers: WSW "lumber wing" and SSE "fish wing"
1957	330-m main breakwater extension realigned (dogleg)
22 May 1960	M_w 9.5 S. Chile tsunami, 1.7 m tsunami at Crescent City, US $30 million damage; two ships destroyed, others damaged
28 March 1964	M_w 9.2 Alaska tsunami, 4.85 m tsunami at Crescent City, US $15+ million damage, 10 deaths, 29 blocks flooded, Citizens Dock severely damaged.
26 May 1964	Crescent City redevelopment project approved
June 1964	Citizens Dock rebuilt, fish wing repaired, new lumber wing and bridge, tide gauge relocated 87 m NE to bridge
July 1964	137-m dogleg extension to inner breakwater completed
1964–1967	Redevelopment of inundation zone, area south of Front Street elevated 3 m
1972	Citizens Dock area redevelopment project completed, small boat basin, dredging of the eastern dock area
16 May 1968	M_w 8.2 Honshu, Japan tsunami, 0.6 m at Crescent City
25 April 1992	M_w 7.2 Cape Mendocino tsunami, 0.6 m at Crescent City; first recorded "near-source" tsunami
4 October 1994	M_w 8.4 S. Kuril Islands tsunami, 0.5 m at Crescent City. Boats left harbor for offshore after Pacific-wide tsunami warning
20 September 2002	Crescent City designated "tsunami ready" by the National Weather Service
15 June 2005	M_w 7.2 Gorda plate tsunami, 0.1 m at Crescent City. Tsunami warning for US West Coast; Crescent City activated tsunami siren, $\sim$4,000 people evacuated.
15 November 2006	M_w 8.3 C. Kuril Islands tsunami, 0.88 m at Crescent City. US $20 million in damage to docks and boats in small boat basin

basins by the NOAA Pacific Marine Environmental Laboratory (GICA *et al.*, 2008). Subduction zones have been broken up into fault segments, or unit sources, each measuring 100 km long by 50 km wide. The propagation database is created from each of these discrete earthquake ruptures segments by computing wave propagation throughout the entire Pacific Basin. Complex sources from larger earthquakes are obtained by linear combinations of outputs of each unit segment. The underlying assumption is that the deep-sea evolution is linear, even though the equations used for propagation are nonlinear. This method has been validated by the NOAA Pacific Marine Environmental Laboratory for recent events (WEI *et al.*, 2008; TANG *et al.*, 2010). Given the typical range of tsunami amplitudes in the deep ocean, this is a reasonable assumption, as in deep water the contributions of the nonlinear terms in the wave evolution are negligible. Once in shallow water, the tsunami dynamics become nonlinear, so the linear superposition method is no longer applicable, hence a site-specific inundation model is constructed to assess coastal tsunami impact (USLU, 2008; USLU *et al.*, 2007; DENGLER *et al.*, 2008, 2009). As the wave transits the fluid body, evolution from propagation to inundation occurs by transference of water level and flow velocities through the grid boundaries of the propagation database to the three nested grids.

To model the tsunami using the present bathymetry, the Crescent City model from the USLU *et al.* (2007) study was used. This model was benchmarked using the 1964 Alaska tsunami inundation distances and 1952 Kamchatka, 1960 Chile, 1964 Alaska, 1994

Table 2

The depth and coordinates of the six locations studied in Crescent City Harbor

	Longitude	Latitude	Depth (m) 1965	Depth (m) 2006
Tide gauge	235.815	41.745	3.1	5.6
Guage 1 small boat basin inlet	235.8155	41.7462	0.9	6.9
Guage 2 coast guard station	235.8146	41.7421	3.5	5.0
Guage 3 Citizen Dock	235.818	41.744	1.1	2.4
Gauge 4 Citizen Dock	235.816	41.7418	3.3	5.0
Inside the small boat basin	235.8152	41.7473	Overland	5.0

Kuril Islands, and 2006 Kuril Islands tsunami tide gauge records. The grid assumes mean high water for vertical datum, WGS 1984 for the horizontal datum, and 0.027 for Manning roughness coefficient for friction. To look at the response of the basin prior to the construction of the basin, we obtained the original Army Corps of Engineers soundings for the harbor. At that time, the Army Corps would typically run soundings for portions of the harbor area twice a year. We selected the October 1964 and the January 1965 soundings, as they were the most recent data to cover the entire harbor area before construction of the boat basin began. We digitized soundings maps and compiled a contour map of the basin bathymetry (Fig. 2a) and used $1''$ (30 m) grid resolution to predict water levels in the harbor for both the 1965 and 2006

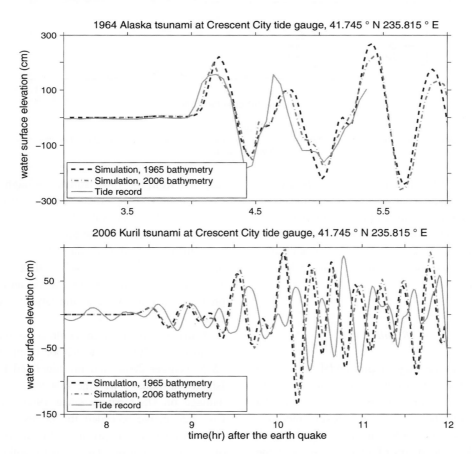

Figure 3
Comparison of the modeled water heights using the 1965 and 2006 grids with the actual tide gauge recording of the 1964 tsunami

217

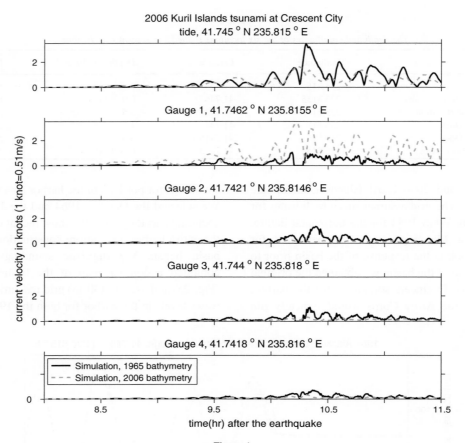

Figure 4
Comparison of modeled current velocities for the 2006 Kuril Islands tsunami at Crescent City at the synthetic tide gauge locations using 1965 and 2006 bathymetric grids

grids (Fig. 2b, c). MOST can output water height and water velocity data at prespecified locations. We selected the location of the 2006 tide gauge and five additional locations listed in Table 2. Four of them are in the Citizens Dock area, including an additional site within the small boat basin that was onshore in the 1965 grid.

4. Results

To verify the accuracy of the model output and look at the sensitivity of water heights to harbor modifications, we compared the water height model simulations with the actual water levels recorded during the 1964 and 2006 tsunamis (Fig. 3). Both simulations do a good job of reproducing both the amplitude and period of the actual tide gauge response from the 1964 tsunami through the first 2.5 cycles that were recorded. There is very little difference in the peak water heights between the two simulations. Both simulations from the 2006 Kuril tsunami agree well with the tide record. The wave phase is computed fairly well with a small discrepancy in arrival of the first wave and the model predicts the sixth wave as the largest instead of the eighth.

Current velocities, in contrast to water height, are more sensitive to the harbor configuration. The 15 November 2006 tsunami generated by the Kuril Islands earthquake was the first to cause significant damage on US territory since 1964. The Crescent City tide gauge recorded the largest water heights (1.76 m peak to trough) in the Pacific Basin outside of the source region. Three docks within the small boat basin were destroyed and others damaged

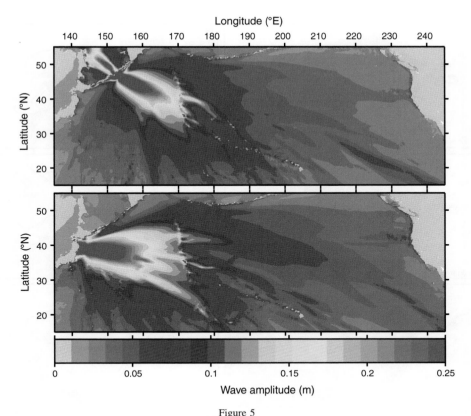

Figure 5
The computed peak water height distribution from 2006 and hypothetical scenario from the Sanriku coast, Japan over Pacific Ocean, after DENGLER *et al.* (2008). Note amplification for both events along the Northern California coast

when strong currents forced dock pile rings against piles, allowing water to flow over the surface (DENGLER *et al.*, 2008, 2009). There was no damage to any boats or structures outside of the small boat basin.

Figure 6 compares the currents at the actual tide gauge location (top graph in Fig. 4) and five synthetic gauge locations (1–5) using the 1965 (pre-boat basin) and 2006 bathymetry. At the tide gauge location, our modeling suggests that the currents would have been about twice as strong in 1965 as they were in 2006. At the synthetic locations distributed in the inner harbor away from the boat basin (2–5), the model output gives water velocities between 0.5 and 3 knots and all values are larger using the 1965 bathymetry. At site 1, at the entrance to the boat basin, the 2006 bathymetry gives velocities three times larger than they would have been in 1965, and the largest values of any of the modeled output sites. This is not surprising. In 1965, this site was in shallow water near shore. Today, all of the water within the boat basin is forced in and out of the 67-m-wide mouth.

The 2006 Kuril source was close to optimum orientation for similar-sized events originating in the Japan, Kuril Islands area to produce impacts at Crescent City (DENGLER *et al.*, 2008). Modeling suggests that only a rupture along the Sanriku coast of Northern Honshu is likely to give as large or larger response in the Crescent City Harbor area (Fig. 5). Figures 6 and 7 compare the model outputs for the *M* 8.3 Kuril event and a hypothetical 8.3 event on the Sanriku coast using both 2006 and 1965 bathymetry. The 2006 Kuril and the Sanriku events are compared in Fig. 7 for the entire harbor for 1965 and 2006 models. The maximum computed currents in Fig. 7 illustrate the sensitivity of the current velocities to harbor modifications. The Sanriku event shows a very

219

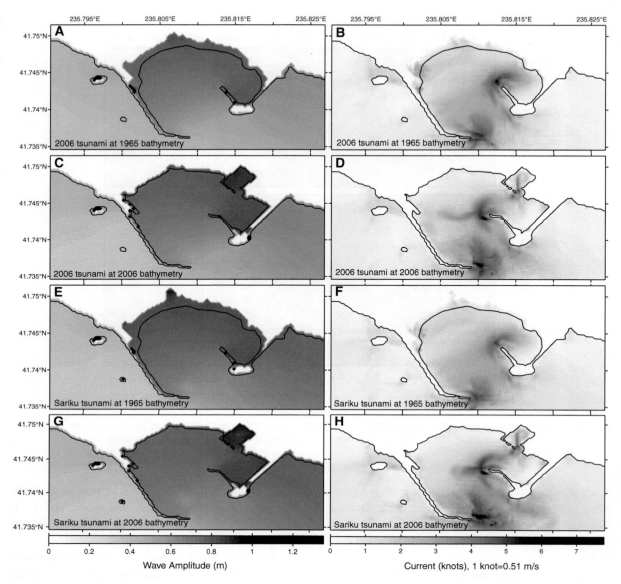

Figure 6
Computed maximum wave amplitudes and current velocities from Sanriku, Japan scenario and 2006 Kuril Islands tsunami for 1965 and 2006
Crescent City bathymetries

similar response to the 2006 Kuril's tsunami at the tide gauge location. The peak 1933 currents are about half as strong with the 2006 configuration as they would have been in 1965. At location 1 at the mouth of the small boat basin, the currents produced by the Sanriku tsunami are nearly three times stronger with 2006 bathymetry and comparable to the 2006 Kuril event. The strongest currents occur within the small boat basin (Fig. 7, bottom graph), an area which was dry land in 1965, where the modeling suggests the currents produced by the Sanriku event would exceed 4 knots and be slightly stronger than the 2006 Kuril event. Note that the depth at location 1 in 1965 is less than 1 m in Table 2, and computed currents at this location are zero during a drawdown shown in Figs. 4 and 7.

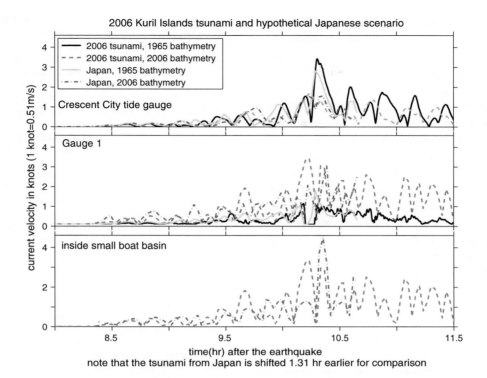

Figure 7
Comparison of computed current velocities from synthetic Sanriku, Japan scenario with 2006 Kuril Islands tsunami at the synthetic tide gauge locations in Crescent City Harbor

5. Discussion

Our results suggest that modifications to the Crescent City Harbor have increased the peak currents produced by a modest tsunami such as the 2006 Kuril Island's tsunami by a factor of at least three within the small boat basin and near its entrance over the peak currents in the inner basin where boats were anchored before the basin was built. This may have been sufficient to push the velocities over the threshold of damage.

In 1933, only 5 weeks before the Crescent City tide gauge was installed, an earthquake of $M_w \geq 8.4$ occurred close to the hypothesized Sanriku source shown in Figs. 5, 6, and 7. The earthquake produced a tsunami that killed over 3,000 people in Japan and produced trace recordings at six locations in California (National Geophysical Data Center (NGDC) 2009). The amplitude of the 1933 tsunami recorded at Hilo, Hawaii (0.5 m) was identical to the 2006 Kuril tsunami amplitude, suggesting that the 1933 tsunami at Crescent City should have been comparable to that of 2006. This earthquake was most likely a normal faulting outer rise event and may have been as large as M_w 8.6–8.7 (KANAMORI, 1971; OKAL, 1992). However, there is no mention of the tsunami or any damage in the Crescent City newspapers during the week after the event. Our modeling suggests that the currents produced in the inner basin where boats were anchored in 1933 before the small boat basin was constructed were not strong enough to produce damage. We have obtained soundings from the early 1930s and are constructing a bathymetric grid for that time period to further examine the likely impacts of the 1933 event in Crescent City.

The harbor master at Crescent City estimated the peak currents during the 2006 tsunami between 10 and 12 knots (5.1–6.2 m/s) (YOUNG, 2007). The peak model output values are less than 40% of his estimate. It should be noted that the model results are an average value over the entire water column and assume no contribution from tidal currents. They were also run assuming conditions of mean high water. The strongest currents during the 2006

Reprinted from the journal

event coincided with low tide. Without direct measurements of the currents during a tsunami, it is impossible to reconcile the model output with eyewitness observations. Two current meters are expected to be deployed in Crescent City Harbor in 2010, which should help to resolve this apparent discrepancy. However, even if the absolute values of the currents predicted by MOST have high uncertainty, the relative computed current speed values are likely to be accurate enough for the purpose of this study. Note that the accuracy of the current velocity prediction depends on the accuracy of the bathymetric data inside the harbor, and this study suggests that the prediction of currents depends on a high-resolution and very accurate harbor model, since the results differ for minor modifications.

Acknowledgments

We thank Thomas Kendall of the San Francisco Army Corps of Engineers office for providing the microfiche records of Crescent City soundings and Richard Young, Crescent City Harbor Master, for his recollections of the 2006 tsunami. Thanks to Costas Synolakis, Orville Magoon, Vasily Titov, and Aggeliki Barberopoulou for their ideas and comments as this project developed.

REFERENCES

DENGLER, L. A., and MAGOON, O.T. (2006), Reassessing Crescent City, California's tsunami risk, in Proceedings of the 100th Anniversary Earthquake Conference, [CD-ROM], 18–22 April 2006, San Francisco, paper R1577.

DENGLER, L., B. USLU, A. BARBEROPOULOU,, J. BORRERO, C. SYNOLAKIS (2008), *The vulnerability of Crescent City, California to tsunamis generated by earthquakes in the Kuril Islands region of the northwestern Pacific*, Seismological Research Letters, **79**(5), 608–619.

DENGLER, L., USLU, B., BARBEROPOULOU, A., YIM, S. C. and KELLEY, A. (2009), Tsunami damage in Crescent City, California from the November 15, 2006 Kuril event, in Tsunami Science Four Years After the 2004 Indian Ocean Tsunami, Part II: Observation and Data Analysis, PHIL R. CUMMINS, LAURA S. L. KONG eds, *Pure and Applied Geophysics* (PAGEOPH) topical volume, 166, 37–53, 2009.

GICA, E., SPILLANE, M., TITOV, V., CHAMBERLIN, C., AND NEWMAN, J. (2008). Development of the forecast propagation database for NOAA's Short–term Inundation Forecast for Tsunamis (SIFT).

Tech. Memo. OAR PMEL–139 NTIS: PBB2008- 109391, NOAA/Pacific Marine Environmental Laboratory, Seattle, WA.

GODDARD, P. E., KROEBER, A. L., & VALORY, D. (1992). Tolowa tales and texts: With free and interlinear translations. Berkeley, CA: California Indian Library Collections [distributor].

HORRILLO, J., KNIGHT, W., KOWALIK, Z. (2008), Kuril Islands tsunami of November 2006: 2. Impact at Crescent City by local enhancement, J. Geophys. Res., 113, C01021, doi:10.1029/2007J C004404.

KANAMORI, H., 1971. *Seismological evidence for a lithospheric normal faulting-the Sanriku earthquake of 1933*. Phys. Earth Planet. Inter. 4, pp. 289–300.

KELLY, A., DENGLER, L., USLU, B., BARBEROPOULOU, A., YIM, S., AND BERGEN, K. (2006), *Recent tsunami highlights need for awareness of tsunami duration*, EOS Transactions American Geophysical Union 87(50), 566–567.

KEULEGAN, G. H., HARRISON, J., and MATTHEWS, M.J. (1969), *Theoretics in The Design or the Proposed Crescent City Harbor Tsunami Model, US Army Corps of Engineers, Waterways Experiment Station, Vicksburg, MS*, Tech. Rept. H-69-9, 1969, 127 pp.

KOWALIK, Z., HORRILLO, J., KNIGHT, W., LOGAN, T. (2008), *Kuril Islands tsunami of November 2006: 1. Impact at Crescent City by distant scattering*, J. Geophys. Res., 113, C01020, doi: 10.1029/2007JC004402.

LANDER, J.F., LOCKRIDGE, P.A., and KOZUCH, M.J., (1993), Tsunamis Affecting the West Coast of the United States 1806-1992, NGDC Key to Geophysical Record Documentation No. 29, NOAA, NESDIS, NGDC, 242 pp.

National Geophysical Data Center (NGDC) (2009), NOAA/WDC Historical Tsunami Data Base, Boulder, Colorado http://www.ngdc.noaa.gov/hazard/tsu_db.shtml.

OKAL, E.A. (1992), *Use of the mantle magnitude Mm for the reassessment of the seismic moment of historical earthquakes. I: Shallow events*, Pure Appl. Geophys., 139, 17–57.

ROBERTS, J. A., and E. K. KAUPER (1964), The effects of wind and precipitation on the modification of South Beach, Crescent City, California. Including an appendix on the focusing of tsunami energy at Crescent City, prepared by C.W. CHIEN: Final Report, prepared for Environmental Sciences Div., Dept. of the Army, Contr. No. DA-49-092-ARO-38, 98 pp.

SATAKE, K., SHIMAZAKI, K., TSUJI, Y., and UEDA, K. (1996). *Time and size of a giant earthquake in Cascadia inferred from Japanese tsunami records of January 1700*. Nature, 379:246–249.

SYNOLAKIS, C. E., E. N. BERNARD, V. V. TITOV, U. KÂNOĞLU, and F. I. GONZÁLEZ, 2008. *Validation and verification of tsunami numerical models*, Pure Appl. Geophys., 165(11–12), 2197–2228.

TANG, L., V.V. TITOV, and C.D. CHAMBERLIN (2009): *Development, testing, and applications of site-specific tsunami inundation models for real-time forecasting*. J. Geophys. Res., 114, C12025, doi:10.1029/2009JC005476.

TANG, L., V.V. TITOV, AND C.D. CHAMBERLIN (2010): A Tsunami Forecast Model for Hilo, Hawaii. NOAA OAR Special Report, PMEL Tsunami Forecast Series: Vol. 1, 94 pp.

TITOV, V., and GONZALEZ, F. (1997). Implementation and testing of the method of splitting tsunami (MOST) model, NOAA Technical Memorandum ERL PMEL-112.

TITOV,V., and SYNOLAKIS, C.E., (1998). *Numerical modeling of tidal wave runup*, J. Waterw.,Port, Coastal, Ocean Eng. 124, 157-171.

USLU, B., BORRERO, J. C., DENGLER, L., AND SYNOLAKIS, C. E. (2007). *Tsunami inundation at Crescent City generated by earthquakes* along the Cascadia Subduction Zone. Geophys. Res. Lett., 34:L20601.

USLU, B. (2008). Deterministic and Probabilistic tsunami studies in California from near and farfield sources. PhD thesis, University of Southern California, Los Angeles, California.

WEI, Y., E. BERNARD, L. TANG, R. WEISS, V. TITOV, C. MOORE, M. SPILLANE, M. HOPKINS, AND U. KÂNOĞLU (2008): *Real-time experimental forecast of the Peruvian tsunami of August 2007 for U.S. coastlines.* Geophys. Res. Lett., 35, L04609, doi:10.1029/2007GL032250.

WIEGEL, R.L. (1965), Protection of Crescent City, California from tsunami waves, Report for the Redevelopment Agency of the City of Crescent City, 5 March 1965 Berkeley, California 114 pp.

WILSON, B.W., TORUM, A. (1968), The Tsunami of the Alaskan Earthquake, 1964: Engineering Evaluation Tech. Memo No. 25, Coastal Engineering Research Center, U.S.. Army Corps of Engineers, Washington, D.C., 401 pp.

WILSON, B. W. AND TORUM, A. (1972), Effects of the tsunamis: an engineering study, in: The Great Alaska earthquake of 1964, National Academy of Sciences, Washington, D.C., 361–523, 1972.

YOUNG, R., (2007). Personal communication, Crescent City Harbor District, Crescent City, CA 95531.

(Received December 31, 2009, revised May 14, 2010, accepted June 17, 2010, Published online January 11, 2011)

Reprinted from the journal

Pure Appl. Geophys. 168 (2011), 1187–1198
© 2010 Springer Basel AG
DOI 10.1007/s00024-010-0225-7

Calculations of Asteroid Impacts into Deep and Shallow Water

GALEN GISLER,[1] ROBERT WEAVER,[2] and MICHAEL GITTINGS[3]

Abstract—Contrary to received opinion, ocean impacts of small (<500 m) asteroids do not produce tsunamis that lead to world-wide devastation. In fact the most dangerous features of ocean impacts, just as for land impacts, are the atmospheric effects. We present illustrative hydrodynamic calculations of impacts into both deep and shallow seas, and draw conclusions from a parameter study in which the size of the impactor and the depth of the sea are varied independently. For vertical impacts at 20 km/s, craters in the seafloor are produced when the water depth is less than about 5–7 times the asteroid diameter. Both the depth and the diameter of the transient crater scale with the asteroid diameter, so the volume of water excavated scales with the asteroid volume. About a third of the crater volume is vaporised, because the kinetic energy per unit mass of the asteroid is much larger than the latent heat of vaporisation of water. The vaporised water carries away a considerable fraction of the impact energy in an explosively expanding blast wave which is responsible for devastating local effects and may affect worldwide climate. Of the remaining energy, a substantial portion is used in the crown splash and the rebound jet that forms as the transient crater collapses. The collapse and rebound cycle leads to a propagating wave with a wavelength considerably shorter than classical tsunamis, being only about twice the diameter of the transient crater. Propagation of this wave is hindered somewhat because its amplitude is so large that it breaks in deep water and is strongly affected by the blast wave's perturbation of the atmosphere. Even if propagation were perfect, however, the volume of water delivered per metre of shoreline is less than was delivered by the Boxing Day 2004 tsunami for any impactor smaller than 500 m diameter in an ocean of 5 km depth or less. Near-field effects are dangerous for impactors of diameter 200 m or greater; hurricane-force winds can extend tens of kilometers from the impact point, and fallout from the initial splash can be extremely violent. There is some indication that near-field effects are more severe if the impact occurs in shallow water.

Key words: Asteroid ocean impacts, seafloor craters, tsunamis, hydrodynamic calculations.

[1] Physics of Geological Processes, University of Oslo, PO Box 1048, Blindern, 0316 Oslo, Norway. E-mail: galen.gisler@fys.uio.no

[2] Los Alamos National Laboratory, MS T086, Los Alamos, NM 87545, USA. E-mail: rpw@lanl.gov

[3] Science Applications International, 3900 North Ocean Dr, #11A, Lauderdale by the Sea, FL 33308, USA. E-mail: mgittings0314@mac.com

1. Introduction

Oceans cover three-quarters of the Earth's surface, yet there is little geological evidence for deep ocean impact events (DAVISON and COLLINS, 2007; GERSONDE *et al.*, 2002; GERSONDE *et al.*, 1997; GERSONDE *et al.*, 2003; JANSA, 1993; ORMÖ and LINDSTRÖM, 2000; SHUVALOV and TRUBESTKAYA, 2002). Tectonic subduction has wiped away essentially all of the oceanic crust older than 120 million years, so older impact craters would not be preserved anyway. Water absorbs the energy of an impact very effectively, so it takes a very large event to produce even a modest crater on the abyssal plain, and the mobilisation of sediment following an impact tends to obscure such a signature except in cases where the impactor diameter is comparable to the ocean depth. Confirmed ocean impact craters are only observed on the continental shelf. Examples of these are the Mjølnir impact structure north of Norway from the late Jurassic (TSIKALAS, 2005; TSIKALAS *et al.*, 2002), the Chesapeake Bay impact structure (COLLINS and WÜNNEMANN, 2005; GOHN *et al.*, 2008), and the Montagnais crater off Nova Scotia (DYPVIK and JANSA, 2003; JANSA *et al.*, 1989), the latter two both from the Eocene. The Chicxulub crater, associated with the Cretaceous-Tertiary extinction event, was caused by a very massive impact on a carbonate platform possibly sloping down to depths of 650 m (GULICK *et al.*, 2008). The Eltanin deep-water impact event, on the abyssal plain of the southern Pacific Ocean, has no crater (GERSONDE *et al.*, 1997; GERSONDE *et al.*, 2003).

Tsunamis are often considered the most likely signature of deep-water impacts. Yet evidence for tsunamis from oceanic asteroid impacts is also scarce, and fierce debates accompany the suggestions that have been presented (MASSE *et al.*, 2006; PINTER and

ISHMAN, 2008). The known shallow-water impacts of Mjølnir and Montagnais should have left tsunami deposits on nearby shores, yet the search for these has been inconclusive (DYPVIK and JANSA, 2003; DYPVIK et al., 2006). In the geological record, only the Chicxulub event, also a continental-shelf event, has confirmed associated tsunami deposits, and these could have been produced by massive continental slope failures triggered by impact-associated earthquakes in the hours or days subsequent to the impact or by resurge (MATSUI et al., 2002). Because ocean impacts should be about three times as frequent as land impacts, the absence of confirmed evidence for tsunamis from these events suggests that tsunamis resulting from oceanic impacts are rare.

Among the planetary defence community, much attention has focused on teletsunamis as being the principal danger from the impact of asteroids with diameters of a few hundred metres (CHESLEY and WARD, 2006; HILLS et al., 1994; WARD and ASPHAUG, 2000, 2002). Others (CRAWFORD, 1998; GUSIAKOV, 2007; MELOSH, 2003; WÜNNEMANN et al., 2007) have urged a more tempered view. In this paper we argue, based on numerical simulations, that the tsunami danger for locations far from the impact site is less than the dangers posed by the atmospheric effects of small impacts. Instead, it is the near-field effects that pose the greatest danger in small oceanic impacts, just as in land impacts. Our calculations differ from most previous calculations of impact tsunami in using the full hydrodynamic equations for the generation phase and including a fully realistic equation of state for water and air. Preheating of the atmosphere due to the passage of the asteroid through the atmosphere is also included.

2. Simulations with the SAGE Hydrocode

The SAGE hydrocode is a multi-material adaptive-grid finite-volume Eulerian code with a high-resolution Godunov scheme originally developed by Michael Gittings (GITTINGS et al., 2008) for Science Applications International (SAIC) and subsequently adopted at Los Alamos National Laboratory (LANL). The grid refinement is continuous, cell-by-cell and cycle-by-cycle throughout the problem run. Refinement occurs when gradients in physical properties

(density, pressure, temperature, material constitution) exceed user-defined limits, down to minimum cell sizes specified by the user. With the computing power concentrated on the regions of the problem which require higher resolution, very large computational volumes and substantial differences in scale can be simulated at relatively low cost. A variety of equations of state are available for use with the code, including tabular equations of state from the LANL Sesame library (HOLIAN, 1984; LYON and JOHNSON, 1992) and the SAIC equation of state for water.

We have used the SAGE code for simulations of tsunami generation by subaerial and submarine landslides, undersea volcanoes, and earthquakes (GISLER, 2008; GISLER et al., 2006a, b; MADER and GITTINGS, 2002) and have reported previously on oceanic asteroid impact simulations performed with this code (GISLER, 2007; GISLER et al., 2003). In these papers, we presented calculations of oblique impacts in three dimensions and of vertical impacts in axisymmetric geometry, and demonstrated that the essential features of oceanic impacts are adequately covered by two-dimensional axisymmetric calculations. The reason for this is that the transient crater is very effectively symmetrised through the vaporisation of water encountered on impact. The kinetic energy per unit mass of an impacting asteroid is many times greater than the latent heat of vaporisation of water, hence many times the asteroid mass is vaporised on impact. The subsequent development of a propagating wave occurs through the collapse of the transient crater, the formation of a central jet rising many kilometres above the initial water surface, and finally the collapse of that jet and its subsequent rebounds.

The initial splash and the near-field waves formed in this manner can be of extremely high amplitude. The splash can rise up tens of kilometers before falling back to the ocean surface with considerable violence. The subsequent waves produced in the near-field can have heights that are substantial fractions of the total ocean depth. As such, they are strongly nonlinear; they break in the open ocean over the abyssal plain, and decay rapidly to form trains of much smaller waves. When coastlines are nearby, these highly nonlinear waves can be extremely dangerous. Their effects at great distances are more difficult to compute, and have been greatly overstated in the past.

Table 1

Input and output characteristics of asteroid impact simulations in deep water

	DwCe	DwFe	DwHe	DwIe	DwJe	DwKe	DwLe
Input parameters							
Asteroid diameter (m)	1,000	700	500	400	300	200	100
Kinetic energy (Megatons TNT eq.)	65,800	22,600	8,220	4,210	1,780	526	66
Transient crater characteristics							
Depth (m)	6,208	5,375	4,375	3,708	3,000	2,208	1,208
Diameter (km)	17.5	12.2	9.0	7.2	5.5	4.1	2.2
Wave characteristics							
Amplitude (m) at 30 km from impact point	477	285	231	179	133	56	37
Wave speed (m/s)	166	160	149	143	138	114	86
Wavelength (km)	28.7	20.5	17.9	15.7	13.6	9.5	4.9
Extent of near-field atmospheric effects							
Fallout from crown splash (km)	67	55	47	36	20	17	7
Hurricane force winds (km)	95	81	75	57	49	36	22
Air temperature above 100°C (km)	55	34	26	13	4	–	–

If a classical tsunami is defined as a wave with amplitude small compared to the ocean depth and wavelength very much greater than the depth, asteroid ocean impacts do not generate classical tsunamis. Classical tsunamis are generated by undersea earthquakes and landslides, often by dipole couples having lever arms tens to hundreds of kilometres in dimension. The very long waves that are produced can propagate very effectively, with little energy loss, over long distances at the so-called shallow-water speed $\sqrt{gD}$, where g is the acceleration due to gravity and D is the ocean depth. In our calculations, we have obtained speeds for the waves produced in asteroid ocean impacts are considerably smaller than $\sqrt{gD}$, and the wavelengths of these waves are less than twice the diameter of the transient crater as shown previously (GISLER, 2007, 2008; GISLER *et al.*, 2003) and in Sect. 3. For example, a 1 km diameter asteroid at vertical impact into a 5 km deep ocean produces a transient crater about 17 km in diameter; the wave that results from the collapse of this crater has a crest-to-crest length that is larger than this by a factor of only 1.5 (this ratio trends slightly larger for smaller impactors). By comparison, the wavelength of the Indian Ocean tsunami on 26 December 2004 was ~120 km. The shallow-water speed in this 5 km deep ocean is 221 m/s; the wave produced by the 1 km impact has a speed of 166 m/s.

The calculations reported earlier (GISLER, 2007) were done for a range of compositions, diameters, and speeds, from 250 m diameter icy bodies to 1,000 m diameter iron bodies at speeds from 10 to 20 km/s. All simulation data were eventually collapsed onto curves of wave amplitude versus kinetic energy at various distances from the impact point, from which we concluded that the ocean-wide tsunami danger from likely impactors of less than 500 m diameter was negligible. In this paper, we therefore turn greater attention to near-field and atmospheric effects of ocean impacts. In addition, we examine the effects of sediment transport and entrainment in the jet and waves.

3. The New Calculations

We present two new parameter studies in this paper. In the first, presented below in Table 1 and Figs. 1, 2, 3, 4, 5, 6, we vary the projectile diameter from 100 m to 1,000 m, holding the speed at 20 km/s and the water depth at 5 km. In the second, presented in Table 2, we hold the projectile diameter at 200 m, and vary the depth of water and sediment.

The deep-water runs are listed in Table 1. Run names, input asteroid diameter, and kinetic energy in Megatons TNT equivalent are the input parameters, followed by outputs of wave characteristics and near-field atmospheric effects. All runs are axisymmetric, computed in a domain of 100 km horizontal extent and 50 km vertical. The vertical space is homogeneously divided into 37 km air (Sesame material

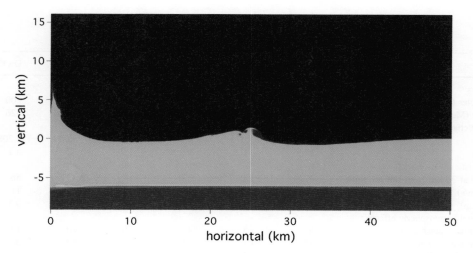

Figure 1
Snapshot, in *vertical* cross-section, of a wave produced by the vertical impact of a 1 km stony asteroid into a 5 km deep ocean (run DwCe in Table 1), 225 s after impact. *Deep blue* is air, *cyan* is water, *green* is ocean-bottom sediment (a layer 1 km in initial thickness), and *red* is the basalt oceanic crust. The domain illustrated here is from 9 km below sea level to 60 km above, and from the impact point out to 50 km radial distance. The computational domain for all simulations is larger than this window, extending out to 100 km radial distance, down to 13 km below sea level and up to 37 km above. The single wave shown here is 1.4 km high (above original sea level) and breaking. It is preceded by a negative trough of 800 m depth, and the trough-to-crest distance is 8 km. The ocean-bottom sediments have been disturbed in the vicinity of the impact point (at *left*), and some of this material has been lofted in the now-collapsing jet to stratospheric levels. The basalt has been dimpled to 200 m depth over a crater diameter of 2.5 km

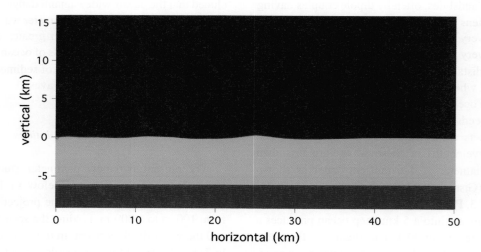

Figure 2
Snapshot of waves produced by the impact of a 400 m stony asteroid into a 5 km deep ocean (run DwIe of Table 1), 329 s after impact. *Colours* and *geometry* are as in Fig. 1. The *central* wave shown here has a height 275 m above original sea level. There are three detectable wave crests at this time, with crest-to-crest distance 12 km. Though there has been some disturbance of the ocean bottom sediments, there is no dimpling of the basalt beneath. The maximum depth of the transient crater in this case was 1.3 km above the *top* of the sediment layer, or 3.7 km *beneath* the original water surface

#5030, dry air, density 0.00129 g/cc), 5 km ocean (SAIC water, density 1 g/cc), 1 km unconsolidated sediments (Sesame material #7111 alluvium, distended and mixed with water to density ~1.5 g/cc),

and 7 km basalt crust (Sesame material #7530, density 2.87 g/cc). The basalt is treated with an elastic–plastic strength model; all other materials in the problem, including the stony asteroid (Sesame

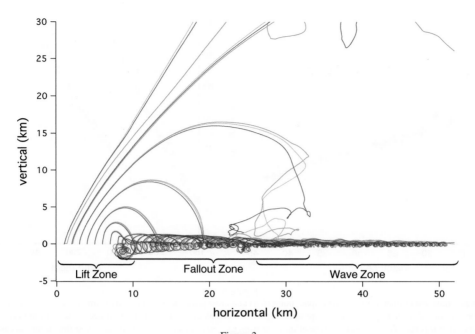

Figure 3

Trajectory plot of Lagrangian tracer particles from run DwFe (700 m diameter impact). Trajectories for 150 particles are shown; in *green* are particles that started 50 m above the initial water surface, in *cyan* those that started on the water surface, and in *blue* those that started 50 m below. The lift zone is somewhat larger than the transient crater, whose radius is 6.1 km; and the pure wave zone begins around 25 km. The fallout zone, as seen in this figure, goes out to at least 32 km; from analysis of other tracers, placed below the water surface within the transient crater and omitted here, the fallout zone extends out to 55 km

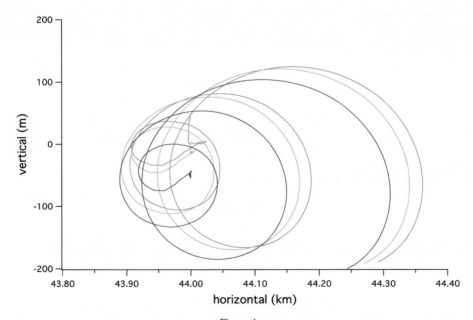

Figure 4

Trajectory plot for three vertically offset tracers in run DwIe (400 m diameter impact). After a period of initial drift, these three particles are hit by the initially regressive wave from the decay of the transient crater, and are then taken in three successive oscillations about a centre that drifts away from the impact site. In this case each of the three oscillations is of greater amplitude (*vertical* and *horizontal*) than the previous. For some other particles the first or the second oscillation is larger

229   Reprinted from the journal

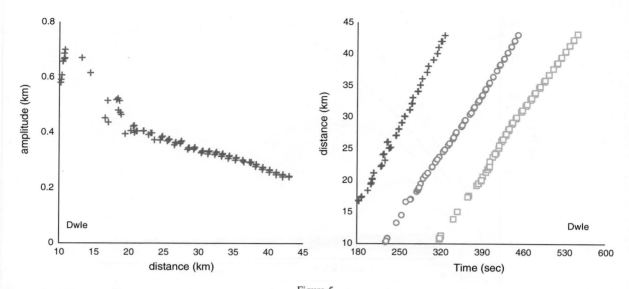

Figure 5
Wave amplitude as a function of distance from the impact point (*left*) and crest position as a function of time for three successive waves (*right*) for run DwIe, the 400 m diameter impact. These were obtained from analysis of 92 tracer particle trajectories from the original 150 water-surface tracers placed in this run. The tracers that were eliminated from the analysis were those that had fewer than three successive crests and troughs within the 600 s of the simulation, and those with excessive temperatures. Plots like these were generated for all runs, and the wave characteristics listed in Table 1 were obtained from these

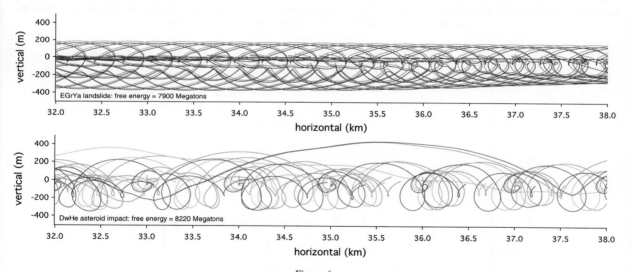

Figure 6
Tracer particle trajectories in the wave zone for a simulation of the tsunami induced by the El Golfo landslide in the Canary Islands (*top*) and for the wave produced by the impact of a 500 m diameter asteroid (run DwHe, *bottom*). These events are of comparable source energy

material #7391, granite, density 2.63 g/cc) are strength-less. The full domain was initialised in hydrostatic equilibrium, and then the asteroid was inserted with a downward velocity of 20 km/s at 15 km above the ocean surface.

All runs were performed with a minimum resolution of 12.8 cells per projectile diameter. The actual minimum cell sizes varied from 7.8 m for run DwLe to 31.3 m for run DwCe. The runs were performed on an Opteron cluster at the University of Tromsø in

Table 2

Input and output characteristics of asteroid impact simulations in water of varying depth

	TwKe	TwKf	TwKg	TwKh	Twki	TwKj
Input parameters						
Water depth (m)	5000	2000	1500	1000	700	500
Sediment depth (m)	30	75	100	150	214	300
Transient crater characteristics						
Depth (m)	2175	1912	1562	1200	988	913
Diameter (km)	2.325	2.45	2.488	2.538	2.65	2.688
Wave characteristics						
Amplitude (m) at 30 km from impact point	47	55	50	50	30	14
Wave speed (m/s)	126	106	96	86	79	72
Wavelength (km)	11	9	8	7	7	7
Extent of near-field atmospheric effects						
Fallout from crown splash (km)	12	12	10	10	9	8
Hurricane force winds (km)	38	43	41	41	39	40
Air temperature above 100°C (km)	2.7	3.7	6.7	7.8	4.1	10.1

Norway, using 32 or 64 processors per run over several weeks. The duration of all runs was 600 s physical time (this is the time necessary for a tsunami, initiated at the time of the maximum transient crater for a 1 km impact and travelling at the shallow-water speed of 221 m/s, to exit the 100 km long computational box).

An illustrative frame from the DwCe run is illustrated in Fig. 1. The wave shown has arisen from the collapse of the central jet, which is undergoing its first rebound at the time shown. The wave has a leading trough, the last remnant of the transient crater. The wave is strongly nonlinear, turbulent, and dissipative, with a breaking crest at 1.4 km above the initial ocean surface. A later stage from the more lightweight DwIe run is shown in Fig. 2. Three wave crests are visible, each from a collapse-rebound cycle of the central jet. The jet collapse and rebound cycle evidently determine the wavelength and period of the waves produced in the impact. In this lower-energy impact, no wave breaking is observed at the scale of these snapshots.

Wave characteristics are diagnosed from the trajectories of Lagrangian tracer particles within the simulation domain. In each of these simulations, we placed water surface tracers evenly along the surface and 50 m above and below, from 1 km out to 50 km from the point of impact. A sample trajectory plot is shown in Fig. 3, for run DwFe. In this plot, it is possible to distinguish a lift zone somewhat larger than the transient crater size, a fallout zone, and a wave zone, partially overlapping. The wave characteristics themselves can be obtained by zooming in on the wave-zone tracers, as shown in Fig. 4 for three vertically offset tracers placed initially 44 km from the impact point in run DwIe. An automated procedure was devised to extract amplitude, period, and wavelength measurements from the tracers used in each run. The procedure required the location of three successive crests and troughs, so particles for which less than three were found were rejected, as were particles with excessive temperatures.

Sample plots of amplitude against distance, and of distance against time for three successive wave crests, are shown in Fig. 5 for run DwIe. The wave amplitude decays with distance, rapidly at first because of wave breaking and other nonlinear effects, and subsequently more slowly. We have not followed waves in these calculations beyond slightly more than 50 km, but we obtain approximate power-law decays at that distance with index -0.7 for all impactors.

To illustrate the difference between classical tsunamis and asteroid impact waves, in Fig. 6 we show a comparison of tracer-particle plots from run DwHe and a run done for a study (GISLER *et al.*, 2009) of a tsunami produced by the prehistoric El Golfo landslide from the island of El Hierro in the Canaries (MASSON, 1996). These two simulations are comparable to one another in terms of the available free energy. For DwHe, this free energy is the initial kinetic energy of the asteroid, 8.2 Gigatons, and for the El Golfo run it is the difference in gravitational potential energy between the initial position of the slide mass and its final position, ~7.9 Gigatons.

The difference between particle trajectories in the El Golfo simulation (top panel) and the asteroid impact simulation (bottom panel) could hardly be more striking. The particle motion in the top panel is orderly, with each particle's motion closely resembling that of its neighbours. The coupling of rock motion to water motion occurs at speeds slow compared to the speed of sound in either medium, and a coherent wave is produced. The much more violent collision between rock and water that occurs in an asteroid impact at hypersonic speed has produced considerably more disorder in the bottom panel. Many of the particles have trajectories that are partly wave-like, but they are jerked from one mode to another as the complex and turbulent wave train passes. At least four particles in this panel are on very long looping trajectories that originated within the fallout zone, less than 15 km from the impact point. These are moving at particle speeds up to 200 m/s, comparable to the wave speed. Normally, particles participating in transverse wave motion have particle speeds much less than the wave speed, and particle oscillation lengths much smaller than the wavelength. This is the case for all particles in the top panel.

If we apply the same analysis to the El Golfo tracers as we applied to the asteroid impact tracers, we get a wavelength of ~40 km and a wave speed of ~170 m/s. These numbers are consistent with the interpretation of this wave structure as a classical tsunami. The water depth 35 km from El Hierro is 3.3 km, giving a shallow-water-wave speed of 178 m/s. On the other hand, the wave speed in DwHe is ~150 m/s, inconsistent with the shallow-water wave speed of 221 m/s in the 5 km deep ocean, and the wavelength of 18 km is only slightly more than 3 times the depth. This asteroid impact wave structure is not a classical tsunami.

Results from the second parameter study are presented in Table 2. All these runs simulated the vertical impact of a stony asteroid of 200 m diameter at 20 km/s. In these runs, we focussed attention on the ability of the projectile to produce a remnant crater in the seafloor crust. Because sediment accumulation is generally higher in shallower seas (on the continental shelf or slope, for example), we made the layer of unconsolidated sediment progressively thicker in the runs with shallower water depth. These runs show a tendency for near-field effects to be more dangerous in shallower water, which would be of considerable concern to coastal populations in the event of a near-shore strike.

From both the parameter studies conducted here, we come to a better understanding of why undersea craters are rare. In Table 1, only runs DwCe and DwFe have transient crater depths greater than the water depth, so for vertical impacts our calculations would predict that a stony asteroid would have to be greater than 600 m in diameter in order to produce a dimpling of the oceanic crust under 5 km of water. In Table 2, only the shallow-water runs TwKi and TwKj produced a transient crater depth great enough to dimple the oceanic crust. The wave characteristics computed from the tracers are consistent with the waves produced in run DwKe of Table 1, which was a 200 m impact into deep water.

The results from Tables 1 and 2 are portrayed graphically in Fig. 7. In the top panel, we show transient crater depth and *radius* (not diameter, in order to use the same ordinate scale) as a function of asteroid diameter for vertical impacts into a 5,000 m deep ocean at 20 km/s. To the seven runs of Table 1 are added three additional runs. As indicated by the arrows, craters on the seafloor are possible only for asteroid diameters greater than about 700 m. In the lower panel we show transient crater depth and radius as a function of the combined depth of water and unconsolidated sediment for the six runs of Table 2 and twelve additional runs, all with vertical impacts at 20 km/s of a 200 m diameter asteroid. As indicated in this plot, craters on the seafloor are possible only for combined sediment–water depths less than about 1,200 m. These two plots support our conclusion that, in vertical impacts at 20 km/s, the asteroid diameter must be greater than 15–20% of the water (or combined water and unconsolidated sediment) depth in order to produce a permanent crater on the seafloor.

A separate paper currently in preparation considers the fate of the unconsolidated sediment and its role in the aftermath of the impact.

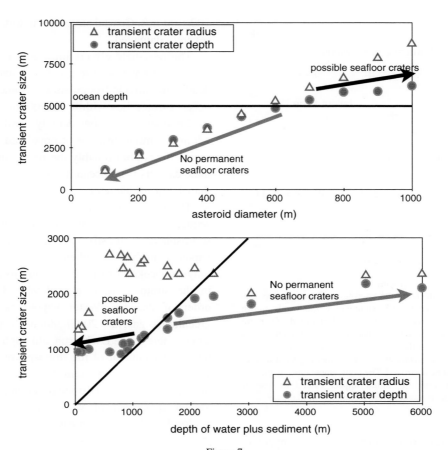

Figure 7

Transient crater depth and radius for the simulations of Tables 1 and 2 plus additional runs. *Top panel* constant ocean depth (5,000 m), variable asteroid diameter. *Bottom panel* constant asteroid diameter (200 m), variable depth of water and unconsolidated sediment. All runs are vertical impacts at 20 km/s. From the ten constant ocean depth and variable asteroid diameter runs (the 7 runs of Table 1 plus 3 additional runs) we get permanent seafloor craters only if the asteroid diameter is greater than about 700 m. From the 18 constant asteroid diameter and variable ocean depth runs (the six runs of Table 2 plus 12 additional runs) we get permanent seafloor craters only if the combined depth of water and unconsolidated sediment is less than about 1,200 m. From these two parameter studies we draw the conclusion that for vertical impacts at 20 km/s the asteroid diameter must be at least 15–20% of the ocean depth in order to make a crater on the seafloor

4. The Dangers from Oceanic Asteroid Impacts

We argue here, as we have previously done, that the long-distance tsunami danger from the impact of a (say) 200 m diameter asteroid is not as great as others (HILLS *et al.*, 1994; WARD and ASPHAUG, 2000, 2002) have supposed. Such impacts do not produce classical tsunamis; the waves they produce are of shorter length and lower speed. They are more disorderly and chaotic, will decay more rapidly, and will not propagate efficiently over long distances. Nevertheless, the prospect of such an impact is not to be taken lightly.

An impact of a 200 m stony body at 20 km/s, whether on land or on water, releases energy equivalent to a >500 Megaton nuclear device. If this occurs in or near a populated region, significant loss of life would occur unless efficient evacuation occurs. But such an impact in the deep ocean will not produce a global tsunami of unprecedented size and devastation.

The real dangers from water impacts are mainly atmospheric. The most immediate of these are concentrated in the near field, just as for land impacts. The extent of the near-field effects is shown in Fig. 8 as a function of impactor diameter. These immediate dangers include the blast wave from the explosive vaporisation of water, followed by hurricane force winds out to tens of kilometres and high

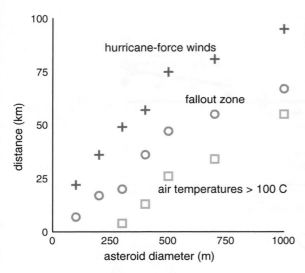

<figure>Figure 8
Extent of near-field effects for the asteroid impact simulation runs of Table 1. In the axisymmetric simulations, the winds shown circulate outward close to the surface and back at altitude. On Earth these would probably generate cyclonic flows. The fallout zone is where water, expelled in the crown splash as the transient crater forms, falls back to the surface at terminal velocity. Any structures in this region would be destroyed. The high temperatures generated in the blast wave from the initial impact extend to tens of kilometers for impactors greater than 400 m diameter</figure>

temperatures over similar distances. For impactors of diameters greater than 500 m, air temperatures may exceed the boiling point of water over tens of kilometres. The fallout zone, where water excavated from the transient crater falls back to the surface in enormous quantities at terminal velocity, extends out to 50 km for a 500 m asteroid impact. An impact in deep water close to a narrow continental shelf (as on the west coast of the Americas or the east coast of Asia) could produce massive destruction from this fallout.

Deep-water tracers in the initial area of the transient crater show us where the excavated water goes. Analysis of the deep-water tracers in the DwKe run suggests that, of the 58 Gigatonnes of water excavated in this impact, roughly a third is catapulted into the stratosphere above 20 km altitude, another third is shoved out laterally, and a final third is splayed out in the crown splash to come down to earth in the fallout zone. In run DwKe, the fallout zone extends out to 17 km. If the fallout occurs evenly, every square metre would receive 22 tonnes of water, falling at speeds of

100–300 m/s. Coastal structures in this zone would be severely damaged.

The near-field effects illustrated in Fig. 8 extend out to 100 km from the point of impact and can be deadly for affected populations. Some 2–5% of the ocean surface lies within 50–100 km of continental land masses, and a considerably greater fraction lies within a similar distance of populated islands. These local effects are probably the most important immediate dangers from ocean impacts of asteroids smaller than 1 km in diameter.

The water injected into the stratosphere has consequences of longer term and more global nature. The stratosphere is mostly dry; most of Earth's water vapour is in the troposphere and cycles fairly rapidly (days to weeks) back to the ground. Its residence time in the stratosphere is considerably longer, on the order of decades. Water vapour is an important greenhouse gas: the 20 Gigatonnes injected into the stratosphere in the DwKe run, although only 0.1% the total water content of the troposphere, is a factor of 100 greater than the present-day water vapour content of the stratosphere (ROSENLOF et al., 2001). Much greater quantities of water are injected into the stratosphere for larger impacts, and for a 1 km bolide may exceed the total water content of the present atmosphere.

Because of the much longer residence time for water vapour in the stratosphere, oceanic impact events may have serious implications for weather and climate. Whether such a sudden injection of water would lead to a warming (because of greenhouse effects) or a cooling (because of the formation of albedo-increasing ice clouds in the stratosphere) is beyond the scope of this study, as is the duration of such weather/climate perturbations.

5. Conclusions

We have performed numerical calculations of oceanic impacts to understand wave generation and energy deposition from these events. We have used tracer particles to measure the characteristics of asteroid impact waves, and find them to be of shorter period and wavelength than expected for tsunamis. The waves are disorderly, and subject to dissipation and decay. We have further examined near-field effects from such impacts, and find that these mainly atmospheric effects can be deadly up to 100 km away from the impact point. In addition the injection of water vapour into the stratosphere may have consequences for weather and climate.

Craters from asteroid oceanic impacts should be very rare. For vertical impacts at 20 km/s, craters do not form in water depths greater than 5–7 times the asteroid diameter. In shallow water, where sediments can be deep, mobilisation of such sediments may obscure the craters that do form.

Strategies for mitigation of the effects of meteor impacts on Earth are being studied by the planetary defence community (see, for example, the web page of the 2009 Planetary Defence Conference, http://www.congrex.nl/09c04/). Small meteors that burn up in the atmosphere can be safely ignored, while large asteroids should be deflected, generally years in advance. Programs to detect all potential threats to the Earth are underway. The minimum size for which the action must be taken is not accurately known, but widely considered to be in the range 100–500 m diameter. Based on the work presented here, the ocean impact of an asteroid of size less than about 500 m in diameter will not lead to a global catastrophe, though it could cost significant loss of life if it landed in the wrong place. For impactors smaller than this, warnings and evacuations may be a more cost-effective strategy than a space mission designed to deflect or disrupt the asteroid.

Acknowledgments

We gratefully acknowledge the support of the Norwegian Research Council for the establishment and funding of the Centre for the Physics of Geological Processes, a Norwegian Centre of Excellence at the University of Oslo. The computing reported here has been done mostly through resources provided by NOTUR, the Norwegian distributed supercomputing network, based on earlier work done at Los Alamos National Laboratory. The comments of two referees have also been helpful in improving this paper.

REFERENCES

CHESLEY S. R. and WARD S. N. (2006) A Quantitative Assessment of the Human and Economic Hazard from Impact-generated Tsunami. *Natural Hazards* 38, 355–374.

COLLINS G. S. and WÜNNEMANN K. (2005) How big was the Chesapeake Bay impact? Insight from numerical modeling. *Geology* 33, 925–928.

CRAWFORD D. A. (1998) Modeling asteroid impact and tsunami. *Science of Tsunami Hazards* 6, 21–30.

DAVISON T. and COLLINS G. S. (2007) The effect of the oceans on the terrestrial crater size frequency distribution: insight from numerical modeling. *Meteoritics and Planetary Science* 42, 1915–1927.

DYPVIK H. and JANSA L. F. (2003) Sedimentary signatures and processes during marine bolide impacts: a review. *Sedimentary Geology* 161, 309–337.

DYPVIK H., SMELROR M., SANDBAKKEN P. T., SALVIGSEN O., and KALLESON E. (2006) Traces of the marine Mjølnir impact event. *Palaeogeography, Palaeoclimatology, Palaeoecology* 241, 621–636.

GERSONDE R., DEUTSCH A., IVANOV B. A., and KYTE F. T. (2002) Oceanic impacts—a growing field of fundamental geology. *Deep-Sea Research II* 49, 951–957.

GERSONDE R., KYTE F. T., BLEIL U., DIEKMANN B., FLORES J. A., GOHL K., GRAHL G., HAGEN R., KUHN G., SIERRO F. J., VÖLKER D., ABELMANN A., and BOSTWICK J. A. (1997) Geological record and reconstruction of the late Pliocene impact of the Eltanin asteroid in the Southern Ocean. *Nature* 390, 357–363.

GERSONDE R., KYTE F. T., FREDERICHS T., BLEIL U., and KUHN G. (2003) New data on the late Pliocene Eltanin impact into the deep southern ocean. In *Third International Conference on Large Meteorite Impacts*, Nördlingen, Germany.

GISLER G. R. (2007) Tsunamis from asteroid impacts in deep water. *Planetary Defense Conference 2007*.

GISLER G. R. (2008) Tsunami simulations. *Annual Review of Fluid Mechanics* 40, 71–90.

GISLER G. R., WEAVER R. P., and GITTINGS M. L. (2006a) Sage calculations of the tsunami threat from La Palma. *Science of Tsunami Hazards* 24, 288–301.

GISLER G. R., WEAVER R. P., and GITTINGS M. L. (2006b) Two-dimensional simulations of explosive eruptions of Kick-em Jenny and other submarine volcanos. *Science of Tsunami Hazards* 25, 34.

GISLER G. R., WEAVER R. P., and GITTINGS M. L. (2009) Calculations of tsunamis from submarine landslides. In *Submarine Mass Movements and Their Consequences* (ed. D. C. Mosher). Springer, Berlin

GISLER G. R., WEAVER R. P., MADER C. L., and GITTINGS M. L. (2003) Two and three dimensional simulations of asteroid ocean impacts. *Science of Tsunami Hazards* 21, 119.

GITTINGS M. L., WEAVER R. P., CLOVER M., BETLACH T., BYRNE N., COKER R., DENDY E., HUECKSTAEDT R., NEW K., OAKES W. R., RANTA D., and STEFAN R. (2008) The RAGE radiation-hydrodynamic code. *Computational Science and Discovery* 1, 015005.

GOHN G. S., KOEBERL C., MILLER K. G., REIMOLD W. U., BROWNING J. V., COCKELL C. S., HORTON J. W., JR., KENKMANN T., KULPECZ A. A., POWARS D. S., SANFORD W. E., and VOYTEK M. A. (2008) Deep Drilling into the Chesapeake Bay Impact Structure. *Science* 320(5884), 1740–1745.

Reprinted from the journal

GULICK S. P. S., BARTON P. J., CHRISTESON G. L., MORGAN J. V., MCDONALD M., MENDOZA-CERVANTES K., PEARSON Z. F., SURENDRA A., URRUTIA-FUCUGAUCHI J., VERMEESCH P. M., and WARNER M. R. (2008) Importance of pre-impact crustal structure for the asymmetry of the Chicxulub impact crater. *Nature Geosciences* 1, 131–135.

GUSIAKOV V. K. (2007) Tsunami as a destructive aftermath of oceanic impacts. In *Comet/asteroid impacts and human society* (eds. P. T. Bobrowsky and H. Rickman), pp. 247–263. Springer, Berlin

HILLS J. G., NEMCHINOV I. V., POPOV S. P., and TETEREV A. V. (1994) Tsunami generated by small asteroid impacts. In *Hazards due to comets and asteroids* (ed. T. Gehrels), pp. 779–790. University of Arizona Press, Tucson

HOLIAN K. S. (1984) T-4 Handbook of material properties data bases: Vol 1c: equations of state. In *Los Alamos National Laboratory Reports*, Los Alamos, NM.

JANSA L. F. (1993) Cometary impacts into ocean - their recognition and the threshold constraint for biological extinctions. *Palaeogeography, Palaeoclimatology, Palaeoecology* 104, 271–286.

JANSA L. F., PE-PIPER G., ROBERTSON P. B., and FREIDENREICH O. (1989) Montagnais, a submarine impact structure on the Scotian shelf, eastern Canada. *Geological Society of America Bulletin* 101, 450–463.

LYON S. P. and JOHNSON J. D. (1992) Sesame: the Los Alamos National Laboratory equation of state database. In *Los Alamos National Laboratory Report*, Los Alamos, NM.

MADER C. L. and GITTINGS M. L. (2002) Modeling the 1958 Lituya Bay mega tsunami, II. *Science of Tsunami Hazards* 20, 241–250.

MASSE W., BRYANT E., GUSIAKOV V. K., ABBOTT D., RAMBOLAMANA G., RAZA H., COURTY M., BREGER D., GERARD-LITTLE P., and BURCKLE I. (2006) Holocene Indian Ocean cosmic impacts: the megatsunami chevron evidence from Madagascar. *EOS Trans. AGU Fall Meet. Suppl.* 87, Abstract PB43B-1244.

MASSON D. G. (1996) Catastrophic collapse of the volcanic island of Hierro 15 ka ago and the history of landslides in the Canary Islands. *Geology* 24, 231–234.

MATSUI T., IMAMURA F., TAJIKA E., NAKANO Y., and FUJISAWA Y. (2002) Generation and propagation of a tsunami from the Cretaceous/Tertiary impact event. In *Catastrophic events and mass extinctions: Impact and beyond* (eds. C. Koeberl and G. Macleod), pp. 69–77.

MELOSH H. J. (2003) Impact generated tsunamis: An over-rated hazard. In *Lunar and Planetary Science Conference XXXIV*, pp. 2013.

ORMÖ J. and LINDSTRÖM M. (2000) When a cosmic impact strikes the sea bed. *Geological Magazine* 137, 67–80.

PINTER N. and ISHMAN S. E. (2008) Impacts, megatsunami, and other extraordinary claims. *GSA Today* 18, 37–38.

ROSENLOF K. H., OLTMANS S., KLEY D., RUSSELL J. M. I., CHIOU E.-W., CHU W. P., JOHNSON D. G., KELLY K. K., MICHELSEN H. A., NEDOLUHA G. E., REMSBERG E. E., TOON G. C., and MCCORMICK M. P. (2001) Stratospheric water vapor increases over the past half century. *Geophysical Research Letters* 28, 1195–1198.

SHUVALOV V. V. and TRUBESTKAYA I. A. (2002) Numerical modeling of marine target impacts. *Solar System Research* 36, 417–430.

TSIKALAS F. (2005) Mjølnir Crater as a result of oblique impact: asymmetry evidence constrains impact direction and angle. In *Impact Studies (Impact Tectonism)* (eds. C. Koeberl and H. Henkel), pp. 285–306. Springer, Berlin

TSIKALAS F., GUDLAUGSSON S. T., FALEIDE J. I., and ELDHOLM O. (2002) The Mjølnir marine impact crater porosity anomaly. *Deep-Sea Research II* 49, 1103–1120.

WARD S. N. and ASPHAUG E. (2000) Asteroid impact tsunami: a probabilistic hazard assessment. *Icarus* 145, 64–78.

WARD S. N. and ASPHAUG E. (2002) Impact tsunami—Eltanin. *Deep-Sea Research II* 49, 1073–1079.

WÜNNEMANN K., WEISS R., and HOFFMAN K. (2007) Characteristics of oceanic impact-induced large water waves—reevaluation of the tsunami hazard. *Meteoritics and Planetary Science* 42, 1893–1903.

(Received December 22, 2009, revised March 11, 2010, accepted March 15, 2010, Published online November 12, 2010)

Pure Appl. Geophys. 168 (2011), 1199–1222
© 2010 Springer Basel AG
DOI 10.1007/s00024-010-0231-9

Pure and Applied Geophysics

Validation and Verification of a Numerical Model for Tsunami Propagation and Runup

D. J. NICOLSKY,[1] E. N. SULEIMANI,[1] and R. A. HANSEN[1]

Abstract—A robust numerical model to simulate propagation and runup of tsunami waves in the framework of non-linear shallow water theory is developed. The numerical code adopts a staggered leapfrog finite-difference scheme to solve the shallow water equations formulated for depth-averaged water fluxes in spherical coordinates. A temporal position of the shoreline is calculated using a free-surface moving boundary algorithm. For large scale problems, the developed algorithm is efficiently parallelized employing a domain decomposition technique. The developed numerical model is benchmarked in an exhaustive series of tests suggested by NOAA. We conducted analytical and laboratory benchmarking for the cases of solitary wave runup on simple beaches, runup of a solitary wave on a conically-shaped island, and the runup in the Monai Valley, Okushiri Island, Japan, during the 1993 Hokkaido-Nansei-Oki tsunami. In all conducted tests the calculated numerical solution is within an accuracy recommended by NOAA standards. We summarize results of numerical benchmarking of the model, its strengths and limits with regards to reproduction of fundamental features of coastal inundation, and also illustrate some possible improvements.

Key words: Numerical modeling, tsunami, inundation.

1. Introduction

The Alaska-Aleutian subduction zone has the greatest earthquake potential in the Pacific Ocean and coseismic crustal deformations in this zone have recently produced several major teletsunamis. For example, the historic 1946, 1957 Aleutian, and 1964 Alaska tsunamis resulted in damage and loss of life not only in Alaska, but in numerous locations around the Pacific Ocean. To mitigate tsunami hazard along the Alaska coast and around the Aleutian islands, the Alaska Tsunami Inundation Mapping project aims to predict inundation of coastal areas by future tsunamis in the Pacific Ocean. A challenging step in this task is

to simulate propagation of tsunami waves in the open ocean and then to predict runup on a complex beach topography. In the 1980s when substantial advances in understanding tsunami evolution occurred, this task became attainable (SYNOLAKIS and BERNARD, 2006). The goal of this work is to develop a robust, validated, and parallelized numerical algorithm for computation of inundation of coastal areas and prevent possible loss of life in Alaska.

Currently, there is a series of approaches suitable for simulation of tsunami wave propagation and runup, ranging from application of primitive threshold-type models (e.g. SHUTO, 1991) to computation of the water dynamics by the 3-D Navier–Stokes equations (e.g. DALRYMPLE and ROGERS, 2006). Unfortunately, simulation of the entire tsunami wave from its generation by an earthquake to runup by solving the 3-D Navier–Stokes equations is impractical due to limitations in modern computational resources. However, the classical non-linear shallow water equations—an approximation to the 3-D Navier–Stokes equations—is widely and successfully exploited to simulate propagation of tsunami waves (LIU *et al.*, 1991; YEH *et al.*, 1994; TITOV and SYNOLAKIS, 1998). The shallow water approximations have proven to be robust enough not only to simulate propagation of the tsunami but also to predict runup of both non-breaking and mildly breaking waves (SYNOLAKIS, 1986). This property of the shallow water equations is useful in modeling of tsunami in most geophysical conditions.

Due to non-linearity, shallow water equations do not have an analytical solution for an arbitrary initial and boundary conditions, and its solution is typically computed by numerical methods. A great variety of numerical methods of solving the shallow water equations exist and are utilized in many scientific fields including atmospheric and ocean flows, river and coastal flows, tides, storm surges, and tsunamis.

---
[1] University of Alaska Fairbanks, Fairbanks, AK 99709, USA. E-mail: djnicolsky@alaska.edu

Next, we briefly review some numerical methods applicable to simulate tsunamis.

Development of the finite difference methods for computation of linear long waves descends to attempts by HANSEN (1956) and FISCHER (1959), an interested reader is referred to (KOWALIK and MURTY, 1993a; IMAMURA, 1996) where a detailed review of finite difference schemes is given. Based on these initial attempts, a currently exploited numerical method TUNAMI is suggested by IMAMURA (1995). In this work, the authors propose to compute water level dynamics near the shoreline, by parameterizing a water flux quantity—the so-called "discharge"—that can significantly affect the shoreline dynamics (IMAMURA, 1996). Another numerical model extensively used for tsunami modeling is COMCOT (LIU et al., 1998), where a certain moving boundary algorithm is proposed to find a shoreline location. In both TUNAMI and COMCOT models, the shallow water equations are formulated in the flux-conservative form, which helps to preserve water mass through out the computations. At the same time TITOV and SYNOLAKIS (1995) presented the VTCS, now MOST, model that can compute runup without adding artificial viscosity or friction factors. An innovative idea of the MOST model is its ability to track the shoreline by adding new temporal grid points.

Later, in a series of papers, e.g. KIRBY et al. (1998) and LYNETT et al. (2002), several numerical methods, based on Boussinesq-type approximation (PEREGRINE, 1967), were developed. Despite resolving the wave dispersion, the models utilizing the Boussinesq approximation have no appreciable advantage over classical shallow water methods in matching field observation of runup (LYNETT et al., 2003; SYNOLAKIS and BERNARD, 2006). In total, more than ten numerical methods including (MADER and LUKAS, 1984; KOWALIK and MURTY, 1993b; GEORGE and LEVEQUE, 2006; ZHANG and BAPTISTA, 2008) for the simulation of tsunamis have developed in the last 20 years.

Some of the above-mentioned methods have been rigorously tested while other are currently being tested. In a series of workshops on long-wave runup models (LIU et al., 1991; YEH et al., 1996; LIU et al., 2007), a number of tests has been suggested to validate numerical models simulating propagation and runup of tsunami waves. These tests are summarized by SYNOLAKIS et al. (2008) and form a basis for verification of algorithms, used for modeling propagation and runup of long waves. SYNOLAKIS et al. (2008) propose a uniform suite of tests for validation and verification of the numerical method by comparing numerical solutions to analytical predictions and certain laboratory measurements. SYNOLAKIS et al. (2008) further argues that no testing of a tsunami runup algorithm in idealized laboratory experiments can ensure robust model performance, nor can such testing substitute for field data benchmarking. Therefore, an important step in tsunami model evaluation is validation of numerically computed tsunami propagation and runup against observations gathered in real settings.

Unfortunately, developed and tested runup algorithms (e.g. in TUNAMI) are notoriously hard to parallelize in order to achieve efficient prediction of inundation areas. In this work, we present an efficient parallelization of a numerical method for the simulation of tsunami propagation and runup. Exploiting ideas of IMAMURA (1995) and LIU et al. (1998), we formulate our numerical method, implementing the so-called "wetting and drying" algorithm. This approach is based on the fictitious domain method (MARCHUK et al., 1986). Our method exploits a domain decomposition technique (PAGLIERI et al., 1997) that allows for efficient parallelization of the runup algorithm. To validate the developed finite-difference scheme according to requirements in SYNOLAKIS et al. (2008), we compare computed numerical solutions to analytical predictions and laboratory measurements. The analytical solution to the non-linear shallow water equations is derived by SYNOLAKIS (1987) for the special case of a long wave runup on a uniformly sloping beach. The laboratory data used to validate the numerical model are provided by SYNOLAKIS (1986) and BRIGGS et al. (1995). In this work, we model the 1993 Okushiri tsunami and compare its runup around Okushiri island against collected observations. While comparing the solutions of the proposed model with the analytical predictions and collected measurements, the numerical calculations of our model are within the tolerated validation errors proposed by SYNOLAKIS et al. (2008). In all comparisons, the presented model captures the main characteristics of the runup process for a variety of initial conditions specified by laboratory experiments and real geophysical events.

The presented article is organized as follows. In Sect. 2, we introduce the numerical method for solving the shallow water equations. In Sect. 3, we test the numerically computed solution against analytical predictions that describe 1-D runup a solitary wave on a simple beach. In the same section, we also validate our method by comparing the numerical solution to laboratory measurements collected by SYNOLAKIS (1987). In Sect. 4, we compare the numerical solution to observations collected during a laboratory experiment, simulating runup of a tsunami wave on a conically shaped island (BRIGGS et al., 1995). In Sect. 5, we simulate runup of tsunami wave on a complex beach. First, we simulate the water dynamics in the wave tank, in which the 1:400 scale model of beach near the village of Monai is constructed. Then, we present modeling of 1993 Okushiri tsunami and comparison of runup prediction around Okushiri island to field observations. Finally, in Sect. 6, we state conclusions.

2. Mathematical Formulation

2.1. Numerical Implementation

Non-linear shallow water theory is commonly used to predict propagation of long waves in the ocean and inundation of coastal areas (SYNOLAKIS and BERNARD, 2006). In many engineering and scientific applications (YEH et al., 1996), the water depth η and the horizontal water velocity $v = (v, u)$ in the ocean, occupying the domain

$$\Omega_t = \{(x, y) : \eta(x, y, t) \geq 0\}, \tag{1}$$

shown in Fig. 1, are described in the spherical coordinates by the mass conservation principle

$$\frac{\partial \eta}{\partial t} + \nabla \cdot (\eta v) = 0, \tag{2}$$

and the linear momentum conservation law

$$\frac{\partial(\eta v)}{\partial t} + \nabla \cdot (v \eta v) = -g \eta \nabla \zeta - f \eta (e_r \times v) + \eta \tau. \tag{3}$$

Here, $\zeta = h + \eta$ is the water level, h is the bathymetry, g is the acceleration of gravity, f is the Coriolis

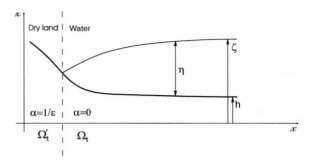

Figure 1
A sketch of a sloping beach profile. The *vertical dashed line* represents the shoreline location and divides the computational domain into two regions. The first region Ω_t is associated with water, while the second region Ω_t', within which $\eta = 0$, is related to the dry land

parameter, e_r is the outward unit normal vector on the sphere, and the term τ represents the bottom friction:

$$\tau = \frac{v}{2\eta} v \|v\|, \quad \mu^2 = \frac{v}{2g} \eta^{1/3}. \tag{4}$$

The constants v and μ are called the friction coefficient and Manning's roughness, respectively. Typical values of μ are compiled from (CHOW, 1959; CHAUDHRY, 1993) and are listed in Table 1.

To compute the water level dynamics, the Eqs. 2 and 3 are supplemented with the initial conditions: $\eta_0 = \eta(x, y, 0)$, and $v_0 = v(x, y, 0)$. Note that from a mathematical point of view, we solve the system of equations 2 and 3 on domain Ω_t, a region which geometry depends on time according to (1). It is thus necessary to find not only the dynamics of η and v, but the evolution of Ω_t as well. One way to handle the time-dependent computational domain Ω_t is to implement the fictitious domain method (GLOWINSKI et al., 1994) described below.

At any time t, water occupies a domain Ω_t that changes its geometry due to the water motion. We embed Ω_t into a larger fixed-in-time rectangular domain Ω (BUZBEE et al., 1971). The complement of Ω_t in Ω is called the fictitious domain: $\Omega_t' = \Omega \backslash \Omega_t$. From a physical point of view, Ω_t' represents dry land which can be potentially inundated. Figure 1 illustrates a typical sloping beach and the fictitious domain associated with the dry land. Some points in Ω_t' initially representing land become associated with the water domain Ω_t when inundated. Therefore, for geophysical applications, the geometric dimensions of

Table 1

Values of the Manning's roughness coefficient (LINSLEY and FRANZINI, 1979)

Bottom material	μ	Bottom material	μ
Smooth metal	0.010	Firm gravel	0.020
Rubble masonry	0.017	Natural channels in good condition	0.025
Smooth earth	0.018	Natural channels with stones	0.035
Corrugates pipe	0.022	Very poor natural channels	0.060

Ω have to be larger than the maximum predicted inundation. An advantage of implementing the fictitious domain method is that the equations are solved on the fixed-in-time computational grid covering Ω, which does not have to be re-gridded to track the water boundary $\partial\Omega_t$.

For implementation of the fictitious domain method, the governing system of equations must have the same set of equations in both the water domain Ω_t and the dry land domain Ω_t'. For the sake of convenience, we introduce a new variable $V = \eta v$, commonly referred to as the water flux. We note that along the shore line, the water-land boundary $\partial\Omega_t$, the water depth $\eta = 0$, and hence water flux $V = 0$. Therefore, variables V and η can be continuously extended outside Ω_t into Ω_t', by being equated with zero. This extension of variables leads us to modify the original equations by adding the so-called penalty terms $-\alpha\eta$ and $-\alpha v$ to the right hand side of (2, 3). We obtain the new system

$$\frac{\partial \eta}{\partial t} + \nabla \cdot V = -\alpha\eta, \tag{5}$$

$$\frac{\partial V}{\partial t} + \nabla \cdot (vV) + g\eta\nabla(\eta + h) + f(e_r \times V) - \tau\eta = -\alpha V. \tag{6}$$

We re-emphasize that Eqs. 5 and 6 are defined over the entire computational domain Ω. The penalty terms $-\alpha\eta$ and $-\alpha V$ vanish in the water domain Ω_t, and have negligible effect on the water dynamics, compared with the effects of other terms. At the same time, the penalty terms impose no velocity over the dry land domain Ω_t'. A mathematical justification of a fictitious domain model, based on the L^2-penalized Navier-Stokes equation, is derived in ANGOT et al. (1999). An interested reader is also referred to KHADRA et al. (2000), where a similar approach is used in numerical modeling.

The coefficient α is called the penalty parameter (DISSEZ et al., 2005) and is defined by KHADRA et al. (2000) as

$$\alpha = \begin{cases} 0 & x \in \Omega_t^\delta \\ 1/\varepsilon & x \in \Omega/\Omega_t^\delta \end{cases}, \tag{7}$$

where $\Omega_t^\delta = \{(x,y) : \eta(x,y,t) \geq \delta\}$. The parameters δ, ε are such that $0 < \varepsilon \ll 1$ and $0 < \delta \ll 1$. We conclude that the system (5, 6) together with (7) is an implementation of the fictitious domain method to solve the non-linear shallow water equations 2 and 3, and that the system (5, 6) can be easily solved by present day finite difference or finite element solvers.

We approximate the system (5, 6) in spherical coordinates by finite differences on Arakawa C-grid (ARAKAWA and LAMB, 1977) spanning the entire domain Ω. The spatial derivatives are discretized by central difference and upwind difference schemes (FLETCHER, 1991); the friction term τ is discretized by a semi-implicit scheme according to GOTO et al. (1997). Equations 5 and 6 are solved semi-implicitly in time using a first order scheme (KOWALIK and MURTY, 1993a). The finite difference scheme is coded in FORTRAN using the Portable, Extensible Toolkit for Scientific computations (BALAY et al., 2004) and the MPI standard (GROPP et al., 1999). Scaling properties of the MPI code are shown in Fig. 2. To generate this figure, a code simulates the 1993 Okushiri tsunami on a series of five telescoping grids covering a part of the Pacific ocean west of Hokkaido and focusing on the village of Monai. Spacial resolution of the coarsest grid is 24-arcs, while the finest grid has a resolution of approximately 5 m. The water level dynamics are simulated over 1 h with 0.2 s time steps. Further details of the simulation of 1993 Okushiri tsunami are described in Sect. 5 Several numerical experiments were conducted with a different number of processors on a parallel computer cluster at the Arctic Region Supercomputing Center, University of Alaska, Fairbanks. The numerical results show the efficient parallelization occurs with a serial portion Δ_s of the numerical code at least 100 times less than the parallelized portion Δ_p.

Utilization of the fictitious domain method requires determination of the water domain Ω_t^δ. In

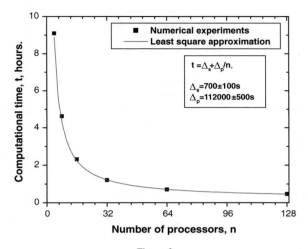

Figure 2

The time t, spent to simulates 1 h of the 1993 Okushiri tsunami on a series of five telescoping grids covering a part of the Pacific ocean west of Hokkaido and focusing on the village of Monai, is marked by rectangles. The *solid line* marks the best fit to estimate serial Δ_s and parallel Δ_p portions of the numerical code

the next section, we propose an algorithm for computing the extent of the water domain Ω_t^δ and for determining the value of α.

2.2. Calculation of the Boundary Location Between the Water and Dry Land

A general review of techniques for determining whether a certain grid cell becomes wet/dry during the runup/rundown of a tsunami wave is thoroughly discussed by BALZANO (1998). Our model exploits some ideas from BALZANO (1998) while introducing a certain symmetry principle. For clarity, we illustrate our approach in the 1-D case. Calculations in the 2-D case are completed by applying the 1-D algorithm first along the x-coordinate and then along the y-coordinate.

As mentioned previously, we solve the shallow water equations 5 and 6 by a finite difference method in which the state variables ζ, V are staggered on an Arakawa C-grid. For the 1-D case, The water depth η is defined at grid cell centers $\{i\}_{i=1}^n$, while the flux V is defined at cell boundaries $\{i + 1/2\}_{i=1}^{n-1}$. The penalty parameter α is defined both at cell centers and boundaries. To compute the parameter α according to (7), it is necessary to find a finite difference approximation $\overline{\Omega}_t^\delta$ to the region $\Omega_t^\delta = \{x : \eta \geq \delta\}$.

All cell centers and cell boundaries that are included in $\overline{\Omega}_t^\delta$ are typically called wet. Otherwise, they are called dry.

When the ith cell center satisfies $\eta_i \geq \delta$, it is wet and we set $\alpha_i = 0$ as prescribed by (7). For any dry cell center, one at which the inequality does not hold, we set $\alpha_i = 1/\varepsilon$. To compute the penalty parameter α at a cell boundary, e.g. $i + 1/2$, we assume that the cell boundary $i + 1/2$ is wet, and $\alpha_{i+1/2} = 0$ if at least one of the following two conditions is satisfied. (a) The water level at a low elevated cell is high enough to inundate an adjacent higher elevated cell, or (b) there is some water at a high elevated cell to flow to an adjacent lower elevated cell.

To mathematically formulate those two conditions, we introduce the notion of left and right cell boundaries. The cell boundary $i + 1/2$ is called left if the bathymetry/topography at cell $i + 1$ is lower than at cell i, i.e. $h_i \geq h_{i+1}$. Otherwise, the cell boundary is called the right one. We provide an example of left and right cell boundaries in Fig. 3. Depending on whether a cell boundary is left or right, the conditions (a) and (b) are formulated differently by inequalities. For brevity, we formulate inequalities representing the conditions only for left cell boundaries. The inequalities associated with right cell boundaries are similarly formulated by taking into account the left-right symmetry.

The condition (a) for the left cell boundary is satisfied if $\zeta_{i+1} \geq \zeta_i$, as illustrated in the left plot in Fig. 4. Recall that the condition (b) for the left cell boundary is satisfied if there is some water on the upper side to flow to the lower side, i.e. $\eta_i \geq \delta > 0$, as illustrated by the central plot in Fig. 4. However, if

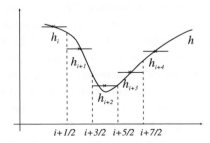

Figure 3

A typical basin in which interfaces $i + 1/2$ and $i + 3/2$ are associated with the left cell boundary, while interfaces $i + 5/2$ and $i + 7/2$ are associated with the right cell boundary

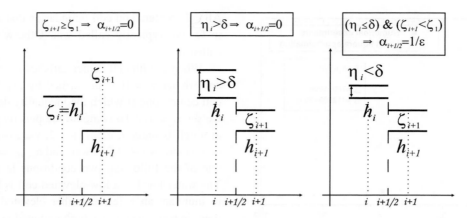

Figure 4

Left plot the water column can inundate the boundary. *Central plot* there is enough water to flow downhill. *Right plot* there is not enough water to flow downhill

there is a negligibly small amount of water, i.e. $\eta_i < \delta \ll 1$, no water may flow over the left cell boundary, as depicted by the right plot in Fig. 4.

The next section tests robustness of the fictitious domain method for solving equations 2 and 3 and efficiency of the proposed technique for determining Ω_t through comparative analysis of numerical and analytical solutions.

3. Runup of a Solitary Wave on a Simple Beach

In this section, we follow guidelines of SYNOLAKIS *et al.* (2008) and compare our numerical solution to analytical predictions of long-wave runup on a sloping beach. Additionally, we compare the numerical solution to laboratory measurements, collected during experiments in a 32-m long wave tank at the California Institute of Technology. The geometry of the tank and laboratory equipment used to generate long-waves are described by HAMMACK (1972); GORING (1979) and SYNOLAKIS (1986). Figure 5 displays a non-scale sketch of the canonical beach, constructed in the wave tank. The bathymetry consists of an area of constant depth d, connected to a plane sloping beach of angle $\beta = \mathrm{arccot}(19.85)$. Note that the x coordinate increases monotonically seaward, $x = 0$ is the initial shore location, and the toe of the beach is located at $x = X_0 = d \cot \beta$.

More than 40 experiments with solitary waves of varying heights were performed (SYNOLAKIS, 1986). The height-to-depth ratio H/d in these experiments ranged from 0.021 to 0.626. The water level profiles at several time moments were measured for the waves with $H/d = 0.019$, $H/d = 0.04$, and $H/d = 0.3$. According to observations, the breaking of a solitary wave occurs when $H/d > 0.045$. The wave with $H/d = 0.019$ did not break in the laboratory experiments, and this case is used to compare numerical and analytical solutions to the collected data.

3.1. Comparison to Analytical Solution

In this section we verify our numerical method by comparing numerical and analytical solutions that describe 1-D solitary wave runup. The analytical solution to a specific solitary wave runup on the sloping beach was derived by SYNOLAKIS (1986). In this problem, the wave of height H is initially centered at distance L from the beach toe and is schematically shown in Fig. 5. The value of $L = \mathrm{arccosh}(\sqrt{20})/\gamma$ is the half-length of the solitary wave, and the initial depth profile is given by

$$\eta(x, 0) = H\mathrm{sech}^2(\gamma(x - X_1)/d), \qquad (8)$$

where $X_1 = X_0 + L$, and $\gamma = \sqrt{3H/4d}$. The initial wave-particle velocity in the computer experiments is set, following TITOV and SYNOLAKIS (1995) as:

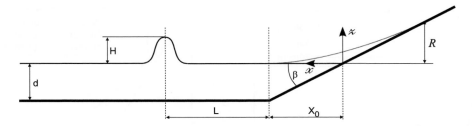

Figure 5
Non-scaled sketch of a canonical beach with a wave climbing up

$$u(x,0) = -\sqrt{g/d}\,\eta(x,0).$$

First, we check the ability of the method, presented in Sect. 2, to model runup on a beach by simulating the runup of a solitary wave when $d = 1, 100$, and 500 m, and then comparing the numerical and analytical solutions. In these numerical experiments, the 1-D domain, with total length $400d$, is discretized with spacing $\Delta x = d/20$. The parameters used to define Ω_t^δ are selected such that $\delta = d/10^6$ and $\varepsilon = 0$. The computational time step $\Delta t = 10^{-3}\sqrt{d/g}$ satisfies the Courant–Friedrichs–Levy stability criterion (COURANT et al., 1928). The results suggest that the computed non-dimensional variables such as η/d, $v/\sqrt{gd}$ do not depend on the value of d, and further that the numerical predictions are in good agreement with analytical solutions for $H/d = 0.019$. We discuss comparison of numerical and analytical solutions for $H/d = 0.019$ in greater detail later in this section. For error analysis, the water mass before and after wave reflection from the beach is calculated, finding a total mass decrease of $<0.01\%$ in each case. This negligibly small error in the mass conservation is well within established criteria (SYNOLAKIS et al., 2008).

A focus in developing a tsunami modeling algorithm is to simulate extreme positions of the shoreline—the maximum runup and rundown. Figure 6 shows computed water surface profiles at the maximum runup and rundown of a solitary wave in the case of $H/d = 0.019$. The maximum runup in the numerical simulation occurs at $t \approx 55\sqrt{d/g}$ and this solution has a 15% error with respect to the derived analytical solution. After refining the computational grid from $\Delta x = d/20$ to $\Delta x = d/200$, the analytically and numerically computed maximum runup values differ by $<2\%$, which is within the recommended criteria (SYNOLAKIS et al., 2008). We additionally

checked convergence of numerically computed maximum rundown to its analytical prediction. For the computational grid with $\Delta x = d/20$, the difference between the numerical and analytical rundown values is at most 16%. After the grid refinement to $\Delta x = d/200$, the difference is $<3\%$. The results show that the numerical solution converges to the analytical prediction at the extreme locations of the shoreline, and that the recommended 5% error in numerical solution is achieved.

Figure 7 shows numerically and analytically computed water level dynamics at locations $x/d = 0.25$ (near the initial shoreline) and $x/d = 9.95$ (between the beach toe and initial wave crest) during propagation and reflection in the case $H/d = 0.019$. During rundown, both numerical and analytical solutions show that water retreats from $t = 67\sqrt{d/g}$ to $t = 82\sqrt{d/g}$, and the point $x/d = 0.25$ temporally becomes dry, while the point $x/d = 9.95$ remains wet throughout the entire length of the computer experiment. Comparison of the analytical and numerical solutions at these two points reveals that the computational error is typically $<2\%$ for $\Delta x = d/20$, and that the agreement between two solutions is quite good even on the coarse grid.

Next, we compare numerically computed wavefront dynamics with certain analytical predictions. As mentioned in (SYNOLAKIS and BERNARD, 2006) a and observed, in e.g. the Sumatra tsunami, the wave first slows as it climbs the sloping beach due to shoaling, then considerably slows further as it hits the shoreline, but then accelerates, before reaching its ultimate onland penetration point. In the rest of this section, we verify that the model captures this particular phenomenon.

As a wave propagates towards the beach, the wavefront location is the place $x_w = x_w(t)$ defined

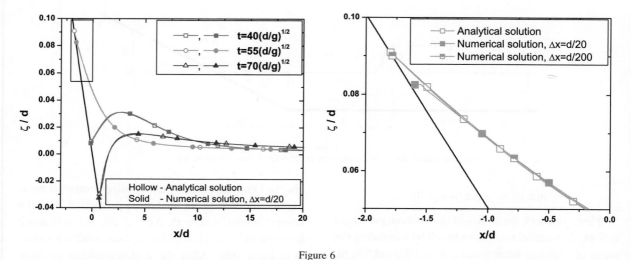

Figure 6

Left plot comparison between the analytically and numerically computed solutions simulating runup of the non-breaking wave in the case of $H/d = 0.019$ on the 1:19.85 beach. *Right plot* an enlarged version of the *left plot* within the rectangle region. Two numerical solutions computed on grids with $\Delta x = d/20$ and $\Delta x = d/200$ are shown at $t = 55\sqrt{d/g}$. The numerical solution is shown to be converging to the analytical one as the spatial discretization is refined. The analytical solution is according to Synolakis (1986)

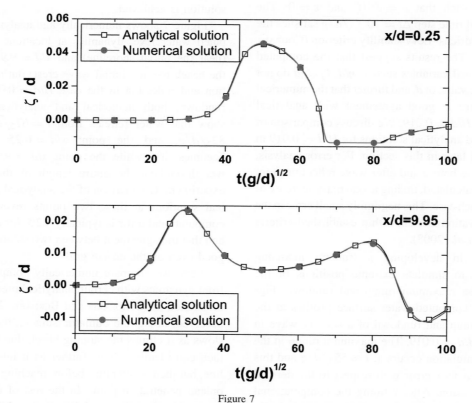

Figure 7

Comparison between the analytical solution (*hollow symbols*) and the finite difference solution (*filled symbols*) during the runup of the non-breaking solitary wave with $H/d = 0.019$ on 1:19.85 beach. The *top and bottom plots* represent comparisons at $x = 0.25d$ and $x = 9.95d$, respectively. The analytical solution is according to Synolakis (1986)

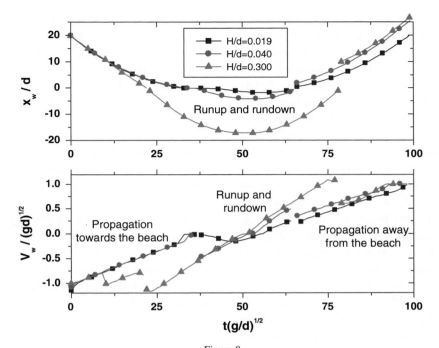

Figure 8
Top and bottom plots show the waterfront path x_w and velocity v_w, respectively. The *lines with rectangles, circles,* and *triangles* are associated with cases $H/d = 0.019$, $H/d = 0.04$, and $H/d = 0.3$, respectively. The propagation phase is associated with the time interval during which $x_w > 0$ and $v_w < 0$. The runup and rundown occurs when $x_w < 0$. The reflection phase is related to the time interval when the wave is completely reflected from the shore i.e. $x_w > 0$ and $v_w > 0$

implicitly by $\zeta(x_w, t) = H/20$, where the quantity ζ is the water level. Throughout, the time interval when water inundates initially dry land, x_w is defined as the shoreline location, i.e. $\eta(x_w, t) = 0$. Note that $x_w < 0$ for this interval because $x > 0$ describes $\Omega_{t=0}$, the initial submerged domain. When the solitary wave is reflected from the beach, x_w is defined on the tail of the reflect wave such that $\zeta(x_w, t) = H/20$.

In the theory of shallow water approximation, the phase velocity $v = \sqrt{gh}$. Hence, a solitary wave propagating towards the beach has the wavefront velocity $v_w = Dx_w/Dt = \sqrt{gh(x_w)}$ in the case of $H \ll d$. The symbol D/Dt stands for the total derivative with respect to time. Since initially $x_w = X_0$ and $h(x) = xd/X_0$ for $0 \leq x \leq X_0$, we obtain the particular analytical solution

$$v_w = \frac{gd}{2X_0}t - \sqrt{gd}. \tag{9}$$

Another analytical solution describing runup of a bore on a sloping beach is derived by SHEN and MEYER (1963). According to MEYER and TAYLOR

(1972), an important peculiarity of this solution is that upward flow of water on the slope weakly depends on the seaside boundary condition after the initial collapse of the bore. This particularly applies to the region near the tip of flow where the water layer becomes thin. For a low-grade sloping beach, it is possible to neglect the hydrostatic pressure term at the tip and to assume that water particles near the tip move only under the influence of gravity. Thus, the wavefront velocity is approximately

$$v_w = \frac{gd}{X_0}t \cos\beta - U_0 \cos\beta. \tag{10}$$

This idealized solution is referred to as the ballistic solution, and its derivation is beyond the scope of the present article. An interested reader is referred to PEREGRINE and WILLIAMS (2001); SVENDSEN (2005).

In a series of computer experiments, we model runup of several solitary waves and plot the computed wavefront location $x_w(t)$ and velocity $v_w(t)$ in the top and bottom graphs in Fig. 8, respectively. The wavefront location and velocity in the cases

$H/d = 0.019$, $H/d = 0.040$, and $H/d = 0.3$ are shown by lines marked with solid rectangles, circles, and triangles, respectively. In computer experiments with $H/d = 0.019$ and $H/d = 0.040$, the modeled waves do not break during propagation towards the beach, and the assumption $H \ll d$ used to derive formula (9) is satisfied. In Fig. 8, we observe that the wavefront velocities for the cases $H/d = 0.019$ and $H/d = 0.04$ are well approximated by straight lines, as predicted by formula (9). For these cases, we analyze the graph of v_w and estimate that the rate of change of v_w on time interval $[0, 35\sqrt{g/d}]$, corresponding to wave propagation towards the beach, is $0.026g \pm 0.002g$, and agrees with analytical prediction of $0.025g$. We emphasize that during a computer experiment with $H/d = 0.3$, the simulated wave propagates towards the beach as a bore, so formula (9) is not applicable to describe $v_w(t)$. Figure 8 shows that the graph of $v_w(t)$ for $t \in [0, 22\sqrt{g/d}]$, the interval over which the wave approaches the beach, has a strong irregularity during formation of the bore at $t \approx 9\sqrt{g/d}$, and hence the graph is not well approximated by a straight line.

Only in computer experiments related to the cases $H/d = 0.04$ and $H/d = 0.3$ water forms a bore that runs up on the slope. Recall that during the runup and rundown, the waterfront location is $x_w < 0$. For example, the runup and rundown for $H/d = 0.04$ and $H/d = 0.3$ cases occur during $[36\sqrt{g/d}, 60\sqrt{g/d}]$ and $[23\sqrt{g/d}, 75\sqrt{g/d}]$ time intervals, respectively, as shown in the top plot in Fig. 8. For these cases, the wavefront velocity $v_w(t)$ is well approximated for the time when water runs up and down from the beach by linear function as predicted by formula (10). The estimated rate of change in the computed velocity v_w is $0.044g \pm 0.002g$ which is $\approx 10\%$ smaller than the analytically predicted rate of $0.050g$. As noted by YEH (1991), the initial bore velocity U_0 differs from the wavefront velocity just before the runup. In the case $H/d = 0.019$, the bore does not form and assumptions necessary to derive the ballistic solution (10) are not satisfied. During the interval $[36\sqrt{g/d}, 60\sqrt{g/d}]$, the velocity $v_w(t)$ graph for $H/d = 0.019$ is a curve, marked by rectangles in Fig. 8.

Finally, we analyze waterfront characteristics $x_w(t)$ and $v_w(t)$ when the wave propagates away from the shore during the reflection phase. Here, x_w is defined as the point on the wave tail such that $\zeta(x_w, t) = H/20$ and $x_w > 0$. The reflection phases for $H/d = 0.019$, $H/d = 0.04$, and $H/d = 0.3$ are also shown in Fig. 8 and occur after $t > 60\sqrt{g/d}$, $t > 60\sqrt{g/d}$, and $t > 75\sqrt{g/d}$, respectively. Note that according to computer experiments, the reflected wave does not break, so the wavefront velocity v_w is well described by formula (9). The wavefront velocity graphs during the reflection phase are well approximated by straight lines, also predicted by (9).

In this section, we thoroughly compared the numerical and analytical solutions as recommended by SYNOLAKIS et al. (2008) and showed good agreement between them. In the next section, we test the numerical solution against certain laboratory measurements and analyze the effect of bottom friction on simulated water dynamics.

3.2. Comparison to Laboratory Measurements

More than 40 laboratory experiments were conducted in the wave tank by SYNOLAKIS (1986). In this subsection, we perform numerical modeling of the water dynamics observed during these experiments. In the computer experiment, we assume that the wave tank is $400d$ in length and discretized by a uniformly spaced grid with $\Delta x = d/200$. To model common geophysical conditions, we assume that $d = 500$ m, although scalability shows that appropriately scaled results do not depend on d. Additionally, we assume that there is no bottom friction, i.e. $v = 0$. We analyze the effects of bottom friction on water dynamics later in this section.

In the first series of laboratory experiments, the runup of a non-breaking solitary wave with $H/d = 0.019$ is studied. We plot laboratory measured water level by black rectangles in Fig. 9. In the same figure, the numerical and analytical solutions are plotted by lines with solid and hollow triangles, respectively. Agreement between analytical and numerical computed solutions is more than sufficient for all snapshots; the discrepancy between the solutions is much smaller than the discrepancy between any one of the solutions and the laboratory data. The computed solutions have slightly higher

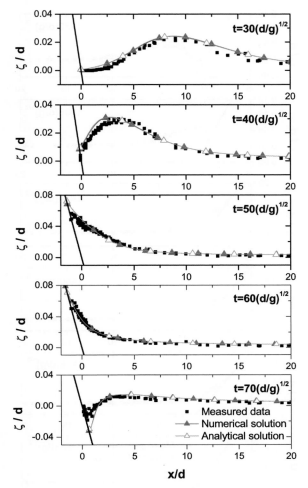

Figure 9
Comparison of observed and simulated water profiles during runup of a non-breaking wave in the case of $H/d = 0.019$. Observations are shown by *dots*. The analytical predictions and numerical calculations are marked by *hollow* and *filled symbols*, respectively. The measurements are provided courtesy of SYNOLAKIS (1986)

runup than observations, and the computed maximum runup also exceeds the physical measurements, visible in Fig. 10 where we show the numerically modeled and observed waterfront path $x_w(t)$. Here, the measured data is plotted by rectangles while the computed path is plotted by a line with hollow triangles. With the difference in computed and measured runup, prescribed to the zero friction assumption in computer modeling, we refer an interested reader to SYNOLAKIS (1986) for detailed analysis of discrepancy between the analytical solution and laboratory data.

In the second series of laboratory experiments, a solitary wave with the initial amplitude $H/d = 0.04$ propagates and inundates the sloping beach. We display laboratory data by black rectangles, and results of numerical modeling by lines with solid triangles in Fig. 11. According to analytical predictions derived using the zero bottom friction assumption, the solitary wave breaks only if its initial height satisfies $H/d \geq 0.029$ (SYNOLAKIS, 1987). The ratio of $H/d = 0.04$ for which the laboratory data are collected satisfies this condition, so a breaking is expected. Laboratory experiments, however, show that this wave does not break. This lack of breaking in laboratory experiment is explained by bottom friction and dispersion effects on wave dynamics. Further, the numerically simulated wave also fails to break, but is on the verge of breaking at $t = 38\sqrt{d/g}$ during runup and at $t = 62\sqrt{d/g}$ during rundown. This behavior in the numerical solution is explained by numerical dispersion and dissipation, introduced by the finite difference discretization of the partial derivatives. The slight numerical dissipation brings stability into the calculations and produces computational results that are in good agreement with laboratory measurements.

Finally, in the third series of laboratory experiments, the runup in the $H/d = 0.3$ case is studied. We compare the measured wave profiles to our finite difference solution and also to the finite element solution of ZELT (1991). Both in computer and in laboratory experiments, the wave severely breaks. The leading front of the solitary wave steepens and becomes singular shortly after beginning of computations. The numerical singularity propagates towards the beach until it meets the shoreline where the singularity dissipates. Figure 12 shows our numerical solution, plotted by a line with solid triangles. Existence of strong wave breaking does prevent a good agreement of our solution with the laboratory measurements. We observe that between moments $t = 15\sqrt{d/g}$ and $t = 20\sqrt{d/g}$, the computed wave propagates faster than the measured wave, since the numerical solution is computed using the primitive shallow water approximation (2, 3) where dispersive terms are neglected. Inclusion of the wave dispersion leads to Boussinesq-type equations, the numerical solutions of which have better agreement with measurements (LYNETT et al., 2002).

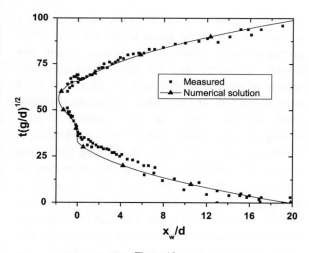

Figure 10

Laboratory measured and simulated waterfront path x_w of a solitary wave running up on a canonical beach. Measurements are represented by *squares* and numerical simulations by a *line*. The measurements are provided courtesy of SYNOLAKIS (1986)

In all previous computations both for breaking and non-breaking waves, the computed maximum runup, denoted by $\mathcal{R}$, is found to be higher than its laboratory-measured value. One possible explanation for this discrepancy is the assumption of zero bottom friction in the model. Additionally, according to ZELT (1991) and KENNEDY *et al.* (2000), higher values of $\mathcal{R}$ for breaking waves are caused by neglecting wave breaking effects and eddy viscosity in computer simulations. In the following sensitivity study, we examine whether the bottom friction can effectively parameterize wave breaking and eddy viscosity to accurately predict the maximum runup height $\mathcal{R}$ both for breaking and non-breaking waves. We begin with a discussion of non-breaking waves.

In several series of computer experiments, we model inundation of the sloping beach by waves with different H/d ratios. In each series, the bottom water friction is parameterized as can be seen through formula (4), where the Manning friction coefficient v is a certain fixed number. In Fig. 13, we plot the computed maximum runup $\mathcal{R}/d$ versus H/d for $v = 0$, $v = 0.02$, and $v = 0.04$. In the same plot, we also display laboratory measurements (SYNOLAKIS, 1987). We observe that for small non-breaking waves with $H/d \leq 0.01$, numerically simulated maximum runup heights do not

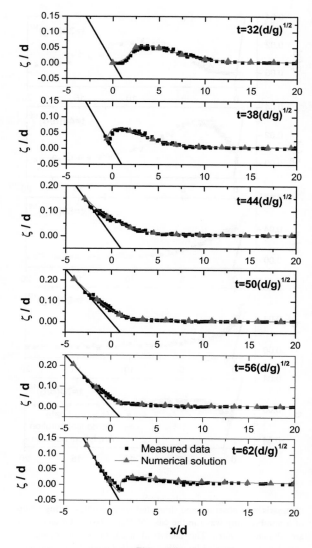

Figure 11

Comparison of measured and simulated water profiles during runup of a non-breaking wave in the case of $H/d = 0.04$. Observations are shown by squares. The analytical predictions and numerical calculations are marked by *hollow* and *filled symbols*, respectively. The measurements are provided courtesy of SYNOLAKIS (1986)

depend on v and are in good agreement with laboratory data. For intermediate non-breaking waves $0.01 \leq H/d \leq 0.03$, the computed runup heights show little dependence on the bottom friction coefficient v; similar results were reported by LIU *et al.* (1995) and LYNETT *et al.* (2002). In the case of breaking waves, those with $H/d > 0.03$, the maximum runup height strongly depends on v since a wave becomes a thin layer of liquid

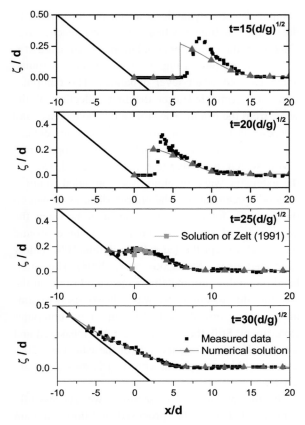

Figure 12
Comparison of measured and simulated water profiles during runup of a breaking wave in the case of $H/d = 0.3$. Observations are shown by *squares*. The analytical predictions and numerical calculations are marked by *hollow* and *filled symbols*, respectively. The measurements are provided courtesy of SYNOLAKIS (1986)

traveling up the slope after breaking, and friction is inversely proportionally to the water depth (4). Analyzing our computer experiments, we conclude that the measured runup height can be well approximated in case of the Manning friction coefficient $v = 0.03$.

By comparing numerical solutions to analytical predictions and available laboratory data, we fully tested our implementation of the fictitious domain method for modeling propagation and runup of non-breaking and breaking waves in the 1-D case. In the next section, we continue testing our method in the 2-D case of a "steep geophysical tsunami" (e.g. a wave height is comparable with the still water depth) inundating a circular island.

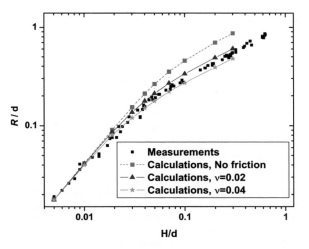

Figure 13
Non-dimensional maximum runup of solitary waves on the 1:19.85 sloping beach versus the height of the initial wave. The measured runup values (SYNOLAKIS, 1986) are marked by dots. The *dashed line* represents maximum runup values computed without an effect of bottom friction, i.e. $v = 0$. The *solid lines* represent maximum runup values computed with the effect of bottom friction, i.e. $v = 0.02$ and $v = 0.04$. The measurements are provided courtesy of SYNOLAKIS (1986)

4. Runup of a Solitary Wave on a Conically Shaped Island

In this section, we simulate propagation and runup of a solitary wave on a conically shaped island. To validate our numerical method, we use a laboratory experiment focused on studying inundation of the Babi island by the 12 December 1992 tsunami. The tsunami attacked the conically shaped Babi island from the north, but extremely high inundation was observed in the south. A model of the conical island island was constructed in a wave tank at the US Army Engineer Waterways Experimental Station (BRIGGS et al., 1995). Figure 14 shows a sketch of the conical island and location of several sensors that recorded the water level dynamics. Along one side of the tank, a wave generator directed plane solitary waves toward the island. An interested reader is referred to LIU et al. (1995) where the laboratory experiments and measured data are described in detail.

Experiments with different wave heights were conducted in the wave tank. A goal of the experiments was to demonstrate that after the tsunami hits the island, it splits into two waves traveling with their

249

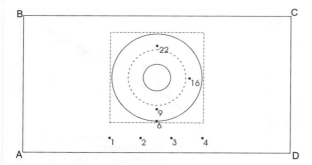

Figure 14

Top-down non-scaled sketch of a conically shaped island. The *solid circles* represent exterior and interior bases of the island. The *dotted line* shows an initial location of the shoreline. The *dash-dotted line* shows the extent of the high resolution computational grid. The *dots* mark gauge locations where laboratory measured water level is compared to numerical calculations. The in-flow boundary condition is simulated on the segment *AD*, while the open boundary condition is modeled on the segments *AB*, *BC*, and *CD*. Location of gauges 1, 2, 3, and 4 is schematic, while locations of the rest of gauges are precise

crests perpendicular to the shoreline. Once these waves meet behind the island, they collide and produce a local extremum in runup. In this work, we model the highest generated wave. This is a formidable test of the numerical algorithm since the modeled wave is steeper than most realistic tsunamis (TITOV and SYNOLAKIS, 1998).

In our computer experiment, we discretize the entire basin with a coarse resolution grid with spacing $\Delta x/d = \Delta y/d = 5/32$, where the undisturbed water depth $d = 0.32$ m. However, in the vicinity of the conical island, we also construct a fine resolution grid with a cell size $\Delta x/d = \Delta y/d = 1/32$ to include the entire island and its exterior base. To couple these two grids, we use an algorithm described by KOWALIK and MURTY (1993a) and GOTO et al. (1997) in which the water flux V from the coarse resolution grid is passed to the fine resolution grid, and the water level η from the fine resolution grid is returned back to the coarse grid at each time step. To simulate the incident wave, the water level at the boundary *AD* is set according to measurements at gauges 1–4, instead of modeling action of generator paddles. On all other sides of the computational domain, we define open boundary conditions. The choice of boundary conditions in the model differs from conditions imposed by horsehair-type absorbers along the tank wall, so the

computed water dynamics can not model laboratory data after the time τ when wave crest reaches *BC*. Therefore, the computer simulation is terminated at τ.

On the top plot in Fig. 15, we compare computed and measured water level dynamics. The computations are terminated after the first reflection of the wave from the island. The simulated wave breaks and steepens faster than in laboratory measurements, a well-known effect of the shallow water approximation in which dispersive terms are neglected. Despite the extensive wave breaking, the computed runup is in good agreement with laboratory data, as shown on the bottom plot in Fig. 15. The error between the measured and simulated runup everywhere around the island, except the lee side, is within 10%, below suggested errors (SYNOLAKIS et al., 2008). The simulated runup does not match the measured runup at the lee side, due to low order wave theory used to simulate the vertical velocity in the computer experiment. Still, the error between the measured and simulated runup at the lee side of the island is <20% and is within acceptable criteria (SYNOLAKIS et al., 2007).

In the previous two sections we successfully demonstrated that the proposed fictitious domain method and implemented wetting/drying algorithm together accurately simulate propagation and runup of waves in 1-D and 2-D cases. However, a further important test is to check the ability of the proposed method to simulate realistic tsunami events. Past tsunamis serve as potential or hypothetical scenarios for future events, and the ability to simulate them is a priority to successfully mitigate tsunami hazards. In the next section, we model a tectonic tsunami and compare numerical results to collected observations.

5. Runup of a Tsunami Wave on Okushiri Island

On the 12th of July, 1993, the $M_w = 7.8$ Hokkaido-Nansei-Oki earthquake generated a tsunami that severely inundated coastal areas in northern Japan. Most of the damage was concentrated around Okushiri island located west of Hokkaido. The tsunami runup around Okushiri island was measured by the HOKKAIDO TSUNAMI SURVEY GROUP (1993) which reported up to 31.7 m runup near Monai village. The

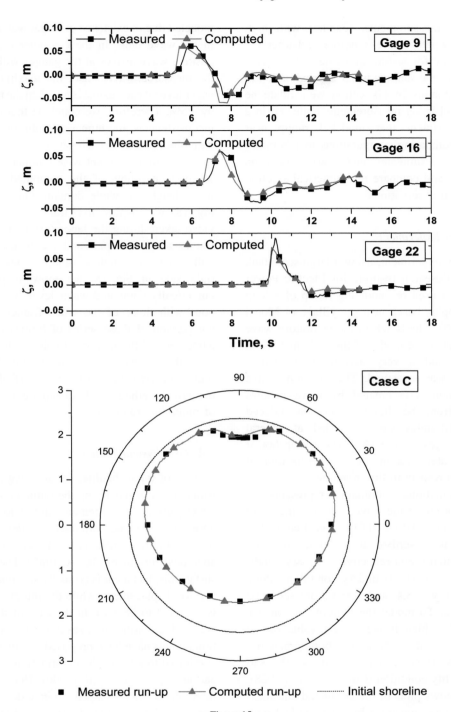

Figure 15

Top plot comparison between the computed (*triangles*) and measured (*rectangles*) water level at gauges shown in Fig. 14 in the case of incident solitary wave in the case of $H/d = 0.2$. *Bottom plot* comparison between computed (*triangles*) and measured (*rectangles*) inundation zones. Top view of the island, with the lee side at $90°$. The *dotted line* represents the initial shoreline. The measurements are provided courtesy of Briggs *et al.* (1995)

detailed runup measurements, together with high resolution bathymetry surveys before and after the earthquake, allow for testing of numerical methods and validation of the shallow water approximation to simulate real tsunamis. In this section, we validate the numerical model using measurements collected in a laboratory experiment that modeled runup near Monai. After comparing computations to laboratory measurements, we simulate tsunami wave runup on Okushiri island and compare the numerical solution to available field observations.

5.1. Laboratory Experiment

A laboratory experiment, using a large-scale tank at the Central Research Institute for Electric Power Industry, was focused on modeling runup of a long wave on a complex beach near the village of Monai (LIU et al., 2007). The beach in the laboratory wave tank was a 1:400 scale model of the bathymetry and topography around a very narrow gully, where extreme runup was measured. The incoming wave in the experiment was created by wave paddles located away from the shoreline, and the induced water level dynamics were recorded at several locations by gauges. Figure 16 shows a snapshot of the simulated water level and the relative location of the gauges with respect to the shoreline.

The computational domain represents a 5.5×3.4 m portion of the wave tank near the shore and is divided into 0.014×0.014 m grid cells. The incident wave is prescribed at $x = 0$ for the first 22.5 s, after which a non-reflective boundary condition is set at $x = 0$. The boundary conditions along segments $y = 0$, $y = 3.4$, and $x = 5.5$ are set to be totally reflective. To model the bottom friction, we select $v = 0.01$, which is the closest value of the Manning's coefficient for the smooth bottom material of the wave tank. The time step is set to 5×10^{-4} s to satisfy the stability condition (COURANT et al., 1928).

Figure 17 shows plots of the computed and measured water surface dynamics by lines marked with triangles and rectangles, respectively. The water level dynamics are shown at channels 5, 7, and 9 for the first 25 s, during which the maximum runup occurs. As noted by (ZHANG and BAPTISTA, 2008), the observed water elevation for the first 10 s cannot be accurately

modeled due to existence of initial water disturbances in the wave tank. In the computer experiment, the positive wave arrives at the gauges with <0.3 s after the measured wave. Also, the maximum computed water level at each gauge is less than the measurements by <5%. Therefore, we conclude that despite minor inconsistencies, the numerical solution matches well with observations at each gauge.

In addition to point-wise comparison at gauges, we plot snapshots of the computed and observed water height of whole domain. On the left side in Fig. 18, we display five frames extracted from a video taken during the laboratory experiment. These frames are 0.5 s apart and are focused on narrow gully where the highest runup is observed. On the right side in Fig. 18, we show snapshots of the numerically computed water level at times synchronous with those of the video frames. Side-by-side comparison of these series of frames reveal a good agreement of the numerical solution to the observations throughout the domain, where the maximum runup occurred. Furthermore, Fig. 18 shows that the numerical method is able to capture a rapid sequence of runup and rundown.

5.2. Geophysical Tsunami

One of the difficulties in modeling a geophysical tsunami lies in specifying the initial conditions of the water surface displacement and velocities. In the absence of detailed earthquake models, deformation in the Earth's crust is commonly computed by analytical formulae (OKADA, 1985). The initial water surface displacement is typically set equal to the crust surface displacement, while the initial water velocity is assumed to be zero. In the case of the Hokkaido-Nansei-Oki earthquake, several earth crust deformation models have been proposed. An interested reader is referred to a list of the deformation models for this earthquake in YEH et al. (1996). Here, we exploit a three-plane dipole-shaped ground deformation proposed by TAKAHASHI et al. (1995) and later suggested by SYNOLAKIS et al. (2008) to verify numerical algorithms. Figure 19 shows the contours of the crust surface deformation around Okushiri and Hokkaido islands and locations of several towns, at which we compare computational results to observations.

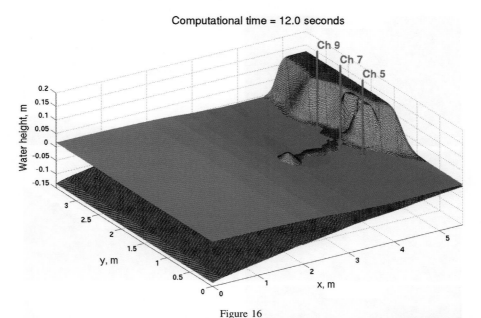

Figure 16
The 3-D view of the computational domain and numerical solution at 12 s. Locations of gauges, at which the modeled and measured water level dynamics are compared, are shown by *arrows*. Abbreviations *Ch*5, *Ch*7, and *Ch*9 stand for Channel 5, 7, and 9, respectively. The inlet boundary is modeled at $x = 0$. At $y = 0$ and $y = 3.4$, the reflective boundary conditions are set

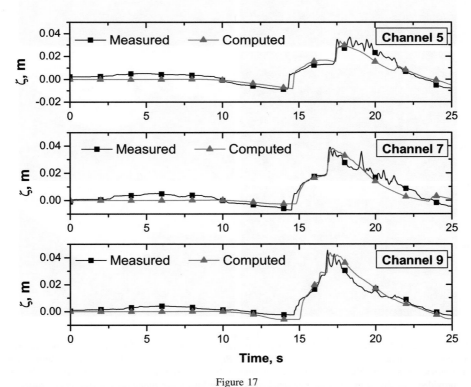

Figure 17
Comparison of the computed water height with the laboratory measurements at water gauges *Ch*5, *Ch*7, and *Ch*9. The measurements are provided courtesy of the Third International Workshop on Long-Wave Runup Models (Liu *et al.*, 2007)

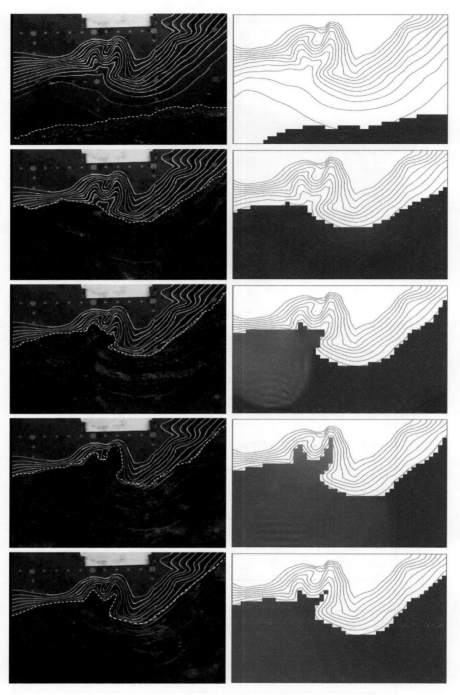

Figure 18
Left side frames 10, 25, 40, 55, and 70 from the overhead movie of the laboratory experiment. The time interval between frames is 0.5 s. The *dashed yellow line* shows the instantaneous location of the shoreline. *Right side* snapshots of the numerical solution at the time intervals corresponding to the movie frames. The *blue shaded area* corresponds to the water domain, Ω_t, and is considered to be wet. The frames are provided courtesy of the third international workshop on long-wave runup models (LIU *et al.*, 2007)

The bathymetry/topography digital elevation model (DEM) for Okushiri island is provided by the Disaster Control Research Center (DCRC) at Tohoku University, Japan. The data consists of several nested grids of increasing spacial resolution ranging from 450 to 5 m. The grids are focused on the Monai and Aonae regions where the maximum runup and devastation was reported in 1993.

We begin to analyze computational results by comparing the numerically computed water level dynamics to tidal gauge records of the first hour after the earthquake. Figure 20 shows the computed and observed water level dynamics at the stations, marked in Fig. 19 by triangles. The arrival time of the computed wave matches well with the arrival of the leading tsunami wave. The correlation of positive and negative phases between the computed and observed waves is rather good, although the computed wave at both locations has a larger range and frequency of variability than the observed wave. The discrepancies between the measured and observed waves can be explained by the lack of detailed bathymetry near tide stations,

limitations of the shallow water approximation model, and inaccuracy of the specified initial conditions.

Figure 21 shows the locations on Okushiri island, where the runup was measured shortly after the 1993 tsunami. To compare the computed and observed runup, we discretize the shoreline into several regions, with each region enclosing the part of the shoreline lying closer to a certain observation point than to any other. Within each region, we compute the maximum and minimum values of the simulated runup and compare this variability to the observations at each point. We note that almost everywhere around the island, the observed values lie within the modeled range of variability. There are, however, several exceptions where the modeled runup underestimates the observations. For example, the modeled runup in the narrow gully near the village of Monai is underestimated partially because of the reasons discussed below.

We recall that we model runup near the Monai village using 5 m resolution computational grids. The bathymetry/topography data within the 5 m grid is based either on the DEM provided by the DCRC, or on the DEM used to construct a wave tank in the laboratory experiment discussed in the previous sub-section. In both DEMs, the narrow gully is identical, but there is small difference in elevation near the shoreline. The numerical computations using DCRC DEM show that the computed maximum runup in the narrow gully is 13.7 m. Mean while, the resulted runup, utilizing the wave tank DEM, is 18.8 m in the gully. We emphasize that model parameters as well as bathymetry/topography in computational grids coarser than 5 m are the same in both simulations. The difference between the maximum runup values in these two simulation reveals high sensitivity of the runup to nearshore bathymetry/topography, and underlines importance of the near-shore bathymetry data for accurate runup predictions. Therefore, the discrepancy between the measured and computed runup values may be explained by the lack of accurate bathymetry/topography data near Monai, uncertainties in the initial water surface displacement, or finally by limitations of the shallow water approximation to model 3-D flows.

In Fig. 22, we show a sequence of snapshots depicting the simulated waves inundating the city of

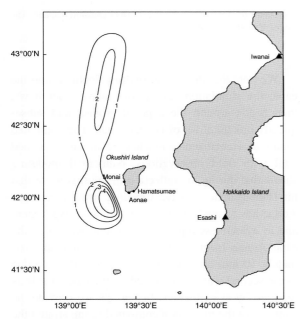

Figure 19

The computational domain used to simulate 1993 Okushiri tsunami. The *triangles* mark locations of tide gauge stations that observed water level to which we compare model dynamics. The *contours* mark the seafloor displacement caused by Hokkaido-Nansei-Oki earthquake (TAKAHASHI et al., 1995)

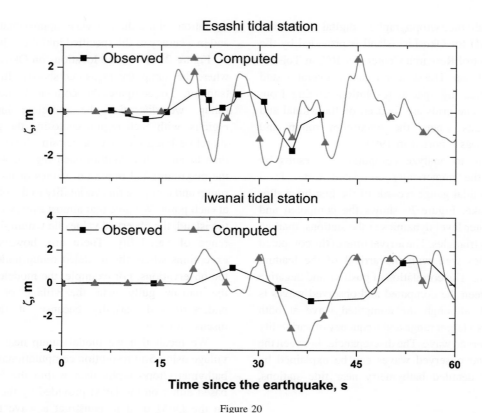

Figure 20
Computed and observed water level at two tide stations located along the west coast of Hokkaido island during 1993 Okushiri tsunami. The observations are provided courtesy of YEH et al. (1996)

Aonae. The 0, 5, and 10 m ground elevations contours are shown by thick lines. The first snapshot corresponds to 280 s after the earthquake, and each snapshot is 60 s after the previous one. In the first snapshot, it is easy to observe the approaching 5 m high wave via water level contours shown by the dashed lines. While the wave approaches the Aonae cape, it drastically steepens over the shallow areas as shown in the second snapshot, shown upper right. The wave runs-up on the eastern side on the cape of Aonae and reaches the 10 m high mark. In the third snapshot, shown lower left, the wave sweeps across the cape. The speed of the water traveling across the tip of the cape, coincide with the primary areas of destruction, is numerically estimated at up to 12 ± 3 m/s, which is in good agreement with observations. In the last snapshot, shown lower right, we show the cape Aonae after the retreat of the computed wave.

We note that due to the shallow depth around the cape, the simulation reveals that wave front bows, then bends around the cape of Aonae, and subsequently hits the town of Hamatsumae. The computed runup at Hamatsumae reaches 15 m and matched well with field observations. Numerical modeling shows that during the reflection of the first wave that hit Hamatsumae, a wave traveling toward the cape Aonae has formed. Both in the computer experiment and in eyewitness reports, this second wave hits the cape Aonae from the south-east direction approximately 10 min after the first wave. The damage due to the second wave is localized on the eastern side as reported by eyewitnesses. In Fig. 23, we provide the contours of the maximum computed runup around the cape Aonae. This computer experiment shows that the numerical algorithm is stable and successfully models the overland flow as well as captures runup of reflected waves.

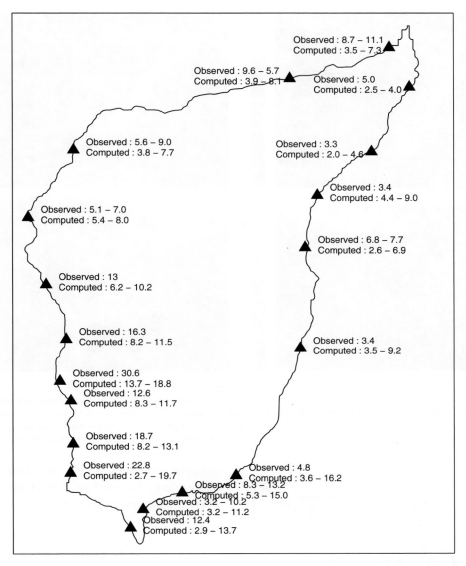

Figure 21
The computed and observed runup in meters at 19 locations along the coast of Okushiri island after 1993 Okushiri tsunami. The observations are provided courtesy of KATO and TSUJI (1994)

6. Conclusions

A numerical model for simulation of tsunami propagation and runup is presented. The model is verified and validated using NOAA standards and criteria—the numerical solution is tested against analytical predictions, laboratory measurements, and field observations SYNOLAKIS et al. (2008). In computer experiments modeling propagation and runup of a solitary wave on a canonical beach and on conically

shaped island, numerical calculations are within established errors proposed by (SYNOLAKIS et al., 2008).

To test the model against field observation, we perform simulation of the 1993 Okushiri tsunami. The computed runup around Okushiri island is within the variability of field observations. However, the local extreme runup, e.g. in the narrow gully near the village of Monai, is sensitive to the near shore interpolation of bathymetry/topography. The

257

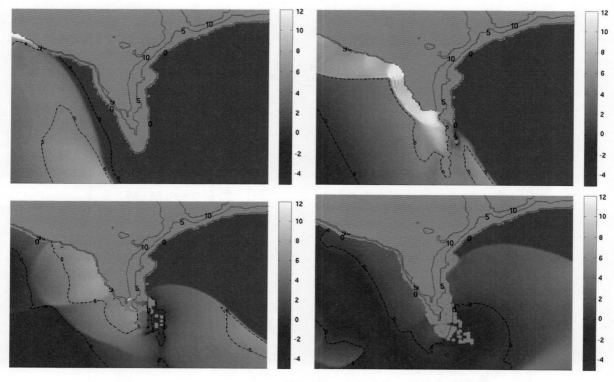

Figure 22

Numerical modeling of a tsunami wave overflowing the cape of Aonae, viewed from above. The *black dashed* and *red solid contours* represent the water level and land elevation, respectively. The upper left plot show an approaching ≈ 5 m high wave. As wave approaches, it steepens and overtops the cape as illustrated by the upper right plot. In the lower left plot, the wavefront bends around the cape and propagates in the direction Hamatsumae. The lower right plot, water retreats and the seabed became partially dry

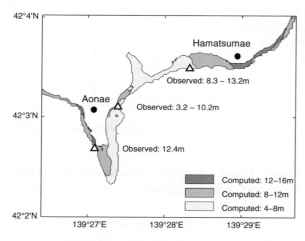

Figure 23

The computed and observed runup in the vicinity of Aonae cape after 1993 Okushiri tsunami. The *triangles* mark locations, where the observations were conducted. The computed runup distribution has a local maximum near Hamatsumae as observed by eyewitnesses. The observations are provided courtesy of KATO and TSUJI (1994)

computer simulation of the 1993 Okushiri tsunami also captures the overland flow at the cape Aonae, where the maximum destruction was reported.

Acknowledgments

We would like to thank C.E. Synolakis, V.V. Titov, J. Stroh and others for all their valuable advice, critique and reassurances along the way. We are thankful to reviewers and the editor for valuable suggestions making the manuscript easier to read and understand. This study was supported by NOAA grants 27-014d and 06-028a through Cooperative Institute for Arctic Research. Numerical calculations for this work are supported by a grant of High Performance Computing resources from the Arctic Region Supercomputing Center at the University of Alaska Fairbanks as part of the US Department of Defense HPC Modernization Program.

REFERENCES

ANGOT, P., BRUNEAU, C., FABRIE, P., 1999. *A penalization method to take into account obstacles in incompressible viscous flows.* Nümerische Mathematik 81(4), 497–520.

ARAKAWA, A., LAMB, V., 1977. Computational design of the basic dynamical processes of the UCLA general circulation model. In: Methods in Computational Physics. Vol. 17. Academic Press, pp. 174–267.

BALAY, S., BUSCHELMAN, K., EIJKHOUT, V., GROPP, W. D., KAUSHIK, D., KNEPLEY, M. G., MCINNES, L. C., SMITH, B. F., ZHANG, H., 2004. PETSc Users Manual. Tech. Rep. ANL-95/11 - Revision 2.1.5, Argonne National Laboratory.

BALZANO, A., 1998. *Evaluation of methods for numerical simulation of wetting and drying in shallow water flow models.* Coastal Engineering 34, 83–107.

BRIGGS, M., SYNOLAKIS, C., HARKINS, G., GREEN, D., 1995. *Laboratory experiments of tsunami runup on a circular island.* Pure and Applied Geophysics 144, 569–593.

BUZBEE, B., DORR, F., GEORGE, J., GOLUB, G., 1971. *The direct solution of the discrete poisson equation on irregular regions.* SIAM Journal on Numerical Analysis 8, 722–736.

CHAUDHRY, M., 1993. Open-Channel Flow. Prentice-Hall, 483 pp.

CHOW, V., 1959. Open Channel Hydraulics. McGraw-Hill, 680 pp.

COURANT, R., FRIEDRICHS, K., LEWY, H., 1928. *"Uber die partiellen differenzengleichungen der mathematischen physic.* Mathematische Annalen 100, 32–74.

DALRYMPLE, R., ROGERS, B., 2006. Numerical modeling of water waves with the SPH method. Coastal Engineering 53, 141–147.

DISSEZ, A., SOUS, D., VINCENT, S., CALTAGIRONE, J., SOTTOLICHIO, A., 2005. *A novel implicit method for coastal hydrodynamics modeling: application to the Arcachon lagoon.* Comptes Rendus Mecanique 333, 796–803.

FISCHER, G., 1959. *Ein numerisches verfahren zur errechnung von windstau und gezeiten in randmeeren.* Tellus 11, 60–76.

FLETCHER, C., 1991. Computational Techniques for Fluid Dynamics 1. Springer-Verlag, 401 pp.

GEORGE, D. L., LEVEQUE, R. J., 2006. *Finite volume methods and adaptive refinement for global tsunami propagation and inundation.* Science of Tsunami Hazards 24(5), 319–328.

GLOWINSKI, R., PAN, T.-W., PERIAUX, J., 1994. *Fictitious domain method for dirichlet problems and applications.* Computer Methods in Applied Mechanics and Engineering 111, 283–303.

GORING, D., 1979. Tsunamis—the propagation of long waves onto a shelf. PhD Thesis, California Institute of Technology, Pasadena, California.

GOTO, C., OGAWA, Y., SHUTO, N., IMAMURA, F., 1997. Numerical method of tsunami simulation with the leap-frog scheme. Manuals and Guides 35, UNESCO: IUGG/IOC TIME Project.

GROPP, W., LUSK, E., SKJELLUM, A., 1999. Using MPI: Portable Parallel Programming with the Message-Passing Interface. The MIT press, 406 pp.

HAMMACK, J., 1972. Tsunamis—A model for their generation and propagation. Tech. Rep. KH-R-28, W.M. Keck Laboratory of Hydraulics and Water Resources, California Institute of Technology.

HANSEN, 1956. *Theorie zur errechnung des wasserstands und der stromungen in randemeeren.* Tellus 8, 287–300.

IMAMURA, F., 1995. Tsunami numerical simulation with the staggered leap-frog scheme. Tech. rep., School Disaster Control Research Center, Tohoku University, Manuscript for TUNAMI code, 33 pp.

IMAMURA, F., 1996. Review of tsunami simulation with a finite difference method. In: Yeh, H., Liu, P., Synolakis, C. (Eds.), Long-Wave Runup Models. World Scientific, pp. 25–42.

KATO, K., TSUJI, Y., 1994. Estimation of fault parameters of the 1993 Hokkaido-Nansei-Oki earthquake and tsunami characteristics. Bulletin of the Earthquake Research Institute 69, 39–66, University of Tokyo.

KENNEDY, A., CHEN, Q., KIRBY, J., DALRYMPLE, R., 2000. Boussinesq modeling of wave transformation, breaking, and runup, Part I:1D. Journal of Waterway, Port, Coastal and Ocean Engineering 126(1), 39–47.

KHADRA, K., PARNEIX, S., ANGOT, P., CALTAGIRONE, J., 2000. *Fictious domain approach for numerical modelling of Navier-Stokes equations.* International Journal for Numerical Methods in Fluids 341, 651–684.

KIRBY, J., WEI, G., CHEN, Q., KENNEDY, A., DALRYMPLE, R., 1998. FUNWAVE 1.0, fully nonlinear boussinesq wave model documentation and users manual. Tech. Rep. Research Report No. CACR-98-06, Center for Applied Coastal Research, University of Delaware.

KOWALIK, Z., MURTY, T., 1993a. Numerical modeling of ocean dynamics. World Scientific, 481 pp.

KOWALIK, Z., MURTY, T., 1993b. Numerical simulation of two-dimensional tsunami runup. Marine Geodesy 16, 87–100.

LINSLEY, R., FRANZINI, J., 1979. Water Resources Engineering. McGraw-Hill, New York, 716 pp.

LIU, P.-F., CHO, Y.-S., BRIGGS, M., KANOĞLU, U., SYNOLAKIS, C., 1995. *Runup of solitary waves on a circular island.* Journal of Fluid Mechanics 302, 259–285.

LIU, P.-F., WOO, S., CHO, Y., 1998. Computer programs for tsunami propagation and inundation. Tech. rep., Cornell University, 104 pp.

LIU, P. L.-F., SYNOLAKIS, C., YEH, H., 1991. *Report on the international workshop on long-wave runup.* Journal of Fluid Mechanics 229, 675–688.

LIU, P. L.-F., YEH, H., SYNOLAKIS, C., 2007. Advanced Numerical Models for Simulationg Tsunami Waves and Runup. Vol. 10 of Advances in Coastal and Ocean Engineering. World Scientific, Proceedings of the Third International Workshop on Long-Wave Runup Models, Catalina, 2004 Benchmark problems, pp. 223–230.

LYNETT, P., BORRERO, J., LIU, P.-F., SYNOLAKIS, C., 2003. *Field survey and numerical simulations: a review of the 1998 Papua New Guinea earthquake and tsunami.* Pure and Applied Geophysics 160, 2119–2146.

LYNETT, P., WU, T.-R., LIU, P.-F., 2002. *Modeling wave runup with depth-integrated equations.* Coastal Engineering 46(2), 89–107.

MADER, C., LUKAS, S., 1984. SWAN-A Shallow Water, Long Wave Code. Tech. Rep. HIG-84-4, Hawaii Institute of Geophysics, University of Hawaii.

MARCHUK, G. I., KUZNETSOV, Y. A., MATSOKIN, A. M., 1986. *Fictitious domain and domain decomposition methods.* Soviet Journal of Numerical Analysis and Mathematical Modelling 1(1), 3–35.

HOKKAIDO TSUNAMI SURVEY GROUP, 1993. *Tsunami devastates Japanese coastal regions.* EOS, Transactions AGU 74 (37), 417–432.

MEYER, R., TAYLOR, A., 1972. Waves on beaches and resulting sediment transport. Academic Press, Ch. Run-up on beaches, pp. 357–411.

OKADA, Y., 1985. *Surface deformation due to shear and tensile faults in a half-space*. Bulletin of the Seismological Society of America 75, 1135–1154.

PAGLIERI, L., AMBROSI, D., FORMAGGIA, L., QUARTERONI, A., SCHEININE, A., 1997. *Parallel computation for shallow water flow: A domain decomposition approach*. Parallel Computing 23, 1261–1277.

PEREGRINE, D., 1967. *Long waves on a beach*. Journal of Fluid Mechanics 27(4), 815–827.

PEREGRINE, D., WILLIAMS, S., 2001. *Swash overtopping a truncated plane beach*. Journal of Fluid Mechanics 440, 391–399.

SHEN, M., MEYER, R., 1963. *Climb of a bore on a beach. Part 3. Run-up*. Journal of Fluid Mechanics 16, 113–125.

SHUTO, N., 1991. Tsunami Hazard. Kluwer Academic Publishers, Netherlands, Ch. Numerical simulation of tsunamis, pp. 171–191.

SVENDSEN, I., 2005. Introduction to Nearshore Hydrodynamics. World Scientific Publishing Company, 722pp.

SYNOLAKIS, C., 1986. The Runup of Long Waves. Ph.D. thesis, California Institute of Technology, Pasadena, California, 228 pp.

SYNOLAKIS, C., 1987. *The runup of solitary waves*. Journal of Fluid Mechanics 185, 523–545.

SYNOLAKIS, C., BERNARD, E., 2006. *Tsunami science before and beyond Boxing Day 2004*. Philosophical Transactions of the Royal Society A 364, 2231–2265.

SYNOLAKIS, C., BERNARD, E., TITOV, V., K\^ANOĞLU, U., GONZÁLEZ, F., 2007. Standards, criteria, and procedures for NOAA evaluation of tsunami numerical models. OAR PMEL-135 Special Report, NOAA/OAR/PMEL, Seattle, Washington,, 55 pp.

SYNOLAKIS, C., BERNARD, E., TITOV, V., K\^ANOĞLU, U., GONZÁLEZ, F., 2008. *Validation and verification of tsunami numerical models*. Pure and Applied Geophysics 165, 2197–2228.

TAKAHASHI, T., TAKAHASHI, T., SHUTO, N., IMAMURA, F., ORTIZ, M., 1995. *Source models for the 1993 Hokkaido-Nansei-Oki earthquake tsunami*. Pure and Applied Geophysics 144, 747–768.

TITOV, V., SYNOLAKIS, C., 1995. *Evolution and runup of breaking and nonbreaking waves using VTSC-2*. Journal of Waterway, Port, Coastal and Ocean Engineering 121(6), 308–316.

TITOV, V., SYNOLAKIS, C., 1998. *Numerical modeling of tidal wave runup*. Journal of Waterway, Port, Coastal and Ocean Engineering 124, 157–171.

YEH, H., 1991. *Tsunami bore runup*. Natural Hazards 4, 209–220.

YEH, H., Liu, P.-F., Synolakis, C., 1996. Long-Wave Runup Models. World Scientific, 403 pp.

YEH, H., LIU, P. L.-F., BRIGGS, M., SYNOLAKIS, C. E., 1994. *Propagation and amplification of tsunamis at coastal boundaries*. Nature 372, 353–355.

ZELT, J., 1991. *The runup of breaking and nonbreaking solitary waves*. Coastal Engineering 125, 205–246.

ZHANG, Y., BAPTISTA, A., 2008. *An efficient and robust tsunami model on unstructured grids. Part I: Inundation benchmarks*. Pure and Applied Geophysics 165, 2229–2248.

(Received November 27, 2009, revised April 22, 2010, accepted June 26, 2010, Published online November 10, 2010)

Pure Appl. Geophys. 168 (2011), 1223–1237
© 2010 Springer Basel AG
DOI 10.1007/s00024-010-0226-6

Optimal Initial Conditions for Simulation of Seismotectonic Tsunamis

MIKHAIL A. NOSOV[1] and SERGEY V. KOLESOV[1]

Abstract—Numerical simulation of seismotectonic tsunamis usually starts with specification of the initial elevation of the water surface in the tsunami source. The initial elevation is traditionally set equal to the vertical residual bottom deformation resulting from earthquakes. We discuss the imperfectness of the traditional approach and suggest an improved practical method of calculating the initial elevation from the solution of the 3D problem in the framework of potential theory. The method takes into account horizontal and vertical components of bottom deformation and bathymetry in the source area. Within the assumption of instant tsunami generation the suggested method represents the optimal way to specify the initial condition in the tsunami propagation problem. The tsunamis in the Central Kuril Islands on 15 November 2006 and 13 January 2007 are taken as examples to demonstrate the efficiency of the new method.

Key words: Tsunami generation, residual bottom deformation, potential theory, initial elevation, long-wave theory.

1. Introduction

The simple majority ($\sim 80\%$) of all known tsunamis is related to strong bottom earthquakes (Historical Tsunami Database for the World Ocean, http://tsun.sscc.ru/nh/tsunami.php). The number of works devoted to investigating the tsunami formation mechanism by a seismotectonic source is incredibly large. Without claiming to present a full list, we shall only mention several publications. Mechanisms of tsunami generation by a moving bottom have been investigated analytically and numerically (AIDA, 1969; HWANG AND DIVOKI, 1970; KAJIURA, 1970; VOIT et al., 1981; MARCHUK et al., 1985; KOSTITSYNA et al., 1992; DOTSENKO AND SOLOVIEV, 1995; DOTSENKO, 1996; NOSOV, 1992, 1996, 1998; DUTYKH et al., 2006;

DUTYKH AND DIAS, 2007, 2009; KERVELLA et al., 2007). Some publications are devoted to laboratory simulations of the generation process (TAKAHASHI 1934, 1963; HAMMACK, 1973; NOSOV AND SHELKOVNIKOV, 1995, 1997).

In practice, numerical simulation of tsunamis is normally based on the shallow water theory, which deals with the equations of hydrodynamics, averaged over the vertical coordinate (TITOV AND GONZALEZ, 1997; KOWALIK et al., 2005; LEVIN and NOSOV, 2008; FUJII AND SATAKE, 2008; GISLER, 2008). As for the description of tsunami generation, an earthquake is considered to instantly cause residual deformations of the ocean bottom. Then, the assumption is made that the displacement of the bottom is simultaneously accompanied by formation at the surface of the ocean of a perturbation (initial elevation), the shape of which is fully similar to the vertical residual deformations of the bottom. The initial elevation thus obtained is then applied as the initial condition in resolving the problem of tsunami propagation. The initial field of flow velocities is assumed to be zero.

The approach described above more or less adequately reproduces the main effect responsible for seismotectonic tsunami generation—ousting of the water. However, though easy to use in practice, the approach is not accurate due to at least the following few reasons. First, the approach implies total separation of hydrodynamic and seismological parts of the problem, whereas physical processes taking place at a seismotectonic tsunami source and at an earthquake fault area represent a unique whole (ALEXEEV and GUSYAKOV, 1976; POD'YAPOLSKY, 1978). Second, the dynamics of rupture formation and the relevant time-dependent process of bottom deformations remain beyond our consideration, i.e., earthquake and tsunami generation are assumed to be an instant process. Third, the vertical structure of water flux in a tsunami

---

[1] Faculty of Physics, M.V. Lomonosov Moscow State University, Leninskie Gory, Moscow 119991, Russia. E-mail: nosov@phys.msu.ru

source is neglected, whereas this very structure is responsible for effects of water compressibility (Nosov, 1999; Nosov and Kolesov, 2007; Gisler, 2008) and for smoothing of perturbations of the water surface as compared with the bottom deformations (Kajiura, 1963; Tanioka and Seno, 2001; Rabinovich et al., 2008; Saito and Furumura, 2009; Nosov and Kolesov, 2009). Finally, the horizontal deformation components, which can also contribute to ousting of the water in the case of a sloping bottom, are neglected (Iwasaki, 1982; Tanioka and Satake, 1996; Nosov and Kolesov, 2009).

Separation of hydrodynamic and seismological parts of the problem means, on the one hand, that the presence of the water column does not influence the earthquake and, in particular, formation of co-seismic bottom deformations. On the other hand, it means that the bottom can be considered as an absolutely rigid medium for all kinds of waves propagating in the water column. The huge energy of an earthquake, as compared with the energy of tsunami waves generated by this earthquake, may serve as a good reason in favor of the separation. Moreover, the slow variations of hydrostatic pressure that are associated with a tsunami wave obviously cause negligibly small elastic deformations of the bottom. So, finite elasticity of the bottom certainly does not play a noticeable role for gravitational waves.

Being absolutely rigid for long gravitational waves, the bottom turns out to be an elastic medium for hydroacoustic waves generated by bottom earthquakes along with gravitational waves (Nosov and Kolesov, 2007). However, even in case of a compressible water column, an essential difference that exists in the acoustic stiffness of the water and bottom (more than an order of magnitude) allows consideration of the model of an absolutely rigid bottom as a quite reasonable first assumption for hydroacoustic problems.

For understanding the role of the dynamics of bottom deformations, it is useful to present a description of the character of the linear response of a water column to movements of the ocean bottom (Levin and Nosov 2008). In reality, seismic movements of the bottom are characterized by a wide frequency spectrum ranging mostly within 0.001–100 Hz. The low limit of the spectrum is due to the maximum duration

of rupture formation. The upper limit is due to intensive attenuation of high frequency seismic waves. Let us consider the characteristic frequencies for a water column: $\sqrt{g/H}$ and $c/4H$, where g is acceleration due to gravity, H is thickness of the water column (ocean depth), and c is the sound velocity in water. The characteristic frequencies are shown on the plane "Ocean Depth Frequency" in Fig. 1. The curves determine three subareas: "gravitational waves," "forced oscillations" and "hydroacoustic waves." Bottom motions of low frequency ($v < \sqrt{g/H}$) generate gravitational waves that are radiated from the source. Bottom motions of intermediate frequency ($\sqrt{g/H} < v < c/4H$) give rise to forced oscillations of the water layer localized in the tsunami source, whereas gravitational waves are not radiated from the source. Bottom motions of high frequency ($v > c/4H$) radiate hydroacoustic waves. Thus, the concept of "instant tsunami generation" turns out to be rather shaky. Indeed, very short bottom movements, which are really instantaneous in respect to the gravitational waves, exhibit a finite duration in respect to the hydroacoustic waves.

Fortunately, hydroacoustic waves, owing to the cutoff frequency (Tolstoy and Clay 1987), can not

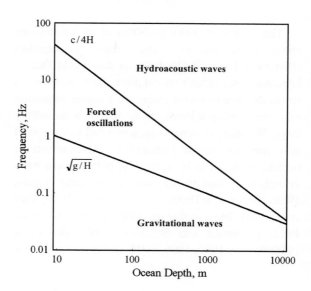

Figure 1
Characteristic frequencies of a water column as functions of ocean depth. Character of linear response of a water column to oscillations of the ocean bottom of a given frequency

provide a direct contribution to the height of the tsunami run-up. In addition, as is seen from Fig. 1, long gravitational waves (tsunamis) and hydroacoustic waves, in the condition of the planet earth, always exhibit essentially different frequency ranges. Therefore, in linear approximation, tsunamis and hydroacoustic waves are not coupled, i.e., one can describe them separately.

In substantiating the application of linear theory in the tsunami generation problem, one usually quotes the condition that the amplitude of the ocean bottom deformation is small compared to the depth of the basin, $A << H$. Indeed, this condition is quite fulfilled in reality. But even when the amplitude of the ocean bottom displacement is small, the velocity of its movement may turn out to be sufficiently high for the manifestation of non-linear effects. Strong earthquakes may give rise to very intensive elastic oscillations of the water column. The non-linear mechanism of tsunami generation is related to the non-linear transfer of energy from elastic oscillations to gravitational waves. The usual tsunami generation mechanism, related to residual displacements substituting the water naturally remains in force, and in most cases it plays the leading role. However, in some cases a non-linear hydroacoustic mechanism can provide an additional contribution to a tsunami wave (Novikova and Ostrovsky, 1982; Nosov and Kolesov, 2005; Nosov et al., 2008; Levin and Nosov, 2008). At present, the non-linear mechanism is still under investigation; thus, let us leave it as beyond the scope of this paper.

From the reasoning above, one can conclude that, in linear approximation, effects of water compressibility exist separately from the long gravitational waves—tsunamis. This is why generation of a tsunami can be considered as a problem of the theory of incompressible fluids.

In the present study, we suggest an optimal method of specification of the initial conditions in the problem of tsunami propagation. Remaining within the approach of "initial elevation," we neglect the dynamics of bottom deformation. Our method is based on the potential fluid theory. First, we discuss the general evolutionary problem in terms of the Laplace equation and reduce it to a simpler static one. After that, an effective analytic-numerical algorithm

for the solution of the static problem is described. Then, taking the Central Kuril Islands tsunami sources of 15 November 2006 and 13 January 2007 as examples, we demonstrate the efficiency of the new method. Finally, we provide a brief description of our numerical model of tsunami propagation and discuss the results of the Central Kuril Islands tsunami simulations.

2. Initial Elevation

In this section we shall focus on a practical method of specification of the initial conditions in the tsunami problem. First, we shall describe the mathematical statement of the problem of tsunami generation within the framework of incompressible fluid theory. Then, the full time-dependent 3D problem will be reduced to a static one. Finally, we shall propose a semi-analytic practical method for resolving the static problem.

2.1. Mathematical Model

Consider a layer, infinite in the horizontal $0xy$ plane, of an ideal incompressible homogeneous liquid of variable depth $H(x, y)$ in the field of gravity. We shall put the origin of the Cartesian reference frame, $0xyz$, in the unperturbed free surface and direct the $0z$ axis vertically upward. The liquid is at rest until the time moment $t = 0$. To find the wave perturbation $\xi(x, y, t)$, formed on the surface of the liquid, and the velocity field, $\vec{v}(x, y, z, t)$, throughout the thickness of the layer in the case of dynamic deformation of the basin floor, occurring in accordance with the law $\vec{\eta}(x, y, t) = (\eta_x, \eta_y, \eta_z)$, we shall solve the problem with respect to the velocity potential $F(x, y, z, t)$ (LANDAU and LIFSHITZ, 1987):

$$\Delta F = 0, \tag{1}$$

$$\frac{\partial^2 F}{\partial t^2} = -g \frac{\partial F}{\partial z}, \quad z = 0, \tag{2}$$

$$\frac{\partial F}{\partial \vec{\mathbf{n}}} = \left(\frac{\partial \vec{\eta}}{\partial t}, \vec{\mathbf{n}} \right), \quad z = -H(x, y), \tag{3}$$

where $\vec{\mathbf{n}}$ is the unit vector normal to the bottom surface. We restrict ourselves to small bottom deformations, $|\vec{\eta}| << H$; thus depth H as well as vector $\vec{n}$ do not depend on time. The small-amplitude restriction gives us ground to specify the linearized free-surface boundary condition 2.

The bottom boundary condition 3 is a mathematical statement of the following principle of classical hydrodynamics (LAMB, 1945; LANDAU and LIFSHITZ, 1987): In case of non-viscous fluid, at an impermeable boundary, the flow of fluid relative to the boundary must be tangential to it. If the boundary is fixed in space, this means that the component of fluid velocity normal to the boundary must be zero. However, if the boundary is moving, then the normal component of the fluid velocity must be equal to the velocity of the boundary normal to itself.

Displacement of the free surface and the flow velocity vector are related to the velocity potential by the following known formulae (LANDAU and LIFSHITZ, 1987):

$$\xi(x,y,t) = -\frac{1}{g}\frac{\partial F}{\partial t}\bigg|_{z=0}, \tag{4}$$

$$\vec{v}(x,y,z,t) = \vec{\nabla} F. \tag{5}$$

In case of liquid of constant depth H_0, problem 1–3 is solved by the method of separation of variables. The general analytical solution of the problem in terms of Laplace and Fourier expansions over time and space coordinates can be written out in the following form (NOSOV and SHELKOVNIKOV, 1996; NOSOV, 1998; LEVIN and NOSOV, 2008):

$$\xi(x,y,t) = \frac{1}{8\pi^3 i}\int\limits_{s-i\infty}^{s+i\infty} dp \int\limits_{-\infty}^{+\infty} dm$$

$$\times \int\limits_{-\infty}^{+\infty} dn \frac{p^2 \exp(pt - imx - iny)\Psi(p,m,n)}{\cosh(kH_0)[gk\tanh(kH_0) + p^2]}, \tag{6}$$

$$\Psi(p,m,n) = \int\limits_0^\infty dt \int\limits_{-\infty}^{+\infty} dx \int\limits_{-\infty}^{+\infty}$$

$$dy \exp(-pt + imx + iny)\,\eta_z(x,y,t),$$

$$k^2 = m^2 + n^2,$$

where $\vec{k} \equiv (m,n)$ is the wave vector.

As is seen from formula 6, the spatial spectrum of the free surface displacement is always modulated by a rapidly damped function, $1/\cosh(kH_0)$, so that inhomogeneities of bottom deformations of scale $\lambda < H_0$ are not manifested on the water surface. All such inhomogeneities turn out to be smoothed out by the liquid column. It is worth emphasizing that direct transfer of bottom deformations up to the water surface artificially enriches the spectrum of the tsunami at the expense of unrealistically short waves. Being a sort of noise, these short waves may lead to artificial resonances in bays and finally to incorrect estimations of runup heights or even to instability in the numerical calculations. Anyway, the numerical description of the short wave components requires very fine grids and, therefore, very small time steps. Ultimately, the imperfectness of the traditional approach may also result in a significant increase in the calculating time in numerical simulations of tsunamis.

It was KAJIURA (1963) who first pointed out the necessity to take into account the "smoothing effect," especially in the cases where the oceanic depth is comparable to the horizontal extension of the source. It must be noted that the just-mentioned paper by K. Kajiura was published before the "era" of numerical simulation of tsunamis. Nevertheless, at the present time, there are only a few works where authors attempted to take this effect into account under real tsunami calculations (TANIOKA and SENO, 2001; RABINOVICH et al., 2008; DUTYKH and DIAS, 2007; SAITO and FURUMURA, 2009). We also developed the idea of smoothing in our recent publications (LEVIN and NOSOV, 2008; NOSOV and KOLESOV, 2009).

The imperfectness of the traditional approach, within which the initial elevation is set equal to the vertical residual bottom deformation, is also due to the second reason. In the case of a sloping (non-horizontal) bottom the horizontal deformation components can also contribute significantly to the displacement of the water surface. The role of horizontal displacement in tsunami generation had been discussed earlier in some publications (e.g., IWASAKI, 1982; TANIOKA and SATAKE, 1996; NOSOV and KOLESOV, 2009).

A logical development of the traditional approach is to calculate the initial elevation from the solution of the 3D problem 1–3 taking into account all three components of the bottom deformation vector and the distribution of depths in the vicinity of the source. Let us introduce, instead of the velocity potential, a new quantity

$$\Phi = \int_0^\tau F \, dt, \qquad (7)$$

where τ is the duration of bottom deformations. Integrating Eqs. 1–3 with respect to time, we reduce the evolutionary problem to a simpler static problem

$$\Delta\Phi = 0, \qquad (8)$$

$$\Phi = 0, \quad z = 0, \qquad (9)$$

$$\frac{\partial\Phi}{\partial \mathbf{n}} = (\vec{\boldsymbol{\eta}}_0, \vec{\mathbf{n}}), \quad z = -H(x,y), \qquad (10)$$

where $\vec{\boldsymbol{\eta}}_0 \equiv (\eta_{0x}, \eta_{0y}, \eta_{0z})$ is the residual bottom deformations. The vertical component of the Eq. 5, after being integrated over time, gives the following expression for the initial elevation:

$$\xi_0 = \left.\frac{\partial\Phi}{\partial z}\right|_{z=0}. \qquad (11)$$

Equations 8 and 10 are obvious consequences of the Eqs. 1 and 3, respectively. The boundary condition 9 is derived from the free-surface boundary condition 2 in the following way. Let us introduce dimensionless variables that are suitable for the tsunami generation process

$$t* = t/\tau,$$

$$z* = z/H.$$

Equation 2 can be rewritten in terms of the dimensionless variables:

$$\frac{\partial^2 F}{\partial t*^2} = -\frac{g\tau^2}{H}\frac{\partial F}{\partial z*}. \qquad (12)$$

In case of instant bottom deformation, i.e.,

$$\tau << \sqrt{H/g}, \qquad (13)$$

the right-hand member of Eq. 12 vanishes. Assuming zero initial conditions for the velocity potential (the liquid is initially at rest) we integrate Eq. 12 with the zero right-hand part with respect to time. Finally, we obtain the boundary condition 9. It is worth noting that the condition of instantaneity 13 is stricter in comparison with the traditional one

$$\tau << L/\sqrt{gH}, \qquad (14)$$

where L is the horizontal scale of a tsunami source.

In the CMT earthquakes catalog (http://www.globalcmt.org/) a temporal characteristic termed 'half duration' is presented, which corresponds to half the duration of the process at an earthquake source. Generally, the half duration increases with the earthquake magnitude. Analysis of all seismic events of magnitude $M_w > 7$, presented in the CMT catalog for the period between January 1976 and March 2005 (370 events), permitted us to obtain the following regression relationship (LEVIN and NOSOV 2008):

$$\lg T_{hd}[s] = (0.42 \pm 0.02) \cdot M_w - (1.99 \pm 0.14).$$

In accordance with the regression, as the moment magnitude M_w varies within the range from 7 to 9, the half duration T_{hd} increases from 9 to 62 s.

At first sight, the duration of bottom deformations τ can be estimated as the duration of the process at an earthquake source. However, deformation of the seafloor in the case of strong earthquakes does not proceed simultaneously over the entire area of the tsunami source, but propagates horizontally following the fault that forms at the earthquake source. Therefore, the duration of the seafloor deformation at a certain point may turn out to be shorter than the total duration of the fault formation. It is important to realize that in many cases, especially if a tsunami source is situated in a shallow water region, condition 13 may be broken, whereas condition 14 is virtually always satisfied.

If condition 13 is broken, a full time-spatial history of bottom deformations $\vec{\eta}(x,y,t)$ should be considered while solving the dynamic problem of tsunami generation 1–3. If one considers tsunami generation as an instant process, which is not obviously true in many real cases, *the optimum way of calculating the initial elevation consists of solving the static problem 8–10*. By optimum here we mean the best way to determine the initial elevation within the framework of the assumption of instant tsunami generation. Indeed, this way first provides a naturally (not artificially) smoothed initial elevation. Second, the account of vertical and horizontal deformations of inclined bottoms gives a correct estimation of the water volume ousted by bottom deformation. Third, this way provides correct upper estimation of tsunami energy-potential energy of the initial elevation. Ultimately, this method does not violate the traditional scheme of tsunami simulation.

2.2. Analytic-Numerical Algorithm

In what follows we restrict ourselves to consideration of instantaneous bottom deformation only. A direct numerical solution of the 3D static problem 8–10 requires huge computational capability. We suggest a simplified approach based on an exact analytical solution of the problem in case of an ocean of constant depth, H_0. Let us consider the rectangular source area of size $2a \times 2b$ described by the following formula:

$$\eta_{0z}(x,y) = B_0[\theta(x+a) - \theta(x-a)][\theta(y+b) - \theta(y-b)],$$

$$(15)$$

where B_0 is the amplitude of residual uplift and θ is the Heaviside step function. The exact analytical solution of problem 8–10 in terms of Fourier expansion over space coordinates has the following form:

$$\xi_0(x,y) = \frac{4B_0}{\pi^2} \int\limits_0^{+\infty} dm \int\limits_0^{+\infty} dn$$

$$\times \frac{\cos(mx)\cos(ny)\sin(ma)\sin(nb)}{m\, n\, \cosh(kH_0)}. \qquad (16)$$

In formula 16 we keep the same notation as in formula 6.

An example of initial elevation due to the residual bottom deformation of rectangular shape 15 calculated using formula 16 is shown in Fig. 2. As was expected, displacement of the free surface is much smoother compared to the bottom deformations: the initial elevation has a smaller amplitude and spreads over a rather wide area. Moreover, the free surface disturbance $\xi_0(x, y)$ turns out to be an exponentially decreasing function outside the source area, so that already at the distance of $4H_0$ from the border of the source its influence vanishes completely. This important feature, together with assumption that oceanic depth and amplitude of bottom deformations are slowly varying functions of

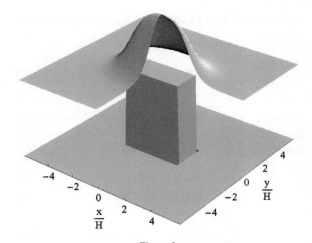

Figure 2
Free surface disturbance caused by residual bottom deformation of rectangular shape with parameters $a = 2H_0$, $b = H_0$. Calculations are performed using formula 16. Surface disturbance and bottom deformation are shown in the same scale

horizontal coordinates, gives us ground to suggest the following algorithm.

The calculation domain is divided into small rectangular subdomains of size $2a \times 2b$. Contributions of each subdomain are calculated with use of analytical solution 16 in which amplitude, η_0, and ocean depth, H_0, are considered as functions of horizontal coordinates. In order to take into account contributions of horizontal and vertical components of bottom deformations, we also assume in formula 16

$$B_0 = (\vec{\eta}_0, \vec{n}) \equiv \eta_{0x}n_x + \eta_{0y}n_y + \eta_{0z}n_z.$$

Resultant initial elevation at a given point (x, y) represents a sum of contributions of subdomains within a circular area of radius of $4H_0 + \text{Max}(a, b)$. Remote subdomains, situated outside of the circular area, are excluded from calculations because of their negligible contribution in the resultant initial elevation. In what follows we shall speak of the method described above as a "Laplace smoothing algorithm."

Input data for tsunami simulation (bathymetry and vector field of bottom deformation) are always a discrete set of values on a grid with certain space increments, i.e., $\Delta x = 2a$ and $\Delta y = 2b$. We introduce critical isobath $H_c = 1/4 \cdot \text{Min}(a, b)$, which separates calculating domain into shallow- and deep-water areas. Within the shallow-water area the Laplace smoothing algorithm will exhibit a smoothing on a space scale smaller than original space increments of input data; such a smoothing obviously does not make any practical sense. Within the deep-water area, the algorithm will effectively smooth spatial inhomogeneities of input data.

3. Central Kuril Islands Tsunami Sources: Bottom Deformations and Initial Elevations

In November 2006 and January 2007, two strong earthquakes occurred to the east of Simushir Island (Central Kuril Islands) with epicenters in the area of the Kuril Trench (15 November 2006, $M_w = 8.3$, and 13 January 2007, $M_w = 8.1$, respectively). Both seismic events induced tsunami waves, recorded over the entire Pacific Ocean and registered by many coastal and deep-ocean tide gauges (TANIOKA et al., 2008; RABINOVICH et al., 2008; FUJII AND SATAKE, 2008; LOBKOVSKY et al., 2009). The coast of the Central Kuril Islands, closest to the tsunami sources is not equipped with tide gauges, and additionally this is an uninhabited and difficult to access region. During the expedition survey of this area, carried out in the summer of 2007, a run-up height of wave up to 20 m was observed (LEVIN et al., 2008; MACINNES et al. 2009a, b).

In calculations of the vector field of residual bottom deformations in the sources of the Central Kuril Islands tsunamis, we rely on the USGS slip distribution data (Finite Fault) that are presented on the site http://earthquake.usgs.gov/regional/world/historical.php. In what follows we shall put the characteristics related to the second event (13 January 2007) in parentheses. The fault plane for the earthquake of 15 November 2006 (13 January 2007) had dimensions of 400 km (200 km) along the strike by 137.5 km (35 km), which was further divided into 220 (175) subfaults: 20 km by 12.5 km (8 km by 5 km). The bottom deformation, caused by each of these subfaults, is calculated by Okada formulae (OKADA 1985). Then, the contributions of all elements are summed up. The Lamé constants λ and μ enter into the Okada formulae in the form of a combination, which is expressed via velocities of longitudinal and transverse seismic waves, c_p and c_s,

$$\frac{\mu}{\lambda + \mu} = \frac{c_s^2}{c_p^2 - c_s^2}.$$

This ratio varies within the range 0.3–0.5. In our calculations we use a value of this ratio averaged along the fault plane. Values of c_p and c_s were taken from the CRUST2.0 model (BASSIN et al., 2000).

Figure 3 shows vector fields of residual bottom deformation calculated for the tsunamigenic Central

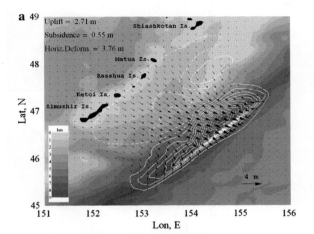

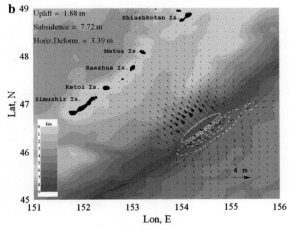

Figure 3

Bottom topography and vector fields of residual bottom deformation for the tsunamigenic Central Kuril Islands earthquakes of 15 November 2006 (**a**) and of 13 January 2007 (**b**). The isobaths are drawn with an interval of 1 km. Vertical bottom deformation is shown by isolines drawn in steps of 0.2 m (**a**) and 1 m (**b**). *Black arrows* stand for horizontal bottom deformation; *scale arrow* (4 m) is depicted in the *right lower corner*

Kuril Islands earthquake of 15 November 2006 (13 January 2007). The maximum uplift and subsidence of bottom deformation amounted to 2.7 m (1.9 m) and −0.6 m (−7.7 m), respectively. The maximum horizontal bottom deformation amounted to about 3.8 m (3.4 m). It is worth noting that significant bottom deformations were confined to the Kuril Trench, i.e., a region of large depths and essential slope of the bottom; so one can expect a noticeable smoothing effect of the water column and non-zero contribution of the horizontal component of bottom deformation in the initial elevation.

Figure 4 shows the initial elevation determined according to the following formulae:

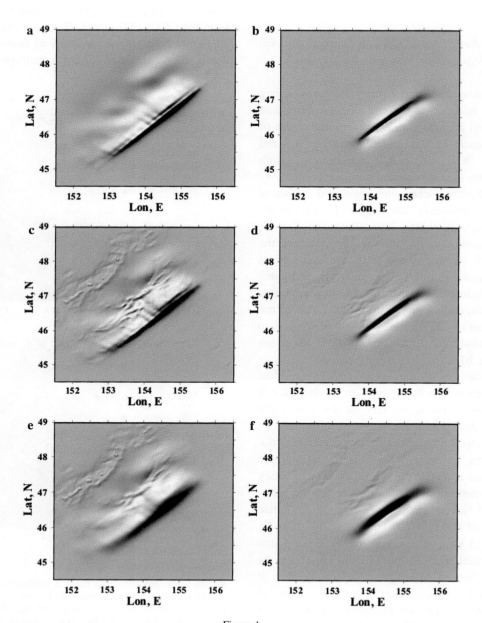

Figure 4

Initial elevation of the water surface in tsunami sources of 15 November 2006 (*left column*) and of 13 January 2007 (*right column*).
a, b Vertical bottom deformation: η_{0z}; **c, d** contributions of vertical and horizontal bottom deformation: $(\vec{n}, \vec{\eta}) \equiv n_x\eta_x + n_y\eta_y + n_z\eta_z$; **e, f** the Laplace smoothing algorithm: $\xi_0(x, y)$

1. η_z (the traditional approach);
2. $(\vec{n}, \vec{\eta}) \equiv n_x\eta_x + n_y\eta_y + n_z\eta_z$ (contribution of all components of bottom deformation vector);
3. $\xi_0(x, y)$ from the solution of the problem 8–10 via the Laplace smoothing algorithm.

From Fig. 4 it is seen that the horizontal deformations of the bottom provide a noticeable contribution to the initial elevation. In terms of amplitude of the initial elevation this contribution is relatively small from -0.28 m (-1.66 m) to 0.58 m (1.98 m). However, in terms of displaced volume of water, the contribution of horizontal displacements amounted to 30% (17%). The complexity of problem 8–10 does not obviously depend on how many components of the bottom deformation vector are taken into account. In spite of the fact that the contribution of the horizontal components in the cases under consideration is not dominant, it makes sense, in order to avoid possible errors, to consider all three components of deformation in calculating the initial elevation in tsunami source.

As for results obtained via the Laplace smoothing algorithm, the calculated amplitude of uplift and subsidence of water surface in the tsunami source amounted to 2.55 m (0.83 m) and -0.50 m (-4.45 m), respectively.

In case the event occurred on 15 November 2006, the initial elevation and vertical bottom deformation are not very different. On the contrary, for the second event (13 January 2007) the amplitude of initial elevation turns out to be nearly two times smaller than the vertical bottom deformation. So the traditional approach of specification of the initial conditions, within which the initial elevation is set equal to the vertical residual bottom deformation, can lead to significant overestimation of tsunami amplitude.

4. Numerical Model of Tsunami Propagation

The numerical model of tsunami propagation is based on the linear long-wave theory. Neglecting the Coriolis force, nonlinearity and bottom friction, we write the set of equations in spherical coordinates in the following form:

$$\frac{\partial U}{\partial t} = -\frac{g}{R\cos\varphi}\frac{\partial\xi}{\partial\psi}, \tag{17}$$

$$\frac{\partial V}{\partial t} = -\frac{g}{R}\frac{\partial\xi}{\partial\varphi}, \tag{18}$$

$$\frac{\partial\xi}{\partial t} + \frac{1}{R\cos\varphi}\left[\frac{\partial(UH)}{\partial\psi} + \frac{\partial(VH\cos\varphi)}{\partial\varphi}\right] = 0, \tag{19}$$

where ψ is the longitude, φ is the latitude, U and V are the flow velocity components, averaged over the depth, along the parallel (west-east) and along the meridian (north-south), respectively, ξ is the free-surface displacement from the equilibrium position, $R \approx 6371$ km is the mean radius of the earth, and $H(\psi, \varphi)$ is the thickness of water column.

In the set of Eqs. 17–19 it is possible to exclude the flow velocity components U and V. As a result we obtain the classical wave equation:

$$\frac{\partial^2\xi}{\partial t^2} = \frac{1}{R^2\cos^2\varphi}\frac{\partial}{\partial\psi}\left(gH\frac{\partial\xi}{\partial\psi}\right)$$
$$+ \frac{1}{R^2\cos\varphi}\frac{\partial}{\partial\varphi}\left(gH\cos\varphi\frac{\partial\xi}{\partial\varphi}\right). \tag{20}$$

Application of the wave Eq. 20 for the computation of tsunami propagation has a number of advantages, as compared with the initial set of Eqs. 17–19. First, the properties of the wave equation and the methods for its numerical solution have been thoroughly investigated. Second, for estimation of the tsunami danger it is the wave amplitudes that are of primary importance, while the flow velocity field serves as auxiliary information. Third, the initial conditions are also formulated precisely as the initial displacement of the free surface.

The wave Eq. 20 is solved with initial conditions consisting of an initial elevation of the free surface

$$\xi|_{t=0} = \xi_0(\psi, \varphi). \tag{21}$$

The initial field of flow velocities is assumed to be zero; therefore, the following additional condition is required:

$$\left.\frac{\partial\xi}{\partial t}\right|_{t=0} = 0. \tag{22}$$

The interaction of waves with the coast is described as the full reflection from the coast (e.g., MEI, 1983; TINTI et al., 2003; YAMAZAKI et al., 2006;

BELLOTTI *et al.*, 2008). The full-reflection boundary conditions arise from the assumption that the flow velocity component normal to the coastline vanishes, $V_n = 0$. The equality to zero of the derivative normal to the coastline of the displacement of the free surface is a direct consequence of this condition:

$$\frac{\partial \xi}{\partial \vec{n}} = 0. \qquad (23)$$

Free pass boundary conditions are specified on the ocean-crossing outer borders of the computational domain.

The wave Eq. 20, supplemented with the initial 21, 22 and boundary 23 conditions, was approximated by the traditional explicit scheme of finite differences (a rectangular net). The time step was determined by the Courant condition

$$\Delta t < \frac{R}{\sqrt{gH_{max}}} \mathrm{Min}[\Delta \varphi, \Delta \psi]. \qquad (24)$$

The computational domain extends from 151°E to 158°E in longitude and from 44°N to 50°N in latitude (approximately 530×670 km). Bathymetric data extracted from the 1-min digital atlas General Bathymetric Chart of the Oceans (GEBCO) and SRTM data were employed to build the computational grid. The grid was obtained from the original data with use of triangulation with the linear interpolation gridding method. In calculations the following values of space increments were used: $\Delta \psi = \Delta \varphi = 0.25$ min (approx. 0.46 km). The time increment was $\Delta t \approx 0.75$ s. For specification of the boundary condition 23 the isobath of $H_{min} = 10$ m was chosen. The period of tsunamis under consideration was longer than $T \approx 200$ s, so in the shallowest area of the computational domain the minimal wave length amounted to $\lambda_{min} = T\sqrt{gH_{min}} \approx 2000$ m. The chosen space increments provided approximately 5 grid points per the minimal wave length.

5. *Results of Numerical Simulations*

We performed numerical simulations of the tsunamis of 15 November 2006 and 13 January 2007 using model 20–23. Three different definitions of the initial elevation, described in Sect. 3, were considered; all other parameters of the model were kept constant.

Examples of numerical simulations shown in Fig. 5 are related to the 13 January 2007 event. Snapshots of tsunami propagation correspond to the time moment 3,000 s from the earthquake. The traditional method of specification of the initial condition, within which the initial elevation is assumed to be equal to the residual vertical bottom deformation, gives the result shown in Fig. 5a. Wave disturbance from the initial elevation calculated using

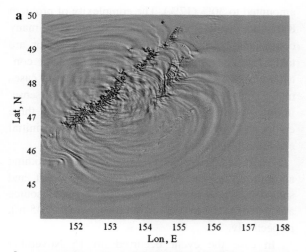

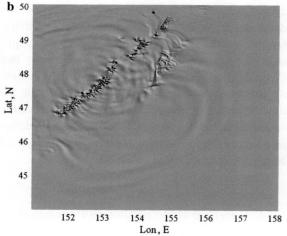

Figure 5

Snapshots of the simulated propagation of the 13 January 2007 tsunami at time moment 3,000 s after the earthquake. The initial elevation was assumed to be equal to the vertical bottom deformation (**a**), calculated with use of the Laplace smoothing algorithm (**b**)

the Laplace smoothing algorithm is presented in Fig. 5b. Figure 5 shows that wave fields are strongly dependent on the method of specification of the initial elevation. In the first case the wave field contains noise-like short wave components. It is worth remembering here that waves shorter than ocean depth cannot be generated by any bottom motions (Sect. 2). Thus, the short waves, as one can readily observe in Fig. 5a, represent artifacts that distort the realistic tsunami wave field. In contrast to the traditional method of specification of the initial condition, the Laplace smoothing provides a natural, not artificial, filtering of the short wave components. As a result one obtains smoothed wave disturbance, which is presented in Fig. 5b.

In order to reveal distinctions in the near-shore amplitude of waves that spring from different initial elevations, we estimate run-up heights as maximum water levels at a hypothetical vertical wall established along the coastline (along a certain isobath close to the coastline). Synthetic run-up heights plotted along the coast line (isobath) are presented in Fig. 6. We restrict the presentation of the run-up data to Simushir and Ketoi Islands, which represent the closest land to the epicenters of the seismic events under consideration. Relief maps of the islands that show the starting points where the distance along the coast is equal to zero, and the direction of "traveling" along the coasts (black arrows), are depicted in Fig. 6.

Figure 6 shows well that applying the Laplace smoothing algorithm always results in a decrease of simulated run-up heights. In the case of the tsunami of 15 November 2006, the difference between the curves is clearly visible but still insignificant. As for the second event (13 January 2007), one can observe a dramatic difference in run-up heights calculated using the traditional method and by means of the suggested Laplace smoothing. So the traditional approach in some cases may lead to an essential overestimation of the run-up heights (more than two times).

The essential difference in efficiency of the Laplace smoothing algorithm between the tsunamis of 2006 and 2007 can be easily explained. The first event was characterized by a rather extensive area of bottom deformations, whereas the second event had a very narrow source area, which was comparable with the ocean depth (see Fig. 3). In the first case, the Laplace smoothing algorithm just filters fine structure of the bottom deformations. As for the second case, the smoothing diminishes the main peak of bottom deformation by a factor of 2 or so.

Gray curves, denoted in Fig. 6 as "$(\vec{\eta}, \vec{n}) - \eta_z$", show difference in run-up heights of synthetic tsunamis originating from the initial elevation calculated as $\xi_0 = (\vec{\eta}, \vec{n})$ and as $\xi_0 = \eta_z$, i.e., taking into account the horizontal and vertical components of bottom deformation and of the vertical component only. For the tsunami of 2006 the horizontal components provide a relatively small contribution, and the polarity of the contribution varies along the coast line. In the event of 2007, the contribution amounted to 4 m and has definite negative polarity, which can be explained as a result of the motion of the west slope of the Kuril trench toward the northwest.

Along with the general purpose of this paper, to demonstrate the advantages of the Laplace smoothing algorithm, we shall compare simulated run-ups with measurements collected during post-disaster expeditions (LEVIN et al., 2008; MACINNES et al., 2009a, b). One should not anticipate an exact coincidence of calculated and observed run-up heights for the following reasons. First, we consider a simplified run-up onto a hypothetical vertical wall established along a fixed isobath. Second, we neglect non-linear effects in the shallow water area. Third, the quality of bathymetric data we used (GEBCO), especially on the shelf of the Central Kuril Islands, is rather poor. During the post-disaster expedition we carried out series of depth measurements by means of an echo sounder. Comparison of our measurements and GEBCO bathymetry is shown in Fig. 7. For the majority of the points the difference is really dramatic. So the last reason probably turns out to be the most important one.

In situ measured run-up heights are depicted in Fig. 6 by gray squares. The time interval between the tsunamis of 15 November 2006 and of 13 January 2007 was rather short, which made it difficult to differentiate manifestations of these two events. So each of the in situ measured run-ups represents the maximum value reached during the tsunamis of 2006 and of 2007. It can be seen from Fig. 6 that for

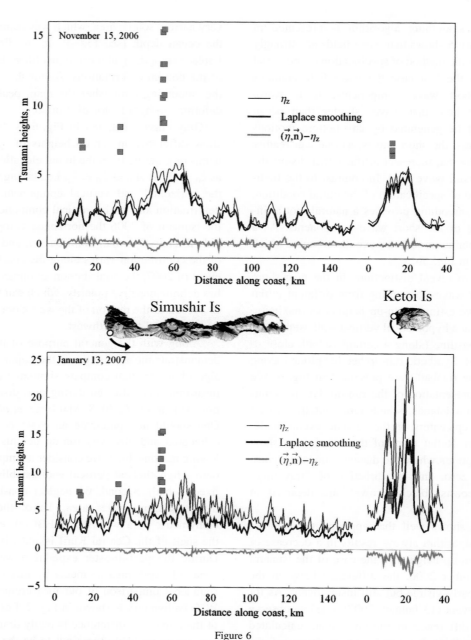

Figure 6

Synthetic (*curves*) and in situ measured (*gray squares*) run-up heights along the coasts of Simushir and Ketoi Islands. *Thin black curves* stand for the traditional method of specification of the initial elevation; *thick black curves* represent the Laplace smoothing method. *Gray curves* denote the difference in run-up heights of tsunamis originated from the initial elevation calculated taking into account the horizontal and vertical components of bottom deformation and taking into account the vertical component only. Relief maps of the islands; starting points (*white circles*) where the distance along the coast is equal to zero and the direction of "traveling" along the coasts (*black arrows*)

Simushir Island the in situ measured run-ups exceed the synthetic data. However, in case of Ketoi Island (Fig. 6b), synthetic run-ups calculated with use of the Laplace smoothing algorithm turn out to be in acceptable agreement with the in situ data, whereas the traditional method of specification of the initial elevation leads to a significant overestimation of the run-up heights.

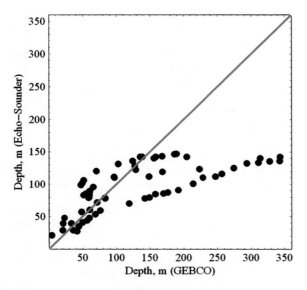

Figure 7
Direct measurements of ocean depth using an echo-sounder on the Central Kuril Islands shelf versus GEBCO bathymetry data

6. Conclusions

The suggested method of calculation of the initial elevation in tsunami source does not violate the traditional scheme of tsunami simulation, but only optimizes it. The first point of optimization consists of the removal from tsunami spectrum of the short-wave components that are not peculiar to real tsunami waves. In particular, it allows a shortening of the calculation time at the expense of increasing the space and time increments. The second point of optimization consists in taking into account not only vertical bottom deformation, but all three components of the deformation vector and bathymetry in the source area. It is important to note here that realization of these two optimizations is based on rigorous hydrodynamic theory. Moreover, the suggested Laplace smoothing algorithm can be easily applied in practice, because it does not require a huge number of computations and specific codes that are necessary for a numerical solution of the 3D Laplace problem in a domain of a complicated shape.

Comparison of the traditional method of specification of the initial condition, within which the initial elevation is assumed to be equal to the residual vertical bottom deformation, with the Laplace smoothing method using the example of the Central Kuril

Islands tsunamis confirms its efficiency. It is shown that the traditional method may lead to significant overestimation of tsunami run-up heights.

Finally, it has been noted that the shortest wave length that can be exited by seismic bottom motions at a given point is approximately equal to the ocean depth at this point. The Laplace smoothing allows the presence of this wave length in the spectrum. Waves of $\lambda \sim H$ length are strongly dispersive waves. Thus, further enhancement of tsunami simulations is certainly associated with dispersive propagation models.

Acknowledgments

This work was supported by the Russian Foundation for Basic Research, projects 07-05-00414 and 10-05-00562. We are grateful to USGS for providing the Finite Fault data.

References

AIDA, I. (1969), *Numerical experiments for tsunami caused by moving deformation of the sea bottom*, Bull. Earthq. Res. Inst. Tokyo Univ., 47, 849–862.

ALEXEEV, A.S., and GUSYAKOV, V.K. (1976), *Numerical Modeling of Tsunami and Seismic Surface Waves Generation by Submarine Earthquake*, Tsunami Research Symposium Bulletin Royal Society New Zealand, 15, 243–251.

BASSIN, C., LASKE, G. and MASTERS, G. (2000), *The Current Limits of Resolution for Surface Wave Tomography in North America*, EOS Trans AGU, 81, F897.

BELLOTTI, G., CECIONI, C., GIROLAMO, P. (2008), *Simulation of small-amplitude frequency-dispersive transient waves by means of the mild-slope equation*, Coastal Engineering, 55, 447–458.

DOTSENKO, S. F. (1996), *The excitation of tsunamis in oscillations of a floor area*, Izvestiya Akademii Nauk Fizika Atmosfery i Okeana, 32 (2), 264–270.

DOTSENKO, S. F., SOLOVIEV, S. L. (1995), *On the role of residual shifts of ocean-bottom in tsunami generation underwater earthquakes*, Okeanologiya, 35 (1), 25–31.

DUTYKH, D., DIAS, F. (2007), *Water waves generated by a moving bottom*, Tsunami and nonlinear waves, Springer (Geo. Sc.), 63–94.

DUTYKH, D., DIAS, F. (2009), *Tsunami generation by dynamic displacement of sea bed due to dip-slip faulting*, Mathematics and Computers in Simulation, 80, 837–848.

DUTYKH, D., DIAS, F., KERVELLA, Y. (2006), *Linear theory of wave generation by a moving bottom*, C. R. Acad. Sci. Paris, Ser. I, 343, 499–504.

FUJII, Y. and SATAKE, K. (2008), *Tsunami Sources of the November 2006 and January 2007 Great Kuril Earthquakes*, Bulletin of the Seismological Society of America, 98(3), 1559–1571.

273

GISLER, G. R. (2008), *Tsunami simulations*, Annu. Rev. Fluid Mech. 40, 71–90.

HAMMACK, J. L. (1973), *A note on tsunamis: their generation and propagation in an ocean of uniform depth*. J. Fluid Mech., 60, 769–799.

HWANG, L. S., and DIVOKI, D. J. (1970), *Tsunami Generation*, J. Geophys. Res. 75, 6802–6817.

IWASAKI, S. (1982), *Experimental study of a tsunami generated by a horizontal motion of a sloping bottom*. Bulletin of the Earthquake Research Institute, *University of Tokyo*, 57, 239–262.

KAJIURA, K. (1963), *The leading wave of a tsunami*, Bulletin of the Earthquake Research Institute, University of Tokyo, 41(3), 535–571.

KAJIURA, K. (1970), *Tsunami source, energy and directivity of wave radiation*, Bulletin of the Earthquake Research Institute, University of Tokyo, 48 (5), 835–869.

KERVELLA, Y., DUTYKH, D., DIAS, F. (2007), *Comparison between three-dimensional linear and nonlinear tsunami generation models*, Theoretical and Computational Fluid Dynamics, 21, 245–269.

KOSTITSYNA, O. V., NOSOV, M. A., SHELKOVNIKOV, N.K. (1992), *A study of nonlinearity in the process of tsunami generation by sea floor motion*. Moscow Univ. Phys. Bull., 47(4), 83–86.

KOWALIK, Z., KNIGHT, W., LOGAN, T., and WHITMORE, P. (2005), *Numerical modelling of the global tsunami: Indonesian tsunami of December 26 2004*, Science of Tsunami Hazard, 23(1), 40–56.

LAMB, H., *Hydrodynamics, 6th ed.* (New York: Dover 1945).

LANDAU, L.D., and LIFSHITZ, E. M. *Fluid Mechanics, V.6 of Course of Theoretical Physics, 2nd English edition. Revised.* (Pergamon Press, Oxford-New York-Beijing-Frankfurt-San Paulo-Sydney-Tokyo-Toronto 1987).

LEVIN, B.W., and NOSOV, M.A., *Physics of Tsunamis* (Springer 2008).

LEVIN, B.W., KAISTRENKO, V.M., RYBIN, A.V., NOSOV, M.A., PINEGINA, T.K., RAZZHIGAEVA, N.G., SASOROVA, E.V., (...), FITZHUGH, B. (2008), *Manifestations of the tsunami on November 15, 2006, on the central Kuril Islands and results of the runup heights modeling*, Doklady Earth Sciences, 419 (1), 335–338.

LOBKOVSKY, L.I., RABINOVICH, A.B., KULIKOV, E.A., IVASHCHENKO, A.I., FINE, I.V., THOMSON, R.E., IVELSKAYA, T.N., BOGDANOV, G.S. (2009), *The Kuril Earthquakes and tsunamis of November 15, 2006, and January 13, 2007: Observations, analysis, and numerical modeling*, Oceanology, 49 (2), 166–181.

MACINNES, B.T., BOURGEOIS, J., PINEGINA, T.K., KRAVCHUNOVSKAYA, E. (2009a), *Tsunami geomorphology: erosion and deposition from the 15 November 2006 Kuril Island tsunami*, Geology, 37, 995–998.

MACINNES, B.T., PINEGINA, T.K., BOURGEOIS, J., RAZZHIGAEVA, N.G., KAISTRENKO, V.M., KRAVCHUNOVSKAYA, E.A. (2009b), *Field survey and geological effects of the 15 November 2006 Kuril tsunami in the middle Kuril Islands*, Pure and Applied Geophysics, 166 (1–2), 9–36.

MARCHUK, AN. G., CHUBAROV, L. B., SHOKIN, YU. I., *Numerical modelling of tsunami waves* (LA-Tr-85-40 USA- Los Alamos National Laboratory, Univ. of California 1985).

MEI, C.C., *The applied dynamics of ocean surface and waves* (World Scientific 1983).

NOSOV, M. A. (1992), *Generation of tsunami by oscillations of a sea floor section*, Moscow Univ. Phys. Bull. 47(1), 110–112.

NOSOV, M. A. (1996), *A comparative study of tsunami excited by piston-type and traveling-wave bottom motion*, Volcanol. Seismol. 17, 693–698.

NOSOV, M. A. (1998), *On the directivity of dispersive tsunami waves excited by piston-type and traveling-wave sea-floor motion*, Volcanol. Seismol., 19, 837–844.

NOSOV, M. A. and KOLESOV, S. V. (2005), *Nonlinear tsunami generation mechanism in compressible ocean*, Vestnik Moskovskogo Universita, Ser. 3 Fizika Astronomiya, (3), 51–54.

NOSOV, M. A., KOLESOV, S. V., and DENISOVA, A.V. (2008), *Contribution of nonlinearity in tsunami generated by submarine earthquake*, Advances in Geosciences, 14, 141–146.

NOSOV, M. A., SHELKOVNIKOV, N. K. (1995), *Tsunami generation by traveling sea-floor shoves*, Moscow Univ. Phys. Bull., 50 (4), 88–92.

NOSOV, M. A., SHELKOVNIKOV, N. K. (1996), *On directivity of radiation of dispersing tsunami waves by asymmetric sources*, Moscow University Physics Bulletin, 51 (3), 77–82.

NOSOV, M. A., SHELKOVNIKOV, N. K. (1997), *The excitation of dispersive tsunami waves by piston and membrane floor motions*, Izvestiya, Atmos. Ocean. Phys. 33 (1), 133–139.

NOSOV, M.A. (1999), *Tsunami Generation in Compressible Ocean*, Phys. Chem. Earth (B), 24(5), 437–441.

NOSOV, M.A. and KOLESOV, S.V. (2007), *Elastic oscillations of water column in the 2003 Tokachi-oki tsunami source:* in situ measurements and 3-D numerical modeling, Natural Hazards and Earth System. Sciences, 7, 243–249.

NOSOV, M.A., and KOLESOV, S.V. (2009), *Method of Specification of the Initial Conditions for Numerical Tsunami Modeling*, Moscow University Physics Bulletin, 64(2), 208–213.

NOVIKOVA, L. E., and OSTROVSKY, L. A. (1982), *On an acoustic mechanism of tsunami wave generation*, Oceanology. 22(5), 693–697.

OKADA, Y. (1985), *Surface deformation due to shear and tensile faults in a half-space*, Bulletin of the Seismological Society of America, 75(4) 1135–1154.

POD'YAPOLSKY, G. S. (1978), *Tsunami excitation by an earthquake*, Methods for calculating tsunami rise and propagation (in Russian), 30–87, Nauka, Moscow.

RABINOVICH, A.B., LOBKOVSKY, L.I., FINE, I.V., THOMSON, R. E., IVELSKAYA, T. N., and KULIKOV, E. A. (2008), *Near-source observations and modeling of the Kuril Islands tsunamis of 15 November 2006 and 13 January 2007*, Advances in Geosciences, 14, 105–116.

SAITO, T., and FURUMURA, T (2009), *Three-dimensional tsunami generation simulation due to sea-bottom deformation and its interpretation based on the linear theory*, Geophys. J. Int., 178, 877–888.

TAKAHASHI, R. (1934), *A model experiment on the mechanism of seismic sea wave generation, Part 1*, Bull. Earthq. Res. Inst. Tokyo Univ., 1, 152–181.

TAKAHASI, R. (1963), *On some model experiment on tsunami generation*, Intern. Union Geodesy and Geophys. Monogr., 24, 235–248.

TANIOKA, Y., and SATAKE, K. (1996), *Tsunami generation by horizontal displacement of ocean bottom*, Geophys. Res. Lett., 23(8), 861–864.

TANIOKA, Y., and SENO, T. (2001), *Sediment effect on tsunami generation of the 1896 Sanriku tsunami earthquake*, Geophysical Research Letters, 28(17), 3389–3392.

TANIOKA, Y., HASEGAWA, Y., KUWAYAMA, T. (2008), *Tsunami waveform analyses of the 2006 underthrust and 2007 outer-rise Kurile earthquakes*, Advances in Geosciences. 14, 129–134.

TINTI, S., PAGNONI, G., and PIATANESI, A. (2003), *Simulation of tsunamis induced by volcanic activity in the Gulf of Naples (Italy)*, Natural Hazards and Earth System Sciences, 3, 311–320.

TITOV, V.V., and GONZALEZ, F.I. (1997), *Implementation and testing of the Method of Splitting Tsunami (MOST) model*, NOAA Technical Memorandum ERL PMEL-112.

TOLSTOY, I., and CLAY, C. S., *Ocean acoustics – theory and experiment in underwater sound, 2nd ed.* (American Institute of Physics, New York 1987).

VOIT, S. S., LEBEDEV, A. N., SEBEKIN, B. I. (1981), *On a formation of a directed tsunami wave in the generation domain*, Izvestiya Akademii Nauk SSSR Fizika Atmosfery i Okeana, 17 (3), 296–304.

YAMAZAKI, Y., WEI, Y., CHEUNGW, K.F., and CURTIS, G.D. (2006), *Forecast of Tsunamis from the Japan–Kuril–Kamchatka Source Region*, Natural Hazards, **38**, 411–435, doi:10.1007/s11069-005-2075-7.

(Received October 30, 2009, revised April 1, 2010, accepted April 3, 2010, Published online November 9, 2010)

Reprinted from the journal

Pure Appl. Geophys. 168 (2011), 1239–1249
© 2010 Springer Basel AG
DOI 10.1007/s00024-010-0232-8

Runup of Tsunami Waves in U-Shaped Bays

IRA DIDENKULOVA[1,2] and EFIM PELINOVSKY[2]

Abstract—The problem of tsunami wave shoaling and runup in U-shaped bays (such as fjords) and underwater canyons is studied in the framework of 1D shallow water theory with the use of an assumption of the uniform current on the cross-section. The wave shoaling in bays, when the depth varies smoothly along the channel axis, is studied with the use of asymptotic approach. In this case a weak reflection provides significant shoaling effects. The existence of traveling (progressive) waves, propagating in bays, when the water depth changes significantly along the channel axis, is studied within rigorous solutions of the shallow water theory. It is shown that traveling waves do exist for certain bay bathymetry configurations and may propagate over large distances without reflection. The tsunami runup in such bays is significantly larger than for a plane beach.

Key words: Tsunami wave runup, narrow bays, abnormal amplification, shallow water theory.

1. Introduction

Entry of sea waves into narrow bays, such as fjords, and river mouths usually leads to an intensification of wave regimes, which is well-known by various photos of tidal and tsunami bores (STOKER, 1957; TSUJI *et al.*, 1991). Significant wave amplification also occurs along underwater canyons, like it was during the 2004 tsunami in the Indian Ocean (IOUALALEN *et al.*, 2007). In contrast to open and wide bays, the wave dynamics in such narrow geometries (the water depth and the bay width are much smaller than the wave length) has many specific features. The wave flow in the first approximation can be considered as uniform in the cross-section that allow using

simplified 1D shallow water equations (STOKER, 1957; PELINOVSKY and TROSHINA, 1994, WU and TIAN, 2000). The cross-section of these bays is assumed to be U-shaped. This type of bays and canyons is rather common in the nature. For example, Fig. 1 shows the transverse profile of the Sognefjoren fjord in Norway, which has a triangular shape (NESJE *et al.*, 1992). The bathymetry of the Scripps Canyon in California, which is presented in Fig. 2, has a quasi-parabolic cross-section (DARTNELL *et al.*, 2007).

Even for uniform in longitudinal direction channels, it is not easy to find the solution for the nonlinear traveling waves (solitons, cnoidal waves) analytically. This problem requires solving the 2D Laplace equation in cross-section domain with curvilinear boundary (PEREGRINE, 1968; 1969; FENTON, 1973; SHEN and ZHONG, 1981; DAS, 1985; MATHEW and AKYLAS, 1990; TENG and WU, 1992, 1994, 1997; CAPUTO and STEPANYANTS 2003). At the same time approximation of a rectangular cross-section does not correspond to natural narrow bays, which bottom configuration varies in both longitudinal and transversal directions. The runup of long nonlinear waves in narrow basins of special geometries is analyzed in (ZAHIBO *et al.*, 2006; CHOI *et al.*, 2008).

Usually the wave propagation in bays with variable bathymetry (bottom slope, curvilinear seawalls) leads to significant reflection and diffraction effects and, as a result, the wave energy can not be transferred over large distances. Meanwhile for certain bathymetry configurations the wave can propagate without internal reflection even in the cases, when the depth varies strongly along the wave path. Such effects have been studied early for 1D wave propagation (CLEMENTS and ROGERS, 1975; DIDENKULOVA *et al.*, 2008; 2009) and recently for channels of a parabolic cross-section (DIDENKULOVA and PELINOVSKY, 2009). When applied to a tsunami problem, it

---

[1]   Department of Wave Engineering, Institute of Cybernetics, Tallinn, Estonia. E-mail: ira@cs.ioc.ee
[2]   Department of Nonlinear Geophysical Processes, Institute of Applied Physics, Nizhny Novgorod, Russia. E-mail: pelinovsky@hydro.appl.sci-nnov.ru

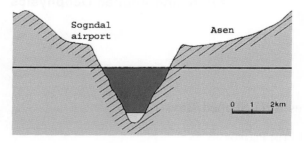

Figure 1
The transverse profile of the Sognefjoren fjord (Norway)

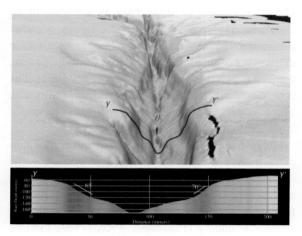

Figure 2
The bathymetry of the Scripps Canyon (California)

means that a destructive tsunami wave can propagate over large distances without reflection and transfers all its energy to the coast that leads to an abnormal wave amplification and runup. That is why the analysis of possibility of such events is extremely important for tsunami forecast and mitigation.

This study is aimed to inspect the existence of traveling waves which can propagate without reflection in the bays, when the depth varies strongly along the wave path, and study the tsunami wave dynamics above such bottom profiles, focusing on processes of wave shoaling and runup. Basic equations of the shallow water theory adapted to the case of tsunami wave propagation along the U-shaped bay of a variable depth in the longitudinal direction are given in Sect. 2. The analogue of the Green's law for wave amplitude in narrow channels is derived in Sect. 3. The existence and properties of traveling waves in such channels with certain variations of water depth

along the wave path ("non-reflecting" depth profiles) is discussed in Sect. 4. Runup of tsunami waves in U-shaped bays is studied in Sect. 5. The main results are summarized in the Sect. 6.

2. Basic equations

The basic model for long waves is 2D shallow water theory:

$$
\begin{aligned}
\frac{\partial \vec{u}}{\partial t} + (\vec{u} \cdot \nabla)\vec{u} + g\nabla \tilde{\eta} &= 0, \\
\frac{\partial \tilde{\eta}}{\partial t} + \left(\nabla \cdot [\tilde{h} + \tilde{\eta}]\vec{u} \right) &= 0,
\end{aligned}
\tag{1}
$$

where $\vec{u} = (u, v)$ is a vector of depth-averaged velocity, $\tilde{\eta}(x, y, t)$ is a water displacement, $\tilde{h}(x, y)$ is an unperturbed water depth in the channel, g is a gravity acceleration and t is time.

Let us consider tsunami wave propagation in a U-shaped bay of a geometry shown in Fig. 3, where $h(x)$ and $\eta(x,t)$ are an unperturbed water depth and a water displacement along the main axis of the bay and $H(x, t) = h(x) + \eta(x, t)$ is a total water depth. With the use of an assumption of the narrow bay, where a velocity component along the bay is much larger, than a cross-section velocity component $v \ll u$ (classical hydraulic approximation), Eq. (1) can be simplified to (STOKER, 1957; ZAHIBO et al., 2006).

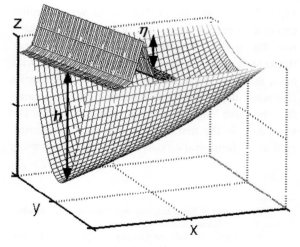

Figure 3
The geometry of the problem

$$\frac{\partial S}{\partial t} + \frac{\partial}{\partial x}(Su) = 0, \quad \frac{\partial u}{\partial t} + u\frac{\partial u}{\partial x} + g\frac{\partial H}{\partial x} = g\frac{dh}{dx}, \quad (2)$$

where $S(H)$ is the water cross-section of the bay and $u(x, t)$ is the cross-section averaged flow velocity. Eq. (2) represent the 1D basic nonlinear mathematical model for long water waves in narrow bays.

In our study we assume that the bay has a symmetric transverse profile with the geometry of sidewalls described by the power law $z \sim |y|^m$ with arbitrary exponent $0 < m < \infty$. In this case $S(H) \sim H^{\frac{m+1}{m}}$ and the system (2) can be rewritten for water flow u and total depth H

$$\frac{\partial H}{\partial t} + u\frac{\partial H}{\partial x} + \frac{H}{q}\frac{\partial u}{\partial x} = 0, \quad \frac{\partial u}{\partial t} + u\frac{\partial u}{\partial x} + g\frac{\partial H}{\partial x} = g\frac{dh}{dx}.$$
$$(3)$$

This system (3) contains a coefficient $q = \frac{m+1}{m}$ depending on the shape of the bay cross-section $1 < q < \infty$, and this differs from the classical 1D shallow water equations ($q = 1$), which are usually applied for water waves in the coastal and surf zones.

The linearized version of shallow water equations follows from Eq. (3) for $\eta \ll h$ and $u \ll \sqrt{gh/q}$

$$\frac{\partial \eta}{\partial t} + u\frac{dh}{dx} + \frac{h}{q}\frac{\partial u}{\partial x} = 0, \quad \frac{\partial u}{\partial t} + g\frac{\partial \eta}{\partial x} = 0, \quad (4)$$

can be easily reduced to the variable-coefficient wave equation for a water displacement

$$\frac{\partial^2 \eta}{\partial t^2} - g\frac{dh}{dx}\frac{\partial \eta}{\partial x} - \frac{gh}{q}\frac{\partial^2 \eta}{\partial x^2} = 0. \quad (5)$$

Equations (3) and (5) can be used as a simplified model for long water waves propagating in the narrow U-shaped bay of arbitrarily varying depth along the wave path.

3. Wave shoaling in U-shaped bays with smoothly varying depth along the wave path

First of all, let us consider the linear wave dynamics in a narrow bay, when the depth varies smoothly with a distance. In this case the asymptotic methods can be used and similar to (DIDENKULOVA et al., 2009) an approximated solution of Eq. (5) can

be found. For a monochromatic wave $\eta \sim \exp(i\omega t)$ Eq. (5) is the second-order ODE and its solution is sought in the following form

$$\eta(x) = A(x)\exp[i\omega\tau(x)], \quad (6)$$

where $A(x)$ and $\tau(x)$ are real functions (local amplitude and travel time, respectively), which should be determined, and ω is the wave frequency. After substituting Eq. (6) into the Eq. (5) we obtain a system for functions $A(x)$ and $\tau(x)$

$$\frac{d^2 A}{dx^2} + \frac{q}{h}\frac{dh}{dx}\frac{dA}{dx} + \left[\frac{q}{gh} - \left(\frac{d\tau}{dx}\right)^2\right]\omega^2 A = 0, \quad (7)$$

$$A\frac{d^2\tau}{dx^2} + 2\frac{dA}{dx}\frac{d\tau}{dx} + \frac{q}{h}\frac{dh}{dx}A\frac{d\tau}{dx} = 0. \quad (8)$$

The first two terms in Eq. (7) are relatively small, if the depth varies smoothly along the wave path and can be neglected, and therefore

$$\frac{d\tau}{dx} = \frac{1}{c(x)}, \quad \tau(x) = \int\frac{dx}{c(x)}, \quad c(x) = \sqrt{gh(x)/q}.$$
$$(9)$$

The function $\tau(x)$ here determines the travel time of tsunami wave propagation in the bay. If the x axis is directed offshore (to the left in Fig. 3) Eq. (9) corresponds to the wave moving onshore (to the right in Fig. 3), for the offshore-going wave we should take the sign "−" for $\tau(x)$. After integrating and using Eq. (9) and (8) is expressed in the form

$$A^2 h^{q-1/2} = const \text{ or } A \sim h^{-\left(\frac{1}{4}+\frac{1}{2m}\right)}. \quad (10)$$

In the case of a plane beach ($m \to \infty$) Eq. (10) represents the well-known Green's law $A \sim h^{-1/4}$ (DINGEMANS, 1997; MEI et al., 2005), which describes the sea wave shoaling in the coastal zone. Equation (10) can also be obtained from the generalized Green's law $A \sim h^{-1/4}B^{-1/2}$ for waves in the rectangular channel of variable depth $h(x)$ and width $B(x)$ (MILES, 1979; DINGEMANS, 1997; MEI et al., 2005), taking into account the characteristic width of a "power" channel $B \sim S/H \sim h^{1/m}$. Thus, shoaling effects depend on the shape of the bay and they are stronger for bays with small values of m. For example, in fiords of triangular shape $A \sim h^{-3/4}$ they are significantly stronger, than in parabolic bays $A \sim h^{-1/2}$. It

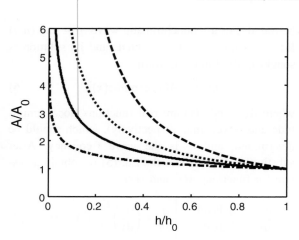

Figure 4
Shoaling effects in the U-shaped bays with $m = 0.5$ (*dashed line*), $m = 1$ (*dotted line*) and $m = 2$ (*solid line*) and the bay of rectangular cross-section (*dash-dotted line*)

is shown in Fig. 4 with respect to the wave amplitude A_0 at the depth h_0.

In a similar way from the second equation in Eq. (4) variations of the velocity field, vertically integrated and averaged over the cross-section of the bay, can be found

$$u(x) = U(x)\exp[i\omega\tau(x)] \quad U \sim h^{-\left(\frac{3}{4}+\frac{1}{2m}\right)}. \quad (11)$$

It follows from Eq. (11) that variations of currents in narrower bays (smaller values of m) are greater.

The obtained approximated solution describes traveling waves with variable amplitude and phase in U-shaped bays of smoothly varied depth along the wave path. The reflection of water waves from the beach is minor and it is less for smaller bottom slopes. Since the reflection of the wave energy in such bottom configuration is negligible, shoaling effects there are significant. Thus, we confirm analytically that narrow bays of decreasing cross-section lead to a strong amplification of tsunami waves at the coast, which is often observed in real conditions.

4. Traveling waves in U-shaped bays with a arbitrary varying depth along the wave path

An approximated solution obtained in Sect. 3 can also be an exact solution of Eqs. (7) and (8) if wave amplitude A satisfies to the following equation:

$$\frac{\mathrm{d}^2A}{\mathrm{d}x^2} + \frac{m+1}{mh}\frac{\mathrm{d}h}{\mathrm{d}x}\frac{\mathrm{d}A}{\mathrm{d}x} = 0, \quad (12)$$

which follows from Eq. (7) after substituting Eq. (9). The system of Eqs. (8), (9) and (12) is an overdetermined system for wave amplitude $A(x)$ and travel time $\tau(x)$. At the same time Eq. (12) can be considered as an equation for unknown longitudinal depth profile $h(x)$ and after integration it gives

$$\frac{\mathrm{d}A}{\mathrm{d}x}h^{1+1/m} = \text{const.} \quad (13)$$

Equation (13) together with Eq. (10) gives the depth profile

$$h(x) \sim x^{\frac{4m}{3m+2}} \quad (14)$$

and wave amplitude

$$A(x) \sim h^{-\left(\frac{1}{4}+\frac{1}{2m}\right)} \sim x^{-\frac{m+2}{3m+2}}. \quad (15)$$

As a result, for a certain bottom profiles (14) the approximated solution coincides with the exact one, which is valid for any values of the bottom slope along the wave path and does not assume a smoothly varying depth. Thus, traveling waves do exist in U-shaped bays [for example, if their cross-section is described by the power law with arbitrary exponent m and the longitudinal component represented by Eq. (14)] and can propagate without reflection and transfer wave energy over large distances.

In the limited case of $m \to \infty$, which corresponds to a channel of rectangular cross-section or a case, when the depth does not depend on y-coordinate, Eq. (14) transforms to $h \sim x^{4/3}$, that coincides with a "non-reflecting" bottom profile (CLEMENTS and ROGERS, 1975; DIDENKULOVA et al., 2008b; 2009). The exponent in Eq. (14) varies monotonically from 0 ($m \to 0$) to 4/3 ($m \to \infty$). Thus, bottom profiles in longitudinal direction can be concave ($m < 2$), convex ($m > 2$), or constant slope ($m = 2$) depending on the shape of the bay, they are presented in Fig. 5 with respect to the water depth h_0 at the distance L from the shoreline. It can be seen that the difference between depth profiles for bays with $m \geq 1$ is relatively small and such profiles can be estimated by a constant slope. At the same time profiles for $m < 1$ change significantly especially for $m \ll 1$. Figure 6 demonstrates the shapes of such "non-reflecting"

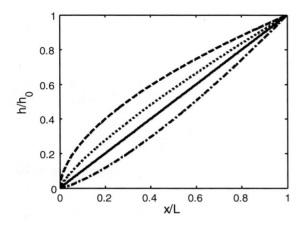

Figure 5
"Non-reflecting" bottom profiles in longitudinal direction for U-shaped bays with $m = 0.5$ (*dashed line*), $m = 1$ (*dotted line*) and $m = 2$ (*solid line*) and the channel of rectangular cross-section (*dash-dotted line*)

bays. They look realistic and similar to those shown in Figs. 1 and 2 for Sognefjoren Fjord and Scripps Canyon.

The exponent in the amplitude Eq. (15) also varies monotonically with an increase in m from -1 ($m \to 0$) to $-1/3$ ($m \to \infty$). Its variations are

absolutely the same as in bays with slowly varying depth along the wave path (Fig. 4).

Thus, the wide class of bottom topographies of the coastal zone satisfies to the condition of the "non-reflecting" propagation which can provide abnormal amplification of tsunami waves at the coast.

Let us discuss the structure of traveling waves in U-shaped bays. Using the solution for a monochromatic wave (6) and Eqs. (14) and (15) the general traveling wave solution can be written as the sum of two progressive waves propagating in opposite directions

$$\eta(x,t) = \eta_+[t - \tau(x)] + \eta_-[t + \tau(x)], \quad (16)$$

where the traveling wave is

$$\eta_\pm(x,t) = A_\pm \left[\frac{h_0}{h(x)}\right]^{\frac{1}{4}+\frac{1}{2m}} \exp\{i\omega[t \mp \tau(x)]\},$$
$$\tau(x) = \frac{(3m+2)L}{(m+2)c_0}\left|1 - \left[\frac{x}{L}\right]^{\frac{m+2}{3m+2}}\right|, \quad (17)$$

where $A_\pm$ are amplitudes of each wave, c_0 and h_0 are a wave speed and water depth at the location $x = L$, respectively, and $\tau(x)$ represents a travel time from the location $x = L$ to the current position. In the

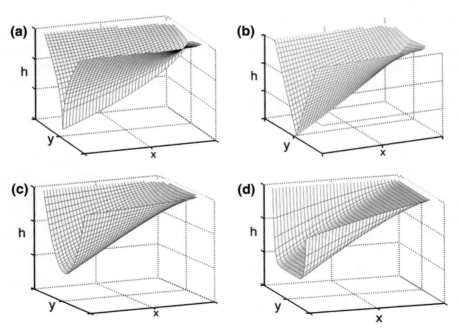

Figure 6
Shapes of "non-reflecting" bays for **a** $m = 0.5$, **b** $m = 1$, **c** $m = 2$ and **d** $m = 10$

linear framework the principle of superposition holds and these waves do not interact with each other.

An obvious generalization of the existing results is with the use of Fourier analysis to obtain the superposition of such sine waves with different frequencies, the technique obviously being applicable in this linear framework. With the use of the Fourier integral of spectral components (17), the traveling wave of an arbitrary shape can be presented in a general form

$$\eta_\pm(x,t) = A_\pm \left[\frac{h_0}{h(x)}\right]^{\frac{1}{4}+\frac{1}{2m}} f_\pm[t \mp \tau(x)], \qquad (18)$$

where $f_\pm(t)$ describes the wave shape at a fixed point $x = L$. An important feature is that representation (18) allows consideration of wave pulses of finite temporal duration being generalized solutions of the wave Eq. (5).

With the use of traveling wave solutions (18) it is possible to analyze long wave dynamics in the basins of "non-reflecting" configurations. This approach has been used in (DIDENKULOVA et al., 2009) for study of wave dynamics and runup along a concave beach, when the depth does not depend on y-coordinate. The approach suggested in (DIDENKULOVA et al., 2009) is also valid for all "non-reflecting" configurations of narrow U-shaped bays and we do not reproduce it here.

"Non-reflecting" bay configurations described above are obtained in the framework of the linear theory. In the nonlinear theory the same effects can be found for a particular case of the linearly inclined bay with a parabolic cross-section $m = 2$ (DIDENKULOVA and PELINOVSKY, 2009). The solution of the nonlinear problem in this case can be obtained with the use of the Legendre (hodograph) transformation, which has been very popular for long wave runup on a plane beach (CARRIER and GREENSPAN, 1958; PEDERSEN and GJEVIK, 1983; SYNOLAKIS, 1987; TADEPALLI and SYNOLAKIS, 1996; LI, 2000; LI and RAICHLEN, 2001; CARRIER et al., 2003; KÂNOĞLU, 2004; TINTI and TONINI, 2005; KÂNOĞLU SYNOLAKIS, 2006; DIDENKULOVA et al., 2006; 2008a; ANTUONO and BROCCHINI, 2007; PRITCHARD AND DICKINSON, 2007) and is valid for non-breaking waves. In this case the nonlinear system (3) can be reduced to the linear equation (CHOI et al., 2008; DIDENKULOVA and PELINOVSKY, 2009)

$$\frac{\partial^2 \Phi}{\partial \lambda^2} - \frac{\partial^2 \Phi}{\partial \sigma^2} - \frac{2\partial \Phi}{\sigma \partial \sigma} = 0, \qquad (19)$$

where

$$\eta = \frac{1}{2g}\left[\frac{2}{3}\frac{\partial \Phi}{\partial \lambda} - u^2\right], \quad u = \frac{1}{\sigma}\frac{\partial \Phi}{\partial \sigma}, \qquad (20)$$

$$x = \frac{\eta}{\alpha} - \frac{\sigma^2}{6g\alpha}, \quad t = \frac{\lambda - u}{g\alpha}. \qquad (21)$$

Equation (19) has a general solution in a simple form

$$\Phi(\lambda, \sigma) = \frac{\Theta(\lambda + \sigma) - \Theta(\lambda - \sigma)}{\sigma}, \qquad (22)$$

which represents a superposition of two traveling waves. Thus, the existence of the nonlinear traveling waves in the linearly inclined bay with a parabolic cross-section becomes evident. An example of the nonlinear traveling wave propagating onshore is presented in Fig. 7 qualitatively.

The nonlinear traveling wave, when it is far from the shoreline, has a symmetrical shape. As it follows from Eqs. (20)–(22) such wave propagating onshore becomes steeper with distance and always breaks near the shore if the boundary condition of the full absorption is applied. As it has been pointed out in (DIDENKULOVA and PELINOVSKY, 2009) the variation of the wave amplitude with distance, which represents the "nonlinear" Green's law, differs from the prediction of the linear theory near the shoreline. The negative wave amplitude grows faster than positive

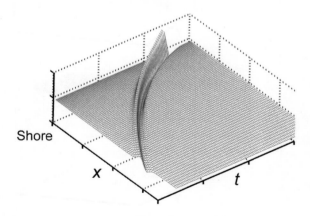

Figure 7
Nonlinear traveling wave in the uniformly inclined channel of a parabolic cross-section

amplitude in shallow waters, demonstrating the difference in the total depth, which is less under the wave trough than under the wave crest. The travel time of a nonlinear wave is described well by the linear theory. At the same time waves propagating offshore do not break.

Tsunami waves, which have a large wavelength, usually reflect from the coast without breaking (MAZOVA et al., 1983), and in this case the boundary condition of the full reflection should be applied. It is discussed in Sect. 5.

Thus, traveling "non-reflecting" waves exist in both linear and nonlinear theories, and therefore, an abnormal amplification of tsunami waves at the coast should be taken into account for evaluation of tsunami risk.

5. Runup of tsunami waves in U-shaped bays of "non-reflecting" configurations

As it has been mentioned above, an existence of traveling waves is especially important for the problem of tsunami wave runup. In this case a tsunami wave can propagate over large distances without reflection and transfer all its energy to the coast that usually leads to abnormal wave amplification on the beach. In this section we study the tsunami wave runup in narrow bays and give estimations for the maximum runup height in such extreme cases. Since tsunami waves are mostly non-breaking (MAZOVA et al., 1983), the tsunami wave energy should fully or partially reflect from the coast. Here we consider the boundary condition of the full reflection at the shoreline.

Let us study this problem in the framework of the linear shallow water theory first. If the wave approaches the beach from an infinitely remote region, the wave solution of Eq. (5) also satisfying the boundary condition of the full reflection, has the following form:

$$\eta(x,t) = A_0 \left(\frac{x}{L}\right)^{-\frac{m+2}{3m+2}} \{f[t + \tau(x)] - f[t - \tau(x)]\},$$

(23)

where $f[t + \tau(x)]$ is the shape of an incident wave with an amplitude A_0 approaching the shoreline

$x = 0$ ($\tau = 0$) and τ represents the time that it takes the wave to propagate from the shoreline to the observation point

$$\tau(x) = \frac{(3m + 2)L}{(m + 2)c_0}\left(\frac{x}{L}\right)^{\frac{m+2}{3m+2}}.$$

(24)

With the use of Taylor's series in the vicinity of the shoreline $\tau = 0$ in Eqs. (23) and (24), the tsunami wave runup (vertical displacement of the water surface at $x = 0$) can be found

$$R(t) = 2\tau_0 \frac{d\eta_{in}(t - \tau_0)}{dt}, \quad \tau_0 = \frac{(3m + 2)L}{(m + 2)c_0}.$$

(25)

where τ_0 is a travel time from a fixed point $x = L$ (chosen far offshore) to the coastline.

Thus, the tsunami wave runup is proportional to the vertical velocity of water particles in the incident wave. If the incident wave has the form of a solitary crest, the water level on the shoreline experiences first runup, followed by rundown. The amplification on the beach and the runup height are determined by the ratio of the travel time τ_0 to the wave period (duration) T, that indicates how many tsunami wavelengths fit into the distance to the shore L. Therefore, it is bigger if the bay is longer along the wave path.

For analysis of the influence of the transverse shape-factor m on the travel time and, therefore, on the tsunami runup height, various estimations can be used. One option is to compare the travel time in the bay of a variable depth along the wave path τ_0 with the travel time in the bay of constant depth along the wave path L/c_0 (Fig. 8).

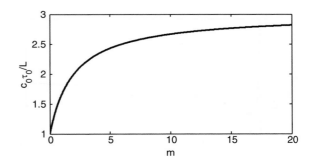

Figure 8
Travel time to the shore in channels of various cross-sections (different values of m) regarding to the travel time in the channel of constant depth along the wave path

It follows from Fig. 8 that tsunami travel time to the shore increases with an increase in the exponent m. For example, for the bay with concave longitudinal projections ($m < 2$, Fig. 6a, b) the travel time to the shore is close to the one in a channel of constant depth. If the same wave propagates in the linearly inclined bay of a parabolic cross-section ($m = 2$, Fig. 6c), the travel time is twice larger. And for the bay with a convex profile ($m > 2$, Fig. 6d) the travel time can be three times larger in comparison with a channel of constant depth.

Another option is to compare various U-shaped bays of the same length L and the same water depth h_0 at the location where we specify parameters of the incident wave. In this case another parameter can be found

$$\frac{\tau_0 \sqrt{gh_0}}{L} = \frac{3m + 2}{m + 2} \sqrt{\frac{m + 1}{m}}, \qquad (26)$$

which characterizes the influence of the bay geometry. This parameter [Eq. (26)] has nonmonotonic character regarding exponent m with its minimum at $m = 2/\sqrt{5} \approx 0.9$. It is shown in Fig. 9.

It follows from Eq. (25) that for the same tsunami wave propagating in bays of different geometries the difference in tsunami runup height is defined by the parameter (26). Therefore, we can expand our conclusions made for the parameter (26) to the analysis of the maximum tsunami runup height

$$R_{\max} = \mu \frac{L}{\sqrt{gh_0}} \max\left[\frac{d\eta_{in}}{dt}\right], \quad \mu = 2\frac{3m + 2}{m + 2}\sqrt{\frac{m + 1}{m}}, \qquad (27)$$

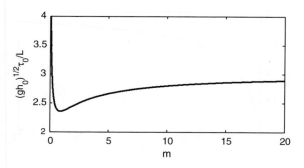

Figure 9
Travel time to the shore in channels of various cross-sections (different values of m) regarding to the travel time in the rectangular channel

where parameter μ represents an influence of the bathymetry configuration of the bay.

It means, for example, if a tsunami wave propagates along the bay with convex longitudinal projections ($m > 2$, Fig. 4d) the expected maximum tsunami runup grows slowly with an increase in m and it is limited by $\mu < 6$ in Eq. (27). If the same wave propagates in the inclined narrow bay ($m = 2$, Fig. 4c), the expected runup height in Eq. (27) has $\mu \approx 4.9$. At the same time for fjords with concave profiles the situation can be different. For $0.2 < m < 2$ the maximum tsunami wave runup on a beach still stays in the range of the parameter $\mu < 6$ and has its minimum value $\mu \approx 4.7$ for $m = 2/\sqrt{5} \approx 0.9$, that represents a bay of almost triangular transverse profile (Fig. 4b), similar to the transverse profile of Sognefjoren fjord in Norway (Fig. 1). If we continue decreasing the parameter $m < 0.9$, that corresponds to the bay of a concave longitudinal profile (Fig. 4a), the maximum tsunami runup increases. Thus, the largest amplification occurs in bays with the largest deviations from the linearly inclined longitudinal profile of both convex and concave shapes.

As an example, let us calculate the runup height analytically for the case when the incident wave is the solitary wave solution of the Korteweg-de Vries (KdV) equation

$$\eta(t) = A_0 \operatorname{sech}^2\left[\sqrt{\frac{3A_0 g}{4h_0^2}}t\right]. \qquad (28)$$

The maximum runup heights induced by an approaching solitary wave in narrow bays, resulted from substituting Eq. (28) into Eq. (27), are

$$R_{\max} = \frac{2}{3}\mu L\left(\frac{A_0}{h_0}\right)^{3/2}. \qquad (29)$$

As it has been pointed out early, the dependence of the maximum runup height on the transverse shape-factor m has nonmonotonic character. The runup height strongly depends on the amplitude of the soliton and is proportional to $A_0^{3/2}$ for any "nonreflecting" bottom configuration.

Comparison of this result with the asymptotic formula for runup of a solitary wave on the plane beach (SYNOLAKIS, 1987)

$$R_{max} = 2.8312\sqrt{Lh_0}\left(\frac{A_0}{h_0}\right)^{5/4} \qquad (30)$$

is presented in Fig. 10 and 11 for the case, when the ratio h_0/L, which also represents the bottom slope of a plane beach, is equal to 0.1.

It can be seen that maximum runup heights of solitary waves in channels of "non-reflecting" configurations are significantly higher than for a plane beach and maximum amplifications are greater. Variations of maximum runup heights for different

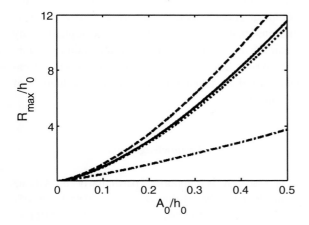

Figure 10
Maximum runup of solitary waves [Eq. (29)] in narrow bays with $m = 1$ (*dotted line*), 2 (*solid line*) and 20 (*dashed line*); *dash-dotted line* corresponds to the runup on a plane beach [Eq. (30)]

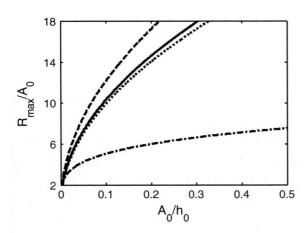

Figure 11
Maximum amplification of solitary waves [Eq. (29)] in narrow bays with $m = 1$ (*dotted line*), 2 (*solid line*) and 20 (*dashed line*); *dash-dotted line* corresponds to the runup on a plane beach [Eq. (30)]

"nonreflecting" bottom configurations regarding transverse shape-factor m reflect the dependence discussed above (Fig. 9). The largest amplification occurs in the bays with the largest deviations from the linearly inclined longitudinal profile of both convex and concave shapes.

The runup height discussed above is computed in the framework of the linear theory. At the same time in the case of the parabolic bay with linearly inclined bottom profile in longitudinal direction it is possible to find the solution of the nonlinear problem using the Legendre transformation (19)–(22) (see ZAHIBO *et al.*, 2006; CHOI *et al.*, 2008). The maximum runup height for an incident wave of a soliton-like shape (28) can be found as [see Eq. (27) in CHOI *et al.* (2008)[1]]

$$R_{max} = \frac{8}{3}\sqrt{\frac{3}{2}}L\left(\frac{A_0}{h_0}\right)^{3/2}, \qquad (31)$$

which coincides with Eq. (29) in the linear theory for $m = 2$. As it can be expected Eq. (28) gives good estimation of the maximum runup height for bays with non-reflecting bottom configurations, even when we do not have an exact analytical solution of the nonlinear shallow water equations ($m \neq 2$). However, in the case of the rigorous nonlinear solution for $m = 2$ (DIDENKULOVA and PELINOVSKY, 2009) nonlinear effects are manifested in the asymmetry of the vertical displacement of the moving shoreline, but not in the maximum runup height. The same can also be expected for a general case of $m \neq 2$.

6. Conclusions

The shoaling and runup of tsunami waves in narrow bays and underwater canyons is studied analytically in the framework of shallow water theory for different types of bay bathymetries. The cross-section of the bay is assumed to be U-shaped and described by the power law $z \sim |y|^m$ with $0 < m < \infty$ and the longitudinal projection can be arbitrary. Such shape is rather typical for narrow bays, such as fjords, and also for underwater canyons.

---

[1] Eq. (29) for the soliton runup height in Choi et al. (2008) has a misprint in the numerical coefficient.

The processes of wave shoaling in these bays, when the longitudinal bottom profile varies smoothly, are studied with the use of asymptotic approach. The reflection of such waves from the beach is minor and it is less for smaller bottom slopes. At the same time shoaling effects are significant. For bays of any transverse shape-factor m, the variations of wave amplitude are stronger than it is predicted from the classical Green's law $\left(h^{-1/4}\right)$ and described by $h^{-1/4-1/2m}$.

Usually tsunami wave propagation in bays with variable bathymetry (bottom slope, curvilinear seawalls) leads to significant reflection and diffraction effects and, as a result, the wave energy can not be transferred over large distances. However, for certain bottom configurations waves can propagate without internal reflection even in the bays of strongly varying depth along the wave path. It is shown here that such traveling (progressive) waves do exist for monotonic longitudinal depth profiles $h \sim x^{4m/(3m+2)}$. As a result, such waves transfer all its energy to the coast and cause abnormal wave amplification and runup. Tsunami wave runup in such bays is significantly larger in comparison with a plane beach.

It is important to mention that the expression for the tsunami runup height at the coast is universal for all "non-reflecting" configurations. It is determined by the ratio of the travel time to the wave period (duration) that indicates the number of tsunami wavelengths, which fit into the distance to the shore. Since the wave travel time to the shoreline for different "non-reflecting" bays is nonmonotonic regarding to the transverse shape-factor m, the maximum tsunami wave height in such bays also has nonmonotonic character regarding to m. The largest amplification occurs in the bays with the largest deviations from the linearly inclined longitudinal profile of both convex and concave shapes.

Characteristic widths of fjords and canyons are usually about a few hundreds meters, while the typical tsunami wave length is about $\lambda = 10$ km. Therefore, the assumption of narrow bays is valid for tsunami waves. Let us consider the water depth $h = 50$ m and amplitude of tsunami waves $A_0 = 1$ m. In this case the parameter of nonlinearity has a weak but finite value $A_0/h = 0.02$, while the frequency dispersion parameter $h^2/\lambda^2 = 2.5 \times 10^{-5}$

is much smaller than the parameter of nonlinearity that demonstrates that shallow water theory is an adequate model for describing tsunami waves. It is also known that very often tsunami waves climb the beach without breaking, thus described here theory can be applied.

It should be noted, that most of the results here are obtained in the framework of the linear shallow water theory. However, we have demonstrated that in the case of a linearly inclined channel with a parabolic cross-section, two analytical solutions for the maximum runup height derived using both linear and nonlinear frameworks, are identical. Therefore, it is expected that obtained formulas can be applied to any basin of the "non-reflecting" bottom configuration. Such basins lead to the significant wave amplification and should be taken into account for evaluation of tsunami hazard.

Acknowledgments

This research is supported particularly by Grants from RFBR (08-05-00069, 08-05-91850, 09-05-91222), Marie Curie network SEAMOCS (MRTN-CT-2005-019374) and EEA Grant (EMP41). Authors thank Utku Kânoğlu, Elena Suleimani and the anonymous reviewer for their useful comments and suggestions.

REFERENCES

ANTUONO, M., and BROCCHINI, M. (2007), *The boundary value problem for the nonlinear shallow water equations*, Stud. Appl. Maths. *119*, 71–91.

CAPUTO, J.-G., and STEPANYANTS, Yu.A. (2003), *Bore formation, evolution and disintegration into solitons in shallow inhomogeneous channels*, Nonlin. Processes Geophys. *10*, 407–424.

CARRIER, G.F., and GREENSPAN, H.P. (1958), *Water waves of finite amplitude on a sloping beach*, J. Fluid Mech. *4*, 97–109.

CARRIER, G.F., WU, T.T., and YEH, H. (2003), *Tsunami run-up and draw-down on a plane beach*, J. Fluid Mech. *475*, 79–99.

CHOI, B.H., PELINOVSKY, E., KIM, D.C., DIDENKULOVA, I., and WOO, S.B. (2008), *Two- and three-dimensional computation of solitary wave runup on non-plane beach*, Nonlin. Processes Geophys. *15*, 489–502.

CLEMENTS, D.L., and ROGERS, C. (1975), *Analytic solution of the linearized shallow-water wave equations for certain continuous depth variations*, J. Australian Math. Soc. B *19*, 81–94.

DARTNELL, P., NORMARK, W.R., DRISCOLL, N.W., BABCOCK, J.M., GARDNER, J.V., KVITEK, R.G., and IAMPIETRO, P.J. (2007),

Multibeam bathymetry and selected perspective views offshore San Diego, California. Scientific Investigations Map 2959, USGS.

DAS, K.P. (1985), A Korteweg-de Vries equation modified by viscosity for waves in a channel of uniform but arbitrary cross section, Phys. Fluids 28, 770–775.

DIDENKULOVA, I., and PELINOVSKY, E. (2009), Non-dispersive traveling waves in inclined shallow water channels. Phys. Lett. A. 373(42), 3883–3887.

DIDENKULOVA, I.I., ZAHIBO, N., KURKIN, A.A., LEVIN, B.V., PELINOVSKY, E.N., and SOOMERE, T. (2006), Runup of nonlinearly deformed waves on a coast, Doklady Earth Sci. 411, 1241–1243.

DIDENKULOVA, I., PELINOVSKY, E., and SOOMERE, T. (2008a), Run-up characteristics of tsunami waves of "unknown" shapes, Pure Appl. Geophys. 165, 2249–2264.

DIDENKULOVA, I., ZAHIBO, N., and PELINOVSKY, E. (2008b), Reflection of long waves from a "non-reflecting" bottom profile, Fluid dyn. 43(4), 590–595.

DIDENKULOVA, I., PELINOVSKY, E., and SOOMERE, T. (2009), Long surface wave dynamics along a convex bottom. J. Geophys. Res.Oceans 114, C07006.

DINGEMANS, M.W. (1997), Water wave propagation over uneven bottoms, World Sci., Singapore.

FENTON, J.D. (1973), Cnoidal waves and bores in uniform channels of arbitrary cross-section, J. Fluid Mech. 58, 417–434.

IOUALALEN, M., PELINOVSKY, E., ASAVANANT, J., LIPIKORN, R., and DESCHAMPS, A. (2007), On the weak impact of the 26 December Indian Ocean tsunami on the Bangladesh coast, Nat. Hazards Earth Syst. Sci. 7, 141–147.

KÂNOĞLU, U. (2004), Nonlinear evolution and runuprundown of long waves over a sloping beach, J. Fluid Mech. 513, 363–372.

KÂNOĞLU, U., and SYNOLAKIS, C. (2006), Initial value problem solution of nonlinear shallow water-wave equations, Phys. Rev. Lett. 97, 148–501.

LI, Y. (2000), Tsunamis: Non-breaking and breaking solitary wave run-up, PhD Thesis, California Institute of Technology.

LI, Y., and RAICHLEN, F. (2001), Solitary wave runup on plane slopes. J.W.P.C.O.E. 127(1), 33–44.

MATHEW, J., and AKYLAS, T.R. (1990), On three-dimensional long water waves in a channel with sloping sidewalls, J. Fluid Mech. 215, 289–307.

MAZOVA, R.Kh., PELINOVSKY, E.N., and SOLOVYEV, S.L. (1983), Statistical data on the tsunami runup onto shore, Oceanology 23(6), 698–702.

MEI, C.C., STIASSNIE, M., and YUE, D.K.-P. (2005), Theory and applications of ocean surface waves, World Sci., Singapore.

MILES, J.W. (1979), On the Korteweg-de Vries equation for a gradually varied channel, J. Fluid Mech. 91, 181–190.

NESJE, A., DAHL, S.O., VALEN, V., and OVSTEDAL, J. (1992), Quaternary erosion in the Sognefjord drainage basin, western Norway, Geomorphology 5, 511–520.

PEDERSEN, G., and GJEVIK, B. (1983), Run-up of solitary waves, J. Fluid Mech. 142, 283–299.

PELINOVSKY, E.N., and TROSHINA, E.N. (1994), Propagation of long waves in straits, Phys. Oceanogr. 5, 43–48.

PEREGRINE, D.H. (1968), Long waves in a uniform channel of arbitrary cross section, J. Fluid Mech. 32, 353–365.

PEREGRINE, D.H. (1969), Solitary waves in trapezoidal channels, J. Fluid Mech. 35, 1–6.

PRITCHARD, D., and DICKINSON, L. (2007), The near-shore behaviour of shallow-water waves with localized initial conditions, J. Fluid Mech. 591, 413–436.

SHEN, M.C., and ZHONG, X.G. (1981), Derivation of K-dV equations for water waves in a channel with variable cross section, J. Mech. 20, 789.

STOKER, J.J. (1957), Water waves, Interscience, Wiley, New York.

SYNOLAKIS, C.E. (1987), The runup of solitary waves, J. Fluid Mech. 185, 523–545.

TADEPALLI, S., and SYNOLAKIS, C.E. (1996), Model for the leading waves of tsunamis, Phys. Review Lett. 77, 2141–2144.

TENG, M.H., and WU, T.Y. (1992), Nonlinear water waves in channels of arbitrary shape, J. Fluid Mech. 242, 211–233.

TENG, M.H., and WU, T.Y. (1994), Evolution of long water waves in variable channels, J. Fluid Mech. 266, 303–317.

TENG, M.H., and WU, T.Y. (1997), Effects of channel cross-sectional geometry on long wave generation and propagation, Phys. Fluids 9, 3368–3377.

TINTI, S., and TONINI, R. (2005), Analytical evolution of tsunamis induced by near-shore earthquakes on a constant-slope ocean, J. Fluid Mech. 535, 33–64.

TSUJI, Y., YANUMA, T., MURATA, I., and FUJIWARA, C. (1991), Tsunami ascending in rivers as as undular bore, Nat. Hazards 4, 257–266.

WU, Y.H., and TIAN, J.-W. (2000), Mathematical analysis of long-wave breaking on open channels with bottom friction, Ocean Eng. 26, 187–201.

ZAHIBO, N, PELINOVSKY, E, GOLINKO, V, and OSIPENKO, N. (2006), Tsunami wave runup on coasts of narrow bays, Int. J. Fluid Mech. Res. 33, 106–118.

(Received October 5, 2009, revised May 7, 2010, accepted June 15, 2010, Published online November 11, 2010)